Lecture Notes in Information Systems and Organisation

Volume 78

Lecture Notes in Information Systems and Organization (LNISO) is a series of scientific books that explore the current state of information systems studies, in particular in the context of organizations, as well as behavioral and design aspects of information systems. The series offers an integrated publication platform for high-quality conferences, symposia and workshops proceedings. Books accepted for publication are selected based on a double-blind peer-review evaluation made by invited reviewers. The series is indexed in Scopus.

Fei Tao • Thippa Reddy Gadekallu
Vikas Kumar • Victoria Akberdina
Evgeny Kuzmin
Editors

Artificial Intelligence and Digital Transformation

From Innovation to Implementation

Springer

Editors
Fei Tao
Digital Twin International Research Center, International Institute for Interdisciplinary and Frontiers
Beihang University
Beijing, China

Vikas Kumar
University of Portsmouth
Portsmouth, UK

Evgeny Kuzmin
Department of Regional Industrial Policy and Economic Security
Institute of Economics of the Ural Branch of the Russian Academy of Sciences
Ekaterinburg, Russia

Thippa Reddy Gadekallu
College of Mathematics and Computer Science
Zhejiang A&F University
Hangzhou, China

Victoria Akberdina
Department of Regional Industrial Policy and Economic Security
Institute of Economics of the Ural Branch of the Russian Academy of Sciences
Ekaterinburg, Russia

ISSN 2195-4968 ISSN 2195-4976 (electronic)
Lecture Notes in Information Systems and Organisation
ISBN 978-3-032-00117-7 ISBN 978-3-032-00118-4 (eBook)
https://doi.org/10.1007/978-3-032-00118-4

This Springer imprint is published by the registered company Springer Nature Switzerland AG
The registered company address is: Gewerbestrasse 11, 6330 Cham, Switzerland

Contents

Editors and Contributors

About the Editors

Fei Tao is a Professor at the School of Automation Science and Electrical Engineering and the Dean of the International Institute for Interdisciplinary and Frontiers at Beihang University, Beijing, China. His research focuses on smart manufacturing and digital twins. He has served as PI for over 30 national research and industry projects. He has published seven books and over 100 peer-reviewed journal articles as the first/corresponding author in *Nature*, *CIRP Annals*, and *IEEE/ASME Transactions*, with over 30 of them being ESI highly cited papers. His publications have over 50,000 citations. He was elected as the Global Highly Cited Researcher (2019–2024) and one of the 20 Most Influential Academics in Smart Manufacturing by SME in 2021. Currently, he serves as an Associate Editor for *Robotics and Computer-Integrated Manufacturing* (RCIM), a CIRP Associate Member, and an IEEE Senior Member. He is the founding Editor-in-Chief of *Digital Twin* in the Taylor & Francis Group and *Digital Engineering* in Elsevier, and he also initiated the Digital Twin Global Forum (DTGF) and the Digital Twin International Conferences (DigiTwin).

Thippa Reddy Gadekallu is currently working as Chief Engineer at Zhongda Group (Jiaxing City, China). He has more than 15 years of experience in teaching and research and over 350 international/national publications in reputed journals and conferences. Currently, his areas of research include machine learning, Internet of things, deep neural networks, blockchain, and computer vision. He serves as an editor for several publishers, including Springer, Hindawi, PLOS ONE, Scientific Reports (Nature), and Wiley. He also acted as a guest editor for several reputed publishers, such as IEEE, Elsevier, Springer, Hindawi, and MDPI. He is recently recognized as one of the top 2% scientists in the world as per the survey conducted by Elsevier in the years 2021, 2022, 2023, and 2024. He is also recognized as a highly cited researcher, young scientist category, by Clarivate (Web of Science) for the period 2017–2022 in the year 2023.

Vikas Kumar is a Deputy Vice Chancellor for Research and Innovation at the University of Portsmouth, UK. Professor Kumar is a distinguished academic and researcher with over 15 years of experience in the operations and supply chain management domain. Professor Kumar has significantly contributed to areas, such as sustainable supply chains, circular economy, operational excellence, and supply chain 4.0. As a prolific author, Professor Kumar has published over 300 papers in top-tier journals and regularly presents his findings at international conferences. Prof. Kumar serves on the editorial board of several international journals and regularly edits special issues in high-ranked international journals. His research has been extensively cited. He has over 19,000 citations and an h-index of 75 on Google Scholar. He was featured among the top 1% of the Highly Cited Researchers 2024 list, which draws on data from the Web of Science Core Collection citation index and is published by Clarivate. He also featured in the world's top 2% scientists list in 2024.

Victoria Akberdina is the Deputy Director of the Institute of Economics of the Ural Branch of the Russian Academy of Sciences and Head of the Department of Regional Industrial Policy and Economic Security. She conducts fundamental and applied research on problems concerning industrial policy formation, forecasting methodologies, modeling the evolution of the economic and technological development of industrial complexes, and the structural dimensions of economic development. In 2019, she was selected as a Corresponding Member of the Russian Academy of Sciences.

Evgeny Kuzmin is a researcher in the Department of Regional Economic Policy and Economic Security at the Institute of Economics of the Ural Branch of the Russian Academy of Sciences. He serves as a reviewer for several high-impact international journals, including the *Journal of Cleaner Production*, *PLOS ONE*, *Sustainability* (*Switzerland*), *Heliyon*, *Business Strategy*, and the *Environment*, among others. Kuzmin has authored over 150 scientific publications. He has participated in the execution of more than 10 research projects (grants) funded by scientific foundations. His research interests encompass risk and uncertainty, economic crises, sustainability, public–private partnerships, industrial policy, economic growth, and entrepreneurship.

Contributors

António Abreu Polytechnic University of Lisbon, Lisbon, Portugal

Victoria Akberdina Institute of Economics of the Ural Branch of the Russian Academy of Sciences, Ekaterinburg, Russia

Vitor Anes Polytechnic University of Lisbon, Lisbon, Portugal

Andrea Appolloni University of Rome Tor Vergata, Rome, Italy

Anastasia Babanskaya Financial University Under the Government of the Russian Federation, Moscow, Russia

Irina Baskakova Ural Federal University, Ekaterinburg, Russia

Moisés Batista University of Cadiz, Puerto Real, Cádiz, Spain

Viktoriia S. Bondareva Kyrgyz-Russian Slavic University named after B.N. Yeltsin, Bishkek, Kyrgyz Republic

Laura Bravi Carlo Bo University of Urbino, Urbino, Italy

Alberto Cerezo-Narváez University of Cadiz, Puerto Real, Cádiz, Spain

Ilia Chernenko Ural Federal University, Ekaterinburg, Russia

Nima Rahmani Choubeh Politecnico di Milano, Milan, Italy

Aleksei Demin Shenzhen MSU-BIT University, Shenzhen, Guangdong, China

Kürşat Demiryürek Ondokuz Mayıs Üniversitesi, Samsun, Turkey

Valentina Derbeneva Ural Federal University, Ekaterinburg, Russia

Nadezhda Efimenko Financial University Under the Government of the Russian Federation, Moscow, Russia

Daria Ermoleva Financial University Under the Government of the Russian Federation, Moscow, Russia

Anna Evseeva Bauman Moscow State Technical University, Moscow, Russia

Luca Fumagalli Politecnico di Milano, Milan, Italy

Thippa Reddy Gadekallu College of Mathematics and Computer Science, Zhejiang A&F University, Hangzhou, China

Manuel Inácio Polytechnic University of Lisbon, Lisbon, Portugal

Vepa Kakadzhanov Kazan National Research Technological University, Kazan, Russia

Denis Koleznev Financial University Under the Government of the Russian Federation, Moscow, Russia

Maksim Koliasnikov Ural Federal University, Ekaterinburg, Russia

Natalia A. Kosolapova Southern Federal University, Rostov-on-Don, Russia

Ivan Kotlyarov Financial University Under the Government of the Russian Federation, Moscow, Russia

Svetlana Kudryavtseva Kazan National Research Technological University, Kazan, Russia

Vikas Kumar University of Portsmouth, Portsmouth, UK

Evgeny Kuzmin Institute of Economics of the Ural Branch of the Russian Academy of Sciences, Ekaterinburg, Russia

Daria S. Laskova Southern Federal University, Rostov-on-Don, Russia

Tatiana S. Laskova Southern Federal University, Rostov-on-Don, Russia

Angelo Marguglio Engineering Ingegneria Informatica SpA, Palermo, Italy

Olga Minulina Kazan National Research Technological University, Kazan, Russia

Federica Murmura Carlo Bo University of Urbino, Urbino, Italy

Bernardo Nicoletti Temple University, Rome, Italy

Anastasia Y. Nikitaeva Southern Federal University, Rostov-on-Don, Russia

Rustam Nurgaliev Kazan National Research Technological University, Kazan, Russia

Ilyos Ochilov Tashkent State University of Economics, Tashkent, Uzbekistan

Manuel Otero-Mateo University of Cadiz, Puerto Real, Cádiz, Spain

Hassan Al Ouatiq Altai State Technical University, Barnaul, Russia

Andres Pastor-Fernández University of Cadiz, Puerto Real, Cádiz, Spain

Giada Pierli Carlo Bo University of Urbino, Urbino, Italy

Aleksandr Pobedin Ural Institute of Management - Branch of the Russian Presidential Academy of National Economy and Public Administration (RANEPA), Ekaterinburg, Russia

Sergei Pronin Altai State Technical University, Barnaul, Russia

Walter Quadrini Politecnico di Milano, Milan, Italy

Aizhan A. Rakhmanalieva Kyrgyz-Russian Slavic University named after B.N. Yeltsin, Bishkek, Kyrgyz Republic

Magdalena Ramírez-Peña University of Cadiz, Puerto Real, Cádiz, Spain

Olga G. Romanovich Kyrgyz-Russian Slavic University named after B.N. Yeltsin, Bishkek, Kyrgyz Republic

Boris Safonov Bauman Moscow State Technical University, Moscow, Russia

Kirill Selivanov Bauman Moscow State Technical University, Moscow, Russia

Irina Semenova Ural Federal University, Ekaterinburg, Russia

Umut Ahmet Seyrek Ondokuz Mayıs Üniversitesi, Samsun, Turkey

Liudmila Shabalina Economic Research Institute, Donetsk, Russia

Galina Shavkun Economic Research Institute, Donetsk, Russia

Alla Shcherbina Donetsk National Technical University, Donetsk, Russia

Akbar Shodiyev Termez University of Economics and Service, Termez, Uzbekistan

Tashkent Institute of Irrigation and Agricultural Mechanization Engineers (TIIAME), Tashkent, Uzbekistan

Diplomat University, Tashkent, Uzbekistan

Andrey F. Shorikov Institute of Economics of the Ural Branch of the Russian Academy of Sciences, Ekaterinburg, Russia

Wadim Strielkowski Cambridge Institute for Advanced Studies, Cambridge, UK

Prague Business School, Prague, Czech Republic

Danish Abbas Syed Politecnico di Milano, Milan, Italy

Fei Tao Digital Twin International Research Center, International Institute for Interdisciplinary and Frontiers, Beihang University, Beijing, China

Sofia Temperoni Carlo Bo University of Urbino, Urbino, Italy

Mark Timko Economic Research Institute, Donetsk, Russia

Irina Turgel Ural Federal University, Ekaterinburg, Russia

Gaia Verrocchio Carlo Bo University of Urbino, Urbino, Italy

Andrey Vlasov Bauman Moscow State Technical University, Moscow, Russia

Riccardo Zanetti Engineering Ingegneria Informatica SpA, Palermo, Italy

Veronika Zemzyulina Ural Federal University, Ekaterinburg, Russia

List of Figures

Using Artificial Intelligence to Combat Fraud: Asian Experience, Russian Prospects

AI-Driven Predictive Maintenance of Industrial Gearboxes

Digital Agents and Generative Artificial Intelligence in Support of Logistics 5.0

Digitalization of Procurement Processes: Application of Lean Methods to Improve Efficiency

Reference Architecture to Exploit Data as a Product Through the Cloud-Edge Continuum

Integration of Embedded Components into Cyber-Physical Systems: Design, Analysis, and Applications

Regional Trajectories of Digital Transformation: A Systematic Review

Digital Pathways of Russian Regions and Their Interaction with the Local Human Capital Markets: An Evolutionary Perspective

Management Strategies for Creative Reindustrialization in Secondary-Tier Cities in the Context of Digital Transformation

Building Health Capital Through Digital Skills: Healthcare Satisfaction and Well-Being in Russian Regions

Digitalization, Innovation, and Competitiveness: Insights from a Cross-Country Analysis of Labor Productivity Effects

Sustainable Industrial Development: An Analysis of Trends in the Case of Russia

Strengthening Digital Trade Integration within BRICS Countries Based on an International Digital Communication Platform

Support for Scientific and Technical Cooperation of the EAEU Countries Through the Creation of a Digital Technological Platform

List of Tables

Digitalization of Procurement Processes: Application of Lean Methods to Improve Efficiency

Digital Transformation and Last-Mile Logistics in Food Delivery: A Comparative Analysis of Urban and Peripheral Models

Integration of Embedded Components into Cyber-Physical Systems: Design, Analysis, and Applications

Digital Pathways of Russian Regions and Their Interaction with the Local Human Capital Markets: An Evolutionary Perspective

Management Strategies for Creative Reindustrialization in Secondary-Tier Cities in the Context of Digital Transformation

Building Health Capital Through Digital Skills: Healthcare Satisfaction and Well-Being in Russian Regions

Digitalization, Innovation, and Competitiveness: Insights from a Cross-Country Analysis of Labor Productivity Effects

Organizational Challenges in Digital Transformation: A Review Through the Lens of Organizational Innovation

Sustainable Industrial Development: An Analysis of Trends in the Case of Russia

Strengthening Digital Trade Integration within BRICS Countries Based on an International Digital Communication Platform

Support for Scientific and Technical Cooperation of the EAEU Countries Through the Creation of a Digital Technological Platform

Editorial: The Role of AI in Digital Transformation. Are We Ready for an AI-Powered Future?

Fei Tao, Evgeny Kuzmin, Thippa Reddy Gadekallu, Vikas Kumar, and Victoria Akberdina

Abstract This chapter summarizes the most prominent studies presented at the International Scientific Conference "Digital Transformation in Industry: Trends, Management, Strategies" (DTI2024), organized by the Institute of Economics of the Ural Branch of the Russian Academy of Sciences on December 16–17, 2024. It serves as an integrative introduction to the collective volume devoted to key trends and challenges of digital transformation amid the rapid proliferation of artificial intelligence technologies. The primary objective of the book is to analyze the transition from technological innovation to the practical implementation of digital solutions across various economic sectors. The editors provide the contextual background underpinning research in this field. In conclusion, a brief overview of the chapters is offered, highlighting their contributions to the conference themes and underscoring the diversity of research approaches. It is our hope that this volume will serve as a valuable resource for scholars, policymakers, and practitioners by offering a conceptual framework and recommendations for navigating a rapidly evolving world where digital transformation is deeply intertwined with AI technologies.

F. Tao
Digital Twin International Research Center, International Institute for Interdisciplinary and Frontiers, Beihang University, Beijing, China
e-mail: ftao@buaa.edu.cn

E. Kuzmin (✉) · V. Akberdina
Department of Regional Industrial Policy and Economic Security, Institute of Economics of the Ural Branch of the Russian Academy of Sciences, Ekaterinburg, Russia
e-mail: kuzmin.ea@uiec.ru; akberdina.vv@uiec.ru

T. R. Gadekallu
College of Mathematics and Computer Science, Zhejiang A&F University, Hangzhou, China
e-mail: thippa@zafu.edu.cn

V. Kumar
University of Portsmouth, Portsmouth, UK
e-mail: Vikas.Kumar@port.ac.uk

F. Tao et al. (eds.), *Artificial Intelligence and Digital Transformation*, Lecture Notes in Information Systems and Organisation 78,
https://doi.org/10.1007/978-3-032-00118-4_1

Keywords Industry 4.0 · Industry 5.0 · Digital economy · Artificial intelligence · Innovation · Digital transformation

The modern economy has entered a phase of profound transformation driven by the rapid development of digital technologies. Artificial Intelligence (AI) plays a leading role in this process and is justifiably regarded as one of the most breakthrough technological trends of the last decade, with its impact being felt across all domains.

The integration of AI into socio-economic systems is radically reconfiguring the mechanisms of human–technology interaction, giving rise to discussions about the future of Industry 6.0. Importantly, digital transformation extends beyond mere technology adoption and necessitates systemic changes in managerial approaches, the restructuring of production and distribution chains, the revision of customer interaction models, and the development of fundamentally new forms of human–machine collaboration. Despite considerable progress in algorithmic solutions such as machine learning, natural language processing, and computer vision, the practical deployment of AI remains complex and fragmented across industries. The book thus pays particular attention to the conditions under which AI technologies can create sustainable value. Which factors enhance the effectiveness of AI integration? How do organizational culture, digital infrastructure, and workforce preparedness affect implementation outcomes? And what are the accompanying risks of accelerated AI adoption? By exploring these questions, the authors contribute to the current scientific and policy discourse.

The chapters included in this volume illustrate a wide range of approaches to the topic, from theoretical modeling and comparative analysis to empirical case studies and implementation practices. The thematic section Artificial Intelligence for Industrial Transformation showcases the multifaceted application of AI. A review of relevant literature conducted by the authors confirms the central role of AI in the industrial digital transformation agenda and highlights the exponential growth of publications on this subject. AI is increasingly used in project-based industries to enhance industrial safety. The implementation of AI-based systems enables predictive risk assessments, real-time compliance monitoring, and automated safety management.

Going beyond industrial applications, AI is becoming a pivotal tool in the fight against corporate fraud. The use of generative models, customer behavior algorithms, anomaly detection systems, and intelligent monitoring technologies facilitates both the identification of fraudulent schemes and the development of proactive risk prevention mechanisms. Empirical findings indicate that businesses' trust in AI is strongly associated with enterprise size, technological awareness, and workforce qualification. Many firms are ready to delegate to AI creative problem-solving and customer-facing automation. However, barriers remain, including high implementation costs, skill shortages, and the opacity of AI decision-making. Thus, social acceptance and trust are viewed as essential conditions for the widespread adoption of AI technologies.

One of the most promising areas of AI deployment is logistics and procurement, the focus of the subsequent thematic section. Particular attention is given to the intelligentization of supply chains, the development of platform-based solutions, and enhancing logistical system adaptability to global challenges.

The digitalization of logistics and procurement is one of the most dynamic vectors of industrial transformation, affecting both tactical aspects (inventory control, supply optimization) and strategic dimensions (the creation of sustainable digital ecosystems and transformation of business models). The chapters illustrate how digital technologies improve operational efficiency and foster rethinking of interactions among organizations, suppliers, consumers, and infrastructure. Research demonstrates how lean management, when integrated with digital tools, transforms internal material supply processes, significantly reducing fulfillment time and operating costs. This confirms the high effectiveness of the digital lean approach, which combines continuous improvement principles with digital transformation—especially relevant for small and medium-sized enterprises striving for agility and adaptability.

Different models show how digitalization affects last-mile logistics development depending on the territorial context. The authors emphasize the potential of crowdshipping—platform-based logistics models leveraging flexible labor—as a cost-optimization and sustainability solution in small towns. Another study develops a theoretical and practical framework for Logistics 5.0 based on the integration of generative AI and digital agents (GAI-DA). The authors highlight not only technological advantages but also the strategic role of GAI-DA as enablers of resilient, human-centered logistics systems. Furthermore, a methodological framework is proposed to address institutional, technical, and regulatory barriers to the integration of AI solutions into existing logistics architectures.

Effective implementation of digital solutions requires a well-developed architectural framework, appropriate platform selection, coordination of hardware–software solutions, and methodological support for transformation processes. The subsequent thematic section—Architecture, Systems, and Methods of Digitalization—focuses on foundational principles of digital architecture, system formalization approaches, and methods for scalable and sustainable implementation of digital solutions. These aspects underpin the long-term effectiveness of digital transformation across economic sectors.

The authors demonstrate that successful digital transformation is grounded in distributed computing, end-to-end digital continuity, high-efficiency analytics, and intelligent quality management systems. Studies emphasize that data product–oriented architectures enhance the economic value of edge-processed data. Such architectures ensure data representation unification, multi-vendor interoperability, and resilience to digital fragmentation. On the practical side, the synthesis of hardware and software is essential. The potential of embedded components for building compact, reliable, and energy-efficient devices in industrial IoT systems is elaborated. The research also develops a network-based model for managing digital industrial ecosystems. It enables scheduling of auxiliary projects through calendar planning and critical path analysis and supports the selection of optimal implementation scenarios considering resource constraints and agent goals. Special focus is placed on algorithmic formalization of decision-making processes—from technology and agent configuration selection to multi-criteria optimization based on cost, time, and quality. This model is applicable to the development of digital platforms that facilitate multivector management of industrial coalitions and supply chains based on Industry 5.0 principles.

The development of digital architectures, systems, and methods creates a foundation for large-scale digital initiatives, ensuring technological and methodological coherence. Yet, the success of digital transformation is determined not only by technical capacity but also by the context of its implementation—especially regional specificities. Therefore, regional aspects of digital transformation must be examined to understand how local conditions influence the success and direction of digital development and how regions adapt to the challenges and opportunities of the digital economy. The next thematic section explores regional trajectories of digital transformation and analyzes trends and approaches at the regional level.

Studies underscore that regional digitalization paths are largely shaped by path dependence and the institutional environment. The authors propose a novel history-friendly modeling approach to identify stable regional development configurations and their impact on human capital reproduction. They find that regions with prolonged digital lag exhibit low levels of innovation activity and foundational digital competencies, while digital frontrunners rely on well-developed human capital.

Another study reveals the role of digital transformation in advancing creative industries as a driver of economic revitalization in small and medium industrial cities. The authors highlight the importance of tailoring strategies to local identities and institutional particularities and the need to establish digital platforms for interaction among government, business, and society. The study emphasizes that digital infrastructure is foundational for social capital and spatial justice amid uneven urbanization. At the same time, digital inequality becomes a dominant factor of regional differentiation, influencing access to essential services. These and other findings underscore the value of an interdisciplinary approach for a comprehensive understanding of regional digital transformations and for developing integrated policies that consider socio-cultural and economic-geographic contexts.

To fully realize the potential of digital technologies at the national and regional levels, a coherent and targeted digital policy is required. Digital policy sets strategic priorities, establishes institutional frameworks, and ensures infrastructure for integrating digital innovation into sustainable development and economic growth. The next thematic section is devoted to analyzing digital policy, its role in economic development and competitiveness, and mechanisms for achieving long-term socio-economic outcomes from digital technology deployment.

Research suggests that digital competitiveness and AI investment do not always produce direct positive effects; in countries with insufficient digital maturity, their impact may be statistically unstable or even negative. The Global Competitiveness Index emerges as the most consistent predictor of labor productivity. Authors emphasize the need for differentiated digital policies tailored to structural characteristics and institutional readiness. Another study establishes a link between the growing share of high-tech products in GDP and reduced energy intensity of the economy. The findings show that the manufacturing sector contributes most significantly to sustainability, maintaining positive dynamics even under sanctions and structural shifts. The constructed model identifies relationships among productivity, energy efficiency, and structural modernization, offering insights for strategic industrial policy planning.

A meta-analysis of organizational challenges in digital transformation identifies core barriers, including digital skill shortages, managerial inertia, fragmented supply chains, and weak coordination of change. In response, the authors propose an analytical framework based on three components—labor, management, and supply—which facilitates the design of organizational innovations to overcome internal resistance to digitalization.

Platform-based solutions integrating diverse processes are becoming essential tools. The formation of unified digital trade policy and the need for international science and technology cooperation necessitate the creation of a global digital communication platform. A central thesis is the dialectic between innovation and implementation. The platform approach is seen as a tool for removing barriers in e-commerce, technology and idea transfer, regulatory harmonization, and cross-border data flows.

These and other critical issues were addressed at the International Scientific Conference "Digital Transformation in Industry: Trends, Management, Strategies" (DTI2024) organized by the Institute of Economics of the Ural Branch of the Russian Academy of Sciences. This book integrates the results of interdisciplinary research on the major milestones and challenges of digital transformation across various economic sectors and levels of socio-economic organization. We hope this volume serves as a source of new ideas and practical solutions for researchers, policymakers, business leaders, and all those committed to sustainable digital development.

Artificial Intelligence for Industrial Transformation

Digital Transformation of Industry Through Using AI: A Bibliometric Analysis Approach

Wadim Strielkowski

Abstract This paper focuses on the theoretical literature overview and bibliometric network analysis of the recent trends in digital transformation and artificial intelligence (AI) in industry. This transformation is characterized by the adoption of digital technologies that reshape modern business processes, organizational strategies and approaches, the role of human capital in industry, as well as value creation. It is very well portrayed by the raising interest in these topics in the academic research literature: from just 2 papers published in 2018 to more than 200 papers in 2024 (according to the Web of Science (WoS), the world renown academic citation and abstract database). This paper identifies major themes, technological advancements, and future research directions based on text and bibliometric network analyses, including the network text and bibliographic data from the 550 papers selected from the WoS database using the keywords "digital transformation of industry" and "AI in industry". Our main results highlight the progression from Industry 4.0 towards Industry 5.0 paradigms emphasizing human-centric, sustainable, as well as resilient approaches. It appears that topics such as Industry 4.0, digital twins, AI-enabled operational excellence, and supply chain optimization are already entrenched. At the same time, topics such as ethical AI usage, workforce development, and the integration of cutting-edge AI such as generative models are quite new and are still evolving. Our results might be of special importance for the relevant stakeholders, entrepreneurs and industry pioneers, as well as policymakers interested in the digital transformation of industry.

Keywords Digital transformation · Industry · Artificial intelligence · Bibliometric network analysis

W. Strielkowski (✉)
Cambridge Institute for Advanced Studies, Cambridge, UK

Prague Business School, Prague, Czech Republic
e-mail: strielkowski@cantab.net

F. Tao et al. (eds.), *Artificial Intelligence and Digital Transformation*, Lecture Notes in Information Systems and Organisation 78,
https://doi.org/10.1007/978-3-032-00118-4_2

1 Introduction

Digital transformation has emerged as a defining trend in modern industry. It reshaped the ways in which organizations operate and compete in the era of advanced technologies [1, 2]. This concept refers to the comprehensive adoption of digital technologies to fundamentally improve business processes, organizational capabilities, and value delivery [3].

Most recently, the research on the digital transformation of industry and the role of AI within it has expanded rapidly across multiple disciplines. Scholars in engineering, computer science, operations management, and information systems have examined topics ranging from technical developments (e.g., new AI algorithms for industrial applications) to managerial and strategic aspects (e.g., how firms implement digital strategies, the impact on business models, and workforce implications) [4, 5]. This interdisciplinary body of literature spans various industrial sectors, including manufacturing, supply chain and logistics, healthcare, energy, and finance.

As the academic community has sought to make sense of these fast-moving developments, numerous literature reviews and bibliometric studies have been undertaken to synthesize current knowledge [6, 7]. Nevertheless, given the accelerating pace of innovation, there is a continuous need to take stock of recent trends and emerging themes in this domain.

The *purpose and the main scientific value added of this paper* is to provide a comprehensive theoretical review of recent trends in the digital transformation of industry, with a special focus on the integration of artificial intelligence. We adopt a bibliometric and thematic analysis approach to identify key research themes, conceptual clusters, and knowledge gaps in the current literature. By analyzing a broad set of most recent and relevant academic publications on "digital transformation" and "AI in industry," we select the dominant topics and highlight how AI is being leveraged across different industrial domains. Diagrams summarizing the results of the bibliographic analysis are presented to support this analysis: a word cloud of frequently occurring terms in relevant paper titles, and two network maps generated via VOSviewer that visualize thematic clusters based on textual data and bibliographic coupling of the vast body of research literature. Through this approach, we discuss how core themes such as Industry 4.0, digital twins, AI-driven process innovation, and supply chain digitalization interconnect, and we examine emerging areas including human-centric Industry 5.0 paradigms. This paper is organized as follows: The next section provides an overview of the relevant academic research literature and conceptual background. We then present the identified thematic clusters of research with in-depth discussion of each cluster. Finally, we discuss the implications of these findings for current trends and future research directions, before concluding with a summary of insights and recommendations.

2 Literature Review

Digital transformation in industry is driven by a confluence of advanced technologies and strategic initiatives aimed at modernizing industrial operations [8–10]. Industry 4.0 serves as the foundational framework for this technological revolution. Introduced in 2011 as a strategic initiative, Industry 4.0 encapsulates the vision of highly automated and interconnected industrial systems [11]. At its core, Industry 4.0 is characterized by the deployment of cyber-physical systems—integrations of computation, networking, and physical processes—enabled by ubiquitous sensor connectivity (the Industrial Internet of Things (IIoT)) and real-time data exchange across the value chain [12].

This paradigm facilitates "smart factories" in which machinery, warehousing systems, and production facilities are digitally linked and can autonomously coordinate and optimize their activities [13]. The goal is to create tailored, versatile manufacturing solutions by leveraging data-driven insights. Key enabling technologies of Industry 4.0 include IoT, cloud computing for scalable data storage and processing, big data analytics, robotics and automation, additive manufacturing (3D printing), and importantly, artificial intelligence and machine learning algorithms to interpret data and drive intelligent decision-making [14–17].

Figure 1 above shows the evolution of the number of publications on digital transformation of industry and AI in industry indicating the gradually rising interest in these topics. It is apparent that the number of publications has increased hundredfold: from merely 2 publications in 2018 to 212 publications in 2024.

A recent systematic literature review found an increasing number of studies leveraging AI-integrated digital twins to tackle diverse industrial problems,

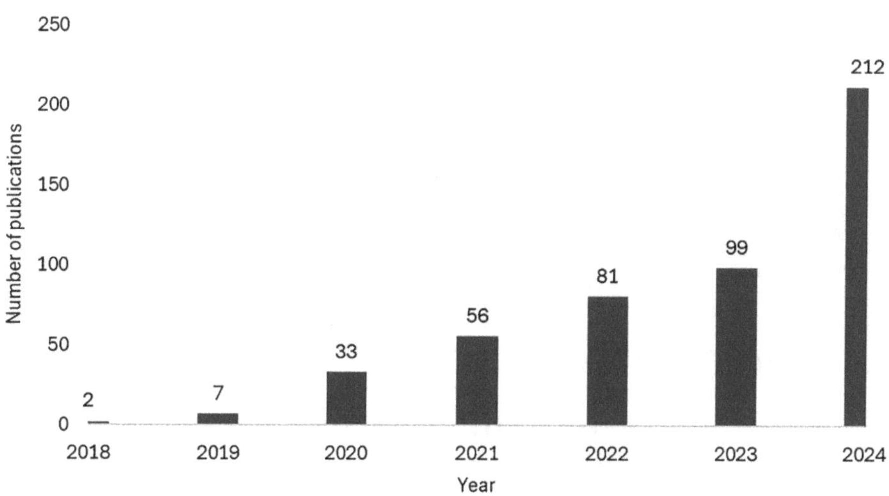

Fig. 1 Evolution of the number of publications on digital transformation of industry and AI in industry

demonstrating applicability across multiple domains [18–20]. It also appears that Industry 5.0 is seen as an evolution that complements Industry 4.0 by focusing on leveraging advanced technologies (including AI) to augment human capabilities rather than replace them, and to ensure production systems align with societal goals for sustainability and worker well-being [21–23].

All the above reflects a growing theme in current research and policy discourse: how to balance the efficiency gains from AI and automation with the need for human oversight, ethical AI use, and sustainable practices [24, 25]. Indeed, ethical considerations, such as data privacy, algorithmic bias, and job impact, have become noticeable and the frameworks for responsible AI deployment in industry are now being discussed alongside technical innovations [26, 27].

In order to synthesize the breadth of literature on these topics, bibliometric analyses can be useful. Researchers employ tools like VOSviewer software package to map the intellectual structure of the field, highlighting major thematic clusters and how they interrelate [28–30].

In this paper, we have collected a large sample of recent publications to perform such an analysis. Figure 2 above provides a high-level overview of the key topics in the literature by visualizing a word cloud of the most frequent words appearing in the titles of 100 relevant academic papers (selected from the Web of Science database) on "digital transformation of industry" and "AI in industry." Larger words in the cloud indicate higher occurrence in titles, thus representing focal points of research.

The size of each word corresponds to its frequency in the paper titles, highlighting prominent topics in the discourse. Notably, terms such as "Industry 4.0", "Artificial Intelligence", "Digital Transformation", and "Smart Manufacturing" appear in large fonts, indicating their centrality to recent research. Other significant terms include "IoT" (Internet of Things), "Digital Twin", "Innovation", "Supply

Fig. 2 WordCloud diagram of the titles of 100 most relevant papers on "digital transformation of industry" and "AI in industry"

Chain", "Management", and "Sustainability", reflecting common themes explored by scholars. This visualization suggests that much of the literature converges on integrating advanced technologies (AI, IoT, digital twin) with strategic transformation objectives (innovation, efficiency, sustainability) in industrial contexts.

3 Methodology

In order to systematically identify the major research themes, we conducted a network analysis of the research literature. Using VOSviewer software, we analyzed two aspects of 550 relevant papers from the Web of Science (WoS) database (2018–2025) that matched the search criteria using the keywords "digital transformation of industry" and "AI in industry".

First, a text analysis of titles and abstracts was performed to find frequently co-occurring terms, which are visualized in a network graph where nodes represent keywords and links indicate co-occurrence in the same documents. Second, we examined the bibliographic coupling among these papers (how papers cite common references or each other), which reveals clusters of papers that form coherent research streams. The whole methodology is presented in Fig. 3 that is depicted above.

4 Results

4.1 Network Map of Key Terms

The resulting maps from the analyses described above and using the methodology presented in the previous section are shown in Figs. 4 and 5 that are shown below. Each cluster has been interpreted and labeled based on the prominent keywords or the thematic focus of the papers in that group.

In Fig. 4, nodes represent terms extracted from titles and abstracts, and node size reflects the frequency of the term. Terms that co-occur frequently in the same publications are grouped into clusters indicated by different colors. Several distinct thematic clusters are evident. For example, one cluster (colored red in the figure) revolves around core Industry 4.0 concepts (e.g., "cyber-physical systems", "IoT", "smart manufacturing"), another cluster (blue) highlights artificial intelligence applications and techniques (e.g., "machine learning", "data analytics", "predictive maintenance"), while another (green) focuses on business and organizational aspects (e.g., "digital strategy", "innovation", "capabilities"). Additional clusters capture themes like supply chain and logistics (e.g., "supply chain management", "optimization", "Blockchain"), sector-specific transformation (terms related to industries like "healthcare", "construction", "finance"), and sustainability (e.g., "sustainable manufacturing", "circular economy"). The term network highlights

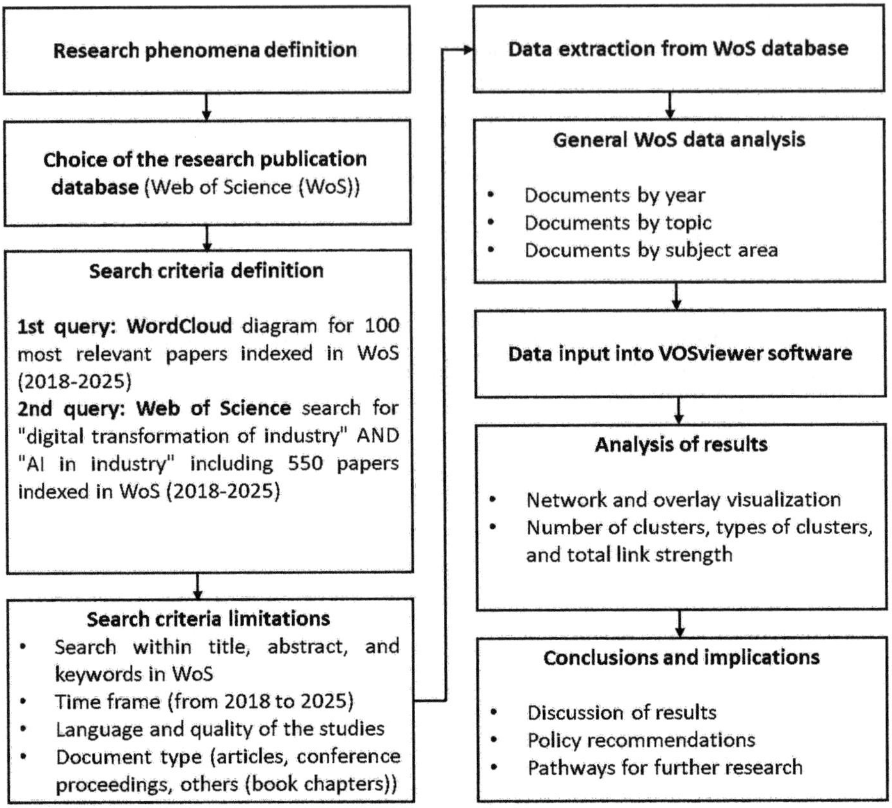

Fig. 3 Research methodology

certain concepts, such as Industry 4.0, AI, and digital strategy, serve as central hubs that connect to many other topics, reflecting their integrative role in the relevant academic literature.

In Fig. 5, each node represents an individual publication, and links indicate the strength of bibliographic coupling (i.e., the extent to which two papers cite a common set of references). Nodes are colored by cluster, and major research streams can be inferred by examining representative papers in each cluster. The clustering largely aligns with the thematic grouping from the text analysis. Notably, one cluster consists of papers establishing frameworks and overviews of Industry 4.0 and digital transformation (often highly cited review articles and conceptual papers). Another cluster contains studies focusing on AI-driven manufacturing and maintenance, including works on digital twins and smart factories. A distinct cluster corresponds to supply chain digital transformation, linking research on AI in logistics, inventory management, and procurement. There is also a cluster oriented towards organizational transformation and business model innovation, comprising

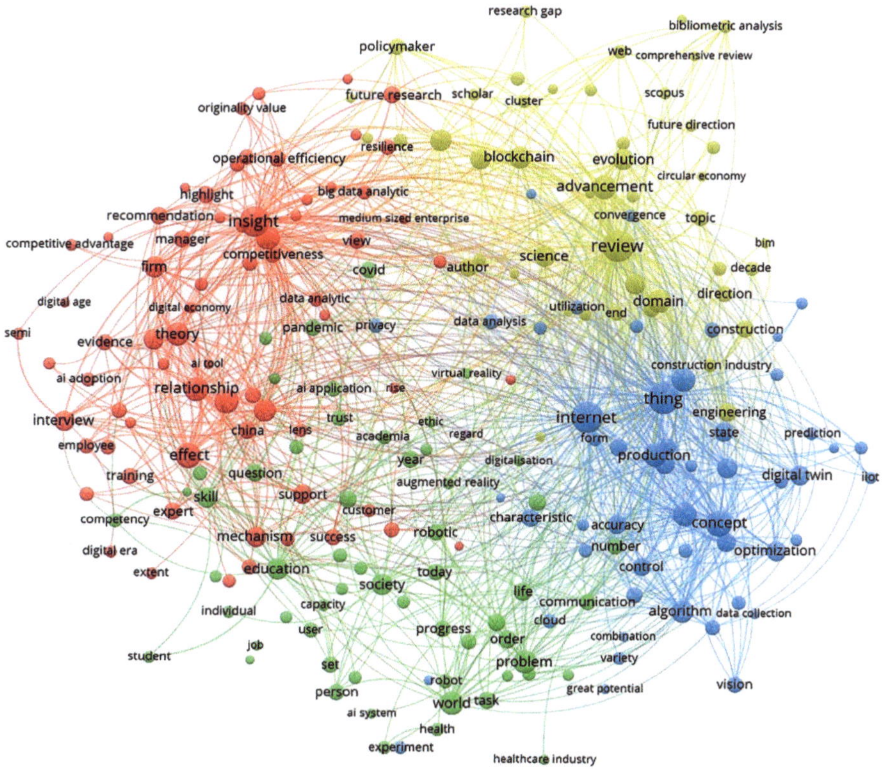

Fig. 4 Network map of key terms from the text data of 550 publications on digital transformation and AI in industry

management studies on strategy, leadership, and competencies required for successful digital transformation. Further clusters highlight research in specific sectors (such as healthcare's digital transformation, fintech applications in finance, or agriculture 4.0), as well as a smaller emerging cluster addressing ethical and societal implications (AI ethics, workforce impact, and sustainability of Industry 4.0 initiatives). The bibliographic network reveals that while the field is interdisciplinary, there are coherent sub-communities of scholars focusing on these topical areas, with relatively dense citation linkages within each cluster. From the combination of these analyses and a qualitative review of representative papers in each cluster, we identify several major thematic areas in the research literature. These thematic clusters and their key characteristics are discussed below.

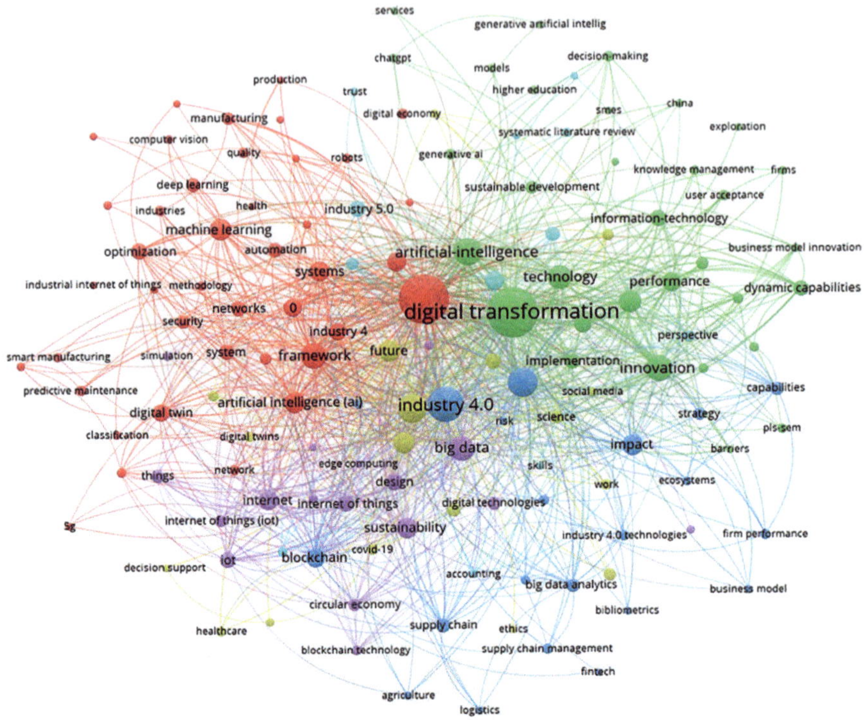

Fig. 5 Bibliographic coupling network of the same 550 publications, illustrating how the literature divides into clusters of closely related studies

4.2 Industry 4.0 Foundations and Enabling Technologies

One prominent cluster of literature centers on the foundational frameworks and technologies of Industry 4.0 itself. These works often provide overarching conceptual models, definitions, and implementation roadmaps for the digital transformation of manufacturing and related industries. Many are broad surveys or structured literature reviews that attempt to synthesize the state of the art. For example, researchers have identified multiple dimensions (technological, organizational, social, etc.) that constitute digital transformation and noted the need to integrate new elements like sustainability into these frameworks.

Studies in this cluster typically discuss the key enabling technologies driving the Fourth Industrial Revolution including IoT, cyber-physical systems, cloud computing, big data, and AI and how their convergence is reshaping industrial systems.

A common theme is the development of readiness and maturity models to assess how prepared organizations are to implement Industry 4.0. Such models break down digital transformation into components (e.g., technology infrastructure, skills, strategy alignment) and provide diagnostic tools for companies. Numerous papers describe case studies or national initiatives aimed at promoting Industry 4.0

adoption, reflecting a global interest in these foundations. Notably, this cluster demonstrates that Industry 4.0 is not viewed as a single technology, but as an ecosystem of interconnected innovations. Authors emphasize the importance of integration—for instance, IoT sensors collecting shop-floor data, which AI algorithms then analyze in cloud platforms, feeding insights back to operators in real time. The cluster's publications often serve as starting points for scholars and practitioners to understand the breadth of digital transformation, the vocabulary of emerging technologies, and reference architectures guiding implementation. By mapping out the landscape of enabling technologies and their interdependence, these studies lay the groundwork for more specialized research in subsequent clusters.

4.3 *Smart Manufacturing and Digital Twin Applications*

Another major cluster covers the application of AI and digital technologies within core manufacturing and operational processes—essentially the realization of "smart factories." Here, topics like intelligent automation, real-time process control, and advanced manufacturing systems are prevalent.

Self-driving vehicles and drones, guided by AI, have also been explored for automating parts of the logistics chain. Another important thread in this cluster is the utilization of blockchain and AI for supply chain transparency and trust—for example, using blockchain to immutably record transactions and AI to detect anomalies or inefficiencies in the chain. The integration of AI is seen to improve not only efficiency but also agility: supply chain AI systems can rapidly re-optimize plans in the face of disruptions (such as sudden supplier failures or transport delays), enhancing resilience. Recent literature in this cluster has also embraced the concept of Supply Chain 4.0 (and even "Industry 5.0" in supply chains), which extends Industry 4.0 principles across the entire value network. Findings consistently show that AI-enabled supply chains yield significant performance improvements; one systematic review concluded that AI integration leads to better demand forecasting, leaner inventory, and superior decision-making capabilities across the supply chain.

These improvements contribute to cost savings and customer service enhancements. However, the cluster also discusses challenges: data silos between supply chain partners, concerns over data privacy/security when sharing information, and the need to upskill logistics personnel to work with AI-driven systems are frequently noted hurdles. Overall, the supply chain cluster underscores that digital transformation is not confined within the factory walls but extends to the coordination of entire ecosystems of production and distribution, with AI acting as a catalyst for a more synchronized and intelligent supply network.

4.4 Strategy, Management, and Business Model Innovation

Beyond the technical domains, a substantial portion of the literature is devoted to the strategic and organizational aspects of digital transformation in industry. This cluster includes research in fields like management, organizational studies, and innovation management, examining how firms plan and execute digital transformation and how it impacts their business models, workforces, and competitive dynamics. There is also literature on organizational structures and processes (e.g., creating cross-functional digital teams, incubating innovation units, and redesigning workflows) that support the integration of AI and digital tools. In summary, this cluster underscores that technology alone does not guarantee transformation; aligning technological capabilities with strategy, reinventing business practices, and effectively managing people and processes are equally crucial. These studies complement the technical research by highlighting the socio-technical nature of digital transformation—success emerges from synchronizing technological change with organizational evolution.

The drive for digital transformation with AI spans across many industrial sectors, and some clusters of research are defined by their sectoral focus. These studies dive into how the general principles of Industry 4.0 and AI adoption manifest in specific contexts such as healthcare, transportation, agriculture, energy, construction, and finance. Although manufacturing is the epicenter of Industry 4.0, other industries have developed their own analogous transformation journeys (sometimes termed with labels like "Healthcare 4.0" or "Construction 4.0"). For example, in healthcare, digital transformation involves AI-driven diagnostics, telemedicine platforms, and smart hospital systems. One can find case studies of hospitals using AI for predictive patient flow management or medical image analysis as part of healthcare's digital evolution. In agriculture (often branded Agriculture 4.0 or smart farming), IoT sensors combined with AI help optimize irrigation, crop monitoring, and yield prediction. The finance sector's transformation, often discussed under fintech, sees AI in algorithmic trading, fraud detection, and personalized financial services, illustrating how even service industries are part of this digital wave. Research focusing on logistics and transportation might examine smart ports or autonomous shipping (maritime 4.0), while energy sector studies look at smart grids and AI for predictive maintenance of utility infrastructure. Each sector brings its unique challenges and priorities: for instance, regulatory compliance is a major theme in healthcare and finance when implementing AI, whereas in construction, the focus might be on integrating AI with Building Information Modeling (BIM) systems for project management. This sector-specific cluster often provides rich detail through case studies and domain-specific frameworks. They reveal that while the fundamental technologies (AI, IoT, cloud, etc.) are similar across sectors, the applications and impact can be very different. Supply chain optimization means one thing in agriculture (managing perishable goods and weather uncertainties) and another in pharmaceuticals (ensuring drug traceability and security). By examining these contexts, the literature underscores that digital transformation is a pervasive phenomenon but not a one-size-fits-all endeavor. Each industry adapts the tools of AI and digitalization to its environment, sometimes even coining new terminology (like "Industry 4.0 for healthcare") to mark the confluence of digital tech and sector practice. These studies collectively broaden the perspective beyond manufacturing, demonstrating how AI-enabled transformation is taking shape in various corners of the economy and providing cross-industry learnings. Notably, they often identify sector-specific benefits—such as improved patient outcomes in healthcare or enhanced sustainability in smart agriculture—alongside general benefits like efficiency and agility.

Emerging from the literature is a cluster that explicitly addresses the human and environmental dimensions of digital transformation—aligning with what is increasingly framed as Industry 5.0. This research stream recognizes that technological advancement must go hand-in-hand with human-centric values and sustainable practices. On the human side, a number of studies explore the impacts of AI and automation on employment, job design, and worker skills. Rather than viewing technology as purely a substitute for labor, these works emphasize human-AI collaboration, seeking ways to augment workers' capabilities with AI tools. Concepts such as the "augmented operator" or "collaborative robotics" appear in this cluster, focusing on how to design systems where humans remain in the loop and benefit from AI assistance (for example, wearable AR devices that guide workers, or AI decision support systems that improve human decision quality). The importance of continuous training and lifelong learning for employees is often stressed, as roles evolve due to digitalization. In fact, some papers in this cluster propose educational frameworks or partnerships to ensure the workforce is prepared for the digital era—a reflection of Industry 5.0's aim to put people at the heart of industrial innovation.

On the sustainability side, this cluster engages with how digital transformation can contribute to or detract from sustainability goals. Industry 4.0 technologies are frequently touted as enablers of more efficient resource use—for instance, AI algorithms optimizing energy consumption in factories, or smart logistics reducing fuel use and emissions through better routing. Several studies provide evidence of environmental performance improvements through such digital interventions. Moreover, the notion of the circular economy is linked in: digital tracking and data analytics can facilitate recycling, remanufacturing, and better product lifecycle management, thereby reducing waste.

Data privacy is another concern, especially when industrial transformation overlaps with handling personal data (like in smart healthcare or customer analytics in service industries). The cluster devoted to these topics is relatively newer and smaller than the technology-focused clusters, but it is growing as companies and regulators alike emphasize responsible innovation. In summary, the human-centric and sustainable transformation cluster broadens the discourse beyond efficiency and profit metrics, urging consideration of worker welfare, societal impacts, and environmental stewardship as core elements of the digital transformation journey. It resonates strongly with the Industry 5.0 vision of technology that empowers workers and is sustainable, and it foreshadows an evolution of research priorities to include these critical dimensions.

4.5 Emerging Frontiers: Generative Ai and Future Technologies

The fast pace of technological advancement means that new tools and paradigms continue to appear on the horizon of industrial digital transformation. A nascent but quickly expanding cluster of recent papers is exploring generative AI and large language models (LLMs) in the context of industry. The release of advanced LLMs (like GPT-3.5 and GPT-4) and generative models (for images, designs, etc.) has prompted questions about their potential uses in manufacturing and enterprise operations. Early studies and thought pieces suggest that generative AI could enhance human-machine interaction on the shop floor—for instance, intelligent chatbots (powered by models like ChatGPT) that can assist engineers and technicians by answering complex questions, retrieving technical documentation, or guiding troubleshooting processes using natural language. This could make expert knowledge more accessible in real time, especially for less experienced staff, thereby flattening the learning curve in industrial settings. Another prospective application is in design and engineering: generative algorithms can help create optimized component designs or suggest innovative solutions by exploring vast design spaces (a process known as generative design). This aids engineers in product development by providing AI-generated design options that meet specified constraints and objectives, accelerating the innovation cycle. Beyond generative AI, this cluster also monitors other frontier technologies that could shape the next wave of industrial transformation. For example, the integration of edge AI computing (deploying AI algorithms on edge devices for real-time control), advancements in 5G/6G communications for ultra-reliable low-latency connections in factories, and the potential of quantum computing for solving complex optimization problems are topics starting to appear in literature. These discussions are largely forward-looking, recognizing that while Industry 4.0 is maturing, continuous innovation is pushing towards new paradigms sometimes referred to as Industry 5.0 and beyond. Industry 5.0, as previously noted, emphasizes human-centric and sustainable use of these technologies, and some authors conjecture about an Industry 6.0 characterized by even deeper integration of artificial and human intelligence and hyper-connected systems.

The emerging frontiers cluster is inherently speculative but important. It indicates the research community's awareness that the landscape of digital transformation is dynamic. As companies begin to experiment with generative AI tools or next-gen technologies in pilot projects, academic studies will follow, documenting benefits and pitfalls. Early indications point to significant interest—for example, industry surveys show a growing number of firms exploring ChatGPT-like systems for knowledge management and process automation tasks. Nevertheless, caution is evident: experts highlight risks such as the accuracy and reliability of generative AI outputs, cybersecurity implications, and the need for new skill sets to effectively use these tools. In capturing these dialogues, this cluster offers a preview of possible future research directions and helps stakeholders prepare for the disruptions and opportunities that emerging AI technologies may soon bring to the industrial domain.

5 Discussion

The analysis presented above illuminates several overarching trends in the digital transformation of industry, as well as revealing gaps and opportunities that chart directions for future research. Figures 4 and 5 collectively show a research landscape that is both broad and segmented. Established topics like Industry 4.0, AI-driven manufacturing, and digital strategy form the core around which much of the literature coalesces. At the same time, newer themes—notably sustainability, human-centric design, and the advent of generative AI—are emerging at the periphery, indicating growing scholarly interest but comparatively fewer studies to date. This suggests that while the foundational aspects of digital transformation (e.g., implementing core technologies and optimizing processes) are well represented in current research, there is still an evolution underway as attention shifts to more holistic and forward-looking concerns. One evident trend is the convergence of formerly distinct disciplines. Traditionally, studies of manufacturing technology and studies of management or strategy were separate silos. However, the cluster analysis (Fig. 2) shows significant linkages between technical terms (like IoT, machine learning, automation) and organizational terms (like innovation, capabilities, strategy). This reflects a recognition that technological innovation in industry cannot be divorced from organizational context. Indeed, recent research increasingly adopts a socio-technical perspective, examining not just how to develop or implement an AI system, but also how it alters workflows, how employees interact with it, and how it creates business value. As a result, one can observe a trend toward integrative frameworks and case studies that involve interdisciplinary collaboration—for example, engineering researchers teaming up with management scholars to study a factory's transformation both in terms of technical performance and change management. Future research is likely to deepen this integration. We can expect more holistic studies that simultaneously address technical efficacy, economic feasibility, and human factors of industrial AI deployments. Another key theme is the identification of success factors and bottlenecks in digital transformation efforts. Relevant research literature has moved beyond simply promoting new technologies to critically evaluating what enables or hinders their adoption. Across multiple clusters (supply chain, smart manufacturing, and strategy), researchers point to common enablers such as top management support, employee training, robust data governance, and incremental implementation approaches. Correspondingly, frequently cited barriers include cybersecurity concerns, lack of interoperability between legacy and new systems, workforce skill gaps, and cultural resistance to change. The prominence of these topics in Fig. 3 clusters (for instance, the cluster on organizational transformation) indicates that understanding the conditions for effective transformation is a priority in current research. This focus will likely persist and strengthen, as companies still report mixed outcomes from their digital initiatives. Future research could provide more quantitative evidence on the impact of certain practices—for example, quantifying the return on investment of training programs or the performance differential between firms that undertake comprehensive process reengineering versus those that layer new technology onto old processes. Implications for industry practice emerging from these trends are significant. The strong interest in AI applications like predictive maintenance, quality control, and supply chain optimization confirms that many companies see immediate value. The literature's findings—such as documented reductions in downtime and inventory via AI–provide an evidence base that practitioners can leverage to make the case for investments in these areas. On the other hand, the growing research on sustainability and human-centric approaches serves as a caution that the next stage of digital transformation will require balancing efficiency goals with broader responsibilities. Industrial firms are increasingly advised, both in literature and in practice, to adopt "responsible AI" and sustainable tech strategies—ensuring that AI deployments are transparent, fair, and aligned with environmental goals. The discussion around Industry 5.0, as seen in our thematic clusters, underscores that companies may gain competitive advantage by proactively addressing worker empowerment and sustainability, rather than treating them as afterthoughts. From an academic perspective, the clustering suggests several future research directions. Firstly, there is a clear opportunity to strengthen the bridge between the technical and managerial domains—for example, developing integrated models that link technical performance metrics (like predictive model accuracy or production throughput) with business metrics (like return on investment, market responsiveness, or employee satisfaction). Such research would help demonstrate more concretely how AI-driven improvements translate (or fail to translate) into business success, thereby addressing a gap in understanding the value realization of digital transformation. Secondly, the relatively smaller clusters related to ethics, workforce, and policy implications point to the need for more scholarship in those areas. As AI systems become more autonomous and pervasive in industry, questions around safety, liability, and ethics (for instance, how to ensure an AI's decision logic in a factory is transparent and does not inadvertently cause harm) will become more pressing.

Researchers can contribute by developing frameworks for ethical AI use in industry and studying the impact of AI on work (e.g., how job roles evolve when certain decisions are automated, and how to design AI systems that complement rather than replace human labor in beneficial ways). Furthermore, the emergence of generative AI and advanced analytics tools opens a new frontier that current literature is only beginning to explore. In the coming years, we anticipate a surge of studies testing these technologies in industrial settings—for example, investigating how chatbots like ChatGPT can serve as on-demand support for engineers and operators, or how generative models might revolutionize product design. Early discussions suggest both high potential and significant challenges, so future research must critically evaluate these tools' practical utility and risks on the factory floor.

Another area for future inquiry is the digital transformation of small and medium-sized enterprises (SMEs) and in developing economies. Much of the current research and many case studies focus on large, advanced manufacturing firms. Extending the knowledge to understand constraints faced by smaller actors (like resource limitations, different skill profiles, or scalability of solutions) will be important for making the digital revolution inclusive across the industrial spectrum. In summary, the current state of research, as visualized and reviewed in this paper, portrays a field that has rapidly progressed in mapping out the technological and managerial blueprint of digital transformation. The discussion highlights that to continue this progress, research must increasingly tackle complex interdisciplinary questions and address emerging challenges. By doing so, scholars can provide insights that ensure the digital transformation of industry not only advances productivity and innovation but also aligns with human values and sustainable development goals.

6 Conclusion

Overall, it appears that digital transformation of industry (powered by AI and similar frontier technologies) has become a multifaceted domain of research and practice. This theoretical review of relevant research literature has outlined how recent literature converges on several dominant themes: the foundational Industry 4.0 frameworks that set the stage for smart factories, the deployment of AI-driven solutions in manufacturing and supply chains that deliver efficiency and agility gains, the imperative of organizational change and business model innovation to truly harness digital technologies, and the rising importance of human-centric and sustainable approaches as we move toward Industry 5.0. Using the thorough analysis of academic literature on the topic, the themes and their interconnections have been depicted and analyzed. The results confirm that topics like Industry 4.0, digital twins, AI-enabled operational excellence, and supply chain optimization are well-established, whereas areas such as ethical AI usage, workforce development, and the integration of cutting-edge AI like generative models are emerging only recently and need further exploration.

All in all, the trajectory of research suggests that the coming years is going to witness a deepening of integration—both in technology (e.g., more seamless integration of AI, IoT, and digital twins in live industrial systems) and in research focus (blending technical, economic, and social analyses). Major key trends have been identified including the widespread adoption of AI for predictive maintenance and decision support, innovations in supply chain digitization, and the push toward embedding sustainability into digital transformation initiatives. Equally, challenges that constitute avenues for future research can be identified. It is important to ensure that digital transformation efforts would result in tangible business value, addressing the human and ethical implications of ubiquitous AI in the workplace, and extending digital benefits beyond early adopters to a wider range of industries and company sizes. In essence, the state of the art in this field reflects both significant progress and ongoing evolution. Industrial enterprises are leveraging AI to become more data-driven, interconnected, and intelligent, fundamentally redefining processes that have existed for decades. Yet, as this study reveals, digital transformation is not a one-time leap but a continuous journey—one that requires balancing technological potential with strategic foresight and societal responsibility. By synthesizing recent contributions, this review would be able to provide scholars and practitioners with a coherent understanding of current knowledge and clear signposts toward the unresolved questions and future directions. The digital transformation of industry, underpinned by AI, would undoubtedly remain a vibrant and critical area of inquiry as industries worldwide attempt to innovate and evolve in the face of rapid technological changes and innovations.

References

1. Omol, E. J. (2024). Organizational digital transformation: From evolution to future trends. *Digital Transformation and Society, 3*(3), 240–256. https://doi.org/10.1108/DTS-08-2023-0061
2. Kraus, S., Jones, P., Kailer, N., Weinmann, A., Chaparro-Banegas, N., & Roig-Tierno, N. (2021). Digital transformation: An overview of the current state of the art of research. *SAGE Open, 11*(3), 21582440211047576. https://doi.org/10.1177/21582440211047576
3. Gao, P., Wu, W., & Yang, Y. (2022). Discovering themes and trends in digital transformation and innovation research. *Journal of Theoretical and Applied Electronic Commerce Research, 17*(3), 1162–1184. https://doi.org/10.3390/jtaer17030059
4. Aldoseri, A., Al-Khalifa, K. N., & Hamouda, A. M. (2024). AI-powered innovation in digital transformation: Key pillars and industry impact. *Sustainability, 16*(5), 1790. https://doi.org/10.3390/su16051790
5. Brauner, P., Dalibor, M., Jarke, M., Kunze, I., Koren, I., Lakemeyer, G., & Ziefle, M. (2022). A computer science perspective on digital transformation in production. *ACM Transactions on Internet of Things, 3*(2), 1–32. https://doi.org/10.1145/3502265
6. Strielkowski, W., Samoilikova, A., Smutka, L., Civín, L., & Lieonov, S. (2022). Dominant trends in intersectoral research on funding innovation in business companies: A bibliometric analysis approach. *Journal of Innovation & Knowledge, 7*(4), 100271. https://doi.org/10.1016/j.jik.2022.100271
7. Hallinger, P. (2021). A meta-synthesis of bibliometric reviews of research on managing for sustainability, 1982–2019. *Sustainability, 13*(6), 3469. https://doi.org/10.3390/su13063469
8. Tolstykh, T., Shmeleva, N., Boev, A., Guseva, T., & Panova, S. (2024). System approach to the process of institutional transformation for industrial integrations in the digital era. *Systems, 12*(4), 120. https://doi.org/10.3390/systems12040120
9. Vrana, J., & Singh, R. (2023). Modeling digital penetration of the industrialized society and its ensuing transfiguration. *Digital Society, 2*(3), 54. https://doi.org/10.1007/s44206-023-00084-w
10. Lisin, E., & Strielkowski, W. (2014). Modelling new economic approaches for the wholesale energy markets in Russia and the EU. *Transformations in Business & Economics, 13*(2B), 566–580.
11. Dabic-Miletic, S. (2023). Advanced technologies in smart factories: A cornerstone of industry 4.0. *Journal of Industrial Intelligence, 1*(3), 148–157. https://doi.org/10.56578/jii010302
12. Kebande, V. R. (2022). Industrial internet of things (IIoT) forensics: The forgotten concept in the race towards industry 4.0. *Forensic Science International: Reports, 5*, 100257. https://doi.org/10.1016/j.fsir.2022.100257

13. Soori, M., Arezoo, B., & Dastres, R. (2023). Internet of things for smart factories in industry 4.0, a review. *Internet of Things and Cyber-Physical Systems, 3*, 192–204. https://doi.org/10.1016/j.iotcps.2023.04.006
14. Nica, E., & Stehel, V. (2021). Internet of things sensing networks, artificial intelligence-based decision-making algorithms, and real-time process monitoring in sustainable industry 4.0. *Journal of Self-governance and Management Economics, 9*(3), 35–47. https://doi.org/10.22381/jsme9320213
15. Haghnegahdar, L., Joshi, S. S., & Dahotre, N. B. (2022). From IoT-based cloud manufacturing approach to intelligent additive manufacturing: Industrial internet of things—An overview. *The International Journal of Advanced Manufacturing Technology, 119*(3), 1461–1478. https://doi.org/10.1007/s00170-021-08436-x
16. Bousdekis, A., Lepenioti, K., Apostolou, D., & Mentzas, G. (2021). A review of data-driven decision-making methods for industry 4.0 maintenance applications. *Electronics, 10*(7), 828. https://doi.org/10.3390/electronics10070828
17. Soni, G., Kumar, S., Mahto, R. V., Mangla, S. K., Mittal, M. L., & Lim, W. M. (2022). A decision-making framework for industry 4.0 technology implementation: The case of FinTech and sustainable supply chain finance for SMEs. *Technological Forecasting and Social Change, 180*, 121686. https://doi.org/10.1016/j.techfore.2022.121686
18. Huang, Z., Shen, Y., Li, J., Fey, M., & Brecher, C. (2021). A survey on AI-driven digital twins in industry 4.0: Smart manufacturing and advanced robotics. *Sensors, 21*(19), 6340. https://doi.org/10.3390/s21196340
19. Miller, T., Durlik, I., Łobodzińska, A., Dorobczyński, L., & Jasionowski, R. (2024). AI in context: Harnessing domain knowledge for smarter machine learning. *Applied Sciences, 14*(24), 11612. https://doi.org/10.3390/app142411612
20. Strielkowski, W., Rausser, G., & Kuzmin, E. (2022). Digital revolution in the energy sector: Effects of using digital twin technology. In V. Kumar, J. Leng, V. Akberdina, & E. Kuzmin (Eds.), *Digital transformation in industry. Lecture notes in information systems and organisation* (Vol. 54). Springer. https://doi.org/10.1007/978-3-030-94617-3_4
21. Alojaiman, B. (2023). Technological modernizations in the industry 5.0 era: A descriptive analysis and future research directions. *PRO, 11*(5), 1318. https://doi.org/10.3390/pr11051318
22. Horvat, D., Jäger, A., & Lerch, C. M. (2025). Fostering innovation by complementing human competences and emerging technologies: An industry 5.0 perspective. *International Journal of Production Research, 63*(3), 1126–1149. https://doi.org/10.1080/00207543.2024.2372009
23. Kovari, A. (2024). Industry 5.0: Generalized definition key applications opportunities and threats. *Acta Polytechnica Hungarica, 21*(3), 267–284. https://doi.org/10.12700/APH.21.3.2024.3.17
24. Akinrinola, O., Okoye, C. C., Ofodile, O. C., & Ugochukwu, C. E. (2024). Navigating and reviewing ethical dilemmas in AI development: Strategies for transparency, fairness, and accountability. *GSC Advanced Research and Reviews, 18*(3), 050–058. https://doi.org/10.30574/gscarr.2024.18.3.0088
25. Qudus, L. (2025). Leveraging artificial intelligence to enhance process control and improve efficiency in manufacturing industries. *International Journal of Computer Applications Technology and Research, 14*(2), 18–38.
26. Anagnostou, M., Karvounidou, O., Katritzidaki, C., Kechagia, C., Melidou, K., Mpeza, E., & Peristeras, V. (2022). Characteristics and challenges in the industries towards responsible AI: A systematic literature review. *Ethics and Information Technology, 24*(3), 37. https://doi.org/10.1007/s10676-022-09634-1
27. Radanliev, P., Santos, O., Brandon-Jones, A., & Joinson, A. (2024). Ethics and responsible AI deployment. *Frontiers in Artificial Intelligence, 7*, 1377011. https://doi.org/10.3389/frai.2024.1377011

28. Marchiori, D. M., Popadiuk, S., Mainardes, E. W., & Rodrigues, R. G. (2021). Innovativeness: A bibliometric vision of the conceptual and intellectual structures and the past and future research directions. *Scientometrics, 126*, 55–92. https://doi.org/10.1007/s11192-020-03753-6
29. Alkathiri, N. A., Said, F. B., Meyer, N., & Soliman, M. (2024). Knowledge management and sustainable entrepreneurship: A bibliometric overview and research agenda. *Journal of Innovation and Entrepreneurship, 13*(1), 38. https://doi.org/10.1186/s13731-024-00387-3
30. Klarin, A. (2024). How to conduct a bibliometric content analysis: Guidelines and contributions of content co-occurrence or co-word literature reviews. *International Journal of Consumer Studies, 48*(2), e13031. https://doi.org/10.1111/ijcs.13031

Business and Artificial Intelligence: To Trust or Not to Trust

Natalia A. Kosolapova, Daria S. Laskova, Anastasia Y. Nikitaeva, and Tatiana S. Laskova

Abstract The study shows that the implementation of Industry 4.0 requires achieving a sufficient level of trust in intelligent technologies. The article analyzes scientific papers devoted to the issue of trust in artificial intelligence (AI). With this in mind, a questionnaire was developed to survey business entities on the use of intelligent technologies in their activities. The purpose was to determine the level of business trust in intelligent technologies, taking into account the practice of their application. The sample of respondents, whose opinion revealed the factors influencing the decision on the use of intelligent technologies and the choice of intelligent technologies used by organizations in Rostov region (Russia), amounted to 132 people. In addition to the traditional frequency analysis of data, methods of analyzing conjugacy tables were used. An analysis of the responses on the AI use frequency revealed their relationship with the scale of the company. Most of the answers about the extremely rare use or non-use of such technologies belong to representatives of medium-sized businesses. Large companies are ready to entrust artificial intelligence with a wider range of tasks. According to respondents, it is necessary to use AI to automate internal and external processes, including interaction and customer service. The majority of respondents are ready to entrust the search for new ideas and the solution of creative tasks to intelligent technologies. There is a convergence of opinions among respondents about barriers to the introduction of intelligent technologies. Such barriers include high cost, insufficient staff competence, as well as a lack of information about AI capabilities in various fields. The significance of the obtained results lies in the fact that understanding businesses' attitudes towards intelligent technologies enables a deeper comprehension of the potential and effective pathways for utilizing artificial intelligence within organizations.

Keywords Artificial intelligence · Industry 4.0 · Trust · Decision-making factors

N. A. Kosolapova · D. S. Laskova (✉) · A. Y. Nikitaeva · T. S. Laskova
Southern Federal University, Rostov-on-Don, Russia
e-mail: nakosolapova@sfedu.ru; laskova@sfedu.ru; aunikitaeva@sfedu.ru; tslaskova@sfedu.ru

F. Tao et al. (eds.), *Artificial Intelligence and Digital Transformation*, Lecture Notes in Information Systems and Organisation 78,
https://doi.org/10.1007/978-3-032-00118-4_3

1 Introduction

In the modern world, trust is a factor determining the success of digital transformations, technological innovations, and economic development in the imperatives of Industry 4.0. This statement is supported by a number of arguments. First of all, research shows that trust is a pro-cyclical factor of economic growth and is directly correlated with economic dynamics [1, 2].

Trust is currently assigned a central role in economic development [3], although achieving this status for this concept required a serious evolution [1, 4, 5]. Trust has a positive impact on economic development both directly (through a positive impact on innovation, reduction of transaction costs, faster achievement of economic convergence, reduction of risks of opportunistic behavior, etc.) [6, 7] and indirectly (for example, through a positive input into human development) [8, 9].

At the same time, different studies conducted at different times for various countries demonstrate the different nature of the influence of trust on economic development. Thus, Safina [10] notes that in 2010–2013 in Russia there was a moderate dependence between trust and GDP per capita, which did not allow the researcher to establish a direct causal relationship and a direct impact of the level of trust on economic growth. Conversely, Coyle and Lu [11] found that trust has a significant positive relationship with the growth of aggregate factor productivity in a sample of 23 European countries over the period 2000–2016. This is especially important in the context of a slowdown in economic growth for these regions. In any event, scholars concur that trust has a major influence on economic progress.

Accordingly, a sufficiently high level of trust is necessary to ensure the technological transition and practical implementation of Industry 4.0 as a key modern vector of economic development. In this context, it should be noted that the spread of the Fourth Industrial Revolution directly corresponds to the use of cutting-edge digital technologies (Artificial Intelligence, Big data, the Internet of Things, blockchain, mobile technologies, etc.). That is, trust in Industry 4.0 can be interpreted through trust in digital technologies.

Artificial intelligence (and a whole stack of intelligent technologies or their various combinations) occupies a special place in the list of digital technologies. In this study, we are talking, first of all, about weak artificial intelligence, which has become widespread in the economic activities of enterprises and organizations and allows solving a whole range of organizational tasks [12]. Fosso-Wamba and Guthrie [13] note that artificial intelligence (AI) is an important factor in the Fourth Industrial Revolution, as it is able to expand the capabilities of intelligent production systems, which are central to this industrial revolution. In turn, Alenizi et al. [14] point out that Industry 4.0 is transforming the manufacturing sector by creating dynamic, networked, and complex industrial environments. These environments generate huge amounts of data. In this regard, AI technologies are required to ensure intelligent, efficient, and sustainable production processes in new environments with large amounts of data to be processed.

Artificial intelligence is gradually opening up new opportunities to create additional functionality, new functions, and trends in the industrial landscape in line with the Industry 4.0 paradigm. In the industry, AI specializes in the development, validation, and implementation of various intelligent algorithms for industrial applications with sustainable performance [15]. Wang et al. [16] connect AI with the revolutionary transformations of the economy. Similarly, Uctu et al. [17] emphasize that AI is a key factor in the nascent sixth wave of technological progress, which has profound economic consequences.

According to scientists, the emergence of artificial intelligence has caused major disruptions in a variety of fields, the reorganization of already-existing companies and industries, and the demise of conventional business methods. This transformative force is consistent with Schumpeter's [17] theory of creative destruction, according to which innovations lead to the obsolescence of old technologies and business models, resulting in significant economic shifts. Jan et al. [18] also believed that artificial intelligence technologies, combined with huge amounts of data collected using modern digital technologies, are becoming one of the cornerstones of cyber-physical systems underlying Industry 4.0. In the economy, AI provides advantages in terms of reducing energy consumption, increasing economic efficiency, reducing operational risks, and increasing productivity [19].

Significant financial resources, technological advancements, staff skills, and management systems are needed for the development, advancement, and adoption of artificial intelligence in order to create and execute new business models. It should be mentioned that business entities and decision-makers have the final say and the resources when it comes to innovations, investments, and management techniques. However, in practice, the level of realization of such opportunities depends on the extent to which business entities trust intelligent technologies and artificial intelligence directly.

The issue of trust in digital and, more specifically, intelligent technologies and artificial intelligence has been the focus of researchers' attention in recent years. Capestro et al. [20] suggested considering the theory of diffusion of innovations, the concept of "technology-organization-environment," the model of technology adoption, and the theory of planned behavior as theoretical foundations for the adoption of digital technologies by companies and the implementation of technological innovations (with a focus on the factors motivating appropriate behavior). At the same time, researchers distinguish cognitive trust and emotional trust in accordance with the McAllister scale [21]. The cognitive dimension of trust is based on rational judgments about partners [22], while the affective dimension is based on the emotional side of the relationship [23]. Scientists also note that in order to obtain deeper results of empirical analysis, it is necessary to take into account the specific context and focus of the study. Thus, Capestro et al. [20] demonstrated the predominant role of cognitive trust, rather than emotional trust, in facilitating effective knowledge exchange within the framework of inter-firm relations in industrial districts (using a structural equation model).

A large-scale study of a wide range of issues of trust in artificial intelligence was conducted by Gillespie et al. [24]. The results of this study showed that in different countries, three out of five people (61%) are wary of trust in artificial intelligence systems, reporting either an ambivalent attitude or an unwillingness to trust. It is noteworthy that people in countries with large developing economies—Brazil, India, China, and South Africa—have the highest level of trust, and most people trust artificial intelligence systems [24, p. 3]. According to these studies, an ambivalent attitude towards trust in artificial intelligence is associated with an assessment of the ratio of positive effects and risks from the use of AI. Most people (85%) believe that artificial intelligence brings a number of advantages, and the advantages of "processes" (increased efficiency, innovation, efficiency, resource use, and cost reduction) exceed the advantages of "people" (associated with improving the decision-making process and end results for people). However, on average, only one in two people believes that the benefits of artificial intelligence outweigh the risks [24, p. 3]. Separately, the result of this study should be emphasized, according to which trust strongly influences the acceptance of AI and, therefore, is crucial for the sustainable acceptance and support of AI in society [24, p. 6]. Similarly, Sutrop [25] emphasizes the role of trust as the cornerstone of the adoption of artificial intelligence.

This is consistent with the results of other studies, according to which trust is an important factor determining the willingness to implement various artificial intelligence systems (from product recommendation agents to banking services with artificial intelligence support), but we are only at an early stage of understanding the prerequisites for trust in artificial intelligence systems [26]. Five primary issues with AI trust have been highlighted by scientists based on the literature [26]: (1) explainability and transparency, (2) accuracy and reliability, (3) automation, (4) anthropomorphism, and (5) mass data extraction.

Li et al. [27] consider trustworthy AI as an AI that is legitimate, ethical and reliable in several changes (interpersonal trust, trust in automation, human trust in artificial intelligence) from the theoretical positions of social cognition. The authors divide the factors influencing trust in AI into three categories: human-related, AI-related, and context-related. They note the significant influence of social, organizational, and institutional factors on the formation of AI perception in the interactive context of trust. A similar allocation of AI confidence factors is observed in Kaplan et al. [28]

A comprehensive, theoretically solid methodological framework for the study of trust in artificial intelligence is developed by Lukyanenko, Maass and Storey [29] (Foundational Trust Framework). The concept proposed by these authors considers trust in AI as a problem of interaction between systems and applies systems thinking and general systems theory to trust in AI. Human trust in AI is understood as a mental and physiological process that takes into account the properties of a specific AI-based system, a class of such systems, or other systems in which it is embedded or with which it interacts, to control the degree and parameters of interaction with these systems.

It can be concluded that the recognition of the decisive role of trust in the adoption and use of artificial intelligence in the field of theoretical research requires empirical verification of the level of trust in relevant technologies in specific spatial and temporal conditions. With this in mind, the purpose of this study is to determine the level of business trust in intelligent technologies, taking into account the practice of their application.

With this in mind, the subsequent structure of the article is organized as follows. The second section outlines the research methodology, including the methods of data collection, processing, verification, and analysis, as well as the characteristics of the sample population. The third section presents the key findings of the study, focusing on the practical application of and issues related to trust in intelligent technologies. The fourth section provides the main conclusions and recommendations.

2 Materials and Methods

The research is based on a logical transition from the content analysis of scientific papers to the development and conduct of a questionnaire survey of business entities on issues of trust in intelligent technologies.

The purpose of the survey was to identify the intelligent technologies used by regional businesses, as well as to assess the degree of trust in them and willingness to entrust AI with solving certain business tasks. Based on the authors' vision of the research construct formed by the results of literary review, a questionnaire was developed using the Google Forms tool to conduct an online survey of the management of companies, enterprises, and organizations of the Rostov region (Russia). This region was chosen to fix specific spatial and temporal conditions since a national project has been adopted and implemented in Russia for the development of artificial intelligence, but the regions of the country are characterized by a high level of differentiation. The questionnaire included 21 questions grouped into three sections. The first part of the questions with the form of a discrete answer belongs to the category of identification questions that characterize the company's field of activity, career position and the respondents' age. Based on the research of the authors highlighting cognitive and emotional trust [21–23], the questionnaire was divided into two substantive parts. The first part focuses on examining the cognitive aspect of trust, which is rooted in the practices and objectives of using intelligent technologies. The second part is dedicated to exploring the emotional dimension of trust. Given that the ambivalent attitude towards trust in artificial intelligence is linked to the assessment of the balance between positive effects and risks [24], the questionnaire incorporates questions related to evaluating both the risks and benefits of AI adoption. Additionally, considering the significant influence of social, organizational, and institutional factors on shaping perceptions of AI [27], questions addressing these factors were included to identify the prerequisites and barriers to AI implementation. Since the research adopts a novel perspective, the structure of the questionnaire, as well as the types and content of the questions, were developed by the authors. Thus, the second set of questions with discrete and textual answers (80%) related to the use of intelligent technologies. The questions in this part are aimed at identifying the list of AI technologies (AIT) specific to a particular field of activity, the frequency of their application, and the range of tasks that the company trusts artificial intelligence to solve. The third section of the questionnaire included questions with the possibility of ranking answers that directly related to the degree of respondents' trust in intelligent technologies and barriers preventing their implementation. The questionnaire is designed in a way to clarify the focus of regional business on a certain class of intelligent technologies, identify factors influencing the choice of AIT, and determine limitations and barriers to the use of intelligent technologies.

Data processing included editing and encoding of information, as some of the questions involved textual answers. The responses were measured in nominal and ordinal scales, and therefore, in some cases, scale reduction was required to assess the relationship. In addition to the traditional frequency analysis of data, methods of analyzing conjugacy tables were also used.

The questionnaire developed during the study aimed at identifying the level of confidence in artificial intelligence of decision-makers was sent to management representatives of more than 200 organizations operating in the Rostov region. The contact details of the companies were selected from the publicly available directory of organizations in the Rostov region by mechanical random selection based on a ranking by type of economic activity presumably interacting with AI. This may be a limitation of the study due to the heterogeneity of the sample without considering industry specifics. However, we will consider this circumstance as an assumption of bias, since the purpose of the study is to identify all possible opinions about AI trust. Another limitation is the inability to cover all organizations in the region. And the 20-unit step for randomly selecting the general population of the study is taken from standard rationing considerations and is not so significant. The survey period covered 3 weeks in November, 2024.

In the questionnaire, the term "artificial intelligence" was replaced by intelligent technologies, since the category of artificial intelligence is still controversial in its interpretation. The sample of respondents, whose opinion revealed the factors influencing the decision on the use of intelligent technologies and the choice of intelligent technologies used by organizations, amounted to 132 people. The resulting sample fits perfectly into the required sample size with a total population of 200 units and confidence probabilities and errors of 95% and 5%, respectively. The sample can be considered representative according to the calculations of the confidence interval without considering the general population. With the standard confidence probability, the size of the confidence interval is ±2.39%. That is, when conducting 100 studies with such a sample (132 supervisors), in 95% of cases, the answers received according to the laws of statistics will be within ±2.39% of the initial ones. Their distribution by age, career position in the company, its scale, and field of activity is shown in Table 1.

Table 1 Identification characteristics of the sample

Parameter	Criterion	Meaning
Age	27–35 years	18.2% (24)
	36–44 years	57.6% (76)
	45–50 years	22.7% (30)
	Over 50 years	1.5% (2)
Position in the organization	Owner	6.1% (8)
	Top manager	27.3% (36)
	Middle manager	34.8% (46)
	Line manager	31.8% (42)
The organization's field of activity	Production	13.7% (18)
	Service sector	19.7% (26)
	Construction	9.1% (12)
	Finance	3.0% (4)
	State and municipal administration	4.5% (6)
	Education and science	16.7% (22)
	Healthcare	4.5% (6)
	Culture	1.5% (2)
	Mass media	4.5% (6)
	Agriculture	4.5% (6)
	IT sector	6.2% (8)
	Transport	1.5% (2)
	Production of utility resources	10.6% (14)
The scale of the organization's activities	Small	21.2% (28)
	Medium	42.4% (56)
	Large	36.4% (48)

3 Results

The majority of respondents (92.4%) noted a certain level of influence of digital technologies on the companies' activities, and only 7.6% chose the answer "Has absolutely no impact." More than half of the respondents, 63.6%, note the great impact of digital transformation on the companies' activities. It was not possible to identify the correlation of the scale of the company or its field of activity with the degree of influence of digital transformation. Answers about the enormous impact were found among respondents from various career positions representing companies of different scales and fields of activity; however, more than half of such answers belong to representatives of large businesses related to the service sector (Table 2).

Analysis of answers about the frequency of AI use revealed their relationship with the scale of the company. Most of the answers about the extremely rare use or non-use of such technologies belong to representatives of medium-sized businesses.

The question of the frequency of using intelligent technologies to solve business problems of varying degrees of complexity allowed us to divide the answers into two categories and, according to respondents with extensive experience in using AI, identify preferences in technologies, and for respondents who do not use technologies or use them extremely rarely, assess the degree of readiness to use them.

At the moment, virtual agents, chatbots, and devices with an intelligent assistant are especially popular in the activities of eighty-two organizations that often use intelligent technologies (Fig. 1).

Table 2 Distribution of respondents' answers on the degree of influence and frequency of use of intelligent technologies

Parameter	Criterion	Meaning
The degree of influence of digital transformation on the organization	1 (has absolutely no effect)	7.6% (10)
	2	1.5% (2)
	3	13.6% (18)
	4	13.6% (18)
	5	21.2% (28)
	6	19.7% (26)
	7 (has a tremendous impact)	22.7% (30)
The frequency of application of intelligent technologies	Every day	36.4% (48)
	Several times a week	18.2% (24)
	Several times a month	7.6% (10)
	Several times every 6 months/year	10.6% (14)
	Not used	27.3% (36)

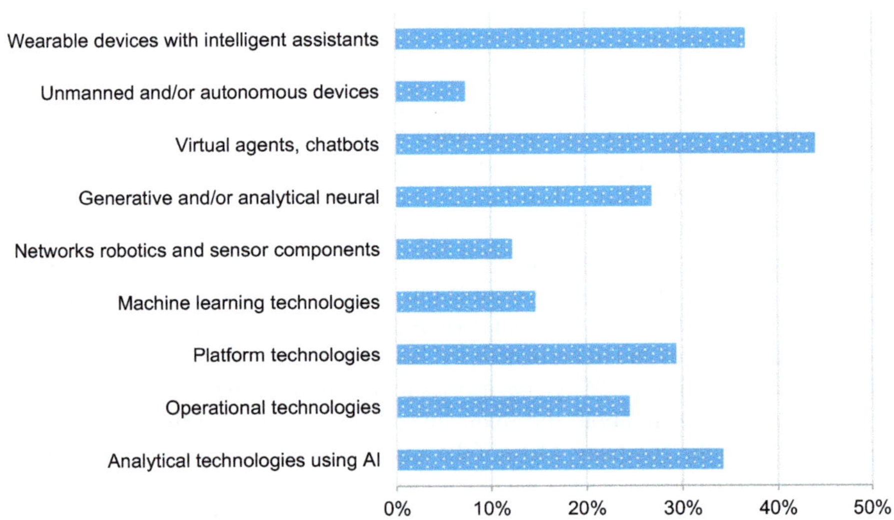

Fig. 1 Preferences in the use of intelligent technologies

At the same time, for organizations that rarely or never use artificial intelligence (50 organizations), the level of internal readiness to use intelligent technologies is very high (Fig. 2).

The goals of using intelligent technologies in organizations are extremely diverse. The most popular area of AI use is business process automation and customer interaction, and more than a third of respondents apply AI for pattern recognition. Automation of business processes and customer interaction is typical for large companies that use technology daily or several times a week. The use of artificial intelligence to generate new ideas is typical for representatives of small businesses in the field of education. The unpopular answer was the use of intelligent technologies for personnel training; such an answer was chosen by representatives of large companies in the manufacturing sector, which, as a rule, is characterized by the presence of virtual simulators (Table 3).

The most popular answer about the tasks that can be entrusted to intelligent technologies was the search for ideas. Moreover, respondents are ready to entrust creative tasks to artificial intelligence, regardless of the type of activity, scale, and scope of the company's activities. It is extremely rare that intelligent technologies are entrusted with the task of evaluating people's decisions. At the same time, almost all respondents noted the need for experts to assess the solutions offered by AI (Fig. 3).

None of the respondents is ready to fully entrust business security to artificial intelligence. The analysis of the answers to the question of respondents' trust in security systems embedded in intelligent technologies did not reach the highest value in any questionnaire (Fig. 4).

Those who expressed their willingness to increase the volume of work tasks delegated to intelligent technologies are interested in using the capabilities of these

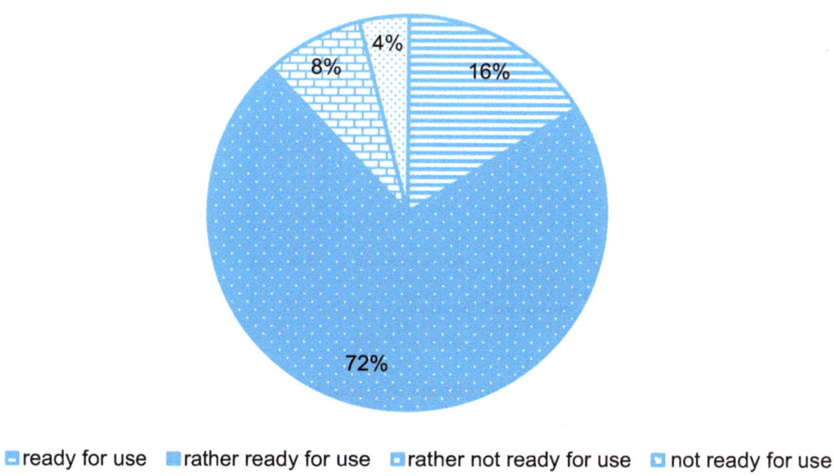

Fig. 2 The level of readiness for the use of intelligent technologies

Table 3 Distribution of responses by purpose of use AI technologies

Purpose of using intelligent technologies	% of answers
Automation of internal and external processes, including customer interaction and customer service	53.7
Text, speech, and image recognition	34.1
Decision-making support to improve the efficiency of management activities	29.3
To protect data, increase information security and reduce the risks of cyber attacks	29.3
To collect and analyze marketing data	26.8
Creation/generation of new ideas and transformation of existing products	24.4
Using virtual assistants to increase customer satisfaction and speed of response to their requests	24.4
For the purposes of analytics in a broad sense	19.5
Product lifecycle management and reduction of time to market	17.1
Optimization of business processes, including through intelligent analysis of sensory data using the industrial internet of things	17.1
Expert systems application to simulate and solve complex problems	14.6
Development and implementation of promotion programs and interaction with consumers	14.6
Optimization and distribution of supply chains	9.8
Complementing existing production practices with network capabilities	9.8
Development and implementation of effective predictive solutions	7.3
Applying digital twins for effective modeling	4.9
Use for electronic and distance learning of personnel	2.4

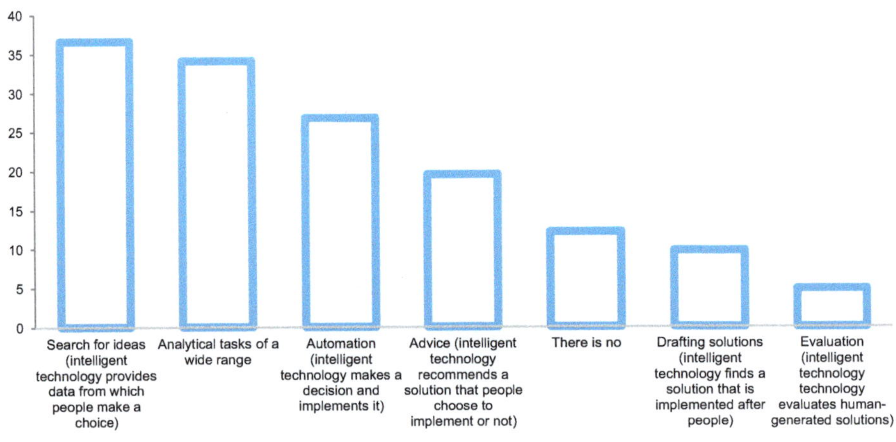

Fig. 3 Tasks that respondents are ready to entrust to intelligent technologies, %

technologies in the "processes" element of the organization's business model (Fig. 5).

The distribution of goals for which intelligent technologies embedded in the business model of an organization would be used for companies that are just starting to implement intelligent technologies practically does not differ from the responses

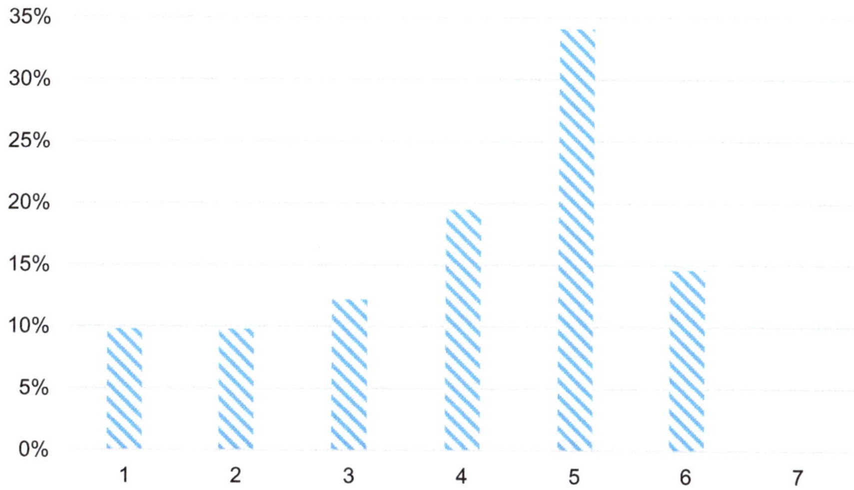

Fig. 4 Distribution of trust ratings for intelligent technology security systems

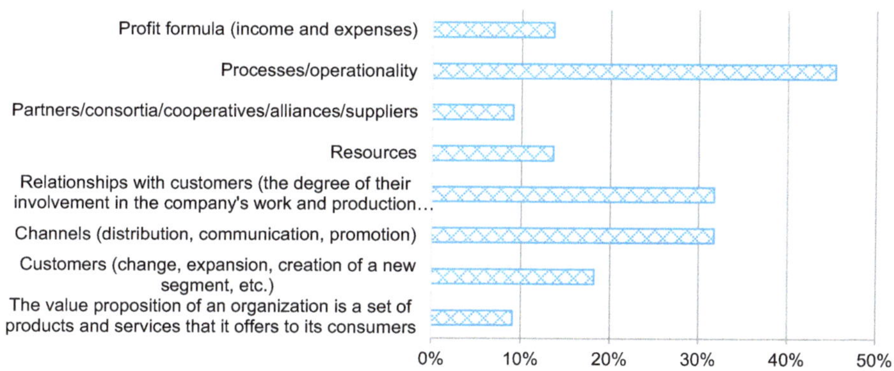

Fig. 5 Distribution of responses about the elements of the business model in which companies are willing to delegate the work of AI

of organizations that often use AI capabilities. New companies are also characterized by answers regarding the automation of internal and external processes, including customer interaction and customer service (Table 4).

Those who are not ready to use intelligent technologies more often or at all in the organization's activities note several barriers. The most popular responses were lack of information, insufficient staff competence, and the high cost of implementing systems, but non-compliance with the security policy of any technology is not considered a problem. The answer to this question showed the agreement between the majority of respondents (Fig. 6).

Table 4 Distribution of responses by the purpose of using technologies of respondents-representatives of companies starting to implement AI

Purpose of using intelligent technologies	%
Automation of internal and external processes, including customer interaction and customer service	45.5
Text, speech, and image recognition	40.9
Decision-making support to improve the efficiency of management activities	36.4
To protect data, increase information security and reduce the risks of cyber attacks	36.4
Using virtual assistants to increase customer satisfaction and speed of response to their requests	27.3
Development and implementation of promotion programs and interaction with consumers	22.7
Expert systems application to simulate and solve complex problems	18.2
For the purposes of analytics in a broad sense	18.2
Product lifecycle management and reduction of time to market	13.6
Complementing existing production practices with network capabilities	13.6
Optimization of business processes, including through intelligent analysis of sensory data using the industrial internet of things	13.6
Development and implementation of effective predictive solutions	13.6
To collect and analyze marketing data	13.6
Optimization and distribution of supply chains	9.1
Applying digital twins for effective modeling	9.1
Creation/generation of new ideas and transformation of existing products	4.5

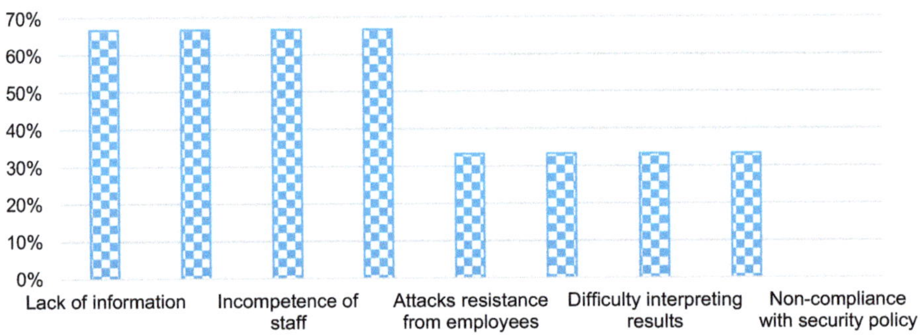

Fig. 6 Barriers to the use of intelligent technologies

Respondents' opinions on what influences the decision-making on the use of intelligent technologies in the organization are similar, regardless of whether these technologies are used often or not, but new companies are characterized by greater attention to employee competencies (Table 5).

Table 5 Distribution of responses on the degree of influence of factors on decision-making on the use of intelligent technologies

Factors influencing the decision on the use of intelligent technologies in the activities of a company/enterprise/organization	A group of respondents whose organizations	
	Often use intelligent technologies (%)	Rarely use/do not use intelligent technologies (%)
Appropriate employee competencies	65.9	100.0
Availability of resources	63.4	66.7
Ability of technology to effectively solve current problems	56.1	66.7
Trust in technology	36.6	33.3
Organizational culture	36.6	33.3
Availability of complementary technologies that do not contradict the existing ones	22.0	33.3

4 Conclusion

The presence of trust in intelligent technologies confirms the bias of respondents' responses towards the high impact of digital technologies on the activities of companies of various scales and fields of activity and does not depend on the age and career position of the respondent. The analysis of the responses on the frequency of AI use revealed their relationship with the company scale. Most answers about the extremely rare use or non-use of such technologies belong to representatives of medium-sized businesses. Large companies that have already implemented such technologies are ready to entrust artificial intelligence with a wider range of tasks. It should be noted that the opinions of representatives of these companies and those beginning to implement AI coincide with the elements of the business model that primarily need the use of intelligent technologies. There are also no significant differences in the purpose of using intelligent technologies. First of all, according to respondents, it is necessary to use AI to automate internal and external processes, including interaction and customer service. Interestingly, the majority of respondents are ready to entrust the search for new ideas and the solution of creative tasks to intelligent technologies. There is also a convergence of opinions among respondents from different groups about barriers to the introduction of intelligent technologies. Such barriers include high cost, insufficient staff competence, as well as a lack of information about AI capabilities in various fields.

However, due to the fact that no respondent is ready to fully entrust business security to artificial intelligence, we cannot state a high level of trust, and decision-making, according to the majority of respondents, despite the development of intelligent technologies, should be carried out in a hybrid format.

Thus, the results of the survey suggest that there is a certain level of trust in intelligent technologies in business structures. Moreover, the level of business trust in artificial intelligence is, on the one hand, linked to the accumulated experience in using intelligent technologies, and, on the other, it varies depending on the specific tasks that organizations are willing to delegate to AI.

The obtained results are consistent with previous studies, which indicate that trust and acceptance depend on AI application [24]. Furthermore, this study demonstrates that perceptions of AI risks are similar across countries, with cybersecurity rated as the top risk globally [24, p. 5]. In line with this, our survey reveals that, as noted earlier, none of the respondents are willing to fully entrust business security to AI. The findings regarding the use of intelligent technologies and trust in AI also align with the results of a study published by Forbes [30], which indicates that AI is becoming increasingly accessible and applicable across organizations, regardless of their size or resources. This trend reflects the growing confidence among employees that investments in AI tools and training will yield tangible benefits. Thus, the present study aligns with previously obtained results and expands the understanding of how trust in intelligent technologies is formed.

In this study, we not only determined whether or not business trusts intelligent technologies, but also identified the factors influencing such trust. The specification of AI functions that are more or less trusted by the heads of organizations has also been defined. In addition, the very act of using AI already confirms that the decision to use it has been made. Certain limitations of the study are related to the questionnaire as a method of obtaining information about the confidence of decision-makers in intelligent technologies. To remove this limitation, the addition of the survey approach presented in this paper with experimental and analytical approaches should be noted as a direction for further research. The experimental approach involves conducting in-depth interviews with two groups of respondents: leaders who actively use artificial intelligence in their activities and outsiders who either do not use intelligent technologies or use them extremely rarely or have a negative experience in their implementation. The data obtained at this stage will allow us to form a base of best practices for the implementation of intelligent technologies, a matrix of the most typical errors and problems of their use with possible solutions, as well as to provide recommendations for the implementation of intelligent technologies, taking into account regional characteristics, the scope of activity, and the scale of the company. The purpose of the analytical approach in the next step is to assess the impact of the level of trust in intelligent technologies and their implementation on regional development. At this stage, using the TOPSIS method (the technique for order of preference by similarity to ideal solution) developed by Hwang and Yun [31], it is proposed to build a monitoring system to assess the level of implementation of intelligent technologies by regional companies.

References

1. Algan, Y., & Cahuc, P. (2014). Trust, growth, and well-being: New evidence and policy implications. In P. Aghion & S. Durlauf (Eds.), *Handbook of economic growth* (Vol. 2, pp. 49–120). Elsevier. https://doi.org/10.1016/B978-0-444-53538-2.00002-2
2. Kosolapova, N. A., Nikitaeva, A. Y., & Laskova, D. S. (2023). Trust risks and industrial development: Framework of the joint analysis. *State and Municipal Management. Scholar Notes, 1*, 18–26. https://doi.org/10.22394/2079-1690-2023-1-1-18-26
3. Galstyan, A. G., & Alaverdyan, A. G. (2024). Analysis of the impact of trust on economic growth. Bulletin of the Russian-Armenian (Slavic) university. *Series: Humanities and Social Sciences, 1*, 16–34. https://doi.org/10.24412/1829-0450-2024-1-16-34
4. Knack, S., & Keefer, P. (1997). Does social capital have an economic payoff? A cross-country investigation. *Quarterly Journal of Economics, 112*(4), 1251–1288. https://doi.org/10.1162/003355300555475
5. Zak, P. J., & Knack, S. (2001). Trust and growth. *The Economic Journal, 111*(470), 295–321. https://doi.org/10.1111/1468-0297.00609
6. Fetchenhauer, D., & van der Vegt, G. (2001). Honesty, trust and economic growth. *Zeitschrift für Sozialpsychologie, 32*(3), 189–200.
7. Fang, M., Cai, L., Park, K., & Su, M. (2024). Trust (in)congruence, open innovation, and circular economy performance: Polynomial regression and response surface analyses. *Journal of Environmental Management, 358*, 120930. https://doi.org/10.1016/j.jenvman.2024.120930
8. Zahid, P., & Chaudhary, A. R. (2015). Does trust matter for economic growth and human development? Empirical evidence from a panel of countries. *Pakistan Journal of Commerce and Social Sciences, 9*(3), 916–927. https://doi.org/10.2139/ssrn.3201504
9. Peiró-Palomino, J., Gianmoena, L., Picazo-Tadeo, A. J., & Rios, V. (2024). Social trust and the advanced aspects of social progress: Evidence for the European regions. *European Journal of Political Economy, 83*, 102547. https://doi.org/10.1016/j.ejpoleco.2024.102547
10. Safina, D. (2015). Trust and economic growth in Russian society. *Procedia Economics and Finance, 24*, 563–567. https://doi.org/10.1016/S2212-5671(15)00634-6
11. Coyle, D., & Lu, S. (2020). *Trust and productivity growth: An empirical analysis (Bennett Institute Working Paper)*. University of Cambridge.
12. Nikitaeva, A. Y., & Salem, A.-B. M. (2022). Institutional framework for the development of artificial intelligence in the industry. *Journal of Institutional Studies, 14*(1), 108–126. https://doi.org/10.17835/2076-6297.2022.14.1.108-126
13. Fosso-Wamba, S., & Guthrie, C. (2024). Artificial intelligence and industry 4.0 and 5.0: A bibliometric study and research agenda. *Procedia Computer Science, 239*, 718–725. https://doi.org/10.1016/j.procs.2024.06.228
14. Alenizi, F. A., Abbasi, S., Mohammed, A. H., & Rahmani, A. M. (2023). The artificial intelligence technologies in industry 4.0: A taxonomy, approaches, and future directions. *Computers & Industrial Engineering, 185*, 109662. https://doi.org/10.1016/j.cie.2023.109662
15. Leng, J., Zhu, X., Huang, Z., Li, X., Zheng, P., Zhou, X., Mourtzis, D., Wang, B., Qi, Q., Shao, H., Wan, J., Chen, X., Wang, L., & Liu, Q. (2024). Unlocking the power of industrial artificial intelligence towards industry 5.0: Insights, pathways, and challenges. *Journal of Manufacturing Systems, 73*, 349–363. https://doi.org/10.1016/j.jmsy.2024.02.010
16. Wang, X. Q., Chen, P., Chow, C. L., & Lau, D. (2023). Artificial-intelligence-led revolution of construction materials: From molecules to industry 4.0. *Matter, 6*(6), 1831–1859. https://doi.org/10.1016/j.matt.2023.04.016
17. Uctu, R., Tuluce, N. S. H., & Aykac, M. (2024). Creative destruction and artificial intelligence: The transformation of industries during the sixth wave. *Journal of Economy and Technology, 2*, 296–309. https://doi.org/10.1016/j.ject.2024.09.004

18. Jan, Z., Ahamed, F., Mayer, W., Patel, N., Grossmann, G., Stumptner, M., & Kuusk, A. (2023). Artificial intelligence for industry 4.0: Systematic review of applications, challenges, and opportunities. *Expert Systems with Applications, 216*, 119456. https://doi.org/10.1016/j.eswa.2022.119456
19. Malik, S., Muhammad, K., & Waheed, Y. (2024). Artificial intelligence and industrial applications: A revolution in modern industries. *Ain Shams Engineering Journal, 15*(9), 102886. https://doi.org/10.1016/j.asej.2024.102886
20. Capestro, M., Rizzo, C., Kliestik, T., Peluso, A. M., & Pino, G. (2024). Enabling digital technologies adoption in industrial districts: The key role of trust and knowledge sharing. *Technological Forecasting and Social Change, 198*, 123003. https://doi.org/10.1016/j.techfore.2023.123003
21. McAllister, D. J. (1995). Affect- and cognition-based trust as foundations for interpersonal cooperation in organizations. *Academy of Management Journal, 38*(1), 24–59. https://doi.org/10.2307/256727
22. Denize, S., & Young, L. (2007). Concerning trust and information. *Industrial Marketing Management, 36*(7), 968–982. https://doi.org/10.1016/j.indmarman.2007.06.004
23. Dowell, D., Morrison, M., & Heffernan, T. (2015). The changing importance of affective trust and cognitive trust across the relationship lifecycle: A study of business-to-business relationships. *Industrial Marketing Management, 44*, 119–130. https://doi.org/10.1016/j.indmarman.2014.10.016
24. Gillespie, N., Lockey, S., Curtis, C., Pool, J., & Akbari, A. (2023). *Trust in artificial intelligence: A global study*. The University of Queensland and KPMG Australia. https://doi.org/10.14264/00d3c94
25. Sutrop, M. (2019). Should we trust artificial intelligence? *Trames: Journal of the Humanities and Social Sciences, 23*(4), 499–522. https://doi.org/10.3176/tr.2019.4.07
26. Lockey, S., Gillespie, N., Holm, D., & Someh, I. A. (2021). A review of trust in artificial intelligence: Challenges, vulnerabilities and future directions. In *Proceedings of the 54th Hawaii international conference on system sciences* (pp. 5463–5472). HICSS. https://doi.org/10.24251/HICSS.2021.664
27. Li, Y., Wu, B., Huang, Y., & Luan, S. (2024). Developing trustworthy artificial intelligence: Insights from research on interpersonal, human-automation, and human-AI trust. *Frontiers in Psychology, 15*, 1382693. https://doi.org/10.3389/fpsyg.2024.1382693
28. Kaplan, A. D., Kessler, T. T., Brill, J. C., & Hancock, P. A. (2021). Trust in artificial intelligence: Meta-analytic findings. *Human Factors: The Journal of the Human Factors and Ergonomics Society, 63*(7), 1208–1225. https://doi.org/10.1177/00187208211013988
29. Lukyanenko, R., Maass, W., & Storey, V. C. (2022). Trust in artificial intelligence: From a foundational trust framework to emerging research opportunities. *Electronic Markets, 32*, 1993–2020. https://doi.org/10.1007/s12525-022-00605-4
30. Ladd, T. (2023). *For AI, does company size matter? Forbes*. Retrieved from https://www.forbes.com/sites/tedladd/2023/08/25/for-ai-does-company-size-matter/
31. Hwang, C. L., & Yoon, K. (1981). *Multiple attribute decision making: Methods and applications*. Springer-Verlag. https://doi.org/10.1007/978-3-642-48318-9

AI-Enhanced Safety in Project-Based Production: A New Era in Workplace Risk

Magdalena Ramírez-Peña, Alberto Cerezo-Narváez, Manuel Otero-Mateo, Andres Pastor-Fernández, and Moisés Batista

Abstract In project-based production models, which typically adopt a fixed-position layout, occupational safety is a key challenge due to the unique characteristics and high degree of customization of each project. This approach involves the constant mobilization of equipment, materials, and workers, which increases the risk of accidents and requires precise safety management. The integration of Artificial Intelligence (AI) in this context represents a transformative tool for enhancing safety and optimizing workflow. This study has been conducted using a review of literature and case studies in industrial sectors such as aerospace, construction, and shipbuilding industries. Through this methodology, key AI applications have been identified including real-time monitoring, predictive risk analysis and the automation of compliance evaluation. The results indicate that AI implementation significantly enhances workplace safety by enabling early risk detection, the customization of safety protocols, and the optimization of resource utilization. In the aerospace industry, for example, improvements have been observed in component condition monitoring and fault diagnosis. In construction, AI has facilitated the detection of regulatory non-compliance and accident prevention through real-time monitoring systems. In shipbuilding, the integration of sensors and IoT networks has enabled more efficient control of working conditions and employee safety. These findings suggest that AI not only contributes to reducing the incidence and severity of workplace accidents but also optimizes operational efficiency, ensuring a safer working environment adapted to the challenges of the industry today.

Keywords Artificial intelligence · Occupational safety · Project-based production

M. Ramírez-Peña · A. Cerezo-Narváez (✉) · M. Otero-Mateo · A. Pastor-Fernández · M. Batista
University of Cadiz, Puerto Real, Cádiz, Spain
e-mail: magdalena.ramirez@uca.es; alberto.cerezo@uca.es; manuel.otero@uca.es; andres.pastor@uca.es; moises.batista@uca.es

F. Tao et al. (eds.), *Artificial Intelligence and Digital Transformation*, Lecture Notes in Information Systems and Organisation 78,
https://doi.org/10.1007/978-3-032-00118-4_4

1 Introduction

Project-based production is understood as a production model in which work is organized around specific projects, characterized by being unique and of limited duration. A fixed type of distribution is usually used, i.e., the project remains in a fixed location, and the necessary resources, workers and materials are moved to it for processing or assembly. This type of distribution is particularly useful when the product is too large, heavy or complex to move easily during the production process [1]. Project-based production systems generate unique products since the considering the workforce indispensable nowadays for the operation of any company. It influences the choice of personnel, its correct location for optimum performance, training, updating of workers, if necessary, supervision of work, effective distribution of jobs, remuneration, objectives, and incentives and of course, their safety and health at work. This workforce management becomes even more critical in large-scale, project-based industries where delays, inefficiencies, or safety issues can significantly impact overall costs and timelines. Ensuring seamless coordination among teams is a priority to achieve high productivity while maintaining safety standards.

The aerospace sector belongs to this type of production and distribution. This sector has optimized production and assembly times and has also improved its production from an ergonomic point of view [2]. Another sector is the construction industry, where site layout planning is crucial to manage space and reduce internal transportation costs, demonstrating how the combination of fixed layout and project-based production helps to minimize costs and optimize workflow [3]. And the shipbuilding industry is also looking to improve efficiency through the use of systematic layout planning methods [4]. In addition, the automotive sector has begun adopting similar approaches, where project-based workflows support the assembly of custom or large-scale components, ensuring precision and reducing waste in production lines.

One of the characteristics of fixed distribution is that it requires careful management of the arrival of resources and personnel at specific times in the process to avoid delays, as well as specialization of the work team, which allows greater concentration on the project. This approach involves the constant mobilization of equipment, materials, and workers, which increases the risk of accidents and the need for precise safety management. This management of occupational safety used to depend on human expertise through compliance with applicable procedures and regulations; however, technological progress has changed this management and new types of occupational risks have appeared in the context of digitalization [5]. The integration of emerging technologies, such as Artificial Intelligence (AI), the Internet of Things (IoT), and predictive analytics, has redefined traditional safety practices, offering new possibilities for risk mitigation and real-time monitoring. AI-powered systems predict hazards by analyzing historical data, while IoT devices monitor workplace conditions.

Artificial Intelligence emerges as an effective ally for occupational safety, being able to anticipate, evaluate and mitigate risks, reducing their incidence and severity while improving operational efficiency [6]. This study seeks to address, first, to identify how AI can improve safety in project-based production models, to exploring what are the most effective AI-driven techniques for monitoring and preventing workplace hazards in industries with fixed-position layouts and what are the challenges and limitations of AI implementation for occupational risk management in these industries. Therefore, this study aims to analyze the current state of occupational safety in project-based production environments and identify key AI applications that enhance safety management. In this way, it is possible to assess the challenges and limitations of AI adoption in these environments and propose strategies for effective implementation.

2 Materials and Methods

This study is based on a literature review combined with case studies of industries where project-based production predominates. This combination will cover two key aspects. Firstly, emerging AI technologies applied to risk assessment, predictive maintenance, and real-time hazard detection, and secondly, case studies demonstrating the successful adoption of AI in industrial safety management.

As mentioned above, Artificial Intelligence has revolutionized traditional methods of operation and management in the industry, redefining standards of productivity, efficiency, and occupational safety. Advanced AI tools, such as predictive analytics, allow for anticipating machinery failures and workplace vulnerabilities, optimizing preventive measures, and reducing risks. Examples include the implementation of predictive risk indexes to foresee incidents before they occur, significantly enhancing safety management in industrial plants [7], and models that predict critical equipment failures by analyzing historical and real-time data [8].

Another crucial aspect is real-time monitoring through intelligent sensors that collect data on temperature, pressure, vibration, and harmful gases. These systems predict failures and issue early warnings, as seen in wireless sensor networks applied to industrial monitoring using RFID smartwatches [9], or platforms integrating multiple sensors and actuators to improve real-time control [10]. Technologies like rotating machinery monitoring also enable preventive maintenance before failures occur, extending equipment lifespan [11].

AI also significantly impacts employee training and education, using simulations and augmented reality to replicate high-risk scenarios without exposing workers to real dangers. This makes training programs more accessible and effective [12]. Furthermore, the personalization of preventive measures tailors interventions to individual worker characteristics, maximizing their effectiveness, as demonstrated by behavior-based safety approaches [13].

Automation in risk assessment is another growing area, using AI, machine learning, and natural language processing tools to analyze large datasets quickly and accurately, as seen in advanced systems for modern industrial environments [14]. Finally, AI-based compliance monitoring systems excel at analyzing real-time operational data and detecting deviations, such as frameworks that allow for dynamic visualization and understanding of violations [15]. The integration of these technologies not only ensures a safer workplace but also enhances operational efficiency across industries.

In the following, different sectors whose production models are project-based and with fixed distribution will be analyzed, based on the techniques and tools mentioned above, as shown in Fig. 1.

The first to be analyzed will be the aerospace sector. In this sector, real-time compliance assessment plays a crucial role in managing and optimizing safety, efficiency and regulatory compliance. This industry, known for its strict regulations and high-quality standards, has adopted advanced technologies to continuously monitor operations and ensure regulatory compliance as it faces unique challenges due to the complexity of its systems and the critical importance of safety. The use of technology enables aerospace companies to maintain continuous control over their operations, which is essential to comply with stringent safety and quality regulations. One of the localized options has been a real-time object detection and tracking system using multi-modal sensors at the edge of the network, designed for regulatory compliance audits. This system improves logging efficiency and traceability, minimizing manual intervention [16].

Furthermore, in the interest of detecting, diagnosing and locating damage, as well as predicting the remaining service life of structures or systems, the knowledge-driven approach to real-time condition monitoring, combining data, physical

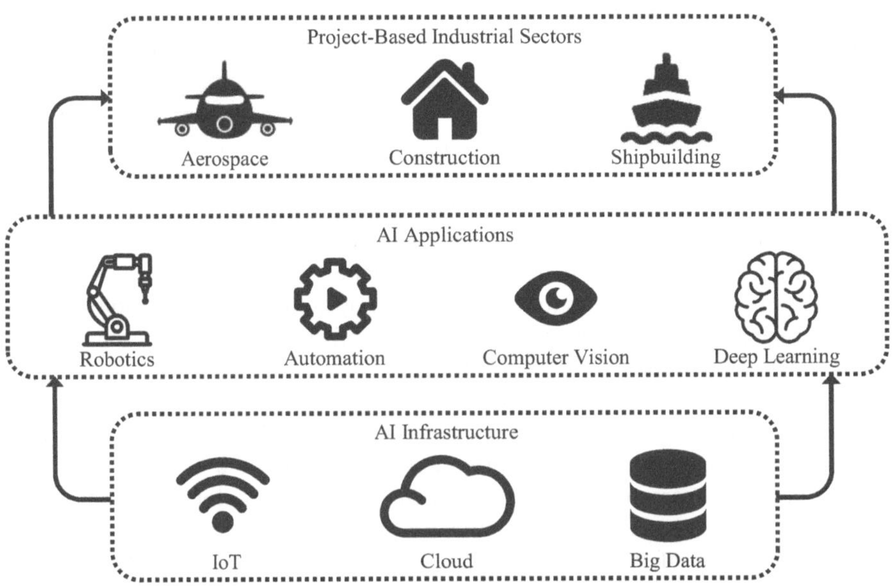

Fig. 1 Application of AI techniques and tools to project-based industrial sectors

modeling and knowledge-based approaches to improve decision making related to aircraft maintenance and safety, has been widely used in the aerospace sector [16].

This real-time monitoring and analysis through sensors in aerospace component manufacturing is also evidenced by a universal platform using readily available hardware, such as robots and Wi-Fi data acquisition systems, focused not only on improving product quality but the safety of the manufacturing process as well [17]. This necessitates that integrated predictive algorithms have had to be developed for anomaly detection in complex system monitoring data in the industry [18]. Figure 2 shows the application of AI for the aerospace sector.

Coming now to the construction industry, real-time assessment of regulatory compliance is an essential tool for ensuring safety and efficiency on construction sites. Construction is an industry that faces unique challenges due to the dynamic and often chaotic nature of work environments. The integration of advanced technologies for real-time monitoring allows construction companies to maintain continuous control over their operations, ensuring that all relevant rules and regulations are met.

One of the greatest benefits of real-time compliance assessment is the ability to detect and correct deviations from regulations immediately. This is particularly crucial in construction, where delays and errors can have serious consequences in terms of both safety and costs so establishing an automated compliance verification

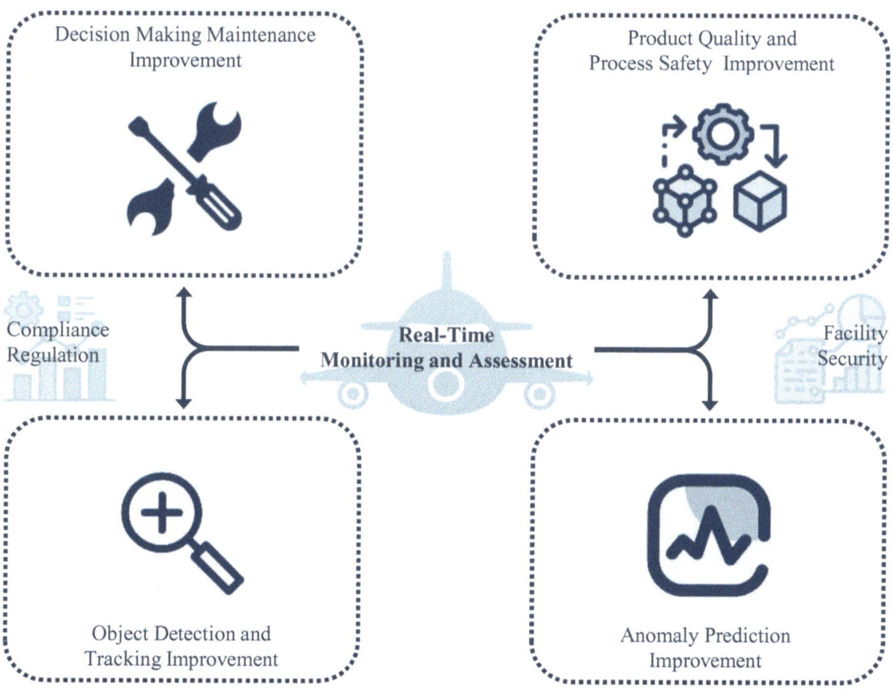

Fig. 2 Integration of AI in the aerospace sector

framework in the construction industry, showing how these systems can improve accuracy and reduce human error in compliance verification [19].

The use of real-time monitoring systems in construction also facilitates the tracking and management of health and safety in the workplace as demonstrated through the application of unsupervised machine learning techniques for monitoring health and safety legislation, demonstrating how these technologies can identify and correct dangerous behaviors before accidents occur [20]. The feasibility of an infrastructure-free real-time monitoring system for monitoring interference between equipment on large construction sites has also been investigated, thus enabling more efficient and safer management of daily activities [21].

Another important aspect is the ability to monitor carbon emissions and other environmental impacts of construction activities, specifically in prefabricated construction, using cyber-physical systems to provide accurate and up-to-date data on emissions throughout the construction life cycle [22]. This approach not only helps to comply with environmental regulations, but also enables companies to make informed decisions to minimize their environmental impact. Figure 3 shows the application of AI for the construction sector.

Finally, in the shipbuilding sector, real-time assessment of regulatory compliance is crucial to ensure that operations are safe, efficient, and compliant with

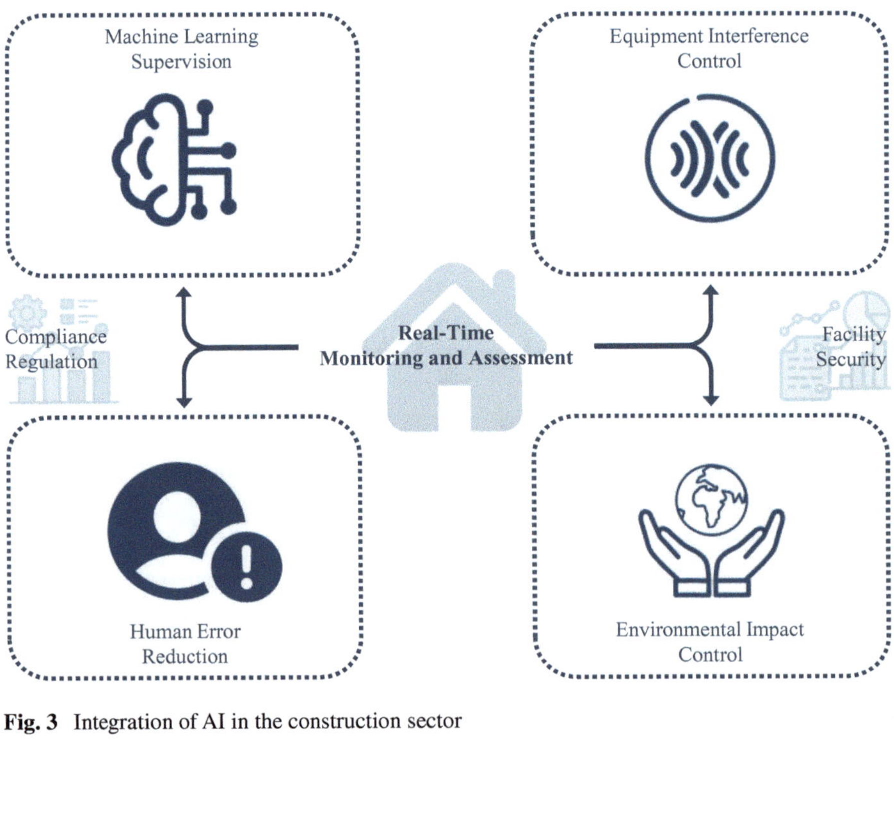

Fig. 3 Integration of AI in the construction sector

environmental and safety regulations. This industry faces unique challenges due to the complexity of working environments, the need to manage large amounts of data and the importance of complying with strict international regulations. One of the advantages that real-time monitoring brings to it is that of ship exhaust emissions in a way that can ensure compliance [17], as well as safety in closed working environments through wireless networks with connections from gas detectors to control stations, providing dynamic reconfiguration in case of network failures [23]. Similarly, using ultrasound technologies, it has been effective in improving productivity and safety by providing continuous updates on the location of workers [24].

Combined with the Internet of Things, AI can use a wireless heterogeneous network to reliably collect and process environmental and worker information, thus improving their safety in the work environment [25]. From the perspective of continuous evaluation of the operational status of propulsion systems, studies focusing on the development trends of condition monitoring and fault diagnosis for power machinery ensure the safety of navigation [26]. Figure 4 shows the application of AI for the shipbuilding sector.

Table 1 summarizes the IA tools used in the sectors studied by their description.

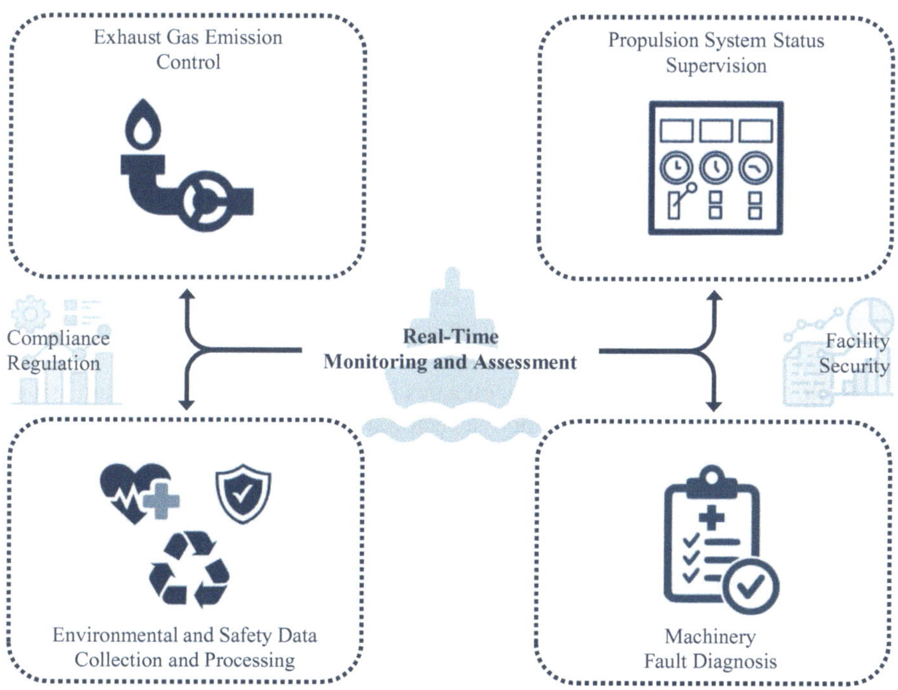

Fig. 4 Integration of AI in the shipbuilding sector

Table 1 Application of AI tools used by project-based industrial sectors

Sector	Description	References
Aerospace	Real-time object detection and tracking system	[27]
	Condition monitoring and fault diagnosis	[16]
	Universal platform for sensor monitoring in manufacturing	[17]
	Predictive algorithm for anomaly detection	[18]
Shipbuilding	Monitoring of ship exhaust emissions	[17]
	IoT-based safety monitoring in shipyards	[25]
	Condition monitoring and fault diagnosis of ship machinery	[26]
	Safety monitoring system using ultrasound	[24]
	Remote toxic gas monitoring in shipyards	[23]
	Automated compliance verification	[19]
Construction	Automated compliance verification	[19]
	Health and safety legislation monitoring using machine learning	[20]
	Real-time monitoring of carbon emissions in precast construction	[22]
	Construction site interference control	[21]

3 Results and Discussion

A first step could be to look at other types of sectors that do not belong to this type of production system to evaluate techniques and tools that are not used in any of the previous case studies with a view to assessing future implementation. For this purpose, we have taken the automotive sector, which belongs to a mass production model with a product-oriented distribution, distinguished by the diversity and depth of its technological applications.

The analysis shows that the automotive sector differs from other sectors by covering a wider range of applications compared to other sectors. It uses predictive analytics not only for maintenance, but also for specific systems such as electronic throttle control [28]. Figure 5 highlights how the automotive sector is leading in integrating AI into workplace safety, suggesting that this trend may soon extend to other applicable sectors, such as project-based ones. This distinguishes it from sectors such as shipbuilding, construction, or aerospace, which focus more on general condition monitoring and fault diagnosis.

While other sectors implement diagnostics in a specific way (e.g., gas emissions or mechanical failures), the automotive sector stands out for employing real-time diagnostics via the Internet and for multiple subsystems such as control and manufacturing systems [29]. Although IoT is used in other sectors, the automotive takes a more advanced approach with cyber-physical systems that integrate real-time monitoring and control. This allows for more precise and adaptive control, especially in manufacturing and maintenance [30]. Moreover, the automotive sector is implementing human presence detectors to avoid collisions, demonstrating a more proactive approach to operational safety during product use, not only in manufacturing [31]. In addition, this sector explicitly includes worker training in its model, reflecting an investment in human capital that is not as evident in other ones [32].

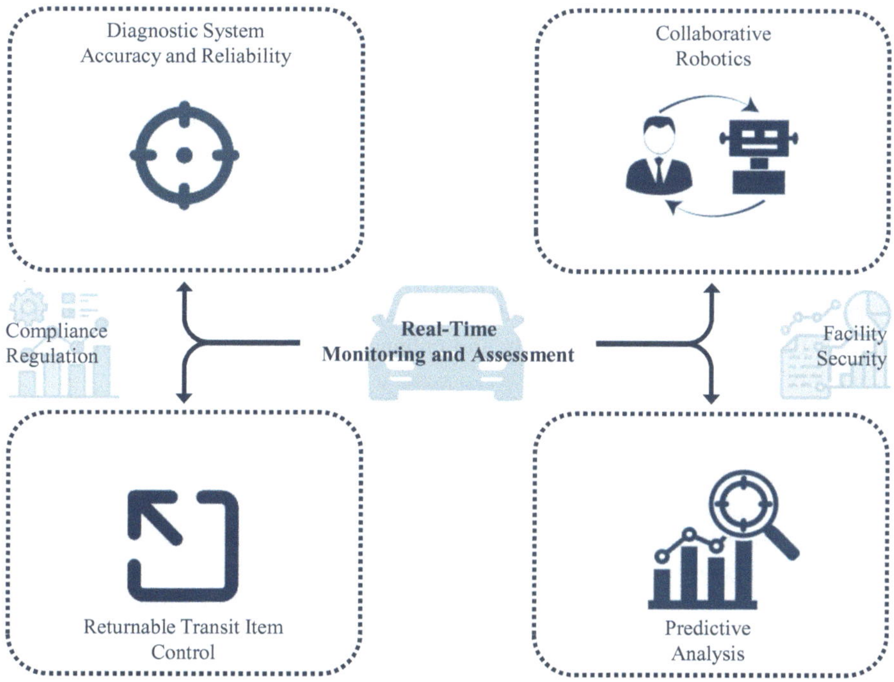

Fig. 5 Integration of AI in the automotive sector

It can be seen how its comprehensive approach, ranging from safety to training, positions it as a leader in the integration of advanced technologies. Whereas the aerospace sector focuses primarily on object detection and sensor monitoring, which is critical for high-risk operations, but does not have the diversity of applications that automotive integrates. Shipbuilding, despite having a strong focus on IoT-based monitoring and environmental safety, lacks advanced tools such as predictive analytics or cyber-physical systems that are essential in automotive. And construction is more focused on regulatory compliance and environmental monitoring, which limits its scope compared to the technical capabilities of automotive.

The adoption of AI-driven safety technologies varies significantly depending on the industrial sector and geographical region. According to recent data published by the OECD AI Policy Observatory [33], large manufacturing companies in several advanced economies have reached an average AI implementation rate of 42% for safety and quality-related applications. In contrast, small to medium-sized enterprises (SMEs) report significantly lower levels of adoption, often citing cost and limited digital infrastructure as the primary barriers. Furthermore, cultural readiness and concerns about workforce re-skilling can hinder AI uptake, particularly in regions where traditional processes remain deeply entrenched. Addressing these challenges may require targeted training initiatives, government incentives, and collaborative approaches involving both industry leaders and policy makers.

Similarly, the McKinsey Global Survey on AI [34] indicates that over 50% of global respondents across industries plan to increase their investment in AI-based safety tools within the next 2 years, with the automotive and aerospace sectors exhibiting the highest projected growth. By integrating AI for tasks such as predictive maintenance, real-time monitoring, and compliance checks, companies can reduce workplace accidents and improve overall operational efficiency. These findings align with the case studies presented in Sect. 3, where organizations in aerospace and shipbuilding have already begun leveraging AI to predict potential hazards and streamline safety management protocols. Moreover, early adopters in these sectors report a noticeable decrease in downtime and incident rates, allowing them to allocate resources more strategically and enhance worker confidence in the effectiveness of safety measures.

Once the tools and techniques offered by AI in the field of occupational safety have been assessed, the challenges and opportunities faced by the sectors with the different tools mentioned will be evaluated. Despite their advantages, the implementation of intelligent sensors faces challenges such as the need for standardization and the management of large volumes of data. However, the integration of these technologies also offers significant opportunities to improve safety and operational efficiency. The adaptability and remote upgradeability of sensors allows companies to keep up with technological advances without the need to completely replace existing systems. For example, in the construction sector, AI is being used to monitor structural stability in real time during large-scale projects. AI-equipped sensors continuously collect data and alert operators to any anomalies that may indicate an imminent risk of collapse or accident, thus enabling timely evacuation and corrective intervention before incidents occur [35].

Moreover, a critical aspect of predictive analytics is its ability to identify emerging risks, which are new and/or increasing and may not be evident without the analysis of large data sets. Such is the case of the approach used to assess the level of emerging risk associated with exposure to hand-arm vibrations in industrial environments under uncertainty conditions, using fuzzy logic and expert systems to integrate uncertainty conditions into risk assessment [36]. In addition, there are some theoretical frameworks in the literature to model these emerging risks in the technological life cycles of industrial processes, allowing their continuous monitoring and the adaptation of mitigation strategies [37], as well as studies on emerging methods in predictive analytics highlighting how these advanced techniques are being applied in risk management and decision making, where it is offered as an interdisciplinary approach that combines business, statistics and information technology for effective decision making in risk management [38].

Similarly, automated decision making for resource allocation aimed at risk mitigation can also be performed using a hierarchical probabilistic model that is calibrated online from safety data according to the method for continuous quantitative analysis of safety risks in dynamic industrial environments [39]. Regarding risk assessment, automation offers multiple benefits, including increased accuracy in assessment, cost and time reduction, and the ability to process and analyze large volumes of data in real time, as demonstrated in the ontological approach conducted to automate cybersecurity risk assessment, which shows how data structure and formalization improve the accuracy and effectiveness of automation [40]. In addition, automation of risk assessment minimizes human error and enables faster response to changing conditions in an industrial environment. An example is the improvement of change management in IT infrastructures where, through risk automation, interruptions are reduced and business continuity is improved [41].

Despite its benefits, automation in risk assessment faces challenges, such as resistance to change by workers and the need to keep systems up to date with emerging threats. In addition, the integration of these technologies requires a significant investment in terms of time and financial resources, but once integrated, security workers can focus on strategic tasks such as planning preventive measures.

Through the personalization of occupational risk prevention, it has been possible to analyze how AI makes it possible to personalize risk prevention according to the specific characteristics and needs of each worker. In the case of personalized medicine, it can be applied in the field of occupational health, using "omics" technologies to adapt preventive measures to individual biological and genetic characteristics [42] or even to identify and treat previously undetected risk conditions, which opens the door to personalized prevention interventions in the workplace [43].

Another application is the perception of risk and the use of personal protective equipment (PPE) by workers, which significantly influences its usage. In this context, it is interesting to note that interventions should be personalized based on how individuals perceive their risks [44]. Personalization in occupational risk prevention also presents challenges, particularly in terms of privacy and potential discrimination. It is crucial to carefully manage personal data and ensure that interventions do not lead to stigmatization or unfair treatment of workers.

Among the benefits offered by real-time compliance evaluation are systems for real-time object detection and tracking at the network edge, demonstrating effectiveness in industrial environments for regulatory compliance audits [27]. Additionally, through the establishment of a framework for real-time business process compliance monitoring, it becomes possible to identify violations and their root causes during process execution [45].

4 Conclusion

Artificial Intelligence is driving a transformation in industrial safety, with smart sensors revolutionizing real-time monitoring, accident prevention, and operational efficiency. These technologies enable industries to identify risks before they escalate, reducing downtime and ensuring business continuity. By enhancing resource allocation and resilience, AI is expected to play an even greater role in industrial safety through continuous monitoring and predictive analysis.

Predictive analytics has emerged as a powerful tool in managing emerging risks, allowing companies to proactively adapt safety strategies. Automation is also redefining risk assessment by improving precision and efficiency. The integration of AI with the Internet of Things (IoT) and machine learning streamlines safety processes, enhancing decision-making and adaptability to unforeseen challenges. Successful implementation requires interdisciplinary collaboration to maintain and optimize these systems.

Personalized occupational risk prevention presents a promising approach to workplace safety. AI-driven monitoring tools and wearable technology allow tailored interventions that enhance worker well-being, productivity, and job satisfaction. However, ethical and practical challenges must be addressed to ensure fair implementation across all employees.

Real-time compliance evaluation has proven essential for maintaining legal, efficient, and transparent industrial operations. AI enables continuous monitoring and adaptation to regulatory changes while fostering organizational integrity. These systems provide actionable insights, allowing managers to implement immediate corrective actions and prevent regulatory breaches, ultimately strengthening workplace safety and corporate reputation.

The benefits of AI extend across multiple industries. In construction, AI enhances monitoring and compliance. Shipbuilding benefits from IoT, ultrasound, and wireless networks for safety management. Aerospace uses predictive analytics and AI-based training to optimize efficiency and protect workers. The automotive industry integrates real-time diagnostics and compliance tools to maintain operational safety.

As AI technologies evolve, their adoption is expected to expand, improving workplace safety, sustainability, and efficiency. Continuous refinement and interdisciplinary collaboration will be crucial to overcoming current challenges and maximizing the impact of AI on industrial safety.

References

1. Brandon-Jones, A. (2015). Fixed position layout. In *Wiley encyclopedia of management* (p. 1). Wiley. https://doi.org/10.1002/9781118785317.weom100228
2. Judt, D., Forster, K., Lockett, H., Lawson, C., & Webb, P. (2016). Aircraft wing build philosophy change through system pre-equipping of major components. *SAE International Journal of Aerospace, 9*(1), 190–197. https://doi.org/10.4271/2016-01-2120
3. Hammad, A. W. A., da Costa, B. B. F., Soares, C. A. P., & Haddad, A. N. (2021). The use of unmanned aerial vehicles for dynamic site layout planning in large-scale construction projects. *Buildings, 11*(12), 600. https://doi.org/10.3390/buildings11120602
4. Tamer, S., Barlas, B., Gunbeyaz, S. A., Kurt, R. E., & Eren, S. (2023). Adjacency-based facility layout optimization for shipyards: A case study. *Journal of Ship Production and Design, 39*(1), 25–31. https://doi.org/10.5957/JSPD.05210013
5. Feng, Z., & Zhu, Y. (2016). A survey on trajectory data mining: Techniques and applications. *IEEE Access, 4*, 2056–2067. https://doi.org/10.1109/ACCESS.2016.2553681
6. Montes, A. A. D., Dominguez, M. L. A., & Algoner, W. C. (2023). On occupational safety and health practices in micro, small and medium-sized companies in the last 4 years: A systematic review. In *Proceedings of the LACCEI international multi-conference* (pp. 1–10). Florida Atlantic University.

7. Chen, J. R., & Yang, Y. T. (2004). A predictive risk index for safety performance in process industries. *Journal of Loss Prevention in the Process Industries, 17*(3), 233–242. https://doi.org/10.1016/j.jlp.2004.03.001
8. Khairuddin, M. Z. F., Hasikin, K., Razak, N. A. A., Mohshim, S. A., & Ibrahim, S. S. (2023). Harnessing the multimodal data integration and deep learning for occupational injury severity prediction. *IEEE Access, 11*, 85284–85302. https://doi.org/10.1109/ACCESS.2023.3304328
9. Sandra, P. S., Sandeep, C. M., Nair, V., Vindhuja, M. V., Nair, S. S., & Raja, M. P. (2017). WSN based industrial parameter monitoring using smartwatch. In *2017 IEEE international conference on circuit, power and computing technologies (ICCPCT)*. IEEE. https://doi.org/10.1109/ICCPCT.2017.8074279
10. Ramamurthy, H., Prabhu, B. S., Gadh, R., & Madni, A. M. (2005). Smart sensor platform for industrial monitoring and control. In *Proceedings of IEEE sensors* (pp. 1116–1119). IEEE. https://doi.org/10.1109/ICSENS.2005.1597900
11. Dinardo, G., Fabbiano, L., & Vacca, G. (2018). A smart and intuitive machine condition monitoring in the industry 4.0 scenario. *Measurement, 126*, 1–12. https://doi.org/10.1016/j.measurement.2018.05.041
12. Dobbe, R. (2022). System safety and artificial intelligence. *Proceedings of the IEEE, 110*(9), 1584. https://doi.org/10.1145/3531146.3533215
13. Geller, E. S. (2005). Behavior-based safety and occupational risk management. *Behavior Modification, 29*(3), 539–561. https://doi.org/10.1177/0145445504273287
14. Varlamova, D. V., Dolzhenkova, A. V., & Korochkina, S. V. (2020). Automation in risk management. *Economics and Environmental Management, 2*, 78–86. https://doi.org/10.17586/2310-1172-2020-13-4-78-86
15. Knuplesch, D., Reichert, M., & Kumar, A. (2017). A framework for visually monitoring business process compliance. *Information Systems, 64*, 381–409. https://doi.org/10.1016/j.is.2016.10.006
16. Phillips, P., & Diston, D. (2011). A knowledge driven approach to aerospace condition monitoring. *Knowledge-Based Systems, 24*(6), 915–927. https://doi.org/10.1016/j.knosys.2011.04.008
17. Wijaya, T., Caesarendra, W., Pappachan, B. K., Tjahjowidodo, T., Wee, A., & Roslan, M. I. (2017). Robot control and decision making through real-time sensors monitoring. In *In: 2017 IEEE PACRIM* (pp. 1–6). IEEE. https://doi.org/10.1109/PACRIM.2017.8121928
18. Song, G., Liang, J., Liu, D., & Peng, Y. (2016). Anomaly detection of condition monitoring. In *In: 2015 IEEE ICEMI* (pp. 248–253). IEEE. https://doi.org/10.1109/ICEMI.2015.7494262
19. Beach, T. H., Kasim, T., Li, H., Nisbet, N., & Rezgui, Y. (2013). Towards automated compliance checking in the construction industry. In H. Decker, L. Lhotská, S. Link, J. Basl, & A. M. Tjoa (Eds.), *Database and expert systems applications. DEXA 2013* (Vol. 8055, pp. 366–380). Springer. https://doi.org/10.1007/978-3-642-40285-2_32
20. Raliile, M. T., & Haupt, T. C. (2020). Machine learning applications for monitoring safety compliance. In *Proceedings of international structural engineering and construction*. ISEC. https://doi.org/10.14455/ISEC.2020.7(2).CON-23
21. Naticchia, B., Vaccarini, M., & Carbonari, A. (2013). A monitoring system for real-time interference control on large construction sites. *Automation in Construction, 29*, 148–160. https://doi.org/10.1016/j.autcon.2012.09.016
22. Liu, G., Chen, R., Xu, P., Fu, Y., Mao, C., & Hong, J. (2020). Real-time carbon emission monitoring in prefabricated construction. *Automation in Construction, 110*, 102945. https://doi.org/10.1016/j.autcon.2019.102945
23. Pérez-Garrido, C., González-Castaño, F. J., Chaves-Diéguez, D., & Rodríguez-Hernández, P. S. (2014). Wireless remote monitoring of toxic gases in shipbuilding. *Sensors, 14*(2), 2981–3000. https://doi.org/10.3390/s140202981
24. Park, J., Kim, H., Yoon, J., Kim, H., Park, C., & Hong, D. (2021). Development of an ultrasound-based indoor-location monitoring system for worker safety. *PRO, 9*(2), 304. https://doi.org/10.3390/pr9020304

25. Zhang, Q., Hua, L., Tian, X., Tang, Z., & Nian, L. (2019). Development of shipbuilding safety information monitoring and management system. *International Journal of Computer Applications in Technology, 61*(4), 297–305. https://doi.org/10.1504/IJCAT.2019.103303
26. Yu, C. (2023). Exploring the current status and development of condition monitoring and fault diagnosis for power machinery of engineering ships. *Applied Science and Innovative Research, 7*(3), 62. https://doi.org/10.22158/asir.v7n3p62
27. Lim, J. S., Wang, Z., Liu, J., Khamis, A., Arablouei, R., Barlow, R., et al. (2023). Real-time multi-modal object detection and tracking on edge. In *Proceedings of the thirty-third international joint conference on artificial intelligence* (pp. 8725–8728). IJCAI. https://doi.org/10.24963/ijcai.2024/1018
28. Arena, F., Collotta, M., Luca, L., Ruggieri, M., & Termine, F. G. (2021). Predictive maintenance in the automotive sector: A literature review. *Mathematical and Computational Applications, 27*(1), 2. https://doi.org/10.3390/mca27010002
29. Syafrudin, M., Alfian, G., Fitriyani, N. L., & Rhee, J. (2018). Performance analysis of IoT-based sensor and machine learning for automotive monitoring. *Sensors, 18*(9), 2946. https://doi.org/10.3390/s18092946
30. Neal, A. D., Sharpe, R. G., van Lopik, K., Tribe, J., Goodall, P., Lugo, H., et al. (2021). Cyber-physical systems for wash monitoring in automotive logistics. *CIRP Journal of Manufacturing Science and Technology, 32*, 461–475. https://doi.org/10.1016/j.cirpj.2020.07.002
31. Polonara, M., Romagnoli, A., Biancini, G., & Carbonari, L. (2024). Collaborative robotics in automotive parts production: A case study. *Machines, 12*(3), 196. https://doi.org/10.3390/machines12030196
32. Osborne, M., & Mavers, S. (2019). Integrating augmented reality in training and industrial applications. In *2019 8th Int. Conf. Of educational innovation through technology (EITT)* (pp. 142–146). EITT. https://doi.org/10.1109/EITT.2019.00035
33. OECD AI Policy Observatory. (2024). *Global AI adoption and industry developments*. OECD.
34. McKinsey Global Institute. (2023). *The state of AI in 2023: Generative AI's breakout year*. Retrieved from https://www.mckinsey.com
35. Pishgar, M., Issa, S. F., Sietsema, M., Pratap, P., & Darabi, H. (2021). Redeca: A framework for AI in occupational safety and health. *International Journal of Environmental Research and Public Health, 18*(13), 6937. https://doi.org/10.3390/ijerph18136705
36. Sánchez, A., González, C., & Brocal, F. (2019). Emerging risk level from hand-arm vibrations under uncertainty. *Safety Science, 114*, 140–147. https://doi.org/10.1016/j.ssci.2019.01.002
37. Brocal, F., Sebastián, M. A., & González, C. (2017). Framework for modeling new occupational risks using technology lifecycle. *Safety Science, 99*, 178–186. https://doi.org/10.1016/j.ssci.2016.10.016
38. Hsu, W. H. (2015). *Emerging methods in predictive analytics: Risk management and decision-making*. FT Press. https://doi.org/10.4018/978-1-4666-5063-3
39. Tewari, A., & Paiva, A. R. (2022). Modeling and mitigation of occupational safety risks in dynamic environments. *Safety Science, 146*, 105531. https://doi.org/10.1016/j.ssci.2021.105531
40. Maunero, N., De Rosa, F., & Prinetto, P. (2023). Towards cybersecurity risk assessment automation: An ontological approach. In *2023 IEEE international conference on dependable, autonomic and secure computing* (pp. 628–635). IEEE. https://doi.org/10.1109/DASC/PiCom/CBDCom/Cy59711.2023.10361456
41. Araujo Wickboldt, J., Armando Bianchin, L., Castagna Lunardi, R., Girardi Andreis, F., Da Costa Cordeiro, W. L., Bonato Both, C., et al. (2009). Improving IT change management processes with automated risk assessment. In *Lecture notes in computer science* (pp. 71–84). Springer. https://doi.org/10.1007/978-3-642-04989-7_6
42. Bollati, V., Ferrari, L., Leso, V., & Iavicoli, I. (2020). Personalised medicine: Implication and perspectives in the field of occupational health. *La Medicina del Lavoro, 111*(6), 425–444. https://doi.org/10.23749/mdl.v111i6.10947

43. Magnavita, N., & Chirico, F. (2020). New and emerging risk factors in occupational health. *Applied Sciences, 10*(24), 8906. https://doi.org/10.3390/app10248906
44. Afolabi, F. J., de Beer, P., & Haafkens, J. A. (2021). Occupational risk perception and the use of personal protective equipment (PPE): A study among informal automobile artisans in Osun state, Nigeria. *SAGE Open, 11*(1), 215824402199458. https://doi.org/10.1177/2158244021994585
45. Ly, L. T., Rinderle-Ma, S., Knuplesch, D., & Dadam, P. (2011). Compliance rule graphs. In *OTM confederated international conferences "on the move to meaningful internet systems"* (pp. 82–99). Springer. https://doi.org/10.1007/978-3-642-25109-2_7

Using Artificial Intelligence to Combat Fraud: Asian Experience, Russian Prospects

Anastasia Babanskaya, Daria Ermoleva, Nadezhda Efimenko, Ivan Kotlyarov, and Denis Koleznev

Abstract The use of artificial intelligence today is more widespread than ever. The areas and opportunities for using AI to combat fraud at all stages are expanding every year. Therefore, it is very important to use the best practices of other countries, especially those following the path of advanced development. The purpose of the article is to study the experience of the UAE and India to pinpoint best practices in using AI and combating corporate fraud. The object of the study is AI-based technological solutions to identify anomalies in financial data sets and prevent fraud. The work uses qualitative methods of analyzing scientific literature, state development programs and national projects, case situations, methods of comparative statistical analysis and analogies. Based on the case studies, it was established that the priority areas for developing AI solutions are the banking sector, government agencies, cybersecurity and transactions of organizations, and interaction with partners. The next stage involved identifying areas for combating corporate fraud for individual AI subtechnologies. As a result, the study comes up with proposals on using individual AI subtechnologies to counter fraud.

Keywords Artificial intelligence · Fraud · Subtechnologies · Monitoring of financial transactions · Risks

---

A. Babanskaya (✉) · D. Ermoleva · N. Efimenko · I. Kotlyarov · D. Koleznev
Departments of Economic Security and Risk Management, Financial University under the Government of the Russian Federation, Moscow, Russian Federation

F. Tao et al. (eds.), *Artificial Intelligence and Digital Transformation*, Lecture Notes in Information Systems and Organisation 78,
https://doi.org/10.1007/978-3-032-00118-4_5

1 Introduction

In the context of digital transformation and globalization of financial systems, the problem of fraud is taking on new dimensions and forms. Organized criminal groups are actively using modern technologies to commit financial crimes, which requires an adequate response from governments and businesses. In the fight against cyber fraud, many scientists [1–3] consider artificial intelligence (AI) to be an indispensable tool, which is capable of analyzing large volumes of data, identifying anomalies and predicting risks, preventing and minimizing fraudulent transactions.

Asian countries such as India and the UAE have already achieved significant success in using AI to combat fraud. For example, the United Arab Emirates (hereinafter referred to as the UAE) is actively attracting investment in the high-tech sector, which allows them not only to develop innovative solutions, but also to move along the trajectory of advanced development. At the same time, India, being one of the leaders in the field of AI, demonstrates impressive results in analyzing large volumes of financial data and identifying suspicious activity. The experience of these countries, especially in using AI to prevent financial crimes, is of significant interest to Russia, which underlines the relevance of its study.

The purpose of the article is to study the experience of the UAE and India to find best practices in using AI and combating corporate fraud. The results are of interest for their application in the activities of Russian companies, and scaling business processes of organizations of all forms of ownership. To attain the stated purpose, we set the following objectives: (1) to review the best practices of using AI in the UAE and India in order to analyze arrays to detect fraud; (2) to analyze the current situation in the IT sector in Russia; (3) to develop recommendations for the use of AI that will be of interest in Russia as well as other countries.

2 Literature Review

Many researchers (see, e.g., Whiting et al. [2], Brown et al. [3], Chiji [4], Shabaany and Ljepava [5], Guo et al. [6]) analyze the effectiveness of using complex digital technologies for security purposes. They point out that AI has a high potential not only in detecting fraud that has already been committed, but also in proactively detecting and preventing financial fraud. Chiji [4] and Shakyawar and Shakya [7] argue that AI-based fraud detection offers numerous benefits to organizations, with the effect being high accuracy and speed of crime detection and prevention, which is many times greater than the capabilities of any human. Fiore et al. [8] and Plakandaras et al. [9] focused on the capabilities of machine learning, one of the most promising solutions for detecting illegal transactions and preventing fraud, especially in the financial sector [8, 9]. Berova and Tutukov [1], Rai and Goyal [10], however, also note ethical, legal, and reputational issues when using AI, which may have negative social consequences.

The experience of using and confirming the effectiveness of AI in international practice is of interest, especially in countries that focus on AI technology as a driver of development. Among such countries, India and the UAE show significant results in the development of AI technologies, which is confirmed by Abu et al. [11], Owusu et al. [12], Agadi and Kinange [13] and Ramos et al. [14].

The works of Shakyavar and Shakya [7], Rai and Goyal [10], Yadav et al. [15] address the issues of AI technologies in India. The authors proved that the use of AI contributed to broader socio-economic progress of the country. The works of Shabaany and Ljepava [5], Mohammed et al. [16], and Mohammed [17] ecplore AI technologies in UAE. In them, the authors put forward recommendations on the demand for increasing the role of AI technologies in UAE corporations in various routine and complex tasks and activities.

However, all the above-mentioned works deal with individual aspects and factors of implementing AI technologies in the anti-fraud system in a particular industry, or study specific narrow cases of implementing AI subtechnologies. However, comprehensive studies with a comparative theoretical analysis of successful practices are scarce. Although non-scientific sources of information (mass media, open Internet sources, official websites, data from press conferences and company briefings) provide numerous examples of successful implementation of various AI technologies in business processes at different stages of countering fraud. Against the background of the investment attractiveness of AI technologies, it is necessary to understand which particular direction can be promising for development and will provide the best result in security.

According to Juniper Research [18], in 2022, global business expenses of leading AI providers in the field of detection and prevention of financial fraud amounted to 6.5 billion US dollars and by 2027 will exceed 10 billion US dollars. At the same time, global spending on AI in the financial sector, according to analysts, will increase from 35 billion US dollars in 2023 to 97 billion US dollars in 2027. The growth of the market for AI-based fraud prevention solutions will grow by an average of 54% over 6 years [18]. Far Eastern countries and China, Western Europe and North America [18] will traditionally bear the most significant costs (more than 90%) for the implementation of AI technologies to prevent fraud. Thus, this study will help businesses discover promising vectors for the development of AI technologies and expand theoretical knowledge in the field of countering fraud.

3 Materials and Methods

The object of the study is artificial intelligence (AI) technologies for combating fraud in the financial and economic spheres. The study examines both international experience (using Asian countries as an example) and the prospects for implementing similar technologies in Russia.

In the study, the authors used qualitative methods of analyzing scientific literature from Asian and Russian countries, state development programs and national projects, case studies, comparative statistical analysis and analogies.

The general course of the study was as follows.

The first stage involved scrutinizing the extensive literature on the subject of the study. Owusu et al. [12] note that in recent years there has been an increase in research on the phenomenon of fraud due to the problem of increasing its scale, especially after the global corporate scandals of 2008. It is worth noting that the vast majority of studies examine developed economies, although the problem of fraud itself is global in nature.

Therefore, we focused on the experience of India and the UAE, because these countries emphasize AI technologies as a driver of economic development, and various academic and corporate sources cover successful practices in using AI to combat fraud.

The second stage involved formulating the theoretical basis and defining the research criteria.

The third stage entailed systematizing the theoretical data and forming the study structure. Afterward, a comparative analysis took place. The authors identified and compared the following parameters as criteria: sector and industry, areas of AI implementation, the type of technology and AI subtechnologies used, and a specific method or method of using them to prevent fraud. The effectiveness criteria included the degree of influence on fraud detection and the difficulties and limitations that arise when using AI. The study also covered the amount of funding for AI technology programs and AI investments focused on safety.

The next stage determines the IT market opportunities for IT technologies in Russia, as well as the demand for technological solutions to prevent fraud. An assessment of the resource and economic potential will allow extrapolating the benefits of the experience of India and the UAE in Russian practice of combating fraud.

The choice of the case study method was due to the insufficient amount of confirmed quantitative data regarding the practice of using AI in the field of anti-fraud. At the same time, this method is useful when one needs to understand a specific problem or situation deeply, and the studies of India and the UAE are rich in information on specific examples. The case study serves as reconnaissance and identification of promising areas that provide competitive advantages and greater opportunities for economic development.

The method allows assessing the effect of the prevalence and level of development of AI technologies, an increase in fraud detection.

The information base included official data on the websites of organizations, regulatory and planning state documentation of Asian countries and Russia on issues of AI development, including national strategies, projects, programs and guidelines for the development of AI technologies, online portals with open information (Government of Russia, CheckMyLink, VisionLabs Luna, National Center for Artificial Intelligence Development under the Government of the Russian Federation).

4 Results

4.1 Experience in Using Artificial Intelligence to Counter Fraud in the UAE

States cooperate and exchange information in the field of AI on the BRISK platform, in accordance with the Beijing Declaration of the XIV Summit, 2022. It expresses concern about the ethical aspect of the use of AI, risks and assesses the use of technology.

The declaration calls for work to eliminate risks, in addition to scaling up experience, and more importantly, joint research to create a unified approach to preventing corporate fraud, which can become a guide for the rest of the BRICS member countries in terms of ethical and responsible use of AI. BRICS has the potential to become a platform for deepening scientific and technological cooperation in areas of AI to counter fraud.

In 2017, the United Arab Emirates (a BRICS member) appointed the world's first Minister of Artificial Intelligence, and the country's leadership is very interested in developing new technologies, including AI.

In addition, government bodies have adopted large-scale key documents, such as the National Strategy in the Field of AI until 2031. The strategy aims to make the UAE a leader in AI technologies. Since 2019, the UAE has had a set of AI principles and ethics in place, an AI Lab, and in 2023, the country opened two AI technology centers. The first center will identify, develop and promote best practices and industry standards for the use of AI in the Middle East. The second center, the Microsoft AI for Good Research Lab in Abu Dhabi, will support AI projects aimed at solving important public problems [5, 12].

We expect new AI-enabled technologies to significantly increase GDP and enable the UAE to continue diversifying into key industries. In 2021, the UAE ranked first in the world in terms of government AI financing strategies, and among the MENA (Middle East and North Africa) countries, and today it leads by a large margin in terms of commercial financing (26th place against 58th place of neighboring Saudi Arabia). This dynamic occurred due to the growth of successfully operating companies from AI startups from 2015 to 2023. These include Group 42 the company has been engaged in AI in the fields of healthcare, oil and gas sector and aviation since 2018.

At the international exhibition of innovations and startups "GITEX Global 2024 Avaya", the introduction of an AI assistant for the Dubai Police was announced aimed at improving interaction with citizens and optimizing internal fraud prevention processes. Computer vision is actively developing to achieve the goal of increasing the number of unmanned taxis by 25% by 2030 [12].

The oil and gas company ADNOC is among the first ones to introduce AI into operational activities to ensure safety. In 2017, the company launched two projects, Thamama and Panorama, and by 2020, the use of AI had generated benefits of $2.1 billion [12, 14].

In 2019, the UAE Federal Tax Service launched a new electronic monitoring system using digital fiscal stamps. This system tracks the facts of payment of excise tax on tobacco products. The idea of its creation is to use modern tools to combat excise tax evasion and corporate fraud. The system includes integrated electronic monitoring tools. Their traces are visible at customs points and throughout the supply chain in the UAE.

In order to reduce fraud, the UAE Cybersecurity Council has created an online CheckMyLink portal (https://staysafe.csc.gov.ae) to check unreliable and fake websites, giving users the ability to check the links of the found websites to scammers. Users of the neural service have the opportunity to enter the address of any website, and the platform will test it for malware, phishing tools or other fraud.

The entire world community is aware of a major corporate fraud in the banking sector. An AI-generated voice imitation helped criminals trick a UAE bank employee. The fraud scheme resulted in the financial institution losing $35 million. Following this precedent, banks and large corporations in the UAE have developed and improved their software tools aimed at countering fraud.

Emirates NBD Bank uses generative AI in its activities to improve customer interaction, which is able to increase the productivity of individual service lines. In addition, Emirates NBD uses neural tools to monitor suspicious transactions. AI tracks not only transactions, but also the behavior of the client, not limited to the amount, frequency and location from which the client usually makes transactions, and also helps to form a sufficiently wide "dossier" on the client in order to protect both himself and the client from fraudulent actions in the future [11, 16, 17].

The ADCB (Abu Dhabi Commercial Bank) case offers its services, including through the WhatsApp messenger. However, in order to conduct its activities through this messenger and reduce the risk of involvement in fraudulent activities, the bank has launched an AI that evaluates and analyzes incoming information and warns about the relevant risks. In addition, ADCB uses artificial intelligence to monitor credit applications and determine the client's solvency and integrity. This mechanism has practically automated the business process of assessing a client upon receipt of a credit application [6].

Deloitte Middle East presents an AI-based technology platform that analyzes the financial data of a client company, identifies anomalies and reports them. Thus, any company implementing this platform will be able to cover several risk profiles at once, including reducing the risk of corporate fraud.

Al-Futtaim Group is the largest conglomerate in the UAE market. It carries out activities in the automotive industry, provides financial services, is engaged in retail trade, as well as real estate trading. To monitor the operations of Al-Futtaim Group, it uses AI in the supply and distribution process, which helps to identify and, in some cases, prevent fraudulent schemes, which directly affects the economic security.

4.2 The Experience of Using Artificial Intelligence to Counter Fraud in India

The Indian experience is no less interesting. The country (a BRICS member) has set a goal—to make an AI revolution. The government of the country recognizes the potential inherent in AI. The Ministry of Commerce and Industry of India has formed a task force to transform the country's economy using AI subtechnologies.

Companies are actively investing in AI training specialists, which has resulted in a significant increase in employees' qualifications. Since 2010, India has been consistently ranked in higher education: fourth in terms of the number of scientific papers on AI, third in terms of the AI personnel reserve, eighth in terms of the number of AI patents (4000 patents in 2020, which is almost 6 times more than in 2011–2015) [13].

In addition, the country's leadership sets goals to become a basic AI laboratory for countries with economies in transition. To achieve this goal, the government has adopted strategic documents targeting five priority sectors of the Indian economy: education, healthcare, agriculture, smart cities and mobility [15].

According to NITI Aayog, the competitive advantage of the country's educational system is a large number of STEM graduates (science, technology, engineering, and math) who can be potential employees in the AI sector (research and practical). At the end of 2022, the penetration rate of AI skills is 3.09, which is the highest value among the OECD and G20 countries. Investments in AI in the country are growing by 30.8% on average annually. Experts estimated the size of the AI market in India at USD 7.8 billion in 2021, which is 22% more than in 2020 [4, 10, 13].

The Pramaan Exchange project has become one of the most innovative solutions in the field of AI. This is the largest gardening exchange, which operates based on Intello Labs. This agrotechnical startup uses a computer vision subtechnology that is based on a database of 300 million images of fruit and vegetable products and analyzes the supplier's products for compliance, thus checking their quality and reducing the risks of supplier fraud.

Artificial intelligence is a serious competitor to the outsourcing industry in India. The introduction of AI is inevitable, but the versatility of the tools reduces jobs. For example, the Indian IT company Dukaan has cut almost 90% of the support staff, entrusting this work to an AI chatbot. The decision not only helped the company save money (customer support costs decreased by 85%), but also increased work efficiency. After the introduction of the chatbot, clients receive a response within seconds after the request, and their issues are resolved much faster (up to 3 min). Before the introduction of AI, it took about 2 h to resolve the issues.

The public sector, with government support, uses artificial intelligence to analyze hot spots, traffic, investigate criminal cases, including fraudulent schemes, for facial recognition, in the agricultural sector, and to protect rare animal species.

Let us consider a number of cases of the banking sector and large corporations.

The HDFC Bank case actively uses AI in the implementation of both projects to improve the quality of customer service and mechanisms in the field of transaction monitoring. The bank has an AI-based electronic virtual assistant that provides information about banking services and products. In order to help with e-commerce and payments, the bank has an interactive platform—HDFC Bank OnChat—in Facebook Messenger. This platform uses AI tools to monitor transactions carried out through the platform and identify suspicious ones. In addition, since 2018, the bank has had a bot recruiter, which carries out its activities based on AI algorithms, and determines whether a particular candidate is suitable for the bank, analyzing his data for compliance with functional and personal requirements [7, 8].

In addition, the bank monitors financial information using neural tools that identify suspicious patterns among all transactions carried out by the bank and react to them. For example, if a customer makes a transaction from an unusual geolocation and for an amount that is unusual for the customer's profile, the AI can freeze the transaction until it clarifies the detailed circumstances. In addition, AI uses the principles of machine learning, so it is able to adapt to new realities and improve.

ICICI Bank's case for interaction with clients and potential employees, this bank uses AI to operate their career chatbot and career platform, the principle of operation is similar to the previous HDFC Bank case. The system checks the functional and personal skills, as well as the candidate's compliance with the bank's security requirements. In addition, the bank has introduced AI technology into its operational activities, which emits employee actions to automate repetitive, voluminous and labor-intensive processes. This, in turn, reduces the risk of accidental and intentional errors, which reduces the risk of fraud in these areas of operational activity [9].

In terms of achieving the goals of ensuring security and compliance with anti-laundering and anti-terrorism legislation, the bank uses AI deep learning technology. The essence of deep learning is that, by self-learning on huge amounts of data, AI can independently find solutions and does not require constant operator intervention when branching the algorithm of action. This helps to reduce the number of false positives of AI when monitoring transactions for suspicious transactions. Such systems help to identify attempts to involve the bank in illegal activities more quickly and efficiently.

TCS (Tata Consultancy Services) is the largest multinational technology company in India, whose main specialization is IT consulting. This company is famous for its technological solutions in the field of risk management. TCS offers its clients a platform and integrates it into the client company's internal ecosystem. The platform is capable of analyzing incoming transaction data and predicting potential fraud cases. A distinctive feature of this case is that the company offers a technological solution to customers for a preventive and proactive response to the risks of corporate and client fraud. In addition, in 2023, to create more affordable fraud protection technological solutions when using communication tools in the field of financial services, TCS entered into a partnership with the American company FundingShield, which specializes in fraud protection in the sphere of housing/mortgage lending.

This technological solution pays great attention to data integrity and prevents their use in fraud, including corporate fraud. A software product for banks that deal with mortgage lending, since the risk profiles that AI responds to in this area are specific. The joint collaboration will allow clients to maintain data integrity, verify suspicious bank accounts and automate the counterparty claims verification system.

Paytm is a popular payment system in India that provides small mobile loans that require prompt verification of the customer's profile and risk level; therefore, the AI implemented in this business process allows reducing fraud risks to an acceptable level. Paytm uses AI to analyze user data, support customers, and improve the accuracy of detecting anomalies in financial information arrays. In addition, the area of AI use in this company certainly affects transaction monitoring, preventing both corporate fraud in order to involve the company in illegal activities, and identifies fraudulent schemes on the part of private clients.

Zomato Case is an Indian, now international, restaurant aggregator for food delivery and restaurant meals. The company introduced AI after it noticed fraudulent reviews of the restaurants it cooperates with. To solve this problem and maintain trusting and reliable relationships with customers, Zomato has launched a neural tool that analyzes the reviews left and identifies those that are part of fraudulent schemes, namely, identifies patterns characteristic of fake reviews.

4.3 Prospects for the Development of Artificial Intelligence in Russia

Against the backdrop of active government regulation and high investment activity in the implementation of AI technologies in India and the UAE, the development pace of technological solutions for protection against fraud in Russia is not keeping up with the leaders. In [19, 20], digital maturity in Russia by industry in 2023 is estimated at just over 74%, which indicates a significant potential for implementing AI solutions in the field of security.

For example, when comparing the share of AI solutions in GDP of countries, a difference is obvious. The share of the AI sector in the Indian economy is very large; experts predict its growth to 20% of GDP in 2028. The UAE ranked first in the world in 2021 in government AI financing strategies, experts forecast that artificial intelligence will account for about 13.6% of the UAE's GDP by 2030. In Russia, the share of AI solutions in GDP stands at 0.8% in 2024, with projections showing growth to 3.6% by 2030 [21].

The Institute for Statistical Research and Economics of Knowledge of the Higher School of Economics, while analyzing the dynamics of economic indicators for the period 2019–2023, emphasizes the steady growth of the IT industry (Table 1). The industry's contribution to GDP reached almost 2% in 2023, against 1.3% in 2019 (Fig. 1).

Table 1 Russian IT industry, key indicators for 2019–2023

IT industry indicators	2023	2023/2022	2023/2019
Contribution to GDP	1.96%	+0.22 p.p.	×1.5
Implementation of own products and services	3.1 trillion rubles	+30.3%	×2.5
Number of employees	857 thousand people	+12.7%	×1.5
Wages	155.9 thousand rubles	+13.3%	×1.7
Investments in fixed assets	0.5 trillion rubles	+46.5%	×4.4

Source: Compiled by the authors based on [19]

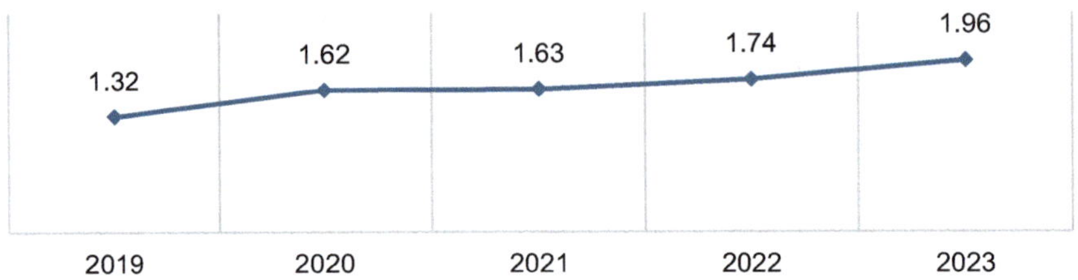

Fig. 1 The share of the IT industry in Russia's GDP for 2019–2023 (%). (Source: compiled by the authors based on [19])

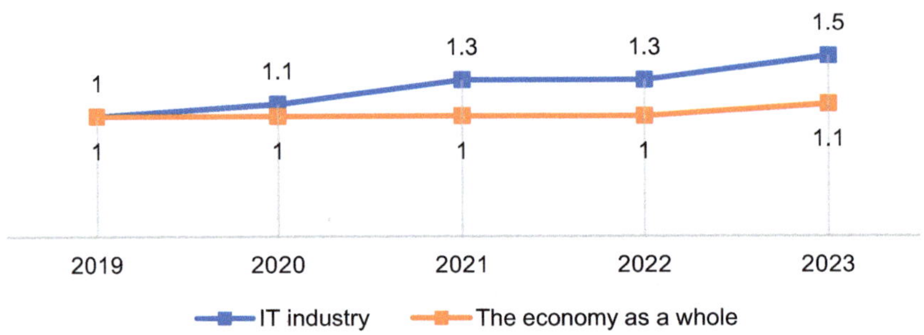

Fig. 2 The growth rate of the Russian GVA in real terms by 2019, times. (Source: compiled by the authors based on [19, 20])

The average annual growth rate of gross value added (GVA) in Russia in comparable prices exceeded 10%, and the average number of employees in the sector increased annually to 11% (Fig. 2). Over a four-year period, the growth dynamics of both indicators increased 1.5 times, in addition, the positive trend persisted throughout the COVID period.

In 2023, according to experts, the volume of the Russian IT market will exceed 2.4 trillion rubles, and in 2022—1.9 trillion rubles (Fig. 3). The fastest growing market segments are IT services and hardware. According to the Association of Software Developers (ARPP) [19], the number of IT companies in the country is more than 100 thousand, and the number of IT specialists is more than 780 thousand people.

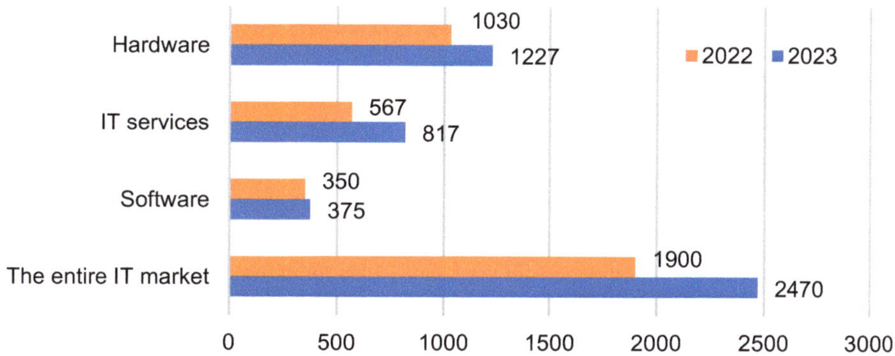

Fig. 3 The Russian IT market in 2022–2023 distributed by large segments, billion rubles. (Source: compiled by the authors based on [19])

Thus, according to the trends and strategic objectives of the domestic IT market, ARPP [19] identifies the most promising areas of activity in 2024:

- the growing role of information security through the introduction of artificial intelligence;
- real, not on-paper import substitution in the fields of software and IT equipment.

These strategic guidelines directly confirm the timeliness of the Federal Artificial Intelligence Project, which aims to increase the efficiency of organizations using mainly domestic AI technologies.

"When analyzing the government's indicative plans, it should be noted that the implementation of the national project Data Economy, namely the IT sphere is the main vector of economic development." Deputy Prime Minister of the Russian Federation Dmitry Chernyshenko announced this forecast on January 17, 2024 [22]. "The total revenue of the 100 largest IT companies in Russia will grow by 2.5 times by 2030 and reach 5.3 trillion rubles." In addition, Chernyshenko emphasized the planned costs of state-owned companies for the development and implementation of IT in 2024, "they will spend more than 1 trillion rubles ..." [22].

The rating positions on the Russian Government's AI Readiness Index are growing, but Russia's position has shifted from 33rd to 40th place in 2023 (Fig. 4).

In 2023, the All-Russian Public Opinion Research Center, on the initiative of the National Center for Artificial Intelligence Development under the Government of the Russian Federation, conducted a survey of 4000 companies on using AI technologies in economic and social sectors. The survey data shows that the level of AI use in Russian companies has increased by 1.5 times since 2021. More than 40% of organizations develop AI solutions on their own, and the leaders in AI use to counter fraud are financial services, ICT, and healthcare. Intelligent support systems, as well as decision-making and computer vision are the most popular areas, 71% and 69%, respectively. In 2 years, out of 4000 respondents, the share of companies that have received multiple effects from the use of AI has doubled. According to the survey,

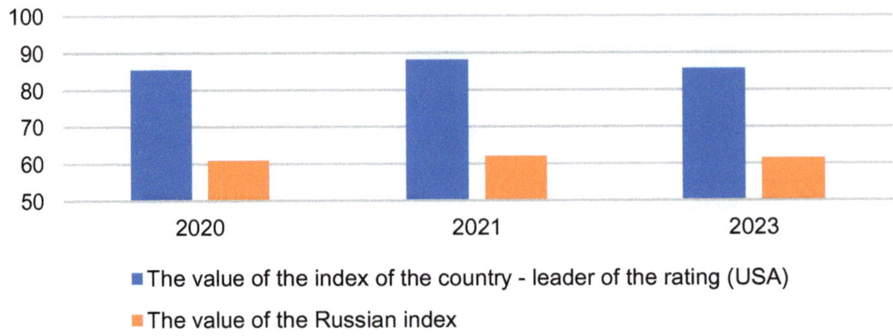

Fig. 4 Government readiness index for Artificial Intelligence (%). (Source: compiled by the authors based on [21])

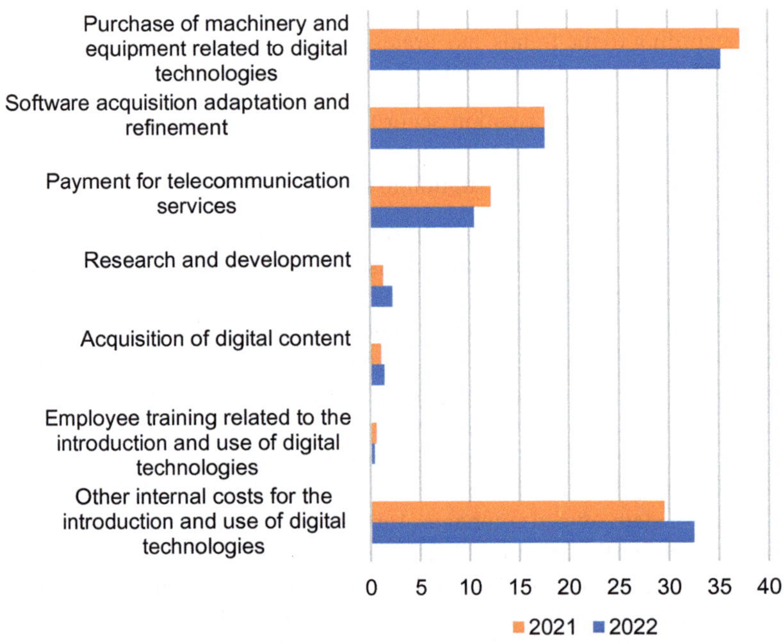

Fig. 5 The structure of the distribution of internal costs of domestic organizations for IT solutions for 2021–2022 (%). (Source: compiled by the authors based on [21])

the introduction of AI allowed increasing the speed and quality of work in individual companies 5–6 times. More than 34% of organizations have approved an AI implementation strategy, 35% plan to implement it within the next 3 years [21].

Having examined the statistical data, we conclude that organizations of all forms of ownership distribute their internal costs mainly on the acquisition of machinery and equipment with digital technologies, software, its adaptation and refinement, as well as other internal costs (Fig. 5).

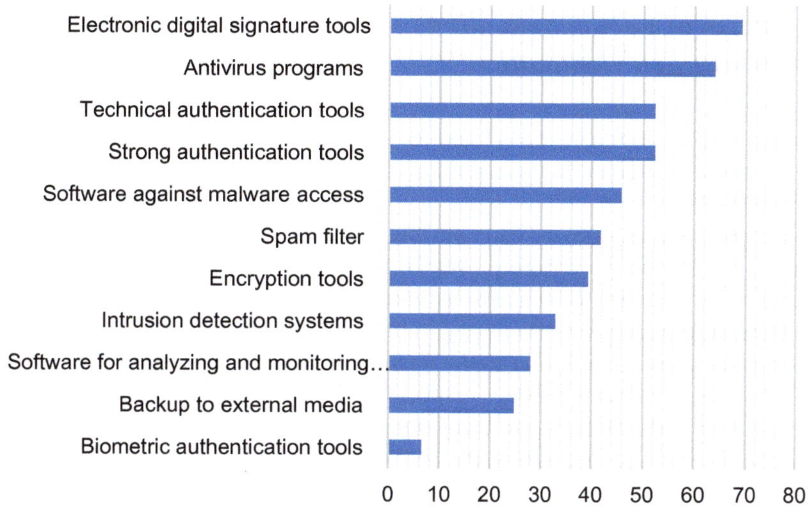

Fig. 6 The use of various information security tools in Russian organizations in 2022 (% of the total number of organizations). (Source: compiled by the authors based on [21])

For the development of the sector and in order to accelerate import substitution in Russia, there are 36 industrial competence centers, which involve over 300 leading companies from different industries.

Competence centers implement about 200 initiatives to introduce advanced programs; they combine the efforts of major customers and developers aimed at creating safe and reliable AI.

Today, companies around the world are using AI methods not only as a scientific and technical tool, but to combat corruption and fraud in a variety of forms and areas. Electronic digital signatures, antivirus programs and authentication tools have become the most widespread as information security tools (Fig. 6). At the same time, the share of AI in information security tools in Russian organizations is not yet large (biometric tools, spam filters, AI-enabled intrusion detection systems, security analysis and control tools).

Fraudsters in the digital economy are increasingly using IT tools to commit illegal actions. Therefore, such a response and prevention of financial fraud, taking into account international experience, is a perfect field for deploying AI capabilities at all stages of illegal activities. Technical solutions based on artificial intelligence that can quickly identify fraudulent schemes, and their scaling is the main task that all countries of the world are solving. The government of the Russian Federation and the Bank of Russia must consider additional mechanisms to combat corporate fraud and theft of funds by December 1, 2024. They will pay special attention to the need to develop AI technologies.

4.4 Practical Recommendations on the Use of AI Technologies for Russian Companies

According to Mohammad [16, 17] and review of successful cases of the UAE and India, the use of AI technologies significantly improves the average fraud detection efficiency (Fig. 7).

Considering the criteria, we can note that AI-based fraud detection systems demonstrate high efficiency averaging over 70% and help reduce the level of fraud by detecting and preventing illegal actions in real time. However, when adapting them to the Russian practice, it is necessary to take into account the limitations and difficulties of their use. In addition to the technical limitations noted in Fig. 7, ethical barriers (issues of citizens' privacy, respect for personal space and citizens' rights to protect personal information) and legal barriers (legislative restrictions on the use of AI in certain areas and operations, the lack of clear regulatory standards in connection with the advanced development of AI) may accompany the introduction of AI.

Having studied statistical data and practical cases on the pace and structure of AI development in the UAE and India, we concluded that the use of AI can improve the efficiency of business processes, and international experience can be used to counter fraud at the corporate level in the following areas.

1. The banking sector. Following the experience of India and the UAE, real-time transaction monitoring through AI yields the greatest impact, significantly enhancing the speed of fraud detection and enabling preventive protection.

   For example, if a client who usually makes small transfers conducts a large transaction, then the AI reasonably considers this an anomaly and reports it to

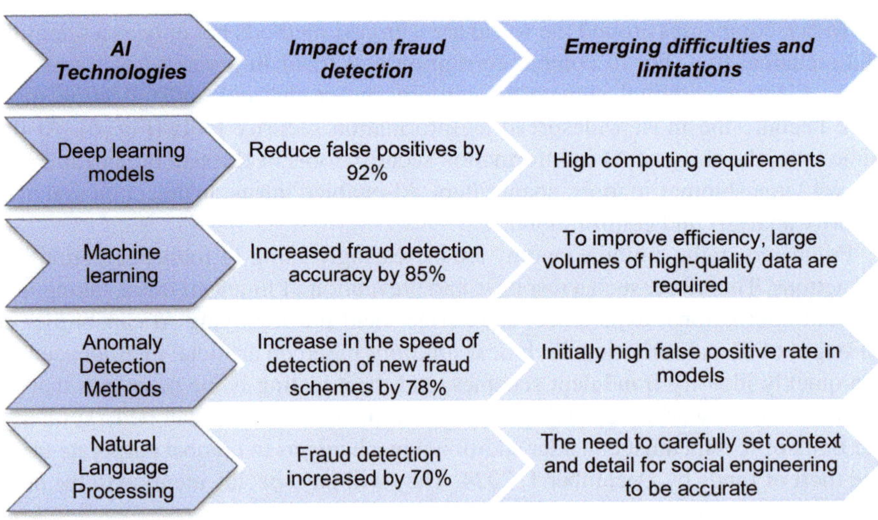

Fig. 7 The effectiveness of AI technologies in detecting fraud. (Source: compiled by the authors based on [16, 17])

the security service. For example, in Russia, Sberbank uses technologies to monitor transactions and detect fraudulent activities, similar to the practice of Paytm in India. Algorithms analyze customer behavior and transaction data in real time, which allows for a quick response to suspicious transactions and timely detection of fraudulent transactions.

2. State financial control bodies. In this area, AI is indispensable for monitoring the targeted use of funds, as well as for detecting abuse and attempts to withdraw funds. This mechanism is especially relevant when monitoring budget spending through the public procurement system. For example, for automatic monitoring of procurement prices, compliance of expense items with project documentation, targeted use of allocated funds.
3. Cybersecurity of organizations. AI helps monitor incoming and outgoing information, including financial information, in order to reduce the risk of information leakage and, as a result, financial losses for the company. In this area, DLP systems are very popular, which are able not only to monitor the activity of incoming/outgoing documentation, but also to block attempts to drain sensitive information.
4. Using AI to monitor company transactions. Therefore, when implementing AI in order to identify suspicious activity and control the approval process, for example, payment orders, the technology will be able to identify and report if the operation performed with the company's accounts differs from the usual profile, and goes against the approval process. For example, if someone tried to make a transaction without the appropriate rights, or the security service did not approve the counterparty to make a transaction. All this can become an effective tool for detecting attempts to withdraw assets and make fictitious transactions.
5. Using AI to interact with customers. This mechanism will reduce the likelihood of collusion on the part of the employee and the client. Despite the fact that this tool does not directly analyze financial information, it helps to detect conflicts of interest and limit the interaction of the parties in order to prevent financial losses due to unfair actions of an employee or supplier. For example, similar to Emirates NBD (UAE), T-Bank (Russia) is developing chatbots to automate customer service and prevent fraud. The AI-based system processes customer requests and analyzes interactions with them to identify potentially fraudulent activities. AI has a great potential in matters of due diligence and assessing the reliability of a client or potential employee, which helps companies avoid financial losses.

Suggestions for using neural tools to combat fraud are given in Table 2.

Today, organizations in the real sector of the economy allocate funds to implement many recommendations. A striking example is T-Bank, which in October 2024introduced the Cybersquall system that has no analogues in Russia to combat financial pyramids. It is a continuation of the Humanoid Robot Factory for talking to scammers, which diverts their resources to itself. The platform scans the Internet in search of sites advertising pseudo-investments with signs of fraudulent schemes. Every week, T-bank identifies 50–60 new pyramid scheme sites. Having discovered such a site, the neural network redirects it to T-Protection employees for manual

Table 2 Possibilities and restrictions for using individual AI subtechnologies to combat fraud

Country experience (developments, solutions, services)	Areas of application of AI	Restrictions, challenges
Computer vision (1, 2), (+)		
India: Pramaan exchange is the world's largest horticulture exchange, powered by Intel labs. A system for controlling an unmanned vehicle from Yandex UAE: UAE immigration authorities scan immigrants' eyes to combat illegal migration	Analysis of recordings from surveillance cameras; document authentication; access control; identification of persons; counterfeit detection: analysis of packaging and condition of goods	AI needs high-quality images and videos to work effectively; development and implementation require significant resources and can only pay off for large companies or government agencies; there are risks of data leakage, difficulties in the ethical aspect
Natural language processing (1, 2), (+)		
Russia: The system for streaming data entry is ABBYY FlexiCapture. The system for text analysis and understanding is ABBYY Compnero. Technical solutions for speech recognition from the company MDG India: Zomato is a neural tool that analyzes the reviews left and identifies those that are part of the fraudulent schemes of the UAE: CheckMyLink online portal-site analysis for phishing and fraud	Analysis of complaints and requests for refunds; analysis of electronic communication; analysis of open sources, including social networks for suspicious patterns of behavior; identification of inconsistencies in the text of documents	A large amount of high-quality information is needed without extraneous noise; expensive implementation into existing operating systems may not pay off for small companies New topics and areas may not have enough data to generate an answer; slang, new words and terms make it difficult to find anomalies
Promising methods and technologies in AI (1, 2, 3, 4), (−)		
UAE: Deloitte Middle East—the platform analyzes the financial data of the client company India: HDFC Bank—transaction monitoring	Detection of anomalies in large amounts of data; detection of suspicious transactions in real time; fraud prevention; detection of fraudulent schemes by the graph method; dynamic risk assessment through implementation into the management system	Training AI requires a large amount of high-quality and representative data; only large companies can afford to increase infrastructure costs due to the need for powerful servers and cloud storage; an ethical issue of impact on workplaces
Intelligent decision support systems (1, 2, 3, 4), (+)		
Russia: The candidate selection software is the Vera robot UAE: ADNOC-decision making system for oil exploration business India: Tata consultancy services—automated risk management	Real-time analysis of financial transactions; risk assessment based on historical data; automation of the loan approval process; monitoring suspicious patterns of employee behavior; optimization of verification processes in terms of KYC and AML	The need for a large amount of high-quality data for training; the technological complexity of integration with existing programs; the threat to cybersecurity

(continued)

Table 2 (continued)

Country experience (developments, solutions, services)	Areas of application of AI	Restrictions, challenges
Speech recognition and synthesis (1, 2, 3, 4), (+)		
Russia: The project of the T-Bank "Cybersquall" The virtual voice assistant from Yandex is Alice UAE: Voice-controlled virtual assistants (medicine and finance) India: Accurate and localized speech recognition solutions. Features—diversity of languages and accents in India	Identifying suspicious patterns when analyzing conversations with customers; biometric voice authentication; monitoring calls for keywords; recognition of the client's moods (aggression or nervousness, etc.)	Low accuracy of speech recognition in a noisy environment or in the presence of an accent, slang; language barrier; difficulties in ensuring the confidentiality of processed information; limited usage scenarios
Note:		
Conform (+)	Roadmap for the development of "end-to-end" digital technology "Neurotechnology and artificial intelligence"	
Not conform (−)		
(1)	Fraud risk prevention stage (preventive measures)	
(2)	Stage identification of fraud risks	
(3)	The stage of fraud risk assessment	
(4)	Retaliatory and corrective actions	

verification. On sites with obvious signs of financial pyramids, AI creates a large number of requests free advice or a callback, and then, delaying time in telephone conversations with fake brokers, proactively neutralize them. When fake brokers call back, they end up on bots that mimic potential customers interested in investing. The task of these humanoid robots is to keep the criminal on the line as long as possible and prevent him from getting through to real people. Cybersquall bots receive an average of 1500–2000 fraudulent calls per day, up to 3500 during peak hours. Cybersquall is a working tool that is of interest to all commercial banks [20].

Also, effective tools, according to [11–13], are partnerships with technology companies that already have experience in developing AI systems to combat fraud, investments in employee training, and more active regulatory work in terms of adapting standards and bills to rapidly changing AI practices.

5 Conclusion

Firstly, the initial phase of the study examined the experience of India and the UAE in using AI technologies to prevent fraud. Using qualitative methods of analysis of scientific literature and state development programs, we obtained the following conclusions.

India is actively developing computer vision to combat fraud, creating complex authentication systems based on product recognition, faces and live fingerprints. The country has achieved great success in the field of deep learning, which analyzes incoming transaction data and predicts potential fraud. We have identified features including government support and funding for startups, government regulation of ethical issues in the use of AI to prevent fraud.

The UAE has opened many specialized centers and universities specializing on AI; the state is actively attracting investments in AI programs. Subtechnologies of generative AI are developing, which can increase the productivity of individual service lines, track not only transactions, but also customer behavior, analyze the financial data of the client company, identify anomalies and report them. We have identified features that include funding based on cooperation between the state and private companies, including knowledge sharing and technology partnerships, with an emphasis on the development of AI security tools in various sectors of the economy.

In Russia, AI is also becoming an effective tool in the fight against economic crime. Funding for AI programs increases annually, the state is developing national technology development programs. We have identified features that include the activity of government regulation and cooperation between the state and private companies; AI solutions are developing primarily in the financial sector, where the main capital is concentrated.

Secondly, comparative analysis of economic indicators of AI solutions financing and the degree of use of various information security tools in Russian organizations allow us to conclude that there are significant opportunities to increase high-tech AI-based solutions to prevent fraud. While Russia's GDP shows a considerable lag in AI integration, positive trends are emerging through government initiatives to spur the development of AI security solutions, partly due to the growing problem of cyber fraud affecting Russian citizens. However, it is worth noting that only very large businesses can afford such solutions, making financial sector organizations and large holdings the main drivers of development.

Thirdly, using the case study method, we reviewed the best practices for implementing AI to prevent fraud. This allowed us to highlight the positive effects and assess the priorities for the development of AI in various sectors of the economy and areas of activity. The study shows that the priority areas for the development of AI solutions in Russia are the banking sector, government agencies, cybersecurity, and the priority processes include control of organizational transactions, due diligence, and partner verification.

Fourthly, in the final part of the study, based on a comparison of the best practices of India, the UAE and the directions of the roadmap for the development of the end-to-end digital technology "Neurotechnologies and Artificial Intelligence" in Russia, priority opportunities for the development and limitations of various AI subtechnologies. Technologies based on the development of advanced methods, intelligent decision support systems, speech recognition and synthesis can be used at all stages of countering fraud and almost all comply with the roadmap for the development of the end-to-end digital technology "Neurotechnologies and Artificial Intelligence".

Deep learning and machine learning models show the greatest effect and high probability of detection, so we see the greatest potential as preventive measures, as well as at the stage of identifying fraud risks, in the development of computer vision and natural language processing technologies.

Thus, various approaches and successful practices of using AI to combat fraud in the UAE and India made it possible to answer the question of what promising areas should be strengthened in the use of AI to combat fraud in Russia, as well as what opportunities and limitations the use of individual AI subtechnologies opens up.

This study has some limitations. Due to challenges in quantitative data analysis, we selected the case study method. Future studies should enhance qualitative analysis by adding a quantitative evaluation of implementing AI solutions' effectiveness. There are also large time costs for searching and analyzing cases. The limited volume of the article did not allow us to consider successful cases from other countries actively developing AI technologies the USA, the European Union, China, Israel, Great Britain, etc. At the same time, the study may be of interest to researchers, business representatives and government agencies that form corporate and government strategies to improve economic security and protect against fraud risks.

References

1. Berova, Y. M., & Tutukov, A. Y. (2024). The potential of artificial intelligence in crime investigation: For or against. *Sociopolitical Sciences, 14*, 96–100. https://doi.org/10.33693/2223-0092-2024-14-3-96-100
2. Whiting, D. G., Hansen, J. V., McDonald, J. B., Albrecht, C., & Albrecht, W. S. (2012). Machine learning methods for detecting patterns of management fraud. *Computational Intelligence, 2*(8), 505–527. https://doi.org/10.1111/j.1467-8640.2012.00425.x
3. Brown, N. C., Crowley, R. M., & Elliott, W. B. (2020). What are you saying? Using topic to detect financial misreporting. *Journal of Accounting Research, 5*(8), 237–291. https://doi.org/10.1111/1475-679X.12294
4. Chiji, L. E. (2024). Artificial intelligence for detecting and preventing procurement fraud. *International Journal of Business Ecosystem & Strategy, 6*, 63–73. https://doi.org/10.36096/ijbes.v6i1.477
5. Shabaany, A., & Ljepava, N. (2018). The expected role of artificial intelligence in digital transformation of business and government sector in UAE. In In *2nd AUE international research conference*. https://doi.org/10.13140/RG.2.2.34857.95843
6. Guo, J., Liu, G., Zuo, Y., & Wu, J. (2018). Learning sequential behavior representations for fraud detection. In *IEEE international conference on data mining (ICDM)* (pp. 127–136). IEEE. https://doi.org/10.1109/ICDM.2018.00028
7. Shakyawar, M., & Shakya, K. (2024). Using artificial intelligence to improve banking services in India: A review and prospects for the future. *International Journal for Research in Applied Science and Engineering Technology, 12*, 728–738. https://doi.org/10.22214/ijraset.2024.59549
8. Fiore, U., De Santis, A., Perla, F., Zanetti, P., & Palmieri, F. (2019). Using generative adversarial networks for improving classification effectiveness in credit card fraud detection. *Information Sciences, 479*, 448–455. https://doi.org/10.1016/j.ins.2017.12.030
9. Plakandaras, B., Gogas, P., Papadimitriou, T., & Tsamardinos, I. (2022). Credit card fraud detection with automated machine learning systems. *Applied Artificial Intelligence, 36*(1), 2086354. https://doi.org/10.1080/08839514.2022.2086354

10. Rai, J., & Goyal, M. (2024). Role of the digital India movement to incorporate the digital technologies in the Indian system: Adoption of artificial intelligence. In *Omnichannel approach to co-creating customer experiences through metaverse platforms*. IGI Global. https://doi.org/10.4018/979-8-3693-1866-9.ch011
11. Abu, H. Y., Sierra, L., & Garcia-Benau, M. (2023). A bibliometric review of information technology, artificial intelligence, and blockchain on auditing. *Total Quality Management & Business Excellence, 35*, 1–23. https://doi.org/10.1080/14783363.2023.2256260
12. Owusu, G., Koomson, T., & Donkor, G. (2023). A scientometric analysis of the structure and trends in corporate fraud research: A 66-year review. *Journal of Financial Crime, 31*, 121. https://doi.org/10.1108/JFC-05-2023-0121
13. Agadi, K., & Kinange, U. (2024). A bibliometric review of artificial intelligence in talent acquisition with respect to India. *GBS Impact: Journal of Multi Disciplinary Research, 9*, 162–174. https://doi.org/10.58419/gbs.v9i2.922311
14. Ramos, S., Perez-Lopez, J., & Abreu, R. (2024). Bibliometric analysis of artificial intelligence trends in auditing and fraud detection. *Corporate Governance and Organizational Behavior Review, 8*, 330–342. https://doi.org/10.22495/cgobrv8i2sip8
15. Yadav, N., Sharma, L., & Dhake, U. (2023). Artificial intelligence: The future. *International Journal of Scientific Research in Engineering and Management, 7*, 1–10. https://doi.org/10.55041/IJSREM27796
16. Mohammed, A., Khan, F., Mohammed, A., Abdalla, Y., Mohammed, A., & Ahmad, A. (2024). Impact of AI applications on corporate financial reporting quality: Evidence from UAE corporations. *Qubahan Academic Journal, 4*, 785–795. https://doi.org/10.48161/qaj.v4n3a860
17. Mohammad, R. (2024). Generative AI in fintech: Advancing risk assessment and fraud detection in digital payment technologies. *International Journal for Research in Applied Science & Engineering Technology, 12*(8), 1318–1326. https://doi.org/10.22214/ijraset.2024.64110
18. Mayanard, N. (2022). *AI in financial fraud detection: Key trends, competitor leaderboard & market forecasts 2022–2027*. JUNIPER Research. Retrieved from https://www.juniperresearch.com/research/fintech-payments/fraud-identity/ai-financial-fraud-detection-trends-report/
19. Institute for Statistical Studies and Economics of Knowledge. (2024). *IT industry: Key indicators 2019–2023*. National Research University Higher School of Economics. Retrieved from https://issek.hse.ru/mirror/pubs/share/914035925.pdf
20. National Center for Artificial Intelligence Development. (2023). *Index of readiness of priority sectors of the Russian economy for the implementation of artificial intelligence (analytical report, IV, 68)*. Government of the Russian Federation. Retrieved from https://ai.gov.ru/upload/iblock/921/w0g8hixh4wxppikl2hu4j2vwv4tprjes.pdf
21. Abashkin, V. L., Abdrakhmanova, G. I., Vishnevsky, K. O., Gokhberg, L. M., et al. (2024). Digital economy indicators: 2024. In *Statistical digest* (p. 276). National Research University Higher School of Economics. Retrieved from https://issek.hse.ru/mirror/pubs/share/892389163.pdf
22. Medvedev, Y. (2024). How Russian artificial intelligence catches scammers. *Rossiyskaya Gazeta—Stolichnyy Issleduya, 68*, 9310. Retrieved from https://rg.ru/2024/03/27/sledstvie-vedet-nejroset.html

AI-Driven Predictive Maintenance of Industrial Gearboxes

Hassan Al Ouatiq and Sergei Pronin

Abstract This study develops a predictive maintenance framework for industrial gearboxes that employs CWT and XGBoost algorithms to improve early fault detection. Compared with the traditional method for detecting gearbox faults, the proposed approach can extract more useful time-frequency domain features from the vibration signals using CWT to accurately diagnose slight faults which are usually not detected by universal methods. XGBoost, a machine learning classifier, then uses these extracted features to classify the data to determine if the operation is normal or fault states, including early-stage gear cracks. To alleviate common problems such as imbalanced data, the framework incorporates Bayesian optimization and SMOTE (Synthetic Minority Oversampling Technique), attaining a considerable classification accuracy of 94.49%. This methodology has practical benefits such as minimizing downtime of the equipment, reducing maintenance costs, and improving the reliability of industrial operations, thus making it appropriate for real-world industrial applications to better meet the goals of Industry 4.0. Further research will aim to generalize fault detection to more types of gear faults and to determine how this could be integrated into industrial IoT systems to increase autonomous maintenance capabilities.

Keywords Industry 4.0 · Predictive maintenance · Fault detection · Wavelet transform · XGBoost · Digital transformation

1 Introduction

In a modern industry, the operational reliability of critical machinery is of paramount importance due to the costly financial and operational consequences of unplanned downtime. Industrial gearboxes, common in applications ranging from wind turbines to manufacturing systems, are especially susceptible due to their

H. Al Ouatiq (✉) · S. Pronin
Altai State Technical University, Barnaul, Russia

F. Tao et al. (eds.), *Artificial Intelligence and Digital Transformation*, Lecture Notes in Information Systems and Organisation 78,
https://doi.org/10.1007/978-3-032-00118-4_6

complex designs and challenging operating environments. Common faults such as cracks, misalignment and wear can significantly raise maintenance costs, hinder production timelines and cause catastrophic failure if not detected.

Instead of being based on scheduled inspections, predictive maintenance uses real-time data to continuously assess the health and condition of machines, and represents an effective approach to reducing the risks associated with production downtimes. This method is favorable for gearbox, since for the vibration signals of the gearbox, they are complex and instantaneous signals, so it is difficult to detect fault in its early stage.

The latest trends in AI especially in the area of machine learning have empowered predictive maintenance systems to be better and have a wider scope. In line with the former assumption, one of the most powerful tools for fault classification is Extreme Gradient Boosting (XGBoost), especially when combined with more advanced signal processing techniques (e.g., wavelet transforms). Wavelet transforms enable detailed time-frequency analysis enabling detection for transient events and subtle anomalies embedded in vibration data—which often goes unnoticed in frequency-domain domains relying on traditional Fast Fourier Transform (FFT) based methods.

In this study, the conformity of Continuous Wavelet Transform (CWT) and XGBoost provides multiple merits in addressing against traditional fault detection filters. First, this hybrid approach works well with noisy and non-stationary data, yielding consistent fault detection capabilities in terms of load variations and dynamic operational states. Moreover, its capacity to detect early-stage failures—like tiny gear cracks—far outclasses that of traditional techniques, which have difficulty with low-amplitude, time-varying signals. Finally, the proposed method can achieve even better performance in predictive maintenance, where data imbalance is widely observed by applying one available data balancing approach, SMOTE and Bayesian optimization.

This study builds upon our previous works, where we explored hybrid deep learning models and synthetic vibration data generation for wind turbine gearboxes. These earlier studies laid the groundwork for improving fault detection sensitivity and data diversity, which we further develop here using a wavelet-XGBoost-based predictive maintenance framework [1, 2].

The main goals of the current study are:

- Propose an advanced predictive maintenance architecture that integrates wavelet transforms with XGBoost to systematically improve the precision of fault detection.
- Prove the efficiency of the framework in dealing with noisy data, dynamic loads, and incipient gearbox faults compared to the conventional detection methods.
- Refine the system to appropriately handle class imbalance while achieving generalizable performance combined across varying operational conditions.

The next sections of this paper are organized as follows: In Sect. 2, we review the state-of-the-art of predictive maintenance and AI-based fault visibility methods. In Sect. 3, we provide the proposed methodology, including data preprocessing, wavelet feature extraction, and training procedure of XGBoost model. In Sect. 4, the results are presented and discussed, with emphasis on the practical consequences for industry. Section 5 presents challenges, broader impacts, and future directions for research. Finally, Sect. 6 wraps up the contributions made by this study and indicates directions for future research.

2 Literature Review

2.1 Predictive Maintenance in Industry

Over the last 10 years, there has been great development in predictive maintenance thanks to the introduction of artificial intelligence (AI) and data-driven approaches to the industrial processing chain. With these advancements, fault detection has evolved with the base of early identification of the possible region for the machinery issues which can positively lower the unplanned downtime optimizing maintenance plan, and minimizing overall costs for operations. This type of preemptive measures is crucial in economic and environment-critical industry in particular when a machine breaks down.

Industrial gearboxes, essential components for mechanical power transmission across diverse sectors such as energy, manufacturing, and transportation, have been central to predictive maintenance research. Given their complex mechanical interactions and frequent exposure to harsh operational conditions, gearboxes are especially prone to faults like cracks, misalignments, and wear (Fig. 1). Undetected, these issues can severely disrupt production processes, inflate maintenance costs, and potentially result in catastrophic equipment failures. While vibration-based monitoring remains the most widely adopted technique, alternative approaches such as current-based analysis have also shown promise in gearbox fault detection, particularly in wind turbine applications, as demonstrated by Qiao and Gong [3]. A comprehensive review of such data-driven condition monitoring frameworks is provided by Aburakhia [4]. Therefore, robust predictive maintenance practices are not just beneficial—they are essential.

Furthermore, good predictive maintenance contributes directly to wider sustainability goals. Fault prediction and maintenance optimization not only help industries save resource consumption such as energy; they also prolong the life of equipment and reduce the environmental impacts.

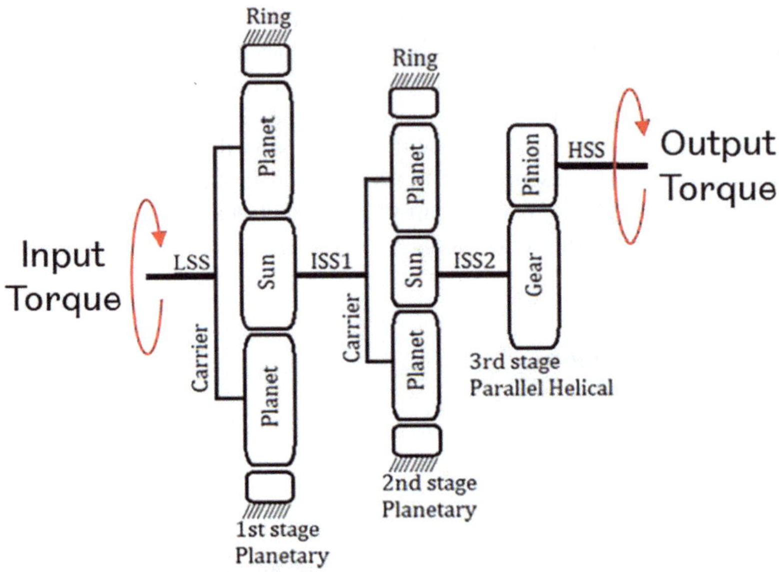

Fig. 1 Diagram of Gearbox and Key Components in Fault Detection. This schematic illustrates the structure of a multi-stage planetary gearbox, including input and output torque pathways through various components, such as the sun, planetary gears, and the helical stage

Predictive maintenance is further accelerating with the alignment of principles of Industry 4.0. As per the latest trends, firms have created smart, automated maintenance systems by incorporating advanced technologies like AI, the Internet of Things (IoT), and real-time analytics that provide holistic, real-time monitoring and diagnostics. This also ensures that these sophisticated systems also dovetail nicely with Environmental, Social, and Governance (ESG) principles, fostering sustainable industries, improving worker safety and minimizing the planetary impact of operations.

Therefore, integrating predictive maintenance approaches ensures not only continuity and reliability of operation, but also relevant positioning of industries into an evolving digital transformation of industries aimed to satisfy both operational and sustainability needs.

2.2 *Machine Learning in Fault Detection*

Machine learning (ML) has become central to predictive maintenance by providing powerful methods for fault detection and classification. Among these methods, ensemble models such as Extreme Gradient Boosting (XGBoost) have shown particular promise due to their robustness and adaptability to industrial datasets. Wang et al. [5] notably pioneered the application of XGBoost for monitoring wind turbine gearboxes, highlighting its strength in capturing complex, non-linear patterns within vibration data more effectively than traditional classifiers. Similarly, Su et al. [6] demonstrated the successful application of XGBoost in vibration-based monitoring of wind turbine towers, further supporting its reliability in real-world predictive maintenance scenarios.

Why XGBoost? The decision goes well beyond just computation speed. Its major benefit is interpretability; the decision-tree-based setup lets users understand how the model arrives at its predictions, an important consideration in fields in which there is a need for clear understanding of and trust in automated systems. Finally, compared to other machine learning algorithms, XGBoost is also quite robust to the angry data of the real world, and can naturally tackle class imbalance issues which is a common problem in industry when handling fault detection problems, where faulting conditions usually only occupy a small number of cases.

Signal processing techniques can be further combined with other machine learning models to improve the detection abilities. For instance, the combination of XGBoost and wavelet transform greatly enhances the capacity of extracting features from vibration signals. Ogaili et al. [7] showcased this synergy with significant improvements in classification accuracy, especially for subtle or early-stage faults.

Though alternative machine learning techniques, including support vector machines (SVMs) and neural networks have also been extensively investigated, these approaches also have limited capacity. Guo et al. [8] combined sound and vibration features with the support vector machine (SVM) model to obtain classification results. However, with large datasets, SVMs can be computationally expensive and may not be practical in real-time industrial applications. Similarly, even though deep learning models can achieve high accuracy, they usually require large datasets and computational resources, and thus are not a feasible option for many industrial use cases. These shortcomings illustrate the practical benefits of XGBoost, which achieves a good trade-off among high predictive performance and the feasibility to implement and operate in the real-world. Vives [9] also demonstrated the potential of ML-based vibration analysis in wind turbines, supporting the broader applicability of such techniques.

2.3 *Artificial Intelligence in Industrial Digitalization*

Artificial intelligence (AI) has become a driving force of the digitalization of industrial maintenance failure detection and predictive maintenance. AI can analyze key patterns in vast datasets to predict faults at an early stage, which is an area that conventional methods fail to work on. For example, the combination of machine learning algorithms like XGBoost and well-outlined signal processing techniques based on wavelets has proved to be a powerful method for providing accurate predictive maintenance evaluation results.

2.4 Wavelet Transforms for Feature Extraction

The wavelet transform is a powerful mathematical tool widely used for non-stationary signal analysis (rotation machinery signals) since it is capable of analyzing the signal on the time and frequency levels at the same time. This allows them to be particularly useful for detecting transient characteristics and slight anomalies in vibrations signals that reflect initial faults. In contrast to Fourier transforms, which do not possess time localization, wavelet transforms provide the means to decompose signals into scale and translation invariant components, providing the ability to detect complex signal patterns. For example, Continuous Wavelet Transform (CWT) improves fault detection capabilities by focusing on specific variations in the nature of signals, which is essential for detecting faults during their early stage.

Recent extension of feature extraction to the time-frequency domain with wavelet transforms has shown particular success in industrial applications. In particular, Toma and Kim [10] show that when combined with ensemble learning models, discrete wavelet transforms (DWT) improve fault diagnosis accuracy for induction motors. In the same vein, wavelet-based feature extraction outperforms traditional time-domain methods by a significant margin in the detection of subtle, transient anomalies, Das and Bagci Das [11] demonstrating this feature in their study.

2.5 XGBoost in Fault Detection

Machine learning algorithms, such as Extreme Gradient Boosting (XGBoost) have become essential tools in the detection of industrial faults due to their remarkable performance and versatility. Focused on, an ensemble algorithm based on decision trees called XGBoost poses significant advantages over other machine learning methods. Especially handling the structural, tabular data that is typical of industrial settings. Its capacity to efficiently handle the imbalanced datasets of predictive maintenance scenarios—which are so common—makes it particularly valuable.

One of the key advantages of XGBoost is its interpretability. As opposed to more complex models like deep neural networks, XGBoost allows practitioners to easily understand decision-making reasoning within the model thanks to transparent tree structures. This interpretability is especially important in industrial applications where trust and explainability justify routine decisions or maintenance strategies.

Moreover, XGBoost's performance is inherently robust even with noisy and incomplete real-world data, effectively capturing non-linear relationships and subtle fault signatures. We should be particularly careful with interpreting statistical results that suggest something contrary to common sense. It is observed that XGBoost is better than the shallow learning methods in extracting features, and it outperforms the deep learning approach. Such patterns are hard to understand without sufficient domain knowledge; deep learning model fitting as we know makes no sense because any combination of parameters can pass as an interpretation. Wang et al. [5] highlighted XGBoost's superior capability in analyzing vibration data from wind turbine gearboxes, showcasing its adaptability and predictive strength for detecting faults early and reliably.

Integrating XGBoost with advanced signal processing techniques, particularly Continuous Wavelet Transform (CWT), further enhances its effectiveness. This combination of methods enables XGBoost to exploit rich, detailed time-frequency features obtained from vibration signals, tremendously boosting fault classification accuracy. Ogaili et al. [7] verified the benefits resulting from this synergy, achieving superior classification performance even in complicated and changing operational environments.

XGBoost, as compared to alternative methods such as Support Vector Machines (SVMs), neural networks, even LightGBM, stands out for its optimal blend of computational efficiency, accuracy, interpretability, and practical applicability. For instance, Tang et al. [12] proposed an enhanced LightGBM-based approach for online gearbox fault detection in wind turbines, demonstrating good results in real-time scenarios. However, XGBoost has consistently shown superior generalization performance and robustness when handling noisy, imbalanced industrial datasets—making it a particularly reliable choice for real-world deployment in predictive maintenance systems.

2.6 Broader Industrial Impact

While the impact of AI-powered solutions such as wavelet-XGBoost could scale beyond an individual machine diagnostic, and their applications are relevant for both industrial and sustainability perspectives, it is clear that AI applications can scale much further than simple burning of machinery. These innovations resonate with current industrial policy trends that are focused on digital sovereignty, sustainability, and technological self-sufficiency. AI-powered predictive maintenance frameworks maximize resource use and minimize energy use; core drivers to improve operational efficiency while meeting requirements for sustainable manufacturing and ESG compliance.

By forming alternate systems to network equipment in a manner, industries can minimize energy wastage, thereby reducing their carbon footprint. Moreover, extending the operational lifetimes of hardware helps to use resources more sustainably, in line with planetary sustainability goals.

In addition, these improvements support Industry 4.0 directly, creating interconnected and responsive operational systems. Predictive maintenance within the Industrial Internet of Things (IIoT) infrastructures improves the ability to continuously monitor conditions in real time and to decide when to act automatically. End-to-end systems not only improve fault detection, but also strengthen operational resilience and competitive advantage in ever more digitized industrial landscapes.

Thus, the use of AI tools such as XGBoost and wavelet transforms transform predictive maintenance while maintaining technical solvability and strategic demands for sustainability as well as digitalization in industry—these factors make it supportive and maintainable.

2.7 Hybrid Models in Predictive Maintenance

Hybrid models combining signal processing techniques and machine learning algorithms for enhanced fault detection. Such models leverage from both methodologies by allowing for important features to be extracted in a high dimensional domain representation, leading to better classification rates. Aburakhia et al. [13] proposed a hybrid model for rolling bearing fault diagnosis by integrating wavelet decomposition and neural networks to provide low delay for the system. Although effective, the high computational needs of neural networks can still be a challenge for real-time hardware applications.

In our previous work (see, [2]), we explored a hybrid deep learning approach that combines time-frequency features with neural networks to enhance fault detection in wind turbine gearboxes, demonstrating the potential of such methods for improving early fault sensitivity and system reliability.

On the other hand, XGBoost provides a practical solution thanks to its speed and performance. Zhang et al. [14] used a deep graph convolutional network to diagnose gearbox faults, finding the accuracy of their approach to be high, but offering no practical suggestions for the implementation in industrial settings due to the computation intensive nature of their work. This study also emphasizes the importance of balancing model complexity with real-time operational needs, a balance achieved by gradient-boosting methods (XGBoost). The most recent works on this subject by Chen et al. [15] have used XGBoost to perform fault detection with vibration signals which have shown high accuracy, nevertheless they fail to take advantage of the time-frequency domain analysis techniques such as wavelet transformation. Apeiranthitis et al. [16] further explored CNN-based models for rotating parts, reinforcing their role in predictive maintenance.

2.8 Addressing Data Imbalance in Fault Detection

Data imbalance is a common challenge in fault detection, as drive normal operational states often far outweighs drivers' faulty states in the dataset. This class imbalance can result in biased models that overfit the majority class, and affect fault detection accuracy negatively. To tackle this problem, Synthetic Minority Oversampling Technique (SMOTE) is widely used to create additional samples of the minority class. Tang et al. [17] proved that employing SMOTE together with

LightGBM enhanced wind turbine gearbox fault detection by equalizing class distributions.

In this study, SMOTE is applied on the wavelet transformed dataset prior to the XGBoost model training. This guarantees the classifier remains sensitive to such rare fault cases, especially in the crack state in gearboxes [18]. Using SMOTE with Bayesian hyperparameter optimization also makes it possible to finetune the model so that a balance is maintained between sensitivity to fault detection and overall classification results [19].

2.9 Research Gap and Contribution

Although machine learning approaches and wavelet transformation techniques have independently made significant progress in the field of fault detection, there is limited research that combines these approaches through the use of ensemble models such as XGBoost. Integrated use of XGBoost and wavelet-based feature extraction has not been extensively studied either for complex fault detection tasks, whereas previous work has independently confirmed the validity of each approach. Thus, the innovative contribution of this study is the implementation of a hybrid approach for gearbox fault detection by integrating CWT with XGBoost.

This fused model is believed to improve fault detection capability, in particular, for earlier faults, while ensuring high level of performance without relying on the heavy computation overheads of typical deep learning models. The proposed model is applied to imbalanced datasets which are common in fault detection applications by applying SMOTE and Bayesian optimization methods, so it is ultimately much more suitable to industrial applications in real time.

To summarize, this work adds to the literature in the following ways:

1. Demonstrating the efficacy of CWT in extracting fault-relevant features from gearbox vibration signals.
2. Validating the application of XGBoost as a classifier optimized for high sensitivity in detecting multiple gearbox fault states.
3. Addressing class imbalance through SMOTE and improving model generalizability via Bayesian optimization.

This literature review highlighted the significance of an integrated wavelet-XGBoost framework in predictive maintenance, providing a necessary base for the methodology and findings addressed in the paper.

3 Methods and Analysis

3.1 Dataset Description

In this paper, synthetic vibration data was collected in controlled laboratory environments to simulate real-world operating conditions and evaluated. Fiber-Optic sensors that use Fiber Bragg Grating (FBG) technology were used for precise collection of high-quality vibration data. As a result, these sensors excel for vibration monitoring thanks to their high sensitivity, excellent resolution and immunity to electromagnetic interference, making them especially well-suited for harsh industrial environments.

The signals collected belong to two major conditions: normal (healthy) and faulty (gear with a crack). The sampling frequency of each vibration signal was 50 Hz and it was 60 Hz, which can ensure capturing the key time-series features of the condition of the gear-box.

The dataset includes these specific columns:

- Vibration_Normal_50Hz_Stage_I: Vibration data representing normal operating conditions, recorded at 50 Hz.
- Vibration_Cracked_50Hz_Stage_I: Vibration data from gearboxes with known cracked gear faults, recorded at 50 Hz.
- Vibration_Normal_60Hz_Stage_I: Normal operating condition data recorded at 60 Hz.
- Vibration_Cracked_60Hz_Stage_I: Cracked gear fault condition data recorded at 60 Hz.

The dataset consists of thousands of vibration cycles, which ensures enough training data for robust training and reliable validation of the model. In particular, although real normal condition data was obtained with Fiber-Optic sensors, synthetic data was also generated to complement the training dataset with realistic variations as explained in our former paper named "Generating synthetic vibration data for a gearbox in a wind turbine" [1]. This method provided a balanced and diverse dataset, improving the model's performance in accurately identifying minute variances between normal and faulty gears.

3.2 Data Preprocessing

Before we extract any feature from the raw vibration signals, we do some preprocessing of the signals (cleaning and standardizing the data) to ensure accurate and reliable fault detection; this is one of the most important steps in the whole process. First, each vibration signal is normalized, i.e., the data for each vibration signal has a zero mean and unit variance. It normalizes various signals which allows to make a fair comparison over vibration features across different operational states.

We then low-pass the signal to remove undesired high frequency noise. Now, we are left with only the parts of the vibration data that are useful in the detection of gearbox faults. And for your information, good noise reduction improves the aquosity for the next post-processing.

These steps are for pre-processing of data which is returned as a matrix. The matrix contains several rows (representing distinct observations of a vibration cycle) and columns (representing different signal points over the course of the time). This format helps to make it easier for the following process based on wavelets to extract useful features.

Table 1 summarizes some characteristics of our dataset and provides a brief description of the signal processing (noting data class distribution, sample size, and other the most important parameters):

Here we used synthetic data generated with methods explained in our previous publication [1], to complement real collected data with Fiber-Optic (FBG) sensors. The dataset, structured and augmented, lays an excellent base for sound, reliable fault detection.

3.3 *Wavelet Transformation for Feature Extraction*

Detection of anomalous vibration signatures is an important part of ensuring the reliability of machinery and determining the most effective method of obtaining transient and steady-state features. The conventional frequency-domain approaches such as Fast Fourier Transform (FFT) have shortcomings, especially in recognizing ephemeral anomalies which may act as vital signs of incipient faults. The Continuous Wavelet Transform (CWT) was chosen for this purpose, being the best in recording the time and frequency of non-stationary signals.

CWT in its basic form is just performing a signal sweep using the wavelets of increasing scale (frequency resolution) and position (time localization). Mathematically this can be expressed as:

$$W(a,b) = \int_{-\infty}^{\infty} x(t)\psi^{*}\left(\frac{t-b}{a}\right)dt$$

Table 1 Dataset characteristics and preprocessing details

Parameter	Description
Total samples	Approximately 4000
Class distribution	Balanced (normal vs. faulty)
Sampling rates	50 Hz, 60 Hz
Signal duration per cycle	Consistent intervals
Data augmentation	Synthetic data generation (see previous work)

where $x(t)$ represents the original vibration signal as a function of time t (measured in s); ψ^* denotes the complex conjugate of the mother wavelet function, which serves as a localized time-frequency basis; a is the scale parameter that controls the frequency resolution. A larger a corresponds to a lower frequency (wider wavelet), while a smaller a corresponds to a higher frequency (narrower wavelet). The scale is unitless but is linked to frequency through the wavelet function. b is the translation parameter, which determines the time localization of the wavelet function (measured in s). It shifts the wavelet function along the time axis to analyze different time instances of the signal. $W(a, b)$ represents the wavelet coefficient, which indicates the correlation between the signal and the scaled and translated wavelet at a given scale a and position b.

In this research, the selection of the db4 wavelet was intentional as the mother wavelet. The reason for this selection is not random. db4 faults are well-known to catch abrupt discontinuities indicating mechanical functions, which are original signals [10]. By being compact-support it ensures that we capture events that are significant without getting superimposed over the signal and being smooth by definition helps us reliably extract meaningful features. While alternative wavelets (Haar, Morlet, etc.) were explored, preliminary results indicated that db4 consistently showed higher sensitivity to transient gearbox faults.

The signal was decomposed in four different levels using db4. This is a compromise—low enough decomposition to reveal a nuanced, high frequency fault, yet high enough not to tax computation. At each level of decomposition, sets of wavelet coefficients are produced reflecting specific frequency bands. Individual means for all coefficients at each level were obtained rather than dynamically analyzing each of their coefficients, enabling the extraction of key diagnostic information. Subsequently, to facilitate the analysis, we average these marks because even small variations and noise in signals can deliver strong extracted patterns.

Overall, the choice of utilizing CWT with the Daubechies db4 wavelet was not merely about technical convenience—this was a targeted strategy designed to reliably capture the subtle characteristics of gearbox faults that other techniques often fail to detect, and the ensuing sections clearly showcase the advantages of this approach, highlighting the practical importance and application of wavelet transforms in the field of predictive maintenance.

3.4 Synthetic Minority Oversampling Technique (SMOTE)

Since, in the dataset, the number of normal states is significantly more than the faulty (cracked) state, SMOTE was used to create a synthetic sample of minority class. A new method of generating data from minority samples is implemented here by generating samples of minority samples based directly on the k-nearest neighbors of the minority samples, thus making the classifier more sensitive to fault conditions. SMOTE works to counter model bias against the majority class and improve fault detection accuracy.

3.5 XGBoost Model for Classification

For the classification task, we chose Extreme Gradient Boosting (XGBoost), primarily due to its excellent performance with structured data, interpretability, and strong track record in predictive maintenance scenarios [13]. While several methods could have been suitable—such as LightGBM or neural networks—we specifically opted for XGBoost for a few critical reasons.

Firstly, XGBoost's ensemble architecture, where multiple decision trees are built sequentially, each aiming to minimize errors of preceding trees, provides a robust mechanism for capturing complex, nonlinear relationships in the data. This is particularly valuable for detecting subtle faults, which might not have straightforward, linear signatures. The objective function of XGBoost encapsulates this approach mathematically:

$$\mathcal{L}(\theta) = \sum_{i} l(y_i, \hat{y}_i) + \sum_{k} \Omega(f_k)$$

where y_i is the true label of the *ith* sample (typically binary or categorical for classification problems), and $\hat{y}_i$ is the predicted label from the model. The function $l(y_i, \hat{y}_i)$ represents the loss function, which quantifies the error between the predicted and actual values. Common choices include logarithmic loss for classification or squared error for regression, measured in dimensionless units.

The term $\Omega(f_k)$ is the regularization function, which penalizes model complexity to prevent overfitting. It typically depends on parameters like the number of trees, leaf weights, and split penalties, all of which influence the generalization ability of the model. The hyperparameters controlling regularization, such as L1 and L2 penalties, are typically measured in arbitrary units that depend on dataset normalization.

It's worth noting that we considered alternative models like LightGBM and neural networks. LightGBM offers slightly faster training speeds due to its histogram-based decision tree algorithm, but preliminary evaluations indicated XGBoost provided better classification accuracy, particularly for our imbalanced dataset. On the other hand, neural networks—especially deep learning architectures—could potentially capture very complex patterns but at the cost of significantly increased training time and resource consumption. In practical terms, neural networks required roughly three to four times the training duration of XGBoost for similar or only slightly improved results.

Additionally, XGBoost inherently handles imbalanced data more effectively through built-in mechanisms like weighting and regularization strategies, an advantage critical to fault detection where normal states frequently outnumber fault conditions. Computational efficiency was also a decisive factor. Our initial tests showed that XGBoost could reliably train on our dataset within minutes (typically 10–15 min for full hyperparameter tuning), whereas comparable neural network approaches took substantially longer (up to 40–50 min per training cycle).

Therefore, XGBoost emerged as the optimal choice, providing a balance of high accuracy, interpretability, efficient computation, and effective management of class imbalance, making it particularly suitable for practical industrial predictive maintenance applications.

3.6 Hyperparameter Optimization

To achieve optimal model performance, Bayesian optimization is employed to fine-tune the XGBoost hyperparameters. Key parameters optimized include the learning rate, which controls the contribution of each new tree to the ensemble—lower values generally improve accuracy but require more trees. The max depth parameter determines the maximum depth of each tree, influencing model complexity. The subsample ratio defines the fraction of samples used to train each tree, balancing accuracy and computational efficiency. Finally, the number of estimators sets the total number of trees in the model.

3.7 Performance Evaluation Metrics

To assess model effectiveness, several performance metrics are calculated. Accuracy measures the overall correctness of classification between normal and faulty states. Precision reflects the proportion of correctly identified fault cases, while recall indicates the proportion of actual faults detected by the model. The F1 score, a harmonic mean of precision and recall, represents a balance between false positives and false negatives. Additionally, the area under the ROC curve (AUC) provides an aggregate measure of model performance across all classification thresholds, capturing both sensitivity and specificity. A confusion matrix and ROC curve are generated to visually inspect classification performance across different fault types, ensuring a comprehensive evaluation of the model's fault detection capabilities.

3.8 Implementation Details

The solution was implemented in Python, using widely-used machine learning libraries, such as scikit-learn and XGBoost, for the data cleaning task. The wavelet transformation was performed using PyWavelets and the implementation of the SMOTE algorithm (to tackle data imbalance. The model was trained and evaluated on the high performance computing system (Intel Core i9 with 32GB of RAM) to process high-dimensional, wavelet-transformed dataset.

It is important to clarify that Fig. 2 presents a confusion matrix with approximately 100 examples for simplicity, whereas the actual training dataset contained

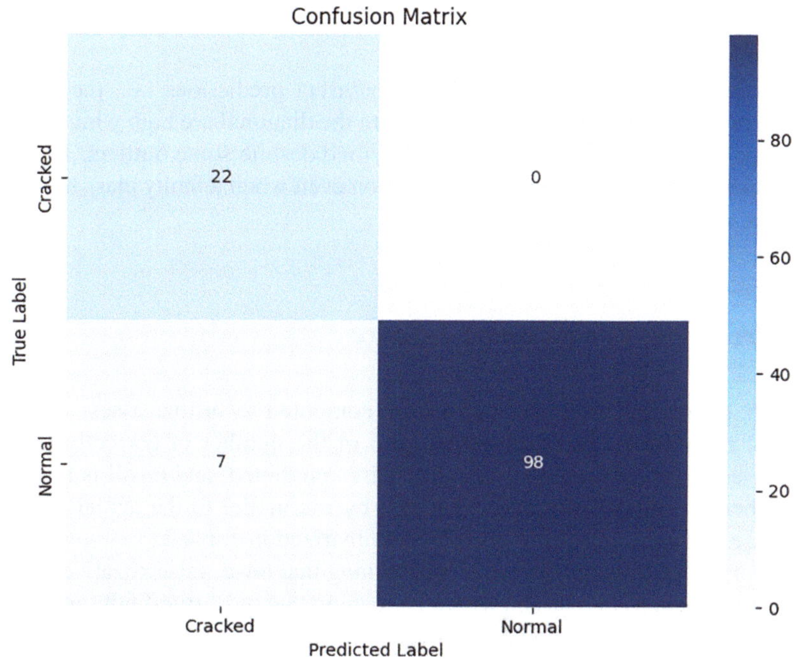

Fig. 2 Confusion matrix for fault classification

around 4000 samples. This dataset size was intentionally chosen to ensure sufficient diversity and volume for robust and reliable fault classification. However, since the data was generated under controlled laboratory conditions using synthetic inputs, validating the model with more diverse real-world operational data would further enhance its generalizability.

The entire implementation consisting of data preprocessing, feature extraction and model training scripts are publicly available at a public repository to promote reproducibility and enhance the opportunity for further development and validation by the research community.

4 Results

4.1 Classification Accuracy

The overall classification accuracy of the proposed model was 94.49%, which demonstrates its ability in distinguishing gearboxes in normal and cracked states. One disadvantage of accuracy, however, is that it does not consider the imbalance in the dataset, which can result in biased evaluation. Nevertheless, additional evaluation metrics are investigated to affirm the strength of the model.

4.2 Confusion Matrix

It shows a representation of correct and incorrect predictions i.e., the confusion matrix represented in Fig. 2. The values along the diagonal are high which indicates that normal and cracked states are well classified despite some outliers. This shows that the model is capable of fault identification even when a faulty class has a subtle condition.

4.3 Precision, Recall, and F1-Score

Precision, recall, and F1-score metrics are computed to further assess the performance of the models. Precision is the ratio of the number of correctly identified faulty cases to the total number of faulty cases predicted, and recall is the ratio of the number of actual faulty cases detected by the model to the actual number of faulty cases. These metrics per-class are summarized in Table 2.

The normal class has high precision, meaning that fewer false negatives are present, and the cracked class has high recall, meaning that most true-faults are detected. The F1-score is a harmonic mean of precision and recall, achieving a score of 0.95, indicating balanced model performance in regards to fault detection.

4.4 Receiver Operating Characteristic (ROC) Curve

The Receiver Operating Characteristic (ROC) curve, illustrated in Fig. 3, presents a visual assessment of the model's discriminative power for normal versus faulty instances, evaluated at various classification thresholds. The area under the ROC curve (AUC) is calculated as 0.97 whose result presents the model's high degree of separability as well as the predictive accuracy for the overall model.

The high AUC score demonstrates the model's accuracy and effectiveness in distinguishing between normal and cracked data, even against a potentially weak fault signal or noisy environment.

Table 2 Confusion matrix for fault classification

Class	Precision	Recall	F1-Score
Normal	1.00	0.93	0.97
Cracked	0.76	1.00	0.86
Weighted Avg.	0.96	0.94	0.95

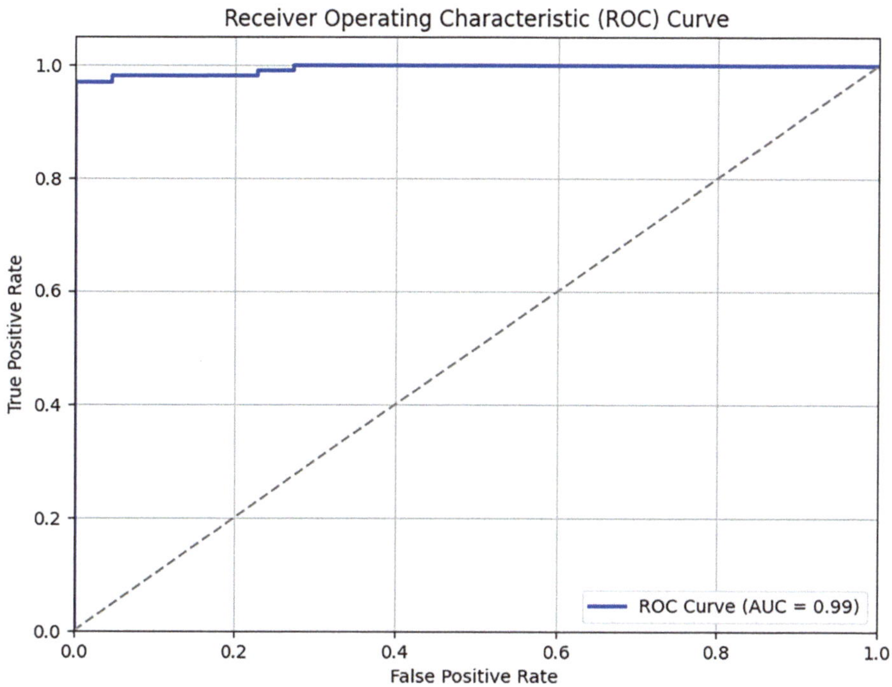

Fig. 3 ROC curve with AUC = 0.97

4.5 Precision-Recall Curve

As shown in Fig. 4, the precision-recall curve reflects the precision-recall trade-off at different thresholds used to define cracking as the detecting state. This indicates that the model is able to maintain high precision and recall across a wide range of thresholds, thus reinforcing that the model is a reliable classifier of the gear-box states under varying conditions.

The Precision-Recall (PR) curve illustrates that the system maintains a stable performance concerning the False Positive Rate (FPR) and False Negative Rate (FNR), which is of utmost importance when implementing real-time predictive maintenance applications.

4.6 Learning Curve

The learning curve, shown in Fig. 5, presents the model's performance as a function of the training data size, demonstrating the model's scalability. The accuracy plateaus as the training set grows, indicating that the model has achieved optimal performance without overfitting.

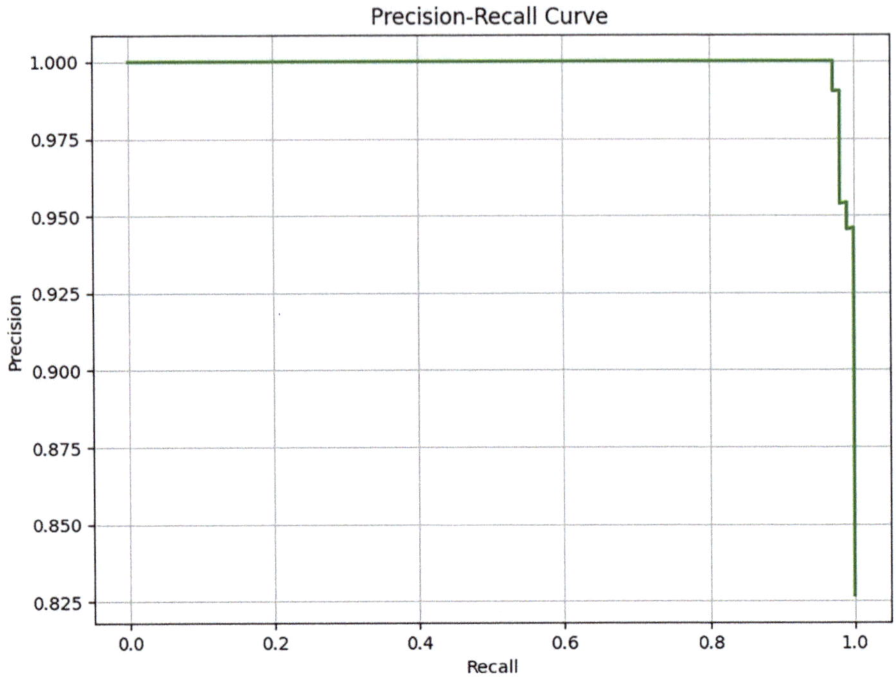

Fig. 4 Precision-recall curve for cracked gearbox detection

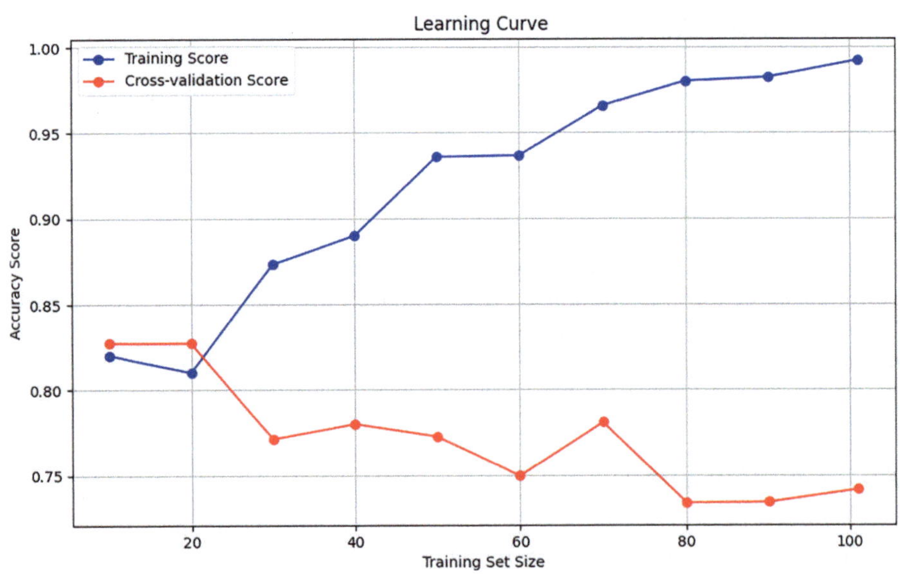

Fig. 5 Learning curve showing model scalability

The experience of successful handling of large datasets also confirms that the model is indeed able to process more extensive datasets that are common to industrial applications and can differ in cardinality by an order of magnitude.

4.7 Model Comparison

To validate the performance of the XGBoost classifier with wavelet-transformed features, a comparison was conducted with traditional classifiers, including Support Vector Machine (SVM) and Random Forest (RF). Table 3 summarizes the accuracy results for each model.

The XGBoost model outperformed both Random Forest and SVM, highlighting its suitability for fault detection in gearboxes when combined with wavelet-transformed features [14]. This result underscores the importance of feature selection and model choice for achieving high fault detection accuracy.

4.8 Interpretation of Results

Experimental results only collected the raw signal from the demo system, showing that wavelet-XGBoost framework has the highest accuracy, recall and precision for distinguishing between normal and faulty states. A robust and reliable model with these performance metrics is vital in scenarios where proactive fault detection can minimize system downtime and save costs. Wavelet transform is used to capture transient fault feature information that could easily be lost through time-domain or frequency-domain analysis.

Hence, when experimenting with leading techniques of classification, the original data and features yield the best results possible, with respect to other classifiers, with XGBoost performing superbly with the feature extraction from wavelets, resulting in a powered approach to real-time predictive maintenance for mass industry capabilities.

Table 3 Confusion matrix for fault classification

Model	Accuracy (%)
XGBoost	94.49
Random forest	88.31
SVM	85.72

5 Discussion

5.1 Implications for Predictive Maintenance

The goal of predictive maintenance is to identify and correct faults before they cause equipment failure, improving operational efficiency and lowering costs [17]. Then, the wavelet-XGBoost model satisfies these objectives together to offer a reliable frame for early fault diagnosis. The high recall in the craked state shows that the model correctly covers a wider variety of fault signatures so that the probability of missed detection is lower [15]. This is particularly important in industrial contexts, where losses from equipment failures can be extremely costly.

The use of wavelet transformation in this study addresses a key challenge in predictive maintenance: the detection of transient faults. Gearbox vibration signals are characterized by high complexity and contain fault signatures buried in the non-stationary signal components. Traditional frequency-domain analyses can miss these momentary characteristics, while time-frequency decomposition using continuous wavelet transform (CWT) can reconstruct the stationary and transient characteristics of the signal. Consequently, the wavelet-XGBoost approach is especially useful in real-time implementations in industrial contexts, which require a model capable of responding to changing fault signatures [17].

5.2 Advantages over Traditional Approaches

The results demonstrated that the developed model outperformed traditional methods like SVM or RF in classifying the gearbox health status, indicating that it was better adapted to the complexity of the vibration data. Conventional approaches, however, suit simpler classification tasks but lack sufficient adaptability to capture non-linear and time-variant characteristics of the vibration data [13]. Additionally, SVMs and RF are extremely sensitive to an imbalance in data, a typical problem in fault detection, where faulty states are often the minority state.

But unlike other algorithms, XGBoost is quite robust against such class imbalances, especially when combined with Synthetic Minority Oversampling Technique (SMOTE) [14]. The findings shown in Sect. 4 validate that the wavelet-XGBoost model outperforms other models, SVM and RF, in all measurements: accuracy, precision, and recall, suggesting that the wavelet-XGBoost is a dominant model in the gearbox fault detection. Moreover, the fine-tuning of hyperparameters in XGBoost using Bayesian optimization maximizes the model performance by achieving optimal sensitivity and accuracy.

5.3 Limitations

Although the proposed model achieves favorable performance, it has several caveats. The model has been tested in conditions of only binary fault states: normal and cracked ones. The relatively narrow scope of fault classification limits the usability of the model to make predictions in diverse and more realistic practical situations in which multiple fault types like wear, misalignment and eccentricity arise at the same time. In order to extend the style to other types of faults, we will need more data and possibly more complex classification algorithms, which will also increase computational requirements.

Another limitation is dependence on laboratory controlled data. While this dataset does simulate real world operating conditions, they do not capture what operational environments behave like, where factors such as temperature, load variation, or operational wear may introduce extra noise. For enhanced generalizability, future work could validate the model on genuine datasets obtained from gearboxes in-field.

Finally, even though the XGBoost model can be lighter than a deep-learning model in the same situation, it still demands a large number of computation resources when it gets to the training and optimization stage. In the case of real-time models where latency matters a lot, some optimizations will be required to run the model efficiently on the related industrial IoT (IIoT) devices.

5.4 Future Research Directions

The limitations of the proposed model already present several research opportunities for future works. The model can be improved by adding more complexity to detect different failure types like bearing wear, gear pitting, and misalignment that would make it more versatile for industrial use. The existing methods of multi-class classification, together with fault-specific feature extraction methods could also allow the model to recognize different fault modes with comparable success.

Moreover, embedding the wavelet-XGBoost model in an industrial IoT based system is an interesting approach to be investigated in order for real-time continuous health monitoring and fault detection for the purpose of predictive maintenance. Such integration would make possible an automated data collection, processing, and analysis and be able to react quickly in the case of detected faults. What is more, the predictive maintenance systems are implemented on the cloud to process the data and update the models with a central common approach capable of ensuring the system adapts according to the operational environment.

We have also seen interest in hybrid approaches that integrate XGBoost with deep learning techniques. For example, this architecture would allow XGBoost to combine both manually extracted wavelet features with automatically extracted features with a Convolutional Neural Network (CNN) model applied on raw vibration signals. This hybrid approach can also improve the sensitivity of the model to the complex fault patterns without affecting the computational size of the overall model [20].

Finally, addressing the issue of data imbalance through advanced resampling techniques, such as Adaptive Synthetic (ADASYN) sampling, could further refine the model's sensitivity to rare fault types. The ADASYN algorithm has an adaptive nature in determining sampling weights according to how challenging the learning process is, which should improve the capability of your model to recognize small but important fault signatures in underrepresented classes.

5.5 *Interpretation of Results*

This study reveals that the proposed wavelet-XGBoost model serves an effective solution for predictive maintenance of industrial gearboxes. The high value of recall and precision scores indicates that the model minimizes both false negatives, meaning it rarely fails to act on an actual fault, and false positives, as it does not raise false alarms [9]. The successful classification of normal and cracked states demonstrates the potential of the model as an effective online monitoring tool, allowing operators to identify potential faults early and carry out appropriate maintenance on time.

Additionally, the AUC (area under the curve) value is significantly high (0.97), reflecting that the model performed well to separate both classes over multivariates, thus ensuring flexibility when applied under varying operational conditions. The learning curve also illustrates the scalability of the model since it handles large datasets without overfitting. The model can also be scaled to larger industrial datasets, and subsequently deployed to production.

Overall, it offers a sound AI-based solution for gearbox fault detection, contributing to the growing body of research on digital transformation in the industrial maintenance space. Wavelet-XGBoost, as a framework is discussed with both high accuracy and addressing predictive maintenance predictions-based challenges like data imbalance and online learning. These results represent an opportunity of AI powered predictive maintenance systems enhancing operational reliability, minimizing maintenance expenses, and aligning with Industry 4.0 objectives.

6 Conclusion

This paper presents a new approach to the industrial gearbox predictive maintenance based on a reliable and novel fault diagnosis, which is an integration of wavelet transformation and XGBoost classification model resulting in a rich high-precision fault diagnostic method. The proposed method demonstrates effective identification of transient faults that are hugely missed by earlier methods by leveraging the symmetry of time-frequency characteristics captured through wavelet-transformed features. Firm validation of the method's performance can be evidenced through 94.49% accuracy, alongside high precision and recall values, and an excellent AUC (0.97), indicating a considerable uplift against existing methodologies and a trustworthy mechanism to discriminate between normal and faulty operation.

The novelty and strength of this study lie not only in its accuracy but also in its practical relevance for industrial settings. Specifically, the framework's integration of SMOTE for handling data imbalance and Bayesian optimization for hyperparameter tuning addresses real-world challenges such as imbalanced datasets and noisy industrial environments. These improvements translate directly into reduced downtime, more precise fault diagnosis, optimized maintenance schedules, and ultimately lower operational costs. By proactively identifying early-stage gearbox faults, industries can achieve significant reductions in maintenance-related disruptions, potentially lowering equipment downtime and associated costs by a considerable margin.

The results provide strong evidence to promote the Industry 4.0 goals at the organizational level, especially in materializing digitized, automated, and intelligent maintenance approaches. The wavelet-XGBoost model proposed in this paper can be easily incorporated in IIoT environments, allowing for continuous real-time monitoring, predictive analytics, and smart decisions. The integrated capabilities can improve operational resilience, enhance productivity, and promote sustainable manufacturing practices in keeping with ESG objectives.

Though the outcome of these studies are encouraging, a few hurdles still stand in our way. Industrial applications take place in a noisy environment where the conditions, at least in part, have never been measured in the laboratory. Thus, the next key step would be to verify and optimize the model on a range of real-world datasets. Also, although the model performs well on crack detection, its generalization to more gearbox fault modes—like wear, misalignment, eccentricity and unexplored fault patterns—brings out novel research challenges and opportunities.

Hence, the next phase should be directed towards widening the diagnostic capabilities of the model and experimenting with high-level hybrid models that tie-up the deep learning methods with XGBoost. Integration of this new method with the existing model could improve the model's ability to interpret complex, high-dimensional vibration data whilst remaining computationally efficient. In addition, extensive field tests and deployment into real industrial environments would yield insights into the framework adaptability and practical barriers that may arise.

Finally, this research contributes to the predictive maintenance knowledge by providing an advanced, data-driven algorithm that has the ability to reliably detect minor faults in the gearbox system. Computer vision is one of the cornerstones of Industry 4.0 and the IIoT, which can significantly enhance operational efficiency and minimize environmental footprints while facilitating the global objectives of digital transformation and sustainable manufacturing.

References

1. Al Ouatiq, H. S. (2024). Generating synthetic vibration data for a gearbox in a wind turbine. In *Proceedings of the conference "problems of scientific and practical activities: Search and selection of innovative solutions"* (pp. 22–26). Springer. Retrieved from https://os-russia.com/SBORNIKI/KON-582.pdf
2. Al Ouatiq, H. S., & Pronin, S. P. (2024). Enhancing wind turbine gearbox reliability: A hybrid deep learning approach for predictive maintenance. In *Proceedings of the conference "modeling nonequilibrium, adaptive, and controlled systems"* (pp. 3–8). Institut Vychislitel'nogo Modelirovaniya So Ran. Retrieved from https://icm.krasn.ru/ftp/conferences/2024/228/Materialy_MNAUS-24.pdf
3. Qiao, W., & Gong, X. (2017). Current-based gear fault detection for wind turbine gearboxes. *IEEE Transactions on Sustainable Energy, 8*(4), 1453–1462. https://doi.org/10.1109/TSTE.2017.2690835
4. Aburakhia, S. A., Myers, R., & Shami, A. (2022). A hybrid method for condition monitoring and fault diagnosis of rolling bearings with low system delay. *IEEE Transactions on Instrumentation and Measurement, 71*, 1–13. https://doi.org/10.1109/TIM.2022.3198477
5. Wang, Y., Zhu, Z., Song, H., & Shi, K. (2017). Wind turbine gearbox condition monitoring based on extreme gradient boosting. In *IECON 2017—43rd annual conference of the IEEE industrial electronics society* (pp. 6017–6023). IEEE. https://doi.org/10.1109/IECON.2017.8217044
6. Su, L., Guo, G., & Li, Y. (2021). Vibration monitoring of wind turbine tower based on XGBoost. *Journal of Physics: Conference Series, 1948*(1), 012075. https://doi.org/10.1088/1742-6596/1948/1/012075
7. Ogaili, A., Hamzah, M., & Jaber, A. (2024). Enhanced fault detection of wind turbine using extreme gradient boosting technique based on nonstationary vibration analysis. *Journal of Failure Analysis and Prevention, 24*(1), 877–895. https://doi.org/10.1007/s11668-024-01894-x
8. Guo, Y., Guo, M., Shen, Y., Peng, Y., & Zhao, S. (2024). Research on radial rotor plunger wear fault monitoring method by fused sound vibration signal features. *IEEE Sensors Journal, 24*(13), 20896–20907. https://doi.org/10.1109/JSEN.2024.3396881
9. Vives, J. (2022). Vibration analysis for fault detection in wind turbines using machine-learning techniques. *Advances in Computational Intelligence, 2*, 15. https://doi.org/10.1007/s43674-021-00029-1
10. Toma, R. N., & Kim, J.-M. (2020). Bearing fault classification of induction motors using discrete wavelet transform and ensemble machine learning algorithms. *Applied Sciences, 10*(15), 5251. https://doi.org/10.3390/app10155251
11. Das, O., & Bagci Das, D. (2023). Smart machine fault diagnostics based on fault-specified discrete wavelet transform. *Journal of the Brazilian Society of Mechanical Sciences and Engineering, 45*, 55. https://doi.org/10.1007/s40430-022-03975-0
12. Tang, M., Zhao, Q., Ding, S., Wu, H., Li, L., Long, W., & Huang, B. (2020). An improved LightGBM algorithm for online fault detection of wind turbine gearboxes. *Energies, 13*(4), 807. https://doi.org/10.3390/en13040807
13. Aburakhia, S. A. (2024). *Data-driven vibration-based condition monitoring: Fundamentals, applications, and challenges* (Publication No. 10109) [Doctoral dissertation, Western University]. Electronic Thesis and Dissertation Repository. Retrieved from https://ir.lib.uwo.ca/etd/10109
14. Yu, X., Tang, B., & Zhang, K. (2021). Fault diagnosis of wind turbine gearbox using a novel method of fast deep graph convolutional network. *IEEE Transactions on Instrumentation and Measurement, 70*, 1–14. https://doi.org/10.1109/tim.2020.3048799
15. Chen, H., Jing, S., & Wang, Z. (2018). Fault diagnosis of wind turbine gearbox based on wavelet neural network. *Journal of Low Frequency Noise, Vibration and Active Control, 37*(4), 977–986. https://doi.org/10.1177/1461348418795376

16. Apeiranthitis, S., Zacharia, P., Chatzopoulos, A., & Papoutsidakis, M. (2024). Predictive maintenance of machinery with rotating parts using convolutional neural networks. *Electronics, 13*(2), 460. https://doi.org/10.3390/electronics13020460
17. Tang, M., Zhao, Q., Ding, S., Wu, H., & Zimin, W. (2021). Cost-sensitive LightGBM-based online fault detection method for wind turbine gearboxes. *Frontiers in Energy Research, 9*, 701574. https://doi.org/10.3389/fenrg.2021.701574
18. Tang, S., Yuan, S., & Zhu, Y. (2020). Deep learning-based intelligent fault diagnosis methods toward rotating machinery. *IEEE Access, 8*, 9335–9346. https://doi.org/10.1109/ACCESS.2019.2963092
19. Bajric, R., Zuber, N., & Miljkovic, N. (2016). Feature extraction using discrete wavelet transform for gear fault diagnosis of wind turbine gearbox. *Shock and Vibration, 2016*, 1–10. https://doi.org/10.1155/2016/6748469
20. Bessaoudi, M., Habbouche, H., Benkedjouh, T., & Mesloub, A. (2024). A hybrid approach for gearbox fault diagnosis based on deep learning techniques. *The International Journal of Advanced Manufacturing Technology*. https://doi.org/10.21203/rs.3.rs-3955773/v1

Digital Technologies in Logistics and Procurement

Digital Agents and Generative Artificial Intelligence in Support of Logistics 5.0

Bernardo Nicoletti and Andrea Appolloni

Abstract This article explores the synergistic integration of generative artificial intelligence (GAI) and autonomous digital agents (DAs) in modern logistics systems, an area of increasing strategic importance. By exploring the convergence of analytical sophistication and operational automation, the study shows how these technologies are redefining the management of resource flows in logistics orchestration, transportation optimization, and intelligent allocation of warehouse space, considering interdependencies from production networks to end-consumer delivery ecosystems. The research systematically explores GAI-DA applications in logistics service innovation and demonstrates its ability to enhance collaboration between organizations and adaptive decision-making in complex multi-stakeholder environments. Through a dual lens of theoretical exploration and empirical analysis, the article advances strategic imperatives for management by highlighting how these technologies catalyze value chain optimization, stakeholder engagement paradigms, and interdisciplinary innovation at the intersection of corporate marketing, operational agility, and technological adoption. Joining the literature on AI-driven organizational transformation, this work goes beyond descriptive analysis by suggesting a holistic business model realignment. It introduces a novel framework that conceptualizes GAI-DA implementations as interdependent systems that require synchronized evolution across four fundamental pillars: precision-engineered processes, highly skilled people capital, strategic partner ecosystems, and purpose-driven technological platforms (the 4Ps). The 'four Ps' framework is a comprehensive approach to GAI-DA implementation, emphasizing the importance of aligning processes, people, partners, and purpose-driven technological architecture for successful integration. The study concludes that successful implementation requires more

B. Nicoletti
Temple University, Rome, Italy

A. Appolloni (✉)
University of Rome Tor Vergata, Rome, Italy
e-mail: andrea.appolloni@uniroma2.it

F. Tao et al. (eds.), *Artificial Intelligence and Digital Transformation*, Lecture Notes in Information Systems and Organisation 78,
https://doi.org/10.1007/978-3-032-00118-4_7

than just the integration of algorithms—it requires redesigning organizational structures to adapt to dynamic logistics ecosystems. As a pragmatic contribution, the work proposes actionable implementation guidelines for embedding GAI-DA solutions into core logistics functions. These include protocols for data management in multi-agent environments, adaptive workflow redesign for human-AI collaboration, and metrics for evaluating performance improvement across the ecosystem. The research advances the scientific approach to smart logistics systems by linking theoretical insights with operational designs. It provides practitioners with a roadmap to exploit GAI-DA organizations at the forefront of innovation while meeting the effective, ethical, economic, and efficiency requirements in an era of hyper-connected logistics.

Keywords Logistics · Artificial intelligence · Digital agents · Industry 5.0

1 Introduction

This study comprehensively introduces generative artificial intelligence (GAI) and digital agents (DA) to support logistics management and operations. As specialized software applications, digital agents are crucial in optimizing logistics tasks. They are essential in route optimization, inventory management, demand forecasting, and customer service. A DA can analyze historical data to predict future demand, optimize inventory levels, and reduce carrying costs. DAs act as virtual assistants, performing tasks that would otherwise require human intervention. By using advanced algorithms and data analytics, they automate processes, improve decision-making, and increase operational efficiency. This combination of analyzing and acting delivers robust solutions that can drive the digital transformation of logistics. The work applies these advanced AI algorithms to the entire logistics cycle, from planning to reverse logistics [1, 2].

We aim to provide a comprehensive and updated overview of the use of GAI and DA and a technical framework for their integrated application. Integrating artificial intelligence (AI) algorithms into the management and operation of logistics services is transforming the industry by increasing operational efficiency, reducing costs, and improving service delivery. The study examines the journey that has transformed logistics from a complementary role to a strategic lever at the center of business strategies. It then discusses the key characteristics of the integration of the transformative era, Logistics 5.0. Logistics 5.0 is not just a change but a profound transformation revolutionizing the industry. It is characterized by integrating advanced technologies such as AI, blockchain, the IoT, and Big Data into logistics, paving the way for a more efficient, effective, ethical, and economic future. This transformative potential of Logistics 5.0 inspires optimism and a brighter future for the industry.

Industry 5.0 (I50) refers to the next phase of the Industrial Revolution, focusing on collaboration between humans and machines. It aims to personalize and humanize the production process using advanced technologies to enhance human capabilities, promote sustainability, and create more resilient and human-centric industries. I50 forms the basis for collaboration between people, automation, and machines, emphasizing the inclusive nature of the industry's future. There are four main factors to consider: improving the environment, collaboration with people, automation and machines, and resilience. As a transformative technology, AI can support all aspects of the design and operation of logistics management. This paper explores these components and how GAI and DA can help digitally in an integrated modeling approach [3]. GAI and DA are critical to Logistics 5.0, enabling highly dynamic and adaptable logistics. GAI can create optimized solutions in real-time, such as generating new delivery routes based on live data. At the same time, DAs automate complex decision-making processes, enabling seamless coordination and improved efficiency across the logistics ecosystem. They provide the logistics industry with more automation, optimization, and real-time adaptability, making the audience feel included and part of its future.

By combining theoretical insights with practical expertise, this research aims to significantly contribute to presenting an integrated architecture that will drive these AI algorithms forward and ultimately increase their potential to foster innovation and growth in logistics. This work combines innovative solutions with the best support from advanced AI algorithms for digital transformation.

2 Literature Review

Literature often considers GAI and DA. GAI creates novel content, such as optimized routes or predictive models, by learning patterns from existing data. DAs are software entities designed to autonomously perform specific tasks, such as managing inventory or coordinating deliveries based on predefined rules and learned behaviors. While GAI creates novel solutions, DAs execute and automate these solutions, often incorporating GAI results into their actions. Essentially, GAI creates, and DA acts. Research highlights the growing potential of GAI and DA in revolutionizing logistics. For example, GAI algorithms can optimize delivery routes by analyzing big data to find the most efficient routes. Organizations have already harnessed this potential and are using AI-powered systems to prioritize deliveries according to urgency and distance, resulting in faster delivery times and lower fuel consumption [4]. A study by Capgemini [4] has shown that DHL's SmartTrucks, which use AI for route optimization, have reduced fuel consumption by up to 15% in pilot programs. GAI also enables predictive maintenance, where systems monitor vehicle performance data to predict maintenance needs, prevent breakdowns, and improve fleet reliability [5, 6]. A study by Volvo Trucks has demonstrated that using

AI-powered diagnostics to predict component failures reduces downtime by up to 40%. The real-time tracking of deliveries made possible by AI provides customers with accurate delivery estimates and increases logistics transparency [7]. The potential of GAI and DA in logistics is promising and offers a brighter future for the industry, making the audience feel hopeful and excited about the future.

GAI is not meant to replace human operators but to empower them and increase their productivity. It can minimize fuel consumption, optimize work schedules, and automate routine tasks so that human operators can focus on complex problems. Studies show that GAI support can increase sales staff's productivity by 20–30% [8, 9]. For example, Salesforce's Einstein AI platform has shown in case studies that automating sales tasks increases sales reps' efficiency in several areas [8]. Big data analytics enable AI to deliver actionable insights, improve decision-making processes, and adapt to market fluctuations [10]. This reassures that AI is not a threat, but a tool that can enhance human capabilities and enable systems to perform better.

Emerging GAI technologies promise to improve traditional logistics operations and significantly reduce environmental impact. These technologies offer more sophisticated routing solutions and automate complex decision-making processes [11]. The industry's focus on sustainable practices drives the development of GAI solutions that optimize logistics while minimizing environmental impact. This is a hopeful sign for the industry's future, as it shows that it is possible to use technology to improve efficiency while reducing the ecological footprint [12, 13]. Projects such as the Green Logistics initiatives, for example, are exploring AI-driven solutions for electric vehicle route planning and load optimization, which have the potential to reduce CO_2 emissions significantly [12].

Integrating DA into logistics operations is not a new trend but a revolution in logistics management. These intelligent systems, powered by advanced algorithms and data analytics, automate processes, improve decision-making, and increase operational efficiency. DA in specialized software applications optimizes a range of logistics tasks, from route planning to inventory management, demand forecasting, and customer service [14]. By analyzing large amounts of data from multiple sources, these agents can predict demand patterns, identify inefficiencies, make informed decisions, and sometimes take direct actions that improve logistics performance. For example, DA can process historical sales data and real-time information to recommend the most efficient delivery routes [14], reducing transportation costs and improving delivery times. For example, Amazon's AI-driven logistics systems dynamically adjust delivery routes based on real-time data, resulting in significant cost savings and shorter delivery times [14]. This is the power of AI in revolutionizing logistics management.

The literature emphasizes the crucial role of predictive analytics in DA algorithms [15]. These systems use historical data to accurately forecast future demand, enabling organizations to maintain optimal inventory levels and mitigate the risk of stock-outs or overstocking. With better insight into inventory management, organizations can better coordinate with partners and streamline procurement processes. For example, research from organizations such as Blue Yonder shows how their AI-powered demand forecasting tools have helped retailers reduce their inventory costs by up to 20% and improve forecasting accuracy [15]. DA contributes significantly to logistics sustainability by optimizing routes and load distribution, reducing fuel consumption, and minimizing transportation-associated carbon emissions. This approach aligns with the increasing importance of sustainable practices in logistics management [16].

GAI and DA offer numerous benefits, but there are also challenges with implementation and integration into existing systems [17]. Organizations address data quality issues, interoperability between different technologies, and the need for ongoing staff training. In addition, collecting and analyzing large data sets raises data privacy issues, and organizations should consider regulatory compliance [18]. Integrating GAI solutions into existing logistics systems can be complex and resource-intensive, and organizations ensure that their infrastructure can support new technologies without disrupting operations [19]. The skills gap in the workforce requires continuous education and training to enable users to utilize GAI tools effectively. Organizations need to develop the digital skills of their employees to maximize the benefits of GAI [20]. For example, McKinsey and the World Economic Forum studies indicate that significant retraining is required to close the gap between the current workforce and the requirements of AI-driven logistics [20].

3 Methodology

This study proposes a structured framework for integrating generative artificial intelligence (GAI) and digital agents (DA) in logistics systems. The methodology uses a three-part analytical approach to comprehensively understand GAI and DA applications in logistics management and operational processes. Underlying this investigation are three interrelated components: (1) a systematic review of academic and industry literature to synthesize conceptual foundations and empirical findings, (2) structured consultations with cross-industry stakeholders that include academic researchers and logistics practitioners, and (3) the formulation of an integrative framework that addresses functional, technical, and normative dimensions to guide the strategic deployment of GAI and DA solutions.

The literature review establishes a theoretical foundation by examining different disciplinary perspectives and operational paradigms documented in academic research and industry case studies. Building on this foundation, a dialogic exchange with subject matter experts is conducted in semi-structured interviews to ensure alignment between conceptual models and practical implementation challenges. The resulting framework emphasizes four critical imperatives: optimizing operational effectiveness, improving process efficiency, ensuring economic viability, and adhering to ethical principles when implementing GAI-DA. This multi-layered methodology advances scientific discourse and industrial practice by providing a robust framework for evaluating and implementing intelligent analytics systems in complex logistics ecosystems. The interviews were conducted with academics from operations studies and managers who apply innovative methods in their areas of responsibility. The managers were selected from various international, national, or local logistics organizations (urban logistics). In parallel, students developed several experimental works to validate the applicability of the proposed framework in actual cases in organizations. After identifying critical potential measures, the authors developed a final ground-breaking framework. This framework utilizes the components to support the essential solutions that comprise the design and operation of GAI and DA logistics support.

3.1 Research Objectives

Given the current limitations of the existing literature on GAI and DA frameworks and their increasing importance, this work pursues two research objectives (ROs) to demonstrate the theoretical justification of the proposed framework:

- RO1: Define and validate an integrated functional framework and technical architecture for GAI and DA using practical use cases centered on supporting logistics applications, active chatbots, and intelligent routing.
- RO2: Comprehensively review, analyze, and clarify the features enabling GAI and DA implementation. Explore the transformative power of these AI algorithms in sustainably reshaping organizations and discuss applications, challenges, and future opportunities related to adopting these AI algorithms in logistics management and operations.

4 Transformation of Logistics: Logistics 5.0

The Council of Supply Chain Management Professionals defines logistics as the planning, execution, and control of the forward and reverse flow and storage of goods, services, and related information between points of origin and consumption to meet customer needs [21]. This function is the foundation of logistics operations. Over time, logistics has evolved from the mechanization of Industry 1.0 to the emerging I50. Logistics has continuously developed and integrated transformative technologies to address pressing social, political, and environmental issues. In line with I50, Logistics 5.0 uses AI as a transformative technology to support human-centered, sustainable, and resilient activity. The role of AI in logistics is not just about mitigating risks, but also about inspiring a new era of innovation and efficiency.

The logistics market has changed profoundly, reshaping its competitive landscape and requirements [2]. The critical role underlying these changes is the technological innovation that enables this evolution. Initially, logistics strategies focused on cost minimization, often at the expense of quality and efficiency [22]. At the same time, modern logistics are increasingly interconnected and globalized, exposing logistics to various operational, environmental, and geopolitical risks. Mitigating these risks has become paramount to organizations, advanced technologies, diversifying partnerships, and regionalizing production to increase resilience.

The emergence of I50 is the foundation of Logistics 5.0, which can integrate mature and emerging technologies such as GAI and DA. Logistics 5.0 emphasizes sustainability and resilience and aims to develop systems that transform operators and customers from cost factors into investments [23]. This human-centric approach reflects a broader trend to align logistics processes with behavioral and societal considerations.

5 GAI and DAs

Different AI branches deal with other tasks and activities. This section is about GAI, a specialized subset of AI capable of generating various forms of data/texts and DAs to support Logistics 5.0.

5.1 GAI

GAI refers to AI models that can generate new content, such as text, images, or music, by learning patterns from existing data [24]. AI programs are intelligent software programs designed to interact with users or other systems and perform tasks autonomously or in collaboration with humans [25]. GAI is a key technology that allows the development of more sophisticated and versatile DA.

Interest in using GAI in the logistics industry is growing [26–28]. Logistics organizations can significantly improve their management and operations by optimizing GAI and DA. One notable impact of GAI is its potential to increase logistics systems' resilience, as requested by I50 [23]. By enabling vehicles to make informed routing decisions, GAI minimizes the impact of disruptions that can occur at any stage of the logistics process [29]. In logistics, GAI can optimize delivery routes by dynamically creating new, efficient paths based on real-time traffic and weather data. It also enables predictive maintenance by creating models anticipating equipment failures, minimizing downtime, and improving fleet reliability. Finally, GAI can help predict demand better and thus optimize the use of resources.

5.2 DAs

DAs (also known as agentic AI) in logistics are sophisticated systems designed to improve operational efficiency, decision-making, and responsiveness in logistics management (Fig. 1). There are five main types of DAs. This taxonomy of DAs

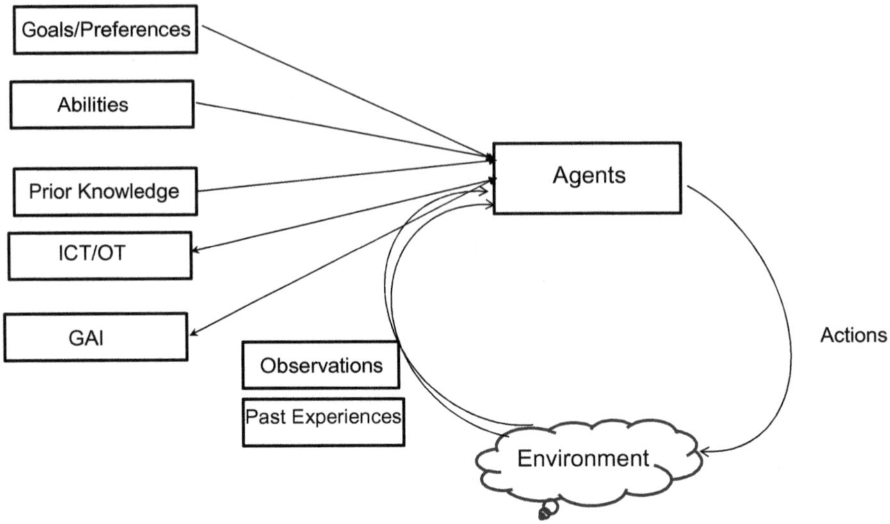

Fig. 1 DAs

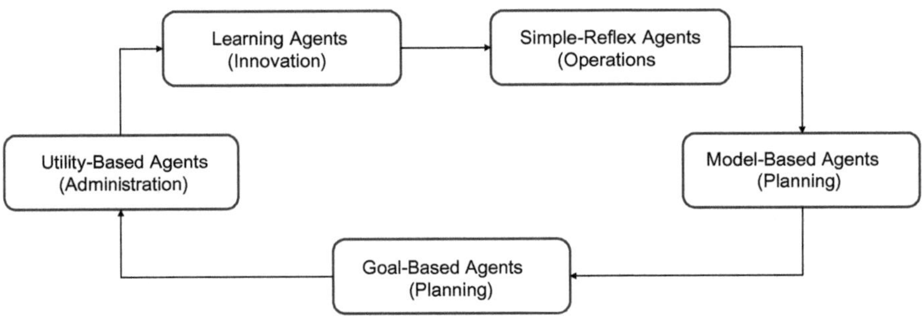

Fig. 2 Agents categorized by the underlined technology

provides a sophisticated epistemological framework that describes the complexity, cognitive capabilities, and operational strategies of computer systems operating in multidimensional technological domains [30]. DA has evolved from simple rule-based systems to sophisticated AI-driven entities. Initially, they performed simple, automated tasks. With advances in machine learning, they have gained the ability to learn, adapt, make complex decisions, and autonomously take the best actions. Combined with GAI, they can now create and execute solutions autonomously and are becoming increasingly intelligent and proactive in dynamic environments.

DA's underlying technology also influences categorization (Fig. 2) [31]. Simple reflex agents react directly to immediate stimuli. Model-based reflex agents consider the state of the environment before responding. Goal-based agents work towards specific goals. Utility-based agents evaluate actions based on risks and rewards. Rule-based agents follow explicit rules. Learning agents adapt and improve through experience. Hybrid agents combine rule-based and learning approaches.

DAs can interact with their environment in different ways [32]. Autonomous agents work independently and make decisions without human intervention. Collaborative agents work together with human decision-makers and provide insights and recommendations.

The scope of a DA's tasks can also be a classification criterion [33]. Micro-level agents focus on specific, granular tasks. Macro-level agents, on the other hand, manage the entire logistics holistically. Another decisive factor is the degree of intelligence that a DA exhibits. Reactive agents respond to immediate stimuli, while deliberative agents can use their advanced cognitive abilities to plan and develop strategies.

These classifications may evolve as technology advances, leading to more sophisticated and versatile DA.

6 Framework of AI

GAI and DA can revolutionize logistics operations and management through sophisticated technological interventions that fundamentally change traditional logistics methods. These AI algorithms use advanced algorithms, machine learning techniques, and real-time data processing capabilities to optimize complex logistics processes in various business areas. The following sections illustrate how GAI and DA can act as intelligent intermediaries, enabling seamless logistics coordination along the SCOR components [34].

6.1 Planning

In an increasingly competitive global logistics landscape, superior planning capabilities are a key strategic differentiator to maintain market leadership. Organizations use AI-based systems to improve operational foresight through advanced demand forecasting, logistics orchestration, and inventory management optimization. GAI combined with machine learning architecture allows organizations to achieve unprecedented accuracy in predicting demand volumes through continuous, real-time data assimilation.

The application of AI in strategic logistics planning occurs across several technological dimensions. Sophisticated predictive analytics engines process massive data sets of historical transaction patterns, consumer behavior metrics, seasonal fluctuations, and macroeconomic indicators to create probabilistic demand models. These smart systems forecast logistics demand, simulate potential disruptions, suggest preventative contingency measures, and independently calibrate inventory parameters to minimize financial risk [35].

In the complicated dynamics of modern logistics ecosystems, operational excellence fundamentally depends on predictive planning mechanisms. GAI facilitates operational cohesion through the cross-functional alignment of procurement and production cycles, which is enabled by the ability to synthesize real-time market signals with enterprise resource data. By processing heterogeneous data streams—from lead times to geopolitical risk factors—GAI systems generate prescriptive recommendations that enable proactive operational adjustments. This analytical capacity, combined with the technology's ability to recognize non-linear relationships within complex data sets, makes GAI a transformative force in logistics. It's potential to derive innovative solutions from data aggregation from multiple sources and pattern recognition heralds a paradigm shift from reactive problem-solving to predictive, intelligence-driven logistics optimization—ultimately redefining competition benchmarks through the synergistic integration of computing power and strategic foresight.

The planning module orchestrates logistics plans based on real-time data. In contrast, the DA executes the tasks derived from the insights.

6.2 Logistics System Design

One area of interest for this framework concerns the design of logistics systems, a set of activities providing fertile ground for AI improvement and optimization [11]. GAI can often feed into the design process and help logistics managers make data-driven decisions to ensure smooth and efficient logistics operations. GAI can help organizations find the best combination of partners, distributors, and operators, and optimize reverse logistics, among many other potential applications.

Regarding system design and optimization, GAI can revolutionize warehouse layout and design by simulating different configurations, considering product turnover rates, storage requirements, and picking patterns. By analyzing historical and real-time operational data, GAI can recommend the appropriate equipment and technology to improve efficiency and reduce costs. In addition, GAI can identify bottlenecks and inefficiencies in logistics processes such as order fulfillment and transportation and suggest process improvements to increase overall performance.

6.3 Warehouse Management

Inventory management is critical in today's competitive and complex business environment [36]. It involves a mix of strategic and tactical decisions that influence the design of logistics systems and the functional design of individual facilities. Excellent warehouse management increases logistics efficiency. The integration of

GAI-driven applications and DA has proven groundbreaking, revolutionizing processes from demand fulfillment to order fulfillment. Intelligent algorithms are crucial in selecting optimal warehouse or distribution center locations and streamlining picking procedures, significantly improving logistics operations.

In inventory management and warehousing, GAI and DA offer significant opportunities to optimize operations and improve efficiency. By accurately predicting demand, GAI minimizes stock-outs and reduces excess inventory, ensuring optimal stock levels. GAI and DA can automate warehouse tasks, including inventory tracking, picking, and packing, improving accuracy and operational productivity. GAI's analytical capabilities enable better use of warehouse space and recommend strategies that maximize storage capacity while minimizing associated costs.

GAI's impact is particularly notable in picking, a traditionally labor-intensive process that accounts for a significant portion of warehouse operating costs. GAI optimizes product placement through real-time data analysis, considering demand patterns, product velocity, and warehouse layout. Frequently picked items are strategically placed in accessible locations, reducing travel time and increasing picker productivity. By grouping similar products in specific zones, GAI minimizes picking errors and ensures greater accuracy in order fulfillment. Seasonal fluctuations in demand are also considered, enabling proactive slotting strategies to optimize inventory placement throughout the year. A DA can automate the processes performed in automated warehouses.

GAI algorithms generate efficient picking paths by analyzing product location and order quantity, minimizing walking distances, and maximizing productivity. GAI-supported, voice-guided systems provide real-time instructions to warehouse operators, reducing errors and streamlining operations. GAI-controlled robotic systems are increasingly used for repetitive or hazardous tasks, significantly improving safety and efficiency in warehouse environments.

GAI-controlled autonomous mobile robots (AMRs) navigate through warehouse spaces to move goods efficiently, reducing labor costs and increasing throughput. GAI also facilitates predictive maintenance by analyzing sensor data to detect potential equipment failures. By identifying risks early, warehouses can schedule timely repairs to minimize downtime and maintain business continuity.

Inventory management systems with GAI and DA offer remarkable improvements in monitoring and decision-making. These systems automatically trigger procurement processes to ensure stock availability while minimizing inventory costs. In manufacturing and retail, GAI's predictive capabilities ensure an optimal balance between supply and demand, avoiding overstocks and stock-outs and increasing customer satisfaction through faster delivery times. A DA can autonomously place orders.

GAI can monitor and maintain stock conditions through advanced computer vision and intelligent sensors. Automated inspection tools provide real-time insight into parameters such as temperature, pressure, and vibration, allowing operators to intervene immediately if anomalies are detected [37]. These systems continuously analyze machine conditions to detect patterns that indicate potential faults. This support enables operators to address problems before they escalate.

As GAI technologies evolve, inventory management and warehousing applications will also increase. From optimizing warehouse configurations and streamlining picking processes to improving predictive analytics and monitoring,

6.4 Transportation

In the transport and logistics sector, GAI and DA can optimize delivery routes by considering traffic conditions, distances, and delivery times, reducing fuel consumption, and minimizing delivery times [38]. GAI can optimize load planning to maximize vehicle capacity and reduce transportation costs. In addition, GAI can track shipments and disruptions in real-time, providing insight into the entire logistics and enabling a proactive response and remediations to potential disruptions in real-time, giving insight into the whole logistics, enabling a proactive response to potential disruptions, and acting thanks to DA.

Route optimization is a critical aspect of transportation management because it largely determines the cost and performance of operations. The American Transportation Research Institute report provides valuable data that underscores the importance of route optimization [39]. According to the report, by implementing route optimization techniques using GAI, organizations can reduce fleet mileage by an average of 20%, reducing overall transportation costs by 10% to 30%. Route optimization has a noticeable impact on delivery speed, customer satisfaction, and sustainability, significantly reducing carbon dioxide emissions [40].

Automated guided vehicles (AGVs) are reliable transportation workhorses. They are used for intralogistics (e.g., within warehouses or factories) and external transport [41]. AGVs rely heavily on GAI and DA for their functionality, including various solutions for navigation and environmental interaction. These vehicles have route planning and optimization algorithms that function similarly to those mentioned in the previous sections.

Delivery drones can change the transportation sector, especially for last-mile deliveries. Depending on various factors, such as the quality of the service, the hazardousness of the materials delivered, and the geographical location, the cost of the last mile ranges from 13% to 73% of total distribution costs [42]. This figure will likely increase in the coming years due to the global growth of e-commerce, increasing customer expectations of delivery speed, and the costs of energy and fuels. This means that products must be delivered to underserved or remote areas where ground transportation is challenging. Transportation management is a critical area in which DA demonstrates its transformative capabilities. Advanced routing algorithms can optimize transport networks. They calculate and implement the most efficient routes, considering multiple variables such as fuel consumption, traffic patterns, delivery times, and environmental constraints.

A key benefit of using DA in logistics is their ability to make autonomous decisions. These agents can perform tasks without human intervention using predefined rules and algorithms, minimizing potential errors. This autonomy is particularly beneficial in scenarios where quick responses are required, such as rerouting shipments in response to unexpected disruptions or changes in demand. DA can improve customer service by providing real-time updates and personalized support. This level of engagement increases customer satisfaction and fosters loyalty in an increasingly competitive market.

6.5 Reporting and Analytics

In reporting and analysis, GAI can analyze large amounts of data to identify trends, patterns, and anomalies and provide valuable insights for decision-making [26]. GAI and DA can automate the creation of detailed reports on key performance indicators (KPIs) such as delivery times, order accuracy, and inventory turnover. With GAI, logistics organizations can achieve new efficiency, agility, and sustainability levels. The application potential of GAI in logistics is enormous.

6.6 Reverse Logistics

Reverse logistics is the "transportation of goods from their typical destination for recycling or proper disposal" [43]. Due to environmental concerns, organizations implement a reverse logistics system. GAI is a strong lever for achieving sustainability goals [44]. Reverse logistics is divided into four phases: network design, collection, storage, and processing.

In reverse logistics, products must be processed safely and efficiently. This requirement means that the most suitable processing option must be selected from several ones, depending on factors such as the product's condition and the materials. GAI can help decision-makers make recommendations based on quantitative and qualitative factors. GAI is used to analyze products and visually develop innovative disassembly processes. In this way, organizations can minimize idle time at each workstation and optimize the disassembly task by, for example, recovering more recyclable parts.

GAI and DA's automation of the return process is a game-changer. It makes return labels, processes return, and issues refunds with unparalleled efficiency. This waste. Waste also saves time and resources, significantly minimizing environmental impact. The system's ability to identify opportunities for product recovery, refurbishment, and recycling further contributes to sustainability, painting a promising picture of the future of logistics management.

6.7 Logistics Outsourcing

GAI and DA algorithms can introduce innovative pricing models for logistics outsourcing [13]. These solutions enable dynamic pricing strategies. GAI also streamlines logistics operations by automating repetitive tasks such as composing and translating messages between logistics partners, improving the clarity and efficiency of communication.

Regarding information management, GAI is not just a tool for operational efficiency. It also plays a crucial role in enhancing customer relationship management and increasing the user-friendliness of logistics organizations' websites for logistics partners. This dual functionality reassures GAI's comprehensive benefits in logistics management.

Risk management is a challenging application of GAI and DA in logistics. Computerized systems can continuously monitor economic indicators, geopolitical developments, and potential disruptions in logistics and create comprehensive risk assessment models. DA can provide predictive insights that enable organizations to develop robust contingency strategies and maintain operational resilience.

GAI can significantly improve the logistics operations of contract logistics providers by optimizing demand forecasting and inventory management. GAI and DA streamlines administrative tasks by automating document generation and providing intelligent insights into contract terms and regulatory compliance, allowing logistics providers to focus on strategic initiatives.

7 High-Level Technical Architecture

After analyzing various innovative technical solutions that can improve logistics organizations through digital technologies such as GAI and agents, DA, the study proposes the following architecture (Fig. 3).

The structure thus defined consists of seven elements: the logistical physical entity, the connections, the shared data book, the information and communication technology (ICT), the operational technology (OT), the virtual entity, and the AI algorithms: GAI and DA.

7.1 Logistic Physical Entity

The framework analyzes an organization's logistics chain from procurement to delivery using three logistics performance evaluation (LPE) functions recorded in the unified blockchain databases. This system provides a clear overview of logistics

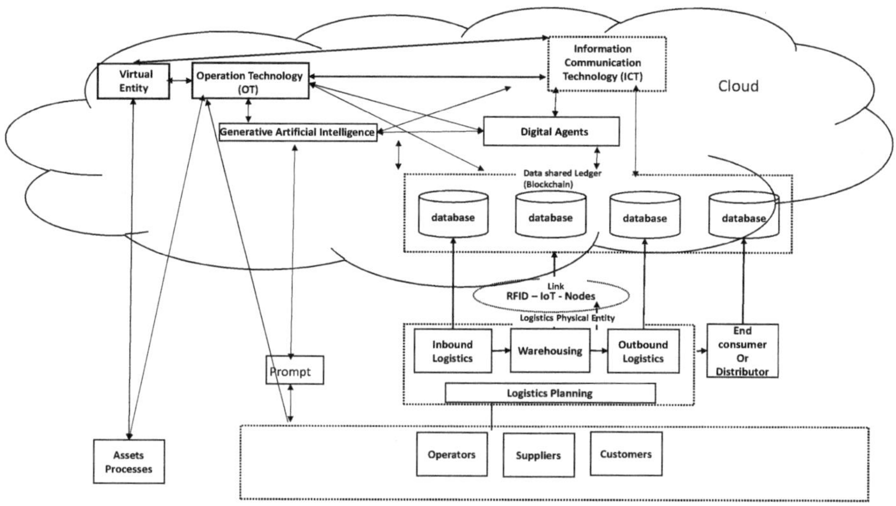

Fig. 3 A technical architecture to optimize the logistic function using the described solutions

performance and covers inbound, outbound, and warehouse management. The LPE is the physical aspect of DT, with immutable, consistent, and easily retrievable data that improves logistics simulation and optimization. This approach helps to identify potential bottlenecks and problems in warehouse management, which is crucial for employee safety. A holistic view of LPE requires integrating data collection and analysis tools.

7.2 Links

The connections in technical architecture are tools that convert information from physical and analog processes into digital data. This digital data is then recorded on the blockchain for the mutual exchange of information. The connections are crucial for the Logistics Performance Evaluation (LPE) process, which comprises various sub-phases, each affecting short- and long-term logistics outcomes, such as equipment failures or security issues. The results of these processes must be recorded in a blockchain register for predictive analysis. In addition, devices from the IIoT, including radio frequency identification (RFID) and sensor nodes, collect data to identify bottlenecks and support strategic decision-making within the organization.

7.3 Data Shared Ledger: DSL (Blockchain)

This DT logistics registration requires separate databases for each function, all connected in a cloud environment for seamless communication. This integration increases the efficiency of information collection, analysis, and logistics planning and requires high interaction between logistics organizations. The reliability of the digital delivery log (DSL) depends on comprehensive data from procurement to distribution that enables accurate diagnostics and forecasting. Data protection, consent mechanisms, and accessibility vary according to user needs and support effective inventory management and logistics planning.

7.4 ICT

ICT applications refer to software and hardware solutions that facilitate digital storage, retrieval, and sharing of information and improve communication and collaboration across different platforms. These applications are beneficial and powerful for resource planning, email, cloud services, and data management systems. They influence the way individuals and organizations interact and work.

7.5 OT

OT refers to hardware and software systems that connect, monitor, and control physical processes. These systems include monitoring and control systems such as Supervisory Control and Data Acquisition (SCADA) and Distributed Control Systems (DCS) that facilitate process automation and optimization. By integrating OT with ICT, organizations can increase operational efficiency, improve safety, and enable real-time data analytics for better decision-making.

7.6 Virtual Entity (VE)

Virtual Entity (VE) is a central hub for various logistics tools and technologies. It uses the digital twin technology [45], a digital environment that closely mirrors the physical logistics assets and processes. This enables continuous control over business processes. For example, it allows organizations to anticipate delivery delays due to external factors such as the weather or international conflicts. Implementing a VE is technically complex and requires time, expertise, and resources that may not be accessible to all organizations.

7.7 Da

The architecture of DA in logistics management includes several key components that increase its effectiveness in performing various tasks. The input module collects and analyzes data from warehouse inventories, transportation data, delivery schedules, and real-time information from IIoT devices. These inputs form the basis for accurate insights and decisions. At the heart of the system is the 'agent,' a crucial component that acts as the system's brain. The agent integrates advanced algorithms, including a profiling module that defines its role (e.g., inventory management), a memory module to store logistics data, and a knowledge module with databases and market trends for informed decisions.

7.8 GAI

The GAI module comprises several essential components that enable convincing text and data generation. As a foundation, the data input layer collects extensive data sets, mainly from internal sources, including text, images, proprietary data, etc. This is complemented by the model architecture, which typically draws on deep learning frameworks such as transformer architectures to enable the understanding and generation of complex data patterns. The training mechanism uses unsupervised or semi-supervised learning and utilizes techniques such as self-supervised learning to improve model performance. The inference engine then processes the user input and generates an output based on the well-trained model. A feedback loop is critical as it continuously incorporates user feedback to refine and improve the model's accuracy, improving the quality of the generated content. The deployment framework facilitates scalability and accessibility, often through APIs and cloud-based services that enable real-time application of GAI in different contexts. People can interact with GAI via prompts. These are specific inputs or instructions given to the model to help it generate text, images, or other content.

8 Results and Discussion

This work is a contribution to RO1. It defines and details the functional and technical architectural framework for using GAI and DA in logistics by explaining the main components, their interaction, and their essential characteristics. It also promotes a standard view of the concept and the underlying terminology. The framework covers all key components and integrates different solutions into a working framework. GAI and DA can significantly improve the organizations' logistics management and operations. GAI optimizes logistics by creating dynamic routes and predictive maintenance schedules, resulting in measurable reductions in delivery times and equipment downtime. DA agents automate inventory management and customer communications, increasing efficiency and customer satisfaction through real-time adjustments and personalized interactions, which is reflected in metrics such as reduced fuel consumption and increased on-time delivery.

This study advances RO2 by demonstrating the critical role of GAI and DA in organizations' multidimensional strategic imperatives for organizations: operational effectiveness, environmental sustainability, process efficiency, economic optimization, ethical compliance, and service quality. The proposed framework functions as an adaptive system that understands digital architectures and operational paradigms as evolutionary reference models that are iteratively refined. These models utilize heterogeneous data streams—including IIoT sensor outputs, transaction histories, and predictive market signals—to generate scenario-based simulations with granular temporal resolution encompassing immediate operational adjustments and long-term strategic planning horizons.

The need for dynamic recalibration of logistics models (whether real-time or *post-hoc*) depends on contextual factors such as demand forecasting cycles, the level of automation of warehouses, the complexity of the transportation network, and the depth of integration of AI-driven decision levels. By embedding GAI-DA systems into organizational workflows, companies can demonstrate measurable improvements in three key areas: (1) sustainability gains through carbon footprint reduction and circular resource utilization, (2) efficiency gains through predictive maintenance and route optimization, and (3) economic resilience through cost-probabilistic risk modeling and lean inventory management.

Case studies illustrate the framework's analytical rigor by demonstrating how hybrid human-AI governance structures increase decision-making precision. For example, GAI's ability to synthesize unstructured data (e.g., geopolitical disruptions and consumer sentiment trends) with AI's quantitative modeling enables proactive mitigation of logistics bottlenecks while maintaining ethical AI deployment standards. This dual technological integration promotes a paradigm shift from isolated process optimization to ecosystem-wide intelligence, where cross-functional data liquidity and algorithmic transparency become organizational cornerstones.

As a strategic concept, the study shows how the 4P framework (Process-People-Partners-Platforms) enables a scalable GAI-DA implementation. It emphasizes that technology implementation must accompany workforce upskilling initiatives, partner ecosystem alignment, and ethical audit protocols. These findings contribute new insights to the literature on supply chain innovation and provide evidence-based guidelines for executives to balance computational sophistication and organizational agility in an era of intelligent, self-optimizing logistics systems.

9 Challenges in Using GAI and Agents in Logistics

Integrating GAI solutions and DA requires careful attention to data privacy and cybersecurity, necessitating robust security frameworks. GAI "hallucinations" can undermine user trust, requiring careful implementation with strategic alignment and benefit assessment. DA designed to reduce human intervention must also be carefully monitored. Successful integration involves process redesign focusing on human-centered workflows, interdisciplinary collaboration, and hands-on operator training. Evaluating return on investment (ROI) and clear career paths are critical to attracting talent. Data quality and interoperability are challenging as AI relies on consistent information; solid data management and API-driven integration can help. Data privacy concerns require strong encryption and regulatory compliance, which requires transparent AI algorithms. Integrating AI into existing systems requires phased implementation and cloud-based platforms to manage infrastructure requirements. Finally, the skills gap requires extensive training and partnerships with educational institutions to equip the workforce for AI-driven logistics. Ultimately, organizations adapt their processes to integrate these innovative technologies seamlessly. The challenge is to combine these GAI and DA with existing ICT and OT applications.

10 Extensions and Limitations

In this study, only the logistics function is considered, as it still needs to be optimized regarding its practicability and thematic coherence. There is no reason why a control and efficiency system based on the architecture described above should not apply to the entire organization's production function or other functions.

Emerging technological paradigms such as blockchain and the IIoT can be integrated with DA and GAI, creating increasingly complex and intelligent ecosystems for logistics management [46]. Blockchain, the IIoT, GAI, and DA can synergistically improve the logistics ecosystem. The IIoT provides real-time data from sensors throughout logistics, which is then secured and immutably recorded by the blockchain, creating a transparent and traceable history of goods. GAI can use this data to optimize routes, predict disruptions, and develop efficient logistics strategies. At the same time, DAs automate the execution of these strategies, ensuring seamless coordination and faster response times. Essentially, the IIoT provides the data, the blockchain secures it, GAI optimizes the processes, and DA executes them, creating a highly efficient, secure provides the data; the blockchain secures it, GAI optimizes the processes, and DA executes them, creating a highly efficient, safe, and responsive logistics network.

It is also necessary to investigate additional implementations of the proposed approach to quantify its benefits, challenges, and remedies. In a broader perspective, integrating systems with other logistics partners guarantees that the organization has control over its processes and can predict possible delivery delays or misplacements due to events that are not attributable to the logistics partner organizations (e.g., unexpected weather events, international conflicts, etc.) [47].

11 Conclusion

The integration of AI into the management of logistics services is changing the industry's landscape. While there are still challenges, the potential benefits—from increased efficiency to improved effectiveness—underscore the need for organizations to adopt these technologies. Future developments in generative GAI and DA applications are likely to strengthen the role of these algorithms in logistics and make them indispensable tools for organizations to succeed in a competitive market [48]. This study examines GAI and DA and their in-depth applications in logistics. It provides a general overview of the currently available solutions, particularly an outlook on specific solutions to support logistics. The paper defines and thoroughly analyzes logistics' evolutionary development path. The characteristics of each phase are characterized by waves of innovation—conceptual, industrial, or both—which ultimately lead organizations into the innovative age of Logistics 5.0. The convergence of blockchain, the IIoT, generative AI, and DAs heralds a fundamental shift towards Logistics 5.0, where logistics become efficient but also resilient and adaptable, paving the way for fully autonomous and intelligent logistics networks. This development promises to revolutionize global trade and enable unprecedented optimization and responsiveness in the face of dynamic market conditions. This progress requires a strong ethical framework, especially regarding transparency, fairness, and data protection [49]. AI-driven decisions in logistics, which impact customers and operators alike, must be rigorously scrutinized to ensure fair outcomes and prevent unintended bias. Ethical AI is not just a consideration but an imperative because the future of Logistics 5.0 depends on building trust and ensuring that technological advances serve the broader interests of society [50].

Algorithmic control is made possible by AI systems organizations' transformative potential for operational control and process optimization. The socio-technical challenges involved in implementing such systems are not trivial. Three critical hurdles are emerging: first, the capital-intensive development and maintenance of sophisticated AI architectures, which presents significant barriers to entry for resource-constrained companies; second, the acute talent shortage in hybrid skills in the areas of data science, supply chain engineering and ethical AI governance and thirdly, the persistent strategic myopia of business leaders regarding the paradigm-shifting capabilities of emerging technologies, as evidenced by Gartner's [51] findings that 68% of executives underestimate the operational transformation potential of AI.

Notwithstanding these implementation challenges, the proposed framework demonstrates technical feasibility for large and medium-size enterprises with sufficient financial, technological, and human resources. When such systems are introduced as part of a structured roadmap, they offer three key benefits: improved process innovation through machine learning and the simulation of alternative operational scenarios, increased inter-organizational collaboration through shared predictive analytics platforms with logistics partners, and improved strategic alignment across the supply chain. This three-part value proposition directly addresses the systemic vulnerabilities created by today's supply chain volatilities—from geopolitical disruptions to demand shocks—by institutionalizing resilience mechanisms based on predictive synchronization, risk-averse optimization, and ethical cohesion [52].

The proposed framework's effectiveness depends on adopting the four-dimensional implementation strategy, which includes process redesign, partnership architectures, platform ecosystems, and workforce upskilling [53]. While technological integration forms the backbone of the infrastructure, success ultimately depends on simultaneous investments in workforce skills development and partner ecosystem incentivization [53]. This multi-dimensional approach transforms AI systems from isolated technical solutions into organizational cornerstones for smart, adaptive logistics governance. This view aligns with recent research from the MIT Center for Transportation & Logistics, which emphasizes that next-generation competitiveness in logistics will be defined by synergistic frameworks for human-AI collaboration, not by technological superiority alone [54, 55].

Acknowledgments Project ECS 0000024 Rome Technopole,—CUP B83C22002820006, NRP Mission 4 Component 2 Investment 1.5, Funded by the European Union—NextGenerationEU.

Use of AI Tools Declaration While preparing this work, the author(s) used ChatGPT 3.5 to brush their English. After using this tool/service, the author(s) reviewed and edited the content as needed and took(s) full responsibility for the publication's content.

References

1. Meidute, I. (2005). Comparative analysis of the definitions of logistics centers. *Transport, 20*(3), 106–110. https://doi.org/10.3846/16484142.2005.9638005
2. Bolatan, G. I. S. (2021). From logistics 4.0 to logistics 5.0: Logistics for digital society. *Academic Studies in Humanities and Social Sciences, 191*, 1–12.
3. Nicoletti, B., & Appolloni, A. (2023). Framework of IoT, blockchain, digital twins, and artificial intelligence solutions in support of the digital business transformation of logistics 5.0. In L. Ferreira, M. Cruz, E. Cruz, H. Quintela, & M. Cunha (Eds.), *Supporting technologies and the impact of blockchain on organizations and society* (pp. 195–219). IGI Global. https://doi.org/10.4018/978-1-6684-5747-4.ch012
4. El Makhloufi, A. (2023). *AI application in transport and logistics: Opportunities and challenges (an exploratory study)* (p. 100). University of Applied Sciences. Retrieved from https://research.hva.nl/en/publications/ai-application-in-transport-and-logistics-opportunities-and-chall

5. Gonçalves, R., & Domingues, L. (2025). Artificial intelligence driving intelligent logistics: Benefits, challenges, and drawbacks. *Procedia Computer Science, 256*, 665–672. https://doi.org/10.1016/j.procs.2025.02.165
6. Liu, G., Huynh, N. V., Du, H., Hoang, D. T., Niyato, D., Zhu, K., Kang, J., Xiong, Z., Jamalipour, A., & Kim, D. I. (2024). *Generative AI for unmanned vehicle swarms: Challenges, applications and opportunities*. arXiv. https://doi.org/10.48550/arXiv.2402.18062
7. Katragadda, V. (2023). Automating customer support: A study on the efficacy of machine learning-driven chatbots and virtual assistants. *IRE Journals, 7*(1), 600–601.
8. Dell'Acqua, F., McFowland, E., Mollick, E. R., Lifshitz-Assaf, H., Kellogg, K., Rajendran, S., & Lakhani, K. R. (2023). *Navigating the jagged technological frontier: Field experimental evidence of the effects of AI on knowledge operator productivity and quality*. Harvard Business School Technology & Operations Management Unit Working Paper (24–013). https://doi.org/10.2139/ssrn.4573321
9. Kanbach, D. K., Heiduk, L., Blueher, G., Schreiter, M., & Lahmann, A. (2024). The GenAI is out of the bottle: Generative artificial intelligence from a business model innovation perspective. *Review of Managerial Science, 18*(4), 1189–1220. https://doi.org/10.1007/s11846-023-00696-z
10. Joel, O. S., Oyewole, A. T., Odunaiya, O. G., & Soyombo, O. T. (2024). Leveraging artificial intelligence for enhanced supply chain optimization: A comprehensive review of current practices and future potentials. *International Journal of Management & Entrepreneurship Research, 6*(3), 707–721. https://doi.org/10.51594/ijmer.v6i3.882
11. Richey, R. G., Jr., Chowdhury, S., Davis-Sramek, B., Giannakis, M., & Dwivedi, Y. K. (2023). Artificial intelligence in logistics and supply chain management: A primer and roadmap for research. *Journal of Business Logistics, 44*(4), 532–549. https://doi.org/10.1111/jbl.12364
12. Kar, A. K., Varsha, P. S., & Rajan, S. (2023). Unraveling the impact of generative artificial intelligence (GAI) in industrial applications: A review of scientific and grey literature. *Global Journal of Flexible Systems Management, 24*(4), 659–689. https://doi.org/10.1007/s40171-023-00356-x
13. Jackson, I., Ivanov, D., Dolgui, A., & Namdar, J. (2024). Generative artificial intelligence in supply chain and operations management: A capability-based framework for analysis and implementation. *International Journal of Production Research, 62*(1), 1–26. https://doi.org/10.1080/00207543.2024.2398583
14. Nimmagadda, V. S. P. (2021). Artificial intelligence for real-time logistics and transportation optimization in retail supply chains: Techniques, models, and applications. *Journal of Machine Learning for Healthcare Decision Support, 1*(1), 88–126.
15. Wissuchek, C., & Zschech, P. (2024). Prescriptive analytics systems revised: A systematic literature review from an information systems perspective. *Information Systems and e-Business Management, 22*, 1–75. https://doi.org/10.1007/s10257-024-00688-w
16. Ferreira, B., & Reis, J. (2023). A systematic literature review on the application of automation in logistics. *Logistics, 7*(4), 80. https://doi.org/10.3390/logistics7040080
17. Rushton, A., Croucher, P., & Baker, P. (2022). *The handbook of logistics and distribution management: Understanding the supply chain* (6th ed.). Kogan Page Publishers.
18. Ajibuwa, O., Hamdaoui, B., & Yavuz, A. A. (2023). *A survey on AI/ML-driven intrusion and misbehavior detection in networked autonomous systems: Techniques, challenges and opportunities*. arXiv. https://doi.org/10.48550/arXiv.2305.05040
19. Yanamala, A. K. Y., & Suryadevara, S. (2024). Navigating data protection challenges in the era of artificial intelligence: A comprehensive review. *Revista de Inteligencia Artificial en Medicina, 15*(1), 113–146.
20. Ajayi, F. A., & Udeh, C. A. (2024). Review of workforce upskilling initiatives for emerging technologies in IT. *International Journal of Management & Entrepreneurship Research, 6*(4), 1119–1137. https://doi.org/10.51594/ijmer.v6i4.1003
21. Council of Supply Chain Management Professionals. (2021). Retrieved from https://www.cscmp.eu

22. Xiao, Z., Yuan, Q., Sun, Y., & Sun, X. (2021). New paradigm of logistics space reorganization: E-commerce, land use, and supply chain management. *Transportation Research Interdisciplinary Perspectives, 9*, 100300. https://doi.org/10.1016/j.trip.2021.100300
23. Nicoletti, B. (2023). *Supply network 5.0: How to improve human automation in the supply chain*. Palgrave Macmillan. https://doi.org/10.1007/978-3-031-22032-6
24. Bandi, A., Adapa, P. V. S. R., & Kuchi, Y. E. V. P. K. (2023). The power of generative AI: A review of requirements, models, input–output formats, evaluation metrics, and challenges. *Future Internet, 15*(8), 260. https://doi.org/10.3390/fi15080260
25. Dolata, M., Katsiuba, D., Wellnhammer, N., & Schwabe, G. (2023). Learning with digital agents: An analysis based on the activity theory. *Journal of Management Information Systems, 40*(1), 56–95. https://doi.org/10.1080/07421222.2023.2172775
26. Doanh, D. C., Dufek, Z., Ejdys, J., Ginevičius, R., Korzynski, P., Mazurek, G., & Ziemba, E. (2023). Generative AI in the manufacturing process: Theoretical considerations. *Engineering Management in Production and Services, 15*(4), 76–89. https://doi.org/10.2478/emj-2023-0029
27. Min, H. (2010). Artificial intelligence in supply chain management: Theory and applications. *International Journal of Logistics: Research and Applications, 13*(1), 13–39. https://doi.org/10.1080/13675560902736537
28. Riahi, Y., Saikouk, T., Gunasekaran, A., & Badraoui, I. (2021). Artificial intelligence applications in the supply chain: A descriptive bibliometric analysis and future research directions. *Expert Systems with Applications, 173*, 114702. https://doi.org/10.1016/j.eswa.2021.114702
29. Mohamed, O. A. M. (2023). *How is generative AI transforming supply chain operations and efficiency?* Politecnico di Milano. Retrieved from https://www.politesi.polimi.it/handle/10589/218912
30. Shapiro, D., Li, W., Delaflor, M., & Toxtli, C. (2023). *Conceptual framework for autonomous cognitive entities*. arXiv. https://doi.org/10.48550/arXiv.2310.06775
31. Wispinski, N. J. (2023). *Adaptive decision making in dynamic environments by artificial and biological agents*. University of Alberta. https://doi.org/10.7939/r3-2bwt-5e85
32. Möllers, M., Berger, B., & Klein, S. (2024). Contrasting human-AI workplace relationship configurations. In *Research handbook on artificial intelligence and decision making in organizations* (pp. 282–303). Edward Elgar Publishing. https://doi.org/10.4337/9781803926216.00025
33. Pan, J., Zhang, Y., Tomlin, N., Zhou, Y., Levine, S., & Suhr, A. (2024). *Autonomous evaluation and refinement of digital agents*. arXiv. https://doi.org/10.48550/arXiv.2404.06474
34. Betti, Q., Khoury, R., Hallé, S., & Montreuil, B. (2019). Improving hyperconnected logistics with blockchains and smart contracts. *IT Professional, 21*(4), 25–32. https://doi.org/10.1109/MITP.2019.2912135
35. Burgess, A., & Burgess, A. (2018). AI in action. In *The executive guide to artificial intelligence: How to identify and implement applications for AI in your organization* (pp. 73–89). Springer. https://doi.org/10.1007/978-3-319-63820-1_5
36. Zaman, S. I., Khan, S., Zaman, S. A. A., & Khan, S. A. (2023). A grey decision-making trial and evaluation laboratory model for digital warehouse management in supply chain networks. *Decision Analytics Journal, 8*, 100293. https://doi.org/10.1016/j.dajour.2023.100293
37. Gupta, S., Iyer, R. S., & Kumar, S. (2024). CyberTwinAI: Enhancing security and efficiency in industry 4.0. In *Digital twins: Advancements in theory, implementation, and applications* (pp. 139–157). Springer. https://doi.org/10.1007/978-3-031-76564-3_6
38. Vilas-Boas, J. L., Rodrigues, J. J., & Alberti, A. M. (2023). Convergence of distributed ledger technologies with digital twins, IoT, and AI for fresh food logistics: Challenges and opportunities. *Journal of Industrial Information Integration, 31*, 100393. https://doi.org/10.1016/j.jii.2022.100393
39. Khan, S. M., Ngo, L. B., Morris, E. A., Ashraf, M. T., Dey, K., & Zhou, Y. (2025). Social media data in transportation. In M. Chowdhury, K. Dey, & A. Apon (Eds.), *Data analytics for intelligent transportation systems* (pp. 317–336). Elsevier. https://doi.org/10.1016/B978-0-443-13878-2.00010-2

40. Chowdhury, M., Dey, K., & Apon, A. (2024). *Data analytics for intelligent transportation systems*. Elsevier. https://doi.org/10.1016/C2022-0-02815-4
41. Vlachos, I. P., Pascazzi, R. M., Zobolas, G., Repoussis, P., & Giannakis, M. (2023). Lean manufacturing systems in industry 4.0: A lean automation plan of AGVs/IoT integration. *Production Planning & Control, 34*(4), 345–358. https://doi.org/10.1080/09537287.2021.1917720
42. Macrina, G., Pugliese, L. D. P., Guerriero, F., & Laporte, G. (2020). Drone-aided routing: A literature review. *Transportation Research Part C: Emerging Technologies, 120*, 102762. https://doi.org/10.1016/j.trc.2020.102762
43. Rogers, D. S., & Tibben-Lembke, R. (2001). An examination of reverse logistics practices. *Journal of Business Logistics, 22*(2), 129–148. https://doi.org/10.1002/j.2158-1592.2001.tb00007.x
44. Cano-Marin, E. (2024). The transformative potential of generative artificial intelligence (GenAI) in business: A text mining analysis on innovation data sources. *ESIC Market, 55*(2), e333. https://doi.org/10.7200/esicm.55.333
45. Zhu, Y., Cheng, J., Liu, Z., Cheng, Q., Zou, X., Xu, H., & Tao, F. (2023). Production logistics digital twins: Research profiling, application, challenges, and opportunities. *Robotics and Computer-Integrated Manufacturing, 84*, 102592. https://doi.org/10.1016/j.rcim.2023.102592
46. Nicoletti, B., & Appolloni, A. (2023). Artificial intelligence for the management of Servitization 5.0. *Sustainability, 15*(14), 11113. https://doi.org/10.3390/su151411113
47. Löffel, M., Schmidt, C. G., & Wagner, S. M. (2025). Supply chain risk management for humanitarian aid delivery: Risk identification and contingency analysis. *The International Journal of Logistics Management, 36*(1), 225–258. https://doi.org/10.1108/IJLM-01-2024-0041
48. Sai, S., Sai, R., & Chamola, V. (2024). Generative AI for industry 5.0: Analyzing the impact of ChatGPT, DALLE, and other models. *IEEE Open Journal of the Communications Society*. https://doi.org/10.1109/OJCOMS.2024.3400161
49. George, A. S., & George, A. H. (2024). Towards a super smart society 5.0: Opportunities and challenges of integrating emerging technologies for social innovation. *Partners Universal International Research Journal, 3*(2), 1–29.
50. Exner, R., & Zunic, A. (2023). *The path to an intelligent enterprise: The art and practice of business intelligence strategy*. Springer. https://doi.org/10.1007/978-3-031-69914-6
51. Tennin, K. L., & Ray, S. (2024). *Cases on economic crisis impact on multinational corporations*. IGI Global. https://doi.org/10.4018/979-8-3693-1544-6
52. Kumar, S. S., Kumar, S. R., & Ramesh, G. (2024). From industry 4.0 to 5.0: Enriching manufacturing excellence through human–robot interaction and technological empowerment. In *Intelligent systems and industrial internet of things for sustainable development* (pp. 24–51). Chapman and Hall. https://doi.org/10.1201/9781032642789-2
53. Challoumis, C. (2024). The imperative of skill development in an AI revolution. In *XIX international scientific conference* (pp. 132–168). WIPO.
54. Sinha, S., & Lee, Y. M. (2024). Challenges with developing and deploying AI models and applications in industrial systems. *Discover Artificial Intelligence, 4*(1), 55. https://doi.org/10.1007/s44163-024-00151-2
55. Karwowski, W., Salvendy, G., Albert, L., Kim, W. C., Denton, B., Dessouky, M., & Tiwari, M. K. (2025). Grand challenges in industrial and systems engineering. *International Journal of Production Research, 63*(4), 1538–1583. https://doi.org/10.1080/00207543.2024.2432463

Digitalization of Procurement Processes: Application of Lean Methods to Improve Efficiency

Manuel Inácio, Vitor Anes, and António Abreu

Abstract This study investigates the application of lean methodologies in optimizing the internal material requisition process within a company, with a focus on waste reduction and operational efficiency. The subject of the study is a small to medium-sized enterprise (SME) based in Greater Lisbon, specializing in industrial machinery maintenance and repair, equipment rental, and accessory manufacturing. Several inefficiencies were identified, including redundancies in the current requisition process, resulting in excessive rework, resource consumption, and operational delays. These inefficiencies disrupt workflows, affect material requisition timelines, and create operational bottlenecks, ultimately hindering business opportunities and service delivery. To address these challenges, the following tasks were undertaken: (1) a detailed analysis of the existing procurement process was conducted, followed by the development of a simulation model to evaluate various improvement scenarios; (2) idle periods were identified and analyzed using Value Stream Mapping (VSM) to highlight areas with potential for efficiency gains; (3) a digitalized process simulation was created to compare against the existing process; (4) a feasibility study for implementing the digitalized process was performed. The results indicate that the proposed improvements will significantly enhance process efficiency, leading to positive impacts on the company's overall operations.

Keywords Material requisition · Industrial processes · Lean · Waste reduction · Digitalization · Simulation

M. Inácio · V. Anes (✉) · A. Abreu
Instituto Superior de Engenharia de Lisboa, Polytechnic University of Lisbon, Lisbon, Portugal
e-mail: A36949@alunos.isel.pt; vitor.anes@isel.pt; antonio.abreu@isel.pt

F. Tao et al. (eds.), *Artificial Intelligence and Digital Transformation*, Lecture Notes in Information Systems and Organisation 78,
https://doi.org/10.1007/978-3-032-00118-4_8

1 Introduction

In today's highly competitive and globalized business environment, organizations increasingly focus on strategic areas such as sustainability, digitalization, and Industry 4.0. The implementation of lean methodologies has become widely recognized as a vital strategy for reducing waste and optimizing production processes, aligning with the evolving industrial landscape. First introduced by John Krafcik in 1988 [1], lean production aims to create a streamlined system—defined as "a set of interconnected elements organized coherently to achieve a specific goal" [2]. By applying lean methodologies, organizations can enhance the efficiency of production systems while minimizing waste, ultimately gaining a competitive advantage through higher productivity [3].

The lean philosophy emphasizes a systemic approach, where all production elements are interconnected and harmonized to achieve common objectives. This holistic perspective is essential for understanding and optimizing the overall performance of production systems [4]. Lean tools such as Value Stream Mapping (VSM) are particularly effective for visualizing and analyzing value streams within organizations, helping to identify inefficiencies and eliminate waste [5]. Additionally, scenario-based simulations play a crucial role in process optimization, allowing companies to model virtual environments, identify bottlenecks, and test improvements without disrupting actual production or making premature investments. Software like Arena facilitates these simulations, driving better process efficiency and decision-making [6].

Beyond operational improvements, lean methodologies align with financial evaluations, enhancing decision-making regarding investments. Financial tools like Net Present Value (NPV), Internal Rate of Return (IRR), and Payback Period (PBP) are instrumental in assessing the feasibility and profitability of projects. NPV calculates the net value of an investment by discounting future cash flows, with a positive NPV signifying value creation [7]. IRR, on the other hand, represents the discount rate at which NPV is zero, effectively indicating the return rate that balances cash flows and investments [8]. PBP, meanwhile, defines the time required to recover the initial investment through net cash flows, highlighting the point where projects start yielding profit [9].

This article explores the holistic benefits of lean production methodologies applied to internal material requisition processes within an organization. By adopting a case study approach, the research develops and validates several waste reduction improvement hypotheses through Arena simulation and financial analysis, demonstrating the potential of lean methodologies to enhance both operational efficiency and economic viability.

2 Background

The optimization of material requisition processes in industrial environments through lean methodologies and digital integration has become a key area of research in recent years. Lean manufacturing principles, initially pioneered by Toyota, focus on reducing waste (muda), improving efficiency, and increasing productivity. These principles have evolved in tandem with the increasing adoption of Industry 4.0 technologies, where the integration of digital tools is seen as pivotal for enhancing the effectiveness of traditional lean techniques.

2.1 *Lean Methodologies in Material Requisition*

Lean methodologies, particularly techniques such as Value Stream Mapping (VSM) and Kanban, have been widely adopted to streamline processes like material requisition. According to Womack and Jones [10], the primary objective of lean is the continuous identification and elimination of waste across all stages of production. These methodologies help identify inefficiencies in material flow, communication, and procurement processes. Recent studies have indicated that integrating lean techniques such as VSM can significantly optimize material requisition processes by reducing lead times, minimizing inventory levels, and improving overall operational flow [11, 12].

2.2 *Digital Integration: A Catalyst for Lean Transformation*

With the rise of digital technologies, the application of lean principles has been enhanced through the integration of tools such as digital twins, the Internet of Things (IoT), and predictive analytics. The fusion of lean practices with digital technologies is referred to as "digital lean." Digital lean transforms traditional methods by providing real-time data analytics and improving decision-making processes, particularly in areas like inventory management and procurement. Studies show that this integration enables more accurate demand forecasting and real-time monitoring of material flow, which leads to reduced waste and improved operational efficiency [13, 14].

Digital lean tools allow organizations to extend traditional lean tools with features such as machine learning and automated decision-making systems. These technologies can predict material shortages or surpluses, thereby reducing over-ordering or stockouts. Moreover, data-driven platforms are crucial in creating flexible and adaptive supply chains, which are essential in optimizing material requisition processes in volatile production environments [15, 16].

2.3 Strategic Waste Reduction Through Lean and Digital Technologies

Waste reduction remains a cornerstone of lean methodology, and recent research has emphasized how digital tools can drive significant improvements in this area. A study by Cifone et al. [17] demonstrates that organizations that implemented a combination of lean and digital technologies saw reductions in material waste by optimizing their ordering systems, reducing lead times, and improving material tracking accuracy. This integration ensures that material requisitions are not only based on accurate forecasts but also on real-time data that accounts for fluctuations in production demands.

Furthermore, the strategic use of technologies such as the IoT enables real-time visibility into the supply chain, which significantly enhances lean's waste reduction capabilities. By reducing manual errors and human intervention in material requisition processes, digital tools streamline workflows and ensure that material demands are met efficiently [18]. These advancements are essential for organizations looking to balance cost reduction with higher levels of productivity and quality.

3 Case Study

3.1 Problem Description

The company in question, a small to medium-sized enterprise (SME) based in Greater Lisbon, specializes in the maintenance and repair of industrial machinery, as well as equipment rental and accessory manufacturing.

The primary issue revolves around the inefficiency of the internal requisition process, which spans from the initial material request to placing orders with suppliers. This process is highly complex, involving numerous stakeholders and a heavy reliance on paper-based documentation, leading to delays, reduced productivity, and the potential loss of new business due to extended workshop occupation by machinery under repair.

3.2 Problem Impact

The inefficiency of the internal requisition process creates several negative outcomes for the company. First, it leads to delays in completing repairs, which can result in customer dissatisfaction and the potential loss of future contracts. Second, the prolonged occupation of workshop space reduces the company's operational capacity, limiting the number of machines that can be repaired simultaneously. This operational bottleneck prevents the company from scaling its revenue and responding effectively to market demand.

3.3 Benefits of Resolving the Problem

Addressing this issue could yield significant benefits for the company:

1. *Cycle time reduction.* Simplifying and digitizing the requisition process could drastically cut down cycle times, enabling quicker repair turnarounds.
2. *Increased operational capacity.* Faster machine turnaround would free up valuable workshop space, allowing the company to handle more machines at once.
3. *Improved customer satisfaction.* Shorter repair times and more efficient service would likely result in higher customer satisfaction, fostering loyalty and attracting new contracts.
4. *Operational cost reduction.* Eliminating inefficiencies and improving processes could lead to a substantial reduction in operational costs, boosting profit margins.
5. *Support for continuous improvement.* A more streamlined system would enable the identification of additional areas for ongoing improvements, in line with lean methodology principles.

Tackling the inefficiencies in the internal requisition process holistically will not only address immediate issues related to delays and capacity but will also provide a solid foundation for sustainable growth and enhanced competitiveness in the industrial market.

4 Improvement Hypotheses

Upon analyzing the company's current purchasing procedure and simulating it using Arena software (Fig. 1), three improvement hypotheses were proposed.

4.1 Improvement Hypothesis 1

The first hypothesis for improving requisition and purchasing management within the company involves standardization. This would be achieved by implementing fixed times for requisition approvals, aimed at reducing variability and dispersion throughout the day, thus optimizing workflow. The assumption behind this hypothesis is that by consolidating requisitions into specific time slots and adopting a Kaizen approach to continuous improvement, the planning and execution of procurement activities will be facilitated. This simplification occurs by eliminating variations in requisition demands and emergency situations [19].

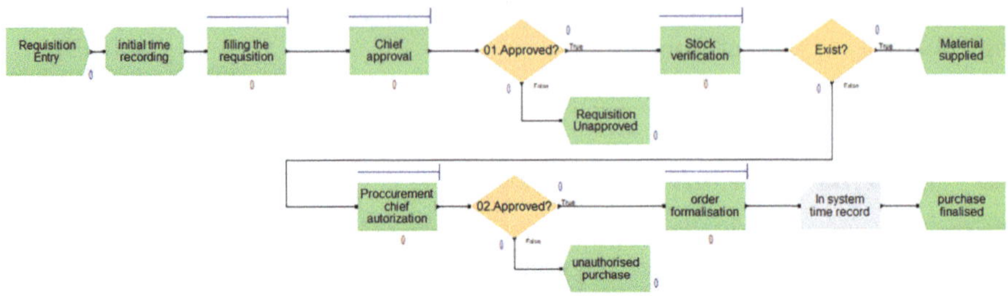

Fig. 1 Current internal requisition process flow simulated in Arena

In this hypothesis, requisitioners would submit their requests to their superior, who would review and determine which follow the established process. The approval times would be set at 10 a.m. and 3 p.m., while the ordering times would be scheduled at 11 a.m. and 4 p.m. This would allow for efficient coordination between stock gathering from suppliers and the courier service, as well as ensuring that all orders are processed within the designated timeframe.

Utilizing the Heijunka approach, the process would be streamlined by reducing the number of orders placed with suppliers, consolidating different requisitions for the same supplier into one order. This approach levels out the ordering process and minimizes fluctuations in demand. Consequently, each participant in the authorization chain would adjust their responsibilities according to the designated times, promoting more effective time management, minimizing interruptions, and optimizing not only the purchasing process but also overall work management throughout the day.

To successfully implement this approach, effective communication and appropriate training will be essential. Employees must understand the objectives and benefits of this change, highlighting the importance of adhering to the established schedules. This will be the primary challenge in implementing this scenario. Furthermore, clear procedures will be necessary to handle emergency situations outside regular hours, ensuring that quick responses do not compromise the efficiency of the process. Regular monitoring of adherence to the established schedules and gathering feedback from employees will be crucial to identify any improvement areas and ensure the sustainability of this approach over time.

Although this hypothesis addresses some of the challenges mentioned earlier—such as the dispersion of requisitions throughout the day—issues related to rework and process management still need to be considered. Nevertheless, operational efficiency is expected to improve with the implementation of this first hypothesis.

The investment for implementing these changes would be minimal, as it would mainly involve informing employees of the new procedure and designating supervisors as responsible for ensuring compliance.

4.2 Improvement Hypothesis 2

The second hypothesis for optimizing requisitions involves digitizing the requisition process, by implementing a system that allows employees to submit their requisitions via a digital platform. Aligned with Industry 4.0 principles, this measure seeks to modernize the process and increase overall efficiency. The system will be implemented gradually, with clear criteria for automatic approvals, utilizing lean tools to simplify and standardize the process [20].

One practical example of such criteria could be setting up automatic approvals for material requisitions destined for scheduled equipment maintenance, where the required materials are always the same for each type of revision, promoting standardization and reducing the need for human intervention.

Digitization of the process will bring tangible benefits, such as a reduction in the time required to complete requisitions and a decrease in rework. For instance, warehouse clerks and procurement employees will receive the material list directly through the software, eliminating the need to input it manually, thus improving operational efficiency. This will integrate Industry 4.0 technologies to automate and enhance processes.

Additionally, notification mechanisms will be established for supervisors to approve pending requisitions at the same times set in the first hypothesis, maintaining the benefits mentioned earlier and supporting production leveling (Heijunka). Supervisors will have real-time visibility of pending requisitions, enabling quick decision-making and reducing waiting times.

Furthermore, a monetary threshold will be defined for requisitions, simplifying the approval process and eliminating bottlenecks. Employees in the department will be able to issue orders up to €500 without supervisor authorization, promoting decentralization of decisions and streamlining workflow, which is consistent with lean principles of autonomy and decentralization.

While system integration is still partial at this stage, the digital requisition system represents a significant step towards more efficient and transparent purchasing management. Digitization will provide more accurate traceability of requisitions, facilitating real-time tracking and analysis of each request, which aligns with continuous improvement (Kaizen) and transparency goals.

The primary challenge to this system's implementation lies in resistance to change and potential technological difficulties that some employees may face when interacting with the software/application. A detailed investment analysis will be necessary, considering software development costs, employee training, and annual software licensing fees to ensure a sustainable and results-oriented approach.

Thus, this second hypothesis aims not only to enhance requisition efficiency but also to prepare the company for future steps toward broader system integration, contributing to more effective and integrated procurement operations.

4.3 Improvement Hypothesis 3

The third hypothesis for optimizing requisitions within the company involves the implementation of traceability technologies by combining automation with integration of the company's current systems. The goal is to improve efficiency, security, and transparency within the process [21].

Assuming that integrating traceability, technologies will enhance the accuracy and efficiency of the process, implementation can be simplified by defining clear protocols for managing urgent situations. In this phase, lean tools, such as standardization of emergency protocols, and Industry 4.0 technologies, such as automated notifications and real-time integration of requisition systems with inventory and purchasing management systems, will be applied. However, direct integration with supplier information systems is not yet considered.

For this scenario, requisitioners would submit requests via a mobile phone, tablet, or PDA. Additionally, a real-time monitoring system would be implemented, allowing users to track the progress of their requests and providing supervisors and managers with instant visibility into the process.

Once a requisition is made, the direct supervisor will receive a notification alerting them of pending approvals, enabling quick decision-making and reducing waiting times. After validating the requisition, the system will automatically manage inventory and forward the request to the purchasing or warehouse section, depending on the nature of the request.

With the mobile application, the material list will already be in digital format, both in the warehouse and purchasing section. This will not only save time and reduce rework—accelerating the process and increasing efficiency—but will also ensure the security and privacy of sensitive company data through robust cybersecurity measures.

However, the challenges to implementing this system include high initial costs and potential compatibility issues with existing systems, as well as resistance to change and technological limitations of some employees. A detailed economic feasibility study will be required, taking into account the high costs associated with software development, hardware acquisition for employees, maintenance expenses, software licenses, and training.

This model, incorporating these additional points, will promote more efficient, transparent, and secure purchasing management in the company, aligning with industry best practices and driving operational excellence.

5 Results and Discussion

5.1 Process Flow Models in Arena

Starting with the current process in Arena (see Fig. 1), and based on the hypotheses described earlier, three models were developed in Arena, as illustrated in Figs. 2, 3, and 4.

The process begins with the Requisition Entry, where new purchase requests are introduced into the system. The Initial Time Recording module captures the entry time for each requisition, providing a basis for analyzing process duration. The requisition is then processed through the Filling the Requisition stage, where necessary details are completed before submission.

Following this, the model aggregates requisitions through the Aggregating Requisitions module before proceeding to Chief Approval. Here, the decision module "01. Approved?" determines whether the requisition is accepted or rejected. If approved, it proceeds to Stock Verification. If not approved, the requisition is categorized as Requisition Unapproved and may either be discarded or escalated for further approval.

If a requisition is not approved initially, it undergoes an additional authorization step in the Procurement Chief Authorization module. The second decision module, "02. Approved?", determines whether the request is ultimately accepted or marked as an unauthorized purchase and removed from the system.

Once a requisition is approved, the model evaluates whether the requested material is available in stock. The Exist? decision module determines if the item exists in inventory. If available, the material is supplied directly, reducing processing time. If unavailable, the requisition proceeds to the Sorting by Supplier module, where the system assigns a supplier based on predefined selection criteria. The model includes

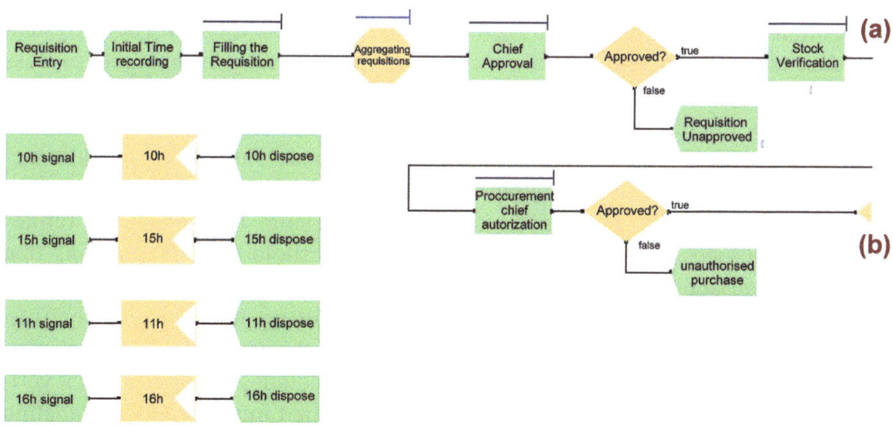

Fig. 2 (**a**) Process flow of Hypothesis 1, in Arena. (**b**) Continuation of process flow for Hypothesis 1, in Arena

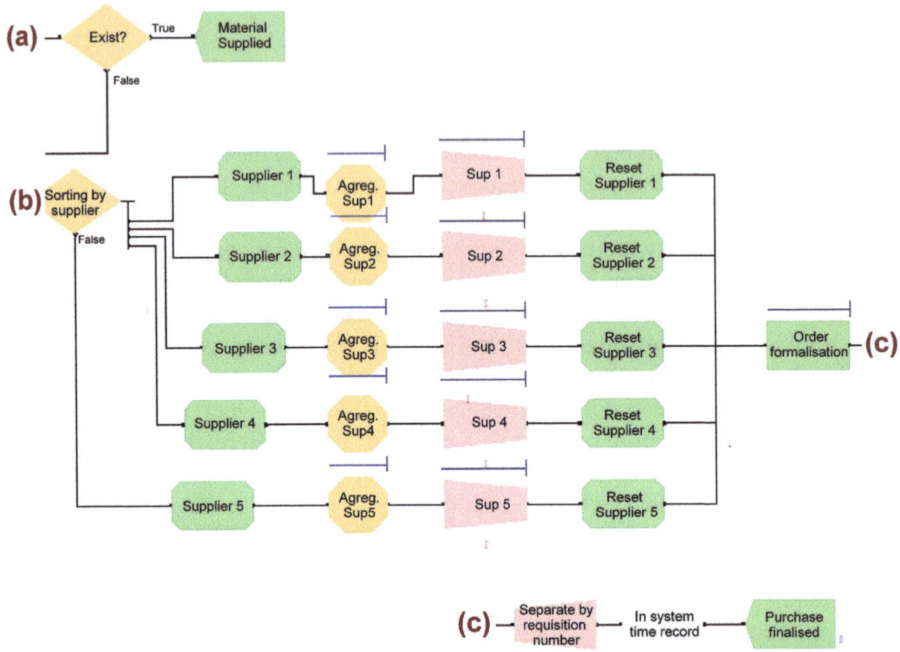

Fig. 2 (continued)

five supplier entities (Supplier 1 to Supplier 5), each associated with an Aggregating per Supplier module to batch similar requisitions. After aggregation, the order is processed through respective supplier modules (Sup1, Sup2, etc.) before being reset through Reset Supplier modules to ensure proper system updates.

After procurement from suppliers, the order reaches the Order Formalization stage, where administrative processes are completed. The system then Separates by Requisition Number to ensure that each request is accurately tracked. The In System Time Record module logs the total processing time, providing insights into process efficiency and potential bottlenecks. Finally, the requisition process concludes with the Purchase Finalized module, indicating the completion of the transaction. Figure 3 shows the process flow of hypothesis 2, the model introduces several structural improvements over the previous version, hypothesis 1, optimizing decision-making, supplier management, and requisition processing. The new model refines the approval process by incorporating a financial threshold of 500€, ensuring that high-value transactions undergo additional scrutiny. This contrasts with the previous model, which had a simpler approval system without financial risk controls. Stock verification is another key enhancement. Unlike the earlier model, which proceeded directly to supplier selection, the new model includes an explicit stock verification step. If materials are available, they are supplied immediately, eliminating unnecessary supplier engagement and reducing procurement costs. Additionally, supplier selection has been significantly improved. While the previous model

Fig. 3 Process flow of Hypothesis 2, in arena

followed a straightforward assignment process, the new model aggregates orders per supplier, enabling batch processing, streamlining operations, and minimizing transaction costs. Requisition tracking and order finalization have also been enhanced. The new model improves traceability by separating orders based on their requisition numbers, ensuring better auditing and reporting capabilities. These improvements lead to several advantages, including greater financial control, optimized inventory utilization, more efficient supplier management, and enhanced traceability. The second hypothesis model provides a more robust and efficient procurement framework by integrating financial oversight and inventory validation. It

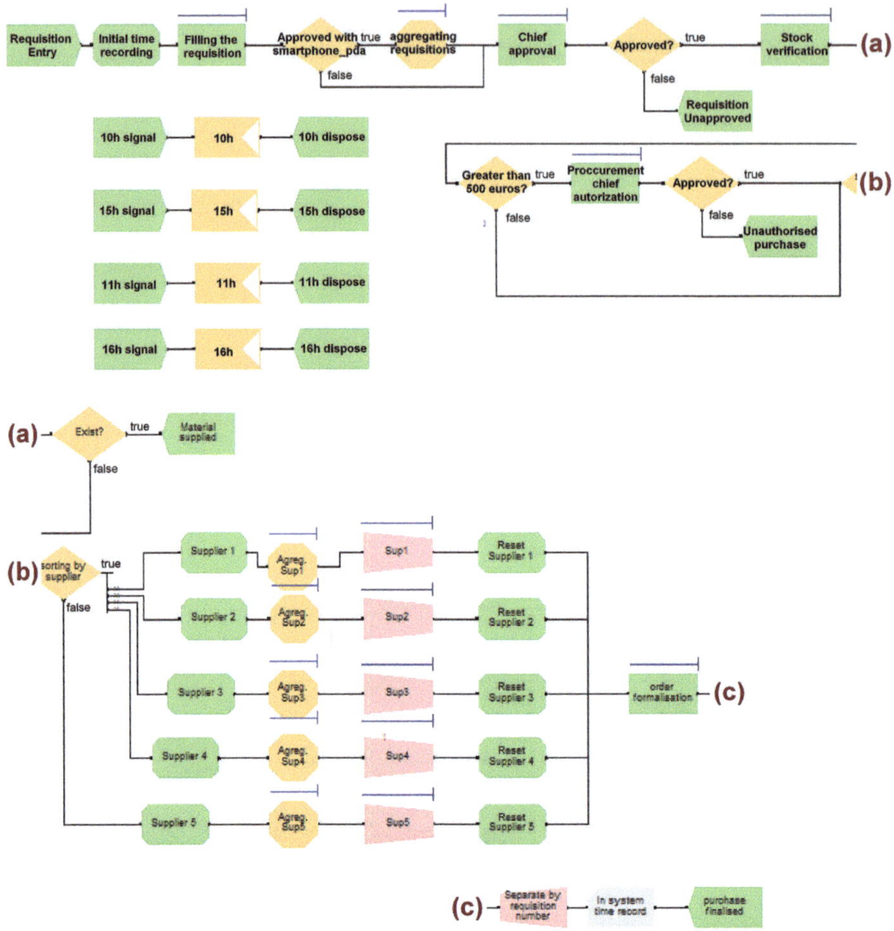

Fig. 4 Process flow of Hypothesis 3, in arena

improves operational efficiency, reduces unnecessary expenditures, and enhances supplier interactions, making the procurement process faster and more cost-effective.

Figure 4 depicts the third hypothesis for the procurement simulation model, introducing an additional layer of approval by incorporating smartphone-based requisition validation. This hypothesis explores a more dynamic and real-time decision-making process as an alternative to previous models. The model begins with the Requisition Entry, where new requests are recorded, followed by Initial Time Recording and Filling the Requisition. A key difference in this version is the Approval with Smartphone Poll, which allows for quicker validation before requisition aggregation. If the smartphone approval fails, the process continues with standard requisition aggregation and chief approval. The requisition then undergoes the 01. Approved? Decision phase, where a rejection moves the process toward

Procurement Chief Authorization, particularly if the requested amount exceeds 500€. If authorization is granted, the requisition proceeds; otherwise, it is categorized as an Unauthorized Purchase and discarded. Stock availability is assessed through the Exist? Decision module. If the required materials are in stock, they are supplied directly, reducing procurement lead time. If unavailable, the system enters the Supplier Sorting phase, where the requisition is allocated to one of five suppliers based on predefined criteria. Aggregation by supplier helps streamline procurement and optimize bulk purchasing. Once processed, each supplier completes the order, and the Reset Supplier module ensures consistency in the supply chain process. The Order Formalization phase finalizes the procurement, ensuring compliance with internal tracking systems. The Separate by Requisition Number module improves traceability, followed by the In-System Time Record, which logs total processing time for performance evaluation. Finally, the Purchase Finalized module completes the transaction, marking the requisition as successfully processed. This hypothesis introduces a more agile approval system, reducing processing delays by leveraging mobile-based validation. Additionally, the integration of supplier aggregation and real-time stock verification ensures better resource utilization and cost efficiency. This third hypothesis presents an alternative approach to procurement, emphasizing improved decision-making, reduced transaction time, and enhanced financial oversight.

To obtain comparable results, and considering that the data available for the simulations are qualitative (as real data and actual times could not be obtained), the author's experience was used to determine the average times of each activity in the current process. Sometimes will remain constant across all simulations, while others will be adjusted based on the improvements adopted, as detailed in the relevant sub-chapters. Additionally, a fixed request arrival mechanism will be used, defined by the expression "expo(6)" in minutes, which assumes that a request arrives every 6 min, following an exponential distribution (Fig. 5).

A total of 40 h will be simulated, distributed over 8-h workdays, representing a workweek. To analyze the results, several indicators were used. First, process efficiency was evaluated by dividing the total number of requests that completed the process by the total number of entries. Additionally, the average time taken for requests to reach the ordering phase was calculated. It is important to note that unauthorized requests or those with immediate delivery due to existing stock were not considered in this average time. Finally, the percentage of time spent on the "Purchase Responsible Authorization" and "Order Formalization" processes was also considered.

5.2 Performance Evaluation Metrics

The results obtained for all the models are presented in Table 1.

Hypothesis 3 demonstrates the best overall performance, with the shortest total system time and highest process efficiency, despite requiring stricter management

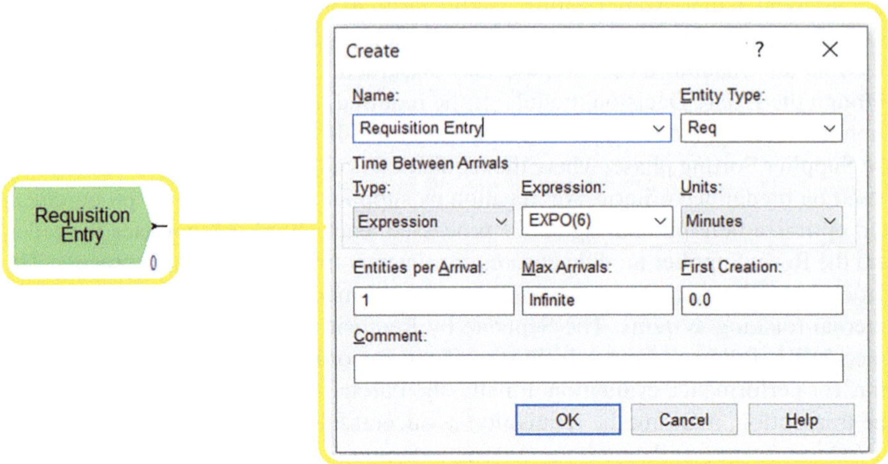

Fig. 5 Parameterization of "request arrivals"

Table 1 Comparison of results

Models/indicators (average values from replications)	Current model	Hypothesis 1	Hypothesis 2	Hypothesis 3
Request arrivals	400	454	438	441
Total requests leaving the process	329	341	409	426
Orders generated	272	45	48	48
Time spent by the purchasing department (%)	55	9	10	10
Number of requests authorized by the requestor's supervisor	396	385	374	384
Time spent by the requestor's supervisor (%)	41	40	39	40
Number of requests arriving at the warehouse	387	363	–	–
Time spent by the warehouse stock checker (%)	78	73	–	–
Number of requests arriving to the purchasing responsible for authorization	286	259	82	83
Time spent by the purchasing responsible in authorizations (%)	99	90	19	20
Total time in system (in hours)	4.08	9.94	4.98	3.78
Process efficiency (%) (total requests leaving the process/request arrivals × 100)	82.25	75.11	93.38	96.60

of requests and authorization time. Hypothesis 2 is also effective, showing good efficiency and reduced authorization time. Hypothesis 1 significantly reduces the time spent by the purchasing department but may lead to more complex request management. The Current Model presents the highest variability and lower efficiency compared to the proposed hypotheses.

5.3 *Comparison of Hypothesis Performance*

Next, an evaluation was carried out for the Second and Third Hypothesis of improvement based on Net Present Value (NPV), Internal Rate of Return (IRR), and Payback Period (PP) to determine the economic viability and financial return of each hypothesis.

To assess the economic feasibility of the improvement proposals, three scenarios were considered: pessimistic, most likely, and optimistic. These scenarios were based on the company's profit. The average annual profit was estimated at €750,000, of which 60% is derived from repair work invoicing, resulting in a base value of €450,000 for the study. For the pessimistic scenario, only 25% of this amount is considered to come from the purchasing process, 30% for the most likely scenario, and 35% for the optimistic scenario.

5.4 *Economic Feasibility and Financial Analysis*

Table 2 estimates the profit corresponding to the purchasing process under each scenario.

The results of the economic feasibility assessment for the second and third improvement hypotheses will now be presented based on Net Present Value (NPV), Internal Rate of Return (IRR), and Payback Period (PP). For the calculation of NPV, a return rate of 4.5% will be considered, based on Portugal's inflation rate, which was 4.3% in 2023 (National Statistics Institute, 2024) but is expected to decrease slightly in 2024. The following costs and benefits were estimated for each hypothesis.

Hypothesis 2:

- Training Costs: Estimated at €3000

Table 2 Estimated profit margins for each scenario

Scenario	Billing profit margin (€)	Percentage applied (%)	Purchasing process profit margin (€)
Pessimistic	45,000,000	25	11,250,000
Likely	45,000,000	30	13,500,000
Optimistic	45,000,000	35	15,750,000

- Software Licenses Costs: For ten new licenses at €210 per license annually, total cost is €2100.

Thus, the initial cost of the Second Hypothesis amounts to €5100, with no other recurring costs beyond the €2100 for software licenses annually (Tables 3 and 4).

Hypothesis 3:

- Training costs: estimated at €3000.
- Software development costs: estimated at €6500.
- Hardware costs: for ten tablets, smartphones, or PDAs at €150 each, total cost is €1500.
- Software licenses costs: for ten new licenses at €210 per license annually, total cost is €2100.

Thus, the initial cost of the Third Hypothesis amounts to €11,000, with no other recurring costs beyond the annual software license cost (Tables 5 and 6). A five-year period was considered, and the following NPV (net present value) was obtained for the second and third improvement hypotheses.

Resulting, for each scenario, an NPV of:

Table 3 Parameterization of the spreadsheet to determine NPV for each scenario of the second improvement hypothesis

			Year					
			0	1	2	3	4	5
Initial investment			−5100					
Annual gains	Scenario	Pessimistic		15,223	15,223	15,223	15,223	15,223
		Likely		18,268	18,268	18,268	18,268,	18,268
		Optimistic		21,312	21,313	21,313	21,313	21,313
Annual costs				2100	2100	2100	2100	2100
Cash-flow	Scenario	Pessimistic		13,123	13,123	13,123	13,123	13,123
		Likely		16,168	16,168	16,168	16,168	16,168
		Optimistic		19,212	19,213	19,213	19,213	19,213
Discounted values	Scenario	Pessimistic		12,558	12,017	11,500	11,005	10,531
		Likely		15,472	14,806	14,168	13,558	12,974
		Optimistic		18,385	17,594	16,836	16,111	15,417
Investment amortization	Scenario	Pessimist		9558	21,576	33,076	44,081	54,611
		Likely		12,472	27,277	41,445	55,003	67,977
		Optimistic		15,385	32,980	49,815	65,926	81,344

Table 4 NPV obtained for each scenario of the second improvement hypothesis

		NPV (€)
Scenario	Pessimistic	54,611
	Likely	67,977
	Optimistic	81,344

Table 5 Spreadsheet parameterization to determine NPV for each scenario of the third hypothesis

			Year					
			0	1	2	3	4	5
Initial investment			−11,000					
Annual gains	Scenario	Pessimistic		19,628	19,628	19,628	19,628	19,628
		Likely		23,553	23,553	23,553	23,553	23,553
		Optimistic		27,479	27,479	27,479	27,479	27,479
Annual costs				2100	2100	2100	2100	2100
Cash-flow	Scenario	Pessimistic		17,528	17,528	17,528	17,528	17,528
		Likely		21,453	21,453	21,453	21,453	21,453
		Optimistic		25,379	25,379	25,379	25,379	25,379
Discounted values	Scenario	Pessimistic		16,773	16,051	15,350	14,698	14,065
		Likely		20,530	19,645	18,799	17,990	17,215
		Optimistic		24,286	23,240	22,239	21,282	20,365
Investment amortization	Scenario	Pessimist		5773	21,823	37,183	51,881	65,946
		Likely		9530	29,175	47,974	65,964	83,179
		Optimistic		13,286	36,526	58,765	80,047	100,412

Table 6 NPV obtained for each scenario of the third improvement hypothesis

		NPV (€)
Scenario	Pessimistic	65,946
	Likely	83,179
	Optimistic	100,412

Considering Tables 3 and 5, and using Formula (1), the Payback Period (PP) was determined for each scenario of both proposals, yielding the following results:

$$PP = n + \frac{CF_n}{CF_n - CF_{n+1}} \tag{1}$$

where, PP is the Payback Period; *n* is the year immediately before the investment amortization shifts from negative to positive, which, for this analysis, is 0 for all scenarios; CF_n is the initial investment (a negative amount, i.e.,—€3000); CF_{n+a} is the amortized value for year n + 1 (in this case, year 1), which, for each scenario, is: €9558 for the pessimistic, €12,472 for the probable, and €15,385 for the optimistic scenarios. Substituting values into the formula for each scenario, we get:

Hypothesis 2.

Pessimistic scenario:

$$PP = 0 + \frac{-3000}{-3000 - 9558} = 0.239\text{years}.$$

Therefore, in the pessimistic scenario, the investment payback occurs in 2 months and 27 days.

Most likely scenario:

$$PP = 0 + \frac{-3000}{-3000 - 12{,}472} = 0.194\text{years}.$$

Thus, in the most likely scenario, the investment payback happens in 2 months and 9 days.

Optimistic scenario:

$$PP = 0 + \frac{-3000}{-3000 - 15{,}385} = 0.163\text{years}.$$

Thus, in the optimistic scenario, the investment payback occurs in 2 months.

Hypothesis 3.

Pessimistic scenario:

$$PP = 0 + \frac{-11{,}000}{-11{,}000 - 5773} = 0.656\text{years}$$

In the pessimistic scenario, the payback period is 7 months and 27 days.

Most likely scenario:

$$PP = 0 + \frac{-11{,}000}{-11{,}000 - 9529} = 0.536\text{years}$$

Therefore, the payback period for the most likely scenario is 6 months and 12 days.

Optimistic scenario:

$$PP = 0 + \frac{-11{,}000}{-11{,}000 - 13{,}286} = 0.452\text{years}$$

Thus, in the optimistic scenario, the payback period is 5 months and 12 days.

Based on Table 7, the following conclusions can be drawn:

Table 7 Comparison of results

	Scenarios								
	Pessimistic			Most likely			Optimistic		
Improvement hypotheses	NPV (€)	IRR (%)	PP (months)	NPV (€)	IRR (%)	PP (months)	NPV (€)	IRR (%)	PP (months)
Hypothesis 2	54,611	437	2.9	67,977	539	2.3	81,343	640	2.0
Hypothesis 3	65,946	158	7.9	83,179	194	6.4	100,412	230	5.4

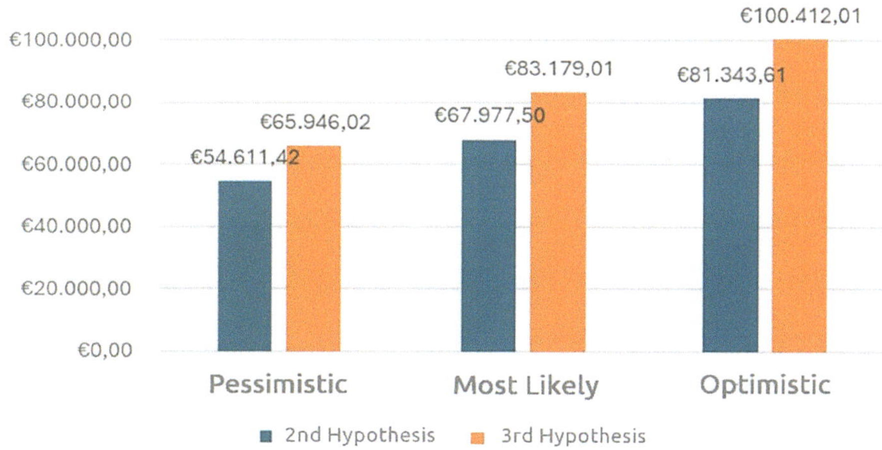

Fig. 6 NPV comparison by hypothesis and scenario

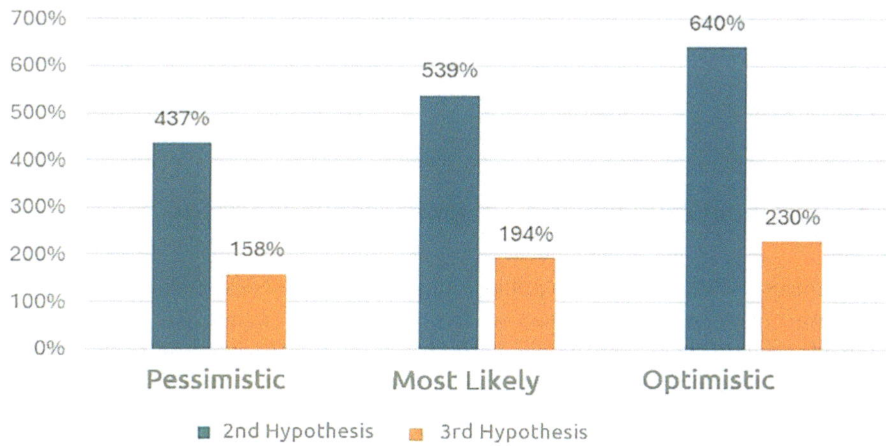

Fig. 7 IRR comparison by hypothesis and scenario

- Net present value (NPV): In all scenarios (pessimistic, most likely, and optimistic), the third improvement hypothesis presents a higher NPV compared to the second hypothesis. This suggests that the third hypothesis could potentially provide a greater financial return, as illustrated in Fig. 6.
- Internal rate of return (IRR): The second hypothesis demonstrates a significantly higher IRR across all scenarios compared to the third hypothesis. A higher IRR indicates that the second hypothesis could yield a higher percentage return on investment, as depicted in Fig. 7.

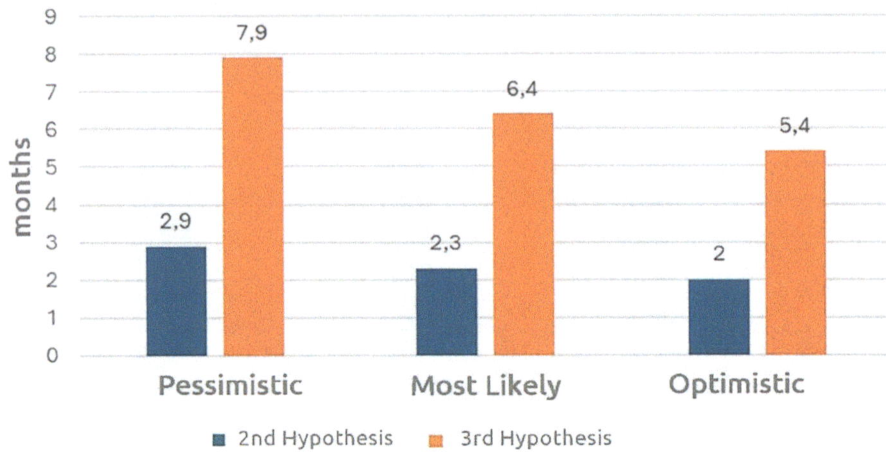

Fig. 8 Payback period by hypothesis

- Payback period (PP): The second hypothesis also shows a shorter payback period in all scenarios. This means that the initial investment would be recovered more quickly with the second hypothesis than with the third, as shown in Fig. 8.

5.5 Practical Implementation and Recommendations

In summary, while the third hypothesis offers a higher NPV, indicating a larger long-term financial return, the second hypothesis has a higher IRR and a shorter payback period. Therefore, the choice between the two depends on the investor's goals and priorities. If the focus is on maximizing financial returns, the third hypothesis may be more appealing. However, if the priority is a higher percentage return and faster investment recovery, the second hypothesis might be preferable.

Given the natural resistance to change within organizations, a phased implementation of both improvement hypotheses could be the most prudent strategy. Initially, the second hypothesis would be adopted. After the company has adjusted to this change, the third hypothesis would be implemented. Since the company provides external support for various types of equipment, the third hypothesis would offer the future advantage of allowing material requisitions to be made during technicians' travel time. This would enable the material request process to start while the technician is en route, optimizing travel time and improving the company's operational efficiency.

5.6 Assumptions and Limitations of the Study

This study is based on a real-world case, with one of the authors being an employee of the company. Due to the unavailability of some data, certain values were estimated based on the author's experience, which introduces an assumption that could impact the accuracy of the results. The study also relies on a fixed request arrival mechanism and simplifies several aspects of the process, such as excluding unauthorized requests and using a standard 40-hour workweek for the simulations. While these assumptions help make the analysis more manageable, they may not fully capture the complexities of real-world operations. The lack of actual data and these simplifications are important limitations to consider when interpreting the findings. Future research could address these limitations by incorporating real data where estimates were used, extending the simulation duration, and accounting for more dynamic factors.

6 Conclusion

This study explored three different ways to improve the internal requisition process of an industrial SME, focusing on digitalization, the implementation of a Production Planning and Control (PPC) system, and the integration of lean methodologies with Industry 4.0 technologies. The results clearly showed that all three approaches helped reduce overall processing time, with the third hypothesis proving to be the most efficient. From a financial perspective, while the second hypothesis had the highest Internal Rate of Return (IRR), the third one offered the best long-term financial stability, as indicated by its superior Net Present Value (NPV) across all scenarios. Although it requires a longer payback period, its long-term benefits outweigh the wait. Given this balance between operational improvements and financial strength, the third hypothesis stands out as the best approach for ensuring sustainable growth and continuous innovation, aligning with both lean principles and Industry 4.0 advancements. Beyond this specific case, the findings of this study can be adapted and applied to other industrial SMEs facing similar challenges in their requisition and procurement processes. Many businesses, regardless of their sector or location, struggle with inefficiencies caused by outdated systems, lack of digital integration, and process variability. By embracing digital tools, automation, and structured methodologies like lean and Industry 4.0, companies can significantly improve efficiency, reduce waste, and enhance decision-making. These improvements are particularly relevant for businesses that rely on well-coordinated procurement and resource management.

6.1 Emerging Trends and Future Directions

The future of material requisition process optimization will likely see further integration of Artificial Intelligence (AI) and machine learning to predict material needs and optimize procurement strategies. Researchers suggest that the use of AI-powered predictive analytics will provide insights into supplier performance, material consumption patterns, and potential disruptions in the supply chain [22]. This could transform how lean methodologies are implemented by enhancing real-time decision-making and further reducing waste.

Moreover, the continuous evolution of Industry 4.0 technologies and the growing importance of sustainability will likely drive further research into the intersection of lean methodologies and digital technologies. Scholars like Perboli et al. [23] have suggested that future research should explore the role of AI, blockchain, and other technologies in improving lean processes for material requisition and supply chain management.

Based on this, one can conclude that optimizing material requisition processes through lean methodologies and digital integration is increasingly seen as a strategic approach to waste reduction and operational efficiency. Lean principles, when combined with digital tools such as the IoT, digital twins, and predictive analytics, not only help reduce material waste but also improve decision-making, supplier collaboration, and overall production performance.

References

1. Holweg, M. (2007). The genealogy of lean production. *Journal of Operations Management, 25*(2), 420–437. https://doi.org/10.1016/j.jom.2006.04.001
2. Meadows, D. H. (2008). *Thinking in systems: A primer*. Chelsea Green Publishing.
3. Souza, R., Ferenhof, H., & Forcellini, F. (2022). Industry 4.0 and industry 5.0 from the lean perspective. *International Journal of Management, Knowledge and Learning, 11*, 145–155. https://doi.org/10.53615/2232-5697.11.145-155
4. Dennis, P. (2009). *Produção lean simplificada [Simplified lean production]*. Bookman Editora.
5. Romero, L. F., & Arce, A. (2017). Applying value stream mapping in manufacturing: A systematic literature review. *IFAC-PapersOnLine, 50*(1), 1075–1086. https://doi.org/10.1016/j.ifacol.2017.08.385
6. de Paula Ferreira, W., Armellini, F., & De Santa-Eulalia, L. A. (2020). Simulation in Industry 4.0: A state-of-the-art review. *Computers & Industrial Engineering, 149*, 106868. https://doi.org/10.1016/j.cie.2020.106868
7. Brealey, R. A., Myers, S. C., & Allen, F. (2014). *Principles of corporate finance* (11th ed.). McGraw-Hill Education.
8. Hillier, D., Ross, S., Westerfield, R., Jaffe, J., & Jordan, B. (2019). *Corporate finance* (4th ed.). McGraw Hill Education.
9. Lefley, F. (1996). The payback method of investment appraisal: A review and synthesis. *International Journal of Production Economics, 44*(3), 207–224. https://doi.org/10.1016/0925-5273(96)00022-9
10. Womack, J. P., & Jones, D. T. (1996). Beyond Toyota: How to root out waste and pursue perfection. *Harvard Business Review, 74*(5), 140–151.

11. Liu, Q., & Yang, H. (2020). An improved value stream mapping to prioritize lean optimization scenarios using simulation and multiple-attribute decision-making method. *IEEE Access, 8*, 204914–204930. https://doi.org/10.1109/ACCESS.2020.3037660
12. Jha, N., & Prashar, D. (2022). Adoption of Industry 4.0 in lean manufacturing. In *Industrial internet of things* (pp. 107–127). CRC Press. https://doi.org/10.1201/9781003102267-6
13. Tay, H. L., & Loh, H. S. (2022). Digital transformations and supply chain management: A lean six sigma perspective. *Journal of Asia Business Studies, 16*(2), 340–353. https://doi.org/10.1108/JABS-10-2020-0415
14. Valamede, L. S., & Akkari, A. C. S. (2020). Lean 4.0: A new holistic approach for the integration of lean manufacturing tools and digital technologies. *International Journal of Mathematical, Engineering and Management Sciences, 5*(5), 851. https://doi.org/10.33889/IJMEMS.2020.5.5.066
15. Zafarzadeh, M., Wiktorsson, M., & Baalsrud Hauge, J. (2021). A systematic review on technologies for data-driven production logistics: Their role from a holistic and value creation perspective. *Logistics, 5*(2), 24. https://doi.org/10.3390/logistics5020024
16. Bechtsis, D., Tsolakis, N., Iakovou, E., & Vlachos, D. (2022). Data-driven secure, resilient and sustainable supply chains: Gaps, opportunities, and a new generalised data sharing and data monetisation framework. *International Journal of Production Research, 60*(14), 4397–4417. https://doi.org/10.1080/00207543.2021.1957506
17. Cifone, F. D., Hoberg, K., Holweg, M., & Staudacher, A. P. (2021). 'Lean 4.0': How can digital technologies support lean practices? *International Journal of Production Economics, 241*, 108258. https://doi.org/10.1016/j.ijpe.2021.108258
18. Wang, C.-N., Vo, T. T. B. C., Hsu, H.-P., Chung, Y.-C., Nguyen, N. T., & Nhieu, N.-L. (2024). Improving processing efficiency through workflow process reengineering, simulation and value stream mapping: A case study of business process reengineering. *Business Process Management Journal, 30*(7), 2482–2515. https://doi.org/10.1108/BPMJ-11-2023-0869
19. van Weele, A. J. (2018). *Purchasing and supply chain management* (7th ed.). Cengage Learning EMEA.
20. Carayannis, E. G., & Popescu, D. (2005). Profiling a methodology for economic growth and convergence: Learning from the EU e-procurement experience for Central and Eastern European countries. *Technovation, 25*(1), 1–14. https://doi.org/10.1016/S0166-4972(03)00071-3
21. Gunasekaran, A., & Ngai, E. W. T. (2004). Information systems in supply chain integration and management. *European Journal of Operational Research, 159*(2), 269–295. https://doi.org/10.1016/j.ejor.2003.08.016
22. Mahi, R. (2024). Optimizing supply chain efficiency in the manufacturing sector through AI-powered analytics. *International Journal of Management Information Systems and Data Science, 1*(1), 41–50. https://doi.org/10.62304/ijmisds.v1i1.116
23. Perboli, G., Musso, S., & Rosano, M. (2018). Blockchain in logistics and supply chain: A lean approach for designing real-world use cases. *IEEE Access, 6*, 62018–62028. https://doi.org/10.1109/ACCESS.2018.2875782

Digital Transformation and Last-Mile Logistics in Food Delivery: A Comparative Analysis of Urban and Peripheral Models

Sofia Temperoni, Gaia Verrocchio, Laura Bravi, Giada Pierli, and Federica Murmura

Abstract This study investigates the impact of digital technologies on the logistics sector, focusing on last-mile delivery in the food delivery industry in Italy. The research specifically compares two cities, Urbino and Milan, highlighting the differences in how Just Eat and Glovo operate in urban and peripheral contexts. In Urbino, small restaurant businesses face significant logistical challenges due to the absence of a robust food delivery network, requiring them to handle delivery services independently. This contrasts with Milan, where both platforms offer more comprehensive delivery solutions. By analyzing variables such as delivery price, minimum order price, delivery times, and customer reviews, the study identifies Glovo's flexible business model as better suited to smaller cities like Urbino, where fluctuating demand and limited resources make managing logistics difficult. The case of Alfonsino, a food delivery platform that has successfully operated in small towns, further supports this conclusion. The findings suggest that adopting a model like Glovo's "Order & Delivery," which offers greater flexibility and lower costs, could enhance delivery services in smaller cities. The research also highlights future opportunities for exploring the environmental impacts of crowdshipping and the role of technological advancements, such as autonomous delivery, in shaping the future of last-mile logistics.

Keywords Last mile delivery · Digital logistic · Food sector · Digital technologies

---

S. Temperoni · G. Verrocchio · L. Bravi (✉) · G. Pierli · F. Murmura
Department of Economics, Society, Politics, Carlo Bo University of Urbino, Urbino, Italy
e-mail: s.temperoni@campus.uniurb.it; g.verrocchio@campus.uniurb.it; laura.bravi@uniurb.it; g.pierli@campus.uniurb.it; federica.murmura@uniurb.it

F. Tao et al. (eds.), *Artificial Intelligence and Digital Transformation*, Lecture Notes in Information Systems and Organisation 78,
https://doi.org/10.1007/978-3-032-00118-4_9

1 Introduction

The Fourth Industrial Revolution is transforming entire production, governance, and management systems through digitalization and automation. Technologies such as artificial intelligence, the Internet of Things, and blockchain are reshaping industries by enhancing connectivity and data-driven decision-making [1]. This shift is particularly evident in logistics, where digital platforms are redefining last-mile delivery models.

One of the most significant transformations in the labor market has been the rise of the platform economy, characterized by digital intermediaries connecting service providers and consumers [2]. In the food delivery sector, companies like Just Eat and Glovo exemplify two distinct operational models: Just Eat primarily acts as an ordering platform, while Glovo integrates delivery logistics through gig workers. This evolution reflects the growing demand for flexibility and cost-efficiency in last-mile delivery, particularly in urban and peripheral areas [3].

The emergence of the gig economy has led to new working dynamics, where workers operate on a contingent basis, enjoying flexibility but facing wage variability [4, 5]. Online platforms for goods and passenger transport have significantly grown, from 6% of transactions in 2013 to 56% in 2018, surpassing other types of platforms [6]. Food delivery services have benefited from this trend, particularly among millennials, who seek convenience and competitive pricing in meal delivery [7].

The objective of this work is to analyze the impact of digital technologies on the logistics sector, particularly focusing on last-mile delivery in the food delivery industry. By exploring emerging technologies and the evolution of labor markets, this paper aims to highlight the opportunities and challenges posed by digitalization and automation, as well as the transformation of business models through a comparative analysis of logistics platforms, such as Just Eat and Glovo, providing insights into how different delivery models can influence efficiency, customer satisfaction, and sustainability in urban and peripheral areas.

The paper is structured as follows: Sect. 2 describes the theoretical background of the research, Sect. 3 explains the methodology used, Sect. 4 presents the main results while Sect. 5 draws the main conclusions of the research.

2 Theoretical Background

2.1 Last Mile Logistic

In the supply chain, which involves the planning and management of all activities related to sourcing, procurement, and logistics, one of the fundamental phases is distribution, which can occur through two main modes: the first is more traditional and involves in-store pickup; the second refers to the direct delivery of the final product to the customer [8].

The second mode, known as last mile delivery (LMD), has undergone significant changes in recent decades due to the increasing demand for delivery services in urban areas. This demand has been driven by two mega-trends: urbanization, the migration from rural to urban areas, and e-commerce, referring to the rise in online shopping (as demonstrated by a 2018 Statista analysis showing a growth rate of 23%). The increased geographic concentration and growing order volume mean that logistics players must manage increasingly smaller parcels, leading to significant challenges, especially in last mile delivery [9].

The final stage of logistics, unlike the earlier ones, is the only one visible to the consumer, and thus becomes a critical success factor, particularly for digital companies [10]. In this context, customer satisfaction becomes increasingly tied to the quality of distribution, especially regarding cost-efficiency and delivery speed [11]. The latter, defined by the time between the confirmation of payment and the arrival of the goods at the destination, can be reduced by acting on lead time, the time it takes for the product to move from production to commercialization [12].

In combination with speed, low costs are the key to LMD's success, given their significant impact on the entire supply chain (41%) [12].

Due to the reasons mentioned above, managing the last mile is becoming increasingly important, and finding innovative ideas is essential. To meet these needs, crowdshipping was born.

2.2 *The Crowdshipping Phenomenon and Its Features*

Given the changes discussed earlier, an innovative way to address the increasing demand for delivery in urban areas is through so-called crowd logistics, literally 'logistics operated by the crowd,' defined as the outsourcing of logistics services to various actors coordinated through a technical infrastructure [13].

Among the most popular paradigms of crowd logistics is crowdshipping, which in the literature does not have a universally recognized definition, but generally, it can be described as a system in which the final stage of the logistics process involves numerous occasional drivers, both professional and non-professional, who are willing to modify their travel routes to deliver goods [14].

A key feature of crowdshipping is the use of collaborative platforms and smartphone applications that connect individuals offering space in their vehicles with companies needing to deliver goods. These drivers are considered 'occasional' because they are not employees but are called upon for one or a few deliveries (receiving a monetary incentive), which also benefits the supplier of the goods by reducing long-term wage costs, insurance, vehicle expenses, etc. [15].

Crowd shippers can be divided into three groups:

1. Traditional logistics carriers, such as DHL and FedEx;
2. Professional drivers who use their free time to make deliveries through crowdshipping;

3. Individuals who are traveling for other reasons (e.g., commuting students).

Some research has shown that crowdshipping represents a more efficient and environmentally friendly type of delivery, particularly in certain urban areas. On one hand, it compensates for the lack of well-organized vehicles in terms of delivery efficiency and speed [16]; on the other, it increases flexibility in managing tasks [13].

Both businesses and consumers benefit from crowdshipping. Businesses, in particular, can handle fluctuating demand without needing to invest in new vehicles and staff, which would otherwise be unnecessary. Consumers benefit from faster delivery times and personalized service (agreeing on the time with the driver), all at reduced costs.

Because crowdshipping is accessible even to smaller businesses, it makes companies without an e-commerce platform more competitive and allows customers to receive products at home that they otherwise could not purchase online.

From an environmental perspective, contrary to what one might think, this method of delivery is not always the ideal solution. To achieve sustainability goals, platforms should promote the optimization of transport by encouraging crowd shippers to improve their already planned trips, as additional trips could result in negative externalities that outweigh the benefits. Among the more sustainable solutions is certainly the use of public transportation, utilizing unused space during off-peak hours [17].

Crowd logistics platforms can connect users with the most suitable resources based on their specific needs. After a customer places a request, the delivery is assigned to a third party. These platforms not only connect companies with riders but also provide logistical support, enabling businesses that cannot independently offer home delivery services to do so [18].

At the core of these platforms is the technology that supports the development of information systems and impacts the consumer experience. For this reason, a crowdshipping platform must have a portal, or better yet, an application, to ensure that the exchange of information is as intuitive and efficient as possible. This is especially important for data collection, which is used by platform owners to make decisions such as which areas to expand into and how to allocate deliveries to riders [19]. The simplest process for shipping through these platforms consists of four steps:

1. The customer requests product delivery via the platform, specifying the desired delivery time and address.
2. The platform verifies the availability of riders in the area and selects one.
3. The rider is asked to accept or decline the job.
4. Based on the rider's decision: (a) if accepted, the rider is committed to collecting and delivering the goods. (b) if declined, the platform returns to the second step.

Some platforms, however, follow different logic: the rider selection is not managed by the platform but is left to the riders themselves, who apply to handle the order.

2.3 The Main Food Delivery Models

The changes previously discussed have also had a strong impact on demand in the restaurant sector, shifting it towards online food delivery. More and more, customers need quick and easy ordering, while also seeking more competitive prices. In this context, food delivery represents an innovation that introduces a service capable of meeting these needs [20]. For this reason, in recent years, the number of dedicated platforms has grown significantly, along with their use by consumers, particularly millennials, who are keen on new trends, curious to try different traditional dishes, but also expect extremely fast delivery [21]. By combining the processes of ordering, preparation, and delivery, four business models in food delivery have been defined [19].

1. The *only order* model. In this model, the delivery company replaces the traditional phone call and acts as an intermediary between restaurants and customers. It also collects various offers, serving as a showcase that allows customers to compare prices, menus, and reviews of partner restaurants. The company only manages the ordering phase, while the preparation and delivery remain the responsibility of the restaurant (usually take-away), which will therefore have a dedicated staff for deliveries, excluding the platform from any possible liability after the order has been received. This can be a limitation if these final phases are not managed correctly, as the customer might project the negative experience onto the platform from which they placed the order [18]. The ordering process through this model is particularly simple, consisting of a first phase where the customer selects and sends the order via the website or app, which then forwards the details to the restaurant via email. The restaurant benefits in two ways: the management of orders becomes simpler, and they can expand their customer base thanks to increased visibility.
2. The *only delivery* model. This model focuses only on delivery service, leaving the ordering and preparation phases to Only Order platforms or the respective restaurants. As in the previous model, the platform managing the delivery has the potential to influence the customer's perceived quality. On one hand, this model allows for reduced delivery times and greater flexibility, as the restaurant can rely on a number of riders proportional to the number of orders. On the other hand, costs are higher than for Only Order platforms (where the fee is around 10%). Therefore, it is advantageous when the number of orders is particularly high, and the delivery locations allow riders to efficiently deliver two or more products in nearby areas [21].
3. The *order & delivery* model. This business model combines two of the three stages of the meal experience: ordering and delivery. Platforms adopting this model pose a threat mainly to Only Order platforms, as delivery is one of the most expensive phases, leading companies to rely on platforms that handle the entire process. In this case, the restaurant is only responsible for preparing the food, outsourcing the entire customer relationship (from order placement to home delivery) to the Order & Delivery company. Once the customer places

their order through the app or website, the platform notifies the closest riders (identified via geolocation), who can choose to accept or decline the job. Many restaurants, by using this platform, have managed to provide home delivery services without investing in their own logistics system [22].
4. Full-integrated model. Companies adopting this model can be considered virtual restaurants through the vertical integration of the delivery, preparation, and ordering processes. This allows them to offer high-quality products at reasonable prices, as the restaurant controls all stages of the meal experience, leading to faster and more lasting customer loyalty. Online restaurants, even without a physical space, can guarantee an infinite number of covers through full-integrated. However, the model is not without disadvantages and limitations, particularly in the choice of menu, which must include only dishes that are most suitable for transportation [22].

3 Methodology

3.1 Case Study Introduction

Following a general study on the food delivery phenomenon, this research aims to conduct a more detailed analysis focusing on the city of Urbino (small city center in Marche Region, Italy). The purpose of this investigation is to understand the absence of a widespread food delivery network in this area and propose a solution tailored to the prevalence of small businesses.

Initially, we conducted a general review of the most commonly used platforms in the sector, determining that Just Eat was the only one operating in Urbino. Based on this finding, we performed a comparative analysis of Just Eat's usage in Urbino against its implementation in Milan, one of Italy's most advanced and developed cities in the food delivery sector.

Analysis of the Just Eat application for riders revealed that it is not possible to apply for this role within the Urbino area (and more broadly, across the entire region). This finding is consistent with direct experiences, where restaurant employees, rather than independent riders, managed deliveries. This model aligns with what has been previously described as the "Only Order" model, which may not be compatible with the limited resources available to restaurants in Urbino, as they are required to invest in both employees and delivery vehicles.

To address these incompatibilities, we examined the model used by Glovo, which offers an alternative solution.

We analyzed both the Just Eat and Glovo platforms in the city of Milan, where both are present and frequently used, created a database, and studied the rider recruitment processes. Finally, the results were analyzed using Excel to assess the data.

3.2 Database Construction

The case analysis started with an observation of the selected food delivery applications. We then identified a random sample composed of restaurants providing delivery services in both central and peripheral areas of the two cities.

The variables considered in this study are:

1. Delivery zone (central/peripheral);
2. Delivery price (P);
3. Delivery times (t): we recorded the maximum delivery time range indicated by the platform;
4. Minimum order price (Pmin);
5. Delivery starts times (O): this variable was subject to change depending on the time of the search. If the service was available at the time of data collection, "00:00:00" was recorded;
6. Number of reviews (R): both applications have limitations on the maximum number of customer reviews visible (Just Eat: 200+; Glovo: 500+), making the analyses approximate.

On April 2, 2024, we simulated fifty orders by entering an address in central Milan, thereby identifying the restaurants willing to deliver within this area. To complete the sample, we selected five restaurants from six peripheral zones: Gratosoglio, Baggio, Rho, Lambrate, Calvairate, and Comasina. This procedure was repeated for both Just Eat and Glovo, resulting in a total of 160 restaurants analyzed in Milan.

For Urbino, we followed the same procedure but built a single database with data from Just Eat (as it is the only platform operating in the area), involving just six participating restaurants.

For each entity, we populated the row with data for the identified variables. The results were then transformed into pivot tables, cross-referencing the coverage zone variable (central/peripheral) with the remaining five. Each variable provided insights into specific characteristics of the city and its service.

4 Results

4.1 Food Delivery in Urbino and Milan: Analysis by Individual City

Before proceeding with the comparison, it is necessary to highlight the different business models used by Just Eat in the two cities: in Urbino, it is limited to order support, while in Milan, it also provides the logistics and delivery service. This creates a challenge for businesses in Urbino, which must recruit riders themselves to offer the service.

Based on this, the initial data analysis aimed to identify the differences in delivery development between the two urban areas.

Milan. The database, constructed through the analysis of Just Eat in the indicated areas of Milan, consists of 80 subjects, 50 of which operate in the central zone and 30 in the peripheral areas.

Regarding the identified variables, we calculated the average for each, distinguishing between the two zones. In Table 1, the situations are very similar, with the minimal differences compensating each other. For example, the average delivery price in the center (average price in the center = €2.22; average price in the periphery = €2.01) is higher, but the delivery time (delivery time in the center = 45 min; delivery time in the periphery = 47 min) is shorter compared to the periphery (Table 1).

The only distinguishing factor emerged from the study of the available ordering time range, as shown in Table 2. Restaurants operating in the central area have no restrictions, making them available for delivery throughout the day; among those in the periphery, we found some (20%) with time restrictions (Table 2).

Urbino. The Urbino database, although much more limited as it consists of only 6 restaurants participating in delivery, still provided sufficient results for the analysis. Before proceeding, it is important to specify that the 'outside the walls (of the town)' category includes two restaurants (specifically 'La Casa del Pane Urbino' and 'Magna Grecia Ristorante') which also operate in the center but under different conditions.

Looking at Table 3, we can observe variations in the 'delivery price' (P) and the 'minimum order price' (Pmin), likely due to their locations: 'La Casa del Pane' is situated outside the city walls, while 'Magna Grecia' is located in the historic

Table 1 Mean value of variables in Milan

Mean	Center	Periphery	Total
T	45 min	47 min	46 min
P	2.22€	2.01€	2.14€
Pmin	5.44€	7.73€	6.30€
R	73.12	100.8	83.5

Table 2 Distribution of delivery start times (O) in Milan

O	Center	Periphery	Total
00:00:00	50	24	74
5:55:00 p.m.	–	1	1
6:10:00 p.m.	–	2	2
6:30:00 p.m.	–	2	2
7:40:00 p.m.	–	1	1
Total	50	30	80

Table 3 Data of Just Eat Urbino

Restaurants	Covering area	P (€)	T	Pmin (€)	O	R
La fenice	Center	2.20	45 min	10.00	18:55	200
Canyon fast	Center	2.50	Nd	8.00	11:30/19:00	200
La casa del pane urbino	Center	3.00	30 min	12.00	12:35/19:30	59
	Outside the walls	2.50	30 min	8.00	12:35/19:30	59
Locanda della stazione	Center	2.00	30 min	10.00	18:55	31
Amici miei	Center	3.50	Nd	15.00	21:55	47
Magna grecia ristorante	Center	2.00	30 min	0.00	19:45	200
	Outside the walls	2.00	30 min	15.00	19:45	200

Nd undetected data

Table 4 Mean values for the Urbino variables

	Center	Periphery	Mean value
T	33 min	30 min	32 min
P	2.53€	2.25€	2.46€
Pmin	9.17€	11.50€	9.75€
R	122.83	129.50	124.50

Table 5 Distribution of delivery start times (O) in Urbino

O	Center/periphery	Total
11:30 a.m./7:00 p.m.	1	1
12:35 a.m./7:30 p.m.	1	1
6:55:00 p.m.	2	2
7:45:00 p.m.	1	1
9:55:00 p.m.	1	1
Total	6	6

center. This could indicate a difficulty in moving between the center and the outskirts and vice versa.

Aside from this detail, we did not find significant differences between the historic center and the peripheral area. On the contrary, as seen in the case of Milan, they seem to balance each other out (a higher average delivery price corresponds to a lower average minimum order price).

To gain a more complete view, we decided to calculate the averages for delivery time (t) and reviews (R), even though we excluded them from the comparison between the center and periphery, as the values (for these variables) from the two restaurants operating in both zones showed no differences (Table 4).

The delivery start time is very fragmented and, from a first observation, there is a tendency to concentrate the service in the evening hours, except for only two of them that are also active during lunch hours although for a very limited time (Table 5).

4.2 Data Comparison Between Urbino and Milan

In the comparative analysis between Just Eat Urbino and Just Eat Milan, we further explored and compared the previously mentioned variables. However, it is important to specify that, for the same reasons stated above, we decided not to repeat the restaurants listed in Table 3 that are present in both the center and periphery.

To create the following pivot tables, we cross-referenced the 'center/periphery' variable with some of the remaining variables that we considered most interesting to analyze.

In the first comparison (Table 6), we analyzed the 'delivery price' variable by examining the cumulative percentage of the values. Looking at the total columns, it immediately becomes apparent that the delivery price in Urbino is consistently above €2.00, a value that corresponds to the median in Milan.

Referring to the average delivery price calculated earlier, we observed only a minimal difference between the two cities. Based on the results from the cumulative percentage analysis, we calculated the standard deviation to better understand the similarity between the averages. It turned out to be lower in Urbino, with a result of 0.54 compared to Milan's value of 1.5. These results indicate a greater dispersion of values around the mean in the metropolis and a higher concentration in Urbino's restaurants, meaning that in the former case, the total frequencies (which include both the center and the periphery) are in the outer ranges, farther from the average value (€2.22).

Subsequently, the comparison (carried out via cumulative %) concerned the minimum order price offered by restaurateurs, in which a greater difference emerges compared to the previous variable. In correspondence with the second row

Table 6 Delivery price in Milan and Urbino

	Milan		Urbino	
P (€)	Total frequency	Cumulative % Milan	Frequency center	Cumulative % Urbino
0.00	15	18.75	0	0.00
1.00	13	35.00	0	0.00
1.49	7	43.75	0	0.00
1.50	1	45.00	0	0.00
1.99	1	46.25	0	0.00
2.00	6	53.75	2	33.00
2.20	0	53.75	1	50.00
2.49	7	62.50	0	50.00
2.50	0	62.50	1	67.00
3.00	0	62.50	1	83.00
3.49	9	73.75	0	83.00
3.50	0	73.75	1	100.00
3.99	21	100.00	0	100.00
Total	80	100.00	6	100.00

Table 7 Minimum order price in Milan and Urbino

	Milan			Urbino		
Pmin (€)	Center (%)	Periphery (%)	Total (%)	Center (%)	Periphery (%)	Total (%)
0.00	14.00	10.00	12.50	17.00	0.00	13.00
5.00	82.00	70.00	77.50	17.00	0.00	13.00
8.00	90.00	73.33	83.75	33.00	50.00	38.00
10.00	94.00	76.00	87.50	76.00	50.00	63.00
12.00	94.00	83.33	90.00	83.00	50.00	75.00
15.00	98.00	90.00	95.00	100.00	100.00	100.00
20.00	100.00	96.67	98.75	100.00	100.00	100.00
30.00	100.00	100.00	100.00	100.00	100.00	100.00

Table 8 Delivery times in Milan and Urbino

	Milan			Urbino		
t (min)	Center (%)	Periphery (%)	Total (%)	Center (%)	Periphery (%)	Total (%)
25	4.00	6.67	5.00	0.00	0.00	0.00
30	6.00	13.33	8.75	50.00	100.00	62.50
35	10.00	16.67	12.50	50.00	100.00	62.50
40	14.00	16.67	15.00	50.00	100.00	62.50
45	62.00	16.67	45.00	66.67	100.00	75.00
50	96.00	56.67	81.25	66.67	100.00	75.00
55	98.00	66.67	86.25	66.67	100.00	75.00
60	98.00	80.00	91.25	66.67	100.00	75.00
65	100.00	80.00	92.50	66.67	100.00	75.00
–	100.00	100.00	100.00	100.00	100.00	100.00

(Pmin = €5.00) in the Milan prospect the third quartile is reached, which in the city of Urbino is reached at a minimum price value equal to €10.00 (double) (Table 7).

An interesting aspect that emerged from the research concerns delivery times. Table 8 shows delivery times in the city of Urbino that are very short, 50.00% of the restaurants analyzed in Urbino declare a maximum time needed of 30 min. On the contrary, the analysis on the metropolis shows a significant number of activities located in the range between "40 min" and "50 min" and more than a tenth with significantly high times (even exceeding an hour's wait).

The fourth variable studied, namely the delivery start time, showed a discrepancy between Urbino and Milan regarding the availability of restaurants to make home deliveries with continuous hours.

From an initial more superficial investigation it emerged that in the small reality of Urbino most restaurants provide service only for evening deliveries. Analyzing the individual pages more in depth it emerged that in some cases they also accept orders at lunch but with a limited time slot (about 1 h).

Comparing the delivery times in Table 9 we can immediately notice a lack in the city of Urbino of restaurants that offer a continuous delivery service (indicated in

Table 9 Delivery times in Milan and Urbino

	Milan			Urbino	
O	Center	Periphery	Total	Center/periphery	Total
00:00	50	24	74	0	0
11:30 a.m./7:00 p.m.	0	0	0	1	1
12:35 a.m./7:30 p.m.	0	0	0	1	1
5:55 p.m.	0	1	1	0	0
6:10 p.m.	0	2	2	0	0
6:30 p.m.	0	2	2	0	0
6:55 p.m.	0	0	0	2	2
7:40 p.m.	0	1	1	0	0
7:45 p.m.	0	0	0	1	1
9:55 p.m.	0	0	0	1	1
Total	50	30	80	6	6

the table with "00:00:00"), unlike the city of Milan where we detected 74 of them. Excluding the latter and observing only the evening openings we can note that in Urbino the first available time to order is at 6:55 p.m., exactly 1 h after the first available time among those in Milan. To this, we must obviously add that most of the restaurants in the latter deliver almost all day, a service that none of the restaurants in Urbino offer. Looking at the table in reverse and taking the last band of both cities, an even wider gap emerges: the last restaurant in the list in Urbino opens deliveries more than 2 h later (9.55 p.m.) than the one in Milan (7.40 p.m.).

The last step of this analysis was dedicated to the study of reviews.

The average of this variable in the case of Urbino, calculated and inserted in Table 4, shows a value of 124.50 reviews; this number can be interpreted as a positive signal from the demand, also considering that it exceeds the average calculated for the city of Milan (Table 1) (83.50) of 41.00 units.

The reviews can be seen as a value proportional to the number of users: ideally, a greater number of them corresponds to a greater number of orders.

4.3 *Just Eat or Glovo?*

Founded in Denmark in 2001, Just Eat arrived in Italy in 2011, and between 2016 and 2017 it grew significantly, covering almost the entire national territory and earning the title of sector leader. At the same time, it managed to expand into twelve additional countries through the use of the Only Delivery model, offering only the ordering service. However, by analyzing the website, we discovered that in some cities a different model is used, where delivery to the final customer is also managed (Order & Delivery).

In the city of Urbino, the original model is applied, but as already noted, it is not well-suited to the small size of local businesses. Ideally, a team of riders would also be provided. For this reason, we found it important to understand the nature of the relationship between riders and Just Eat, which is characterized by remuneration based on a fixed hourly wage of €8.75, additional bonuses for each delivery made, paid vacation, life insurance, and severance pay (TFR).

It is, therefore, a part-time employment contract where working hours are distributed through weekly shifts [23].

Glovo was founded as a food delivery start-up in Barcelona in 2014, later expanding to the 'anything delivery' business model, where couriers handle not only food delivery but also any transportable items (if they don't exceed certain weight and size limits), such as medication, groceries, fresh flowers, and much more. It arrived in Italy 2 years later through the acquisition of Foodinho (a food delivery start-up operating in Milan), and then gradually expanded into the major Italian cities. Through both its app and website, Glovo offers consumers the ability to browse through different restaurants, select products to order, and track the delivery. It also provides a platform for restaurants to manage orders and one for couriers to book deliveries.

It is worth noting the contractual relationship established with the riders, which, unlike Just Eat, is based on greater flexibility. Upon visiting the 'sign up as a rider' section on *Glovoapp.com*, one immediately sees a phrase that clearly expresses this characteristic: *'Do you want to set your own hours and connect whenever it suits you? Earn money by delivering orders with the Glovo Courier app. Sign up now!'*

In this case, riders are free to decide when and how much to work. No weekly schedules are provided, so riders can make themselves available for assignments on the days and times they prefer without being bound to stay available during a set time frame. They are also free to accept or decline any order. Likewise, the company is not obligated to assign delivery tasks to the rider.

Glovo is also innovative in how it evaluates rider performance. Both restaurants and customers can rate the courier, and this score becomes visible on the rider's personal page. Riders with higher ratings can access the schedule earlier to book slots (i.e., the orders placed by consumers that the rider can take on). Consumers can also view the profile of Glovers (riders), where, in addition to reviews, the rider's phone number and a photo are displayed.

The compensation offered to the team of riders varies depending on the city where the delivery takes place. In some cities, there is a variable payment structure, consisting of a fixed part and an additional amount that can vary based on the order preparation wait time and the kilometers traveled. In other cities, a fixed compensation is provided (the courier can view an estimated amount corresponding to the order before booking it). The company is committed to protecting its partners in the event of order cancellations by consumers when the rider is already near the delivery location, guaranteeing a percentage of the compensation or, in some cases, the full amount [24].

Based on the research conducted in the previous sub-sections, we have found that the model adopted by Glovo may be more functional in a context like Urbino, compared to the model currently used by the available application.

To further investigate the results, we created a database using the same criteria as in the previous analyses, which was then compared with the data from Just Eat.

Regarding the first variable analyzed in Table 10, related to delivery price, it was found that Glovo is more economical, with an overall average of €1.76 (compared to the Just Eat average of €2.14). Notably, the difference is most evident in the 'Center' column, where the third quartile corresponds to a price of €1.49 for Glovo, compared to more than double that amount for Just Eat (€3.99). In contrast, in the peripheral areas, Just Eat appears to be slightly more economical, but with only a minimal difference.

The advantage of using Glovo given by lower average prices is strengthened by the absence of a minimum order price constraint (in Table 11, the Glovo columns show that 100% of restaurants have a minimum order price equal to €0.00), which is instead present, although usually not very high, on Just Eat.

Glovo aims to reduce delivery times to a minimum to meet customer satisfaction by trying not to exceed 1 h as the maximum waiting time for delivery. The goal is clear by observing the total column in Table 12 in which approximately 80% of the

Table 10 Delivery prices for Glovo and Just Eat

	Glovo			Just Eat		
P (€)	Center (%)	Periphery (%)	Total (%)	Center (%)	Periphery (%)	Total (%)
0.00	24.00	7.00	18.00	18.00	20.00	18.75
0.99	47.00	7.00	32.00	18.00	20.00	18.75
1.00	47.00	7.00	32.00	36.00	33.33	35.00
1.49	80.00	20.00	57.00	46.00	40.00	43.75
1.50	80.00	20.00	57.00	48.00	40.00	45.00
1.99	82.00	43.00	67.00	50.00	40.00	46.25
2.00	82.00	43.00	67.00	50.00	60.00	53.75
2.49	94.00	57.00	80.00	56.00	73.33	62.50
2.99	100.00	70.00	89.00	56.00	73.33	62.50
3.49	100.00	70.00	89.00	72.00	76.67	73.75
3.99	100.00	100.00	100.00	100.00	100.00	100.00

Table 11 Glovo and Just Eat minimum delivery price

	Glovo			Just Eat		
Pmin (€)	Center (%)	Periphery (%)	Total (%)	Center (%)	Periphery (%)	Total (%)
0.00	100.00	100.00	100.00	14.00	10.00	12.50
5.00	100.00	100.00	100.00	82.00	70.00	77.50
8.00	100.00	100.00	100.00	90.00	73.00	83.75
10.00	100.00	100.00	100.00	94.00	76.67	87.50
12.00	100.00	100.00	100.00	94.00	83.33	90.00
15.00	100.00	100.00	100.00	98.00	90.00	95.00
20.00	100.00	100.00	100.00	100.00	96.67	98.75
30.00	100.00	100.00	100.00	100.00	100.00	100.00

Table 12 Glovo and Just Eat delivery times

	Glovo			Just Eat		
t (min)	Center (%)	Periphery (%)	Total (%)	Center (%)	Periphery (%)	Total (%)
15	6.00	0.00	4.00	0.00	0.00	0.00
20	22.00	3.00	15.00	0.00	0.00	0.00
25	56.00	10.00	39.00	4.00	6.67	5.00
30	82.00	23.00	60.00	6.00	13.33	8.75
35	96.00	33.00	73.00	10.00	16.67	12.50
40	98.00	50.00	80.00	14.00	16.67	15.00
45	98.00	70.00	88.00	62.00	16.67	45.00
50	100.00	87.00	95.00	96.00	56.67	81.25
55	100.00	87.00	95.00	98.00	66.67	86.25
60	100.00	90.00	96.00	98.00	80.00	91.25
65	100.00	100.00	100.00	100.00	80.00	92.50
–	100.00	100.00	100.00	100.00	100.00	100.00

Table 13 Orario di consegna Glovo e Just Eat

	Glovo			Just Eat		
O	Center (%)	Periphery (%)	Total (%)	Center (%)	Periphery (%)	Total (%)
5:55 p.m.	0.00	0.00	0.00	0.00	3.00	1.00
6:10 p.m.	0.00	0.00	0.00	0.00	10.00	4.00
6:30 p.m.	0.00	7.00	3.00	0.00	17.00	6.00
7:00 p.m.	0.00	10.00	4.00	0.00	17.00	6.00
7:40 p.m.	0.00	10.00	4.00	0.00	20.00	8.00
00:00 p.m.	0.00	10.00	4.00	100.00	100.00	100.00
Nd	100.00	100.00	100.00	100.00	100.00	100.00

Nd undetected data

businesses declare a delivery time of no more than 40 min and none more than 60. As happens in the price analysis, also in this case Glovo is more efficient in the center where it reaches 96% in the "35 min" row (percentage corresponding to "50 min" for Just Eat).

The differences regarding the time variable (see Table 12) are minimal; therefore, they did not affect the results shown in Table 13 for delivery times.

5 Discussion

From the comparative analysis between the two cities, restaurants in Urbino face significant difficulties in implementing a logistical service, which can be attributed to several factors, including their small size, which reduces their willingness to invest in such a service. This was particularly evident from the study of the variables 'delivery price,' 'minimum order price' (which were, on average, higher than the data observed for the city of Milan), and 'delivery start time.' The observation of the latter was especially relevant when compared to the actual opening hours of the restaurants. An example is 'Canyon Fast Food,' which is available for delivery from 11:30 a.m. to 2:30 p.m. and again from 7:00 p.m. to 11:30 p.m., despite the physical restaurant's operating hours being from 10:00 a.m. to 12:00 p.m.

The remaining variables can be interpreted as a positive sign: on one hand, the shorter delivery times in Urbino demonstrate the potential to provide a more satisfying service, and on the other hand, the reviews reflect consumers' willingness to use this service. These findings align with previous research indicating that consumer satisfaction in last-mile delivery is highly dependent on delivery speed and service reliability, particularly in smaller urban settings where logistical constraints may be more pronounced [11].

Regarding the second analysis, which compares two platforms based on two different models, it can be concluded that, despite Just Eat being one of the first food delivery platforms in the world and having secured the title of leader in Italy, the analysis shows that it is less efficient than Glovo. This superiority, which could also stem from the type of contractual relationship with the riders, is more evident in central areas across all the variables considered. Studies on the gig economy have highlighted that flexible work arrangements, such as those employed by Glovo, provide businesses with the ability to scale operations dynamically in response to fluctuating demand, making them particularly advantageous in contexts where order volumes vary significantly [6, 7].

Among the findings, the difference in payment methods between the two platforms is noteworthy: while Just Eat offers hourly wages, Glovo pays based on the number of deliveries made, making it much more flexible. This aligns with previous research on digital labor markets, which has shown that performance-based compensation models tend to increase efficiency while reducing costs for platforms [5]. However, these models also introduce income variability for workers, raising concerns about job stability and earnings predictability [4].

We can therefore conclude that the challenges faced by restaurants in Urbino in offering home delivery are not compatible with the model on which Just Eat (Only Order) is based, as it does not include logistical services, which must instead be managed entirely by the restaurant. A possible solution to this issue lies in adopting the Order & Delivery model, which was analyzed in the second part of the case study. The combination of these two studies, aimed at analyzing the difficulties and opportunities in Urbino and comparing two food delivery platforms, has led us to conclude that Glovo could also represent a better solution in Urbino compared to the one currently available. Given the investments that small restaurant owners in Urbino must make to provide an adequate logistical service, they could be among the first to benefit from the advantages of the Order & Delivery model. By not having to manage the recruitment and payment of riders, even restaurants currently excluded from delivery services could be more inclined to join the platform through Glovo, thus increasing the offerings available to consumers.

The difference in compensation identified in previous studies proved to be a crucial factor in these conclusions. In a city like Urbino, characterized by a high percentage of non-resident students, demand is highly unstable, and this is precisely why the piece-rate payment model offered by Glovo is the ideal solution. Prior research has emphasized that cities with a high student population tend to experience fluctuating food delivery demand, making adaptive and flexible delivery models a more sustainable approach for both businesses and workers [10].

6 Conclusions, Implications and Limitations

In summary, the comparative analysis between Urbino and Milan highlights the significant challenges faced by small restaurants in offering home delivery services, particularly in cities like Urbino. The research demonstrates that the Glovo model, with its flexible rider contracts and lower operational costs, offers a more suitable solution for smaller businesses compared to Just Eat's "Only Order" model. This finding could have broader implications for similar small cities, where limited resources and fluctuating demand make it difficult for businesses to manage their own logistics. The case of Alfonsino, a food delivery platform successfully developed in small towns, further supports this conclusion. Alfonsino's model, which offers flexible, delivery-based compensation, similar to Glovo, demonstrates the viability of such platforms in smaller markets where traditional food delivery services struggle.

Moreover, Glovo's crowdshipping approach, which allows riders to work on flexible schedules, presents not only economic benefits but also potential sustainability advantages, especially when considering its use for non-food deliveries and the optimization of transportation resources.

From a theoretical perspective, this study contributes to the growing body of literature on digital transformation in logistics by highlighting the adaptability of platform-based models in small urban centers [16]. It reinforces existing research on the role of gig economy structures in shaping last-mile delivery and extends it by demonstrating how these models can mitigate logistical inefficiencies in low-demand areas. Additionally, the study offers insights into the interplay between flexibility, cost management, and service availability, which are key factors in optimizing digital logistics networks.

In practice, the findings suggest that small restaurant owners in peripheral cities should consider integrating more dynamic delivery solutions, such as the Order & Delivery model, to remain competitive. Policymakers and urban planners could also leverage this research to develop frameworks that support sustainable and tech-enabled last-mile logistics. Furthermore, food delivery platforms may use these insights to refine their expansion strategies, particularly in underserved areas where traditional models struggle.

However, this study has some limitations, notably the smaller sample size in Urbino, which may impact the generalizability of the findings. Future research should expand the dataset to include additional small and medium-sized cities to further validate these observations and assess the scalability of the proposed solutions, as well as explore the environmental impact of different delivery models. Additionally, with the rapid advancement of delivery technologies, including autonomous vehicles and drones, future studies should investigate how such innovations could further enhance the efficiency and sustainability of last-mile logistics.

References

1. Trauth-Goik, A. (2021). Repudiating the fourth industrial revolution discourse: A new episteme of technological progress. *World Futures, 77*(1), 55–78. https://doi.org/10.1080/02604027.2020.1788357
2. Tassinari, A., & Maccarrone, V. (2020). Riders on the storm: Workplace solidarity among gig economy couriers in Italy and the UK. *Work, Employment and Society, 34*(1), 35–54. https://doi.org/10.1177/0950017019862954
3. Fareri, S., Fantoni, G., Chiarello, F., Coli, E., & Binda, A. (2020). Estimating industry 4.0 impact on job profiles and skills using text mining. *Computers in Industry, 118*, 103222. https://doi.org/10.1016/j.compind.2020.103222
4. Domini, G., Grazzi, M., Moschella, D., & Treibich, T. (2021). Threats and opportunities in the digital era: Automation spikes and employment dynamics. *Research Policy, 50*(7), 104137. https://doi.org/10.1016/j.respol.2020.104137
5. Sun, P., Chen, J. Y., & Rani, U. (2023). From flexible labour to 'sticky labour': A tracking study of workers in the food-delivery platform economy of China. *Work, Employment and Society, 37*(2), 412–431. https://doi.org/10.1177/09500170211021570
6. Gramano, E. (2020). Digitalisation and work: Challenges from the platform economy. *Contemporary Social Science, 15*(4), 476–488. https://doi.org/10.1080/21582041.2019.1572919
7. Salmon, P. M., Bhawana, K. C., Irwin, B. G., Brennan, C. J., & Read, G. J. (2023). What influences gig economy delivery rider behaviour and safety? A systems analysis. *Safety Science, 166*, 106263. https://doi.org/10.1016/j.ssci.2023.106263
8. Kiba-Janiak, M., Marcinkowski, J., Jagoda, A., & Skowrońska, A. (2021). Sustainable last mile delivery on e-commerce market in cities from the perspective of various stakeholders: Literature review. *Sustainable Cities and Society, 71*, 102984. https://doi.org/10.1016/j.scs.2021.102984
9. Simoni, M. D., Kutanoglu, E., & Claudel, C. G. (2020). Optimization and analysis of a robot-assisted last mile delivery system. *Transportation Research Part E: Logistics and Transportation Review, 142*, 102049. https://doi.org/10.1016/j.tre.2020.102049
10. Correia, D., Teixeira, L., & Marques, J. L. (2021). Last-mile-as-a-service (LMaaS): An innovative concept for the disruption of the supply chain. *Sustainable Cities and Society, 75*, 103310. https://doi.org/10.1016/j.scs.2021.103310
11. Grant, D. B. (2021). Fulfilling customer needs in the 2020s with marketing and logistics. In D. B. Grant (Ed.), *Global logistics: New directions in supply chain management* (pp. 79–94). Kogan Page.
12. Nguyen, M. H., Pojani, D., Nguyen-Phuoc, D. Q., & Thi, B. N. (2023). What if delivery riders quit? Challenges to last-mile logistics during the COVID-19 pandemic. *Research in Transportation Business & Management, 47*, 100941. https://doi.org/10.1016/j.rtbm.2022.100941

13. Cebeci, M. S., Tapia, R. J., Kroesen, M., de Bok, M., & Tavasszy, L. (2023). The effect of trust on the choice for crowdshipping services. *Transportation Research Part A: Policy and Practice, 170*, 103622. https://doi.org/10.1016/j.tra.2023.103622
14. Mohri, S. S., Ghaderi, H., Nassir, N., & Thompson, R. G. (2023). Crowdshipping for sustainable urban logistics: A systematic review of the literature. *Transportation Research Part E: Logistics and Transportation Review, 178*, 103289. https://doi.org/10.1016/j.tre.2023.103289
15. Mohri, S. S., Nassir, N., Thompson, R. G., & Lavieri, P. S. (2024). Public transportation-based crowd-shipping initiatives: Are users willing to participate? Why not? *Transportation Research Part A: Policy and Practice, 182*, 104019. https://doi.org/10.1016/j.tra.2024.104019
16. Deng, Q., Fang, X., & Lim, Y. F. (2021). Urban consolidation center or peer-to-peer platform? The solution to urban last-mile delivery. *Production and Operations Management, 30*(4), 997–1013. https://doi.org/10.1111/poms.13276
17. Ghaderi, H., Tsai, P. W., Zhang, L., & Moayedikia, A. (2022). An integrated crowdshipping framework for green last mile delivery. *Sustainable Cities and Society, 78*, 103552. https://doi.org/10.1016/j.scs.2021.103552
18. Mittal, A., Marusak, A. A., Krejci, C. C., Sadeghiamirshahidi, N., & Rogers, K. J. (2022). Evaluating the suitability of crowd-shipping platforms for small and medium-sized enterprises. *Sustainability, 14*(21), 14177. https://doi.org/10.3390/su142114177
19. Pourrahmani, E., & Jaller, M. (2021). Crowdshipping in last mile deliveries: Operational challenges and research opportunities. *Socio-Economic Planning Sciences, 78*, 101063. https://doi.org/10.1016/j.seps.2021.101063
20. Cramer, F., & Fikar, C. (2024). Investigating crowd logistics platform operations for local food distribution. *International Journal of Retail & Distribution Management, 52*(9), 836–855. https://doi.org/10.1108/IJRDM-10-2022-0400
21. Mehrolia, S., Alagarsamy, S., & Solaikutty, V. M. (2021). Customers' response to online food delivery services during COVID-19 outbreak using binary logistic regression. *International Journal of Consumer Studies, 45*(3), 396–408. https://doi.org/10.1111/ijcs.12630
22. Troise, C., O'Driscoll, A., Tani, M., & Prisco, A. (2021). Online food delivery services and behavioural intention: A test of an integrated TAM and TPB framework. *British Food Journal, 123*(2), 664–683. https://doi.org/10.1108/BFJ-05-2020-0418
23. Just Eat. (2024). *How do contracts with Just Eat work?* Retrieved September 23, 2024, from https://www.justeat.it/rider/the-inside-track/consegnare-con-noi/contratto-lavoro-rider
24. Glovo. (2021). *National collective labor agreement for the regulation of the activity of delivery of goods on behalf of others, carried out by self-employed workers, so-called riders.* Retrieved September 23, 2024, from https://delivery.glovoapp.com/it/sdde3fsxaqw/

Architecture, Systems, and Methods of Digitalization

Network Modeling Method for Optimizing the Management of Digital Industrial Ecosystem Project Implementation

Andrey F. Shorikov

Abstract The article considers the problem of implementing a digital industrial ecosystem project in the presence of several acceptable technologies for its implementation and corresponding vector objective functions for assessing of their quality. For a formalized description of optimization of project implementation management, a new formalization in the form of a two-level multi-agent hierarchical network economic and mathematical model is proposed. The identification of parameters, structural balanced interaction and optimization of the result of managing the implementation of processes of the studied digital industrial ecosystem project within the framework of the proposed two-level multi-agent hierarchical network model are described. The paper presents a methodology for solving the problem under consideration, which is implemented in the form of one-step operations that allow their algorithmization.

Keywords Digital industrial ecosystem · Project implementation · Network economic · Mathematical modeling · Two-level multi-agent hierarchical control · Control optimization

1 Introduction

The paper considers the problem of implementing *the main project* (MP) of *the digital industrial ecosystem* (DIES) in the presence of several admissible technologies for its implementation and corresponding vector objective functions for assessing of their quality. It is assumed that the DIES carries out the MP, which is implemented by the main production enterprise and its auxiliary production enterprises, which

A. F. Shorikov (✉)
Institute of Economics of the Ural Branch of the Russian Academy of Sciences, Ekaterinburg, Russia
e-mail: shorikov.af@uiec.ru

F. Tao et al. (eds.), *Artificial Intelligence and Digital Transformation*, Lecture Notes in Information Systems and Organisation 78,
https://doi.org/10.1007/978-3-032-00118-4_10

implement *auxiliary projects* (AP) included in the main project and not implemented at the main production enterprise [1–6]. To implement the MP of the DIES, it is possible to use several admissible technologies, the quality of which is assessed by the corresponding vector objective functions. It is necessary to find a solution to the problem of implementing the MP of the DIES by optimizing the choice of an admissible technology for its implementation relative to the corresponding vector objective function.

The article describes the identification of objects of the considered DIES and their structural interaction, information and control links between agents managing system objects, the formation of a vector objective functions to assess the quality of the MP of the DIES implementation by corresponding technologies, and the achievement of the goals of the system agents. To describe the process of optimization of the management of the implementation the MP of the DIES, the article proposes a new formalization in the form of a two-level multi-agent hierarchical network economic-mathematical model in the presence of several technologies for its implementation and corresponding vector objective functions for assessing of their quality, which is based on the results of works [1, 4–6] and the article is adjacent to studies [2, 3, 7–26].

2 Literature Review

Currently, the economy is experiencing intensive implementation of digital technologies, primarily in production systems. At the same time, their efficiency directly depends on the infrastructure in which they operate. The problems of forming various programs and activities aimed at creating a digital space that ensures efficient and sustainable functioning of production enterprises have been considered by many authors, for example, in [2, 8, 9, 11, 13, 17, 27–29]. At the same time, efficient industrial activity within the digital economy is realized only when the production enterprises that form it operate within the framework of the relevant DIES and on the basis of specialized digital platforms. The creation and improvement of the DIES allows enterprises participating in such systems to effectively exchange information, goods and services to achieve their goals in the conditions of competition and risks. Numerous studies are devoted to theoretical and practical issues of development and improvement of the DIES, for example, in [2, 9, 15, 17, 22, 27, 29–32]. The functioning of production enterprises within the DIES is aimed at implementing specific projects, the implementation of which should optimize the specified target functions. Extensive scientific literature is devoted to issues of managing the implementation of production projects and related problems, and various studies have been conducted, the results of which are presented, for example, in [5, 6, 11, 12, 18, 23, 24, 28, 33]. One of the main directions in the study and modeling of production project implementation management problems is the multi-agent approach, which is intensively developing and reflected in numerous works [1, 21, 25, 26, 32, 34, 35]. Theoretical and practical research in the field of application of intelligent computer systems in industry is also developing intensively [1, 2, 5, 20, 26, 31, 32, 34, 36].

When studying the problem of managing the MP of the DIES, there is a need to develop and create a corresponding economic and mathematical model. The basic elements of such a model are: production enterprises included in the DIES and managed by the corresponding agents; the AP of the DIES, the implementation of which allows the implementation the MP of the DIES; control parameters that the DIES agents manage; information and control links between the DIES agents; conditions and restrictions on the implementation the MP of the DIES and the AP of the DIES parameters; objective functions for the DIES agents, as well as the presence of several levels of control of the processes considered in the system.

The main task for each DIES agent managing the implementation of the corresponding production project is to develop a methodology for implementing the project in order to achieve the best (optimal) values for the formed objective function (functions), which is selected as a criterion (or criteria) for the quality of its implementation. To solve this problem, it is necessary to create an appropriate economic and mathematical model. Within the framework of the developed model, an optimization problem is formulated that corresponds to the original problem, the solution of which can be used to create a computer software system. Such a software system should be included in the computer software system of information support and management of the DIES, implementing support for making management decisions by managers of various levels.

The problems of optimal project management within the framework of the DIES must be studied using models and methods of economic and mathematical modeling [1, 4, 6, 16, 19, 36–40]. One of the important approaches to solving such problems is network economic and mathematical modeling, the results of which are presented, for example, in the works [5, 11, 12, 23, 24, 28, 33].

Based on the given brief review of the most typical works related to this study, the following conclusions can be made:

1. The problems of economic and mathematical modeling of the management of the implementation the MP of the DIES are relevant and complex;
2. To solve the problems of managing the implementation the MP of the DIES, the presence in the complex of several levels of management, several technologies for its implementation, several agents for managing system objects is not taken into account;
3. In the DIES models for assessing the quality of project implementation there are no formalizations in the form of a multi-criteria (vector) objective function defined on the system parameters;
4. In the DIES models the organization of information and control links between objects and agents of the system is not formalized;
5. In the scientific literature there is no application of network economic and mathematical modeling tools for solving problems of process optimization within DIES.

3 Methodology

Modeling of the processes of implementation the MP of the DIES involves the development of a special economic-mathematical apparatus that takes into account the features of the objects and processes under consideration. In this case, the development of economic-mathematical models for managing the implementation of complex multiparameter dynamic systems is carried out in two main directions - stochastic and deterministic. Very often, stochastic modeling tools are used to develop such models, without taking into account the rather strict requirements that are imposed on the objects of modeling and the conditions of their functioning (see, for example, [39]). At the same time, studies of the processes of managing complex production systems show that the requirements that are necessary for the implementation of objects in stochastic modeling are usually not met.

One of the important areas of economic and mathematical modeling of the processes of implementation of various socio-economic, technical, military and other complex projects is network mathematical modeling. It should be noted that the models and methods of network mathematical modeling have been well studied and the results of such studies are presented in a huge number of scientific and educational works (see, for example, works [5, 6, 11, 12, 23, 24, 28, 33]). Network mathematical modeling allows one to clearly present a set of APs of the DIES, the implementation of which allows one to implement the MP of the DIES in the optimal time period and to form a calendar schedule [33] for the execution of all APs of the DIES. It should be noted that the conditions for the application of network mathematical modeling are not burdensome for systems of the DIES type and are reduced to standard properties for the AP forming the MP of the DIES and are described, for example, in works [4–6].

For the problem of implementing the MP of the DIES studied in this article, the methodology of deterministic network economic-mathematical modeling presented in the works [1, 4–6] is used, which allows taking into account the presence of APs of the DIES forming the MP of the DIES and the corresponding objects implementing their realization, and the presence of information and control links between agents and objects of the DIES, the existing conditions and restrictions on the implementation of the parameters of the MP of the DIES and the APs of the DIES, objective functions for the agents of the DIES and the presence of several levels of control of the processes considered in the system.

The use of the network economic-mathematical modeling methodology allows us to study the problems of optimizing the management of the implementation of the MP of the DIES and the APs of the DIES as a whole with respect to a given vector objective functions with the possibility of using several technologies for implementing the MP of the DIES within the framework of the considered DIES. The formed network model can serve as a basis for developing a corresponding computer software system for information support and management of the DIES, which is necessary for implementing support for making management decisions by managers at various levels.

In this article, to describe the process of optimization of the management of the implementation of the MP of the DIES, a new formalization has been developed in the form of a two-level multi-agent hierarchical network economic-mathematical model in the presence of several technologies for its implementation and corresponding vector objective functions for assessing their quality. This formalization is based on the results of works [1, 4–6] and the article is adjacent to studies [2, 3, 7–26].

4 Results

4.1 Structure and Information Links Between Objects of a Multi-Agent Digital Industrial Ecosystem

The article examines the proposed two-level multi-agent hierarchical network economic-mathematical model of the DIES, which describes the processes of implementing the MP of the DIES, with the possibility of using a set of admissible technologies for its implementation and corresponding vector objective functions for assessing their quality. Each admissible technology for implementing the MP of the DIES consists of a set of APs of the DIES. In this case, the MP is implemented by *the main production enterprise* (MPE)—Object I, managed by Agent P, in cooperation with n *auxiliary production enterprises* (APEs)—Objects II_i, $i \in \overline{1,n} = \{1,2,\ldots,n\}$ ($n \in \mathbf{N}$; hereinafter, $\mathbf{N}$ is the set of all natural numbers), implementing the APs and managed by the corresponding auxiliary Agents E_i (economic entities in charge of the corresponding production enterprises), subordinate to agent P.

Management entities have their own goals and information support tools for making management decisions.

It is assumed that the multi-agent CPES considers the implementation of the MP in the presence of various technologies for its implementation with the corresponding vector objective functions for assessing their effectiveness. To solve this problem, it is proposed to use network economic and mathematical modeling [5, 6, 11, 12, 23, 24, 28, 33], which allows formalizing the presence of several technologies for implementing the MP of the DIES and the corresponding vector objective functions for assessing their quality.

When solving the problem under study, at the first stage, for each admissible technology for implementing the MP of the DIES, a corresponding optimal network model is formed [33] and on their basis, the optimal technology for implementing the MP of the DIES is selected relative to the specified vector objective function. At the second stage, for the found optimal technology for implementing the MP of the DIES and the corresponding optimal network model, the optimal time period for its implementation and the optimal calendar schedule for implementing the project as a whole are calculated. Taking into account the available information about the capabilities of the MPE and APEs for implementing the MP of the DIES and APs of DIES, respectively, Agent P forms a team under its command consisting of Object I and Objects II_i, controlled by the corresponding auxiliary Agents E_j, $j \in J \subseteq \overline{1,n}$, which is capable of implementing the optimal technology for implementing the MP of the DIES.

Based on the generated optimal schedule for the implementation of the MP of the DIES, data are generated for the implementation of the APs of the DIES, which are transferred to Agents E_j, $j \in J$. Using this data, each Agent E_j, $j \in J$, generates the corresponding optimal network models of the APs of the DIES implementation, which are executed by the APE of the DIES controlled by the Agent E_j, and on their basis develops schedules for their implementation. Thus, the development of a model for optimizing the management of the implementation of the MP of the DIES is based on procedures that use the presence of information and control links between the Agents of the DIES. Such procedures involve the formation of sets of admissible positions of the MP of the DIES and APs of the DIES management processes corresponding to the generated network models and schedules of their implementation.

The paper describes a new method for formalizing and optimizing the management of the implementation of the MP of the CPES in the form of *a two-level multi-agent hierarchical network economic-mathematical model* that takes into account the presence of several technologies for implementing the MP of the DIES and corresponding vector objective functions for assessing of their quality.

4.2 Two-Level Multi-Agent Hierarchical Network Model for Implementing a Digital Industrial Ecosystem Project

A new method for formalizing and solving the problem of optimizing the management of the process of implementing the MP of the DIES using the optimal technology from the class of admissible ones and in the presence of corresponding vector objective functions for assessing their quality can be presented in the form of a methodology, the implementation of which is carried out in the form of the following finite sequence of one-step operations.

1. A given integer time interval is considered—hereinafter, simply an interval $\overline{0,T} = \{0,1,\ldots,T\}$ ($T \in \mathbf{N}$; where, for example, a time period $t \in \overline{0,T}$ is a month, quarter, year, etc.).
2. A natural number n is introduced that determines the number of APE of the DIES—Objects II_i, $i \in \overline{1,n}$, implementing s APs of the DIES over time interval $\overline{0,T}$ under the control of corresponding auxiliary Agents E_i ($s \in \mathbf{N}, s \geq n$), and each APE of the DIES implements at least one AP of the DIES.
3. Agent P and the MPE of the DIES—Object I, and the set of APEs of the DIES—Objects II_i and Agents E_i, $i \in \overline{1,n}$, form *the first (dominant) level of the control system for realization of the* MP of the DIES.

4. The set of APEs of the DIES—Objects II_i and Agents E_i, $i \in \overline{1,n}$, form *the second (subordinate) level of the control system for realization of the* APs *of the* DIES.
5. To implement the MP of the DIES, Agent P forms a tuple $\mathbf{U} = \{U_1, U_2, \ldots, U_l\}$ that describes—initial data, constraints, acceptable technological solutions, parameters of the objective functions, and final results ($l \in \mathbf{N}$).
6. An array $\mathbf{TP}(\mathbf{U}) = \{TP_1, TP_2, \ldots, TP_r\}$ of admissible technologies is introduced that allow the implementation of the considered MP of the DIES, satisfying the specified conditions-constraints $\mathbf{U} = \{U_1, U_2, \ldots, U_l\}$ ($r \in \mathbf{N}$).
7. For each admissible k-th technology $TP_k \in \mathbf{TP}(\mathbf{U})$ $\left(k \in \overline{1,r}\right)$, an array $\mathbf{BR}\left(TP_k\right) = \left\{R_1\left(TP_k\right), R_2\left(TP_k\right), \ldots, R_{m_k}\left(TP_k\right)\right\}$ of APs of the DIES is introduced that implements it ($m_k \in \mathbf{N}$).
8. For each array $\mathbf{BR}\left(TP_k\right) = \left\{R_1\left(TP_k\right), R_2\left(TP_k\right), \ldots, R_{m_k}\left(TP_k\right)\right\}$ $\left(k \in \overline{1,r}\right)$ of APs of the DIES, a corresponding set of quality criteria (functionalities) $\boldsymbol{F}_k = \left\{F_1^{(k)}, F_2^{(k)}, \ldots, F_\tau^{(k)}\right\}$ is introduced ($\tau \in \mathbf{N}$), evaluating the results of the implementation of the considered MP of the DIES, where $F_j^{(k)}$: $\mathbf{R}^{3\times m_k} \to \mathbf{R}^1 \left(j \in \overline{1,\tau}\right)$, and is, for example, a linear or convex function.
9. For each array $\mathbf{BR}\left(TP_k\right) = \left\{R_1\left(TP_k\right), R_2\left(TP_k\right), \ldots, R_{m_k}\left(TP_k\right)\right\}$ $\left(k \in \overline{1,r}\right)$ of APs of the DIES and the corresponding set of functionals $\boldsymbol{F}_k = \left\{F_1^{(k)}, F_2^{(k)}, \ldots, F_\tau^{(k)}\right\}$ —*vector objective function*, the goal of the Agent P in managing the process of implementing the MP of the DIES is the maximization (minimization) of this functional.
10. Each j-th AP of the DIES $R_j(TP_k) \in \mathbf{BR}(TP_k)$ $\left(j \in \overline{1,m_k}\right)$ corresponds to a data array—a real matrix $A_{kj} = \left\|a_{lm}^{(kj)}\right\|_{\substack{l\in\overline{1,p_{kj}}\\ m\in\overline{1,3}}}$ ($p_{kj} \in \mathbf{N}$), in which the values of the set of elements $\left\{a_{l1}^{(kj)}, a_{l2}^{(kj)}, a_{l3}^{(kj)}\right\}$ of each l-th row $\left(l \in \overline{1,p_{kj}}\right)$ are respectively equal to the duration, cost and quality of the possible l-th variant of implementing the given j-th AP of the DIES (their values are real dimensionless quantities), i.e. the number of rows of this matrix p_{kj} is equal to the number of different acceptable variants of implementing the AP of the DIES under consideration.
11. Based on the available data, a solution to the following vector optimization problem is found.

Problem 1 For each k-th technology $TP_k \in \mathbf{TP}(\mathbf{U})$ $\left(k \in \overline{1,r}\right)$ of the implementation of the MP of the DIES and the corresponding to it the set of matrices $\boldsymbol{A}_{kj} = \left\|a_{lm}^{(kj)}\right\|_{\substack{l\in\overline{1,p_{kj}}\\ m\in\overline{1,3}}}$, $j \in \overline{1,m_k}$ ($p_{kj} \in \mathbf{N}$), and a set of numbers $\left\{\lambda_\delta^{(k)}\right\}_{\delta\in\overline{1,\tau}}$ such that $\forall \delta \in \overline{1,\tau}$: $\left(\lambda_\delta^{(k)} \ge 0\right) \wedge \le \left(\sum_{\delta=1}^{\tau} \lambda_\delta^{(k)} = 1\right)$, it is required to find a matrix $\boldsymbol{B}_k^{(e)} = b_{jm}^{(ek)}{}_{\substack{j\in\overline{1,m_k}\\ m\in\overline{1,3}}}$ whose elements are the solution to *the optimization problem* for maximum (minimum) with a scalarized objective vector function $\boldsymbol{F}_k = \left\{F_1^{(k)}, F_2^{(k)}, \ldots, F_\tau^{(k)}\right\}$ (see, for example, [38]), namely, satisfy the following *optimality condition*:

$$F_k^{(e)} = F_k\left(\left\{a_{l_j^{(e)}1}^{(kj)}, a_{l_j^{(e)}2}^{(kj)}, a_{l_j^{(e)}3}^{(kj)}\right\}_{j\in\overline{1,m_k}}\right) =$$

$$= \sum_{\delta=1}^{\tau} \lambda_\delta^{(k)} \cdot F_\delta^{(k)}\left(\left\{a_{l_j^{(e)}1}^{(kj)}, a_{l_j^{(e)}2}^{(kj)}, a_{l_j^{(e)}3}^{(kj)}\right\}_{j\in\overline{1,m_k}}\right) =$$

$$= \min_{l=\{l_1,l_2,\ldots,l_{m_k}\}\in\overline{1,p_{k1}}\times\overline{1,p_{k2}}\times\ldots\times\overline{1,p_{km_k}}} \sum_{\delta=1}^{\tau} \lambda_\delta^{(k)} \cdot F_\delta^{(k)}\left(\left\{a_{l_j 1}^{(kj)}, a_{l_j 2}^{(kj)}, a_{l_j 3}^{(kj)}\right\}_{j\in\overline{1,m_k}}\right), \quad (1)$$

and the scalar value $F_k^{(e)}$ is the *optimal result for Agent P when implementing the k-th technology* $TP_k \in \mathbf{TP(U)}$ $\left(k \in \overline{1,r}\right)$.

Note that the matrix $B_k^{(e)} = b_{jm}^{(ek)}{}_{\substack{j\in\overline{1,m_k}\\ m\in\overline{1,3}}} = a_{l_j^{(e)}m}^{(kj)}{}_{\substack{j\in\overline{1,m_k}\\ m\in\overline{1,3}}}$ contains data on all m_k APs of the DIES that determine the k-th technology $TP_k \in \mathbf{TP(U)}$ $\left(k \in \overline{1,r}\right)$ and that are optimal with respect to the selected three indicators for each AP of the DIES, and to the scalarized vector objective function $F_k = \left\{F_1^{(k)}, F_2^{(k)}, \ldots, F_\tau^{(k)}\right\}$.

12. Based on the solution of r Problems 1, the following problem is solved.

Problem 2 Among all admissible technologies $\mathbf{TP(U)} = \{TP_1, TP_2, \ldots, TP_r\}$ for the implementation of the considered MP of the DIES and a given set of vector objective functions $F_k = \left\{F_1^{(k)}, F_2^{(k)}, \ldots, F_\tau^{(k)}\right\}$, $k \in \overline{1,r}$, from the solution of r optimization Problems 1, it is required to find at least one technology $TP^{(e)} = TP_{k^{(e)}} \in \mathbf{TP}(\mathbf{U})$, $k^{(e)} \in \mathbf{I}^{(e)} \subseteq \overline{1,r}$, which satisfies the following *optimality condition*:

$$\mathbf{K}^{(e)} = \left\{k^{(e)} : k^{(e)} \in \overline{1,r}, F^{(e)} = \min_{k\in\overline{1,r}} F_k^{(e)} = F_{k^{(e)}}\right\}, \quad (2)$$

where $\forall k^{(e)} \in \mathbf{K}^{(e)} : TP^{(e)} = TP_{k^{(e)}} \in \mathbf{TP}(\mathbf{U})$, and $\forall k \in \overline{1,r}$, the value $F_k^{(e)}$ is determined from the solution of the corresponding Problem 1.

We will call the set of technologies $TP^{(e)} = TP_{k^{(e)}} \in \mathbf{TP}(\mathbf{U})$, $k^{(e)} \in \mathbf{K}^{(e)}$, the set of *optimal technologies*, and the number $F^{(e)} = F_{k^{(e)}}$—*the optimal value of the result for the implementation of the considered* MP of the DIES.

Note that from the solution of Problem 1 for a specific $k^{(e)} \in \mathbf{K}^{(e)}$ one it follows that the matrix $B_{k^{(e)}}^{(e)} = b_{jm}^{(ek^{(e)})}{}_{\substack{j\in\overline{1,m_{k^{(e)}}}\\ m\in\overline{1,3}}} = a_{l_j^{(e)}m}^{(k^{(e)}j)}{}_{\substack{j\in\overline{1,m_{k^{(e)}}}\\ m\in\overline{1,3}}}$ contains all the data that are required to describe all the APs of the DIES necessary for the implementation of a specific optimal technology $TP^{(e)} = TP_{k^{(e)}} \in \mathbf{TP}(\mathbf{U})$.

13. Agent P makes a choice of a specific optimal technology $TP_{k^{(e)}} \in \mathbf{TP}(\mathbf{U})$ corresponding to a specific value $k^{(e)} \in \mathbf{K}^{(e)}$.
14. Then, for a set of APs $\mathbf{BR}\left(TP_{k^{(e)}}\right) = \left\{R_1\left(TP_{k^{(e)}}\right), R_2\left(TP_{k^{(e)}}\right), \ldots, R_{m_{k^{(e)}}}\left(TP_{k^{(e)}}\right)\right\}$ ($k^{(e)} \in \mathbf{K}^{(e)}$) of the DIES corresponding to the formed optimal technology

$\boldsymbol{TP}^{(e)} = TP_{k^{(e)}} \in \mathbf{TP}(\mathbf{U})$, in accordance with *the rules for constructing a network model* [33], *the problem of network modeling* [33] is solved—the formation of *an optimal network model* $\boldsymbol{WM}^{(e)} = WM_{i^{(e)}} \in \boldsymbol{WM} = \{WM_i\}_{i \in \overline{1,\beta}}$ corresponding to it for the considered MP of the DIES (where $\beta \in \mathbf{N}$; $\forall i \in \overline{1,\beta}: WM_i$ is an admissible network model corresponding to the optimal technology $\boldsymbol{TP}^{(e)}$).

15. For the formed network model $\boldsymbol{WM}^{(e)} = WM_{i^{(e)}}\left(i^{(e)} \in \overline{1,\beta}\right)$, based on the found *critical path,* which determines *the optimal (critical) time period for the implementation of the* MP of the DIES, and data from the matrix $\boldsymbol{B}^{(e)}_{k^{(e)}} = b_{jm}^{\left(ek^{(e)}\right)}{}_{\substack{j \in \overline{1,m_{k^{(e)}}} \\ m \in \overline{1,3}}}$, the problem of *calendar planning* [33] is solved—the formation of *an optimal calendar schedule* [33] $\boldsymbol{TG}^{(e)} = TG_{k^{(e)}} \in \boldsymbol{TG} = \{\boldsymbol{TG}_k\}_{k \in \overline{1,r}}$—a description of the deadlines for the execution of all optimal APs $\boldsymbol{R}(\boldsymbol{TP}^{(e)}) = \{R_1(\boldsymbol{TP}^{(e)}), R_2(\boldsymbol{TP}^{(e)}), \ldots, R_s(\boldsymbol{TP}^{(e)})\}$ of the DIES that form the network model $\boldsymbol{WM}^{(e)}$, in the form of *a Gantt chart (diagram)* [33] or in the form of a corresponding *data table* (where $s \in \mathbf{N}: s \geq n; \forall k \in \overline{1,r}: \boldsymbol{TG}_k$ is the calendar schedule corresponding to the implementation of the k-th admissible technology $TP_k \in \mathbf{TP}(\mathbf{U})$).
16. Based on the generated optimal set of APs $\boldsymbol{R}(\boldsymbol{TP}^{(e)}) = \{R_1(\boldsymbol{TP}^{(e)}), R_2(\boldsymbol{TP}^{(e)}), \ldots, R_s(\boldsymbol{TP}^{(e)})\}$ of the DIES ($s \in \mathbf{N}: s \geq n$) and the available data on the capabilities of the APEs included in the DIES, Agent P forms a team consisting of $n^{(e)}$ Objects I and II$_j$, controlled respectively by Agents P and E_j, $j \in J \subseteq \overline{1,n}$, which *has the capabilities and resources to fully implement this set of* APs of the DIES *within the specified time periods determined by the generated calendar schedule* $\boldsymbol{TG}^{(e)}$.
17. Let the set of APs $\tilde{\boldsymbol{R}}\left(\boldsymbol{TP}^{(e)}\right) = \left\{\tilde{R}_1\left(\boldsymbol{TP}^{(e)}\right), \tilde{R}_2\left(\boldsymbol{TP}^{(e)}\right), \ldots, \tilde{R}_{\tilde{s}}\left(\boldsymbol{TP}^{(e)}\right)\right\} \subseteq$ $\subseteq \boldsymbol{R}(\boldsymbol{TP}^{(e)})$ of the DIES consist only of those APs, defined by $\boldsymbol{R}(\boldsymbol{TP}^{(e)})$, *which can be implemented by the* MPE, i.e. by Object I, in specified time periods determined by the generated calendar schedule $\boldsymbol{TG}^{(e)}$.
18. Agent P generates a calendar schedule $\tilde{\boldsymbol{T}}\tilde{\boldsymbol{G}}^{(e)}$ corresponding to the optimal set of APs $\tilde{\boldsymbol{R}}\left(\boldsymbol{TP}^{(e)}\right) = \left\{\tilde{R}_1\left(\boldsymbol{TP}^{(e)}\right), \tilde{R}_2\left(\boldsymbol{TP}^{(e)}\right), \ldots, \tilde{R}_{\tilde{s}}\left(\boldsymbol{TP}^{(e)}\right)\right\}$ of the DIES, which is described by the data set $\tilde{\boldsymbol{T}}\tilde{\boldsymbol{G}}^{(e)} = \left\{\tilde{\boldsymbol{T}}\tilde{\boldsymbol{B}}_j^{(e)}, \tilde{\boldsymbol{T}}\tilde{\boldsymbol{E}}_j^{(e)}\right\}_{j \in \overline{1,\tilde{s}}}$, where $\tilde{\boldsymbol{T}}\tilde{\boldsymbol{B}}_j^{(e)}$ is the earliest acceptable deadline, and $\tilde{\boldsymbol{T}}\tilde{\boldsymbol{E}}_j^{(e)}$ is the latest acceptable deadline for the execution of the j-th AP $\tilde{R}_j\left(\boldsymbol{TP}^{(e)}\right)$.
19. Based on the calendar schedule $\tilde{\boldsymbol{T}}\tilde{\boldsymbol{G}}^{(e)}$ for the APs of the DIES from the set $\tilde{\boldsymbol{R}}\left(\boldsymbol{TP}^{(e)}\right)$, Agent P forms a set of corresponding network models $\left\{\tilde{\boldsymbol{W}}\tilde{\boldsymbol{M}}_j^{(e)}\right\}_{j \in \overline{1,\tilde{s}}}$

for execution in the specified optimal timeframes $\left\{\tilde{T}\tilde{B}_j^{(e)}, \tilde{T}\tilde{E}_j^{(e)}\right\}_{j\in\overline{1,\tilde{s}}}$ of the APs $\tilde{R}_j\left(\boldsymbol{TP}^{(e)}\right)$, $j \in \overline{1,\tilde{s}}$, prescribed to him.

20. Agent P, based on a set of network models $\left\{\tilde{W}\tilde{M}_j^{(e)}\right\}_{j\in\overline{1,\tilde{s}}}$ and the corresponding prescribed deadlines $\left\{\tilde{T}\tilde{B}_j^{(e)}, \tilde{T}\tilde{E}_j^{(e)}\right\}_{j\in\overline{1,\tilde{s}}}$ for the execution of each AP $\tilde{R}_j\left(\boldsymbol{TP}^{(e)}\right)$ of the DIES, $j \in \overline{1,\tilde{s}}$, based on the found critical path and data from the matrix $\tilde{\boldsymbol{B}}_{k^{(e)}}^{(e)} = \tilde{b}_{jm}^{\left(ek^{(e)}\right)}{}_{\substack{j\in\overline{1,m_{k^{(e)}}}\\ m\in\overline{1,3}}}$ corresponding to the AP $\tilde{R}_j\left(\boldsymbol{TP}^{(e)}\right)$, solves the problem of scheduling—the formation of an optimal (critical) time period $\tilde{\boldsymbol{T}}_j^{(e)}$ for the execution of the j-th AP $\tilde{R}_j\left(\boldsymbol{TP}^{(e)}\right)$, and optimal schedule $\tilde{T}\tilde{G}_j^{(e)}$—a description of the deadlines for the execution of all operations included in this AP and forming the network model $\tilde{W}\tilde{M}_j^{(e)}$, in the form of a Gantt chart (diagram) or in the form of a corresponding data table.

Note that the implementation of all APs $\tilde{R}_j\left(\boldsymbol{TP}^{(e)}\right)$ of the DIES, $j \in \overline{1,\tilde{s}}$, controlled by Agent P, is carried out in the optimal time $\boldsymbol{T}^{(e)}$.

21. Let the set of APs $\bar{\boldsymbol{R}}\left(\boldsymbol{TP}^{(e)}\right) = \left\{\bar{R}_1\left(\boldsymbol{TP}^{(e)}\right), \bar{R}_2\left(\boldsymbol{TP}^{(e)}\right), \ldots, \bar{R}_{\bar{s}}\left(\boldsymbol{TP}^{(e)}\right)\right\} \subseteq \boldsymbol{R}(\boldsymbol{TP}^{(e)})$ of the DIES consist only of those APs of the DIES, defined by $\boldsymbol{R}(\boldsymbol{TP}^{(e)})$, which cannot be realized by the MPE, i.e. by Object I, and therefore it is true: $\boldsymbol{R}\left(\boldsymbol{TP}^{(e)}\right) = \tilde{\boldsymbol{R}}\left(\boldsymbol{TP}^{(e)}\right) \cup \bar{\boldsymbol{R}}\left(\boldsymbol{TP}^{(e)}\right)$; $s = \tilde{s} + \bar{s}$. It is assumed that each j-th Object II_j ($j \in J$), realizes the set of APs $\left\{\bar{R}_k\left(\boldsymbol{TP}^{(e)}\right)\right\}_{k\in K_j}$ of the DIES $\left(K_j \subseteq \overline{1,\bar{s}}, \bigcup_{j=1}^{J} K_j = \overline{1,\bar{s}}\right)$ under the control of the j-th Agent E_j ($j \in J$) subordinate to Agent P, and *has the ability and resources to fully realize them within in specified time periods determined by the generated calendar schedule* $\boldsymbol{TG}^{(e)}$.
22. Agent P forms a calendar schedule corresponding to the optimal set of APs $\bar{\boldsymbol{R}}\left(\boldsymbol{TP}^{(e)}\right) = \left\{\bar{R}_1\left(\boldsymbol{TP}^{(e)}\right), \bar{R}_2\left(\boldsymbol{TP}^{(e)}\right), \ldots, \bar{R}_{\bar{s}}\left(\boldsymbol{TP}^{(e)}\right)\right\}$ of the DIES, which is described by the data set $\bar{T}\bar{G}^{(e)} = \left\{\bar{T}\bar{B}_j^{(e)}, \bar{T}\bar{E}_j^{(e)}\right\}_{j\in\overline{1,\bar{s}}}$, where $\bar{T}\bar{B}_j^{(e)}$ is the earliest acceptable deadline, and $\bar{T}\bar{E}_j^{(e)}$ is the latest acceptable deadline for the execution of the j-th AP $\bar{R}_j\left(\boldsymbol{TP}^{(e)}\right)$ of the DIES, $j \in \overline{1,\bar{s}}$.
23. Based on the calendar schedule $\bar{T}\bar{G}^{(e)}$, each Agent E_j, $j \in J$, forms a set of corresponding optimal network models $\left\{\bar{W}\bar{M}_k^{(e)}\right\}_{k\in K_j}$ for execution within the optimal timeframes $\left\{\bar{T}\bar{B}_k^{(e)}, \bar{T}\bar{E}_k^{(e)}\right\}_{k\in K_j}$ specified by Agent P for the execution of the APs $\bar{R}_k\left(\boldsymbol{TP}^{(e)}\right)$ of the DIES, $k \in K_j$, prescribed to him.

24. Each Agent $E_j, j \in J$, based on a set of network models $\left\{\overline{\overline{\boldsymbol{WM}}}_k^{(e)}\right\}_{k \in K_j}$ and the corresponding specified deadlines $\left\{\overline{\boldsymbol{TB}}_k^{(e)}, \overline{\boldsymbol{TE}}_k^{(e)}\right\}_{k \in K_j}$ for the execution of the AP $\overline{R}_k\left(\boldsymbol{TP}^{(e)}\right)$ of the DIES, $k \in K_j$, based on the found critical path and data from the matrices $\overline{\boldsymbol{B}}_{k^{(e)}}^{(e)} = \overline{b}_{j \in \overline{1, m_{k^{(e)}}}, m \in \overline{1,3}}^{\left(ek^{(e)}\right)}$ corresponding to the AP $\overline{R}_k\left(\boldsymbol{TP}^{(e)}\right)$ of the DIES, solves the problem of scheduling—the formation of the optimal (critical) time period $\overline{\boldsymbol{T}}_k^{(e)}$ for the execution of the k-th AP, the optimal calendar schedule $\overline{\boldsymbol{T}}\overline{\boldsymbol{G}}_k^{(e)}$—a description of the deadlines for the execution of all operations included in this AP and forming the network model $\overline{\overline{\boldsymbol{WM}}}_k^{(e)}$, in the form of a Gantt chart (diagram) or in the form of a corresponding data table.

Note that the implementation of all AP $\overline{R}_k\left(\boldsymbol{TP}^{(e)}\right)$ of the DIES, $k \in K_j$, controlled by Agents $E_j, j \in J$, is carried out in the optimal time period $\boldsymbol{T}^{(e)}$ prescribed by Agent P.

25. Agent P generates the obtained optimal results for control level I in the form of data tuples: $\{\boldsymbol{TP}^{(e)}, \boldsymbol{R}(\boldsymbol{TP}^{(e)}), \boldsymbol{WM}^{(e)}, \boldsymbol{TG}^{(e)}, \boldsymbol{T}^{(e)}\}$, $\left\{\tilde{\boldsymbol{T}}\tilde{\boldsymbol{P}}^{(e)}, \tilde{\boldsymbol{R}}\left(\boldsymbol{TP}^{(e)}\right), \tilde{\boldsymbol{W}}\tilde{\boldsymbol{M}}^{(e)}, \tilde{\boldsymbol{T}}\tilde{\boldsymbol{G}}^{(e)}, \tilde{\boldsymbol{T}}^{(e)}\right\}$ and $\left\{\overline{R}_k\left(\boldsymbol{TP}^{(e)}\right), \boldsymbol{WM}_k^{(e)}, \overline{\boldsymbol{T}}\overline{\boldsymbol{G}}_k^{(e)}, \overline{\boldsymbol{T}}_k^{(e)}\right\}_{k \in K_j}$, $j \in J$.
26. Agents $E_j, j \in J$, generate the obtained optimal results for control level II in the form of a set of data tuples $\left\{\overline{R}_k\left(\boldsymbol{TP}^{(e)}\right), \boldsymbol{WM}_k^{(e)}, \overline{\boldsymbol{T}}\overline{\boldsymbol{G}}_k^{(e)}, \overline{\boldsymbol{T}}_k^{(e)}\right\}_{k \in K_j}, j \in J$.
27. The obtained results are displayed in a form convenient for use by Agents P, and $E_j, j \in J$.

Taking into account the description of the proposed new method of optimal management of the implementation of the MP of the DIES in the form of a two-level multi-agent hierarchical network economic-mathematical model, taking into account the presence of several technologies for the implementation of the MP of the DIES and corresponding vector objective functions for assessing of their quality, it can be shown that the following statement is true.

Statement 1 Let the time interval $\overline{0, T}$, and the tuple $\mathbf{U} = \{U_1, U_2, \ldots, U_l\}$ describing the initial data, constraints, admissible technological solutions in the form of an array of technologies $\mathbf{TP}(\mathbf{U}) = \{TP_1, TP_2, \ldots, TP_r\}$, parameters of the set of vector objective functions $\boldsymbol{F}_k = \left\{F_1^{(k)}, F_2^{(k)}, \ldots, F_\tau^{(k)}\right\}$, $k \in \overline{1, r}$, and a final results necessary for the implementation of the MP of the DIES be given. Then, from the description of the proposed methodology and the results of the works [1, 4–6], it follows that the formation of optimal results by Agents P and $E_j, j \in J$, for control levels I and II, in the form of data tuples $\{\boldsymbol{TP}^{(e)}, \boldsymbol{R}(\boldsymbol{TP}^{(e)}), \boldsymbol{WM}^{(e)}, \boldsymbol{TG}^{(e)}, \boldsymbol{T}^{(e)}\}$, $\left\{\tilde{\boldsymbol{T}}\tilde{\boldsymbol{P}}^{(e)}, \tilde{\boldsymbol{R}}\left(\boldsymbol{TP}^{(e)}\right), \tilde{\boldsymbol{W}}\tilde{\boldsymbol{M}}^{(e)}, \tilde{\boldsymbol{T}}\tilde{\boldsymbol{G}}^{(e)}, \tilde{\boldsymbol{T}}^{(e)}\right\}$, and $\left\{\overline{R}_k\left(\boldsymbol{TP}^{(e)}\right), \boldsymbol{WM}_k^{(e)}, \overline{\boldsymbol{T}}\overline{\boldsymbol{G}}_k^{(e)}, \overline{\boldsymbol{T}}_k^{(e)}\right\}_{k \in K_j}$,

$j \in J$, is *carried out by implementing a finite set of operations that allow their algorithmization.*

The proposed method for solving the problem under consideration is based on the results presented in [1, 4–6] and the developed methodology for finding a solution to the problem under consideration is implemented in the form of a finite sequence of one-step operations that allow their algorithmization. The results obtained can serve as a basis for developing methods for optimizing the management of the implementation of the MP of the DIES using feedback, as well as for solving practical problems within the framework of specific DIES.

It should be noted that, based on the proposed methodology for solving the considered problem of optimizing the implementation of the MP of the DIES in the presence of several acceptable technologies for its implementation and corresponding vector objective functions for assessing of their quality, it is possible to develop numerical algorithms for creating computer applications that allow implementing support for decision-making by managers of manufacturing enterprises.

5 Discussion

It should be noted that in the scientific literature there are no works that propose deterministic economic and mathematical models for the implementation of projects within the framework of the DIES that take into account the interests of all agents who participate in their implementation. The results presented in this article fill this gap and can serve as a basis for further research in this direction. As a tool for the proposed formalization of the initial problem, the paper uses the apparatus of network economic and mathematical modeling, which is the most adequate to the real processes of implementing projects in the DIES.

In this paper, the proposed economic and mathematical model for solving the problem under study of implementing the MP of the DIES in the presence of several acceptable technologies for its implementation and the corresponding vector objective function for assessing the quality of the process under consideration *is deterministic*. Based on this model, the article describes a *constructive method* for solving it, which can serve as a basis for developing a numerical algorithm and creating a corresponding computer application. The creation of such a computer application will automate the decision-making process when implementing projects within specific DIES. In subsequent works, it is planned to specify the proposed economic and mathematical model for specific types of industrial activity within the framework of the DIES and present the results of computer modeling using meaningful examples.

6 Conclusions

The article studies the problem of optimization of the implementation of the DIES project in the presence of several admissible technologies for its implementation and corresponding vector objective functions for assessing of their quality. For a formalized description of the optimization of the management of the DIES project, a new formalization is proposed in the form of a two-level multi-agent hierarchical network economic-mathematical model in the presence of several technologies for its implementation and corresponding vector objective function for assessing of their quality. The paper describes a new method for solving the problem under consideration in the form of a constructive methodology, which is implemented in the form of one-step operations that allow their algorithmization.

The results obtained in the article are based on the studies [1, 4–6] and the article is adjacent to the studies, are adjacent to the results of works [2, 3, 7–26] and can be used for computer modeling of the implementation of the projects of the DIES and the creation of multi-level intelligent process control systems in economic and technical multi-parameter systems operating in the presence of risks and information uncertainty. Mathematical models of such systems are presented, for example, in works [1, 4–6, 11, 12, 16, 19, 23, 24, 28, 33, 36–38, 40].

Acknowledgments The article was prepared in accordance with the state assignment for the Institute of Economics of the Ural Branch of the Russian Academy of Sciences for 2023–2025.

References

1. Akberdina, V. V., & Shorikov, A. F. (2022). Hierarchical agent-based model of industrial complex management. *Manager, 13*(6), 2–14. https://doi.org/10.29141/2218-5003-2022-13-6-1
2. Makarov, V. L., Bakhtizin, A. R., Beklaryan, G. L., & Akopov, A. S. (2021). Digital plant: Methods of discrete-event modeling and optimization of production characteristics. *Business Informatics, 15*(2), 7–20. https://doi.org/10.17323/2587-814X.2021.2.7.20
3. Makarov, V. L., Bakhtizin, A. R., & Sushko, E. D. (2017). Regulation of industrial emissions based on an agent-based approach. *Economic and Social Changes: Facts, Trends, Forecast, 6*(54), 42–58. https://doi.org/10.15838/esc.2017.6.54.3
4. Shorikov, A. F. (2006). Methodology of modeling multilevel systems: Hierarchy and dynamics. *Journal of Applied Informatics, 1*(1), 136–141.
5. Shorikov, A. F., & Butsenko, E. V. (2015). Construction of a network economic-mathematical model for the implementation of the investment design optimization process. *Journal of Applied Informatics, 10*(2), 80–91.
6. Shorikov, A. F., & Butsenko, E. V. (2017). *Forecasting and optimization of investment design management results*. URSS–LENAND.
7. Adner, R. (2017). Ecosystem as structure: An actionable construct for strategy. *Journal of Management, 43*(1), 39–58. https://doi.org/10.1177/0149206316678451
8. Akberdina, V. V., & Romanova, O. A. (2021). Regional aspects of industrial development: A review of approaches to the formation of priorities and regulatory mechanisms. *Economy of Regions, 17*(3), 714–736. https://doi.org/10.17059/ekon.reg.2021-3-1

9. Asen, R., & Blechschmidt, B. (2016). Making digital real and rewarding. *Cognizanti, 9*(1), 2–13.
10. Barbati, M., Bruno, G., & Genovese, A. (2012). Applications of agent-based models for optimization problems: A literature review. *Expert Systems with Applications, 39*(5), 6020–6028. https://doi.org/10.1016/j.eswa.2011.12.015
11. Bryde, D. J. (1995). Establishing a project organization and a project management process for telecommunications project management. *International Journal of Project Management, 13*(1), 25–31. https://doi.org/10.1016/0263-7863(95)95700-N
12. Cleland, D. L., & Ireland, L. R. (2006). *Project management* (5th ed.). McGraw-Hill Professional.
13. Cheng, W., & Xiao-Bing, L. (2013). Integrated production planning and control: A multi-objective optimization model. *Journal of Industrial Engineering and Management, 6*(4), 815–830. https://doi.org/10.3926/jiem.771
14. Gamidullaeva, L., Shmeleva, N., Tolstykh, T., & Shmatko, A. (2022). An assessment approach to circular business models within an industrial ecosystem for sustainable territorial development. *Sustainability, 14*, 704. https://doi.org/10.3390/su14020704
15. Kalenov, O. E. (2022). Digital ecosystems of organizations. *Vestnik of the Plekhanov Russian University of Economics, 19*(1), 139–147. https://doi.org/10.21686/2413-2829-2022-1-139-147
16. Kantorovich, L. V., & Gorstko, A. B. (1972). *Optimal solutions in economics*. Nauka.
17. Khomenko, E. B. (2021). Infrastructure of entrepreneurship in the context of digital transformation. *Science and Business: Development Paths, 4*(118), 191–194.
18. Lenfle, S. (2008). Exploration and project management. *International Journal of Project Management, 26*(5), 469–478. https://doi.org/10.1016/j.ijproman.2008.05.017
19. Makarov, V. L. (2009). Review of mathematical models of economy with innovations. *Economy and Mathematical Methods, 45*(1), 3–14.
20. Margineanu, C., & Lixandroiu, D. (2021). Optimization of industrial management processes. *IOP Conference Series: Materials Science and Engineering, 1009*, 012039. https://doi.org/10.1088/1757-899X/1009/1/012039
21. Novikova, T. S., & Tsyplakov, A. A. (2020). Social policy in a multi-industry agent-oriented model. *Economic and Social Changes: Facts, Trends, Forecast, 13*(3), 129–142. https://doi.org/10.15838/esc.2020.3.69.9
22. Peltoniemi, M. (2006). Preliminary theoretical framework for the study of business ecosystems. *Emergence: Complexity and Organization, 8*(1), 10–19.
23. Tonnquist, B. (2016). *Project management*. Sanoma Utbildning.
24. Walker, A. (2015). *Project management in construction* (6th ed.). John Wiley & Sons.
25. Windrum, P., Fagiolo, G., & Moneta, A. (2007). Empirical validation of agent-based models: Alternatives and prospects. *Journal of Artificial Societies and Social Simulation, 10*(2), 8. https://doi.org/10.1017/9781108227278.009
26. Wooldridge, M., & Jennings, N. (1995). Intelligent agents: Theory and practice. *Knowledge Engineering Review, 10*(2), 115–152. https://doi.org/10.1017/S0269888900008122
27. Akberdina, V. V., & Vasilenko, E. V. (2021). Innovation ecosystem: Review of the research field. *Russian Journal of Economic Theory, 18*(3), 462–473. https://doi.org/10.31063/2073-6517/2021.18-3.10
28. Pollack, J. (2007). The changing paradigms of project management. *International Journal of Project Management, 25*(3), 266–274. https://doi.org/10.1016/j.ijproman.2006.08.002
29. Zhang, C., & Chen, Y. (2020). A review of research relevant to the emerging industry trends: Industry 4.0, internet of things, blockchain, and business analytics. *Journal of Industrial Integration and Management, 5*(1), 165–180. https://doi.org/10.1142/S2424862219500192
30. Beerepoot, N., & Lambregts, B. (2015). Competition in online job marketplaces: Towards a global labour market for outsourcing services? *Global Networks, 15*(2), 236–255. https://doi.org/10.1111/glob.12051

31. Kusiak, A. (2018). Smart manufacturing. *International Journal of Production Research, 56*(1–2), 508–517. https://doi.org/10.1080/00207543.2017.1351644
32. Madejski, J. (2007). Survey of the agent-based approach to intelligent manufacturing. *Journal Of Achievements In Materials and Manufacturing Engineering, 21*(1), 67–70.
33. Taha, H. A. (2007). *Introduction to operations research*. Williams Publishing House.
34. Aksyonov, K., Bykov, E., Aksyonova, O., Goncharova, N., & Nevolina, A. (2017). Multi-agent simulation of the resource conversion processes with the sample application to the logistical problem. In *UKSim-AMSS 11th European Symposium on Mathematical Modelling and Computer Simulation* (pp. 177–181). IEEE. https://doi.org/10.1109/EMS.2017.39
35. Billari, F. G., Fent, T., Prskawetz, A., & Scheffran, J. (2006). *Agent-based computational modelling: Applications in demography, social, economic and environmental sciences (contributions to economics)*. Physica-Verlag. https://doi.org/10.1007/3-7908-1721-X
36. Emelyanov, A. A., Vlasova, E. A., & Duma, R. V. (2014). *Simulation modeling of economic processes*. Finance and Statistics.
37. Kleiner, G. B., & Rybachuk, M. A. (2017). *Systemic balance of the economy*. Scientific Library.
38. Lotov, A. V. (1984). *Introduction to economic and mathematical modeling*. Nauka.
39. Pervozvansky, A. A. (1975). *Mathematical models in production management*. Nauka.
40. Ter-Krikorov, A. M. (1977). *Optimal control and mathematical economics*. Nauka.

Reference Architecture to Exploit Data as a Product Through the Cloud-Edge Continuum

Nima Rahmani Choubeh, Walter Quadrini, Danish Abbas Syed, Riccardo Zanetti, Angelo Marguglio, and Luca Fumagalli

Abstract The Internet of Things (IoT) computational power and storage requirements are constantly increasing, implying a subsequent rise in the amount of data created by devices at the edge of the network. While cloud computing has been a well-established method of purchasing services for many applications, it may not be enough to handle the amount of data from IoT devices while simultaneously addressing the heterogeneous application needs. The Cloud-Edge-IoT (CEI) continuum, where sensor networks and data coexist with cloud and edge resources, appears then to be a suitable solution to address future data-intensive applications. CEI continuum employs edge computing, cloud computing, and the IoT to boost the Industrial IoT (IIoT) development. However, the distributed nature requirements of digital manufacturing present difficulties for typical cloud-centric techniques: to address some of these issues, an analysis of current Reference Architectures (RAs) has been performed. Consequently, the opportunity for a new RA has been discussed, leading to include capabilities supposed to mitigate some CEI continuum issues, among which the concept of "Data as a Product", supported by specific Data Container. In addition, it has been noticed how Federated Learning services can improve privacy and security issues, as well as computing effort of the CEI.

Keywords Cloud-edge-IoT · Reference architecture · Interoperability

N. Rahmani Choubeh (✉) · W. Quadrini · D. A. Syed · L. Fumagalli
Politecnico di Milano, Milan, Italy
e-mail: nima.rahmani@polimi.it; walter.quadrini@polimi.it; danishabbas.syed@polimi.it; luca1.fumagalli@polimi.it

R. Zanetti · A. Marguglio
Engineering Ingegneria Informatica SpA, Palermo, Italy
e-mail: riccardo.zanetti@eng.it; angelo.marguglio@eng.it

F. Tao et al. (eds.), *Artificial Intelligence and Digital Transformation*, Lecture Notes in Information Systems and Organisation 78,
https://doi.org/10.1007/978-3-032-00118-4_11

1 Introduction

Modern Cyber-Physical Production Systems (CPPSs) are based on composition of systems and components from different suppliers that need to exchange data and integrate services seamlessly at run time [1]. Big data enables industrial firms and organizations to interact and generate new value from data [2]. The IoT allows interconnected industrial devices to sense and control processes, generate data, and interact with each other [3]. Capturing, processing, and analysing large amounts of data from these devices can help companies managing resources, optimizing operations, understanding market demand, and developing business intelligence and analytics [4]. As this strategy is being pursued, mobility support, geo-distribution, as well as location awareness and low-latency have all become requirements that the resource infrastructure should support [5]. Recent advancements in end devices and edge computing have resulted in a new paradigm known as the Cloud-Edge-IoT (CEI) continuum [6]. Fog computing, combined with traditional cloud computing, offers an inherently distributed infrastructure—referred to as the cloud-to-edge continuum—that can be used for the execution of low-latency and location-aware the IoT services [5]. Data processing can happen primarily at the edge, while the cloud would only be accessed when the edge resources do not suffice. Fog computing builds on this idea and extends it by combining and using the different layers of compute, storage and network resources distributed across the edge and the cloud, which are commonly referred to as the cloud-to-edge continuum [7]. This approach has been enabled mainly by economic factors, such as the spread of cloud computing business realities offering computational services with fees lower than the traditional server hosting, and by the increase of Application to Program Interfaces (APIs) disseminated at the different software modules composing these solutions [8]. In addition, the savings on these fees implied by the on-premises allocation of some of these computations led the practitioners' community to investigate software architecture aimed at localizing, as most as possible, the required operations, leaving on the cloud the ones strictly needing the cloud-related requirements (such as the data input from different sources, e.g., the so-called "federated learning"). This approach, furtherly fostered by the technological evolution of the CPPSs and of the so-called edge nodes (computational units located on the field) allows to instantiate control and monitoring loops closer to the process under control, decreasing the time constants while preserving the data analytics-related features enabled by the cloud computing.

From a functional point of view, these architectures include multiple layers of computing and data processing, reflecting the evolving dynamics of data generation, processing, and analysis, with each layer having specialized functions and requirements [6]. Cloud computing is at one end of the continuum and often represents centralized servers, providing vast scalability, storage capacity, and processing power. Proceeding towards the middle, where edge computing comes into play, data is processed closer to its source, which is typically constituted by computing devices that are operating at the edge of the network, to lower latency, improve real-time processing, and increase application responsiveness. The Industrial Internet of things (IIoT) can be seen at the far end, where an endless number of linked devices produces and sends data to cloud servers and to the edge [6]. The IIoT systems leverage on edge computing to preprocess and filter data before sending them to the cloud for further analysis. The Cloud-Edge-IoT continuum shifts from centralized to hybrid computing, focusing on adaptability and scalability, including latency. Data-driven industrial value networks aim to execute their workflows and business processes as quickly and affordably as possible. Rigid and centralized systems and technologies fail in the face of the size, complexity, distributed nature of data, and need for constant intelligence that digital manufacturing demands. Achieving efficient data analysis is a challenge in the pursuit of data-driven operations [9].

Apart from these considerations, which enable new technical approaches for system integrators and software architects, another business-related aspect implied by this technological evolution sits in the data themselves, which, cleaned and processed at the edge level, immobilize an economic value deriving from the processing invested in these edge-operations regardless of the value deriving by the contained information. This aspect led to the concept of "Data as a Product" (DaaP), which has been proposed as the fundamental concept to help implementing digital continuity across digital threads, data spaces, digital twin workflows, and data pipelines. To maximize the potential of distributed data management solutions implemented to address factory resiliency, the DaaP concept leverages resiliency on top of advanced manufacturing digital processes and value ecosystems supporting the development and implementation of digital continuity enablers (e.g., distributed computing and networking [10], digital thread [11], and digital twins [12]). To satisfy the requirements of this concept, the need for developing reference architectures (software architectures provided as a set of interfaceable logical modules typically accomplishing tasks related to data exploitation) has been identified and elaborated. To address the shortcomings of centralized learning and local training in traditional Cloud-Edge Continuum, this model proposes Federated Learning and Services, resulting in decreased data transfer, furthermore, by introducing specific Data Containers, a unified representation of data has been offered which can reduce the data complexity and interoperability issues while ensuring data privacy and security.

This paper has been structured as follows: the analysis of the state of the art as well as explaining the steps to depict the proposed reference architecture has been discussed in Sect. 2. In addition, innovative toolkits and concepts resulting from the RA have been described. Section 3 introduces the proposed RA Computing/Networking Continuum. Finally, conclusion has been presented in Sect. 4.

2 Proposed Reference Architecture

2.1 Methodology

The proposed model has been developed in different steps: initially, a thorough analysis assesses existing architectures focusing on big data technologies in the manufacturing sector. Then, the analysis of various blueprints revealed the need for a new architecture to bridge the gap between these starting points and the desired objectives. Hence, main motivations and needs for a new reference framework have been examined, leading to a new architectural design. Lastly, considerations about the effectiveness of the new architecture towards the aforementioned objectives have been stated.

Knowledgeable on State of the Art

The investigation that was carried out to look at existing architectures that concentrate on big data technologies and the Industrial Internet of Things among several reference frameworks, focused on five industrial blueprints as per a background on digital infrastructure related to the digitalisation of manufacturing sector.

The Reference Architecture Model for Industrie 4.0 (RAMI 4.0) [13] is the convergence of multiple stakeholder visions on how Industry 4.0 might be realized, based on existing communication standards and functional descriptions [14]. The six layers of the vertical axis of RAMI 4.0 define the nature of IT components in the so-called "Industry 4.0" (I4.0) business applications, functional aspects, information handling, communication and integration capability, and ability of the assets to implement I4.0 features [15].

The Industrial Internet Reference Architecture (IIRA) [16] is a standard-oriented open architecture for Industrial Internet Systems and aims at extending interoperability in industry and guiding the technology standards development [15]. The main IIRA categorization is based on ISO/IEC 42010 [17] standard, introducing the four viewpoints Business, Usage, Functional and Implementation [18].

The International Data Spaces Reference Architecture Model (IDS-RAM) [19] consists of five layers to establish interoperability and three crosscutting perspectives for reaching its main target, namely, to ensure end-to-end data sovereignty of the data owner. The syntactic interoperability is accomplished by the IDS Connectors with their standardized interfaces and exchange protocols [18].

The Big Data Value Reference Model (BDV-RM) [20] organises topics according to one vertical and one horizontal dimension: while the latter forms a data management stack, the former contains aspects and challenges. Interoperability, security, or composition are only mentioned to a limited extend. BDV-RM provides a comprehensive overview of concerns at the intersection of big data and cloud platforms [18]. While the IIoT is one use case among RAMI4.0 and IIRA, BDV-RM specifically distinguishes between static and dynamic data. A comparable view is neither part of RAMI4.0 nor IIRA, even though both discuss the impacts of data streams and stream processing. BDV-RM goes further and analyses current gaps and challenges for dynamic data, formulating a list of necessary advancements [18]. Additionally, a more related framework for the IoT sector has further investigated: the Internet of Things-Architecture (IoT-A) [21] presents an extensive list of requirements on many aspects of the IoT architectures, allowing a categorization of technologies, protocols and best practices according to the defined layers and perspectives. With its focus on achieving interoperability in means of communication and information exchange, the IoT-A serves as major step towards internet-based technical integration of heterogeneous systems [18].

Main Motivations for a New Architecture

Despite efforts in I4.0, standardization issues have not been solved. The challenges are indeed not only related to the requirement for data interoperability, but also for interoperability of system architectures and dynamic compositions in their interplay as well as whole ecosystems [1]. The production domain challenges are emphasized by the immature information and communication technologies available for implementing a seamless, open Cloud-Edge-IoT continuum [1, 7, 22]. After investigation of the state of the art, it became evident that a novel architectural framework needed to be developed to bridge the gap between the existing foundations and the desired objectives and ambitions. This disparity can be argued by the four motivations listed below.

1. Functional requirement of centrally managing dynamic system configurations and decentralized information flows, and authorizations of service compositions into applications [1]. Hence, need to reinforce decentralization on infrastructures, services, and data planes. In the context of federation and distributed systems, there is a recognized necessity to strengthen decentralization across infrastructures, services, and data planes. Decentralization refers to the distribution of control, authority, and decision-making to multiple entities or nodes in a network, rather than relying on a centralized authority: basically, it is a principle that promotes resilience, scalability, and autonomy within a federated environment. Reinforcing decentralization on infrastructures, services, and data planes not only enhances fault tolerance and robustness, but also facilitates interoperability among federated entities, e.g., exchanging data as a valuable product.
2. Functional requirement of (pre)processing data and executing advanced data analytics functions on the edge and/or in the cloud, balancing and optimizing where computation is taking place [1]. Therefore, introducing Digital Continuity for computing, networking, and deployment for an exploitation of the digital thread, regardless of where data and applications are. It involves the seamless integration of digital technologies, systems, and data across different stages, such as design, manufacturing, distribution, and maintenance, to ensure the reliable and efficient flow of information, knowledge, and resources [23].

3. Need of exchanging IoT data and other data streams from various sensors and systems in a unified and standardized format, supporting rerouting to different consumers, e.g., AI [1]. The DaaP concept turns data into an asset that can be monetized. Hence, when companies gather and analyse massive amounts of data, they start recognizing the value of this data beyond its immediate application. This value can include insights, predictive analytics models, and data-driven consulting services that they can offer to third parties [18].
4. Ease natural convergence between manufacturing and IT operations by integrating toolkits that cover the entire lifecycle of an industrial data platform, from realization (design and development) to commissioning (integration and validation), and, finally, to operation (management and maintenance) of all software artifacts.

Integration of State of the Art

The reference framework depicted in a previous study [24] has been considered as starting point, as part of its layers and vertical dimensions match the first requirements. In the meanwhile, the proposed RA tries to address shortcomings in existing architectures investigated earlier by considering three elements:

- Decentralized, Scalable Data Processing: RAMI 4.0 and IIRA leverage on a centralized approach, leading to lack of support for distributed computing models across cloud, edge, and IoT layers [25]. In addition, IDS-RAM offers secure data exchange while missing real-time decentralized processing capabilities. The initiated RA in this paper integrates the Cloud-Edge-IoT (CEI) continuum perspective, fostering data processing closer to the edge in comparison to relying on centralized cloud architectures. Furthermore, it exploits Federated Learning (FL), facilitating training of AI models across multiple distributed nodes while maintaining data privacy. Lastly, dynamic system configurations based on computational demand enhance flexibility for resource allocation at edge and cloud making it scalable for data processing tasks.
- Enhanced interoperability: IIRA and IoT-A fail to establish a unified semantic model for data interoperability, making cross-platform data transfer difficult to handle [26]. BDV-RM relies on large data management; however, it does not specify standardized industrial data sharing means. On the other hand, the proposed RA represents Data Containers (DCs) encapsulating manufacturing data into a standardized, self-descriptive container to facilitate sharing, monetization, and interoperability while incorporating Data Connection Profiles (DCPs), which lead to context-aware data integration without custom development, reducing complexity in multi-vendor environments and finally aligning with the Digital Factory Alliance (DFA) model, ensuring compliance with European digital industry standards.
- Integration of Cognitive Digital Twins, and Federated Learning for real-time decision-making: RAMI 4.0 and IIRA do not include real-time AI-based

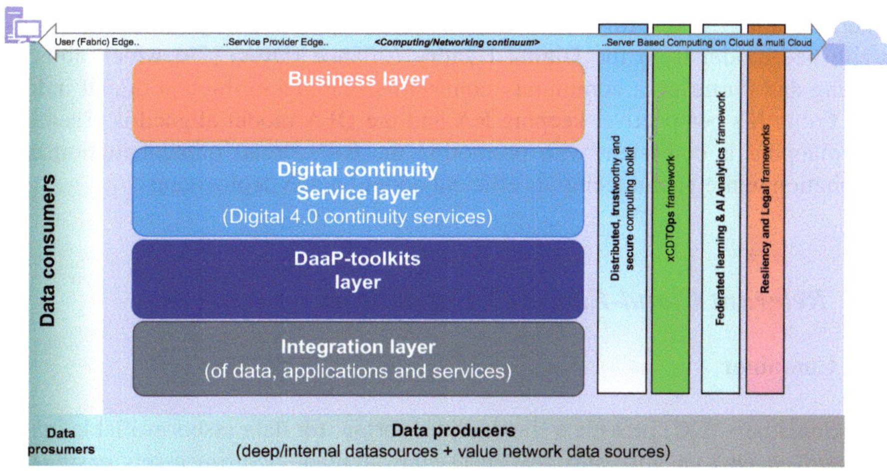

Fig. 1 Reference architecture

decision-making frameworks [27] while IDS-RAM does not support AI-driven federated analytics to offer decision-making at the edge. The proposed RA instead uses Federated Learning Services to train AI models. Additionally, it incorporates Cognitive Digital Twins activating real-time monitoring and closed-loop control of industrial assets while by AI at the edge paves the way for low-latency decision-making reducing network dependency on cloud processing.

Reference Architecture Design

This phase encompasses the design process of the architecture (Fig. 1) which is made up of four layers and as many vertical dimensions, with a double-headed arrow indicating the significance of Digital Continuum in computing and networking. This provides a seamless use of the digital thread, regardless of the location of data and applications. All these dimensions work to establish a model creating a shared and sovereign data space, represented by the purple area encompassing these dimensions. The primary participants engaged in this model are the data consumers and producers. Every layer consists of building blocks that represent the provided functionality.

Exploitability for DaaP

DaaP is a read-optimized, standardized, autonomous data unit including at least one dataset that has been designed to fulfil customer needs. Data should be adequately constructed and maintained in order to assure the value it creates for its users. It also needs to meet certain requirements, such as being discoverable, secure, exploitable, understandable, trustworthy, etc. [28]. The RA has been aligned with a well-established model from the Digital Factory Alliance (DFA) [29] which aims at building and nurturing a community connecting manufacturing and digital industries. From this perspective, keeping RA and the DFA model aligned is essential. This mapping is consistent with promoting the RA's broad implementation and exploitation while guaranteeing its efficient adoption and deployment.

2.2 *Relevant Cloud-Edge-IoT Capabilities*

Data Container

Data Containers (DC) provide a standardized format for data assets available in the marketplace. DCs encapsulate data generated from manufacturing assets, easing the data management and exchange. Specific use cases needs are implemented by Data Connection Profiles (DCPs), which enable simple and context-sensitive integration between complex systems without any custom development. Thus, the marketplace enables users to discover and use data assets, ensuring seamless integration and accessibility of data. Data virtualization is one of the key data integration techniques used in digital thread management: it provides access to information via a virtualized service layer, offering a unified data view from the different sources, and defining a unified way for data access from heterogeneous sources. The introduced DCs provide access to the data following the DaaP approach while creating an abstraction layer that hides the underlying complexity from the users. DCs allow applications to access data in a trusted way, regardless of the location (edge or cloud). The DC (Fig. 2) provides data according to the consumer's requirements in terms of format and quality, including considerations about security, privacy, and performance. A DC has the following functionalities [30]:

- Enable access to the data following the DaaP principles.
- Provision of the needed metadata to ease the data usage by the upper layers and applications, as well as the implementation of the DaaP features.
- Analytics and metadata extraction, which could vary from basic ones to more complex ones.
- Data transformation to a format suitable for the data recipient.
- Composition of processing techniques in pipelines to adapt data to the consumer's requirements.

A DC is composed of the following modules:

- REST API providing data access.
- Data Transformation module converting data to the requested format.
- Data Processing module feeding the lower components. This module may perform additional tasks based on the request, such as querying, parsing and filtering.

DC's objectives aim to:

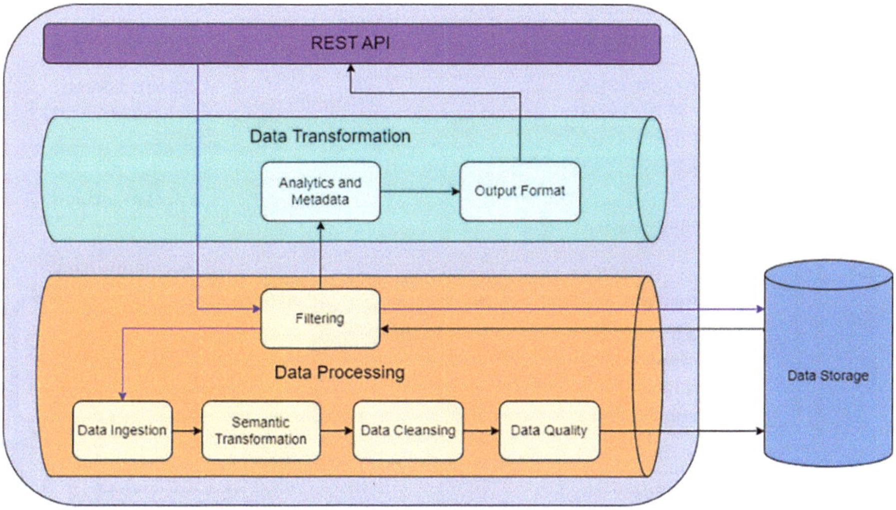

Fig. 2 Data container submodules

- Process datasets (for analytics and metadata extraction).
- Transform data into a more suitable format.
- Apply data filtering to extract required information.
- Integrate with other blocks of the RA to provide data following the DaaP approach regardless of the location (Edge or Cloud) of the data.

Federated Learning Services

One of the key technologies in the IIoT, Machine Learning (ML), exposes privacy and overhead issues in CEI. The amount of data created by various IoT devices has increased exponentially. Despite the features of the ML-based models [31], they are raising significant concerns related to user privacy and heterogeneity [32]. Several regulatory policies highlight the need for user data protection. Federated Learning (FL) emerged as a potentially effective method to address these problems: under FL, machines can work together to build a model while retaining local training data [6]. The capability given by FL services to train machine learning models by leveraging on a wide range of datasets by simultaneously offering privacy guarantees, allows to realize eXecutable Cognitive Digital Twins (xCDT). In other words, technologies that can learn, monitor, and forecast the status of a wide range of assets in real time using AI and data acquired from diverse (even geographically remote) sources. The improvement of data privacy and security is a high-value benefit of federated services, as sensitive data are typically contained within the limits of the service that originates them. FL tools and platforms leverage on a well-defined underlying DaaP toolkits layer to enable this approach for data sharing. This layer ensures data quality through specialized cleansing and quality tools that can bring

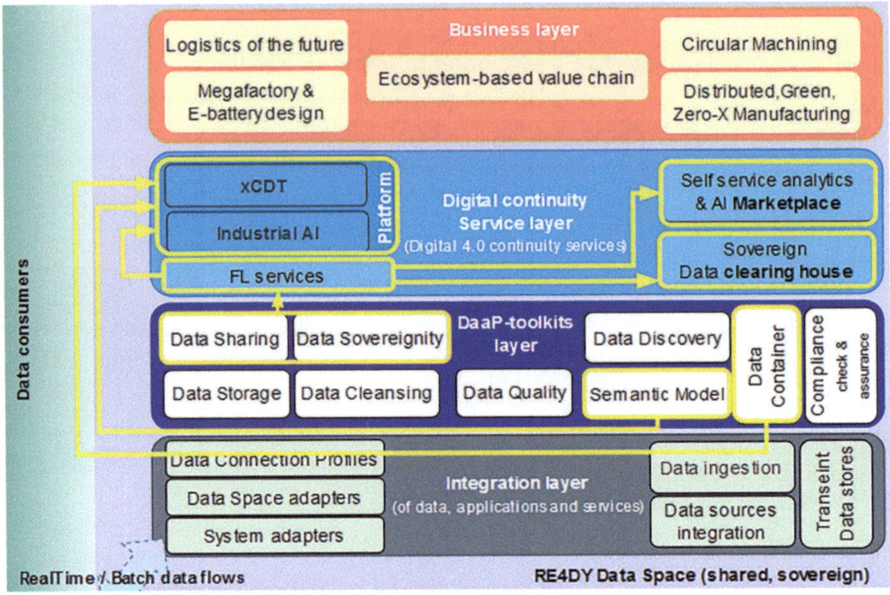

Fig. 3 RA interactions involved in/by FL services

datasets into compliance with pre-established quality standards, as well as the interoperability of datasets and algorithms through DC and semantic models. By using data sovereignty methods in conjunction with clearing house services, data owners retain control over their datasets and the related usage along the whole data pipeline (Fig. 3).

3 RA Computing/Networking Continuum

Fog and edge computing are expected to replace traditional cloud computing for large-scale information processing and knowledge extraction. Despite considerable potential of fog and edge computing, this expectation could be quite naive leading to misinterpreting the interaction of fog, edge, and cloud computing. The computing continuum originates by the adoption of fog and edge computing, which are primarily an extension of cloud services towards the data sources [33]. Consequently, low-latency, privacy-preserving edge computing can be combined with high-performance, scalable infrastructure and high cloud reliability. The computing continuum is composed of up of three fundamental layers: endpoint, edge, and cloud. The endpoint, also known as the Internet of Things layer, includes the devices or things that surround us. They are connected to the edge network as well as to other devices via wired or wireless connections. The edge layer unites edge nodes, which can be any device with computational power. It connects to cloud data centers. The cloud layer consists of large-scale data centers controlled by cloud service providers. A cloud data center is a physical location that stores and processes data employing computing, storage, and networking infrastructure [34].

The networking infrastructure is also critical to achieve the digital continuum, since it enables the interconnection of data sources hosted in the cloud, edge or endpoint systems, and huge networks of intelligent digital twins. Proper planning and commissioning of the network infrastructure is therefore required to ensure performance in terms of capacity and latency, and advance along the digital continuum. Current approaches for the planning and commissioning of factories mostly consider the computing and networking infrastructure as independent to production systems. However, the computing and networking infrastructure must be considered as an additional asset of the factory and, as such, the planning and commissioning of the computing and networking infrastructure must be done jointly with the rest of the factory's assets with the aim of achieving production targets. The Computing/Networking Continuum layer will then include the needed tools and solutions for the joint planning and commissioning of factory and digital twin fabrics with the underlying computing and networking infrastructure which is critical to achieve the digital continuum. One key aspect for the design of these tools and solutions is the integration of the networking infrastructure in the digital twin fabric of the factory. In this context, the Computing/Networking continuum layer of the RA will also contain the Asset Administration Shells (AASs) of the networking infrastructure. The AASs are used to create fully digital versions or digital twins of a factory's asset [35] and it easies the integration of the communication network into a factory management and control system [36], which is key to provide the capacity to support a digital 4.0 continuum efficiently and resiliently.

4 Conclusion

Owing to recent developments in ML and cloud computing, the growth of the IoT has opened up many opportunities for the development of big data applications in recent years. The CEI continuum, where the cloud, edge, network, sensors, and data itself coexist, is essential for these data-intensive applications to operate effectively. The CEI continuum, despite its potential, faces significant challenges, including robustness issues, communication-induced latency, and inconsistent model convergence due to systems and data heterogeneity. However, the distributed nature demands for digital manufacturing pose considerable challenges to conventional cloud-centric approaches. FL addresses these difficulties by distributing ML activities across the CEI continuum, combining Edge and IoT layers directly. Implementing these methodologies in ML processes, including data security and privacy, is a complex and ongoing research topic. To face these challenges, this paper undertook an analysis of existing reference architectures, focusing on big data and the IoT aspects, and identified the need for a new RA capable of addressing the complexities of the CEI continuum. The proposed RA introduces the concept of DaaP, supported by specific DCs, to enhance data management and interoperability within the CEI framework. Furthermore, integrating Federated Learning services within this architecture offers potential solutions to privacy, security, and computational challenges inherent in the CEI continuum. Lastly, the Computing/Networking Continuum of the proposed RA has been described, offering innovative interoperability opportunities offered by AAS.

Acknowledgments This paper is supported by the European Union's HORIZON Research and Innovation Programme under grant agreement No 101058384, project RE4DY (European Data as a PRoduct Value Ecosystems for Resilient Factory 4.0 Product and ProDuction ContinuitY and Sustainability). Views and opinions expressed are, however, those of the authors only and do not necessarily reflect those of the European Union. Neither the European Union nor the granting authority can be held responsible for them.

References

1. Hastbacka, D., Halme, J., Barna, L., Hoikka, H., Pettinen, H., Larranaga, M., Bjorkbom, M., Mesia, H., Jaatinen, A., & Elo, M. (2022). Dynamic edge and cloud service integration for industrial IoT and production monitoring applications of industrial cyber-physical systems. *IEEE Transactions on Industrial Informatics, 18*(1), 498–508. https://doi.org/10.1109/TII.2021.3071509
2. Manyika, J., Chui, M., Brown, B., Bughin, J., Dobbs, R., Roxburgh, C., & Byers, A. H. (2011). *Big data: The next frontier for innovation, competition and productivity*. McKinsey Global Institute. Retrieved from https://bigdatawg.nist.gov/pdf/MGI_big_data_full_report.pdf
3. Quadrini, W., Galparoli, S., Nucera, D. D., Fumagalli, L., & Negri, E. (2021). Architecture for data acquisition in research and teaching laboratories. *Procedia Computer Science, 180*, 833–842. https://doi.org/10.1016/j.procs.2021.01.333
4. Chen, H., Chiang, R. H. L., & Storey, V. C. (2012). Business intelligence and analytics: From big data to big impact. *MIS Quarterly, 36*(4), 1165–1188. https://doi.org/10.2307/41703503
5. Tusa, F., & Clayman, S. (2023). End-to-end slices to orchestrate resources and services in the cloud-to-edge continuum. *Future Generation Computer Systems, 141*, 473–488. https://doi.org/10.1016/j.future.2022.11.026
6. Aouedi, O., & Piamrat, K. (n.d.). Towards a scalable and energy-efficient framework for industrial cloud-edge-IoT continuum.
7. Bittencourt, L., Immich, R., Sakellariou, R., Fonseca, N., Madeira, E., Curado, M., Villas, L., DaSilva, L., Lee, C., & Rana, O. (2018). The internet of things, fog and cloud continuum: Integration and challenges. *Internet of Things, 3-4*, 134–155. https://doi.org/10.1016/j.iot.2018.09.005
8. Salis, A., Marguglio, A., De Luca, G., Razzetti, S., Quadrini, W., & Gusmeroli, S. (2023). An edge-cloud based reference architecture to support cognitive solutions in process industry. *Procedia Computer Science, 217*, 20–30. https://doi.org/10.1016/j.procs.2022.12.198
9. Cheng, B., Zhang, J., Hancke, G. P., Karnouskos, S., & Colombo, A. W. (2018). Industrial cyber-physical systems: Realizing cloud-based big data infrastructures. *IEEE Industrial Electronics Magazine, 12*(1), 25–35. https://doi.org/10.1109/MIE.2017.2788850
10. Sitaram, D., & Manjunath, G. (2012). *Moving to the cloud*. Elsevier. https://doi.org/10.1016/C2010-0-66389-9
11. Margaria, T., & Schieweck, A. (2019). The digital thread in industry 4.0. In T. Margaria (Ed.), *Lecture notes in computer science* (Vol. 11918, pp. 3–24). Springer. https://doi.org/10.1007/978-3-030-34968-4_1

12. Negri, E., Fumagalli, L., & Macchi, M. (2017). A review of the roles of digital twin in CPS-based production systems. *Procedia Manufacturing, 11*, 939–948. https://doi.org/10.1016/j.promfg.2017.07.198
13. Hankel, M., Koschnick, G., & Rexroth, B. (2015). RAMI 4.0—Structure: The reference architectural model industrie 4.0. *ZVEI, 2*, 4–9. Retrieved from https://www.zvei.org/
14. Quadrini, W., Cuzzola, F. A., Fumagalli, L., Taisch, M., De Luca, G., Calderaro, M., Marzano, M. G., & Marguglio, A. (2024). A reference architecture to implement self-X capability in an industrial software architecture. *Procedia Computer Science, 232*, 446–455. https://doi.org/10.1016/j.procs.2024.01.044
15. Pedone, G., & Mezgár, I. (2018). Model similarity evidence and interoperability affinity in cloud-ready industry 4.0 technologies. *Computers in Industry, 100*, 278–286. https://doi.org/10.1016/j.compind.2018.05.003
16. Industry IoT Consortium. (2022). *The industrial internet reference architecture (Version 1.9)*. Retrieved from https://www.iiconsortium.org/IIRA/
17. ISO/IEC/IEEE. (2018). *ISO/IEC/IEEE 15288: Systems and software engineering — System life cycle processes* (2nd ed.). International Standard.
18. Bader, S. R., Maleshkova, M., & Lohmann, S. (2019). Structuring reference architectures for the industrial internet of things. *Future Internet, 11*(7), 1–23. https://doi.org/10.3390/fi11070151
19. International Data Spaces Association. (n.d.). *IDS reference architecture model (IDS-RAM)*. Retrieved from https://docs.internationaldataspaces.org/ids-ram-4/
20. Big Data Value Association. (2017). *European big data value strategic research & innovation agenda*. Retrieved from http://www.edwardcurry.org/publications/BDVA_SRIA_v4_Ed1.1.pdf
21. Kramp, T., van Kranenburg, R., & Lange, S. (2013). Introduction to the internet of things. In H. Bassi et al. (Eds.), *Enabling things to talk: Designing IoT solutions with the IoT architectural reference model* (pp. 1–10). Springer. https://doi.org/10.1007/978-3-642-40403-0_1
22. Khan, W. Z., Ahmed, E., Hakak, S., Yaqoob, I., & Ahmed, A. (2019). Edge computing: A survey. *Future Generation Computer Systems, 97*, 219–235. https://doi.org/10.1016/j.future.2019.02.050
23. Vaño, R., Lacalle, I., Sowiński, P., San Julián, R., & Palau, C. E. (2023). Cloud-native workload orchestration at the edge: A deployment review and future directions. *Sensors, 23*(4), 2215. https://doi.org/10.3390/s23042215
24. INTRA. (2019). *BOOST 4.0 reference architecture specification*. Retrieved from https://boost40.eu/wp-content/uploads/2020/11/D2.5.pdf
25. Velásquez, N., Estevez, E., & Pesado, P. (2018). Cloud computing, big data and the industry 4.0 reference architectures. *Journal of Computer Science and Technology, 18*(3), e29. https://doi.org/10.24215/16666038.18.e29
26. Nagasundaram, D., Manickam, S., & Karuppayah, S. (2022). Semantic interoperability issues and challenges in IoT: A brief review. In *Advances in information and communication* (pp. 16–31). Springer. https://doi.org/10.1007/978-3-031-15063-0_2
27. Bousdekis, A., Lepenioti, K., Ntalaperas, D., Vergeti, D., Apostolou, D., & Boursinos, V. (2019). A RAMI 4.0 view of predictive maintenance: Software architecture, platform and case study in steel industry. *IFIP Advances in Information and Communication Technology, 563*, 95–106. https://doi.org/10.1007/978-3-030-20948-3_9
28. Wang, J., Gao, F., Zhou, Y., Guo, Q., Tan, C.-W., Song, J., & Wang, Y. (2023). Data sharing in energy systems. *Advances in Applied Energy, 10*, 100132. https://doi.org/10.1016/j.adapen.2023.100132
29. Together, T. M. (2021). Digital Factory Alliance (DFA). December.
30. Xia, Y., Jazdi, N., & Weyrich, M. (2022). Automated generation of asset administration shell: A transfer learning approach with neural language model and semantic fingerprints. In *2022 IEEE 27th international conference on emerging technologies and factory automation (ETFA)* (pp. 1–4). IEEE. https://doi.org/10.1109/ETFA52439.2022.9921637

31. Nucera, D. D., Quadrini, W., Fumagalli, L., & Scipioni, M. P. (2021). Data-driven state detection for an asset working at heterogeneous regimens. *IFAC-PapersOnLine, 54*(1), 1248–1253. https://doi.org/10.1016/j.ifacol.2021.08.149
32. Li, Q., Wen, Z., Wu, Z., Hu, S., Wang, N., Li, Y., Liu, X., & He, B. (2023). A survey on federated learning systems: Vision, hype and reality for data privacy and protection. *IEEE Transactions on Knowledge and Data Engineering, 35*(4), 3347–3366. https://doi.org/10.1109/TKDE.2021.3124599
33. Kimovski, D., Matha, R., Hammer, J., Mehran, N., Hellwagner, H., & Prodan, R. (2021). Cloud, fog, or edge: Where to compute? *IEEE Internet Computing, 25*(4), 30–36. https://doi.org/10.1109/MIC.2021.3050613
34. Al-Dulaimy, A., Jansen, M., Johansson, B., Trivedi, A., Iosup, A., Ashjaei, M., Galletta, A., Kimovski, D., Prodan, R., Tserpes, K., Kousiouris, G., Giannakos, C., Brandic, I., Ali, N., Bondi, A. B., & Papadopoulos, A. V. (2024). The computing continuum: From IoT to the cloud. *Internet of Things, 27*, 101272. https://doi.org/10.1016/j.iot.2024.101272
35. Quadrini, W., Cimino, C., Abdel-Aty, T. A., Fumagalli, L., & Rovere, D. (2023). Asset administration shell as an interoperable enabler of industry 4.0 software architectures: A case study. *Procedia Computer Science, 217*, 1794–1802. https://doi.org/10.1016/j.procs.2022.12.379
36. 5G-ACIA. (n.d.). *Using digital twins to integrate 5G into production networks*. Retrieved from https://5g-acia.org/whitepapers/using-digital-twins-to-integrate-5g-into-production-networks/

Integration of Embedded Components into Cyber-Physical Systems: Design, Analysis, and Applications

Aleksei Demin, Andrey Vlasov, Kirill Selivanov, Anna Evseeva, and Boris Safonov

Abstract The adoption of artificial intelligence in industry is inextricably linked to Internet of Things technologies. The development of this technology generates new requirements for the mounting density and reliability of digital devices. Embedded components are becoming one of the solutions to improve the characterization of cyber-physical system elements. This technology allows electronic components to be placed inside printed circuit board, providing micro-miniaturization and increased reliability. The paper proposes intelligent methods to increase the mounting density and reduce the size of elements of cyber-physical systems without a significant complication of production technology. The proposed approach would allow companies that manufacture electronic devices to become more independent of electronic component suppliers. In the long term, these technologies can have an impact on increasing the economic freedom of the entire industry, making it more sustainable in the face of import substitution. Implementation of the proposed technology will allow realizing the integration of inductive and capacitive components in the printed circuit board. The main focus of the paper is on the way in which the embedded inductors and capacitors are implemented. The conclusion provides a comparative analysis of embedded components of cyber-physical systems and assesses promising directions for further development of the technology of embedded elements of cyber-physical systems within the framework of models of digital transformation of industry.

Keywords Embedded components · Cyber-physical systems · Sensors · Energy capacity · Reliability · Inductor · Capacitor · Internet of things · Industry 5.0

A. Demin (✉)
Shenzhen MSU-BIT University, Shenzhen, Guangdong, China

A. Vlasov · K. Selivanov · A. Evseeva · B. Safonov
Bauman Moscow State Technical University, Moscow, Russia
e-mail: vlasov@iu4.ru

F. Tao et al. (eds.), *Artificial Intelligence and Digital Transformation*, Lecture Notes in Information Systems and Organisation 78,
https://doi.org/10.1007/978-3-032-00118-4_12

1 Introduction

Modern strategies and models of digital transformation of industrial companies are inextricably linked with Industrial Internet of Things technologies [1] and cyber-physical systems [2]. There is a lot of research going on in the miniaturization of IoT devices [3–5], including in the area of the printed circuit board (PCB) producing. Current methods require advanced technologies that are unavailable to most companies, preventing electronics modules at the volumes of 5.0. required for Industry. This article examines PCB minimization technologies and provides available methods for reducing their dimensions. The main problem of modern cyber-physical systems is how to minimize the size and power consumption of their components while increasing reliability. One solution to this problem is to build components into the PCB. This decision regarding active and passive components in a multilayer structure should be made early in the design process. This task is particularly relevant in the field of the Industrial Internet of Things. In this field, there is a significant demand for small-sized sensors and electronic modules for serial production, which will not be inferior to classical solutions in terms of reliability, radiation resistance, and power consumption. Printed circuit boards have traditionally served as a platform for connecting active and passive components on its surface. Embedding passive elements in the inner layers will increase the reliability and reduce the size of the devices [6], and hence reduce resistance, inductance, and increase processing speed and improve radiation resistance. The technology under consideration is already widely used in the manufacture of modern electronics, and there are international standards describing models and technologies for the production of embedded elements [7–9]. However, the efficient layout of embedded components within the PCB remains poorly understood. To solve this problem, methods of structural-parametric and generative (intelligent) synthesis of efficient layouts based on libraries of basic topologies are increasingly used.

The work aims to identify the most efficient and available layout solutions of inductive and capacitive component topologies to realize intelligent generative layout methods and to form a database of efficient topologies.

To achieve the stated goal, the classification of the main types of topologies for integrated inductive and capacitive elements is proposed in the paper; their characteristics are summarized and systematized. A comparative analysis of element characteristics has been made, both between different groups of topologies and between representatives of the same group. The most promising methods of forming integrated components of embedded electronic components of cyber-physical systems are summarized.

Using cluster analysis, a comparative analysis of the main topologies of inductors and capacitors has been carried out, and recommendations for the implementation of effective cyber-physical solutions based on embedded electronics technology have been given.

2 Literature Review

The technology of introducing passive components into the PCB was known as early as in the twentieth century [6]. However, it became widespread later, with the growing capabilities of three-dimensional integration technologies. Traditionally, multilayer PCB fabrication techniques have been used to increase layout density [10], and electronic components with a miniaturized form factor, such as BGA packages, have been used. As we approach the limits of the capabilities of these methods, developers have increasingly turned their attention to embedded technology. Today, standards for the design, installation, and control of these components have already been developed and are in active use [7–9].

We use semantic cluster analysis of the literature to analyze the current state of the art of embedded component technology. The main part of the study was carried out using the VOSViewer.1.6.15 software (https://www.vosviewer.com). A bibliometric analysis of the scientific literature on the subject of embedded electronics was conducted. Figure 1 shows a semantic relationship map based on the text of more than 1000 articles in the open-source database Lens.org (https://www.lens.org) containing the keywords "embedded electronics". Blue color indicates discrete embedded component technologies; red color indicates formed embedded component technologies. Discrete components are supplied in housings and mounted by the electronic module manufacturer. Within a cluster of discrete components, clusters of passive and active elements can be distinguished. The active components can

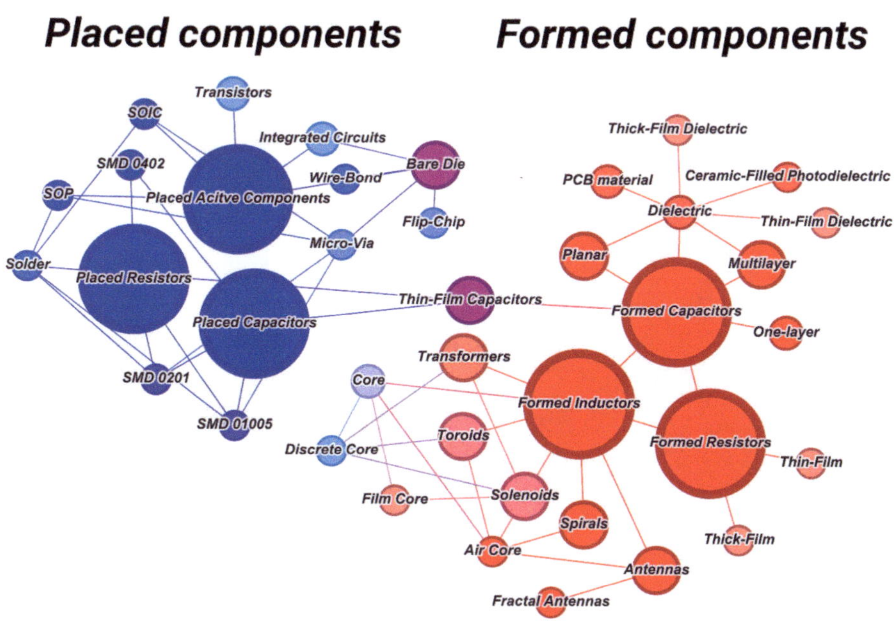

Fig. 1 Major technology clusters in the embedded component field

be supplied as a separate Bare Die. A significant part of the processing and control of the component in this case falls to the PCB manufacturer, so this technology is brought between the discrete and formed component clusters.

The most affordable for today's production facilities are embedded formed components. For capacitors, a planar design [11] is most commonly used (Fig. 2a), which can be extended to a multilayer planar capacitor [12]. For inductor design, the most common architectures are spiral [13, 14] (Fig. 2b), solenoid [15] (Fig. 2c), and toroid [16] (Fig. 2d). However, the set of forms of embedded inductive elements is not limited to these designs alone; their synthesis is a complex, multivariant task realized by specialized methods of automated generative synthesis [17].

The search for new architectures of embedded inductors and capacitors in related fields aims at formalized representation of fractal antennas [18–20]. Pressure sensors based on an embedded capacitor have been developed [21], and passive components for radiation sensors and other integrated structures have been designed [18, 22, 23].

The main current trend in research on embedded components is to improve their performance by using special additionally introduced structures or substances. This area of manufacturing is closely related to the now developing additive technologies [24]. Several types can be attributed to them including a cluster of magnetic core designs and implementation methods should be noted [17, 25, 26]. This technique is especially important for introduced transformers [27]. Since solid-state cores are off-the-shelf products embedded in a PCB with formed inductors, this technology is

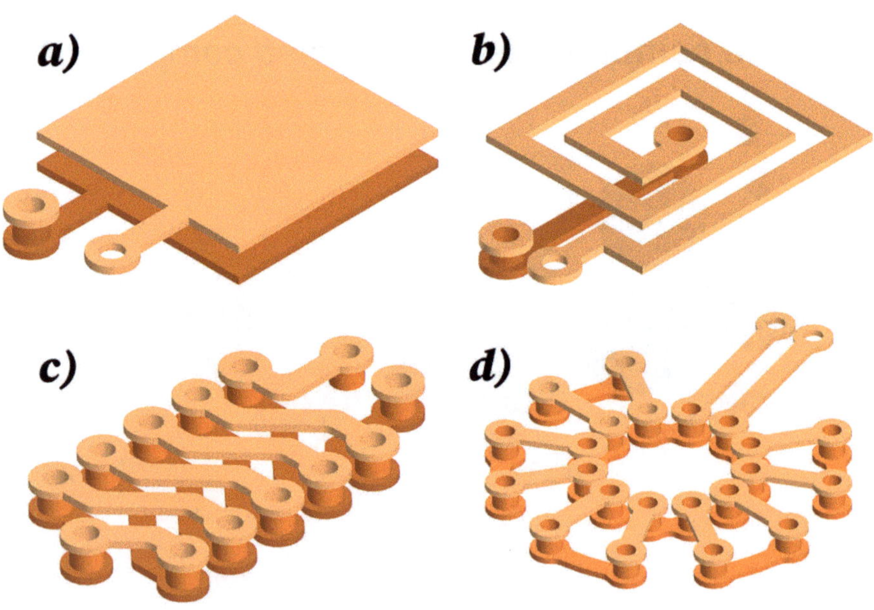

Fig. 2 Classic designs of embedded components: (**a**) planar capacitor; (**b**) helix inductor; (**c**) solenoid inductor; (**d**) toroid inductor

at the intersection of discrete and formed component clusters. For capacitors, different dielectric layer compositions are most often considered [28]. To create advanced cyber-physical systems with high performance properties, further development of topologies and manufacturing processes for embedded components is required. For the purpose of this study, we will focus on methods for synthesizing embedded shaped inductors without magnetic cores and embedded shaped capacitors, which are the most common embedded components.

3 Materials and Methods

In this article, general scientific methods were used, in particular: experimental (experiment, comparison) and experimental-theoretical (analogy, abstraction, induction). The experiment was conducted to investigate the properties of integrated capacitors and inductors under natural conditions and to study the characteristics of different element designs.

The comparison was carried out to identify differences in the properties of the electronic components under consideration, as well as to determine the most efficient architecture.

Using the analogy method, designs were developed representing the main or equal the main groups of built-in elements. Among the models there are representations of the most popular architecture, in addition to this, models of non-classical construction are proposed.

For the practical realization of a device with embedded components, it is necessary to be able to create a PCB with embedded components: inductors and capacitors. As an example, consider an PCB fabricated from 1.5 mm thick FR4 Tg 135 glass-textolite, the conductive pattern was obtained from an 18 μm thick layer of copper foil. The surface of the board, except for the contact pads, is covered with a solder mask on both sides. Openings of the board are metallized; contact pads are covered with POS-63 solder.

The measurements were carried out with a measurement accuracy of 0.05% using the LRC-meter of the GW Instek company, model LRC-816. Two conductive tracks were connected to each element of the PCB, with connected PLS-2 connectors. The LRC-meter was connected to these connectors.

To compare the characteristics of embedded component architectures, we will evaluate the ratio of the inductance or capacitance of an element to the area occupied. We will call this value specific capacitance and specific inductance. The passive elements to be implemented must meet the following requirements:

- Elements formed by a conductive pattern;
- An element can cover an area of no more than 400 mm^2;
- 2 layers of PCB and transition holes can be used for the element;
- The minimum width of the conductive track is0.5 mm;

- The minimum distance between non-overlapping areas of the conductive pattern is0.5 mm;
- The hole diameter is0.5 mm;
- The diameter of the hole contact area is1 mm;
- The minimum angle between the conductive tracks is 85°.

All conductive elements should be arranged as compact as possible, as this improves their electrical characteristics and thus increases the specific capacitance and specific inductance. The conductive elements are therefore located at the minimum permitted distance.

The topology of the spiral inductors is located on both layers of the PCB. The transition hole is in their center. The most common designs of such inductors are square and round spirals. However, due to the fact that most CAD systems do not provide for the design of circular spirals, square and octagonal inductors L4 and L1 will be fabricated, respectively (Table 1). The octagonal spiral was added in order to compare the performance of the square inductor with a model similar to it, but with a shape closer to the round spiral.

Consider an inductor based on the L2 meander (Table 1). To calculate the inductance of a meander-shaped conductor, we can use the formula [29]:

$$L = 0.0026 \cdot a^{0.0603} \cdot h^{0.4429} \cdot N^{0.954} \cdot d^{0.606} \cdot w^{-0.173},$$

where L meander inductance, nHn, a the length of the output of the meander μm, h the height of the meander front μm, N the number of fronts, d the distance between the two fronts μm, w the width of the conductive track, μm.

The parameters of the formula are explained in Fig. 3.

To achieve the maximum inductance of the meander, it is necessary to make the values of the bases of powers with exponents less than one as small as possible. Thus, the best values of the meander parameters under these conditions would be h = 1 mm; d = 1 mm; w = 0.5 mm, since these dimensions are the smallest among those allowed by the design rules for these passive components.

Consider solenoid-based inductors. The representatives of this group will be elements L3 and L6 (Table 1). Their conductive pattern runs across both layers of the PCB and has many transition holes. The L3 component consists of four such solenoids. Element L6 starts with four similar rows, but after that, its pattern continues between the windings of the first four solenoids. Such a design has been called a double solenoid inductor.

Consider the toroidal inductor L5 (Table 1). The prototype of this element was toroidal coils. Like solenoids, a toroid needs many transition holes. This will be the last inductor architecture considered.

Images of the inductor topologies and their brief descriptions are summarized in Table 1.

Consider a flat capacitor C1 (Table 2). It has a classic design consisting of two conductive plates separated by a PCB material acting as a dielectric.

Table 1 Topologies and descriptions of inductive elements

Number	Name	Topology	Description
L1	Octagonal spiral	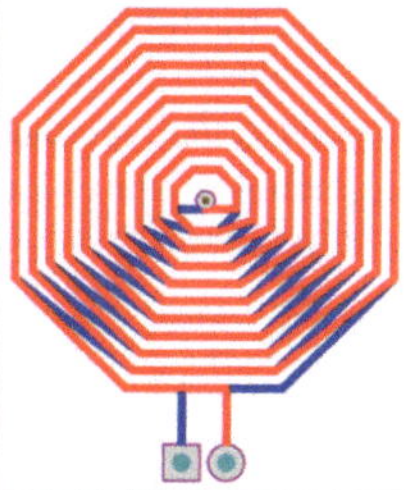	The spiral in the upper layer tends to the center, the conductor passes to the lower layer and unfolds the same spiral from the center hole. The shape is based on an octagon
L2	Meandral inductor		Consists of rows of meanders that are on both layers of the PCB
L3	Solenoid	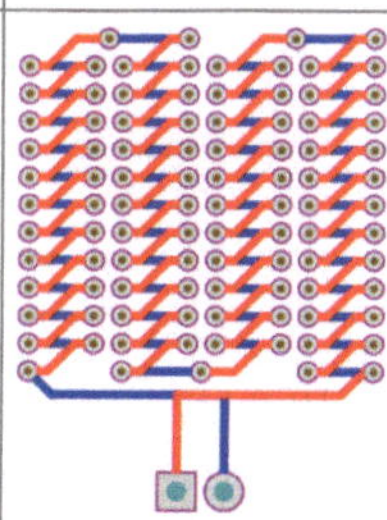	Consists of 4 solenoids, each of which runs on both conductive layers. It has 98 transition holes
L4	Square spiral		The spiral in the upper layer tends to the center, the conductor passes to the lower layer and unfolds the same spiral from the center hole. The shape is based on a square
L5	Toroidal inductor	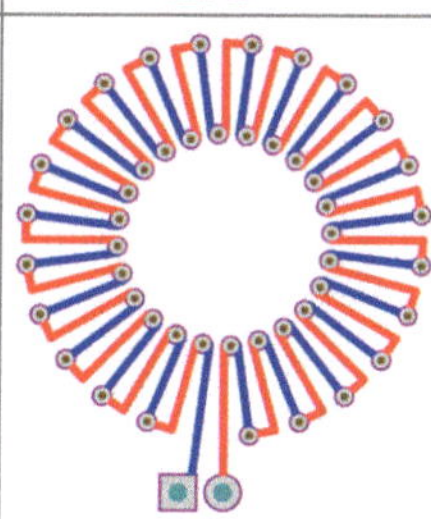	Transitions from layer to layer also require many holes. There are 47

(continued)

Table 1 (continued)

Number	Name	Topology	Description
L6	Double solenoid inductor	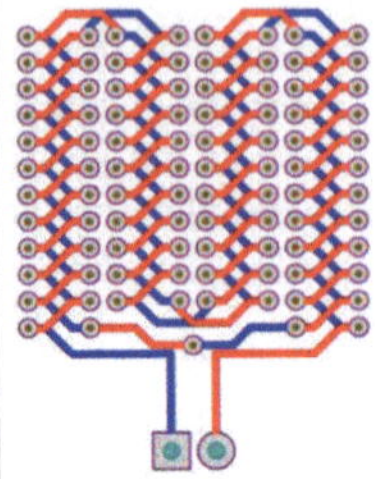	After the formation of 4 solenoids passing through both layers, the conducting circuit goes to the "second circle" of the same solenoids, whose turns pass between the turns of the first solenoids. It has 93 holes

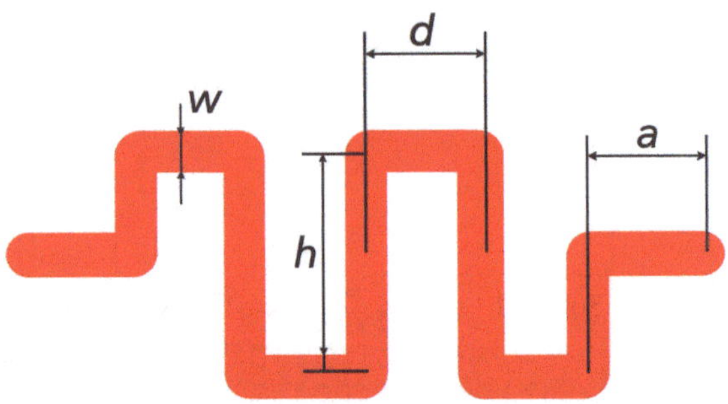

Fig. 3 Parameters of the meander formed by the conductive track of the printed circuit board

Consider a capacitor formed by metallized holes spaced at the nodes of the C2 grid (Table 2). A grid of conductive tracks is formed on both layers of the PCB. Each grid has its own potential. Metallized transition holes are placed at the nodes of each mesh. The alternation of metallized holes with different potentials leads to the formation of capacitance.

Consider a capacitor formed by a row of metallized holes C3 (Table 2). Its capacitive effect is also caused by metallization of holes with different potentials. However, in this architecture, holes of the same polarity are in the same row. The rows alternate with each other.

Images of the capacitor topologies and their brief descriptions are summarized in Table 2.

The presented results illustrate typical topologies of capacitive and inductive elements.

4 Results

Building cyber-physical systems based on embedded components (Tables 1 and 2) requires an evaluation of their functional characteristics. We will conduct experimental investigations of the properties of integrated capacitors and inductors in vivo. The comparative analysis will show the differences in the properties of the

Table 2 Topologies and descriptions of capacitive elements

Number	Name	Topology	Description
C1	Flat capacitor	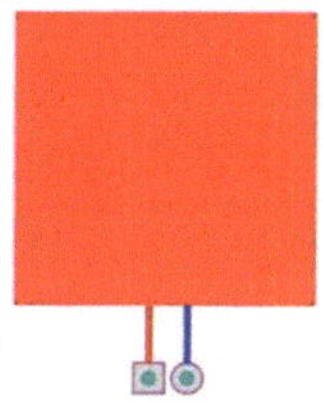	Consists of two square conductor plates separated by a dielectric board base
C2	Capacitor formed by holes arranged in the nodes of the grid	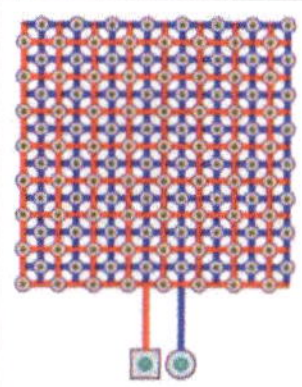	Capacitor formed by holes with metallization. Two neighboring holes in the same row or column belong to different poles of the capacitor. It has 128 transition holes
C3	Capacitor formed by rows of holes	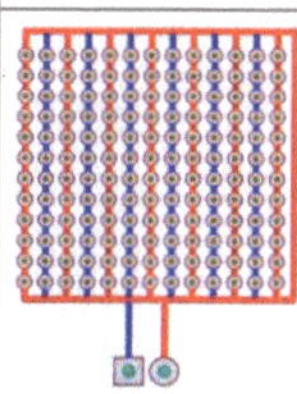	Capacitor formed by holes with metallization. Here the holes belonging to one pole are built in rows, the rows alternating. It has 156 transition holes

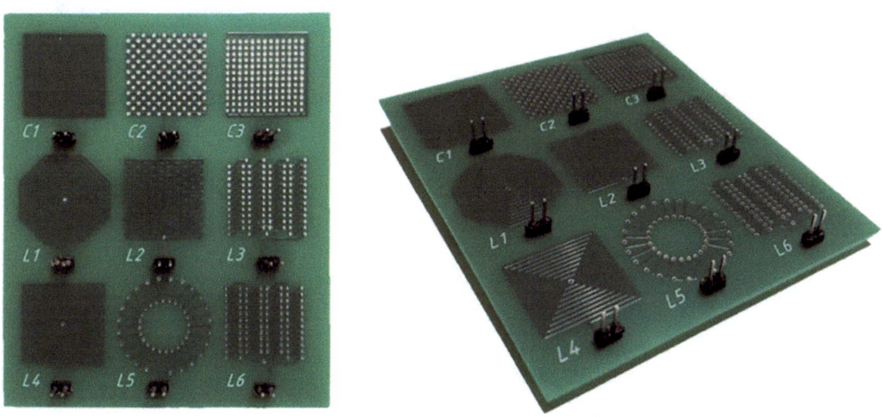

Fig. 4 General view of the test printed circuit board

electronic components under consideration and will also allow justifying the most efficient solutions.

The evaluation of the actual performance of the designs of the considered elements was performed by means of an experiment, in which a test sample PCB with placed typical embedded components was used (Fig. 4).

Table 3 Characteristics of inductive elements

Number	Inductance (μHn)	Area (mm^2)	Specific inductance (μHn/mm^2)
L1	43.84	399.5	0.11
L2	40.53	380.25	0.107
L3	40.58	400	0.101
L4	43.55	380.25	0.115
L5	40.48	400	0.101
L6	40.67	385.125	0.106

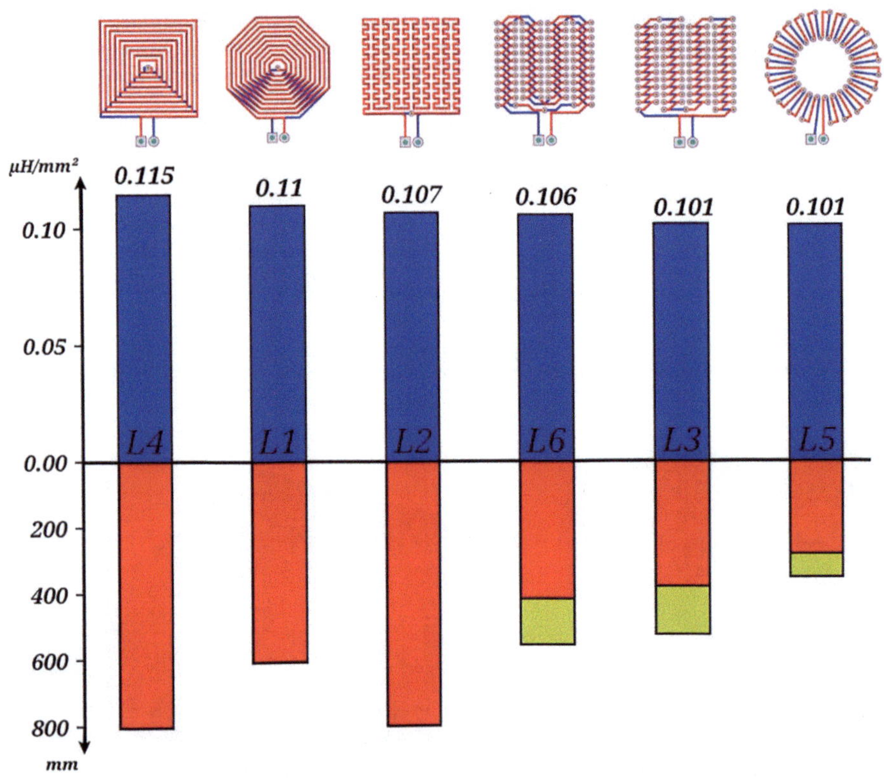

Fig. 5 Characteristics of embedded inductors

The results of comparative evaluations of inductor performance of different inductor designs are presented in Table 3. The measurements were performed using a GW InstekLRC meter, model LRC-816. Two conductive tracks were connected to each PCB element, to which PLS-2 connectors were connected. An LRC meter was connected to these connectors.

Figure 5 shows the characteristics of the embedded inductors based on Table 3 data. The top half of the graph (in blue) shows the specific inductances of the elements. In the lower half are the lengths of the inductors in mm. The red part of the

Table 4 Characteristics of capacitive elements

Number	Capacity (pF)	Area (mm²)	Specific capacity (nF/mm²)
C1	14.874	400	37.185
C2	23.667	390	60.685
C3	20.534	400	51.335

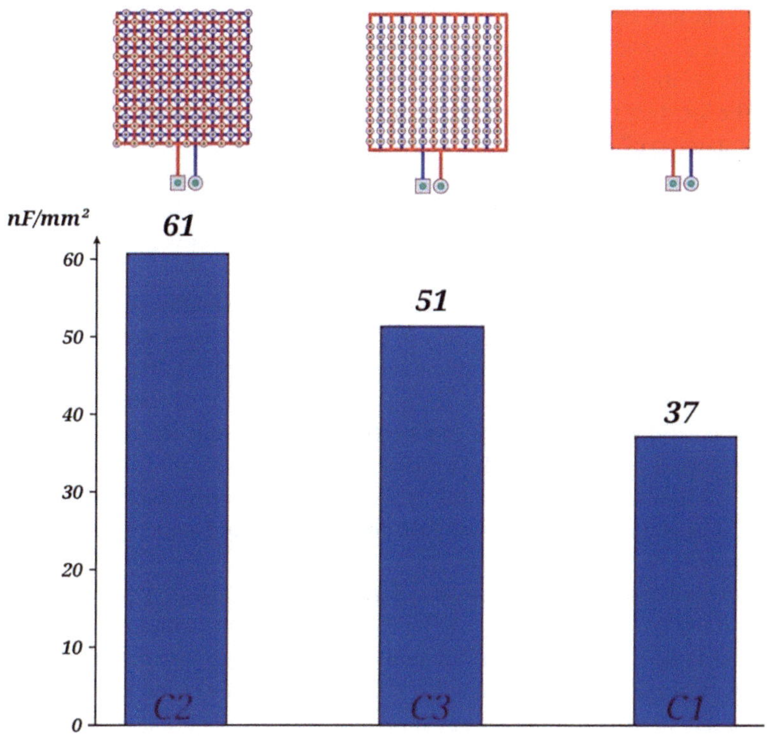

Fig. 6 Specific electrical capacitance of built-in capacitors

column shows how much of the length is occupied by the conductive loop; the yellow part of the length is formed by the holes. The inductors are arranged from left to right in descending order of their specific inductance.

The results of the capacitive element characteristic measurements are presented in Table 4.

The results of Table 4 were also transformed into a graph in Fig. 6 for ease of perception. As can be seen from the graph in Fig. 6, the specific capacitance of capacitors C2 and C3 is larger than that of component C1. Thus, capacitors formed by holes have shown to be more efficient compared to the classical planar design.

From the comparative analysis, it can be concluded that the best inductor models are the L4 and L1 models, which have a spiral design. Next in terms of specific inductance is inductor L2, which is meander based. Inductors based on solenoids running through the thickness of the PCB have performed the worst. Probably under the current constraints, "winding up" in these devices proved to be too rare. Also, a significant advantage of the components formed by the conductive tracks of the board is the small number of holes, which simplifies, speeds up, and reduces the cost of production of these elements.

The results of the study showed the superiority of the hole-formed capacitors over the classical embedded capacitor design. The element C3 has the highest specific electrical capacitance. This design requires far fewer holes than C2. This superiority can be attributed to the role of conductive tracks in increasing capacitance as well as the location of potentials on the holes. In C2, the holes with different polarities are "staggered" and tracks of one polarity regularly overlap tracks of the other polarity on the opposite layer. In C3, the capacitance is formed predominantly by rows of holes with the same potential. Also, the advantage of the C2 capacitor is that it has fewer holes than C3. This makes its manufacturing process faster and cheaper than C3.

The specific electrical capacitance of C1 is 38.7% smaller with respect to the specific capacitance of C2. This means that a capacitor with metalized holes can replace a flat capacitor with the same rating, but using 38.7% less area.

Existing discrete components currently have better specific characteristics. However, considered technology can be further improved, for example, by using special materials or increasing the accuracy level.

These methods, as well as the ability to place these components in the inner layers of PCB, make these elements no less an effective tool for the designer than classic solutions.

The use of embedded elements in design requires sophisticated feature analysis on the part of the designer.

This study does not provide a full analysis of the characteristics of the presented structures dependencies, sufficient for the practical application of these methods, including due to the simultaneous consideration of several architectures based on a comparison of models produced under the same conditions. However, these results demonstrate potential direction for research into embedded passive elements.

The widespread use of this technology should inevitably lead to the emergence of intelligent computer-aided design systems with functions of generative synthesis of embedded components. These tools based on aggregated data in this area will be able to synthesize effective solutions based on embedded components. The emergence of such design systems will provide a wide range of opportunities for the creation of electronic devices [30, 31].

5 Conclusion

The work investigates the principles of implementing embedded components of cyber-physical systems that provide their microminiaturization, reduced power consumption, and increased reliability. The topological design of embedded systems is based on intelligent design methods aimed at increasing the mounting density and reducing the size without significantly complicating the manufacturing technology.

It is shown that embedded electronics technologies are among the promising technologies for energy-efficient and miniaturized Industrial Internet of Things systems and collectively have a significant impact on increasing the flexibility of digital transformation. Implementation of the technologies considered will allow realizing the integration of embedded components, in particular inductive and capacitive, in the PCB of modules of cyber-physical systems. The proposed approach will allow companies manufacturing electronic devices to become more independent from suppliers of electronic components in the context of import substitution.

The results of the comparative analysis of embedded components show that embedded capacitors based on metallized holes have great potential. They have a higher specific electrical capacity. However, the large number of holes required can increase the cost of such components.

Spiral inductors are the best in terms of specific inductance. Inductive components with a substantial portion of their length formed by holes showed worse electrical performance than those formed by a mostly conductive circuit on different sides of the PCB.

The results show differences between fundamentally different passive element architectures, but the experiment also highlights potentially useful areas for studying these components. Practical use of the proposed methods needs a more detailed study of each architecture, as well as a search for mathematical dependencies of the proposed models parameters sufficiently accurate for practical application. This is necessary for automated simulation of capacitors and inductors according to the required characteristics.

Further research in this direction may focus on the study of embedded inductors with fractal design, as well as a deeper investigation of capacitors based on metallized holes.

Such embedded element designs may have great potential in the current design and manufacturing of industrial Internet of Things modules. Widespread adoption of this technology will reduce the dependence of electronic module manufacturers on suppliers of radio parts. Such a trend will be important in the further digital transformation of industry and the widespread adoption of the Industrial Internet of Things and other embedded electronics.

Acknowledgments The results were partially obtained within the project "FSFN_2024_0086".

References

1. Akberdina, V., Kalinina, A., & Vlasov, A. (2018). Transformation stages of the Russian industrial complex in the context of economy digitization. *Problems and Perspectives in Management, 16*(4), 201–211. https://doi.org/10.21511/ppm.16(4).2018.17
2. Vlasov, A. I., Berdyugina, O. N., & Krivoshein, A. I. (2018). Technological platform for innovative social infrastructure development on basis of smart machines and principles of internet

of things. In *2018 global smart industry conference (GloSIC) (no. 8570062)*. IEEE. https://doi.org/10.1109/GloSIC.2018.8570062
3. Hussain, N., Kumar, S., & Cn, D. (2021). MEMS sensors in IoT applications. *Journal of Control & Instrumentation, 12*(1), 37591.
4. Reddy, B. G. (2025). Powering the internet of things: Advances in energy harvesting technologies. *International Journal of Scientific Research in Computer Science Engineering and Information Technology, 11*(1), 1867–1876. https://doi.org/10.32628/CSEIT251112192
5. García, A., Andújar, A., & Anguera, J. (2024). Overview of reconfigurable antenna systems for IoT devices. *Electronics, 13*(20), 3988. https://doi.org/10.3390/electronics13203988
6. Fairchild, K., Morcan, G., Lenihan, T., Brown, W., Schaper, L., Ang, S., Sommers, W., Parkerson, J., & Glover, M. (1997). Reliability of flexible thin-film embedded resistors and electrical characterization of thin-film embedded capacitors and inductors. In *Proceedings of the 47th electronic components and technology conference* (pp. 1–6). IEEE. https://doi.org/10.1109/ECTC.1997.606251
7. IPC. (2015). *IPC-7092: Design and assembly process implementation for embedded components*. Developed by the Embedded Devices Process Implementation Subcommittee (D-55) of the Embedded Components Committee (D-50) of IPC.
8. IPC. (2007). *IPC-2316: Design guide for embedded passive device printed boards*. Developed by the Embedded Devices Design Subcommittee (D-51) of the Embedded Components Committee (D-30) of IPC.
9. International Electrotechnical Commission. (2015). *IEC 62878-1-1: Device embedded substrate—Part 1-1: Generic specification—Test methods*.
10. Chernov, I. E., Kondakov, N. A., Perederin, K. D., Vlasov, A. I., Zhalnin, V. P., & Shakhnov, V. A. (2020). Use of the "via-in-pad" method to ensure the high-density layout of the conductive pattern when designing multilayer switching structures. *International Journal on Advanced Science, Engineering and Information Technology, 10*(3), 1176–1183. https://doi.org/10.18517/ijaseit.10.3.10831
11. Piasecki, T., Nitsch, K., Dziedzic, A., Chabowski, K., Stęplewski, W., & Kozioł, G. (2012). Electrical properties of dielectric foil for embedded PCB capacitors. *Materials Science, 30*(4), 335–341. https://doi.org/10.2478/s13536-012-0057-5
12. Arva, M. C., & Diaconescu, E. (2015). Modeling of stackable embedded capacitors into the PCB layers. In *Proceedings of the 11th international conference on technical and physical problems of electrical engineering (September 10–12, 2015)*. Bucharest, Romania.
13. Kaziz, S., Maamer, B., Delhaye, T., Tounsi, F., Francis, L. A., & Flandre, D. (2020). Tuning range comparison between different planar inductors layouts on PCB. In *2020 IEEE international conference on design & test of integrated micro & nano-systems (DTS)*. IEEE. https://doi.org/10.1109/DTS48731.2020.9196105
14. Bąk, M., Dudek, M., & Dziedzic, A. (2008). Chosen electrical and stability properties of surface and embedded planar PCB inductors. In *2008 31st international spring seminar on electronics technology*. ISSE. https://doi.org/10.1109/ISSE.2008.5276627
15. Li, L., Lee, D. W., Hwang, K. P., Min, Y., & Wang, S. X. (2009). On-package magnetic materials for embedded inductor applications. In *2009 international conference on electronic packaging technology & high density packaging*. ICEPT. https://doi.org/10.1109/ICEPT.2009.5270707
16. Biglarbegian, M., Shah, N., Mazhari, I., & Parkhideh, B. (2015). Design considerations for high power density: Efficient PCB embedded inductor. In *2015 IEEE 3rd workshop on wide bandgap power devices and applications (WiPDA)*. IEEE. https://doi.org/10.1109/WiPDA.2015.7369285
17. Barros, C. A. (2021). *Design and demonstration of embedded inductors for high-voltage integrated voltage regulators*. Georgia Institute of Technology.
18. Mapato, M., Klysuban, P., Kulworawanichpong, T., & Chomnawang, N. (2012). Metal-embedded SU-8 slab techniques for low-resistance micromachined inductors. *International Journal of Electrical and Computer Engineering (IJECE), 8*(6), 4472–4480. https://doi.org/10.11591/ijece.v8i6.pp4772-4780

19. Bjelica, J. M., Djuric, N. M., & Djuric, S. M. (2020). Modeling and performance analysis of planar fractal inductors. *IEEE Transactions on Magnetics, 56*(11), 8400308. https://doi.org/10.1109/TMAG.2020.3018428
20. Vinoy, K. J. (2002). *Fractal shaped antenna elements for wide- and multi-band wireless applications*. Pennsylvania State University.
21. Kasemsin, W., & Boonkirdram, S. (2024). Design of a planar interdigital capacitor for pressure measurement. *EUREKA: Physics and Engineering, 5*, 64–72. https://doi.org/10.21303/2461-4262.2024.003400
22. Yoon, Y. K., & Allen, M. G. (2005). Embedded conductor technology for micromachined RF elements. *Journal of Micromechanics and Microengineering, 15*(6), 25. https://doi.org/10.1088/0960-1317/15/6/025
23. Yoon, Y.-K., Chen, E., Allen, M. G., & Laskar, J. (2001). Embedded solenoid inductors for RF CMOS power amplifiers. In E. Obermeier (Ed.), *Transducers '01 eurosensors XV* (pp. 1034–1037). Springer. https://doi.org/10.1007/978-3-642-59497-7_257
24. Vlasov, A. I., Juravleva, L. V., & Ismagilov, K. (2022). The concept of using additive technologies for digital prototyping of assembly devices. *Journal of Physics: Conference Series, 2373*, 072035. https://doi.org/10.1088/1742-6596/2373/7/072035
25. Sun, X., Lin, H., Velenis, D., Slabbekoorn, J., Talmelli, G., & Bex, P. (2020). 3D heterogeneous package integration of air/magnetic core inductor: 89%-efficiency buck converter with backside power delivery network. In *2020 IEEE symposium on VLSI technology*. IEEE. https://doi.org/10.1109/VLSITechnology18217.2020.9265045
26. Caillaud, R., Buttay, C., Mrad, R., Le Leslé, J., Morel, F., & Degrenne, N. (2018). Design, manufacturing and characterization of printed circuit board embedded inductors for power applications. In *2018 IEEE international conference on industrial technology (ICIT)*. IEEE. https://doi.org/10.1109/ICIT.2018.8352262
27. Ouyang, Z., Thomsen, O. C., & Andersen, M. A. E. (2012). Optimal design and tradeoff analysis of planar transformer in high-power DC–DC converters. *IEEE Transactions on Industrial Electronics, 59*(7), 2800–2810. https://doi.org/10.1109/TIE.2010.2046005
28. Bergstresser, T., Hilburn, R., Obrzut, J., & Phillips, K. (2003). Embedded capacitance materials and their application in high speed designs. In *IPC expo technical conference, March 23–27, 2003, Long Beach, CA*. Retrieved from https://tsapps.nist.gov/publication/get_pdf.cfm?pub_id=852216
29. Damjanovic, M., & Stojanovic, G. (2004). Compact form of expressions for inductance calculation of meander inductors. *Serbian Journal of Electrical Engineering, 1*(3), 57–68. https://doi.org/10.2298/SJEE0403057S
30. Nazarov, A. V., Shakhnov, V. A., Vlasov, A. I., & Novikov, A. N. (2018). Effective algorithm for routing integral structures with two layer switching. *Journal of Physics: Conference Series, 1015*(3), 032098.
31. Zhalnin, V. P., Zakharova, A. S., Uzenkov, D. A., Vlasov, A. I., Krivoshein, A. I., & Filin, S. S. (2019). Configuration-making algorithm for the smart machine controller based on the internet of things concept. *International Review of Electrical Engineering, 14*(5), 375–384. https://doi.org/10.15866/iree.v14i5.16923

Regional Aspects of Digital Transformation

Regional Trajectories of Digital Transformation: A Systematic Review

Aleksandr Pobedin

Abstract The article provides a comprehensive analysis of modern research in the field of digital transformation of regions based on a systematic review of publications from leading scientific journals in the Ural scientific and educational space of Russia. Having performed a systematic review of publications in academic journals for the period of 2019–2024, we identified key trends and directions of scientific discourse. Among the major tendencies revealed is the growing interest in the issue of digitalization of territories covering various socio-economic aspects. It is shown that there is a trend towards interdisciplinary integration and the formation of a new research landscape in the study of digital transformation. The special focus of the paper is on the concept of smart territories, the impact of the digital divide on regional development, and the transformation of educational systems and the labor market within the digital economy. Our analysis indicates the need for formulating integrated approaches to managing digital transformation of regions that would allow for global trends and the local context. The promising avenues for further research are the study of nonlinear effects of digitalization, long-term implications of digital transformation for the spatial organization of the economy, and the development of integrative models of digital development of territories.

Keywords Digital transformation · Digitalization · Region · Smart specialization · Digital divide

---

A. Pobedin (✉)
Ural Institute of Management - Branch of the Russian Presidential Academy of National Economy and Public Administration (RANEPA), Ekaterinburg, Russia
e-mail: pobedin-aa@ranepa.ru

F. Tao et al. (eds.), *Artificial Intelligence and Digital Transformation*, Lecture Notes in Information Systems and Organisation 78,
https://doi.org/10.1007/978-3-032-00118-4_13

1 Introduction

Digital transformation covers all aspects of socio-economic life and has a substantial impact on the development of regions creating new opportunities and challenges for territorial economic systems. Digitalization processes fueled by both technological progress and change in the social and institutional environment inevitably affect the structure of regional economies, forming new development trajectories and transforming existing models of cross-regional interaction.

The risks and opportunities associated with digital transformation are distributed unevenly among different types of regions. While large agglomerations and innovation centers are often the top performers in adapting to the digital economy, traditional industrial regions with a less developed innovation ecosystem face serious challenges. Such territories are more susceptible to negative influences of the digital divide and more prone to structural changes in the economy caused by digitalization [1].

The unevenness of digital transformation processes at the regional level is evidenced by the experience of Russian regions. While Moscow and Saint Petersburg demonstrate high rates of digitalization and advanced innovation infrastructure, many industrial regions have to deal with serious difficulties in adjusting to new technological realities, which entails the risks of increasing interregional disparities and requires differentiated approaches to be employed to stimulate the digital development of territories [2].

In this context, it is becoming increasingly important to examine the models of digital transformation in regions that can ensure sustainable development of territories amid global technological changes. The concept of smart territories, which has been actively developed in recent years, is one of such models designed to integrate digital technologies into various aspects of regional development [3, 4].

The purpose of our study is to comprehensively analyze modern research on digital transformation at the regional level. Based on a systematic review of publications, we detect key trends typical of digital transformation processes in regions.

Within the framework of the stated goal, the following research questions were formulated: what main thematic directions and conceptual approaches dominate in studies of digital transformation of regions in scientific publications of the Ural scientific and educational space; how the scientific discourse on digital transformation of regions evolved during the period under review (2019–2024), especially under conditions of global upheavals (COVID-19 pandemic); whether there are significant differences in the conceptualization of regional digital transformation processes between publications of various disciplinary orientations.

As a working hypothesis, it is suggested that a new interdisciplinary research landscape is forming, within which the traditional boundaries between economic, sociological, and educational research are becoming more permeable, indicating a paradigm shift in understanding the mechanisms of digital transformation of territories.

2 Theoretical Overview

As one of the key factors determining the thrusts of today's socio-economic systems, digital transformation has no single, generally accepted definition in scientific literature. Due to the multifaceted nature of this phenomenon, there exist various approaches to its conceptualization [5]. For instance, researchers adhering to technological determinism define digital transformation as a process of integrating digital technologies into all aspects of economic entities' activity, which results in fundamental shifts in the ways of functioning and creating value [6]. Other authors, who focus on social aspects of digitalization, view this phenomenon as a comprehensive transformation of socio-economic relations caused by the introduction of digital technologies and the formation of new models of interaction between individuals, organizations and institutions [7].

When considering various aspects of digital transformation, it is necessary to highlight its multidimensional nature affecting the technological, economic, social and institutional spheres. In terms of technology, digital transformation lies in the large-scale implementation of innovative solutions, such as artificial intelligence, the Internet of Things, big data, and cloud computing [8]. The economic aspect of digital transformation implies the emergence of new business models, and changes in value chains and the structure of markets [9]. Social effects of digitalization embrace shifts in consumption patterns, communication and social interaction, as well as the transformation of the labor market and the educational system [10]. The institutional influence of digital transformation processes suggests changes in formal and informal rules governing economic activity in the digital environment, as well as the formation of new coordination and management mechanisms [11].

Digital transformation at the regional level has a few peculiarities predetermined by the specificity of territorial socio-economic systems having a unique combination of the natural resource potential, human capital, institutional environment, and the stable structure of the economy [12]. In the regional context, digital transformation can be viewed as a process leading to shifts in the spatial organization of economic activity, the transformation of interregional connections and the creation of new sources of competitive advantages for territories [13]. At the same time, due to digital inequality between regions caused by differences in infrastructure development, the quality of human capital and the institutional environment, there are preconditions for increasing interregional disparities, which requires differentiated approaches to be proposed to stimulate digitalization at the regional level [14].

The concept of smart territories, which has gained in popularity in recent years, is one of the theoretical frameworks for analyzing the processes of digital transformation of regions and cities [15]. This approach, which integrates the ideas of innovation theory, new economic geography and the concept of sustainable development, considers digitalization as a tool for enhancing the effectiveness of territorial development regulation and improving the quality of life of the population. It concentrates on the formation of regional innovation ecosystems that makes it easier to generate and diffuse digital innovations [16].

The above theoretical approaches taken together provide the basis for a comprehensive analysis of digital transformation processes in regions. This interdisciplinary approach not only broadens the understanding of digital transformation mechanisms at the regional level, but also allows devising effective management tools contributing to the sustainable development of territories amid global technological changes.

3 Material and Methods

The Ural region, as a highly industrialized territory largely involved in digital transformation processes, is of particular interest to regional scholarly journals. The object of study was publications from several scientific periodicals, such as *R-Economy,* specializing in regional economics and development; *Changing Societies and Personalities,* examining social changes and their special features; and *The Education and Science Journal,* focusing on the evolution of the educational system. The journals for analysis were selected based on their belonging to the scientific publishing cluster that was formed in the Ural region under the influence of the reform of higher education in the Russian Federation. The selected journals allow proposing three complementary perspectives for studying digital transformation processes. *R-Economy* delves into the economic aspects of regional development and particularly the issues of modeling and projecting economic processes. *Changing Societies & Personalities* concentrates on the transformation of values, moral behavior and social identity in the context of rapidly changing social institutions. *The Education and Science Journal* covers relevant psychological and pedagogical issues, including the introduction of information technologies into the educational process. The selected journals are indexed in international databases: *R-Economy* is part of the Scopus database (SJR 0.174, Q3 in the subject area "Economics, Econometrics and Finance") and DOAJ; *Changing Societies and Personalities* is indexed in Scopus (SJR 0.145, Q2 in the subject area "Cultural Studies"); *The Education and Science Journal* is covered in Scopus (SJR 0.253, Q3 in the subject area "Education") and DOAJ. The institutional and territorial proximity of the journals published in Yekaterinburg (the administrative center of the Sverdlovsk region and the Ural Federal District) allows one to trace how current digitalization processes are comprehended from various disciplinary perspectives within a single regional scientific-educational space.

The time frame between 2019 and 2024 was chosen to analyze the most relevant trends in the field of digital transformation of regions. This time interval encompasses the period before and after the COVID-19 pandemic, which makes it possible to assess the impact of global shocks on digitalization and adaptation of regional economic systems to a new socio-economic environment.

To search and select relevant publications, the Lens platform (https://www.lens.org/) was used. A comprehensive search query was formed, taking into account a wide range of aspects of digital transformation in regions: *region* OR territor* OR* *area* OR district* OR province* OR "local government" OR municipality OR city OR cities OR urban OR rural OR local) AND ("digital transformation" OR digitalization OR digitisation OR "smart city" OR "smart region" OR "digital economy" OR "regional development" OR digital OR smart OR technology OR innovation OR IoT OR "Internet of Things" OR "artificial intelligence" OR AI OR "big data" OR "cloud computing" OR blockchain OR "digital twin*" OR "cyber-physical system*" OR "edge computing" OR 5G OR 6G OR "quantum computing" OR "industry 4.0" OR "industry 5.0" OR "fifth industrial revolution" OR "smart manufacturing" OR "intelligent automation" OR "human-machine collaboration" OR cobotics OR "digital divide" OR "technological gap" OR "digital inclusion" OR e-government OR "digital public services" OR "smart governance" OR "digital skills" OR "digital literacy" OR "workforce development" OR "human-centric technology" OR "innovation ecosystem" OR "digital innovation" OR "technological innovation" OR "open innovation" OR "augmented reality" OR "virtual reality" OR "mixed reality" OR "extended reality" OR XR OR industry OR manufacturing OR "smart factory" OR "predictive maintenance" OR "autonomous systems" OR "self-optimizing production" OR "mass customization".*

The query, which comprised terms related to regional development, key concepts of digitalization, social aspects of technological changes and innovation processes, allowed investigating the topic under review from different angles.

The article selection process consisted of several stages, namely initial search, selection of publications based on title and abstract screening, and a full-text analysis of potentially relevant materials to determine final inclusion in the review. The final sample included 149 articles that formed the empirical framework of the study. The sample covered metadata from the three journals and appears to be representative to detect key trends in the area under study.

The methodological tools used to analyze the selected array of publications encompassed a set of complementary methods. In addition to bibliometric analysis aimed at identifying quantitative patterns in the dynamics of publication activity, distribution of articles across journals and keyword analysis, we also performed content analysis to identify the core thematic areas, methodological approaches and the authors' main conclusions.

To visualize the obtained data, the VOSviewer software tool developed by the Leiden University team was used (official website of the developer of the VOSviewer software package: https://www.vosviewer.com/).

The selection of three journals in one region is methodologically justified as it ensures sample homogeneity through a common sociocultural context. In the Russian Federation, there is high differentiation in socioeconomic indicators, which is also evident when examining publishing practices. Along with socioeconomic differentiation in Russia, there are significant differences between territories in terms of personnel qualification levels and human capital characteristics, including those related to the scientific publishing community, defining the sociocultural context within which the skills and qualifications of editorial board members are formed. The Ural region is characterized by a relatively high level of scientific and educational potential (which positively affects personnel characteristics) and a comparatively high concentration of major university publications, concentrated particularly in Yekaterinburg as the capital of the Ural Federal District. The selected publications allow for creating a sufficiently representative picture of scientific discourse on digital transformation issues within a specific regional context. In the future, a promising direction for continuing the research could be studying the peculiarities of publication activity on digital transformation issues in other Russian regions.

4 Results

The final sample included 149 articles on digital transformation of regions published between 2019 and 2024. The selected works are embedded in a number of research areas, including not only economics (regional economics, in particular), but also management, geography, sociology, psychology, political science, computer science, and engineering (Fig. 1). This diversity of disciplines emphasizes that research into digital transformation at the regional level is of an interdisciplinary nature and highlights the complexity of this phenomenon that affects various components of socio-economic development.

The analysis of publication activity in the three journals demonstrates a steadily growing research interest in the problems of digital transformation of territories.

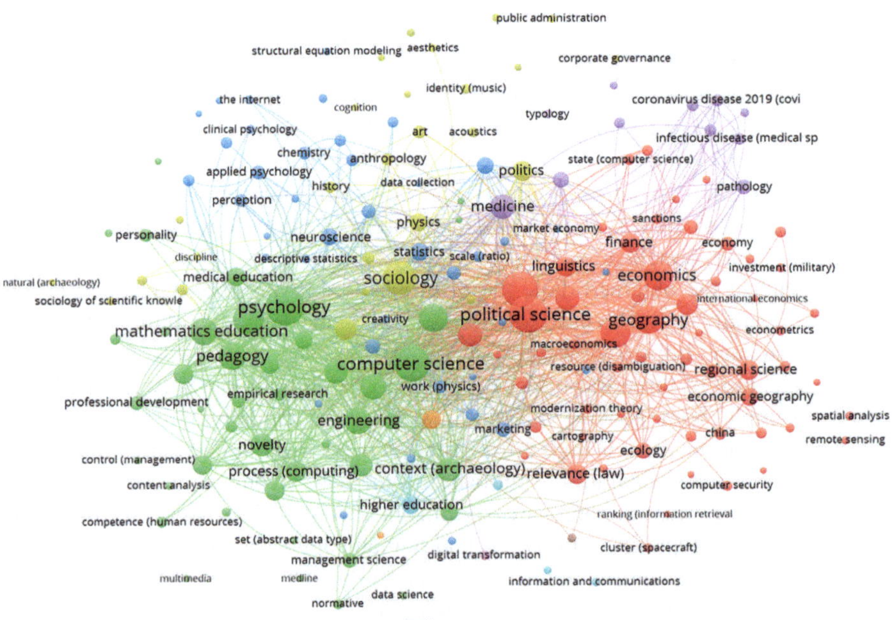

Fig. 1 Network visualization map of key research areas related to digital transformation of regions

The annual volume of publications on the topic increased from 21 to 31 articles, and the highest rise was recorded in *R-Economy*, which is due to the journal's specialization. However, *The Education and Science Journal* also published a significant number of relevant works, which indicates the decisive role of the educational aspect in regional digitalization. *Changing Societies & Personalities,* despite a comparatively smaller number of publications, has been consistently present in the research field throughout the period under review, which proves the importance of socio-psychological factors (Fig. 2).

As for the temporal dynamics, it is worth noting a significant surge in publications in 2020 fueled by the growing relevance of the studied issues in light of global socio-economic transformations, as well as by the increased interest in digitalization processes due to the COVID-19 lockdown. In the following years, some fluctuations were observed, but the overall trend remained positive. The 2024 data are not yet complete, but we can state that researchers' interest in the topic is still strong.

Figure 3 shows the results of frequency analysis of the most popular keywords in the publications under review.

The most popular term used in the articles in 2019–2024 was "artificial intelligence" (AI), while "digital" (and "digitalization" as well) was ranked second. The keywords "technology", "innovation", "digital transformation", "smart" and "smart city" were also consistently mentioned in the works analyzed, which indicates an ongoing scientific discourse on digital transformation and intellectualization of territorial economic systems and, thus, unveils a paradigm shift in the understanding of

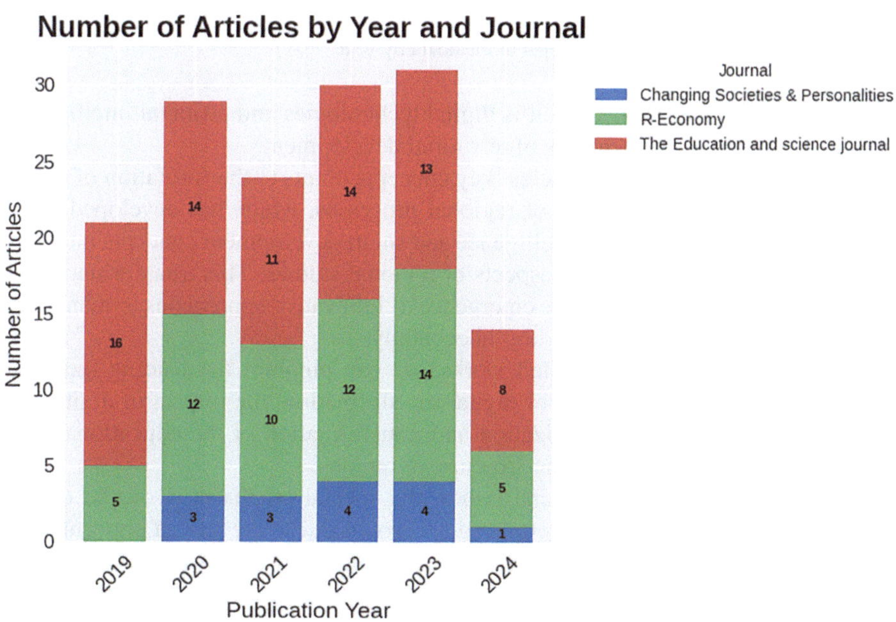

Fig. 2 Number of articles by year and journal

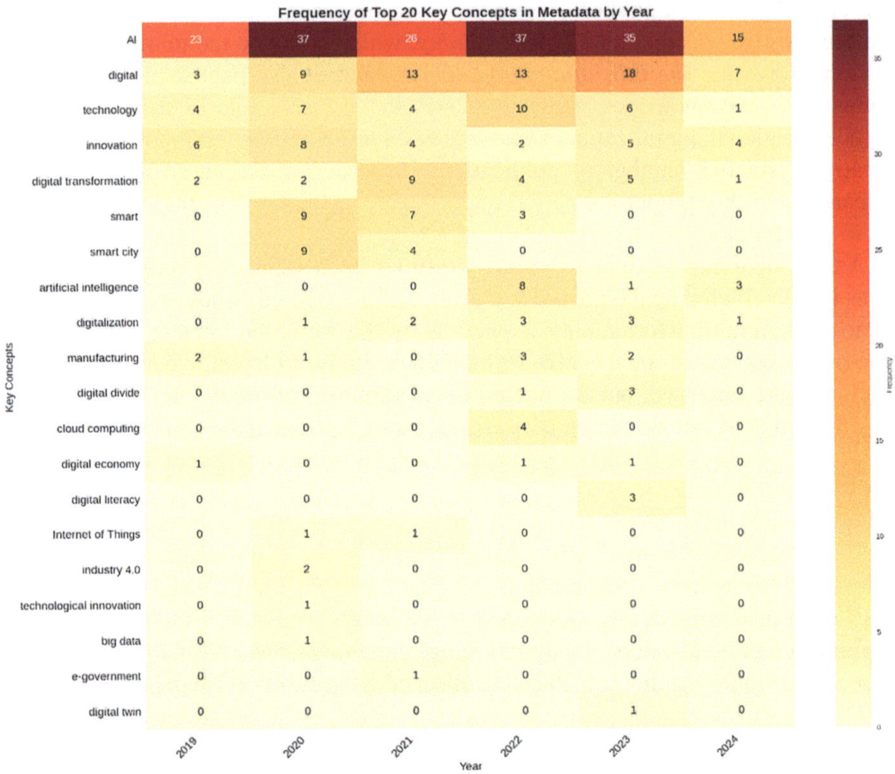

Fig. 3 Frequency of top 20 key concepts in metadata by year

socio-economic processes, since it is digital technologies and artificial intelligence that are becoming the key drivers of territorial development.

Frequency analysis of the articles' key concepts points to the formation of a new research landscape in the study of regional processes, which has developed amid digital technologies, artificial intelligence and smart development concepts integrating into theoretical and applied aspects of regional studies. This transformation of scientific discourse stimulates the emergence of innovative approaches to managing regional development within the digital economy.

When analyzing the most cited works, we can pinpoint the leading thematic blocks covering different facets of digital transformation: the impact of digitalization on social processes, digitalization and transformation of the educational system, and changes in the economic structure of regions.

In the context of general social issues, the special emphasis is on the digital divide (i.e. limitations faced by certain social groups due to the lack of opportunities or conditions to access modern means of communication) and its impact on household behavior, including the planning of family budgets. Studying this phenomenon using the case of China, Kefeng et al. [17] found that the digital divide, which manifests itself in three dimensions—access to modern technologies, the use of these technologies, and digital inequality—has a significant impact on the likelihood of households participating in risky financial investments. Moreover, the reason behind the digital divide is only the traditional differentiation between rural and urban areas, but also social barriers between different generations. It highlights the need to map out strategies to overcome digital inequality that take into account the national context and are aimed at increasing the digital literacy of the population.

However, it is not only older generations that may experience discomfort associated with the digitalization of the social environment. Of special interest is the perception of digital technologies by the young population, in particular the phenomenon of digital fears. Having extensively studied the Russian youth, Abramova et al. [18] identified new types of social fears associated with digitalization. The authors proposed a typology of digital fears, including concerns about control, security, communication and social inequality in the digital environment. The obtained results indicate the need to consider psychological aspects when designing educational programs and policies on digitalization.

Social factors can significantly affect the processes of smart development of territories and cities. In this context, the study by Kostko and Pecherkina [19], dedicated to the analysis of urban identity, is of high importance. Addressing the case study of three Russian cities (Tyumen, Tobolsk, and Khanty-Mansiysk), the authors discovered a significant correlation between residents' perception of their cities (including emotional attachment) and their willingness to take part in smart development processes. The findings illustrate that digitalization of the urban environment cannot be uncoupled from the socio-cultural context and residents' identity.

The development of the cultural environment in the digital age is also a quite relevant issue. Simbirtseva et al. [20] investigated cultural and educational practices in museums and demonstrated how digital technologies can preserve and transmit cultural heritage, which is directly related to the concept of the knowledge economy.

An equally important area of research is the transformation of citizens' involvement in political processes in the digital age. Radina and Belyashova [21] analyze the political activity of western and eastern parts of Germany residents using digital tools, primarily online petitions. The authors find that historical heritage and socio-economic factors exert less influence on civic engagement in the digital environment than previously assumed. This study shows that digitalization can help to level out regional differences in political culture.

Thus, digital transformation can not only provoke a digital divide, but also smooth out the pre-existing imbalances caused by both geographical and socio-cultural factors. On the other hand, under globalization and digitalization, online communication channels are becoming especially important, as they can broadcast not only unifying, but also destructive narratives. Having analyzed the election campaigns of Donald Trump and Jair Bolsonaro, Novoselova [22] established specific patterns and innovations in the transmission of nationalist messages through digital channels. This study highlights the significance of exploring the relationship between digitalization of communications and transformation of political discourse in today's world.

Among social institutions, it was the educational system that experienced perhaps the most powerful impact of digital transformation as it is at the junction of not only different generations, but waves of technological development that is not always gradual and smooth. The shock digitalization of education caused by the COVID-19 pandemic became a catalyst for profound changes in the educational process. Nazarov et al. [23] discuss the complex nature of these transformations and look at both technological and psychological aspects of the transition to distance learning. The authors stress that this transition has revealed a number of significant shortcomings in the digital transformation strategy for education, such as insufficient development of digital infrastructure and the lack of adequate methods for using digital educational tools.

Not only educational organizations, but also students are not always prepared for new digital technologies in education. Alenezi [24] scrutinized the relationship between students' emotional intelligence and their readiness for online learning and concluded that emotional competencies play the key part in successful adaptation to the digital educational environment. These findings correlate with the study by Tsalikova and Pakhotina [25], who note that developing soft skills is a pressing task of modern education, along with acquiring additional hard skills that are instrumental in interacting with the digital environment.

Perminov et al. [26] emphasize the significance of fundamental mathematical training for students, which is in line with the ideas of the new institutional economics about the role of basic knowledge in the formation of effective institutions. Rabinovich et al. [27] propose providing students with a comprehensive training for innovative activities through pre-adaptation of schoolchildren. This study exhibits the tendency towards a proactive approach in education, which corresponds to the principles of an innovative economy.

New technology is a challenge not only for students, but also for teachers. The changing role of a teacher in the digital age is another key aspect of research. Zeer et al. [28] analyze the changing capabilities of higher education teachers in conditions of uncertainty, including those associated with digitalization of education and the educational system.

The issues of graduate employment in the context of the digital economy also attract the attention of researchers. Merenkov et al. [29] focus on changes in orientations to employment among bachelor's graduates, which reflects the digitalization-induced transformation of the labor market. This issue is closely related to HR perspectives of Russian universities considered by Ezrokh [30]. The author underscores the need for the higher education system to adapt to the digital economy requirements. Digitalization of education affects all levels of the educational system—from technological aspects to psychological, pedagogical and socio-economic ones—and requires a comprehensive approach to its study and reform. The discovered trends prove the need to rethink not only the methods and forms of teaching, but also the very paradigm of education in the context of the digital economy and knowledge society.

Digital transformation not only affects socio-cultural development in regions, but also shapes the directions of structural changes in territorial economic systems.

The concept of smart territories as a driver of territorial development, described in by Nikitaeva et al. [31], marks a new stage in understanding regional policy. Drawing on endogenous growth theory, the authors demonstrate how digital technologies can become a key factor in achieving sustainable development goals at the regional level. This approach, echoing the ideas of new economic geography and underlining the role of innovation and human capital in the formation of territories' competitive advantages, is furthered by Choi [32], Myslyakova et al. [33], Komarevtseva [34], Urdabayev and Utkelbay [35]. The study of creative industries by Turgel et al. [36] contributes to the debate on the role of the creative economy in regional development. The authors systematize theoretical approaches to identifying creative industries and emphasize that they can potentially encourage innovative growth and diversification of the regional economy, which directly correlates with the concept of smart specialization of regions. Another option for regulating structural transformation is the implementation of cluster policy [37].

In the context of global economic challenges, the issues of structural stability of the regional economy are gaining in relevance. Romanova and Ponomareva [38] analyzed the impact of the pandemic on the economy of Russian regions and established that the structure of the economy and the quality of public administration are the key factors in ensuring economic sustainability. Akhunov et al. [39], Pobedin et al. [40] and Oykher [41] delve into the pandemic's effects on regional development and discuss various strategies for adapting economic systems to such challenges, including through digital technological solutions. Hennebry's [42] study of the economic resilience of Irish counties allows comprehending the factors underlying regional resilience. The author revealed that there is no correlation between resilience to the financial crisis and resilience to the COVID-19 pandemic, which proves the need for a differentiated approach to the analysis of regional resilience. One more option for implementing external challenges is the tightening of sanctions against the Russian Federation.

Stepanov et al. [43] raise the question of how sanctions influence industrial regions, which demonstrates the relevance of the geoeconomic approach in regional studies. Using the case of the Sverdlovsk region, the authors clarify how external shocks transform the development path of industrial territories, forcing them to adapt strategic priorities and seek new sources of growth. Abramova et al. [44] examine the attractiveness of a city as a factor of territorial mobility in student estimates, which highlights the importance of human capital in regional development. The authors emphasize the role of the urban environment and educational infrastructure in the formation of the human potential in regions.

In general, the selected studies on territorial development employ an interdisciplinary approach that integrates the ideas of economic geography, institutional economics, innovation theory, and the concept of sustainable development. The revealed trends point to the need for a comprehensive approach to regional policy that would consider global trends in digitalization and sustainable development, as well as the specificity of local institutional and socio-economic conditions. Researchers pay special attention to the role of human capital, innovation and the institutional environment in boosting the competitiveness and sustainability of regional economic systems.

5 Discussion

Currently, examining digital transformation processes in regions is one of the main avenues for research on regional economics. It raises a variety of issues that require a deep understanding and an interdisciplinary approach. The tendency to integrate various scientific disciplines, revealed during the analysis of publication activity, indicates the emergence of a new research landscape, where the traditional boundaries between economic, sociological, geographical and technological research are becoming increasingly permeable [31, 36].

Diversification of research interest embodied in the growing array of scientific publications on digital transformation of territories can be seen as an indicator of a paradigm shift in understanding the mechanisms of regional development. This is due to the transition from a highly specialized economic analysis to a comprehensive examination of the socio-economic, technological and institutional aspects of territorial development and, thus, it lies the foundations for new theoretical concepts and methodological approaches in regional economics.

Spatial differentiation in the context of the digital economy deserves special attention of researchers. The revealed patterns in territorial inequality stemming from different development levels of digital infrastructure and the population's digital competencies make it necessary to rethink traditional approaches to regional policy [17].

Transformations in the labor market and the educational system are not only a challenge for regions, but also a potential driver of their innovative development. Digitalization-induced shifts in the employment structure and educational practices foster the development of new approaches to human capital formation at the regional level [23, 24]. In this case, the ratio between universal and specific competencies necessary for successful adaptation to the digital environment come to the fore [25, 26].

An analysis of digitalization-related structural changes in regional economies shows the need for new regional policy instruments that allow for the specificity of innovation ecosystems and the potential of creative industries [36, 37]. In this context, the concept of smart territories can be viewed as a potential tool for smoothing out interregional disparities, but its effectiveness is largely predetermined by the capability of regional authorities to modify this concept according to local socio-economic conditions [19]. Smart specialization suggests unique competitive advantages forming in the regions based on their endogenous potential and technological competencies.

The problem of regional resilience to external shocks, which has become especially acute amid global crises, opens up new research areas focused on assessing territories' adaptive potential within the digital economy. The differences in regions' responses to various types of crises accentuate the need for a differentiated approach to formulating regional development strategies that considers both technological and institutional aspects of digital transformation [38–41].

Spatial factors and their role in the formation of innovation ecosystems under the digital economy occupy a special place in the research agenda. The trends observed in the field of regional innovation concentration make it necessary to reconsider traditional approaches to regional development with a focus on a favorable environment for generating and diffusing innovations, as well as on effective mechanisms for cross-regional interaction in the sphere of innovation [42, 44] based on institutional factors in digital transformation of regions and, in particular, changes in the mechanisms for coordinating economic activity and forms of social interaction [19, 21, 22].

6 Conclusion

Based on the scientometric analysis of Russia's three highly cited regional journals, our study creates a holistic understanding of the current state of research on digital transformation in regions. A progressive growth of research interest in the problems of digital transformation was revealed, with studies focusing on economic consequences of digitalization and the corresponding dynamics of social processes, primarily education. It is worth noting the tendency towards convergence of methodological apparatuses of various scientific disciplines, which, while creating an integrated effect, also identifies a number of areas that require additional research efforts to fully understand the nature and implications of digitalization at the regional level.

The observed research trends can be utilized when introducing measures to regulate digital transformation in regions. Heated academic debates about artificial intelligence, digitalization and the concept of smart territories indicate the need to include these aspects in the strategies and programs of the constituent entities of the Russian Federation. A comprehensive approach to the problems of digital transformation that takes into account both economic-technological and socio-psychological components can be realized through organizing interdepartmental expert groups on digital development, involving competent professionals from both business and the scientific educational community.

Our study differs from other review articles on similar topics (for example, [45–47]) over an interdisciplinary approach, the methodology used, the temporal and territorial coverage, as well as the empirical basis of the study. Based on the analysis of publications from multidisciplinary journals and integration of economic, social and educational aspects, we produced a multifaceted overview of the phenomenon under study. A set of methodological tools, including bibliometric analysis and content analysis using VOSviewer, were applied to recognize quantitative patterns in the publication dynamics and identify the core thematic areas of research. The study covers the most relevant period of 2019–2024, which allows tracing the transformation of scientific discourse under the influence of global shocks, such as the COVID-19 pandemic and subsequent socio-economic changes, with a primary focus on Russian regions, but also deeming global experience and trends. A representative sample of 149 research articles, selected based on a comprehensive search query via the Lens platform, provided sufficient empirical foundations for in-depth qualitative analysis, in contrast to large-scale but less detailed bibliometric studies.

The scientific novelty of the conducted research consists of the following:

- Systematization and comprehensive analysis of scientific discourse on digital transformation of regions within the sociocultural context of the Ural scientific and educational space has been carried out;
- A methodology for multi-aspect analysis of publication activity on digital transformation issues has been developed and tested, allowing identification of changes in the conceptualization of the studied phenomenon;
- The tendency toward convergence of methodological approaches from various scientific disciplines in studying the digital transformation of regions has been identified and substantiated.

The identified research trends are instrumental when implementing measures to regulate digital transformation at the regional level. Vivid scholarly discussion about artificial intelligence, digitalization and the concept of smart territories emphasizes the need to cover these aspects in the strategies and programs of the RF constituent entities. The problems of digital transformation should be tackled in a comprehensive manner, e.g., through forming expert groups with the involvement of business practitioners and academics.

Based on the detected trends, one can assume that research focus on the problems of using artificial intelligence in various areas of the regional economy is expected to intensify. Among the promising avenues for further research are the development of digital transformation integrative models rooted in the local specificity of territories, the study of the long-term effects of digitalization and the search for a balance between technological progress and sustainable development of regions. New knowledge in these fields will enrich the theoretical framework and offer practical recommendations for formulating an effective policy for the digital development of territories that would enhance the quality of life of the population and reduce interregional disparities in the digital age.

References

1. Sanders, C. K., & Scanlon, E. (2021). The digital divide is a human rights issue: Advancing social inclusion through social work advocacy. *Journal of Human Rights and Social Work, 6*, 130–143. https://doi.org/10.1007/s41134-020-00147-9
2. Mironov, V. V., & Kuznetsov, A. O. (2024). Digitalization as a determinant of economic policy choice: Russian realities and world experience. *Voprosy Ekonomiki, 4*, 38–69. https://doi.org/10.32609/0042-8736-2024-4-38-69
3. Shaidullin, A. K. (2024). Smart specialization of regions as a basis for sustainable development of The Russian Federation. *Finance and Management, 1*, 1–11. https://doi.org/10.25136/2409-7802.2024.1.69846

4. Di Cataldo, M., Monastiriotis, V., & Rodríguez-Pose, A. (2022). How "smart" are smart specialization strategies? JCMS. *Journal of Common Market Studies, 60*, 1272–1298. https://doi.org/10.1111/jcms.13156
5. Vial, G. (2019). Understanding digital transformation: A review and a research agenda. *The Journal of Strategic Information Systems, 28*(2), 118–144. https://doi.org/10.1016/j.jsis.2019.01.003
6. Verhoef, P. C., Broekhuizen, T., Bart, Y., Bhattacharya, A., Dong, J. Q., Fabian, N., & Haenlein, M. (2021). Digital transformation: A multidisciplinary reflection and research agenda. *Journal of Business Research, 122*, 889–901. https://doi.org/10.1016/j.jbusres.2019.09.022
7. Mergel, I., Edelmann, N., & Haug, N. (2019). Defining digital transformation: Results from expert interviews. *Government Information Quarterly, 36*(4), 101385. https://doi.org/10.1016/j.giq.2019.06.002
8. Khin, S., & Ho, T. C. (2020). Digital technology, digital capability and organizational performance: A mediating role of digital innovation. *International Journal of Innovation Science, 11*(2), 177–195. https://doi.org/10.1108/IJIS-08-2018-0083
9. Teece, D. J. (2018). Business models and dynamic capabilities. *Long Range Planning, 51*(1), 40–49. https://doi.org/10.1016/j.lrp.2017.06.007
10. Yoo, I., & Yi, C.-G. (2022). Economic innovation caused by digital transformation and impact on social systems. *Sustainability, 14*(5), 2600. https://doi.org/10.3390/su14052600
11. Hinings, B., Gegenhuber, T., & Greenwood, R. (2018). Digital innovation and transformation: An institutional perspective. *Information and Organization, 28*(1), 52–61. https://doi.org/10.1016/j.infoandorg.2018.02.004
12. Götz, M. (2021). *Clusters, digital transformation and regional development in Germany* (1st ed.). Routledge. https://doi.org/10.4324/9781003005506
13. Tranos, E., Kitsos, T., & Ortega-Argilés, R. (2021). Digital economy in the UK: Regional productivity effects of early adoption. *Regional Studies, 55*(12), 1924–1938. https://doi.org/10.1080/00343404.2020.1826420
14. Ragnedda, M., & Kreitem, H. (2018). The three levels of digital divide in east EU countries. World of media. *Journal of Russian Media and Journalism Studies, 1*(4), 5–26. https://doi.org/10.30547/worldofmedia.4.2018.1
15. Ibănescu, B.-C., Pascariu, G. C., Bănică, A., & Bejenaru, I. (2022). Smart city: A critical assessment of the concept and its implementation in Romanian urban strategies. *Journal of Urban Management, 11*(2), 246–255. https://doi.org/10.1016/j.jum.2022.05.003
16. Linde, L., Sjödin, D., Parida, V., & Wincent, J. (2021). Dynamic capabilities for ecosystem orchestration: A capability-based framework for smart city innovation initiatives. *Technological Forecasting and Social Change, 166*, 120614. https://doi.org/10.1016/j.techfore.2021.120614
17. Kefeng, Y., Xiaoxia, Z., & Nedospasova, O. (2023). The impact of digital divide on household participation in risky financial investments: Evidence from China. *Changing Societies & Personalities, 7*(1), 113–129. https://doi.org/10.15826/csp.2023.7.1.221
18. Abramova, S., Antonova, N., Campa, R., & Popova, N. (2022). Digital fears experienced by young people in the age of technoscience. *Changing Societies & Personalities, 6*(1), 56–78. https://doi.org/10.15826/csp.2022.6.1.163
19. Kostko, N., & Pecherkina, I. (2021). Urban identities in Russian cities and the prospects of their "smart" development. *Changing Societies & Personalities, 5*(4), 636–653. https://doi.org/10.15826/csp.2021.5.4.154
20. Simbirtseva, N., Kruglikova, G., & Plaksina, E. (2020). Cultural and educational practices in the museum environment: Transmission of cultural heritage. *Changing Societies & Personalities, 4*(4), 492–507. https://doi.org/10.15826/csp.2020.4.4.113
21. Radina, N., & Belyashova, D. (2021). Digital political participation of western and eastern parts of Germany residents (based on change.org online petitions). *Changing Societies & Personalities, 5*(1), 63–82. https://doi.org/10.15826/csp.2021.5.1.122

22. Novoselova, O. (2020). Peculiarities of modern nationalist messages in online political communication: The analyses of Donald Trump's and Jair Bolsonaro's election campaigns. *Changing Societies & Personalities, 4*(3), 350–371. https://doi.org/10.15826/csp.2020.4.3.105
23. Nazarov, V. L., Zherdev, D. V., & Averbukh, N. V. (2021). Shock digitalisation of education: The perception of participants of the educational process. *The Education and Science Journal, 23*(1), 156–201. https://doi.org/10.17853/1994-5639-2021-1-156-201
24. Alenezi, A. M. (2020). The relationship of students' emotional intelligence and the level of their readiness for online education: A contextual study on the example of university training in Saudi Arabia. *The Education and Science Journal, 22*(4), 89–109. https://doi.org/10.17853/1994-5639-2020-4-89-109
25. Tsalikova, I. K., & Pakhotina, S. V. (2019). Scientific research on the issue of soft skills development (review of the data in international databases of Scopus, web of science). *The Education and Science Journal, 21*(8), 187–207. https://doi.org/10.17853/1994-5639-2019-7-187-207
26. Perminov, E. A., Gadjiev, D. D., & Abdurazakov, M. M. (2019). About relevance of fundamentalisation of mathematical training of students of the pedagogical directions during the digital era. *The Education and Science Journal, 21*(5), 86–111. https://doi.org/10.17853/1994-5639-2019-5-87-112
27. Rabinovich, P. D., Kremneva, L. V., Zavedenskiy, K. E., Shekhter, E. D., & Apenko, S. N. (2021). Preadaptation of students to innovation activity and formation of practices of futures scenario building. *The Education and Science Journal, 23*(2), 39–70. https://doi.org/10.17853/1994-5639-2021-2-39-70
28. Zeer, E. F., Rezer, T. M., & Symaniuk, N. V. (2023). Transformation of the capabilities of higher school teachers in conditions of uncertainty: Problem statement. *The Education and Science Journal, 25*(5), 12–48. https://doi.org/10.17853/1994-5639-2023-5-12-48
29. Merenkov, A. V., Sandler, D. G., & Shavrin, V. S. (2019). The features of changes in orientations to employment among bachelor's graduates. *The Education and Science Journal, 21*(10), 116–142. https://doi.org/10.17853/1994-5639-2019-10-116-142
30. Ezrokh, Y. S. (2019). HR perspectives of Russian universities: Who will teach in the near future? *The Education and Science Journal, 21*(7), 9–40. https://doi.org/10.17853/1994-5639-2019-7-9-40
31. Nikitaeva, A. Y., Chernova, O. A., & Molapisi, L. (2022). Smart territories as a driver for the transition to sustainable regional development and green economy. *R-Economy, 8*(2), 120–134. https://doi.org/10.15826/recon.2022.8.2.010
32. Choi, Y.-S. (2020). Smart city development projects in the Republic of Korea. *R-Economy, 6*(1), 40–49. https://doi.org/10.15826/recon.2020.6.1.004
33. Myslyakova, Y. G., Shamova, E. A., & Neklyudova, N. P. (2021). Key steps to smart specialization development of Russian regions. *R-Economy, 7*(2), 123–132. https://doi.org/10.15826/recon.2021.7.2.011
34. Komarevtseva, O. O. (2020). The modified smart city concept for Russian municipalities in the context of change management. *R-Economy, 6*(4), 292–298. https://doi.org/10.15826/recon.2020.6.4.026
35. Urdabayev, M. T., & Utkelbay, R. E. (2021). SWOT analysis of smart city projects in capital cities of Russia and Kazakhstan. *R-Economy, 7*(4), 235–243. https://doi.org/10.15826/recon.2021.7.4.021
36. Turgel, I. D., Derbeneva, V. V., Baskakova, I. V., & Chukavina, K. V. (2022). Theoretical approaches to identifying creative industries. *R-Economy, 8*(4), 310–326. https://doi.org/10.15826/recon.2022.8.4.024
37. Turgel, I. D., Bozhko, L. L., & Zinovieva, E. G. (2019). Cluster approach to organization of special economic zones in Russia and Kazakhstan. *R-Economy, 5*(2), 71–78. https://doi.org/10.15826/recon.2019.5.2.008

38. Romanova, O. A., & Ponomareva, A. O. (2021). The structural factor of regional economic stability in Russia during the coronacrisis period. *R-Economy, 7*(3), 158–169. https://doi.org/10.15826/recon.2021.7.3.014
39. Akhunov, R. R., Akhunova, L. R., Marichev, S. G., & Nizamutdinov, R. L. (2021). Russian oil and gas regions during the COVID-19 crisis and their digital transformation. *R-Economy, 7*(3), 179–191. https://doi.org/10.15826/recon.2021.7.3.016
40. Pobedin, A. A., Balynskaya, N. R., & Williams, D. (2021). Socioeconomic consequences of the first and second waves of the pandemic in Russian regions. *R-Economy, 7*(3), 146–157. https://doi.org/10.15826/recon.2021.7.3.013
41. Oykher, A. D. (2021). The economic and organizational model of the international admission campaign during the COVID-19 pandemic (the case of the Moscow Institute of Physics and technology). *R-Economy, 7*(3), 170–178. https://doi.org/10.15826/recon.2021.7.3.015
42. Hennebry, B. (2020). The economic resilience of Irish counties for subsequent recessions and the impact of population distribution on resilience. *R-Economy, 6*(3), 146–153. https://doi.org/10.15826/recon.2020.6.3.012
43. Stepanov, A. V., Burnasov, A. S., Valiakhmetova, G. N., & Ilyushkina, M. Y. (2022). The impact of economic sanctions on the industrial regions of Russia (the case of Sverdlovsk region). *R-Economy, 8*(3), 295–305. https://doi.org/10.15826/recon.2022.8.3.023
44. Abramova, S. B., Antonova, N. L., & Pimenova, O. I. (2019). Attractiveness of a city as a factor of territorial mobility in student estimates (on the example of Ekaterinburg). *The Education and Science Journal, 21*(1), 97–123. https://doi.org/10.17853/1994-5639-2019-1-97-123
45. Benner, M. (2022). An institutionalist perspective on smart specialization: Towards a political economy of regional innovation policy. *Science and Public Policy, 49*(6), 878–889. https://doi.org/10.1093/scipol/scac035
46. Cheng, C., Wang, L., Xie, H., & Yan, L. (2023). Mapping digital innovation: A bibliometric analysis and systematic literature review. *Technological Forecasting and Social Change, 194*, 122706. https://doi.org/10.1016/j.techfore.2023.122706
47. Ma, H., & Ismail, L. (2025). Bibliometric analysis and systematic review of digital competence in education. *Humanities and Social Sciences Communications, 12*, 185. https://doi.org/10.1057/s41599-025-04401-1

Digital Pathways of Russian Regions and Their Interaction with the Local Human Capital Markets: An Evolutionary Perspective

Irina Semenova, Veronika Zemzyulina, and Ilia Chernenko

Abstract Digitalization enhances regional competitiveness by optimizing resource utilization, fostering connectivity, and driving innovation. However, the long-term digital evolution of Russian regions remains poorly understood. The digital evolution is uneven and constrained by limitations in dynamic capabilities and digital human capital, often resulting in path dependency and development lock-ins. This study aims to identify the configurations of regional digital technology development and analyze their dynamic trajectories, which shape regional development pathways. We evaluate the interaction between pathways and the dynamics of human capital accumulation. Our approach combines evolutionary economics techniques, such as history-friendly modeling and compartmental methods, with formal statistical tools, including cluster analysis and regression. Using cluster analysis based on Rosstat data, the study identifies three groups of regions (progressive, inertial, and lagging) and their respective pathways from 2011 to 2022, including "leader", "COVID impact", "long disruption", and "developing after 2014". Pioneer regions, such as Moscow and St. Petersburg, demonstrate the "leader" pathway, having maintained high levels of digital maturity since 2011. The "long disruption" pathway, observed in southern regions, highlights persistent digital lag over the study period. Regression analysis reveals that regions following the "long disruption" pathway are characterized by insufficient basic digital skills and low innovation activity. The "leader" pathway is driven by the development of advanced digital skills, particularly in programming. The overall level of human capital positively influences region's long-term digital performance. Practical implications include the need to differentiate regional development policies and increase attention to regions with a long disruption pathway.

I. Semenova · V. Zemzyulina · I. Chernenko (✉)
Ural Federal University, Ekaterinburg, Russia
e-mail: i.i.semenova@urfu.ru; veronika.zemziulina@urfu.ru; i.m.chernenko@urfu.ru

F. Tao et al. (eds.), *Artificial Intelligence and Digital Transformation*, Lecture Notes in Information Systems and Organisation 78,
https://doi.org/10.1007/978-3-032-00118-4_14

Keywords Digitalization · Evolutionary economics · Human capital · Digital skills · Regions

1 Introduction

Technological development driven by innovation and its dissemination has a strong impact on economic growth, transforming existing interactions between agents in the capital, goods and services markets, as well as in the labor market [1]. Contemporary technological developments, notably driven by digitalization, are historically unprecedented due to their rapid pace and extensive impact. Digitalization promotes both product and process innovations and facilitates sustained organizational and individual learning, knowledge exchange, and adaptation [2]. Human capital is reshaped under the influence of the digital environment, some skills become obsolete and are updated, in addition, key competencies such as analytical skills and critical thinking, the ability to justify decisions based on data analysis, programming skills and working with applications become in demand [3]. Understanding and implementing the capabilities of the digital environment becomes a driver of growth, but evolutionary paths are full of uncertainty, which causes significant differences in the results of digital transformation [4, 5]. Investigating regional digital evolution is therefore essential to identifying critical success factors and barriers influencing long-term regional development, particularly highlighting the role of intellectual resources at distinct stages of digitalization.

The social implications of digitalization are central to policies aimed at maintaining well-being and sustaining human capital, particularly in the face of economic shocks. Adopting an evolutionary perspective provides valuable insights into how selected development paths interact with the reproduction of regional knowledge and skills, particularly in the domain of information and computer literacy [6]. Despite significant advancements, the literature still provides limited empirical evidence regarding long-term trends in the evolution of digital human capital, especially considering the unique digitalization regimes within Russian regions. Specifically, there is a knowledge gap concerning the dynamic evolution of distinct regional digital adoption patterns and their subsequent interactions with regional human capital accumulation.

The existing literature provides limited insights into the long-term evolutionary trends of digital human capital under diverse regional digitalization regimes, particularly within the context of Russian regions. Specifically, there is insufficient understanding of how distinct regional patterns of digital technology adoption evolve dynamically over extended periods and how these patterns interact with the accumulation and evolution of human capital. Additionally, despite recognizing digitalization as a critical factor influencing regional growth, prior studies have not comprehensively analyzed how institutional contexts, innovation capacities, and socioeconomic variables collectively shape regional digital trajectories. Given the gaps, this study investigates how regional configurations of digital technology development evolve over time and how these trajectories interact with human capital accumulation within the specific institutional and socioeconomic contexts of Russian regions. The nature of human capital and its manifestations are diverse; in our study we consider such aspects as education and work experience. Key variables considered include gross regional product (GRP), levels of innovative development, basic and advanced digital skills, general and specialized human capital, industry structure, and the extent of government involvement, factors that collectively define the institutional context of digitalization. This study is the first to examine the long-term development of digital technologies in Russian regions using the principles of history-friendly modeling, focusing on the model interpretations based on an understanding of the context and episodes of industrial development, as well as cause-and-effect relationships. The study examines the 12-year period from 2011 to 2022, with a specific focus on the impact of digital development paths on human capital during the more recent period of 2016 to 2022. The latter period is particularly relevant given the increased geopolitical tensions and technological restrictions, and the disruptive effects of the COVID-19 pandemic on regional markets [7]. The primary research objective is to identify critical determinants and barriers shaping regional digital transformation paths, and to elucidate their long-term implications for human capital accumulation and dynamics within the distinctive socioeconomic and institutional contexts of Russian regions.

2 Theoretical Background

Understanding the dynamics of digital transformation from an evolutionary economics standpoint requires a review of its theoretical underpinnings. The evolutionary perspective calls for examining key principles, such as adaptation, path dependence, and the pivotal role of technological innovation, which collectively shape the evolution of digital economies and the development of human capital. The following subsections review these theoretical aspects in detail, including evolutionary perspectives within the digital economy.

2.1 Evolutionary Perspective on Digital Economy

The principles of evolutionary economics pay attention to real empirical evidence within a specific historical context and allow us to form an idea of long-term changes in the adaptive behavior and transformation of agents under the influence of external shocks in the recent decades. These include the pandemic, rising geopolitical tensions, fragmentation of technological exchange and trade, as well as the aggravation of global problems related to ecology, demography and increasing inequality [8, 9]. Offering an alternative to the neoclassical perspective, based on a strict formal theory and a number of restrictive assumptions, evolutionary theory suggests that survival, behavioral change and adaptation of economic agents occur in conditions of disequilibrium and depend on innovation-oriented changes, reconfigurations, the ability to implement radical changes, convergence and catch-up processes [6, 10, 11]. Thus, evolutionary economics pays close attention primarily to the processes of technological change, which are currently transforming the processes of value creation under the revolution of digital technologies, transforming the markets for goods, services, capital and labor [12].

The concept of a path is central to the evolutionary perspective, as it captures the dynamic reconfiguration of agents within a socio-economic environment, which represent specific combinations of parameters: technological, institutional, and economic factors, that are essential for ensuring long-term well-being [6]. Evolutionary economics emphasizes that these development paths are shaped by historical choices and stages of socio-economic and technological change, a concept known as *path dependence* [13]. Path dependence highlights how earlier decisions and established patterns influence the current configurations of agents, often imposing limitations on their future development. Decisions made in the preformation and formation stages of a path can reinforce behaviors and systems, leading to a lock-in phase [12]. During this phase, development trajectories become increasingly constrained, with dominant patterns consolidating and narrowing the range of future opportunities. In the macroeconomic context, this phenomenon is particularly evident in firms, which, as they mature, may become less responsive to change and innovation. By focusing on a specific path and set of opportunities, firms can become entrenched, which eventually drives stagnation, decline, and even market exit [12]. However, the digital economy challenges and reinterprets the traditional understanding of path dependence. Information and communication technologies (ICTs) introduce opportunities to break free from lock-ins by enabling systems to adapt and reconfigure more dynamically [14].

The literature emphasizes emerging periodization in the evolutionary path of digital technology development, related to the understanding of the network and social role of ICT solutions. Industry 3.0 technologies, such as digital computers and the Internet, provided connectivity, storage capacity and computing capabilities, while Industry 4.0 provided complex interaction through the existence of a cyber-physical environment [15, 16]. Recent trends indicate the emergence of Industry 5.0, which supports cyber-social systems focused on full interaction with humans and complementing their intellectual abilities [17, 18]. The latest round of digitalization is associated with inclusive production, human-centric robotics, providing joint real-time interaction between humans and smart robots. Central to Industry 5.0 are the expectations surrounding artificial intelligence, which is intended to help improve productivity and economic growth. However, this also introduces significant risks for human capital, particularly in developing countries, where labor market disruptions and skill mismatches could exacerbate existing inequalities [19]. Thus, at each stage, digitalization creates new elements of the value proposition and leads to changes in the company's business models, ensuring the dynamics of market development.

An essential aspect of the evolutionary perspective is analyzing variables that initiate changes and influence the outcomes achieved by agents. A critical determinant of the digital evolution of regions is the institutional environment, which not only sets the behavioral rules for economic agents but is also shaped by their activities and evolving goals [6]. Institutional variables influencing digital pathways include explicit dimensions such as regional tax structures, technological policies, and socio-economic strategies, alongside implicit elements like cultural norms, values, and shared practices [11]. Dalloshi and Kyqyku [20] find that in European regions, differences in institutions determined the inequality in the digital development of regions, which was also reflected in the skills of the population. However, Ding et al. argue actively promote digitalization, anticipating improvements in institutional quality through direct effects, digital innovation, and externalities [21].

2.2 Digital Pathways in Russian Regions

Previous studies consistently highlight the heterogeneity of development paths across Russian regions, emphasizing disparities in digital development that are closely tied to inequality and gaps in access to resources. Dobrinskaya and Martynenko [22] demonstrate that intensive digitalization exacerbates disparities in access to technology, skills, and life opportunities, with significant implications for quality of life and well-being. In the modern context, such gaps reflect differences in the maturity of processes and elements within economic systems that arise during digital transformation, directly influencing value creation [23, 24]. Empirical evidence suggests that, on average, Russian companies require about 3 years to adapt to complementary digital technologies. However, as digital inequalities increase, the adaptation period extends significantly, further widening developmental disparities [23]. The heterogeneity of development paths is also increased by the combination of various technologies and the transformation of business models, which are becoming increasingly individualized.

From an evolutionary perspective, the digital development paths of Russian regions must be analyzed in the context of the global shocks that have shaped the last decade. The pandemic, according to most studies, has significantly pushed and accelerated digitalization in Russian regions, ensuring their deep integration into social and professional contexts [25–27]. Technologies that previously played a supplementary role have now become central to critical processes such as mass formal education, job recruitment, healthcare services, and advanced production methods like digital twins and big data applications. In sectors like finance, intermediaries developing ICT platforms and networks have emerged as key drivers of digital evolution, facilitating deeper technological integration and innovation [28]. Similarly, the challenges posed by Industry 4.0 during travel restrictions and supply chain disruptions have catalyzed transformative advancements in operational efficiency and strategic integration across various industries [29]. However, the widespread adoption of general-purpose technologies, while instrumental in driving progress, has also introduced complexities, including increased uncertainty and uneven regional impacts, which complicate the digital trajectories of regions and their ability to obtain the full benefits of technological evolution.

In the Russian context, geoeconomic fragmentation has emerged as a significant challenge, driven by intensified sanctions pressure, motivating strategies such as parallel import and import substitution, aimed at fostering national technological sovereignty. Over the past decade, Russian companies have engaged in numerous systemic projects and initiatives to scale digital solutions. However, the overall outcomes have been moderate or limited, as the majority of Russian companies remain at an initial level of digital maturity [25]. Despite the constraints, there is a growing consensus on the role of digitalization as a critical tool for ensuring strategic competitiveness and enhancing the interconnectedness of business and society.

2.3 Human Capital Markets Evolution: The Role of Digital Automation and Disruption

In the long term, the dynamics of technological change ensure the cyclical development of industries and human capital markets, leading to the emergence of opportunities and threats through skill obsolescence and technological unemployment, reskilling and upskilling, and the transformation of the cultural and social environment and policies [20, 30]. The evolutionary trajectory reflects the dynamic interaction between technological changes, institutional structures, regional differences, and policy initiatives. On the one hand, digitalization leads to a surge in demand for a skilled workforce with specific competencies that can, however, be applied in various related industries [31]. Thus, digital evolution complements the workforce and leads to the reproduction of human capital, as companies ensure transformation processes that improve operational efficiency and introduce innovations that change and complement business models [23]. Digital skills serve as a complementary resource, integrating with existing assets and ICT innovations within companies.

On the other hand, digitalization disrupts market equilibrium, leading to the devaluation of human capital in certain professions and a redistribution of labor demand. This phenomenon aligns with the principles of skill-biased technical change (SBTC) theory, which assumes that technological advancements favor workers with high skill levels while reducing demand for less skilled labor [32, 33]. One of the most visible consequences of this disruption is technological unemployment, which is well-documented in the literature. Feldmann, for instance, analyzes the evolutionary labor market model and finds that unemployment typically increases during the first 3 years of technological expansion within industries. However, these negative effects tend to diminish over time, as job creation eventually offsets the initial losses [34]. During the period of technological adaptation, as professions are automated, the human capital market experiences polarization [33], that is, a failure in the segment of mid-level specialists with a simultaneous increase in employees with high and low qualifications [35]. However, empirical studies suggest that this polarization is less pronounced in the Russian labor market, reflecting the catch-up nature of Russia's economic development, where breakthrough innovations and advanced solutions are relatively rare, and changes in labor demand occur more gradually [36]. In particular, professions requiring dexterity, precision, non-routine tasks, or the urgent adoption of complex decisions are less affected by automation and digitalization in the Russian context [37]. Moreover, in recent years, the strengthening of digitalization is associated with long-term demographic changes; it has been empirically shown that robotization is designed to support the aging population and strengthen the demand for middle-aged workers in a number of industries [38].

The development and evolution of specific digital skills during the technological transformation of regional economies have received relatively limited attention in the literature. A major challenge lies in measuring and distinguishing between basic and advanced digital skills while accounting for the influence of educational background and the role of formal and informal training pathways [20]. Digital skill development is shaped not only by employer demand but also by the increasing technologization of contexts where households reproduce human capital. ICTs have become integral to education, healthcare, and the broader institutional environment, acting as critical channels for social interaction, the dynamics of social capital, and the formation of new cultural and value orientations. Automation impacts not only routine physical tasks but also cognitive processes, altering the nature of work and emphasizing the necessity for continuous learning strategies [29]. As employers increasingly seek analytical and derivative skills, the pressure on education systems to adapt grows significantly [3]. The required transformations in education call for specific leadership capacities in regional and corporate governance and the implementation of evidence-based policies grounded in empirical research. Nguyen's analysis of 35 developing economies shows the importance of governance in driving digital skill promotion. Factors such as control of corruption, political stability, and regulatory quality play a crucial role in advancing ICT skills and supporting digital evolution within regions [39].

Digital technologies alone are insufficient to drive the development of human capital in regional labor markets. It is essential to ensure a match between the skills of the workforce and the demands of employers, facilitating access to high-performance jobs that increase individual income and well-being [22]. Over time, digital human capital develops within regional labor markets, encompassing the skills, knowledge, and competencies required for effective engagement with digital technologies across diverse socio-economic contexts [11, 40, 41]. However, the risks of automation for the Russian labor market appear limited. Gimpelson and Kapelyushnikov [32] argue that Russia's labor market structure is characterized by a high prevalence of cognitive and physical non-routine tasks. These tasks, given the current technological capabilities, are not easily automated or displaced, making the threat of widespread job loss due to automation minimal in the foreseeable future.

An analysis of the Russian context highlights significant heterogeneity not only in the development of digital technologies but also in the evolution of human capital

[42, 43]. Research indicates that regions with a developed industrial base tend to adopt digital skills more rapidly, often driven by technological upgrades in manufacturing and services sectors [44, 45]. However, access to digital education and training is highly uneven across Russian regions. Advanced regions such as Moscow and St. Petersburg lead in digital skill acquisition due to better infrastructure and resources, while rural areas lag behind significantly [41, 46]. However, along the evolutionary path of human capital, weak institutional frameworks such as corruption and regulatory inefficiency hinder the scaling of digital skills development initiatives, especially in regions with lower governance quality [44]. In the context of sanctions pressure, access to technology is limited, which defines a new round in the evolution of digital skills in the national labor market [7]. Moreover, the rapid pace of technological change has often outpaced the ability of traditional education systems to adapt, leading to skills mismatches: lifelong learning and retraining programs have been identified as critical to addressing gaps, but their implementation has been inconsistent, particularly in regions with limited institutional capacity [45]. Finally, sanctions pressure creates risks of brain drain from the regions, facilitating the migration outflow of the most qualified personnel from Russian regions after 2022 [47].

Based on the literature review on long-term digital development and its interaction with the labor market, we formulate the following research questions:

1. Are there significant differences in the paths of digital technology development in Russian regions? If so, what is their configuration and comparative development trends in the regional dimension?
2. How do digital technology paths determine changes in human capital markets related to the skills of the population in the regions that ensure competitiveness in the labor market?

3 Materials and Methods

This study adopts the principles of history-friendly modeling, which enriches traditional economic modeling methods with evolutionary assumptions to better understand the long-term dynamics of regional digitalization and human capital development [6]. First, we consider specific episodes in the history of regional development associated with the introduction of technologies, focusing on periods separated by macroeconomic shocks: two turning points of increasing geopolitical tensions in 2014 and 2022, as well as the 2020 pandemic. Second, we provide a representation of regional change agents, such as organizations and households, that are involved in the process of reproduction of specific human capital associated with digitalization. Third, we study the dynamic processes that are influenced by several variables that are considered key in this study, including local labor market configurations, regional specialization, innovation dynamics, and the state of general human capital. Finally, the study places emphasis on changes in configurations and their interpretation. Here, configurations refer to stable combinations of environmental parameters and human capital characteristics within a region over time. Configurations are closely linked to the region's development path. By employing evolutionary analysis and compartmental methods, the study groups economic actors and analyzes their transitions between states over time, offering insights into how configurations evolve in response to internal and external pressures [5]. Thus, the chosen approach allows theoretical and empirical evidence to be integrated, providing an understanding of the main drivers of technological change and their impact on accumulated human capital.

In the study, we identified two areas of digitalization that determine the configurations and paths of regional development, as well as those significant for human capital: access to technology and the accumulation and use of digital skills. Among the variables of the regional context that play a role in shaping development paths, we identified innovation variables and the specialization of regions by economic sectors in accordance with the share of the gross regional product (GRP) distributed according to the Russian OKVED classifier. Previous studies classifying the level of digitalization of regions distinguish a different number of groups, for example, Masoura and Malefaki [11], studying the evolution of European regions from 2014 to 2019, note two clusters with high and low performance and examine the transitions of regions between them. Among the traditional statistical methods for studying evolution, K-means cluster and regression analyses were used. *Cluster analysis* was used to determine configurations and transitions between them, reflecting the development path, and *regression analysis* was used to determine the impact of the technological path on human capital indicators. Each region was classified according to its cluster membership, and classes of regions were also defined according to the types of transitions between clusters.

The empirical basis of the study was the Rosstat Regions of Russia database [48], which became the source of information on the level of implementation of digital technologies in the regions, innovation activity, GRP, as well as the Rosstat microdatabase on the digital skills of the population [49]. To determine the number of accumulated years of education by population cohorts, data from the Labor Force Survey [50] were used. The analysis encompassed data from 82 regions of Russia, for which complete records were available for the period from 2011 to 2022.

4 Results and Discussion

Since 2017, a number of strategic and regulatory acts have emerged in the institutional space of Russian regions, declaring the key role of digitalization in ensuring growth and outlining programs and actions. In Russia, over the past decade, the development of digital human capital has been shaped by initiatives such as the *Digital Economy of the Russian Federation* program, which focuses on education, training, and digital literacy [41]. The significance of this transitional event is emphasized by systemic efforts to integrate not only the concept of digitalization, but also investment efforts in the regions. For comparison, the development and implementation of long-term plans for the development of the digital economy in the European Union (EU) began back in 2010 in order to overcome the consequences of the crisis, use technological advantages in the form of openness, flexibility, inclusiveness, and the creation of digital competencies and jobs in the next decade [11]. EU initiatives also included index and rating methods for measuring the digital economy, considering various socio-economic aspects. In Russia, initial efforts to modernize education and workforce skills between 2011 and 2017 were constrained by uneven regional investment and institutional inefficiencies [46].

Figure 1 illustrates the gradual introduction of digital technologies across Russian regions over a 13-year period. Notable trends include the significant rise in the share of servers in organizations after 2014, which aligns with increased sanctions pressure and the need for greater digital infrastructure. Personal computers remained consistently used by organizations; however, their share declined during the COVID-19 pandemic, when personal devices such as laptops, tablets, and

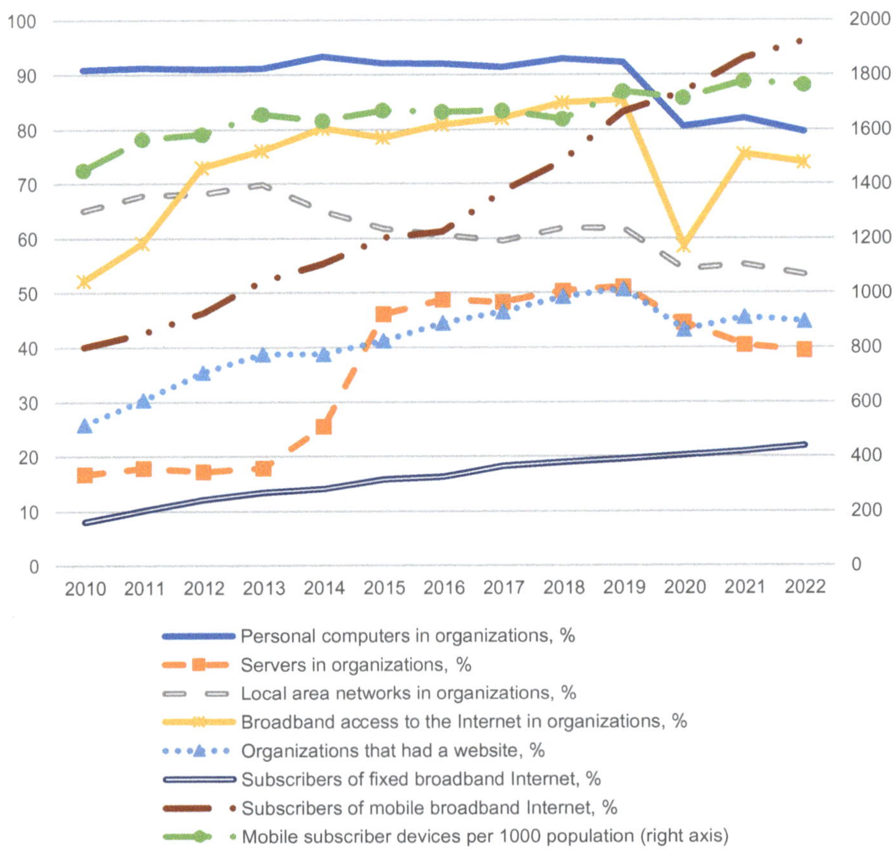

Fig. 1 Dynamics of the use of basic digital technologies in organizations, mobile communications and the Internet by the population. Source: Authors own collaboration based on Rosstat data

smartphones became prioritized for remote work and learning. Over the 30 years considered, the number of mobile Internet users grew steadily, while the number of broadband Internet users didn't change significantly. Thus, changes in the use of basic digital technologies by the population and organizations occurred at turning points, after 2014 and in 2020, associated with sanctions pressure and the pandemic.

The transition to more advanced technologies, statistics for which are available after 2017, involves mastering the Industry 4.0 in the manufacturing and service sectors (Fig. 2). For the period from 2017 to 2022, Russian organizations do not demonstrate any particular dynamics in the implementation of cloud services, and the number of ERP systems fell to 9.5% in the post-pandemic period; this process was somewhat influenced by increased sanctions pressure and the departure of the largest foreign ERP system suppliers in 2022. Thus, for a number of Russian regions, 2020 was a turning point, which increased digital heterogeneity. A similar trend applies to the Internet of Things technologies, such as digital twins and RFID tags, which enable interaction and control over infrastructure objects within cyber-physical systems.

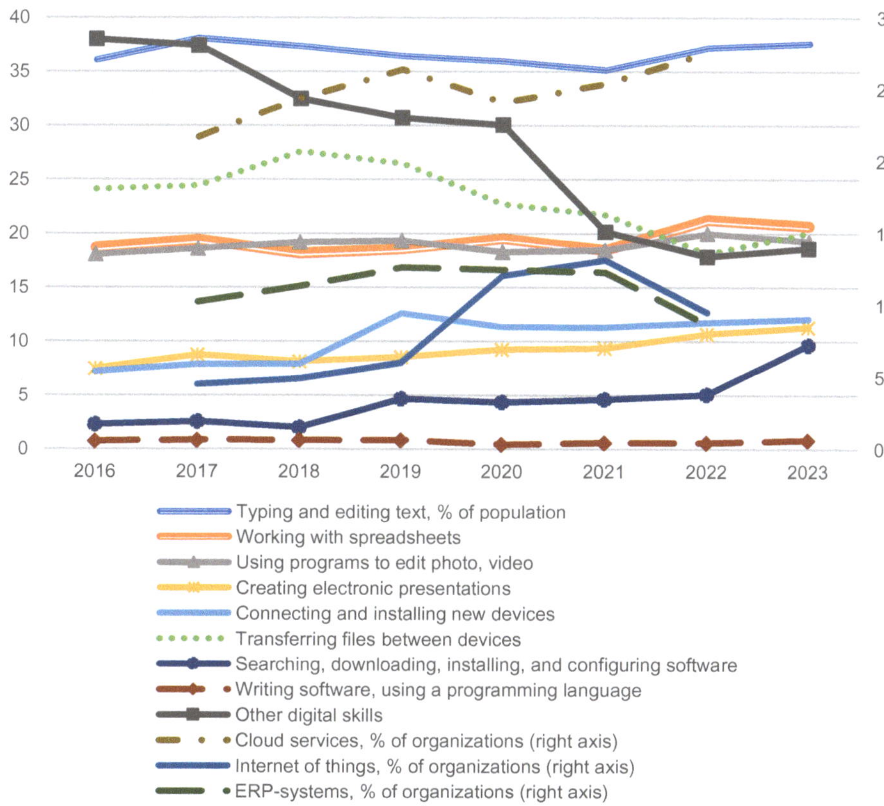

Fig. 2 Evolution of digital skills of the population and the dynamics of the use of Industry 4.0 in organizations from 2016 to 2023. Source: Authors own collaboration based on Rosstat data

Changes in the digital skills of the population in the regions are also moderate, emphasizing the importance of the regions' dependence on already accumulated human capital. Advanced digital skills demonstrated the most noticeable growth, including software installation and applied mastery of programming languages. In addition, the population strengthened the skills of creating electronic interactive presentations, but the skills of manually transferring files between devices became obsolete, which is probably due to the expansion of cloud technologies on mobile devices and the automation of data sharing processes.

The results of the cluster analysis, presented in Fig. 3, illustrate a high degree of differentiation across variables, as confirmed by ANOVA. Clusters include regions and years, i.e. a total of 984 observations were identified for the period from 2010 to 2022, which were combined into 3 clusters based on the K-means method. Regional classification was carried out using k-means clustering with Euclidean distance to group regions based on eight distinct indicators. The optimal number of clusters was determined using the NbClust package in R, which provided robust criteria for cluster selection [11]. Subsequently, regional development trajectories were identified by analyzing transitions between clusters over time. Finally, regression analysis was used to assess the relative impact of various regional parameters on these trajectories and their influence on long-term regional ratings.

The *first cluster* represents lagging regions, which were predominant prior to 2015. Following the introduction of sanctions and the implementation of

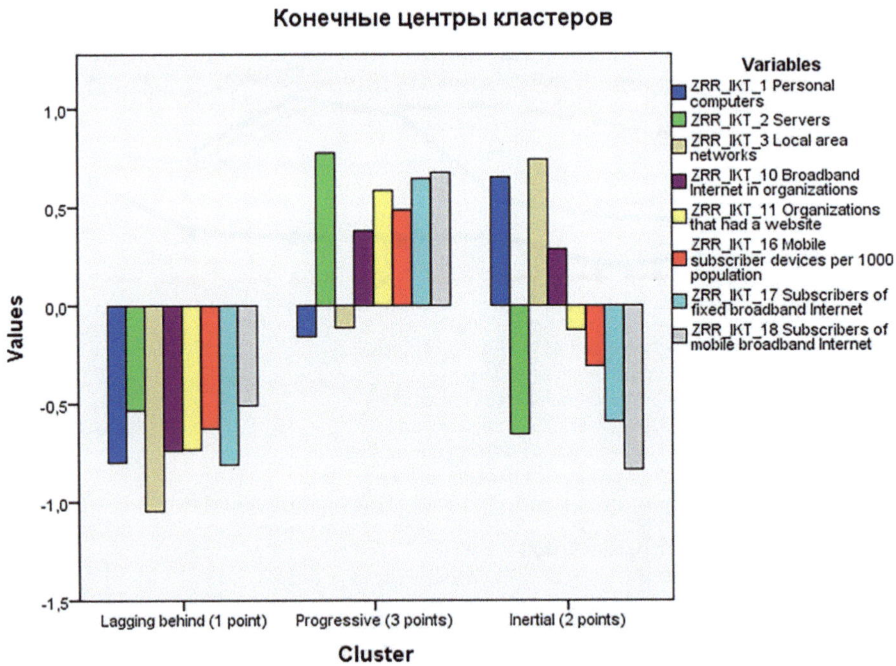

Fig. 3 Results of cluster analysis for standardized variables

digitalization strategies, the number of lagging regions dropped significantly, with only four regions remaining in this cluster by 2019 (e.g. Altai krai, Republic of Tyva and Samara region in 2015). However, the digital divides exacerbated by the COVID-19 pandemic caused the number of lagging regions to rise again, reaching 22 by 2020. The *second cluster* includes progressive regions, characterized by advanced adoption of digital technologies. In these regions, a higher proportion of organizations utilize servers, broadband Internet, and websites, while the population demonstrates active use of broadband Internet and mobile communications (it includes for example such regions as Irkutsk region, Moscow and Saint-Petersburg in 2015). Notably, the number of regions in this cluster has remained stable since 2017, although the specific regions comprising the cluster vary over time, reflecting changes in the socio-economic environment. Finally, the *third cluster* represents regions of inertial development, where progress in digital adoption has been slower. These regions lag behind in implementing personal mobile devices and mobile Internet, and their organizations make relatively less use of broadband Internet for work (Vladimir region, Perm Krai and Tambov region in 2015 belong to this cluster). However, since 2020, the number of regions in this cluster has dropped to zero, indicating a polarization in regional digital development.

Descriptive statistics for each cluster were calculated to compare socio-economic, technological, and innovative development indicators (Table 1). Differences in traditional human capital indicators, except for production experience, are not significant for the clusters, but the level of advanced digitalization varies significantly: in progressive periods, organizations in the regions more often use artificial intelligence and implement ERP systems. Particularly significant differences are observed between the level of digitalization of households, in progressive regions more of them own a computer, use broadband Internet and mobile communications. Some of these effects are certainly associated with the spread of technology over time, since the number of progressive regions has increased significantly since 2014. Digital skills of the population also vary significantly across all clusters, with progressive regions accumulating more of both basic and advanced skills. Using factor analysis based on the data from ICT database, digital skills were classified into two distinct categories. The first category, basic digital skills, was evaluated as the arithmetic mean of self-assessment for abilities related to text editing (e.g., word processing), spreadsheet manipulation (including filtering, sorting, formula creation, and chart construction), multimedia file editing (e.g., photos, videos, audio), electronic presentation creation, and file transfers between various devices, including the use of cloud storage. The second category, advanced digital skills, was defined as the arithmetic mean of self-assessments for more complex tasks such as searching for, downloading, installing, and configuring software and applications; software programming (using programming languages or specific codes/commands); and connecting and installing new hardware devices (e.g., modems, cameras, printers). For example, in lagging regions in various periods less than 34% of the population have basic skills in working with applications, while in progressive regions this figure exceeds 37%. Differences in regional specialization, assessed based on the share of industry, extractive, and service sectors in the GRP, are relatively minor

Table 1 Descriptive statistics for the clusters (mean values for 2010–2022, if not otherwise specified)

Variables	Lagging behind		Inertial		Progressive	
	Mean	S.D.	Mean	S.D.	Mean	S.D.
Human capital Years of education	11.0	0.4	11.0	0.2	11.2	0.4
Years of experience	23.8	2.9	23.4	1.7	27.3	2.5
Basic digitalization in organizations Personal computers (%)	85.4	8.7	95.7	2.8	90.0	6.6
Servers (%)	27.8	12.2	25.9	12.8	48.5	8.5
Local area networks (%)	52.4	9.6	71.0	8.0	62.1	7.4
Cloud services (2015–2022) (%)	20.4	7.6	22.2	5.2	24.4	5.3
Broadband internet in organizations (%)	65.9	11.1	78.8	9.2	80.0	9.3
Organizations that had a website (%)	34.4	8.1	40.6	8.7	47.8	6.6
Electronic data exchange between external information systems (%)	42.3	14.4	39.2	17.4	60.6	7.9
Industry 4.0 in organizations Big data processing (%)	26.7	12.1	n.d.	n.d.	29.8	12.9
Internet of Things (2017–2022) (%)	9.5	5.9	5.0	1.5	8.5	3.9
Artificial intelligence technologies (2017–2022) (%)	1.4	2.7	n.d.	n.d.	2.3	3.1
Digital platforms (2020–2022) (%)	3.6	6.4	n.d.	n.d.	5.9	7.7
ERP systems (2017–2022) (%)	3.5	5.6	0.8	3.2	9.6	5.8
Household digitalization Households with a personal computer (%)	65.8	9.2	68.5	7.6	70.7	8.0
Households that had broadband internet (%)	70.0	13.8	62.8	10.2	73.9	9.4
Population using the internet every day or almost every day (%)	65.3	15.5	52.7	9.1	69.4	11.4
Mobile subscriber devices per 1000 population	1426.7	412.1	1569.4	538.9	1928.7	280.2
Subscribers to broadband internet (%)	11.4	5.8	12.9	5.4	21.7	5.1
Subscribers to mobile internet (%)	57.0	20.4	48.2	19.7	88.5	18.1
Innovation and R&D activities Organizations that performed R&D (%)	26.2	35.9	37.8	51.5	61.8	119.9
Personnel engaged in scientific research per 1000 population	1.6	1.8	2.5	2.9	3.0	3.7
Patent applications for inventions	128.6	256.4	262.0	465.0	388.4	1207.8
Developed advanced manufacturing technologies	8.0	25.4	15.1	28.9	25.8	55.4
Level of innovation activity of organizations	6.3	4.6	7.8	4.9	11.0	5.4
Digital skills of the population Self-assessment of the impact of ICT on an individual's life: positive impact (%)	82.7	19.8	82.0	6.5	81.1	19.6
Typing and editing text (e.g., using a word processor) (%)	33.87	8.67	35.33	9.60	37.22	8.70

(continued)

Table 1 (continued)

Variables	Lagging behind		Inertial		Progressive	
	Mean	S.D.	Mean	S.D.	Mean	S.D.
Working with spreadsheets (e.g., using filtering, sorting, writing formulas etc.) (%)	16.98	7.02	18.63	6.73	19.58	5.72
Using programs to edit photo, video (%)	16.86	6.59	17.93	6.64	19.28	6.32
Creating electronic presentations (e.g., using special programs) (%)	8.16	4.05	8.81	4.53	8.99	3.42
Connecting and installing new devices (e.g., modem, camera, printer, etc.) (%)	8.40	5.16	7.77	4.93	10.44	5.38
Transferring files between devices (computer, digital camera, player, smartphone)	19.41	8.06	22.22	8.80	24.47	8.22
Searching, downloading, installing, and configuring software, applications	3.23	2.59	2.81	2.29	3.78	2.77
Writing software (using a programming language or special codes/commands)	0.53	0.66	0.99	1.51	0.69	0.64
Other skills	26.54	12.93	35.66	10.82	29.62	13.39

N.d. no data available.
Source: Authors' calculations based on Rosstat data

Region name	Path type	11	12	13	14	15	16	17	18	19	20	21	22	Path raiting
Kabardino-Balkarian Republic	Long disruprion													16
Karachay-Cherkess Republic	Long disruprion													16
Volgograd Region	COVID impact													21
Altai Krai	COVID impact													24
Arkhangelsk Region	Developing after 2014													32
Astrakhan Region	Developing after 2014													32
Kaliningrad Region	Leader pathway													34
Saint Petersburg	Leader pathway													34
Moscow	Leader pathway													36
Total number of regions by cluster type	Lagging behind	32	18	10	17	22	16	11	6	4	22	14	14	
	Inertial	49	63	69	60	18	13	8	9	5	0	0	0	
	Progressive	1	1	3	5	42	53	63	67	73	60	68	68	

Fig. 4 Examples of digital path types for the selected sample of regions and values of path rating in 2011–2022. Note: Red is lagging behind period; yellow is inertial period; green is progressive period

across clusters. Progressive regions show a slight advantage in the service sector and derive less income from extractive enterprises compared to lagging and inertial regions, but the gap is less than 5%.

For each region, development episodes were identified, and the overall dynamics over the period were assessed. Transitions between clusters were then interpreted using a contextual understanding of macroeconomic events and the socio-economic conditions of the regions (Fig. 4). A total of four types of development paths were identified. The *"Long disruption" path* is typical for regions that have been at a low level of development throughout the period, slowly introducing technologies. The

"COVID impact" path assumes an episodic but significant decline in digital development during the pandemic, which is caused by the relatively low efficiency of the digitalization policy. The *"Developing after 2014" path* is typical of regions that intensified digitalization programs after the escalation of sanctions pressure. Under the influence of restrictions on access to foreign high-tech markets during the first wave of the geopolitical crisis, many companies in the regions suspended digital transformation. Finally, the *"leader" path* is typical for regions that demonstrate sustainable implementation of digitalization throughout the period under review. For example, Moscow has always belonged to the class of digitalization leaders due to its central position as a financial and distribution region concentrating investments. The same applies to the central regions, e.g., St. Petersburg and Kaliningrad. We also use the conditional *path rating indicator*, which is calculated as the sum of scores assigned to a region's cluster membership over the entire development period. For instance, belonging to the lagging regions cluster is assigned 1 point, while membership in the progressive cluster is assigned 3 points.

To assess the impact of various regional parameters on the development path and long-term rating of the region, a regression analysis was conducted (Table 2). The sample included 82 regions from 2016 to 2022. In the *first model* based on OLS, the factors influencing the path rating values were estimated. The analysis showed that access to advanced technologies, such as cloud services, has a positive impact on the long-term rating, in addition, advanced skills related to searching, installing or writing software play an important role. In addition, human capital plays a positive role in the development dynamics: for each year of study, the digital rating increases by an average of 2.2 points. An increase in the share of the public sector in the regional economy in the long term leads to a decrease in the rating. In the *second and third models* based on logistic regression, the impact of regional variables on the probability of entering a certain development path was estimated. The "long disruption" pathway is associated with a high share of the public sector and significant accumulated human capital, which is inefficiently used in regional ecosystems. Low levels of basic skills of the population and low levels of innovative activity of organizations in the regions also contribute to the long-term lag of the region. Regions with a long lag include the Southern republics, which are slowly accumulating basic digital skills. Progressive regions are few in number at the beginning of 2011, but by the beginning of 2023 their number has grown to 68 over the period. The main factors of competitiveness are the rapid expansion of mobile devices and broadband Internet, while the level of innovative activity and advanced skills of the population play a positive role.

Next, we estimated the parameters of the panel regression; based on the assessment of the quality of the models, a specification with random effects was selected, where the dependent variables were the basic and advanced digital skills of the population in the regions (Table 3), which means that the differences can be estimated both within and between regions. Considering the influence of generation

Table 2 Results of regression analysis

	Path rating (OLS)		Long disruption		Leader pathway	
Variables	B	T	B	Exp(B)	B	Exp(B)
(Constant)	−15.29	−1.30	−15.72	0.00	73.64*	–
LN_GRP log of GRP in 2016 prices	0.14	0.51	−0.15	0.86	−1.86	0.16
RND_ORG_N organizations performed R&D	−0.01**	−4.59	0.03	1.03	0.04*	1.04
RND_PERS_N1 personnel in R&D per 1000	−0.04	−0.49	−0.58	0.56	0.15	1.17
VRP_GOV share of GRP in government sector	−0.22**	−6.24	0.37**	1.44	−0.19	0.83
EDU_YEAR years of education	2.17**	3.47	3.27**	26.39	−2.26	0.10
EXP_YEAR years of work experience	−0.12	−1.29	0.46	1.58	−0.35	0.71
RR_IKT_16 Mobile subscriber devices	0.54**	14.57	−1.72**	0.18	0.3**	1.35
RR_IKT_17 subscribers to broadband internet	0.24**	6.77	−0.06	0.94	0.3**	1.34
RR_IKT_5 cloud services	0.11**	3.31	−0.1	0.91	0	1.00
ERP_sys ERP systems	0.07	1.50	−0.02	0.98	−0.05	0.95
RR_AMT2 advanced manufacturing	0.00	−0.94	0.00	0.00	0.00	0.00
RR_INNOV level of innovation activity	0.04	1.26	−0.25**	1.28	0.33*	0.72
IKT_SK_BAS basic skills on a 100-point scale	0.07	1.63	−0.57**	0.57	−0.17	0.84
IKT_SK_AD advanced skills on a 100-point scale	0.35**	2.59	0.23	1.26	0.9**	2.45
Time fixed effects	Yes		No		No	
R^2 adjusted	0.673		–		–	
Nagelkirk R-squared	–		0.901		0.732	
−2 log-likelihood	–		84.04		69.03	
Percentage correctly predicted obs.	–		97.0		98.4	
F-statistic	59.9**		–		–	
Durbin-Watson	1.757		–		–	
No of obs.	574		574		574	

Note: (**) significant at a level of less than 1%; (*) significant at a level of less than 5%

differences in skills, we determined their level by cohorts based on year of birth in five-year periods (from 1948 to 1997: 11 cohorts in 82 regions over 7 years). Increase in GRP, typical for central or oil and gas regions, positively affects both basic and advanced skills, accumulated formal education also has a positive effect. At the same time increase in quantity of employed population negatively affects both types of skills. The "long disruption" path has a significant negative effect on the basic skills of the population, measured on a 100-point scale. Leading regions, on the contrary, stimulate the accumulation of both basic and advanced skills of the population, creating additional jobs and attracting additional labor force. Regions that have shown "long disruption" pathway also have decreased level of basic digital skills.

Table 3 Results of panel regression by cohorts for the period from 2016 to 2022

Variables	IKT_SK_BAS			IKT_SK_AD		
Control	B	Std. e.	z	B	Std. e.	z
LN_GRP log of GRP in 2016 prices	3.08**	0.21	14.95	0.77**	0.06	12.22
EDU_YEAR years of education	0.71**	0.08	8.61	0.13**	0.03	4.84
EXP_YEAR years of work experience	o.00	0.01	0.45	0.02**	0.00	8.72
ZAN log of employed population	−1.88**	0.22	−8.56	−0.45**	0.07	−6.77
RR_INNOV level of innovation activity	−0.01	0.01	−0.46	−0.03**	0.00	−8.68
Development pathways						
Development after 2014 (dummy)	−0.55*	0.28	−2.01	−0.12	0.08	−1.40
Long disruption (dummy)	−0.92*	0.36	−2.54	−0.02	0.11	−0.19
Leader pathway (dummy)	4.02**	0.59	6.82	1.26**	0.18	7.15
(Constant)	−47.07**	3.71	−12.70	−14.29**	1.13	−12.65
R^2 (overall)	0.24			0.10		
N	6314			6314		

Note: (**) significant at a level of less than 1%; (*) significant at a level of less than 5%

5 Conclusion

The evolutionary perspective offers valuable insights into the mechanisms underlying the interaction of digital development paths in Russian regions, defined through the intensity and depth of implementation of basic ICT, as well as the accumulated digital skills of the population. By combining history-friendly and formal methods, this study provides a statistical assessment and interpretation of these dynamics within their historical and institutional contexts. First, cluster analysis allowed us to differentiate development paths and identify several main types of paths during the period from 2011 to 2022. Central regions, such as Moscow and St. Petersburg, maintain their digital leadership throughout the entire development path. For most Russian regions, however, the main turning point in development was in 2014, when most regions activated digital development strategies under the influence of sanctions pressure. In addition, the pandemic disrupted digitalization processes in a number of southern regions, increasing heterogeneity and uncertainty of their paths. Second, regression analysis confirmed the importance of advanced digital skills related to programming and software installation for the dynamics of digital development. The key drivers of digital development in the regions were broadband Internet and mobile devices, which provided access to digital ecosystems for the population, strengthening both basic and advanced digital skills. Logistic regression confirmed that the lack of basic skills development causes a long-term gap and digital backwardness of the regions.

The study contributes to the *theory of evolutionary economics* by proposing a classification of regional digitalization paths during economic shocks and geoeconomic fragmentation. Our findings align with Martin and Sunley's [51] emphasis on trajectory dependence, but extend their framework by using empirical calculations based on clustering and regression analysis to explain the impact of different regional trajectories on digital skills in Russian regions. Confirming the research of Boschma and Frenken [52], our study empirically validates the co-evolutionary interplay between regional digitalization trajectories and pre-existing institutional-geographic contexts, demonstrating that even in emergent digital sectors, path-dependent dynamics, shaped by heterogeneous skill distributions, episodic shocks (e.g., sanctions, pandemics), and infrastructural legacies, persistently constrain locational neutrality, necessitating adaptive policy designs that account for historically embedded regional asymmetries in human capital and technological absorptive capacity. We also confirmed the co-evolutionary dynamics between regional digitalization trajectories and pre-existing institutional-technological contexts demonstrating that even emergent digital sectors exhibit path-dependent constraints shaped by heterogeneous skill endowments, episodic shocks (e.g., sanctions, pandemics), and infrastructural legacies, aligning with Tödling and Trippl's [53] emphasis on institutional adaptability.

The four types of paths are based on an understanding of the historical context and reflect not only the contextual contribution of episodic crises but also a systemic approach to the impact of external changes on the dynamics of digitalization. *Practical implications* include, firstly, recommendations for the implementation of differentiated regional digitalization policies and the distribution of investment programs in accordance with the identified development paths. Secondly, regulatory policies should consider technological, innovative and social areas that reflect the contribution of digital skills to the speed of ICT adoption: regional programs should be sensitive to skill gaps in the population. Finally, it is advisable to use the proposed dynamic approach to determining the region's path rating over a certain period to assess the effectiveness of digitalization and the interaction of local organizations, authorities and the community.

Despite the identified challenges, digital technologies have significantly impacted the quality of human capital in Russia, offering new ways to access knowledge, expanding economic opportunities, and improving well-being. However, from an evolutionary perspective, this study confirms for the first time that such benefits are also unevenly distributed over the long term. The *limitations of the approach* are related to the shortcomings in the explanatory power of the path dependence concept: the systemic circumstances in which it arises are not fully understood. *Future research* should overcome the limitations of the current approach by selecting a broader set of institutional indicators, including regulatory indicators related to education and the digital transformation of industry. As new statistical data become available, it is also promising to determine the contribution of the second wave of geoeconomic fragmentation in 2022 to changing paths and human capital markets.

Acknowledgments The study was supported by the Russian Science Foundation grant No. 23-78-10165, https://rscf.ru/project/23-78-10165/.

References

1. Laitsou, E., Katsianis, D., Xenakis, A., & Gerogiannis, V. C. (2024). Pacing the digital decade: Digital evolution and its impact on human well-being. *Telecommunications Policy, 2024*, 102868. https://doi.org/10.1016/j.telpol.2024.102868
2. Karavasilis, I., Vrana, V., & Karavasilis, G. (2024). Forecasting the evolution of the digital economy in the industry of the European Union. *Journal of Risk and Financial Management, 17*(9), 393. https://doi.org/10.3390/jrfm17090393
3. World Economic Forum (WEF). (2023). *The future of jobs report 2023*. World Economic Forum. Retrieved from https://www3.weforum.org/docs/WEF_Future_of_Jobs_2023.pdf
4. Xia, Y., Lv, G., Wang, H., & Ding, L. (2023). Evolution of digital economy research: A bibliometric analysis. *International Review of Economics and Finance, 88*, 1151–1172. https://doi.org/10.1016/j.iref.2023.07.051
5. Szalkowski, G. A., & Mikalef, P. (2023). Understanding digital platform evolution using compartmental models. *Technological Forecasting and Social Change, 193*, 122600. https://doi.org/10.1016/j.techfore.2023.122600
6. Nelson, R. R., Dosi, G., Helfat, C. E., Pyka, A., Saviotti, P. P., & Lee, K. (2018). *Modern evolutionary economics: An overview*. Cambridge University Press. https://doi.org/10.1017/9781108661928
7. Akberdina, V. (2023). System resilience of industry to the sanctions pressure in industrial regions: Assessment and outlook. *Journal of New Economy, 23*(4), 26–45. https://doi.org/10.29141/2658-5081-2022-23-4-2
8. Chernenko, I. M. (2024). Risks for the development of the Russian human capital in the context of geoeconomic fragmentation. *Outlines of Global Transformations: Politics, Economics, Law, 17*(2), 31–53. https://doi.org/10.31249/kgt/2024.02.02
9. Aiyar, S., Ilyina, A., Chen, J., Kangur, A., Trevino, J., Ebeke, C., Gudmundsson, T., Soderberg, G., Schulze, T., Kunaratskul, T., Ruta, M., Garcia-Saltos, R., & Rodriguez, S. (2023). Geoeconomic fragmentation and the future of multilateralism. *IMF Working Papers, 1*, 38. https://doi.org/10.5089/9798400229046.006
10. Frolov, D. P. (2020). Evolutionary economics at the peak and in crisis: Prospects for the new paradigm. *Journal of Institutional Studies, 12*(1), 019–037. https://doi.org/10.17835/2076-6297.2020.12.1.019-037
11. Masoura, M., & Malefaki, S. (2023). Evolution of the digital economy and society index in the European Union: A socioeconomic perspective. *TalTech Journal of European Studies, 13*(2), 177–203. https://doi.org/10.2478/bjes-2023-0020
12. Bohnsack, R., Kurtz, H., & Hanelt, A. (2021). Re-examining path dependence in the digital age: The evolution of connected car business models. *Research Policy, 50*(9), 104328. https://doi.org/10.1016/j.respol.2021.104328
13. Liebowitz, S. J., & Margolis, S. E. (1995). Path dependence, lock-in, and history. *Journal of Law, Economics, and Organization, 11*(1), 205–226. https://doi.org/10.2139/ssrn.1706450
14. Yu, P., Shi, J., Sadowski, B. M., & Nomaler, Ö. (2020). Catching up in the face of technological discontinuity: Exploring the role of demand structure and technological regimes in the transition from 2G to 3G in China. *Journal of Evolutionary Economics, 30*(3), 815–841. https://doi.org/10.1007/s00191-020-00673-9
15. Ghobakhloo, M. (2018). The future of manufacturing industry: A strategic roadmap toward industry 4.0. *Journal of Manufacturing Technology Management, 29*(6), 910–936. https://doi.org/10.1108/JMTM-02-2018-0057
16. Grybauskas, A., Stefanini, A., & Ghobakhloo, M. (2022). Social sustainability in the age of digitalization: A systematic literature review on the social implications of industry 4.0. *Technology in Society, 70*, 101997. https://doi.org/10.1016/j.techsoc.2022.101997
17. Li, J., Chernenko, I., & Semenova, I. (2024). Strategic integration of industry 5.0 assistive technologies for cognition in business for human capital development. In *The future of indus-*

try. *Human-centric approaches in digital transformation* (pp. 395–414). Springer. https://doi.org/10.1007/978-3-031-66801-2_26
18. Ghobakhloo, M., Iranmanesh, M., Foroughi, B., Babaee Tirkolaee, E., Asadi, S., & Amran, A. (2023). Industry 5.0 implications for inclusive sustainable manufacturing: An evidence-knowledge-based strategic roadmap. *Journal of Cleaner Production, 417*, 138023. https://doi.org/10.1016/j.jclepro.2023.138023
19. Carbonero, F., Davies, J., Ernst, E., Fossen, F. M., Samaan, D., & Sorgner, A. (2023). The impact of artificial intelligence on labor markets in developing countries: A new method with an illustration for Lao PDR and urban Viet Nam. *Journal of Evolutionary Economics, 33*(3), 707–736. https://doi.org/10.1007/s00191-023-00809-7
20. Dalloshi, P., & Kyqyku, D. (2023). Digital skills as an impetus for the acceleration of economic digitalization: EU perspective. *Corporate Governance and Organizational Behavior Review, 7*(3), 365–374. https://doi.org/10.22495/cgobrv7i3sip11
21. Ding, C., Liu, C., Zheng, C., & Li, F. (2022). Digital economy, technological innovation and high-quality economic development: Based on spatial effect and mediation effect. *Sustainability, 14*(1), 216. https://doi.org/10.3390/su14010216
22. Dobrinskaya, D. E., & Martynenko, T. S. (2019). Defining the digital divide in Russia: Key features and trends. *Monitoring Obshchestvennogo Mneniya: Ekonomicheskie i Sotsial'nye Peremeny, 153*(5), 100–119. https://doi.org/10.14515/monitoring.2019.5.06
23. Shakina, E., Parshakov, P., & Alsufiev, A. (2021). Rethinking the corporate digital divide: The complementarity of technologies and the demand for digital skills. *Technological Forecasting and Social Change, 162*, 120405. https://doi.org/10.1016/j.techfore.2020.120405
24. Pérez-Amaral, T., Valarezo, A., López, R., & Garín-Muñoz, T. (2021). Digital divides across consumers of internet services in Spain using panel data 2007–2019. Narrowing or not? *Telecommunications Policy, 45*(2), 102093. https://doi.org/10.1016/j.telpol.2020.102093
25. Bubnov, V., Kopilevich, V., & Istomina, A. (2021). The evolution of digital capital in organizations: A quantitative assessment. *Journal of Telecommunications and the Digital Economy, 9*(4), 1–22. https://doi.org/10.18080/JTDE.V9N4.435
26. Almeida, F., Duarte Santos, J., & Augusto Monteiro, J. (2020). The challenges and opportunities in the digitalization of companies in a post-COVID-19 world. *IEEE Engineering Management Review, 48*(3), 97–103. https://doi.org/10.1109/EMR.2020.3013206
27. Kucherov, D., & Tsybova, V. (2022). The contribution of e-recruitment practices to e-recruitment outcomes in Russian companies. *Measuring Business Excellence, 26*(3), 366–377. https://doi.org/10.1108/MBE-02-2021-0017
28. Evlakhova, Y. S. (2022). Russian bancassurance perspectives: From path dependence to ecosystem. *Finance: Theory and Practice, 26*(3), 33–49. https://doi.org/10.26794/2587-5671-2022-26-3-33-49
29. Rotatori, D., Lee, E. J., & Sleeva, S. (2021). The evolution of the workforce during the fourth industrial revolution. *Human Resource Development International, 24*(1), 92–103. https://doi.org/10.1080/13678868.2020.1767453
30. Chernenko, I. M., Kelchevskaya, N. R., Pelymskaya, I. S., & Almusaedi, H. K. A. (2021). Opportunities and threats of digitalisation for human capital development at the individual and regional levels. *Economy of Region, 17*(4), 1239–1255. https://doi.org/10.17059/ekon.reg.2021-4-14
31. Rodriguez-Pasquín, M., García-Luque, O., & López-Martínez, M. (2023). Digitalization and skills in Spain: Regional differences and gender gaps. *Sociologia y Tecnociencia, 13*(2), 94–117.
32. Gimpelson, V. E., & Kapeliushnikov, R. I. (2022). Work routines and risks of automation in the Russian labor market. *Voprosy Ekonomiki, 8*, 68–94. https://doi.org/10.32609/0042-8736-2022-8-68-94
33. Afonso, Ó., Lima, P. G., & Sequeira, T. (2022). The effects of automation and lobbying in wage inequality: A directed technical change model with routine and non-routine tasks. *Journal of Evolutionary Economics, 32*(5), 1467–1497. https://doi.org/10.1007/s00191-022-00801-7

34. Feldmann, H. (2013). Technological unemployment in industrial countries. *Journal of Evolutionary Economics, 23*(5), 1099–1126. https://doi.org/10.1007/s00191-013-0308-6
35. Autor, D. H. (2015). Why are there still so many jobs? The history and future of workplace automation. *Journal of Economic Perspectives, 29*(3), 3–30. https://doi.org/10.1257/jep.29.3.3
36. Gimpelson, V. E., & Kapeliushnikov, R. I. (2023). Job structure evolution in Russia: Polarization, upgrading, stalemate. *Voprosy Ekonomiki, 1*, 59–85. https://doi.org/10.32609/0042-8736-2023-1-59-85
37. Frey, C. B., & Osborne, M. A. (2017). The future of employment: How susceptible are jobs to computerisation? *Technological Forecasting and Social Change, 114*(1), 254–280. https://doi.org/10.1016/j.techfore.2016.08.019
38. Acemoglu, D., & Restrepo, P. (2022). Demographics and automation. *Review of Economic Studies, 89*(1), 1–44. https://doi.org/10.1093/restud/rdab031
39. Nguyen, V. B. (2021). The digitalization–economic growth relationship in developing countries and the role of governance. *Scientific Annals of Economics and Business, 68*(4), 481–493. https://doi.org/10.47743/SAEB-2021-0028
40. Untura, G. A. (2023). The knowledge economy and digitalization: Assessing the impact on economic growth of Russian regions. *Regional Research of Russia, 13*(3), 397–406. https://doi.org/10.1134/S2079970523700909
41. Sidorov, A., & Senchenko, P. (2020). Regional digital economy: Assessment of development levels. *Mathematics, 8*(12), 1–23. https://doi.org/10.3390/math8122143
42. Akberdina, V., Naumov, I. V., & Krasnykh, S. S. (2023). Digital space of regions: Assessment of development factors and influence on socio-economic growth. *Journal of Applied Economic Research, 22*(2), 294–322. https://doi.org/10.15826/vestnik.2023.22.2.013
43. Akberdina, V., Naumov, I., & Krasnykh, S. (2023). Regional digital space and digitalisation of industry: Spatial econometric analysis. In *Lecture notes in information systems and organisation* (pp. 7–19). Springer. https://doi.org/10.1007/978-3-031-30351-7_2
44. Zokirov, Y., Yamada, D., & Hiwatari, M. (2023). Innovation and competition under weak institutions: An empirical analysis of Russian firms. *Russian Journal of Economics, 9*(1), 33–56. https://doi.org/10.32609/j.ruje.9.97916
45. Zemtsov, S., Barinova, V., & Semenova, R. (2019). The risks of digitalization and the adaptation of regional labor markets in Russia. *Foresight and STI Governance, 13*(2), 84–96. https://doi.org/10.17323/2500-2597.2019.2.84.96
46. Kuzmenko, N. I., Molchan, A. S., Anichkina, O. A., Ponomarev, S. V., & Osadchuk, L. M. (2023). The "digitalisation trap" of Russian regions. *International Journal of Technology, Policy and Management, 23*(1), 20. https://doi.org/10.1504/ijtpm.2023.10054598
47. Wachs, J. (2023). Digital traces of brain drain. *EPJ Data Science, 12*(1), 14. https://doi.org/10.1140/epjds/s13688-023-00389-3
48. Rosstat. (2024). *Regions of Russia. Socio-economic indicators*. Retrieved October, 2024, from https://rosstat.gov.ru/folder/210/document/13204
49. Rosstat. (2024). *Selective federal statistical observation on the use of information technologies and information and telecommunication networks by the population*. Retrieved October, 2024, from https://rosstat.gov.ru/free_doc/new_site/business/it/ikt23/index.html
50. Rosstat. (2024). *Labor force, employment and unemployment*. Retrieved October, 2024, from https://rosstat.gov.ru/labour_force#.
51. Martin, R., & Sunley, P. (2006). Path dependence and regional economic evolution. *Journal of Economic Geography, 6*(4), 395–437. https://doi.org/10.1093/jeg/lbl012
52. Boschma, R. A., & Frenken, K. (2017). Why is economic geography not an evolutionary science? Towards an evolutionary economic geography. In *Economy: Critical essays in human geography* (pp. 127–156). Routledge. https://doi.org/10.4324/9781351159203-6
53. Tödtling, F., & Trippl, M. (2013). Transformation of regional innovation systems: From old legacies to new development paths. In *Re-framing regional development: Evolution, innovation and transition* (pp. 297–317). Routledge. https://doi.org/10.4324/9780203097489-23

Management Strategies for Creative Reindustrialization in Secondary-Tier Cities in the Context of Digital Transformation

Irina Turgel, Valentina Derbeneva, and Irina Baskakova

Abstract Creative industries are becoming an increasingly important driver of economic growth in Russian industrial cities, which calls for a tailored approach to policy development. This study aims to outline a strategy for managing reindustrialization in secondary-tier cities through creative industries, by focusing on the opportunities presented by digital transformation. The authors propose a modular approach to managing creative industries, which allows for differentiated strategies based on three organizational and economic development models: conservation, transformation, and generation. The choice of a model should be based on two key factors: the level of government intervention and the specific characteristics of the creative industries in each city. To maximize the effectiveness of these strategies, it is crucial to adjust them to the unique needs of each creative cluster. It is also proposed to establish an ecosystem of creative industries in Russian second-tier cities on the basis of a digital platform for effective interaction between institutions and organizations providing the process of their management.

Keywords Second-tier cities · Creative reindustrialization · Digital transformation · Management strategies

I. Turgel · V. Derbeneva (✉)
Department of Theory, Methodology, and Legal Support of Public and Municipal Administration, Ural Federal University, Ekaterinburg, Russia
e-mail: i.d.turgel@urfu.ru; v.v.derbeneva@urfu.ru

I. Baskakova
Department of Economic Theory and Economic Policy, Ural Federal University, Ekaterinburg, Russia
e-mail: i.v.baskakova@urfu.ru

F. Tao et al. (eds.), *Artificial Intelligence and Digital Transformation*, Lecture Notes in Information Systems and Organisation 78,
https://doi.org/10.1007/978-3-032-00118-4_15

1 Introduction

In today's world, culture and creativity have become powerful drivers of the global economic and social development. Digital transformation of modern life has led to a surge in the creative industries, driven by innovative problem-solving in the political, social, cultural, and technological spheres. At the heart of this trend lies the new "creative economic policy". Conceptually, creative industries rely on forward-thinking theories that capture the sweeping changes in technology, management, economy, and society [1]. Seen from this perspective, creative industries play a vital role in fueling economic growth at national and regional levels by harnessing, positioning, and maximizing the unique resources of distinct areas [2].

The first country to create creative clusters was the UK. By implementing the new economic policy, abandoned or derelict industrial sites that made cities less attractive to residents and visitors began to transform into creative cities. The success of such projects largely stemmed from the government's effective prioritization as the development of creative spaces was considered a top policy goal. Early successes enabled authorities to extend these strategies to regional and local economies, sparking a "creative revolution" [3]. This shift transformed creativity into a valuable economic resource, turning cities into dynamic spaces for innovation and expression. Revitalization of abandoned industrial areas, especially in city centers, became one of the most impactful ways to build creative clusters. Globally, this approach has rejuvenated old industrial regions, drawing new investments and infusing these areas with renewed purpose [4].

A wide array of interactive services (various multimedia, computer games, the internet) serve as tools for promoting and expressing human creativity. These tools not only assist people in their daily lives but also activate their creative potential, encouraging them to create something on their own [5]. The advent of new technical means has enabled the mass production of creative products, making them accessible to a broader range of customers [6]. In the creative economy, digital technologies are used as a foundation for developing value chains, significantly increasing the capital value of enterprises [7].

Currently, there is a recognition that the creative sector is Russia's new industrial policy, it is a catalyst that influences other spheres, increasing their efficiency. A new context for the development of creative industries arises from shifts in national priorities, such as strengthening Russia's cultural identity, promoting domestic tourism, improving labor market participation, and unlocking the creative potential of individuals in entrepreneurship [2]. To achieve these goals, it is crucial to establish a creative economic sector and enhance its contribution to the regional economy [8]. Regions, particularly smaller cities, hold vast untapped potential.

The rapid development of creative industries in Ural and Siberian cities requires theoretical and practical reflection, taking into account the world experience of creative reindustrialization in old industrial centers.

These regions are primarily dominated by small towns, often formerly industrial but in need of reindustrialization. Russia is sometimes referred to as the country of small towns, because among more than a thousand Russian cities, small towns with a population of less than 50,000 account for more than 70%, and according to 2023 data, they are home to about 15% of the population, with their share of the total number ranging from 43% in the Southern Federal District to 83% in the Ural Federal District [9]. These towns and cities stitch together the vast expanse of the country into a unified system. Despite the fact that many of these towns and cities have reserves of human capital, rich industrial and cultural heritage, they remain unattractive for living and therefore need revitalization.

This is especially relevant for small regional towns, often former industrial centers in need of reindustrialization. In this regard, creative industries serve as a key tool for fostering sustainable growth in second-tier cities, making them more attractive to both residents and visitors. The process can also be significantly accelerated through well-structured strategies at the national, regional, or municipal levels. The growing emphasis on creative industries in government policy is particularly important, as small and medium-sized enterprises (SMEs) in creative clusters were initially established with minimal government support. Over the past decade, there has been significant progress, marking a turning point with the state's increased focus on the creative economy. However, the development of creative industry clusters in Russian regions remains uneven, progressing at different rates and scales due to factors such as historical, cultural, and socio-economic conditions, as well as available resources and local development priorities [10].

In today's economic landscape, the strategy for developing the creative industry needs to be updated, which includes integrating various elements at different stages of strategy development and implementation [11], while also ensuring proper methodological and legal frameworks. The concept of creative industries, closely tied to regional characteristics that vary across areas [12] and often involving small and micro-enterprises, individual actors [13], and local associations [14, 15], presents a major challenge in identifying which companies should qualify as part of the creative sector. This situation, in turn, has made it difficult to accurately measure the sector's size and impact.

Global experience in developing creative industries clearly shows that urban policy design cannot be a "one-size-fits-all" approach. It is, therefore, essential to avoid simply "copying" models from elsewhere [16]. In order to develop a tailored management policy, it is important to preserve and emphasize the local identity of each region, as the latter serves as a crucial resource for the growth of the creative economy [17].

Russian policy in the field of creative industries is still evolving, as are the academic discussions on this topic, which are currently mostly limited to qualitative assessments and analytical reviews [18].

The subject of our study is second-tier cities, which we define in the broadest sense as "all cities in the region, except for administrative centers and large regional industrial hubs" [19].

Our research focuses on the emerging field of creative reindustrialization (or "creativization") in second-tier cities in the context of digitalization. This approach allows us to address key issues related to both digital and spatial transformation

[20]. At the heart of this field is the concept of "creative reindustrialization," which stands for the transformation of the economy of an industrial city to support its transition to sustainable socio-economic development through creative industries [21].

The successful development of creative industries relies heavily on a unique concept that emphasizes the creative specialization of a region or city. This specialization draws on both established industries and new, innovative ones [22]. In our 2023 article (see, [8]), we formulated a conceptual approach to managing the development of creative industries in second-tier industrial cities.

This concept underlies a strategy, which, in turn, provides recommendations for overcoming challenges and offers support measures to address "the specific issues and characteristics of the creative sector in the region".

This article aims to develop a modular approach to managing creative industries in second-tier industrial cities of the Urals and Western Siberia, differentiated according to the identified organizational and economic models of their development. The realize this goal, the following tasks should be solved: to develop a modular approach to managing creative industries as a tool for reindustrializing second-tier cities; to propose a set of state support measures differentiated for various management strategies in the context of creative reindustrialization under the modular approach; and to devise a system of interaction between organizations involved in managing creative industries in second-tier cities in the context of digitalization.

In our study, we interpret a creative cluster as a community of entrepreneurs and creative industries organizations operating in a certain territory. The specific result of a creative cluster is a synergetic effect due to the interaction of cluster residents, manifested in creating new ideas and projects.

Within the modular approach, we see the strategy as a system for identifying, formulating, and developing a concept that guarantees long-term success through its consistent and full implementation [23]. The development model for strategies in the creative industries should be based on the following theoretical and methodological principles: (1) flexibility of the strategy, supported by "investments in development opportunities" to create and sustain competitive advantages; (2) recognition of the strategy as an "economic and managerial category," meaning it is a set of rules and criteria for making management decisions, particularly in future unstable conditions; and (3) the strategy should result from a long-term focus on the city's unique capabilities.

2 Literature Review

The policy of creative industries managing in the digital era should include several key directions [24], we based our review on this topic.

- *Creation of public service platforms that act as "bridges" between all participants: the state, businesses, and the population.* Grodach [25] advocates for a strategy that focuses on leveraging and supporting the existing creative communities in a city, as well as prioritizing the needs of creative entrepreneurs. He argues that, for the development of creative industries, preference should be given to supporting the already existing networks rather than starting new ones. He also justifies the need to differentiate policies in the creative industries not only in industrial cities and cities with a developed knowledge economy but also in "shrinking" cities and those experiencing overpopulation.
- *Interagency cooperation to jointly promote the development of cultural and creative industries in partnership with universities, research institutions, and businesses.* Most studies on creative sector management policy and the role of institutional development suggest that the number and diversity of creative industries positively impact urban economies [18]. A separate body of literature focuses on the development of creative industries in industrial areas. It is often assumed that a strong industrial sector can hinder the market entry of non-extractive industries at the regional level. However, there is evidence that effective regional institutions can alleviate these negative effects on regional diversification indicators [26].
- *Establishment and improvement of the investment and financing system for cultural and creative industries.* Globally, government financial support of creative industries is not always direct and can also be provided indirectly. For example, in 2018, the European Council supported a VAT reduction on electronic publications, which contributed to the growth in the consumption of cultural goods [27]. In response to the decline in industrial production, the policy of supporting local creative entrepreneurs and organizations gained popularity. Florida's research, which paved the way for creative place-making and urban redevelopment policies, focuses on attracting creative workers [28]. According to Fazlagić and Szczepankiewicz [29], the urban development of a creative city, and consequently its management policies, should be based on an assessment of the city's creative potential, which includes its urban structure, traditions, and cultural climate.
- *Creation of a special fund for cultural and creative industries.* Studies on the management policy of creative industries also highlight the importance of the social aspects of economic development: creating a business-friendly climate, stimulating local leadership, fostering tolerance, and building social capital. The local administration plays a central role in this process, coordinating all activities, including the creation of digital platforms to connect with creative industry entrepreneurs [30–33]. Most often, government institutions are the key figures that determine financial support for creative industries, as the creative business sector is considered high-risk for external investors [34]. In Russia, state grant support depends both on experts from the Presidential Fund for Cultural Initiatives, who play an important role in distributing artistic and cultural funding from the federal budget, and on regional government institutions responsible for grant application processes and co-financing projects. Due to digitalization,

grant applications can be sent to the foundation through the foundation's platform from any municipality in Russia.

The different classifications of creative cities in a technological world are detailed in one of our previous papers [35], where we develop the idea of Hospers [36] that local governments can ensure the creation of different types of creative cities by providing the basic conditions for their emergence. This classification identifies technologically-innovative, culturally-intellectual, culturally-technological and technologically-organizational cities. Each of these towns and cities develops on the basis of digital technologies that support its specificity.

Matovic et al. [37] classifies creative cities by identifying "Creative-Governance Cities". This type of city focuses on multi-level and collaborative governance. In this case, the key decision-making tools are feedback platforms and digital channels of joint decision-making by authorities, business and population.

The issue of reindustrialization in second-tier cities is reflected in Dragan [38], where tourism is considered as one of the promising options for economic development. More case studies on reindustrialization and creative cities are mentioned in our article, where we explore key factors in managing creative reindustrialization strategies.

Globally, government financial support is not always direct and can also be provided indirectly. For example, in 2018, the European Council supported a VAT reduction on electronic publications, which contributed to the growth in the consumption of cultural goods [27]. In response to the decline in industrial production, the policy of supporting local creative entrepreneurs and organizations gained popularity. Florida's research, which paved the way for creative place-making and urban redevelopment policies, focuses on attracting creative workers [28]. According to Fazlagić and Szczepankiewicz [29], the urban development of a creative city, and consequently its management policies, should be based on an assessment of the city's creative potential, which includes its urban structure, traditions, and cultural climate.

There are a number of research centered on the processes of reindustrialization (revitalization) as a fundamental strategy for small towns [2, 39, 40]. The authors highlight that harnessing a territory's creative potential is crucial for restoring and developing historical and cultural heritage sites, promoting domestic and event tourism, establishing economic models for realizing creative potential, and reinforcing Russia's cultural identity and sovereignty.

The second area deals with the practical and methodological aspects of the assessment of regional creative potential, which is vital for shaping or updating development strategies [41–45]. For example, Boos et al. [19] developed the Index of Regional Creative Policies Quality (ICQ) to assess the quality of planning and support for creative industries in Russia's regions. Another issue that researchers focus on is government support for the creative sector of the economy across all regions [46–48].

A significant number of studies analyze and assess creative industries as part of municipal and regional strategies [49, 50]. There are also works examining specific aspects of strategic planning and design in the field of creative industries [51, 52].

There is a surge of scholarly interest in the digitalization of the creative economy sector. Due to digitalization, creative companies grow 3–5 times faster than the overall economy, as digital platforms play a crucial role in processes like product promotion and reputation management [53, 54].

3 Materials and Methods

The empirical base, as part of which data are translated into results of intellectual activity (RIA), was formed in 2022–2024, and includes clusters, the start of which dates back to the mid-2010s. The objects of the study include both established creative clusters and those with the prospect of their creation in small and medium-sized cities in Sverdlovsk region, Chelyabinsk region, Kuzbass and Altai Krai. In total, the study area included 16 creative clusters of old industrial cities of the second tier (Table 1).

It should be noted that the study is based on empirical data, which is not complete and exhaustive due to the dynamic process of creative industries development and cluster formation in the second-tier cities of the Urals and Siberia.

The data were collected from publicly available open sources, the websites of creative clusters and websites of administrations of the relevant regions of the Russian Federation, including the author's database on municipalities (created on the basis of two sources: the site "My City" and Rosstat), case studies of the Agency for Strategic Initiatives (ASI), the author's database "Regulatory legal acts regulating the development of creative and tourist industries in the subjects of the Russian Federation" (certificate number 2023624398). The structuring of social space is based on the territorial principle, and the criterion for selecting cities is the quantitative criterion of population size.

The methodological basis of the study is case study analysis. The method of classification was used to group creative clusters into types according to the criterion of local identity structure (different combinations of material and symbolic components), which allowed forming three models of creative clusters based on the developed typologization, reflecting their mission: conservation, transformation, and generation.

The theoretical basis of the study was formed by articles of Russian and foreign researchers on management and development of creative industries, including the factor of digital transformation.

As a result of case analysis, a modular approach to the management of creative industries was formed. The basis of this approach is a local identity construct, which includes material and symbolic components in various combinations of importance. This allowed us to identify three strategies for managing creative clusters: conservation, transformation, and generation depending on the choice of the local strategy in

Table 1 Creative clusters and creative spaces in the Urals and Siberian cities

City size	City	Object (creative cluster)	Cluster site
Sverdlovsk region			
Settlement	Chernoistochinsk (3.5)	Creative cluster in Chernoistochinsk	Demidov ironworks (not opera Tional)
Small: 10–50	Sysert (20)	Creative cluster Leto na zavode	Turchaninov-Solomirsky iron Works (not operational)
Small: 10–50	Aramil (14)	Creative cluster Razvitie fabriki idej ili pro tekstil v Aramile	Aramil cloth factory (not operational)
Medium-sized: 50–100	Polevskoy (54)	Museum complex *Severskaya Domna*	Seversky pipe plant (operational)
Large: 100–250	Pervouralsk (113)	Innovation culture Centre	Starotrubny factory (not operational)
Large: 250–500	Nizhny Tagil (334)	Creative cluster *Samorodok*	College of Applied Disciplines (not operational)
		Association of museums and heritage sites *Gornozavodskoy Ural*	Building of the former City Council
Chelyabinsk region			
Small: 10–50	Satka (43)	Creative cluster art-Satka	Building of the branch of the South Ural state university
Large: 250–500	Magnitogorsk (418)	Multifunctional park Prityazhenie	Park (free territory)
Kemerovo region			
Medium-sized: 50–100	Mezhdurechensk (95.4)	Eco-resort Mezhdurechensk. Gorod taigi	Mountain Yugus, mountain Cherny Salan, and Podnebesnye Zubia
Largest (500–1000)	Novokuznetsk (544)	Creative cluster KMK hotel (ecosystem)	KMK hotel (not operational)
Largest (500–1000)	Kemerovo (549)	Cultural space *"editorial"*	Publishing and printing enterprise "Kuzbass"
		Prototyping Center for Creative Industries "shop"	Branch of the Russian state Institute of Stage Arts
		Cultural and educational complex of the Siberian arts cluster	At the intersection of Voroshilova St. and Khimikov Ave, Leninsky district

(continued)

Table 1 (continued)

City size	City	Object (creative cluster)	Cluster site
Altai Krai			
Small: 10–50	Zarinsky district of Altai region (13.7)	Sports and tourism cluster Tyagun	On the territory of Tyagunsky selsoviet, Zarinsky District, Altai region
Large: 100–250	Biysk (184)	Creative space Kalendar	Based on the youth Center for Civic Initiatives Vector
		Comprehensive tourist route small Golden ring of Altai	Chuysky Trakt: Biysk, Belokurikha, Biysky, Krasnogorsky, Altaisky, and Smolensky districts

Source: Turgel et al. [8]

achieving the goals of socio-economic development of territories. A differentiated management policy and a set of state support measures are proposed for each strategy.

The choice of the organizational and economic model for the formation and management of creative clusters in second-tier cities is determined based on two basic criteria: (1) the level of government intervention and (2) the specifics of the organization of creative industries.

The method of content analysis of the existing academic and regulatory sources allowed us to develop a system of interaction between organizations that ensure the process of managing creative industries in second-tier cities amid digitalization.

4 Results

4.1 A Modular Approach to Managing Creative Industries in Second-Tier Cities of the Urals and Western Siberia

Strategies for managing creindustrialisation in second-tier cities under conditions of digital transformation on the basis of a modular approach are presented in Fig. 1.

The main premise of the modular approach is that "a smart strategy ... implies a fine tuning to the characteristics of each territory" [35]. This means that creativity-based policies do not inherently guarantee successful territorial development and can, in some cases, have neutral or even negative outcomes. Therefore, it is crucial to consider as many details, processes, and factors as possible that influence the outcome of a creative development strategy in second-tier cities.

We see the modular concept in management as a set of elements that form a unified system for managing a city's creative development while retaining relative autonomy. In this study, the concept implies the use of a "construction set" approach in managing creative industries, where creative industries should serve as a key tool

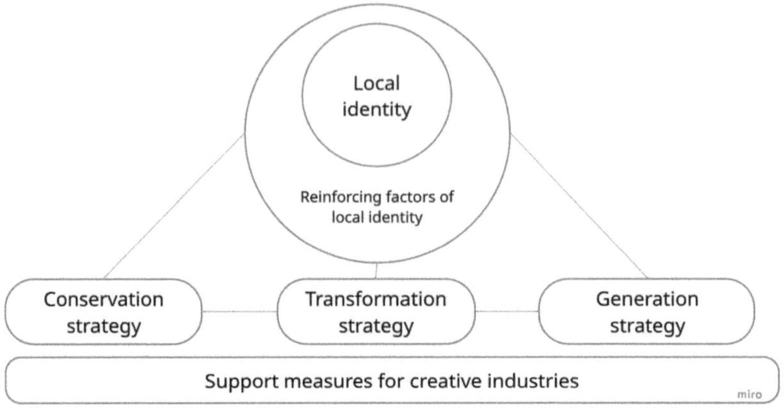

Fig. 1 Strategies for managing creindustrialisation in second-tier cities under conditions of digital transformation on the basis of a modular approach

for preserving and leveraging the tangible and intangible heritage of peripheral cities, transforming this heritage into an economic asset.

The primary mission of the module is to create a customized "construction set" for each city that supports an effective development strategy. The core of this construction set is creativity rooted in local identity. The other elements of the module act as supporting, interconnected components essential for the success of the city's development strategy. These include executive and legislative bodies, infrastructure that fosters the growth of the city's creative economy, human capital, and other factors. These elements constitute a kind of "outer shell" and "protective belt" around the core. Additionally, they include factors that characterize the local environment. In simpler terms, the modular approach seeks to establish a comprehensive management system—built on essential principles, methods, and tools for achieving goals—while also allowing for the strategy to be tailored to the specific needs of industrial second-tier cities as they develop their creative economies.

The first step is to identify the city's unique characteristics to create a tailored strategy for managing its creative space. More specifically, the management of urban space development should start with an analysis of its creative potential and challenges, followed by the development and implementation of "activities of the strategic development plan."

The next step is to select the organizational and economic model that best represents the city in the context of its creative development. For this purpose, we proposed two typologies: one for creative clusters in second-tier cities [8] and the other for organizational and economic management models [55].

The reverse direction involves monitoring the implementation of the strategy and making adjustments when needed. The development of creativity in a city is influenced by various factors, which may sometimes require significant changes in the management process. These changes can affect the core—local identity, which provides coherence to the entire structure. Local identity thus serves both as the source for creating the modular management concept and its ultimate goal. For the creative sector to become an instrument of urban development, it must stem from the city's local identity, which we view as the key "formatting characteristic" that shapes the territorial community.

4.2 A Typology of Creative Clusters in Second-Tier Cities Based on the Two-Component Construct of Local Identity

The identity of a location is the source of dynamic development for any space, including urban areas, due to the actors operating within it. Each new generation not only has its own understanding of the shared living space but also inherits the system of social meanings created by its predecessors, expressed both in spiritual historical heritage and in the tangible objects of material culture. It is local identity that shapes the image (context) of the city as a cohesive, recognizable place, encompassing local traditions, landmarks, the "social profile of residents," and so on. It is clear that the most important role in developing the "politics of identity" falls to local authorities that are responsible for initiating its creation and development in peripheral cities.

The local identity of the second-tier cities in the Urals and Western Siberia is shaped by various processes and factors, yet these cities largely remain "repositories of traditional values," retaining their cultural code. This is why experts believe these cities have "geostrategic significance" and are capable of strengthening the "framework of the state."

The starting point for developing the modular management concept is our understanding of local identity as a construct, which includes two components: material and symbolic. The first component consists of physical objects that reflect the uniqueness of the location (industrial and factory areas, natural landmarks, and the cultural-historical heritage of the region). The second component transforms the city's space into a "symbolic space," which serves as the foundation for the formation and preservation of identity through symbols and meanings that shape the city's context. At the same time, it works in conjunction with the city's creative economy to outline its creative space. If all elements of the urban environment are brought together in this space, it creates opportunities for personal growth and enables every resident to achieve creative self-realization. In other words, it is about creating an economic model in the city that, as Florida [28] suggests, is primarily focused on the residents. The key to developing this model lies in the ideas and innovations of the people who live there.

The distinct combinations and significance of material and symbolic components within the construct allowed us, based on empirical data (case analysis of creative clusters in cities of the Urals and Siberia), to develop an original typology of creative clusters represented by three models: "conservation," "transformation," and "generation" [18]. Schematically, the feature of these typologies is presented in Table 2.

Table 2 Types of creative clusters

Creative cluster model	Creative cluster type	Significance of the material component	Significance of the symbolic component
Conservation	1	High	High
Transformation	2	Average	Low
	3	Low	Average
	4	High	Average
Generation	5	Low	High

This approach, in our view, offers a more effective framework for local strategic planning to achieve the socio-economic development goals of a city by leveraging the creative potential of its residents. Focusing on local identity helps tailor the conditions in accordance with the unique characteristics of a location, which are essential for developing effective policies to manage the city's creative industries.

4.3 Modular Management of Creative Industries Based on Local Identity in Industrial Cities

For second-tier cities in the Urals and Western Siberia, which are characterized by their distinct industrial profiles, manufacturing has long been a defining aspect of their local identity. However, the decline in industrial specialization across many of these cities has triggered a crisis of "factory identity," prompting a shift in local discourse. The success of this transition largely depends on whether local authorities have a clear understanding of the initial conditions, enabling them to identify new symbols and meanings for the city.

Establishing this understanding is crucial for formulating a strategy that fosters growth within the creative sector of these industrial cities. The goal is to revitalize and transform these areas into hubs of growth by expanding the concept of traditional factory symbolism, adapting local identity to reflect contemporary realities, and leveraging the creative potential inherent in these cities.

If a creative space is represented by clusters where both components of local identity, material and symbolic, are equally significant (in our typology, this is the "dynamic conservation" model), the main goal of managing such a location is to preserve the city's old identity while ensuring its continuous adjustment in response to emerging challenges. The brand of such a cluster is shaped by its place of origin, and its successful performance largely depends on its ability to convey the location's symbolic meanings through creative industries. In contrast, for clusters where both components are weakly developed (the "generation" model), management efforts should focus on how the local community interprets its identity, creating new meanings and values. In this case, the creative cluster serves as a key tool to achieve that goal. The "actualization" of local identity can be affected by various processes, such as tourism development or territorial branding, initiated not only by local authorities but also by regional and federal ones. The ultimate goal is to transform the local context in a way that allows for an effective global outcome—preserving national culture.

The choice of an organizational-economic model for developing creative clusters in second-tier cities is based on two key factors: the level of government intervention and the way creative industries are organized [18]. If a city lacks bottom-up initiatives and creative development primarily results from the government's efforts, such as infrastructure creation and funding through state subsidies (the "dependent" model in our classification), then it is clear that local authorities should focus on stimulating local initiatives in the creative space to transform cultural heritage into a valuable urban resource. At the city leadership level, the main focus should be on developing initiative projects that are thoroughly researched and supported by a clear rationale. These projects should have a strong foundation, making them more likely to secure grants and financial support from the regional center. If the government is not directly involved in building the creative urban space, and instead, the initiative comes from large creative enterprises—organized by industry, capable of reaching national and international markets, and with business strategies in place for consuming creative products—this approach is classified as a "mature" organizational-economic model. In this case, the management goal is to support both individual and collective creativity through the use of technological innovations. It should also be noted that the strategy for managing creative industries will be most effective if it is tailored to the specific needs of each type of creative cluster.

Government support should be tailored to suit each development model. For example, if an urban creative space is to be developed under the "dynamic conservation" model, the primary forms of municipal assistance should include funding and informational support. On the other hand, if the city's main strategy is to create a creative cluster, the emphasis should shift toward infrastructure development, project production, and expert evaluation. Additional forms of methodological support, such as organizing consulting and training programs to enhance the skills of creative industry participants and fostering a network of creative entrepreneurs, should also be prioritized. Finally, when it is necessary to transform an already established creative cluster—for example, to increase the "urban creative intensity" or find an unconventional solution to a current urban challenge—the choice of support measures will depend on the planned trajectory of its development. In this case, the most effective form of infrastructure support for creative industries would be "creative clusters of advanced development." These clusters have the potential to establish technological value chains that drive the growth of the creative urban space by producing new, unique products with high added value and opening up new markets for them. Another important approach could involve modifying the territory's "geo-brand," emphasizing not only the city's cultural and natural heritage but also its unique strengths that can attract talented creative individuals. This strategy aims to position the city as an appealing destination for creative talent by showcasing its distinctive attributes and potential.

In all three cases, when implementing any of the three strategies in the city, particular attention should be given to building interactions and establishing dialogue with regional cultural authorities, and, of course, supporting entrepreneurs in protecting their rights and intellectual property. A significant role in this process is assigned to the Regional Standard for the Development of Creative Industries. It serves as a compilation of best practices, organized into 12 recommended steps for establishing and implementing support measures aimed at fostering the growth of creative industries at the regional level (Regional Standard for the Development of Creative Industries, https://asi.ru/library/main/197563).

4.4 Creative Industries Ecosystem in Second-Tier Cities Based on a Digital Platform for Effective Interaction Between Institutions and Organizations

Our analysis of strategic documents has shown the importance of creating a coordinated system to manage creative industries. This system should comprise a clear organizational structure between representative bodies and establish a foundation for both methodological support and legal regulation. It is also essential to define the key roles and functions of development institutions, federal agencies, and both sector-specific and cross-sectoral organizations.

The practice of institutional support is shaped by the creation of anchor organizations in the management of creative industries, which can be broadly divided into two models of operation. Within the first model, support is provided by an already existing regional organization for small business and entrepreneurship. A prime example is the Sverdlovsk Regional Fund for Entrepreneurship Support (SOFPP), which offers a full range of services for entrepreneurs in the creative industries at any stage of development such as startup training programs, concessional lending, and assistance in entering international markets. Within the second model, a separate organization is created, for example, "Krespektiva" in Kaliningrad region.

However, there is a lack of systematic interaction among institutions and intersectoral organizations that should provide the necessary conditions for the growth of creative industries (Fig. 2). The green lines on the diagram represent connections established through legally defined cooperation, without strict organizational subordination:

1—Federal institutions should implement major projects of interregional and national significance and co-finance regional projects;

2—Educational organizations are often established on the basis of sectoral and intersectoral, federal organizations;

3—Project institutes and cross-sectoral organizations can cooperate with the Ministry of Economic Development of the Russian Federation on the elaboration of development directions for individual creative economy industries, and organize joint educational events.

4—Educational institutions such as the Higher School of Economics (HSE) can collaborate with the ASI on research tasks and organize joint educational events;

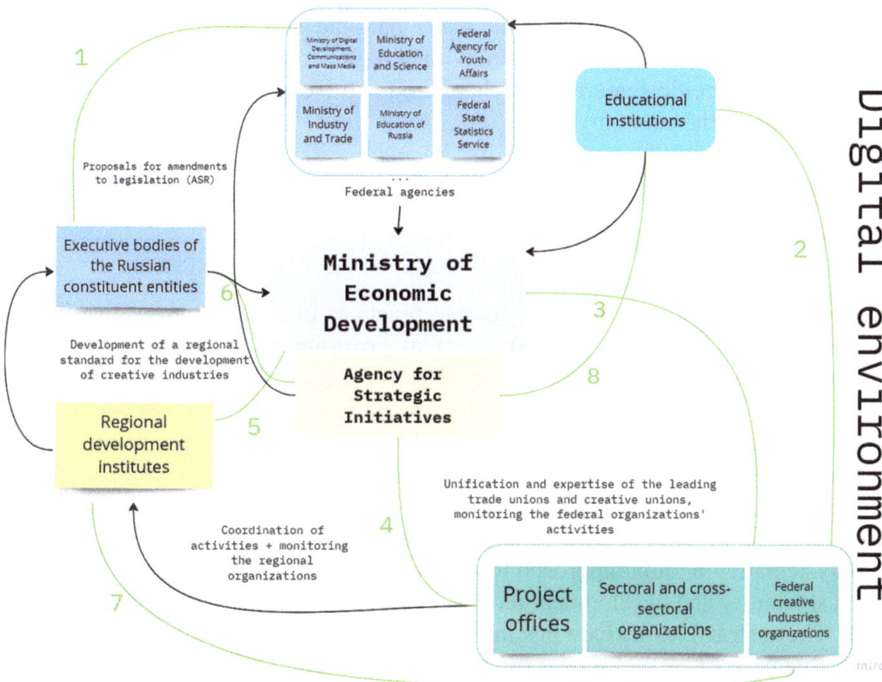

Fig. 2 Key development institutions and intersectoral organizations managing creative industries in the digital environment

5—Development of regional strategic documents (regional standards for creative industries development) with informational and educational functions; Building partnerships with federal centers of creative industries development.

6, 7—Comprehensive information exchange to foster the development of creative industries;

8—Implementation of educational, acceleration, and outreach programs focused on regional development through creative economy tools.

Addressing these issues will promote effective collaboration among all relevant institutions and organizations. At the city level, this involves building an ecosystem for creative industries that takes into account spatial, economic, social, and cultural factors. Such an ecosystem aligns institutional conditions and interaction mechanisms among companies engaged in the creation, development, production, and distribution of creative industry products, as well as in workforce training [56]. The digital environment serves as the foundation for the operation of this ecosystem [56].

Importantly, all relevant stakeholders—government bodies, business representatives, and public and educational organizations—should be involved in developing and implementing an effective national strategy to ensure the economic well-being of regions and individual cities. This collaboration will create optimal conditions for helping regions achieve their strategic socio-economic development goals through creative industries. However, while national strategies focus on general characteristics, the strategy for each individual region, and especially cities, should be tailored to specific features that shape competitive advantages and "potential growth points of the economy" [57].

5 Conclusion

Analysis of both international and Russian practices in supporting creative industries demonstrates that the greatest effect of government regulation is achieved through systematic and sustained efforts [6].

The creative sector comprises, firstly, small enterprises, and secondly, self-employed individuals, which creates a need for virtual spaces that facilitate networking not only with clients and business partners but also with educational, scientific, and urban communities. The digital environment is essential for fostering these connections and establishing strong relationships.

A systematic, modular approach to managing creative industries, which considers local identity and development factors, helps define strategies for secondary-tier cities. These strategies include placing small businesses in city centers, renovating historic central areas, and transforming historical monuments through public and private investment. Most cities located in former industrial areas face a severe shortage of innovative business practices and management solutions. Therefore, it is essential to establish an environment that attracts creative individuals, transforming the urban landscape and fostering the production and commercialization of local entrepreneurs' know-how. The launch of these processes will inevitably lead to the creation of an inclusive "personalized economy," highlighting the uniqueness of the territory.

However, relying solely on the resources of a secondary-tier city will not yield positive results unless the location's unique characteristics are supported externally, with substantial institutional and financial backing, primarily from regional authorities. The municipality's task is, therefore, to maintain an ongoing, active dialogue with residents, businesses, and other potential stakeholders. This will help local authorities preserve the unique atmosphere of small provincial towns, traditionally guardians of cultural values, and prevent them from losing out to megacities. It will also help reduce or eliminate harmful migration trends, primarily the outflow from these areas.

Further development of the topic will have several directions. First, it is the study of the digital transformation process in relation to creative reindustrialization, including the formation of the smart city concept for small and medium-sized provincial locations; the creation of a creative industries management ecosystem on a digital platform. Secondly, a detailed justification of the applied significance of the theoretical and methodological concept proposed by the authors for both Russian regions and other countries that have small and medium-sized cities with industrial heritage requiring revitalization, using a comparative analysis.

Acknowledgements The study was carried out with the support of the Russian Science Foundation grant No. 22-18-00679 "Creative reindustrialization of "second-tier" cities in the context of digital transformation".

References

1. Babina, E. N., Barashkina, E. V., Beganskaya, I. Yu., et al. (2024). *Creative industries as an imperative for economic growth: Cross-innovation and sustainable development*, Samara.
2. Naumova, O. N., & Nikolaeva, N. A. (2023). Revitalization of creative industries as a driver of national and regional economic development. Bulletin of the Volga State University of Service. *Series: Economics, 19*(1), 26–29.
3. Zelentsova, E. V. (2010). *Creative industries: Theories and practices*. Klassika.
4. Bonello, V., Faraone, C., Gambarotto, F., Nicoletto, L., & Pedrini, G. (2020). Clusters in formation in a deindustrialized area: Urban regeneration and structural change in Porto Marghera (Venice). *Competitiveness Review, 30*(4), 417–436. https://doi.org/10.1108/CR-12-2019-0129
5. Hesmondhalgh, D. (2014). *Cultural industries (Russian edition)*. National Research University.
6. Lavrinenko, A. S. (2015). Actual issues of state regulation of creative industries. *Issues of State and Municipal Management, 4*, 135–159.
7. Mikhaylova, A. V. (2018). Digital and creative economy in the modern space. *Journal of Creative Economy, 12*(1), 29–42. https://doi.org/10.18334/ce.12.1.38783
8. Turgel, I., Derbeneva, V., & Baskakova, I. (2023). Conceptual approach to managing the development of creative industries in second-tier industrial cities. *R-Economy, 9*(4), 366–383. https://doi.org/10.15826/recon.2023.9.4.023
9. Rastvortseva, S. N., & Manaeva, I. V. (2022). Modern development of small and medium-sized cities: Trends and drivers. *Economic and Social Changes: Facts, Trends, Forecast, 15*(1), 110–127. https://doi.org/10.15838/esc.2022.1.79.6
10. Musiezdov, A. A. (2010). Local identity as a brand. *V. N. Karazin Kharkiv National University Bulletin, 889*, 116–120.
11. Vasina, A. V., & Glushkova, Y. O. (2020). Creative economy: Prospects of development in the region (on the example of Saratov and Ulyanovsk regions). *Actual Problems of Economics and Management, 3*(27), 35–43.
12. Labaznova, E. V., Glushkova, Y. O., Bashirzade, R. R., & Pakhomova, A. V. (2019). Generation of creative industry development strategy based on planning. *Azimuth of Scientific Research: Economics and Administration, 8*(2), 64–69. https://doi.org/10.26140/anie-2019-0802-0015
13. Abankina, T. A., Boss, V. O., & Bredikhin, S. V. (2022). *Creative (creative) industries*, Moscow.
14. Hearn, G., Cunningham, S., & Ordoñez, D. (2004). Commercialisation of knowledge in universities: The case of the creative industries. *Prometheus, 22*(2), 189–200. https://doi.org/10.1080/0810902042000218364
15. Seixas, J., & Costa, P. (2011). Criatividade e governança na cidade: A conjugação de dois conceitos poliédricos e complementares. *Cadernos Metrópole, 13*, 69–92. https://doi.org/10.7749/citiescommunitiesterritories.dec2010.020-21.art02
16. Dovey, J., Moreton, S., Sparke, S., & Sharpe, B. (2016). The practice of cultural ecology: Network connectivity in the creative economy. *Cultural Trends, 25*(2), 87–103. https://doi.org/10.1080/09548963.2016.1170922
17. Imperiale, F., Fasiello, R., & Adamo, S. (2021). Sustainability determinants of cultural and creative industries in peripheral areas. *Journal of Risk and Financial Management, 14*(9), 438. https://doi.org/10.3390/jrfm14090438
18. Baskakova, I. V., Derbeneva, V. V., Turgel, I. D., & Tsepeleva, A. D. (2023). Local identity as a basis for creative clusters in Urals and Siberian cities. *Kreativnaya Ekonomika, 17*(12), 4729–4748. https://doi.org/10.18334/ce.17.12.119949

19. Boos, V. O., Shubina, V. I., & Kutsenko, E. S. (2023). Russian regions in focus of creative policies quality index. *Regional Studies, 4*, 53–65. https://doi.org/10.5922/1994-5280-2023-4-5
20. Antonova, I. S., & Maleeva, E. A. (2024). Assessing the development potential of creative business in second-tier cities. *Economy of Regions, 20*(3), 671–685. https://doi.org/10.17059/ekon.reg.2024-3-5
21. Turgel, I. D., & Antonova, I. S. (2023). Creative reindustrialisation of the second-tier cities in the digital transformation era: A study using SciVal tools. *Economy of Regions, 19*(3), 629–650. https://doi.org/10.17059/ekon.reg.2023-3-3
22. Antonova, I. S., Pchelintsev, E. A., & Maleeva, E. A. (2023). Second-tier cities of creative reindustrialization: Search for insights. *Tomsk State University Journal of Economics, 61*, 74–95. https://doi.org/10.17223/19988648/61/6
23. Center for Strategic Research Foundation. (2023). *Measures to support the creative economy*. Retrieved from https://www.csr.ru/ru/research/mery-podderzhki-kreativnoy-ekonomiki/
24. Mao, L. J. (2020). Research on the development path of cultural and creative industries in the digital economy era. *American Journal of Industrial and Business Management, 10*(7), 1237–1249. https://doi.org/10.4236/ajibm.2020.107082
25. Grodach, C. (2017). Urban cultural policy and creative city making. *Cities, 68*, 82–91. https://doi.org/10.1016/j.cities.2017.05.015
26. Breul, M., & Nguyen, T. X. (2022). The impact of extractive industries on regional diversification—Evidence from Vietnam. *The Extractive Industries and Society, 11*, 100982. https://doi.org/10.1016/j.exis.2021.100982
27. Borowiecki, K. J., & Navarrete, T. (2016). *The economic and fiscal dimension of cultural heritage*. European Policy Brief. Retrieved from http://hdl.handle.net/1765/115237
28. Florida, R. (2005). *The rise of the creative class: And how it's transforming work, leisure, community and everyday life*. Basic Books.
29. Fazlagić, J., & Szczepankiewicz, E. I. (2020). The role of local governments in supporting creative industries—A conceptual model. *Sustainability, 12*(1), 438. https://doi.org/10.3390/su12010438
30. Van Blitterswijk, D., Haley, C., & Febvre, J. (2019). *Paths to scale: Finance lessons from European entrepreneurs*. NESTA. Retrieved from https://www.nesta.org.uk/report/paths-to-scale/
31. Jiang, Y., Qian, Q., Zhang, X., & Chen, Y. (2019). The formation of government-oriented creative community and its driving mechanisms: A case study of the 39 space art creative Community in Foshan, China. *Sustainability, 11*(3), 625. https://doi.org/10.3390/su11030625
32. Markopoulos, E., Markopoulos, P., Liumila, M., Almufti, Y., & Romano, C. (2019). Digital cultural strategies within the context of digital humanities economics. In V. G. Duffy (Ed.), *Advances in human factors in wearable technologies and game design* (pp. 283–295). Springer. https://doi.org/10.1007/978-3-030-20476-1_29
33. Lee, H.-K. (2020). Making creative industries policy in the real world: Differing configurations of the culture–market–state nexus in the UK and South Korea. *International Journal of Cultural Policy, 26*(4), 544–560. https://doi.org/10.1080/10286632.2019.1577401
34. Cunningham, S., McCutcheon, M., Hearn, G., & Ryan, M. D. (2020). 'Demand' for culture and 'allied' industries: Policy insights from multi-site creative economy research. *International Journal of Cultural Policy, 27*(6), 768–781. https://doi.org/10.1080/10286632.2020.1849168
35. Turgel, I., Baskakova, I., & Derbeneva, V. (2023). Classifications of "second-tier" cities in the context of creative reindustrialisation. *E3S Web of Conferences, 435*, 03004. https://doi.org/10.1051/e3sconf/202343503004
36. Hospers, G. J. (2003). Creative cities: Breeding places in the knowledge economy. *Knowledge, Technology & Policy, 16*(3), 143–162. https://doi.org/10.1007/s12130-003-1037-1
37. Matovic, M., Madariaga, A., Salvador, S., & del Valle, R. (2018). *Creative cities: Mapping creativity*. Deusto Cities Lab Katedra, University of Deusto.

38. Dragan, A., Creţan, R., Jucu, I. S., & Hriţcu, A. (2024). Revitalizing post-communist urban industrial areas: Divergent narratives in the imagining of copper mine reopening and tourism in a Romanian town. *Cities, 154*, 105379. https://doi.org/10.1016/j.cities.2024.105379
39. Amosova, E. V. (2019). Creative clusters as a way to preserve and redevelop industrial heritage sites. *Society, Environment, Development, 3*, 98–102. Retrieved from https://terrahumana.ru/arhiv/19_03/19_03_14.pdf
40. Markova, E. A., & Konovalova, E. V. (2021). Clustering elements of regional economy as a tool of revitalization. In *Creative strategies and creative industries in the economic, social and cultural space of the region* (pp. 270–274). Springer.
41. Vasina, A. V., & Glushkova, Y. O. (2022). Comprehensive model of creative industries development strategy assessment of the region. *Actual Problems of Economics and Management, 2*(34), 57–64.
42. Evseev, A. S., & Urusova, N. N. (2022). Method of assessment of creative economic development of regions. *Bulletin of Volga State Technological University Series: Economics and Management, 3–4*(55), 40–48. https://doi.org/10.25686/2306-2800.2022.3-4.40
43. Mordanov, M. A. (2022). Assessing the level of creativity in Russian regions: Application of the Florida index to current realities. *Creative Economy, 16*(6), 2093–2110. https://doi.org/10.18334/ce.16.6.114829
44. Salikhov, B. V. (2019). Methodological and methodical aspects of evaluation of the region creative potential in behavioral and digital economy. *Information and Economic Aspects of Standardization and Technical Regulation, 3*(49), 2.
45. Glushkova, Y. O. (2019). The approaches to assessing the effectiveness of the economic and management strategy for the development and state support of creative industries. *Creative Economy, 13*(12), 2387–2396. https://doi.org/10.18334/ce.13.12.41477
46. Abankina, T. V. (2022). Creative economy in Russia: New trends. *Journal of the New Economic Association, 2*(54), 222–229. https://doi.org/10.31737/2221-2264-2022-54-2-13
47. Golovina, K. Y., & Zhiharevich, B. S. (2023). Creative industries in municipal and regional strategies of Ivanovo Oblast and Krasnodar Krai. *Regional Economy The South of Russia, 11*(4), 190–200. https://doi.org/10.15688/re.volsu.2023.4.17
48. Kvint, V. L. (2020). Theoretical basis and methodology of strategizing of the private and public sectors of the Kuzbass region as a medial subsystem of the national economy. *Russian Journal of Industrial Economics, 13*(3), 290–299. https://doi.org/10.17073/2072-1633-2020-3-290-299
49. Suminova, T. N. (2023). Art management as a project practice in the sphere of creative industries. *The Bulletin of Moscow State University of Culture and Arts (Vestnik MGUKI), 4*(114), 141–148. https://doi.org/10.24412/1997-0803-2023-4114-141-148
50. Erokhin, G. P. (2022). Novosibirsk creative cluster—Target development indicators. *Creativity and Modernity, 3*(18), 38–43.
51. Imaeva, G. R., Sushko, E. Y., Gildebrandt, I. A., Spiridonova, L. V., & Aymaletdinov, T. A. (2021). *The contribution of digital platforms to the development of creative industries and support of creative entrepreneurship*. NAFI Publishing House.
52. Gushchina, E. G., & Tarabanova, E. V. (2022). Creative industries: New capabilities for the development of Russian cities and regions. *Journal of Volgograd State University Economics, 24*(1), 91–104. https://doi.org/10.15688/ek.jvolsu.2022.1.9
53. Mirolubova, T. V., & Radionova, M. V. (2023). Digital transformation and its impact on the socio-economic development of Russian regions. *Economy of Regions, 19*(3), 697–710. https://doi.org/10.17059/ekon.reg.2023-3-7
54. Domenech, R. B., De Miguel Molina, B., & Rausell, K. P. (2021). The impact of cultural and creative industries on the wealth of countries, regions and municipalities. *European Planning Studies, 29*(10), 1777–1797. https://doi.org/10.1080/09654313.2021.1909540

55. Derbeneva, V., Baskakova, I., Chukavina, K., Turgel, I., Novokshonova, Z., & Tsepeleva, A. (2024). Key factors in managing creative reindustrialization strategies. *R-Economy, 10*(4), 475–494. https://doi.org/10.15826/recon.2024.10.4.029
56. Bogdanova, N. V., & Fieraru, V. A. (2017). Features of strategic planning and development of competitive advantages of urban agglomerations (on the example of St. Petersburg). *Management Consulting, 2*, 121–127.
57. Norilsk Development Agency, & Universal University. (2021). *Strategy for the development of creative industries in Norilsk until 2024*. Norilsk Development Agency, & Universal University.

Building Health Capital Through Digital Skills: Healthcare Satisfaction and Well-Being in Russian Regions

Ilia Chernenko, Maksim Koliasnikov, and Veronika Zemzyulina

Abstract The availability of digital competencies among the population in the regions is one of the critical drivers of technological transformation of the medical sector in the coming decades. This article aims to examine the impact of medical digital skills of the population on self-assessment of personal health, satisfaction with healthcare services, and subjective well-being related to health. Using microdata from Rosstat's 2023 databases on digital competencies and population health status, we calculate indicators of human, health capital, and well-being across population cohorts segmented by five-year age intervals. The findings reveal that medical digital skills positively impact self-assessment of health primarily among individuals aged 50 and older. In contrast, for younger cohorts (aged 20–35), greater engagement with digital health services correlates with poorer health outcomes. Notably, among the various predictors of digital skills, only the use of online platforms for scheduling medical appointments consistently shows a positive impact on both health self-assessment and subjective well-being. While digital support for regional healthcare reforms offers some benefits, its overall effectiveness in enhancing health capital remains limited. Further investments in technological infrastructure and equipment for the healthcare sector are necessary to fully realize the potential of digital transformation.

Keywords Healthcare · Digital skills · E-health · Human capital · Health capital · Subjective well-being

---

I. Chernenko (✉) · M. Koliasnikov · V. Zemzyulina
Ural Federal University, Ekaterinburg, Russia
e-mail: i.m.chernenko@urfu.ru; m.s.koliasnikov@urfu.ru; veronika.zemziulina@urfu.ru

F. Tao et al. (eds.), *Artificial Intelligence and Digital Transformation*, Lecture Notes in Information Systems and Organisation 78,
https://doi.org/10.1007/978-3-032-00118-4_16

1 Introduction

The widespread adoption of digital technologies, driven by advancements in science and technology, has catalyzed digital transformation across all sectors, including business, the public sector, and households [1]. Digital transformation aims to enhance business processes by introducing substantial changes through the integration of information and communication technologies (ICT) and related innovations [2]. Modern technological advances applied within the framework of the Industry 4.0 concept, such as 3D printing, cloud computing, artificial intelligence, digital twins (DT), and the Internet of Things (IoT), have changed the approaches of both business and public institutions to value creation and contribute to enhancing the quality of life across various domains [3]. One of the strategically important areas is healthcare, where digital transformation has gained increased importance largely due to the need for technological convergence across sectors and regions, accelerating the adoption of ICT in response to the challenges caused by the COVID-19 pandemic [4].

Recent literature shows that the COVID-19 pandemic has highlighted the need for digital adoption, particularly in the healthcare sector, where challenges such as staff shortages, inadequate equipment and unstable supply chains have increased dissatisfaction with the quality of healthcare services [5]. In response, many healthcare institutions within the European Union accelerated their digital transformation efforts as early as 2020 [6]. Solutions such as electronic health records (EHRs), telemedicine, and the systematization and intelligent analysis of large patient datasets have shown potential to reduce social inequalities in healthcare, thereby improving the overall well-being of the population [4]. However, the outcomes of many healthcare digital transformation initiatives have been mixed. Projects such as EHR implementation and digital appointment systems have often fallen short of expectations, yielding inconsistent results [7, 8]. Previous research has identified several barriers to digital transformation, including social factors such as the usability of services, fear of new technologies, low levels of digital literacy, and limited access to digital communication infrastructure [9, 10]. Among these barriers, digital literacy, defined as the presence of digital competencies among users of information systems, stands out as a critical factor. Digital literacy is necessary for the effective use of digital tools and technologies and is becoming a decisive factor in mitigating the effects of the pandemic [5, 11, 12].

Over the past two decades, the Russian healthcare system has undergone significant reforms aimed at operational optimization, reducing inefficiencies, and increasing the number of high-tech medical institutions [13]. However, these reforms have also led to several unintended consequences, including a substantial decline in the availability of medical services in remote areas, deteriorating working conditions for healthcare professionals, and an emphasis on economic efficiency at the expense of service quality [14]. The digital transformation of Russia's healthcare sector is confronted by numerous challenges, such as excessive bureaucratization, low motivation among key stakeholders, and insufficient ICT competencies among both practitioners and administrators [13]. Therefore, issues of developing digital competencies of the population are key to improving the quality and accessibility of medical services, increasing health capital and subjective well-being in Russian regions.

A review of the literature reveals that while existing studies predominantly focus on the benefits and barriers associated with implementing digital health technologies [15], as well as the role of digital literacy in enhancing the effectiveness of these technologies [16], insufficient attention has been given to the direct impact of digital competencies on individual health outcomes. Our study expands the current understanding of digital health by examining how medical digital literacy influences health indicators, well-being, and the ability to maintain an active lifestyle among diverse demographic groups in Russia. We address a gap in the literature by evaluating the impact of digital medical skills on self-assessed personal health, satisfaction with healthcare services, and health-related subjective well-being. In our framework, medical digital skills are characterized by individuals' ability to search for health-related information, purchase healthcare products online, and manage access to medical services in a digital environment.

2 Literature Review

2.1 Digital Transformation of Healthcare: Opportunities and Barriers for Social Context of the Regions

Digital transformation has emerged as a key driver of technological and social change, becoming a significant source of economic growth over the past decade. This phenomenon was anticipated by the widespread adoption of the Internet in the mid-1990s, which revolutionized communication across all sectors [17]. The healthcare sector was similarly impacted, with digital technologies gaining attention around the same time through the rise of telemedicine and e-health [18]. The e-health concept includes the development and implementation of digital systems in the activities of medical institutions that provide open access to data, remote access to the medical record system, remote treatment, and monitoring of the patient's condition [19]. As this concept evolved, along with new technological advancements, four primary areas of digital transformation in healthcare have been identified, focusing on different stages of patient interaction: prevention, pre- and during-care procedures, and post-treatment monitoring of recovery [20]. Academic research on the digital transformation of healthcare institutions has concentrated on three main aspects: (I) identifying specific digital technologies, (II) evaluating their potential benefits for healthcare systems and individual stakeholders, and (III) analyzing the social barriers and challenges associated with their implementation and maintenance [21].

The widespread adoption of Industry 4.0 technologies has led to significant advancements in medicine, often referred to as Healthcare 4.0, which has enhanced the healthcare system's ability to adapt more effectively to patients' needs [22, 23]. The most studied technologies of Industry 4.0 that have transitioned to the concept of Healthcare 4.0 today are additive technologies and collaborative robots [4]. One of the earliest and most impactful applications of digital technologies in healthcare is telemedicine. Its integration within the Healthcare 4.0 framework has greatly expanded the capabilities of both patients and healthcare providers [24]. The use of sensors and IoT has made it possible to monitor patients in real time and, without visiting medical institutions, transmit readings such as blood pressure, sleep data, body temperature, etc. As a result, it allows to diagnose and prevent diseases such as heart failure. Additionally, the integration of various technological tools has significantly improved the monitoring of patient recovery in fields such as ophthalmology, neurology, and rehabilitation after injuries or strokes [24].

The integration of advanced technological combinations has enabled the implementation of the DT concept in healthcare. DT offers unique social opportunities for personalized patient care by providing on-demand individual risk profiles, assessing potential reactions to specific medications or combination therapies, and delivering detailed recommendations to minimize side effects and prevent the onset of diseases at early stages [25]. Moreover, the continuous analysis of data from wearable medical devices facilitates the modeling of pathological developments, such as diabetes and cardiovascular diseases, enabling early intervention and more precise management strategies [26].

Artificial intelligence, combined with advancements in telemedicine, has the potential to significantly enhance the training and digital human capital of healthcare professionals [27]. The increased capabilities in this area are also associated with virtual, augmented, and mixed reality technologies, which make it possible to implement simulations of both clinical cases and extreme situations for training medical personnel, as well as more effectively disseminate knowledge on first aid among the population [20]. Virtual reality significantly broadens the scope for performing remote surgeries, particularly in Russian regions [28]. Big data analysis and cloud computing make it possible to implement fault-tolerant electronic recording systems and systematize patient data [29]. These technologies became especially vital during the COVID-19 pandemic, when the rapid redistribution of workloads among medical institutions and personnel was crucial [30]. In recent years, big data analysis has been further enhanced by the machine learning and artificial intelligence, which have been applied in diagnosing complex diseases, supporting surgical decision-making, and transforming patient interaction models [31, 32].

As highlighted in the literature, the digital transformation of healthcare offers numerous social benefits within the regional context, primarily through increased labor automation and connectivity among various stakeholders in the healthcare services market [15]. Key advantages include reduced socially significant financial costs, enhanced diagnostic and preventive capabilities, the development of personalized patient care, improved speed and efficiency of medical services, shortened waiting times, and expanded educational opportunities for medical personnel, industry professionals, and the general public [4]. Despite these promising prospects, the digital transformation of healthcare does not always meet expectations and encounters numerous barriers and potential threats, particularly in regional communities. Notable challenges include information security risks, such as the transmission of personal images and confidential data over the Internet [8], and concerns about unauthorized access to electronic health records [25]. Additional issues include the high cost of implementing digital solutions [33], regulatory complexities that hinder swift adoption, and persistent infrastructure gaps limiting access to digital health services [4], particularly in developing countries [8, 34].

A critical social barrier to eHealth adoption is stakeholder resistance to innovative digital health technologies, as it is particularly evident in the use of digital health services such as mobile health applications (mHealth) [35] and electronic health records [10]. Ngafeeson and Manga [10] show that resistance often stems from dissatisfaction with outcomes and a sense of helplessness during digital service delivery, regardless of confidence in the technology's effectiveness. Furthermore, with the decline of COVID-19 cases and the return to pre-pandemic routines, there is a noticeable reluctance among both healthcare providers and patients to continue the active use of digital health technologies, favoring a return to face-to-face interactions [3]. Social challenges and threats significantly impact the utilization of human capital in regional healthcare systems. A crucial factor underpinning these issues is the insufficient level of digital literacy among both medical personnel delivering digital services and end users accessing them.

2.2 *Digital Literacy for the Effective Digital Transformation of Healthcare*

Resistance to technology often stems from a lack of digital literacy among both healthcare professionals, who may perceive digital healthcare as a threat to their autonomy and professional competence, and patients, who may distrust the effectiveness of new technologies [10]. The term "digital literacy" was first introduced by Paul Gilster in 1997 in his book of the same name, where he defined it as the ability to acquire a set of skills essential for functioning in a society increasingly mediated by digital tools [16]. *Medical digital literacy* is a crucial factor in addressing the digital divide, which limits certain population groups' access to healthcare information and services. In severe cases, the digital divide can result in complete exclusion from some types of healthcare. One of the primary contributors to the digital divide is age, as older individuals are significantly less likely to use ICTs, thereby limiting their access to digital healthcare services [36]. Low digital literacy among older population cohorts in regional areas presents risks beyond limited access to healthcare services, it also increases the likelihood of individuals encountering unreliable or fraudulent information, potentially harming both their physical and mental health [16, 37]. The lack of digital competencies may act as a limiting factor for the population's interaction with public digital platforms.

The digital divide is emerging as a critical determinant of health capital and well-being, particularly in urban contexts where rapid digitalization does not automatically yield inclusive benefits. For example, Vanolo's study on smartmentality in Urban Studies demonstrates that although the smart city paradigm promotes efficiency and technological advancement, it often assumes an ICT competency that many elderly citizens lack. The assumption can marginalize older adults by complicating their ability to navigate the sophisticated digital infrastructures that support modern urban governance and public services [38].

Empirical evidence from Romania further supports the idea of digital divide. Dragan et al. show through spatial analyses that ICT-driven initiatives are unevenly distributed, and peripheral urban areas frequently overlooking the limited digital skills of the poor and elderly. The inequality not only reduces the potential health benefits of digital integration, such as telemedicine and e-governance, but also reinforces existing socio-economic differences by excluding those most in need of accessible digital services [39]. Beyond the challenges faced by older adults, digital exclusion compromises health capital among other vulnerable populations. Malovics et al. highlight that poor Roma communities, already burdened by socio-economic marginalization, face significant barriers to accessing digital tools and resources. The limited digital literacy restricts opportunities for social engagement and access to health-related information, thereby impeding their ability to accumulate both social and health capital [40]. The COVID-19 pandemic has further revealed the consequences of digital illiteracy among vulnerable groups. Jupîneanț et al. [41] document that Roma migrant women in Spain, confronted with challenges of gender, ethnicity, and economic insecurity, struggled with the sudden digital transformation during lockdown. Experiences of migrants illustrate how inadequate digital skills can severely restrict access to essential services, from online education to health information, thus exacerbating health disparities during crises [41]. From an econometric perspective, these case studies collectively suggest that digital literacy should be considered a key explanatory variable in models assessing healthcare satisfaction and overall well-being. Enhancing digital skills among the elderly and other vulnerable groups may also serve as an effective policy lever to boost health capital.

However, previous studies have not found a clear relationship between the level of digitalization and the level of digital skills of the population [42]. Even in highly digitalized public systems, service coverage often remains uneven, arising both from inadequate infrastructure and a lack of requisite digital skills, particularly among the elderly [43]. The use of digital health may be limited for people who do not have the necessary level of digital literacy, which will further exacerbate inequalities and may exclude such users from the healthcare system altogether [37]. For example, Alam et al. [44] found that the availability of eHealth services is closely related to the digital literacy levels of the population. In remote regions with limited access to high-speed communication networks, the availability of digital healthcare services remains particularly low.

In the long term, limited access to quality health care can have serious negative consequences, especially for the health of older people [45]. The *digital divide* is a direct threat to human capital accumulation. It is a set of social differences that result in the benefits of digital transformation being concentrated in the population groups that are able to maximize its benefits, while those lagging behind find themselves in a situation of significant reduction in access to services, or even total exclusion [46, 47]. Addressing the digital divide requires a strong focus on expanding digital literacy education programs to promote equitable access to modern healthcare services [48]. The COVID-19 pandemic has exacerbated concerns about digital dependency in healthcare, intensifying fears that the growing digital divide will further harm vulnerable groups, as they have not only faced limited access to digital health solutions but also experienced more severe illness symptoms and longer recovery times [49, 50]. Lindström et al. [51] found significant associations between unmet health care need and mortality in older adults.

A sufficient level of digital literacy significantly increases the likelihood of patients utilizing remote consultations [52], as well as the use of telemedicine services in general [53]. At the same time, digital literacy acts as a mediator of the effectiveness of online information search on medical topics, including for cancer patients [54]. However, there remains a notable gap in research regarding the direct impact of digital skills on individuals' health outcomes [5]. This study aims to address this gap by examining the relationship between digital literacy levels and patients' satisfaction with healthcare services, as well as their self-assessment of health when engaging with digital health systems. Based on the literature review, we propose the following research questions:

RQ1: How do medical digital skills, such as searching for health information and utilizing digital health services, influence self-assessed health and health-related well-being in Russian regions?

RQ2: How does the age-related digital divide shape the structural relationships between digital competencies and self-assessed health across different population cohorts in Russian regions?

3 Methods and Data

The empirical strategy of this study relies on statistical analysis to identify the determinants of health capital associated with digitalization. Due to the absence of a unified database containing microdata on digital competencies, self-assessed health, and satisfaction with healthcare services in a cross-sectional sample for Russian regions, we employed a cohort approach. It enabled the creation of a statistical observation base for 2023, covering 85 regions of Russia and including 11 population cohorts, each defined by five-year age intervals from 20 to 75 years (1948–2003 years of birth). As a result, 935 observations were obtained, which were used in further econometric analysis. The sources of microdata for calculating regional statistics for each cohort were Rosstat data, including annual observation of the digital skills of the population [55], population health [56], and sample observation of the quality of services in the field of health care and education [57]. To calculate the statistics, the corresponding weights defined by Rosstat for a representative sample were used.

Three groups of variables were identified for the analysis: indicators of health capital, satisfaction with the quality of healthcare services, and digital skills of the population. Average values for each variable were calculated for each cohort within each region. To ensure statistical reliability, data from at least 50 individuals were used for each of the 935 observations. Additionally, individual weights were applied to ensure that the sample was representative of the broader population.

The econometric analysis was conducted in two stages: regression analysis and structural equation modelling. Regression analysis was employed to identify common factors influencing self-assessed health and subjective well-being, yielding coefficients for three models with different dependent variables but an identical set of independent variables. The dependent variables included self-assessed health from two alternative Rosstat databases (KDU_S_HEAL and HEAL_S_SELF) and health-related subjective well-being (HEAL_P_AVE). To calculate the subjective well-being indicator for each cohort within the regions, the arithmetic mean of five variables was determined: cheerfulness (HEAL_P_1), calmness (HEAL_P_2), activity (HEAL_P_3), sleep efficiency (HEAL_P_4), and interest in life (HEAL_P_5). Each indicator was measured on a six-point Likert scale, reflecting the frequency of experiencing these states, ranging from 0 (never) to 5 (all the time). The independent variables included various control factors, such as visiting a doctor (HEAL_T_DOC), satisfaction with medical services (HEAL_S_PMED and HEAL_S_PMED), participation in sports (HEAL_SPOR), alcohol consumption (HEAL_ALCO), smoking (HEAL_SMOK), having a disability (HEAL_INVAL), and undergoing a medical examination within the last 2 years (HEAL_DISPAN).

The key independent variables included indicators related to digital engagement and competencies: time spent on a computer during free time, the perceived influence of ICT on daily life (ICT_IMPT) measured on a 5-point Likert scale, the use of the Internet for purchasing medical products (ICT_M_PUR), the level of digital skills (DIG_SKILLS), and the likelihood of making a digital appointment with a doctor (ICT_APMNT). The DIG_SKILLS variable was calculated as the arithmetic mean of 14 dummy-variables from the Rosstat database, which measured proficiency in using computers, the Internet, and mobile applications. These scores were standardized on a 10-point scale. The ICT_APMNT variable represented the proportion of individuals within each cohort who used the Internet to schedule medical appointments in 2023. A critical indicator for assessing the effectiveness of digitalization was the digital divide (DIS), calculated as the relative difference in digital skills between the youngest cohort (20–24 years) and the oldest cohort (70–74 years). A DIS value of 1 indicates that the older population cohort lacks essential digital skills entirely:

$$DIS = \frac{DIG\_SKILLS_{20-24} - DIG\_SKILLS_{70-74}}{DIG\_SKILLS_{20-24}}$$

Structural equation modeling (SEM) was employed to formulate an empirical model aligned with the research questions. In this model, self-rated health was represented as a latent variable (HEAL_ESTIM), comprising three observable variables: current health status, health compared to 1 year ago, and expected future health. The level of medical digital competencies was captured through another latent variable (INT_ACTIV), which included three observable indicators. Satisfaction with healthcare services (HEAL_SATIS) was assessed using observable variables that measured satisfaction with both private and public healthcare organizations. The final latent variable in the model was subjective health-related well-being (HEAL_ACTIV). Parameters were estimated for four distinct models, corresponding to different age groups: the full sample, cohorts under 35 years, cohorts aged 35–50 years, and cohorts over 50 years. Standardized coefficient estimates allowed for an assessment of age-related differences in the impact on health capital. Covariance-based structural equation modeling was conducted using SPSS AMOS 23 to estimate the standardized coefficients across these four models.

4 Results and Discussion

In the first stage of the study, we evaluated the level of medical digital skills across various regions and assessed the extent of the digital divide in each. The average level of medical digital skills was calculated for all cohorts in each region, based on three indicators: the use of digital appointment systems, online searches for medical information, and the purchase of medical goods and services via the Internet. The results revealed significant regional disparities. The central regions of Russia, such as Moscow and the Moscow Region, exhibited the highest levels of medical digital skills. Western Russia and the Urals demonstrated moderate levels, while Siberia and the Far East lagged significantly behind (Fig. 1). The distribution in 2023 is likely attributable to the intensive healthcare digitalization initiatives implemented as part of pilot projects in the central regions [13].

The digital skills gap among population cohorts reveals distinct trends. The calculated relative indicator has a minimum value of 0.68, indicating that significant skill disparities between age cohorts are prevalent across all regions. This finding is in line with previous research in the international context [36, 46]. The gap is smallest in Moscow and several southern regions of Russia. However, many western regions, while exhibiting higher overall digital skills, also show a widening gap between the younger and older cohorts (Fig. 2). The central regions demonstrate the greatest effectiveness in leveraging digitalization for human capital development, while other regions show smaller cohort skill disparities, albeit with less advanced digital skills overall. Therefore, central regions demonstrate increased effectiveness

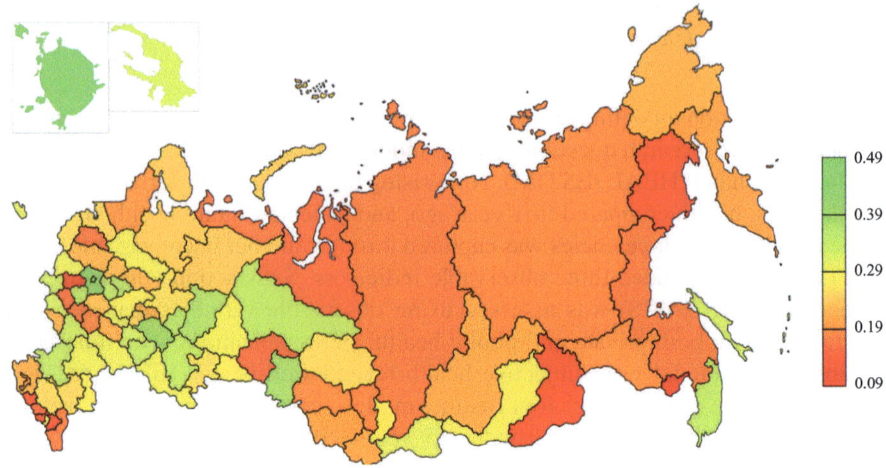

Fig. 1 Average level of medical digital skills of the Russian population in 2023. Regions with no reliable data are colored in grey. *Source:* Authors' own collaboration based on Rosstat data [55–57]

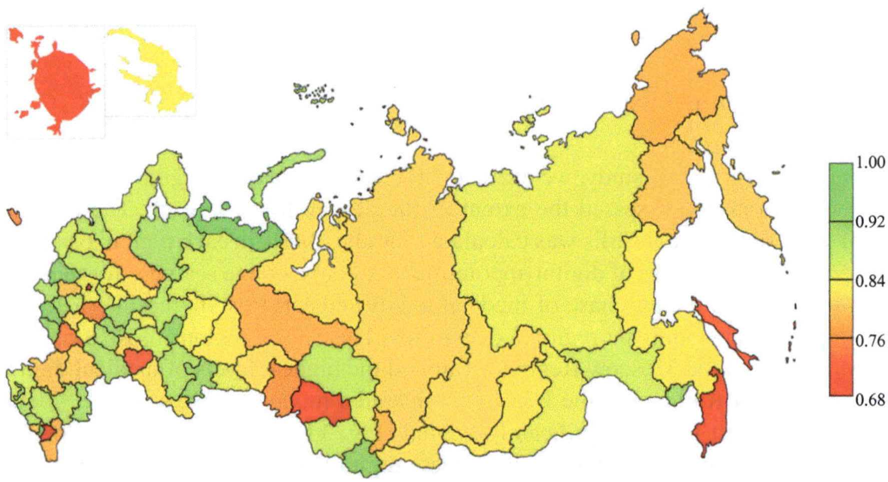

Fig. 2 The level of the relative digital divide (DIS) in ICT skills by regions of Russia in 2023 between cohorts of the population aged 20–24 and 70–74. DIS = 1 means that the 70–74 cohort has no significant digital skills. Regions with no reliable data are colored in grey. *Source:* Authors' own collaboration based on Rosstat data [55–57]

in leveraging digitalization for human capital development, while other regions show smaller cohort skill disparities, though with less advanced digital skills overall.

Table 1 presents descriptive statistics, including the mean values and standard deviations (SD) of the variables. Additionally, skewness and kurtosis indicators were calculated, showing that the distribution of values approaches normality; for all dependent variables, skewness and kurtosis are within 1. As expected, health

Table 1 Descriptive statistics

Variables	Mean	SD
HEAL_P_AVE subjective well-being related to health, 6-point scale	3.45	0.53
KDU_S_HEAL self-assessment of health status of population, 5-point scale	3.51	0.40
HEAL_S_SELF how do you rate your current health status, 5-point scale	3.57	0.43
HEAL_S_YSELF how do you rate your health status compared to a year ago, 5-point scale	3.03	0.22
HEAL_S_OSELF how do you rate your health status compared to people your age, 5-point scale	3.05	0.27
HEAL_S_PMED level of satisfaction with private health services, 5-point scale	4.40	0.31
HEAL_S_GMED level of satisfaction with public health services, 5-point scale	4.12	0.41
HEAL_INVAL have a disability, share of population from 0 to 1	0.06	0.07
HEAL_DISPAN have had a medical examination in the last 2 years, share of population from 0 to 1	0.60	0.14
HEAL_T_DOC have seen a doctor, share of population from 0 to 1	0.92	0.06
HEAL_T_NTR alternative medicine, share of population from 0 to 1	0.03	0.03
HEAL_T_SAMOL self-medication, share of population from 0 to 1	0.51	0.14
HEAL_SPOR actively involved in sports, share of population from 0 to 1	0.30	0.18
HEAL_P_1 cheerful, 6-point scale	3.64	0.52
HEAL_P_2 calm, 6-point scale	3.60	0.48
HEAL_P_3 active, 6-point scale	3.49	0.57
HEAL_P_4 sleep efficiency, 6-point scale	3.45	0.53
HEAL_P_5 things of interest happen every day, 6-point scale	3.08	0.62
HEAL_COMP spend free time on a computer, tablet, phone, share of population from 0 to 1	0.51	0.19
HEAL_SMOK active smokers, share of population from 0 to 1	0.21	0.11
HEAL_ALCO have consumed alcohol in the last 12 months, share of population from 0 to 1	0.53	0.21
ICT_SEAR search for information related to health or health services in the internet, share of population from 0 to 1	0.30	0.13
ICT_APMNT probability of digital appointment with a doctor, share of population from 0 to 1	0.32	0.16
ICT_M_PUR have you purchased medical products and medicines online, share of population from 0 to 1	0.13	0.09
ICT_IMPT impact of ICT on life, 5-point scale	4.31	0.31
DIG_SKILLS level of digital SKILLS of the population on a 10-point scale	2.08	1.11

indicators correlate strongly with age, indicating that cohort fixed effects will be significant across regions: health capital declines noticeably with age. On average, approximately 60% of the population surveyed by Rosstat reported undergoing a medical examination within the last 2 years, and over 90% sought medical assistance. Despite this, self-medication remains prevalent, with more than 50% of the population in Russian regions engaging in it. According to the data, about 21% of individuals aged 20 to 75 are active smokers, while 53% consume alcohol at least once a year.

The population's medical digital skills are moderate: 30% searched for health-related information online, 32% made a digital appointment with a doctor, but only 13% purchased medicines or other medical products online in 2023. Additionally, a majority of respondents reported a strong positive impact of ICT on their lives overall.

The results of the regression analysis are presented in Table 2. All models demonstrated high explanatory power, explaining over 70% of the variance in the dependent variables. Additionally, cohort effects were both strong and significant. The regression analysis addressed the first research question regarding the determinants of health associated with digital skills. To test the robustness of the models, self-assessed health indicators were derived from two alternative Rosstat databases. The models produced similar results, indicating that the determinants of health capital are generally stable. Among the control variables, satisfaction with public healthcare services, which are the key providers in Russian regions, consistently showed a positive effect across all three models. Active participation in sports also significantly improved self-assessed health and subjective well-being, while alcohol consumption had a significant negative impact. Among the digital skills, only the ability to make a digital appointment with a doctor demonstrated a significant positive effect. This variable was significant at the 10% level for self-assessed health and at the 1% level for subjective well-being. However, the overall level of digital skills

Table 2 Results of regression analysis

	HEAL_P_AVE		HEAL_S_SELF		KDU_S_HEAL	
Variables	B	t-stat.	B	t-stat.	B	t-stat.
(Constant)	2.46**	10.39	2.31**	16.77	2.7**	16.50
HEAL_T_DOC	−0.47**	−2.89	−0.01	−0.05	−0.26*	−2.30
HEAL_S_GMED	0.10**	4.27	0.10**	7.07	0.04*	2.54
HEAL_T_NTR	0.19	0.74	0.41**	2.71	0.75**	4.14
HEAL_T_SAMOL	−0.07	−1.00	−0.01	−0.33	−0.01	−0.20
HEAL_INVAL	−0.76**	−3.93	−0.59**	−5.29	−0.06	−0.47
HEAL_DISPAN	0.48**	6.97	−0.05	−1.23	−0.23**	−4.90
HEAL_SPOR	0.19**	2.70	0.23**	5.44	0.12*	2.48
HEAL_SMOK	0.01	0.13	0.02	0.36	0.15[a]	1.85
HEAL_ALCO	−0.52**	−7.92	−0.26**	−6.88	−0.28**	−6.32
HEAL_COMP	0.57**	6.77	0.05	1.01	0.13*	2.19
ICT_IMPT	0.05	1.09	0.12**	4.48	0.14**	4.37
ICT_M_PUR	−0.2	−1.51	−0.08	−1.10	−0.01	−0.09
ICT_APMNT	0.35**	4.70	0.08*	1.96	0.09[a]	1.86
DIG_SKILLS	0.01	−0.18	0.02[a]	1.95	0.01	−0.24
Cohort fixed effects	Yes		Yes		Yes	
R^2 adjusted	0.776		0.881		0.808	
F-statistics	147.7		316.0		180.1	
N observations	935		935		935	

Note: ** significant at the 1% level, * significant at the 5% level
[a] Significant at the 10% level

did not have a significant impact when age effects were controlled for, nor did the online purchase of medical goods and services show a positive effect. Interestingly, the use of free time, particularly in younger cohorts, had a strong positive impact on subjective well-being. The observed result is attributable to greater access to technology and lifestyle changes that integrate ICTs as a fundamental part of leisure activities.

Based on the results of structural modeling, coefficients were estimated for one model segmented into three conditional age groups. The analysis provided insights into the second research question, which explored the mechanisms linking medical digital skills and health capital across different age groups. All four models demonstrated acceptable fit, with normative and actual values presented in Table 3. For cohorts under 35 years, digital skills were associated with lower self-assessed health and reduced satisfaction with medical services, which may be explained by a selection effect: increased digital activity in health-related areas might reflect existing health concerns, leading to relatively lower self-assessments of health among younger individuals. In the 35–49 age group, the use of digital skills in healthcare had weak but positive effects on both self-assessed health and satisfaction with medical services. The strongest impact of digital medical skills was observed in cohorts aged 50 and older. For this group, the use of ICT significantly contributed to maintaining health, as indicated by a path coefficient of 0.38, representing a moderate positive effect.

The general model for all age cohorts (935 observations) is presented in Fig. 3. The direct effect of medical digital skills on self-assessed health is moderate, with a standardized path coefficient of 0.24. The indirect effect of digital skills on self-assessed health, mediated by subjective well-being, is 0.22 (0.24×0.92), indicating a moderately positive impact. These findings suggest that while digital competencies influence health-related subjective well-being through self-assessed health, they do not have a significant effect on satisfaction with medical services. The result likely reflects the relatively low level of medical ICT development in many regions, as well as the ongoing digitalization of Russia's healthcare sector, which may have mixed effects on public satisfaction with services. For the Russian population, the ability to maintain a cheerful and active lifestyle depends primarily on objective health, which is shaped by both the quality of medical services and the population's medical digital skills.

5 Conclusion

This study evaluates the regional spillovers of digital skills development across age cohorts, highlighting their impact not only at the individual level but also at the regional scale. Analyzing data from 11 age cohorts across 85 regions of Russia, we examine the influence of medical digital skills on self-assessed health and health-related subjective well-being, including indicators such as cheerfulness, activity, calmness, sleep quality, and interest in life. While satisfaction with public

Table 3 Results of structural equation modeling for different population cohorts. Standardized coefficients are shown

	All population		20–34 years		35–49 years		50+ years	
Path	Std. B	S.E.	Std. B	S.E.	Std. B	S.E.	Std. B	S.E.
HEAL_SATIS <—ICT_ACTIV	0.03	0.14	−0.20*	0.24	−0.03	0.28	−0.01	0.22
HEAL_ESTIM <—ICT_ACTIV	0.24**	0.19	−0.3**	0.16	0.12*	0.19	0.38**	0.20
HEAL_ESTIM <—HEAL_SATIS	0.44**	0.04	0.31**	0.05	0.37**	0.05	0.34**	0.04
HEAL_ACTIV <—HEAL_ESTIM	0.92**	0.03	0.59**	0.14	0.65**	0.11	0.77**	0.08
HEAL_ACTIV <—HEAL_SATIS	−0.03[a]	0.02	0.04	0.06	0.12*	0.06	−0.03	0.04
HEAL_P_1 <—HEAL_ACTIV	1.02**	n.a.	1.04**	n.a.	0.92**	n.a.	1.06**	n.a.
HEAL_P_2 <—HEAL_ACTIV	1.00**	0.01	0.96**	0.08	1.01**	0.06	0.99**	0.03
HEAL_P_3 <—HEAL_ACTIV	1.02**	0.01	1.01**	0.09	1.01**	0.06	1.01**	0.03
HEAL_P_4 <—HEAL_ACTIV	0.98**	0.01	0.94**	0.10	0.95**	0.07	0.96**	0.04
HEAL_P_5 <—HEAL_ACTIV	0.91**	0.02	0.76**	0.12	0.81**	0.10	0.84**	0.05
HEAL_S_GMED <—HEAL_SATIS	0.79**	0.05	0.93**	0.20	0.95**	0.16	0.85**	0.10
HEAL_S_PMED <—HEAL_SATIS	1.02**	n.a.	0.85**	n.a.	0.87**	n.a.	1.03**	n.a.
HEAL_S_YSELF <—HEAL_ESTIM	0.83**	0.01	0.55**	0.07	0.71**	0.06	0.73**	0.03
HEAL_S_OSELF <—HEAL_ESTIM	0.81**	0.01	0.62**	0.09	0.67**	0.07	0.64**	0.04
HEAL_S_SELF <—HEAL_ESTIM	0.99**	n.a.	0.99**	n.a.	0.91**	n.a.	0.98**	n.a.
ICT_M_PUR <—ICT_ACTIV	0.73**	0.16	0.65**	0.19	0.63	1.04	0.54**	0.10
ICT_APMNT <—ICT_ACTIV	0.94**	0.38	0.8**	0.39	1.02	2.91	0.69**	0.24
ICT_SEAR <—ICT_ACTIV	0.58**	n.a.	0.66**	n.a.	0.46**	n.a.	0.73**	n.a.
CMIN/DF (~3)	3.250		1.518		1.518		2.100	
GFI (>0.9)	0.977		0.962		0.962		0.950	
AGFI (>0.9)	0.954		0.923		0.923		0.899	
PGFI (~0.5)	0.483		0.476		0.476		0.470	
RMSEA (<0.08)	0.049		0.045		0.032		0.066	
PCLOSE (>0.05)	0.551		0.624		0.998		0.079	

Note: ** significant at the 1% level, * significant at the 5% level
[a] Significant at the 10% level

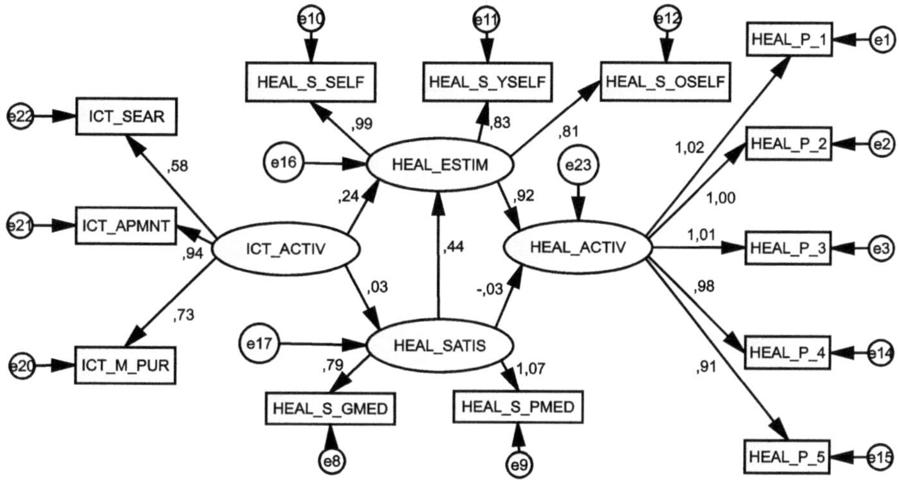

Fig. 3 Path model with standardized coefficients. Ovals denote latent variables, rectangles denote observable variables measured based on Rosstat data. Errors are indicated in circles. *Source:* Obtained by the authors using SPSS AMOS 23

healthcare services, engagement in sports, and alcohol consumption emerged as significant control predictors of health capital, the impact of medical digital skills was found to be moderate or, in some cases, insignificant. Notably, across all age cohorts, only digital appointments with doctors consistently led to improved health outcomes. For younger cohorts (up to 35 years), increased digital activity, such as searching for health information and visiting doctors, was associated with poorer health outcomes. Conversely, digital competencies appear to support the health capital of older cohorts, indicating their potential in mitigating age-related health declines.

The study also quantified the digital skills gap at the regional level, demonstrating that age is the primary driver of this gap, followed by varying levels of access to technology. Regions in Western Russia, which often serve as testing grounds for advanced medical ICT, exhibit strong cohort effects in the digital skills gap. In contrast, Siberia and the Far East face the most significant challenges, with low levels of both digital skills and technology access. From a policy perspective, the findings suggest that the digitalization of healthcare remains a vulnerable area. Despite efforts to optimize the medical industry, including the reduction in the number of institutions, the digital transformation of healthcare has shown only a moderate impact on self-assessed health capital and subjective well-being, indicating the need for more robust regional development strategies to enhance the effectiveness of digital health initiatives.

Our study is subject to several limitations, including its reliance on a sample restricted to the year 2023 and the inherent shortcomings of the cohort approach. Specifically, our analysis does not account for regional technological development or population income levels, both of which may serve as important determinants of health capital. In this paper, the focus was limited to variables associated with individual characteristics and human capital. Future research should explore the impact of regional technological development, particularly in terms of Internet access, and consider the broader effects of human capital utilization. Technological factors could provide a more comprehensive understanding of the dynamics influencing health capital and the effectiveness of digital health initiatives.

Acknowledgments The study was supported by the Russian Science Foundation grant No. 23-78-10165, https://rscf.ru/project/23-78-10165/.

References

1. Verhoef, P. C., Broekhuizen, T., Bart, Y., Bhattacharya, A., Dong, J. Q., Fabian, N., & Haenlein, M. (2021). Digital transformation: A multidisciplinary reflection and research agenda. *Journal of Business Research, 122*, 889–901. https://doi.org/10.1016/j.jbusres.2019.09.022
2. Vial, G. (2019). Understanding digital transformation: A review and a research agenda. *The Journal of Strategic Information Systems, 28*(2), 118–144. https://doi.org/10.1016/j.jsis.2019.01.003
3. Iyanna, S., Kaur, P., Ractham, P., Talwar, S., & Islam, A. K. M. N. (2022). Digital transformation of healthcare sector: What is impeding adoption and continued usage of technology-driven innovations by end-users? *Journal of Business Research, 153*, 150–161. https://doi.org/10.1016/j.jbusres.2022.08.007
4. Raimo, N., De Turi, I., Albergo, F., & Vitolla, F. (2023). The drivers of the digital transformation in the healthcare industry: An empirical analysis in Italian hospitals. *Technovation, 121*, 102558. https://doi.org/10.1016/j.technovation.2022.102558
5. Leporatti, L., & Montefiori, M. (2024). Complex role of individual digital skills and eHealth policies in shaping health policy. *Socio-Economic Planning Sciences, 93*, 101897. https://doi.org/10.1016/j.seps.2024.101897
6. Deloitte. (2020). *Digital transformation: Shaping the future of European healthcare*. Retrieved from https://nor.deloitte.com/rs/712-CNF-326/images/deloitte-shaping-the-future-of-european-healthcare.pdf
7. Kraus, S., Schiavone, F., Pluzhnikova, A., & Invernizzi, A. C. (2021). Digital transformation in healthcare: Analyzing the current state-of-research. *Journal of Business Research, 123*, 557–567. https://doi.org/10.1016/j.jbusres.2020.10.030
8. Preko, M., & Boateng, R. (2020). Assessing healthcare digitalisation in Ghana: A critical realist's approach. *Health Policy and Technology, 9*(2), 255–262. https://doi.org/10.1016/j.hlpt.2020.03.006
9. Alohali, M., Carton, F., & O'Connor, Y. (2020). Investigating the antecedents of perceived threats and user resistance to health information technology: A case study of a public hospital. *Journal of Decision Systems, 29*(1), 27–52. https://doi.org/10.1080/12460125.2020.1728988
10. Ngafeeson, M. N., & Manga, J. A. (2024). User-resistance behaviours toward electronic health records: Uncovering the determinants of perceived threats. *Behaviour & Information Technology, 1–18*. https://doi.org/10.1080/0144929X.2024.2410312
11. Cantor, J. H., McBain, R. K., Pera, M. F., Bravata, D. M., & Whaley, C. M. (2021). Who is (and is not) receiving telemedicine care during the COVID-19 pandemic. *American Journal of Preventive Medicine, 61*(3), 434–438. https://doi.org/10.1016/j.amepre.2021.01.030

12. Longhini, J., Rossettini, G., & Palese, A. (2022). Digital health competencies among health care professionals: Systematic review. *Journal of Medical Internet Research, 24*(8), e36414. https://doi.org/10.2196/36414
13. Sklyar, T., & Sokolova, E. (2019). Driving forces for information and communication technology innovations in smart health in St. Petersburg. *IOP Conference Series: Materials Science and Engineering, 497*(1), 012094. https://doi.org/10.1088/1757-899X/497/1/012094
14. Dvoryadkina, E., & Fechina, A. (2023). Telemedicine services in Russia: Regulation and diversification prospects. *Upravlenets, 14*(2), 62–75. https://doi.org/10.29141/2218-5003-2023-14-2-5
15. Tortorella, G. L., Fogliatto, F. S., Espôsto, K. F., Vergara, M. C., Vassolo, R., Tlapa Mendoza, D., & Narayanamurthy, G. (2022). Measuring the effect of Healthcare 4.0 implementation on hospitals' performance. *Production Planning & Control, 33*(4), 386–401. https://doi.org/10.1080/09537287.2020.1824283
16. Campanozzi, L. L., Gibelli, F., Bailo, P., Nittari, G., Sirignano, A., & Ricci, G. (2023). The role of digital literacy in achieving health equity in the third millennium society: A literature review. *Frontiers in Public Health, 11*, 1109323. https://doi.org/10.3389/fpubh.2023.1109323
17. Suggs, L. S. (2006). A 10-year retrospective of research in new technologies for health communication. *Journal of Health Communication, 11*(1), 61–74. https://doi.org/10.1080/10810730500461083
18. Aceto, G., Persico, V., & Pescapé, A. (2018). The role of information and communication technologies in healthcare: Taxonomies, perspectives, and challenges. *Journal of Network and Computer Applications, 107*, 125–154. https://doi.org/10.1016/j.jnca.2018.02.008
19. Butpheng, C., Yeh, K.-H., & Xiong, H. (2020). Security and privacy in IoT-cloud-based e-health systems—A comprehensive review. *Symmetry, 12*(7), 1191. https://doi.org/10.3390/sym12071191
20. Habeeb, A., & Anaya, L. (2024). Digital technologies in the healthcare industry: Literature review. *Procedia Computer Science, 237*, 363–370. https://doi.org/10.1016/j.procs.2024.05.116
21. Tortorella, G. L., Vergara, M. C., Garza-Reyes, J. A., & Sawhney, R. (2020). Organizational learning paths based upon industry 4.0 adoption: An empirical study with Brazilian manufacturers. *International Journal of Production Economics, 219*, 284–294. https://doi.org/10.1016/j.ijpe.2019.06.023
22. Alloghani, M., Al-Jumeily, D., Hussain, A., Aljaaf, A. J., Mustafina, J., & Petrov, E. (2018). Healthcare services innovations based on the state-of-the-art technology trend Industry 4.0. In *In: 2018 11th International Conference on Developments in eSystems Engineering (DeSE)* (pp. 64–70). IEEE. https://doi.org/10.1109/DeSE.2018.00016
23. Kumari, A., Tanwar, S., Tyagi, S., & Kumar, N. (2018). Fog computing for Healthcare 4.0 environment: Opportunities and challenges. *Computers and Electrical Engineering, 72*, 1–13. https://doi.org/10.1016/j.compeleceng.2018.08.015
24. Biancone, P., Secinaro, S., Marseglia, R., & Calandra, D. (2023). E-health for the future: Managerial perspectives using a multiple case study approach. *Technovation, 120*, 102406. https://doi.org/10.1016/j.technovation.2021.102406
25. Zhang, K., Zhou, H.-Y., Baptista-Hon, D. T., Gao, Y., Liu, X., Oermann, E., Xu, S., Jin, S., Zhang, J., Sun, Z., Yin, Y., Razmi, R. M., Loupy, A., Beck, S., Qu, J., & Wu, J. (2024). Concepts and applications of digital twins in healthcare and medicine. *Patterns, 5*(8), 101028. https://doi.org/10.1016/j.patter.2024.101028
26. Xia, K., & Wang, J. (2023). Recent advances of Transformers in medical image analysis: A comprehensive review. *MedComm - Future Medicine, 2*(1), e38. https://doi.org/10.1002/mef2.38
27. Sharma, D., & Bhaskar, S. (2020). Addressing the COVID-19 burden on medical education and training: The role of telemedicine and tele-education during and beyond the pandemic. *Frontiers in Public Health, 8*, 589669. https://doi.org/10.3389/fpubh.2020.589669
28. Ivanov, V. M., Krivtsov, A. M., Strelkov, S. V., Smirnov, A. Y., Shipov, R. Y., Grebenkov, V. G., Rumyantsev, V. N., Gheleznyak, I. S., Surov, D. A., Korzhuk, M. S., & Koskin, V. S. (2022).

Practical application of augmented/mixed reality technologies in surgery of abdominal cancer patients. *Journal of Imaging, 8*(7), 183. https://doi.org/10.3390/jimaging8070183
29. Evans, R. S. (2016). Electronic health records: Then, now, and in the future. *Yearbook of Medical Informatics, 25*(S1), S48–S61. https://doi.org/10.15265/IYS-2016-s006
30. Hollander, J. E., & Carr, B. G. (2020). Virtually perfect? Telemedicine for COVID-19. *New England Journal of Medicine, 382*(18), 1679–1681. https://doi.org/10.1056/NEJMp2003539
31. Cobianchi, L., Dal Mas, F., & Ansaloni, L. (2022). Editorial: New frontiers for artificial intelligence in surgical decision making and its organizational impacts. *Frontiers in Surgery, 9*, 933673. https://doi.org/10.3389/fsurg.2022.933673
32. Dal Mas, F., Massaro, M., Rippa, P., & Secundo, G. (2023). The challenges of digital transformation in healthcare: An interdisciplinary literature review, framework, and future research agenda. *Technovation, 123*, 102716. https://doi.org/10.1016/j.technovation.2023.102716
33. Flessa, S., & Huebner, C. (2021). Innovations in health care—A conceptual framework. *International Journal of Environmental Research and Public Health, 18*(19), 10026. https://doi.org/10.3390/ijerph181910026
34. Alam, M. Z., Hu, W., & Uddin, A. (2020). Digital transformation in healthcare services sector of Bangladesh: Current status, challenges and future direction. *Journal on Innovation and Sustainability RISUS, 11*(1), 30–38. https://doi.org/10.23925/2179-3565.2020v11i1p30-38
35. Sarradon-Eck, A., Bouchez, T., Auroy, L., Schuers, M., & Darmon, D. (2021). Attitudes of general practitioners toward prescription of mobile health apps: Qualitative study. *JMIR mHealth and uHealth, 9*(3), e21795. https://doi.org/10.2196/21795
36. Lopez de Coca, T., Moreno, L., Alacreu, M., & Sebastian-Morello, M. (2022). Bridging the generational digital divide in the healthcare environment. *Journal of Personalized Medicine, 12*(8), 1214. https://doi.org/10.3390/jpm12081214
37. Piccolo, R. (2024). Digitisation, health literacy and health empowerment of older people. *International Entrepreneurship and Management Journal, 20*(4), 3001–3034. https://doi.org/10.1007/s11365-024-00980-8
38. Vanolo, A. (2014). Smartmentality: The smart city as disciplinary strategy. *Urban Studies, 51*(5), 883–898. https://doi.org/10.1177/0042098013494427
39. Dragan, A., Crețan, R., & Bulzan, R. D. (2024). The spatial development of peripheralisation: The case of smart city projects in Romania. *Area, 56*(1), 1–9. https://doi.org/10.1111/area.12902
40. Málovics, G., Berki, B. M., & Mihály, M. (2021). Policy reform instead of policy transformation? Experiences of participatory action research (PAR) on desegregation policy in Szeged, Hungary. *International Journal of Action Research, 17*(1), 81–101. https://doi.org/10.3224/ijar.v17i1.05
41. Jupîneanț, A. C., Crețan, R., Voiculescu, S., & Doiciar, C. (2024). COVID-19 crisis, Romanian Roma migrant women, and the temporary geographies of lockdown in the Spanish home. *Area, 56*(2), e12910. https://doi.org/10.1111/area.12910
42. Mihai, P. D., Liviu, T., & Maria, N. (2022). E-government and the general population's digital skills in the European Union and OECD member states. In *Digitalization and big data for resilience and economic intelligence* (pp. 41–53). Springer. https://doi.org/10.1007/978-3-030-93286-2_3
43. Lu, X., Yao, Y., & Jin, Y. (2022). Digital exclusion and functional dependence in older people: Findings from five longitudinal cohort studies. *EClinicalMedicine, 54*, 101708. https://doi.org/10.1016/j.eclinm.2022.101708
44. Alam, K., Mahumud, R. A., Alam, F., Keramat, S. A., Erdiaw-Kwasie, M. O., & Sarker, A. R. (2019). Determinants of access to eHealth services in regional Australia. *International Journal of Medical Informatics, 131*, 103960. https://doi.org/10.1016/j.ijmedinf.2019.103960
45. Palmer, K., Monaco, A., Kivipelto, M., Onder, G., Maggi, S., Michel, J. P., Prieto, R., Sykara, G., & Donde, S. (2020). The potential long-term impact of the COVID-19 outbreak on patients with non-communicable diseases in Europe: Consequences for healthy ageing. *Aging Clinical and Experimental Research, 32*(7), 1189–1194. https://doi.org/10.1007/s40520-020-01601-4

46. Cullen, R. (2003). The digital divide: A global and national call to action. *The Electronic Library, 21*(3), 247–257. https://doi.org/10.1108/02640470310480506
47. Litchfield, I., Shukla, D., & Greenfield, S. (2021). Impact of COVID-19 on the digital divide: A rapid review. *BMJ Open, 11*(10), e053440. https://doi.org/10.1136/bmjopen-2021-053440
48. Nutbeam, D., & Lloyd, J. E. (2021). Understanding and responding to health literacy as a social determinant of health. *Annual Review of Public Health, 42*(1), 159–173. https://doi.org/10.1146/annurev-publhealth-090419-102529
49. Scanzera, A. C., Kim, S. J., & Chan, R. V. P. (2021). Teleophthalmology and the digital divide: Inequities highlighted by the COVID-19 pandemic. *Eye, 35*(6), 1529–1531. https://doi.org/10.1038/s41433-020-01323-x
50. Thornton, J. (2020). COVID-19: How coronavirus will change the face of general practice forever. *BMJ, 368*, m1279. https://doi.org/10.1136/bmj.m1279
51. Lindström, C., Rosvall, M., & Lindström, M. (2020). Unmet healthcare needs and mortality: A prospective cohort study from southern Sweden. *Scandinavian Journal of Public Health, 48*(3), 267–274. https://doi.org/10.1177/1403494819863530
52. Hsiao, V., Chandereng, T., Lankton, R. L., Huebner, J. A., Baltus, J. J., Flood, G. E., Dean, S. M., Tevaarwerk, A. J., & Schneider, D. F. (2021). Disparities in telemedicine access: A cross-sectional study of a newly established infrastructure during the COVID-19 pandemic. *Applied Clinical Informatics, 12*(3), 445–458. https://doi.org/10.1055/s-0041-1730026
53. Le, T. V., Galperin, H., & Traube, D. (2023). The impact of digital competence on telehealth utilization. *Health Policy and Technology, 12*(1), 100724. https://doi.org/10.1016/j.hlpt.2023.100724
54. Ferraris, G., Monzani, D., Coppini, V., Conti, L., Pizzoli, S. F. M., Grasso, R., & Pravettoni, G. (2023). Barriers to and facilitators of online health information-seeking behaviours among cancer patients: A systematic review. *DIGITAL HEALTH, 9*, 1–22. https://doi.org/10.1177/20552076231210663
55. Rosstat. (2024). *Selective federal statistical observation on the use of information technologies and information and telecommunication networks by the population*. Retrieved from https://rosstat.gov.ru/free_doc/new_site/business/it/ikt23/index.html
56. Rosstat. (2024). *Selective observation of the health status of the population*. Retrieved from https://rosstat.gov.ru/free_doc/new_site/zdor23/PublishSite_2023/index.html
57. Rosstat. (2024). *Results of the selective monitoring of the quality and availability of services in the spheres of education, health and social services, and employment promotion in 2023*. Retrieved from http://rosstat.gov.ru/free_doc/new_site/GKS_KDU-2023/index.html

Digital Policy in the Context of Development and Economic Growth

Digitalization, Innovation, and Competitiveness: Insights from a Cross-Country Analysis of Labor Productivity Effects

Evgeny Kuzmin, Viktoriia S. Bondareva, Akbar Shodiyev, and Ilyos Ochilov

Abstract The modern economy faces the necessity of continuously reassessing the factors that determine labor productivity growth. This study presents a cross-country analysis of the impact of digitalization, innovation potential, institutional development, and economic structural composition on labor productivity across 17 countries during the period from 2015 to 2024. The primary aim of the research is to identify robust determinants and evaluate the heterogeneity of digital transformation effects depending on the country profile. The analysis incorporates five explanatory variables: digital competitiveness index, artificial intelligence investment as a percentage of GDP, global innovation index, global competitiveness index, and the share of industry in GDP. Labor productivity per hour worked, expressed in USD adjusted for purchasing power parity at constant 2017 prices, serves as the dependent variable. The methodology involves the construction of an ordinary least squares (OLS) regression model, multicollinearity diagnostics using the variance

E. Kuzmin (✉)
Institute of Economics of the Ural Branch of the Russian Academy of Sciences, Ekaterinburg, Russia
e-mail: kuzmin.ea@uiec.ru

V. S. Bondareva
Kyrgyz-Russian Slavic University named after B.N. Yeltsin, Bishkek, Kyrgyz Republic

A. Shodiyev
Termez University of Economics and Service, Termez, Uzbekistan

Tashkent Institute of Irrigation and Agricultural Mechanization Engineers (TIIAME), Tashkent, Uzbekistan

Diplomat University, Tashkent, Uzbekistan

I. Ochilov
Tashkent State University of Economics, Tashkent, Uzbekistan
e-mail: i.ochilov@tsue.uz

F. Tao et al. (eds.), *Artificial Intelligence and Digital Transformation*, Lecture Notes in Information Systems and Organisation 78,
https://doi.org/10.1007/978-3-032-00118-4_17

inflation factor (VIF), dimensionality reduction via principal component analysis (PCA), and country stratification based on k-means cluster analysis. Separate regression models were constructed for each cluster group. The results indicate that the most significant predictors of labor productivity across the full sample are global competitiveness (positive effect), innovation index (negative effect), and digital competitiveness (negative effect). Investments in artificial intelligence and digital competitiveness yielded statistically unstable or paradoxical effects, possibly indicating the presence of time lags, institutional barriers, or structural heterogeneity. The cluster-based models reveal differentiated trajectories of digital transformation. In digitally mature countries, labor productivity is primarily driven by global competitiveness (positive) and a declining share of industry (negative). In contrast, for countries with transitional digital structures, digital and global competitiveness positively influence productivity, while innovation has a restraining effect. These findings underscore the heterogeneity of digitalization effects and highlight the necessity of differentiated digital policy approaches. The conclusions drawn from this study may serve as a basis for developing strategies aimed at enhancing economic performance in the context of a digital economy.

Keywords Digitalization · Labor productivity · Artificial intelligence · Innovation · Competitiveness · Economic structure · Digital effects

1 Introduction

Digitalization has become a defining factor in the transformation of contemporary economic systems [1–3], exerting a fundamental influence on production processes, value-added structures, and employment dynamics. The expansion of investment in digital technologies, the advancement of platform-based solutions, the integration of artificial intelligence (AI), and the transformation of business models are radically altering traditional conceptions of the drivers of labor productivity and sustainable economic growth. Despite a growing body of literature devoted to digital transformation, the academic discourse remains markedly fragmented, with assessments of the economic effects of digitalization still characterized by ambiguity, inconsistency, and strong contextual dependence.

Scholarly research has identified diverse channels through which digital technologies affect labor productivity. The vast potential of digital tools—particularly AI and automation—to boost productivity is often emphasized [4–10]. Numerous studies document a positive correlation between digitalization and productivity growth [11–17]. However, the so-called 'digitalization paradox' [18–22] has been observed in several countries: despite the increasing volume of digital investments, productivity growth remains moderate or stagnant. This paradox is frequently attributed to institutional constraints, skill gaps, or imbalanced implementation of digital initiatives. Other studies [23, 24] suggest that digitalization may temporarily suppress productivity, particularly during transitional phases, due to adaptation costs and labor displacement. Some analyses detect no statistically significant effects at all. Several authors [25] underscore the lagged nature of digitalization outcomes, noting that the economic benefits of digital investments may take time to materialize, as they require organizational restructuring and workforce requalification. Furthermore, digitalization effects may be nonlinear [26–28], becoming apparent only once a certain threshold of digital maturity has been attained. These contradictions reflect the complex and multifaceted relationship between digitalization and economic performance, thereby opening a wide field for further empirical investigation.

This study seeks to reconcile these inconsistencies and clarify the dominant patterns through which digitalization affects labor productivity from a cross-country perspective. To achieve this objective, the following research questions are examined in sequence: Which indicators exert a statistically significant impact on labor productivity? To what extent does the structure of the economy modify the relationship between digital investment and productivity? What are the cross-country differences, and how do they relate to variations in productivity levels?

Answering the first question necessitates a reassessment of productivity growth drivers in the context of contemporary digital transformation, alongside the selection of adequate explanatory variables. In this regard, the direct influence of digital technologies on productivity, as previously discussed, is acknowledged. In parallel, the literature highlights the role of innovation capacity as a long-term growth factor [29, 30]. Classical theories of endogenous growth emphasize the importance of knowledge accumulation, R&D investment, and technological progress as fundamental sources of productivity gains [31]. However, more recent empirical studies demonstrate that the innovation effect is not universal—it depends on a country's ability to translate innovation investments into tangible economic outcomes, which in turn requires a well-developed institutional environment and effective commercialization mechanisms [32]. Another complex variable is investment in artificial intelligence, widely considered a key future productivity driver [33, 34]. Nonetheless, the effects of AI investment may be delayed and contingent on the presence of a conducive application environment [33, 35, 36]. In addition, global competitiveness remains one of the most consistent determinants of macroeconomic performance, reflecting the development level of institutions, infrastructure, education, innovation systems, and the labor market [37, 38]. It functions as a contextual backdrop for effective digital and innovation-driven transformations.

Further attention is directed to the sectoral composition of the economy as a moderator of digital effects [39]. The role of industry is not diminishing in the digital era but is undergoing transformation: sectors with high digitalization potential—such as manufacturing, logistics, and energy—tend to yield greater returns from digital investments. A declining industrial share may indicate either structural modernization or the erosion of a production base, which in turn may limit scalable technological adoption. These theoretical considerations underpin our empirical framework for identifying variables that significantly influence labor productivity. The analysis focuses not only on the direct relationship between digital and institutional indicators and labor productivity, but also on the specificity of these relationships across countries at varying stages of digital development.

Accordingly, this study aims to provide a deeper understanding of the mechanisms through which digitalization and its associated factors influence labor productivity in a cross-national context. The methodological framework is designed to produce robust and comparable findings, contributing both to theoretical generalization and to the formulation of policy-relevant insights. The anticipated scholarly contribution lies in formalizing stable predictors of labor productivity and identifying clusters of countries with similar developmental characteristics.

2 Materials and Methods

2.1 Data and Processing

The empirical foundation of this study is a composite dataset covering the period from 2015 to 2024 and encompassing indicators for 17 countries. The data are structured as a panel with annual observations. The dependent variable is labor productivity, measured as output per hour worked in USD (at 2017 purchasing power parity, constant prices), based on ILOSTAT data. This indicator reflects the average economic output generated per employed person per unit of time.

The independent variables included in the model capture institutional and structural dimensions of digital and innovation-driven transformation within national economies:

- *Digital Competitiveness Index* (sourced from the International Institute for Management Development) reflects a country's ability to harness digital technologies for transforming government, business, and society;
- *Artificial Intelligence Investment* (% of GDP) (based on data from the Emerging Technology Observatory) measures the volume of disclosed inbound AI investments relative to national GDP;
- *Global Innovation Index* (compiled by WIPO Global Innovation) serves as a composite indicator of national innovation capacity;
- *Global Competitiveness Index* (sourced from the International Institute for Management Development) evaluates countries' ability to sustain comparable levels of economic growth;
- *Industry Share in GDP* (according to World Bank data) reflects the degree of industrialization and the economy's orientation toward production sectors, including construction.

Initial data processing involved cleaning and standardization procedures. Countries with incomplete or fragmented time series for the selected indicators were excluded during the final panel construction. Statistical processing tools were applied to ensure consistency and analytical validity. All indicators were harmonized by scale and temporal alignment. This dataset and preparation protocol provide a sufficient empirical basis for conducting regression analysis aimed at identifying the impact of digital and innovation-related transformation factors on labor productivity from an international perspective.

2.2 Research Design

This study employs a quantitative methodological approach, utilizing a combination of complementary statistical techniques to examine the impact of digitalization and associated factors on labor productivity in a cross-country context. The analysis is based on a panel dataset covering the years 2015–2024 and includes the following interrelated steps:

1. *Regression model construction.* The first stage involves estimating a multiple linear regression using the Ordinary Least Squares (OLS) method. The objective is to evaluate the statistical significance and direction of influence of the selected factors on labor productivity.
2. *Model diagnostics and sensitivity analysis.* The regression model was tested for multicollinearity using the Variance Inflation Factor (VIF) method. A VIF threshold of <5 was applied. In addition, influence diagnostics were performed to detect observations with undue leverage on parameter estimates and to account for them during interpretation.
3. *Variable selection.* Stepwise backward elimination was applied to exclude redundant predictors. This approach identifies the smallest subset of variables that explains the maximum variation in the dependent variable with minimal information loss (based on adjusted R^2).
4. *Principal component analysis (PCA).* PCA was implemented to reduce dimensionality and manage multicollinearity among highly correlated predictors. The method identifies latent components that summarize shared information from correlated indicators. Standardized (Z-score) variables were used to extract principal components explaining the greatest proportion of total variance.
5. *Country clustering.* A k-means clustering procedure was conducted to classify countries into robust typological groups based on their digital, innovation, institutional, and structural characteristics. The optimal number of clusters ($k = 3$) was determined empirically through visual analysis and PCA-based explained variance structures, ensuring both stability and interpretability. Clustering was performed on standardized values for all indices. The resulting stratification enabled us to account for economic heterogeneity in the interpretation of digitalization's effects on labor productivity. Separate regression models were subsequently constructed for each cluster to reveal intra-group differences in productivity determinants.

To monitor the temporal evolution of countries' digital profiles, a cluster transition map was created. Each observation (country-year) was assigned a cluster, allowing for the reconstruction of transformation trajectories and the evaluation of cluster membership stability over time. These dynamics provided an additional interpretive layer for analyzing national digital development paths.

2.3 Limitations and Assumptions of the Study

This study is subject to a number of limitations that must be considered when interpreting the results and drawing conclusions. The analysis is based on panel data for 17 countries over the period 2015–2024. Despite relying on reputable sources (WIPO, IMD, World Bank, ILOSTAT, Emerging Technology Observatory), data gaps exist for certain countries. As a result, some observations were excluded, reducing the sample size and potentially affecting the generalizability of the findings.

The indices used—digital competitiveness, global competitiveness, and the global innovation index—are aggregate composite indicators constructed from a broad set of sub-indicators. This creates the potential for multicollinearity and complicates the precise interpretation of individual component contributions. Additionally, variations in index construction methodologies may introduce hidden structural heterogeneity.

The models developed in this study do not incorporate dummy variables, country-specific institutional characteristics, levels of digital literacy, or cultural differences, all of which may influence the pace and effects of digitalization. This omission limits the comprehensiveness of interpretation. Furthermore, the empirical analysis is based on multiple linear regression, which assumes a linear and additive relationship between independent variables and labor productivity. In practice, the effects may be nonlinear and include threshold or synergistic interactions not captured by the current model framework.

The study assumes that the selected variables serve as adequate proxies for digital maturity, innovation potential, and economic structure. The models also presume that digitalization effects manifest within the same time period (annual observation) and do not account for lagged dependencies. The regression framework further assumes that independent variables are not strongly collinear and that they provide sufficient variance to estimate individual contributions. This assumption was validated through VIF diagnostics, which confirmed that variance inflation factors do not exceed empirical thresholds.

It is also assumed that labor productivity appropriately reflects the aggregate impact of institutional, structural, and digital factors, and that it is not distorted by such factors as workforce demographic structure, differences in labor standards, or the presence of exogenous shocks—which are not explicitly modeled in this analysis. These assumptions represent a compromise between theoretical completeness and practical feasibility, given the limited availability of harmonized cross-country data and the high heterogeneity of national trajectories.

In light of these limitations and assumptions, the results should be interpreted as indicative estimates of the direction and strength of the examined factors' influence on labor productivity, rather than definitive causal relationships. Future research may benefit from extending the temporal scope, incorporating lagged variables, applying panel regressions with fixed and random effects, and integrating additional explanatory factors.

3 Results and Discussion

3.1 Indicator Profiles

To substantiate the subsequent empirical modeling and to interpret the impact of digitalization on labor productivity, a step-by-step analysis was conducted to examine the dynamics of key indicators that reflect various dimensions of innovation-digital development and structural transformation across national economies. Cross-country variations in these indicators reveal trends, cycles, and divergences that form the contextual background for evaluating the economic effectiveness of ongoing transformations.

A crucial aspect of economic transformation lies in countries' ability to effectively utilize digital technologies. Digital transformation has become a central vector of structural change, influencing both innovation strategies and productivity enhancement models. Digitalization encompasses not only technical infrastructure, but also the adaptation of businesses, public administration, and society to new technological conditions. Within this context, the assessment of digital competitiveness becomes particularly significant, as it reflects not only the level of digital infrastructure but also societal readiness to adopt digital solutions.

The Digital Competitiveness Index, developed by the International Institute for Management Development (IMD), assesses a country's capacity to adapt and effectively apply digital technologies across sectors. An analysis of cross-country dynamics from 2018 to 2024 reveals a general upward trend in digital competitiveness (Fig. 1). The average index score across all countries increased from 71.9 in 2018 to 80.1 in 2022, indicating a systematic strengthening of digital capacities amid accelerated digital transformation—especially in the post-pandemic recovery period. The greatest dispersion in values occurred between 2020 and 2021, likely reflecting uneven access to digital resources, differences in digitalization strategies, and variation in adaptation speeds.

Between 2020 and 2024, the range of country scores expanded significantly. While in 2018 the minimum value was 57.0 and the maximum 85.6, by 2021–2022 the scores ranged from 43.6 to 100.0, indicating increasing stratification in digital maturity. Countries consistently scoring above 90 points include the United States, Singapore, Sweden, the Netherlands, and Switzerland—global leaders in digital competitiveness. A group of countries with moderate scores (70–85 points) includes

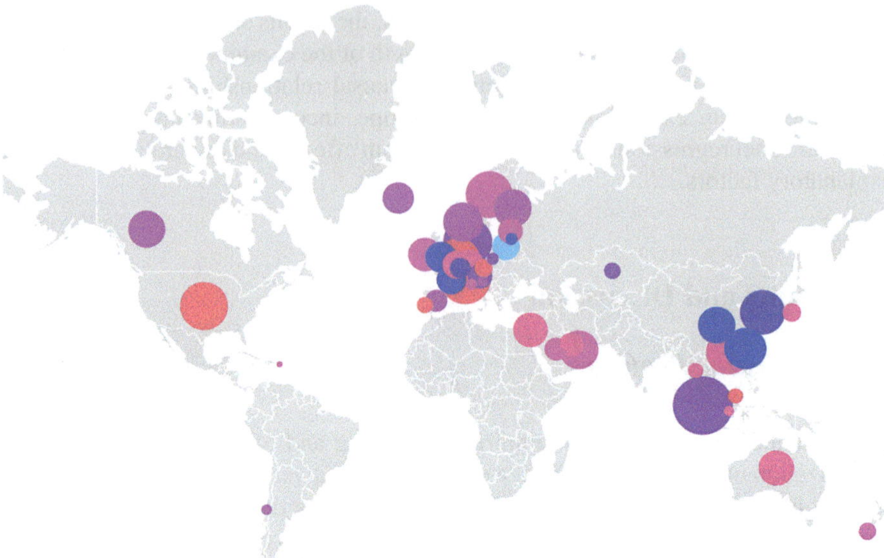

Fig. 1 Digital competitiveness index, 2024. *Source:* International Institute for Management Development

most developed European nations, Canada, South Korea, and Australia. Although countries with the lowest scores (below 60 points) showed some improvement, they continue to lag behind digital leaders. These findings underscore both the overall growth in digital competitiveness and the growing stratification across countries—emphasizing the need for a differentiated approach when assessing macroeconomic effects of digitalization, particularly in terms of productivity and innovation outcomes.

The Global Innovation Index (GII), published annually by the World Intellectual Property Organization (WIPO), serves as an aggregated measure of countries' systemic capacity to generate and implement innovations. The index includes institutional, human capital, and infrastructure dimensions, as well as actual outputs of innovation activity. Between 2015 and 2024, the average index value across the sample was approximately 53 points, with relatively stable trends and minor fluctuations. For instance, average scores ranged from 51.7 (in 2019) to 53.8 (in 2015), suggesting a saturation of innovation potential in many high-income economies and limited cross-country differentiation (Fig. 2).

Nevertheless, the gap between the highest and lowest values remained substantial: in 2016, the index ranged from 41.7 to 66.3 points, and in 2023—from 39.4 to 68.2 points. Long-term trends show no clear increase or decrease in aggregate innovation capacity, potentially due to institutional inertia and methodological differences in indicator construction. The top-performing countries during this period—Switzerland, Sweden, the United States, the Netherlands, and the United Kingdom—consistently scored above 65 points. Countries with lower and

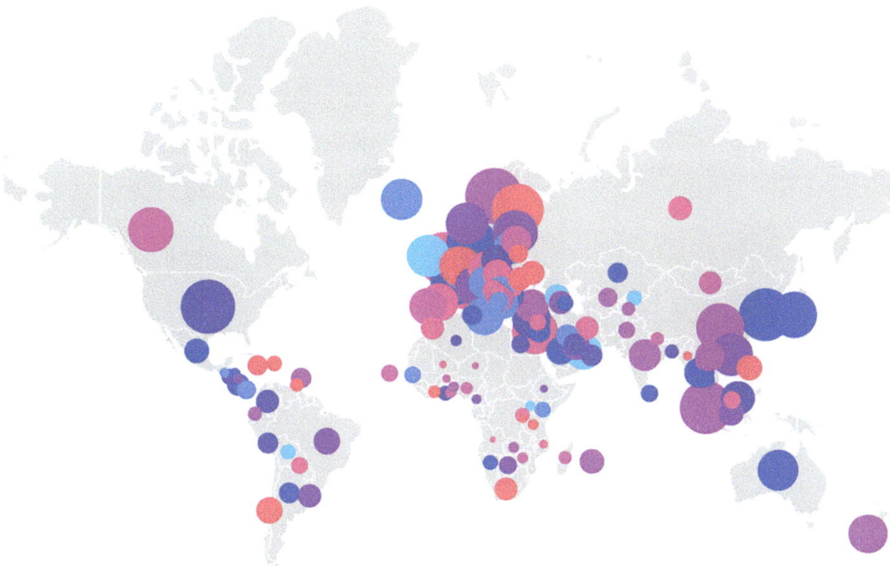

Fig. 2 Global innovation index, 2024. *Source:* WIPO Global Innovation

mid-range scores (below 50) demonstrated limited positive dynamics, pointing to persistent barriers and the need for comprehensive measures to strengthen innovation capacity.

Although global innovation differentiation remains persistent, the innovation landscape is increasingly shifting toward breakthrough digital technologies, with artificial intelligence occupying a central role. In this context, assessing the dynamics of investment in AI technologies becomes essential to understanding the real scale and strategic priorities of technological investment.

Investments in artificial intelligence technologies represent a key indicator of national-level technological transformation. Measuring inbound AI investments as a percentage of GDP enables cross-country comparison adjusted for economic scale and captures the relative intensity of resource allocation to the AI sector (Fig. 3). Average AI investment across the sample rose from 0.014% of GDP in 2015 to a peak of 0.172% in 2019, reflecting heightened global interest in AI. The most significant increases occurred in 2017 and 2019. In some years, exceptionally high values were recorded for individual countries—for instance, Bermuda reached 1.0921% of GDP in 2017, indicative of large one-time investment deals. This was accompanied by high cross-country dispersion (e.g., a standard deviation of 0.33 percentage points in 2017).

Following the 2019 peak, the average investment share began to decline moderately, possibly reflecting market saturation or the shift toward implementing previously funded projects. Disparities across countries remain high, with minimum values ranging from 0.0001% to 0.05% in every year—indicating that some countries maintain very low AI investment levels. The leading countries in terms of AI

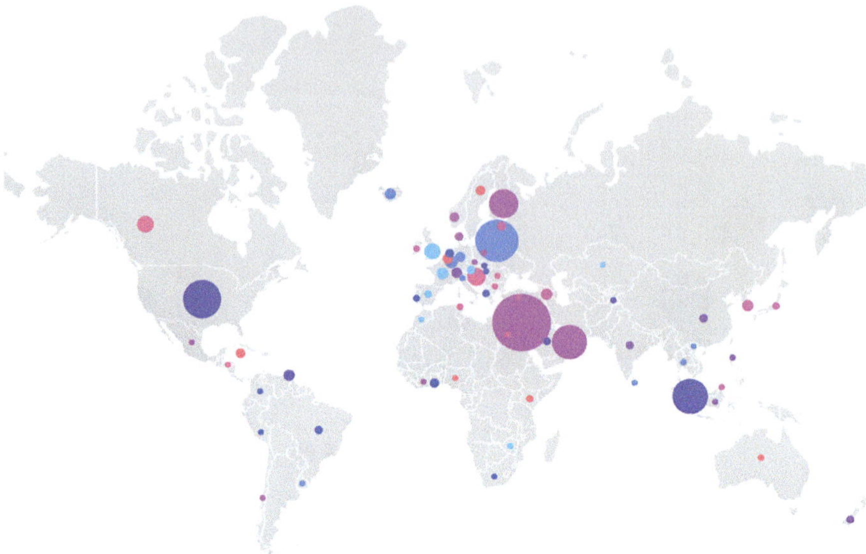

Fig. 3 Artificial intelligence inbound investment, 2024 (% of GDP). *Source:* Emerging Technology Observatory

investment intensity varied year to year, underscoring the volatility of investment patterns. Overall, inbound AI investment is a rapidly growing but unstable indicator, often featuring outlier values. This supports the need to analyze such indicators dynamically and, where possible, to complement them with more stable measures (e.g., domestic investment volume or the number of implemented AI solutions) in regression modeling.

The observed growth in AI investment highlights the increasing global interest in transformative digital technologies. However, investment alone does not guarantee sustained competitive advantage. The critical factor enabling the conversion of technological and financial resources into long-term economic efficiency is global competitiveness.

The Global Competitiveness Index (GCI) provides a comprehensive assessment of a country's ability to maintain conditions for sustainable economic growth and productivity enhancement (Fig. 4). It encompasses a wide range of determinants, including institutional frameworks, macroeconomic stability, infrastructure, labor market dynamics, financial development, innovation capacity, and education quality. Analysis of data from 2015 to 2024 reveals a consistent rise in average GCI scores during the early years of the period. The average increased from 69.87 in 2015 to a peak of 77.51 in 2017, reflecting improvements in institutional and economic conditions in many countries. After 2017, the average stabilized in the 74–77 range, with a moderate decline in 2019 (to 74.23), possibly due to global economic uncertainty and increasing regional disparities.

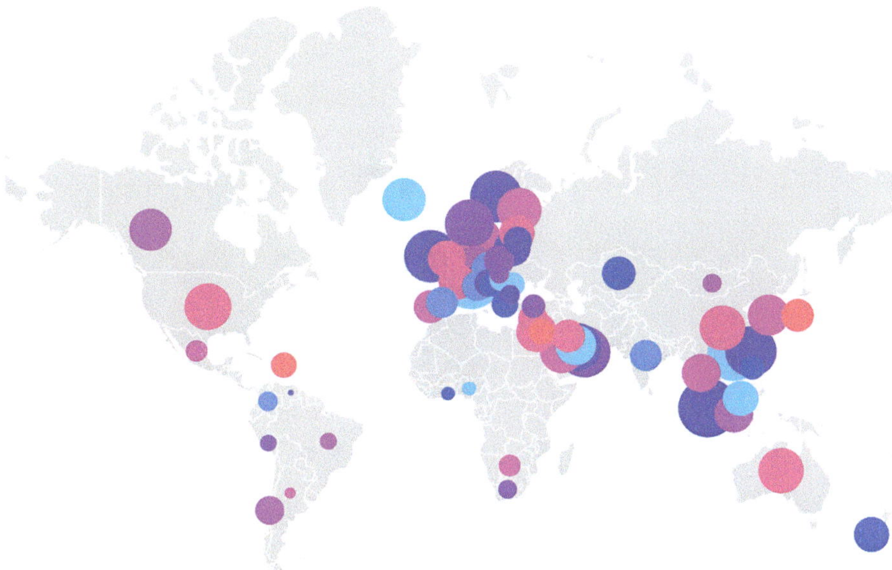

Fig. 4 Global competitiveness index, 2024. *Source:* International Institute for Management Development

Country-level dispersion also widened, signaling a growing gap between nations with strong institutional competitiveness and those lagging behind. Top performers throughout the period included Switzerland, Singapore, the United States, the Netherlands, and Germany—countries with robust institutional frameworks and strong innovation ecosystems, all scoring close to 100 points. The general upward trend among leaders, combined with the increasing disparity, points to widening inequality in global competitiveness.

To better understand these structural dynamics, it is important to consider the production profile of national economies. In this context, the share of industry in GDP serves as a key complementary indicator.

The share of industry in GDP is a critical macroeconomic indicator that reflects the structural composition of national economies, the level of industrialization, and dependence on the production sector. Analyzing this indicator over time allows for the detection of deindustrialization or reindustrialization trends and provides insight into the resilience of industrial value-added. The data reveal a general decline in the industry share globally (Fig. 5). The average share fell from 25.6% in 2014 to 23.2% in 2023, reflecting a broader shift toward service-oriented and digital sectors. The most pronounced decline occurred between 2015 and 2016, with a drop of over 1 percentage point—from 24.5% to 24.1%.

Despite this trend, cross-country variation remains high. In all years observed, values ranged from under 5% in some post-industrial economies (e.g., Luxembourg, Cyprus) to over 60% in countries dominated by manufacturing or extractive industries (e.g., Qatar, the UAE, Brunei). A stable or increasing industrial share in

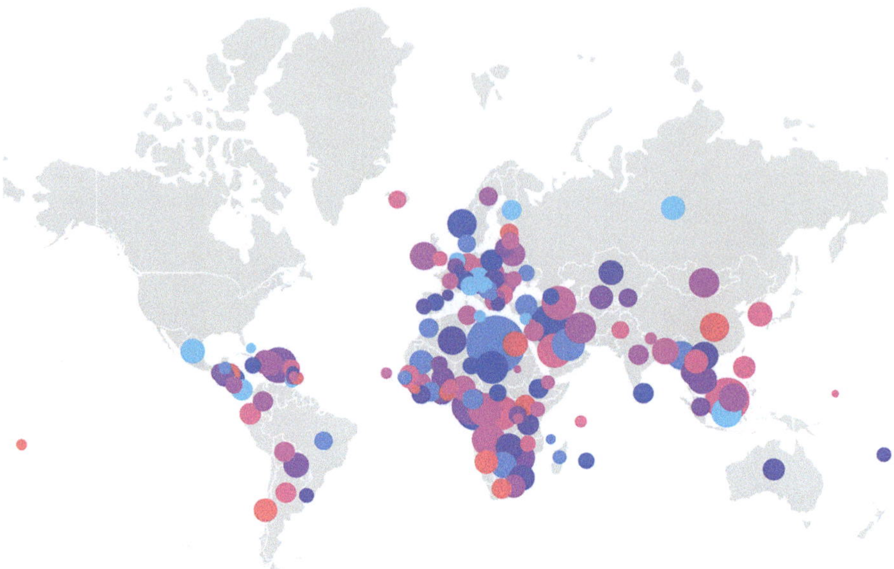

Fig. 5 Share of industry in GDP, 2023. *Source:* World Bank

countries such as Poland, the Czech Republic, and Vietnam may indicate a strategic pivot toward "new industrialization" in the context of Industry 4.0. Thus, although the overall trend points to a decline in industrial share, persistent structural differences across countries reflect varying development strategies, production specializations, and industrial policies. These differences must be accounted for in modeling the impact of digitalization on economic performance and in the typology of national economies.

Labor productivity, measured in constant 2017 PPP-adjusted USD per hour worked, is a key indicator of economic efficiency and technological maturity. It reflects the value added generated by a worker per unit of time and serves as a central metric for analyzing the impact of digital and innovation factors. A moderate increase in productivity was observed across the sample. The average value rose from $71.7/h in 2014 to $76.6/h in 2023, indicating gradual accumulation of technological and organizational gains (Fig. 6). The highest growth rates were recorded between 2017 and 2021, with annual increases of $1.5–2.0/h. Growth slowed in the post-pandemic period (2021–2023).

Maximum productivity levels in 2023 reached $136/h—typical of countries with advanced digital service sectors and high capital intensity (e.g., Ireland, Switzerland, Luxembourg). Minimum values remained within $53–56/h, reflecting lower productivity in labor-intensive or traditional economies. Cross-country dispersion remained high throughout the period, with standard deviations in the range of $19–21/h, confirming persistent productivity gaps among countries with different economic structures, levels of automation, and digital integration. These findings reinforce the importance of accounting for national characteristics when

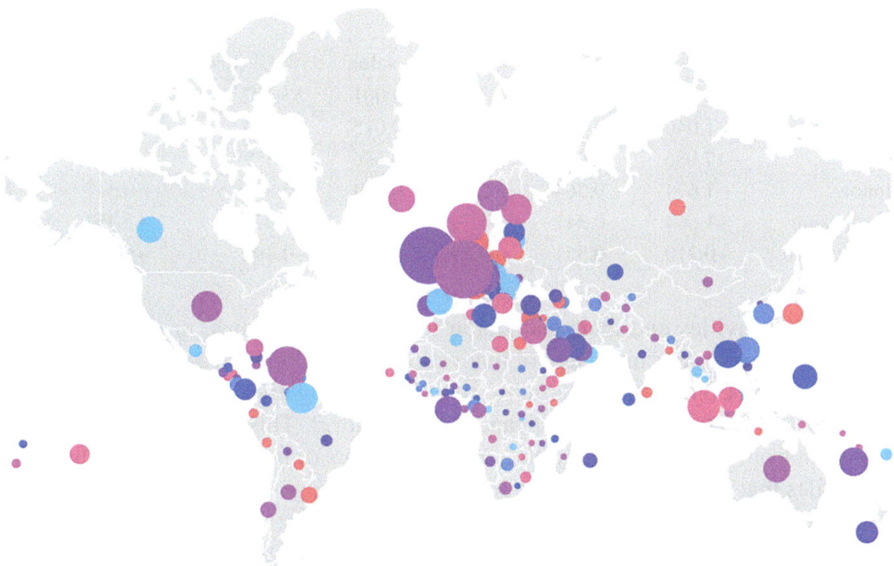

Fig. 6 Labor productivity per hour worked, 2023 (PPP-adjusted USD at 2017 prices). *Source:* ILOSTAT

interpreting the productivity effects of digitalization and support the selection of labor productivity as the dependent variable in econometric modeling.

3.2 Econometric Models

To assess the influence of the selected factors on labor productivity, a multiple linear regression model was constructed using the Ordinary Least Squares (OLS) method. The analytical form of the model is as follows:

$$\begin{aligned} \mathrm{Y}_{it} &= \beta_0 + \beta_1 \times \mathrm{DigiComp}_{it} + \beta_2 \times \mathrm{AIInv}_{it} + \beta_3 \times \mathrm{Innov}_{it} \\ &\quad + \beta_4 \times \mathrm{GlobComp}_{it} + \beta_5 \times \mathrm{IndustShare}_{it} + \varepsilon_{it}, \end{aligned}$$

where Y_{it} is labor productivity in country i at time t; $\mathrm{DigiComp}_{it}$ is Digital Competitiveness Index; AIInv_{it} is AI investment as a percentage of GDP; Innov_{it} is Global Innovation Index; $\mathrm{GlobComp}_{it}$ is Global Competitiveness Index; $\mathrm{IndustShare}_{it}$ is share of industry in GDP; ε_{it} is error term.

Based on the regression results presented in Table 1, the statistically significant predictors of labor productivity are the Global Competitiveness Index and the Global Innovation Index. The former exerts a strong positive effect, supporting the hypothesis that a favorable institutional and market environment enhances economic efficiency.

In contrast, the Global Innovation Index demonstrates a statistically significant negative effect, which contradicts expectations. This may reflect a time lag between

Table 1 Results of the baseline regression model

Variable	Coefficient	Std. error	t-value	p-value	95% CI (lower)	95% CI (upper)
Constant (β_0)	110.216	28.488	3.869	<0.001	53.322	167.110
DigiComp	−1.040	0.417	−2.495	0.015	−1.873	−0.208
AIInv	−17.086	18.011	−0.949	0.346	−53.055	18.884
Innov	−1.674	0.564	−2.967	0.004	−2.801	−0.547
GlobComp	+1.664	0.347	+4.799	<0.001	+0.972	+2.357
IndustShare	+0.210	0.351	+0.596	0.553	−0.492	+0.911

innovation activities and their realization in productivity gains, or structural constraints that hinder the conversion of innovation potential into measurable outcomes.

The Digital Competitiveness Index also shows a negative relationship with productivity and is statistically significant at the 5% level. This counterintuitive result may stem from multicollinearity with other indicators or from country-specific digital profiles that distort the aggregate relationship. It suggests the need for additional analysis, including stratification by country groups.

AI investment, despite its presumed importance in digital modernization, does not show a significant effect. This may be due to delayed impacts or the fact that much of the investment is directed toward long-term research and infrastructure projects.

Similarly, the share of industry in GDP does not exhibit a significant effect, possibly indicating a declining role of the industrial sector as a direct driver of productivity in the digital era.

3.3 *Multicollinearity Diagnostics*

Given the anomalous coefficients observed for certain variables in the baseline regression model—particularly the negative sign of the digital competitiveness index—it was essential to assess the degree of multicollinearity among the independent variables. Multicollinearity can lead to instability in coefficient estimates, overestimation or underestimation of variable effects, and hinder the interpretability of the results.

To diagnose multicollinearity, the Variance Inflation Factor (VIF) was calculated for each predictor. VIF values are derived from the inverse of the tolerance ($1 - R^2$) of an auxiliary regression in which the given predictor is treated as the dependent variable. Empirical guidelines suggest that VIF values exceeding 5 indicate problematic multicollinearity requiring corrective action.

The results (Table 2) indicate that none of the independent variables exceed the VIF threshold of 5. The highest VIF is observed for digital competitiveness (2.46) and global competitiveness (2.23), which points to only moderate intercorrelation. Consequently, the negative coefficients in the model cannot be attributed to high multicollinearity and may instead reflect structural characteristics of the dataset or underlying latent factors.

Table 2 Multicollinearity diagnostics (VIF)

Variable	VIF	Interpretation
Constant (β_0)	162.67	Not evaluated for the intercept
DigiComp	2.46	Moderate correlation with other variables
AIInv	1.15	Low multicollinearity
Innov	1.91	Moderate multicollinearity
GlobComp	2.23	Moderate multicollinearity
IndustShare	1.20	Low multicollinearity

The absence of critical multicollinearity confirms the appropriateness of the model specification and the internal consistency of the included predictors. Nevertheless, considering the potential for latent structural dependencies, subsequent stages of analysis employed dimensionality reduction techniques—namely, principal component analysis (PCA)—to improve interpretability and reveal typologies of digital development.

3.4 *Principal Component Analysis (PCA)*

To enhance model interpretability and identify hidden structural patterns, principal component analysis (PCA) was applied to the set of standardized independent variables. PCA reduces the dimensionality of correlated data by extracting orthogonal linear combinations—principal components—that capture the maximum variance in the dataset. All predictors were z-standardized prior to PCA, ensuring comparability of scales across variables.

The PCA results (Fig. 7) show that the first principal component (PC1) explains 48.7% of the total variance in the dataset. This component is strongly positively loaded on digital competitiveness, global competitiveness, innovation, and AI investment. It represents countries with advanced digital, competitive, and innovation capabilities.

The second principal component (PC2) explains 22.7% of the variance. It has strong positive loadings for global competitiveness and industry share, and negative loadings for innovation and AI investment. PC2 captures a structural-industrial vector, contrasting countries with traditional industrial strength against those focusing on AI and innovation.

The third component (PC3) explains 15.8% of the variance. It is positively associated with AI investment and industry share, and negatively with innovation, reflecting a pattern of technology-driven industrialization—a combination of high AI investment and a strong industrial base.

Each principal component generalizes specific dimensions of techno-economic development: PC1—Digital maturity and global competitiveness, PC2—Economic structure and industrial orientation, PC3—AI-driven industrialization.

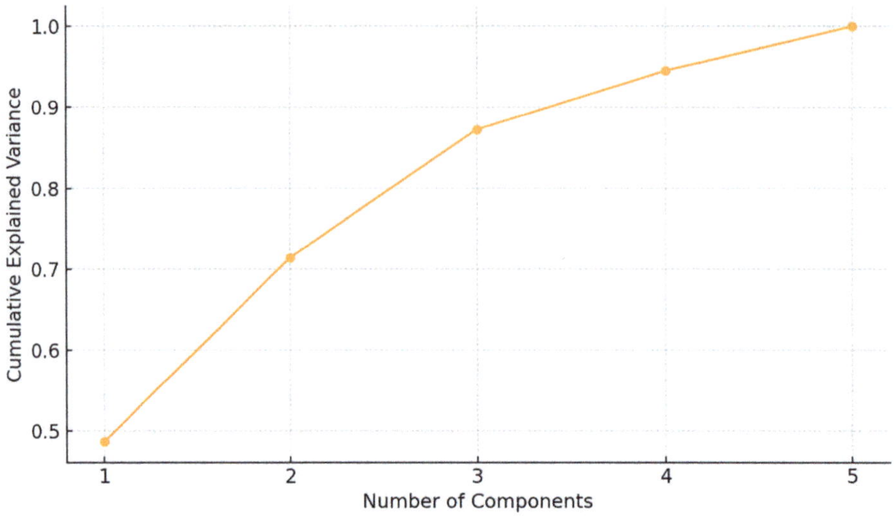

Fig. 7 PCA: cumulative explained variance by number of components

The first two components account for 71.4% of total variance, while the first three explain 87.2%. This high explanatory power justifies the use of the first two or three components in subsequent regression and clustering analyses. The presence of a stable latent structure supports the application of dimensionality reduction to improve data interpretability.

3.5 *Cluster Analysis and Country Typologies*

To further improve model interpretability and reveal latent heterogeneity among countries, a k-means cluster analysis was conducted based on the standardized values of all indicators. The objective was to group countries with similar techno-economic characteristics and digital development trajectories.

The optimal number of clusters was determined empirically as k = 3, based on the interpretability of the results, explained variance structure from PCA, and temporal stability of cluster membership. Individual regression models were constructed for each cluster to reveal differences in the determinants of labor productivity.

Several countries appeared in multiple clusters over different years (e.g., the United Kingdom, Canada, France), indicating dynamic digital transformation processes, possibly characterized by abrupt shifts or structural changes during the observation period.

- Cluster 0 (2 countries): Includes Ireland and Norway in selected years. This group reflects outlier profiles, characterized by exceptionally high or atypical

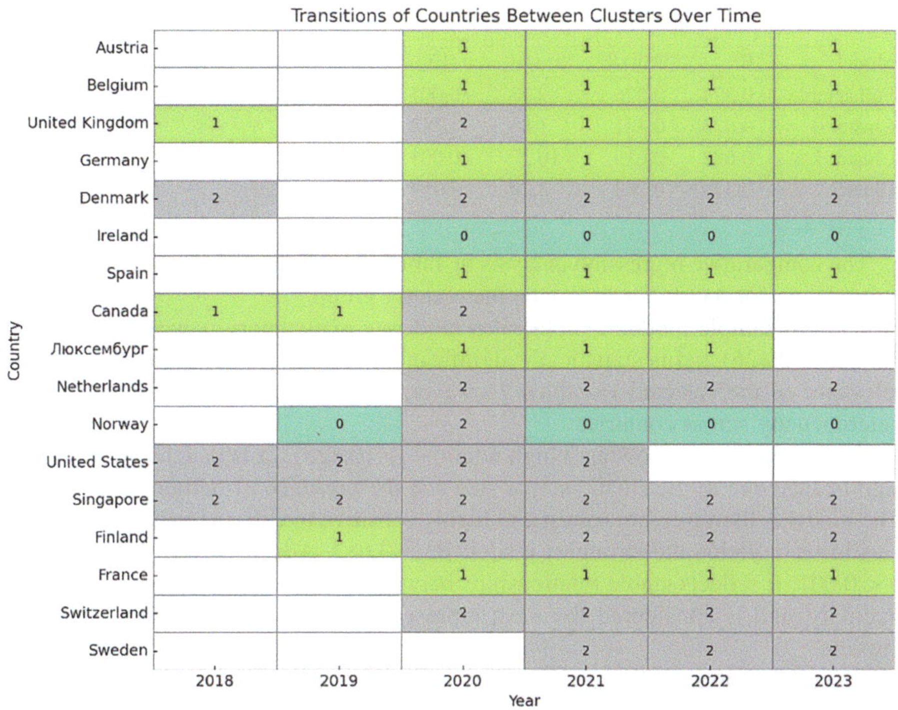

Fig. 8 Transitions of countries between clusters over time

digital indicators — either due to extreme digital saturation or unusual development trajectories. Due to the small sample size and high variability, regression results for this cluster are less stable and should be interpreted with caution.

- Cluster 1 (9 countries): Comprises the United Kingdom, Canada, Finland, Austria, Belgium, Sweden, France, the Netherlands, and Switzerland. These countries are marked by high digital and global competitiveness and a moderate industrial share, reflecting mature digital economies. This group produced the most stable and consistent regression model, with strong associations between digital integration and labor productivity.
- Cluster 2 (10 countries): Represents transitional digital economies, including Denmark, the United States, Singapore, the United Kingdom, Canada, France, Switzerland, Germany, Australia, and Austria. These countries exhibit moderate levels of digital competitiveness and growing interest in AI investment. Digital variables in this cluster showed more gradual and variable effects on productivity.

The cluster transition map (Fig. 8) illustrates how country profiles evolved over time. It reveals countries with volatile cluster affiliations, highlighting the dynamic nature of digital transformation and reinforcing the need for a differentiated approach to analyzing digitalization effects.

Table 3 Comparative analysis of regression models by cluster

Model	R^2	Adj. R^2	F-stat	p (F)	AIC	Observations	Countries
Full sample	0.374	0.326	7.77	<0.001	623.98	71	17
Cluster 0	0.823	0.381	1.86	0.385	71.76	8	2
Cluster 1	0.682	0.615	10.27	<0.001	256.40	30	9
Cluster 2	0.379	0.263	3.29	0.019	209.26	33	10

The comparative regression analysis in Table 3 highlights substantial differences in model performance depending on the country group.

The full sample model demonstrates moderate explanatory power ($R^2 = 0.374$, Adj. $R^2 = 0.326$) and is statistically significant ($p < 0.001$), confirming the general relevance of the selected variables. However, the relatively low R^2 suggests high heterogeneity across countries.

Cluster 0, despite showing a high nominal R^2 (0.823), fails to achieve statistical significance due to the small sample size and the presence of outliers ($p = 0.385$). The model is therefore not robust and highly sensitive to extreme values.

Cluster 1 yields the strongest model: $R^2 = 0.682$, Adj. $R^2 = 0.615$, $F = 10.27$, $p < 0.001$. It reflects stable relationships between global competitiveness and productivity, and is considered the most representative and interpretable among the clusters.

Cluster 2 shows moderate explanatory power ($R^2 = 0.379$, Adj. $R^2 = 0.263$) but remains statistically significant ($p = 0.019$). This suggests the presence of meaningful, albeit less stable, effects of digitalization and competitiveness in transitional economies.

One key insight is that AI investment consistently fails to produce statistically significant effects across all models. This may indicate lagged effects or intervening institutional mechanisms. Meanwhile, global competitiveness emerges as a robust predictor across all clusters, mediating productivity outcomes. Notably, digital competitiveness becomes a significant positive driver in Cluster 2, suggesting that countries in earlier digitalization stages benefit more explicitly from digital investments. The effect of industry share varies by cluster and warrants deeper stratified interpretation. For more details, see Tables 4, 5, and 6.

A comparative analysis of the models demonstrates consistency with the findings of other studies, reaffirming the influence of digitalization and innovation on labor productivity. The baseline model, constructed on the aggregated sample, reveals a statistically significant positive effect of global competitiveness and a negative effect of innovation and digitalization. This ambiguity aligns with previous research, which shows that institutional factors and the degree of market maturity determine the extent to which innovation potential can be converted into productivity growth [40, 41]. At the same time, these results contradict studies emphasizing that digitalization enhances efficiency and labor productivity [14, 42, 43]. Most likely, the influence of digitalization on productivity is nonlinear and depends on a country's level of digital maturity and the scale of AI integration.

Table 4 Baseline model (full sample)

Indicator	Direction of effect	Statistical Significance	Interpretation
Digital competitiveness	Negative (−)	Significant ($p = 0.015$)	Paradoxical effect; may reflect hidden mechanisms or overlaps with other indices
AI investment (% of GDP)	Negative (−)	Not significant ($p = 0.346$)	Possible lagged impact or institutional barriers
Global innovation index	Negative (−)	Significant ($p = 0.004$)	Indicates a mismatch between innovation capacity and productivity realization
Global competitiveness	Positive (+)	Highly significant ($p < 0.001$)	Core predictor of productivity growth
Industry share in GDP	Positive (+)	Not significant ($p = 0.553$)	Structural variable with limited standalone explanatory power

Note. Full sample model includes 17 countries: Austria, Belgium, United Kingdom, Germany, Denmark, Ireland, Spain, Canada, Luxembourg, Netherlands, Norway, USA, Singapore, Finland, France, Switzerland, and Sweden

Table 5 Cluster 1 model

Indicator	Direction of Effect	Statistical Significance	Interpretation
Digital competitiveness	Negative (−)	Not significant ($p = 0.590$)	Likely saturated effect; may overlap with global competitiveness
AI investment (% of GDP)	Negative (−)	Marginally significant ($p = 0.104$)	Impact not directly realized; filtered through institutional conditions
Global innovation index	Negative (−)	Not significant ($p = 0.531$)	Innovation impact absorbed through other channels
Global competitiveness	Positive (+)	Significant ($p = 0.001$)	Key driver of productivity in digitally mature economies
Industry share in GDP	Negative (−)	Highly significant ($p < 0.001$)	Reflects shift to service/digital economy, reducing reliance on industrial base

Note. Cluster 1 includes 9 countries: Austria, Belgium, United Kingdom, Germany, Spain, Canada, Luxembourg, Finland, and France

The model for Cluster 1 demonstrates a stable positive effect of global competitiveness and a negative effect of the industrial share, which corresponds with conclusions in the literature indicating that in economies with high levels of digitalization, there is a shift toward service-oriented structures and a declining dependence on the industrial sector [44, 45].

The Cluster 2 model confirms the positive impact of both digital competitiveness and global competitiveness on labor productivity. These findings are in line with studies suggesting that the effects of digital investment in moderately digitally mature economies become more pronounced as human capital and digital infrastructure accumulate [46–48].

Table 6 Cluster 2 model

Indicator	Direction of Effect	Statistical Significance	Interpretation
Digital competitiveness	Positive (+)	Significant (p = 0.027)	Digitalization becomes an active productivity driver
AI investment (% of GDP)	Negative (−)	Not significant (p = 0.178)	Effects not yet materialized; weak institutional channels
Global innovation index	Negative (−)	Marginally significant (p = 0.111)	Innovations not yet integrated into production processes
Global competitiveness	Positive (+)	Significant (p = 0.018)	Indicator of economic maturity and a stable business environment
Industry share in GDP	Positive (+)	Not significant (p = 0.501)	Industry not yet a decisive factor in labor efficiency

Note. Cluster 2 includes 10 countries: United Kingdom, Denmark, Canada, Netherlands, Norway, USA, Singapore, Finland, Switzerland, and Sweden

Finally, similar results are found in studies focused on countries with emerging digital ecosystems, which argue that only when investment, institutional readiness, and a sufficient human capital base are jointly present, does digitalization provide a noticeable contribution to productivity enhancement.

4 Conclusion

This study quantitatively assessed the influence of digitalization, innovation activity, global and digital competitiveness, and economic structure on labor productivity in an international comparative perspective. The baseline regression model confirmed the significance of global competitiveness (positive effect) and the global innovation index (negative effect). The digital competitiveness index demonstrated a counterintuitive negative relationship with productivity, which may reflect unaccounted structural differences or latent effects not captured in this model. Neither AI investment nor industry share in GDP yielded statistically significant impacts, likely due to temporal lags or neutralizing institutional effects.

Cluster analysis revealed substantial variation in productivity determinants across country groups. The Cluster 1 model, encompassing digitally mature economies, exhibited the highest explanatory power and consistent parameters. For Cluster 2 countries—those undergoing transitional digital development—digital competitiveness emerged as a statistically significant positive predictor of labor productivity, suggesting that the productivity effects of digitalization become more visible as digital infrastructure and human capital accumulate.

The comparative model analysis supports findings from prior research while also offering refinements. Notably, global competitiveness consistently served as a mediating factor, enhancing the efficacy of both digital and innovation investments. The results also confirm that the impact of digitalization is not universal but instead conditional upon a country's institutional maturity, digital readiness, and economic structure. Furthermore, the absence or inversion of effects from certain digital and innovation indicators emphasizes that the shift toward a digital economy is nonlinear, gradual, and contingent upon complementary capacities.

Overall, this study reinforces the need for a differentiated policy approach that tailors digital strategies to the specific developmental stage and structural characteristics of national economies. The results can inform the design of productivity-enhancing policies in the context of ongoing digital transformation.

Conflict of Interest The authors declare that the research was conducted in the absence of any commercial or financial relationships that could be construed as a potential conflict of interest.

Credit Author Statement *E.K.*: Conceptualization, Data curation, Formal Analysis, Methodology, Project administration, Validation, Visualization, Writing—original draft, Writing—review & editing. *V.B.*: Data curation, Formal Analysis, Visualization, Writing—review & editing. *A.S.*: Data curation, Formal Analysis, Visualization, Writing—review & editing. *I.O.*: Data curation, Formal Analysis, Visualization, Writing—review & editing.

Data Availability Statement The original contributions presented in the study are included in the article, further inquiries can be directed to the corresponding author/s.

References

1. Zhuravlev, D. M., & Glukhov, V. V. (2021). Strategizing of economic systems digital transformation: A driver on innovative development. *St. Petersburg State Polytechnical University Journal Economics, 14*(2), 7–21.
2. Demin, S., Mikhaylova, A., & Pyankova, S. (2023). Digitalization and its impact on regional economy transformation mechanisms. *International Journal of System Assurance Engineering and Management, 14*(1), 377–390. https://doi.org/10.1007/s13198-022-01806-y
3. Stroiko, T., Nazarova, L., & Danik, N. (2021). Transformation of economic processes on the basis of digitalisation. *Baltic Journal of Economic Studies, 7*(1), 102–106. https://doi.org/10.30525/2256-0742/2021-7-1-102-106
4. Brynjolfsson, E., & McAfee, A. (2014). *The second machine age: Work, progress, and prosperity in a time of brilliant technologies*. W. W. Norton & Company.
5. Brynjolfsson, E., Rock, D., & Syverson, C. (2021). The productivity J-curve: How intangibles complement general purpose technologies. *American Economic Journal: Macroeconomics, 13*(1), 333–372. https://doi.org/10.1257/mac.20180386
6. Bughin, J. (2020). Artificial intelligence, its corporate use and how it will affect the future of work. In *Capitalism, global change and sustainable development* (pp. 239–260). Springer International Publishing. https://doi.org/10.1007/978-3-030-46143-0_14
7. McKinsey Global Institute. (2023). *The economic potential of generative AI: The next productivity frontier*. Retrieved from https://www.mckinsey.com/capabilities/mckinsey-digital/our-insights/the-economic-potential-of-generative-ai-the-next-productivity-frontier
8. OECD. (2024). *The impact of artificial intelligence on productivity, distribution and growth*. Retrieved from https://www.oecd.org/content/dam/oecd/en/publications/reports/2024/04/the-impact-of-artificial-intelligence-on-productivity-distribution-and-growth_d54e2842/8d900037-en.pdf

9. Bailin, M., & Kane, A. (2023). *How will AI affect productivity?* Brookings Institution. Retrieved from https://www.brookings.edu/articles/how-will-ai-affect-productivity/
10. Czarnitzki, D., Fernández, G. P., & Rammer, C. (2023). Artificial intelligence and firm-level productivity. *Journal of Economic Behavior & Organization, 211*, 188–205. https://doi.org/10.1016/j.jebo.2023.05.008
11. Gal, P., Nicoletti, G., Renault, T., Sorbe, S., & Timiliotis, C. (2019). Digitalisation and productivity: In search of the holy grail—Firm-level empirical evidence from EU countries. *OECD Economics Department Working Papers, 1533*, 1–57.
12. Cette, G., Nevoux, S., & Py, L. (2022). The impact of ICTs and digitalization on productivity and labor share: Evidence from French firms. *Economics of Innovation and New Technology, 31*(8), 669–692. https://doi.org/10.1080/10438599.2020.1849967
13. Varlamova, J., & Larionova, N. (2020). Labor productivity in the digital era: A spatial-temporal analysis. *International Journal of Technology, 11*(6), 4429. https://doi.org/10.14716/ijtech.v11i6.4429
14. Mollins, J., & Taskin, T. (2023). *Digitalization: Productivity (no. 2023-17)*. Bank of Canada. https://doi.org/10.34989/sdp-2023-17
15. Anghel, B., Bunel, S., Bijnens, G., Botelho, V., Falck, E., Labhard, V., & Strobel, J. (2024). *Digitalisation and productivity*. ECB occasional paper series (2024/339). https://doi.org/10.2139/ssrn.4741441
16. Borowiecki, M., Pareliussen, J., Glocker, D., Kim, E. J., Polder, M., & Rud, I. (2021). The impact of digitalisation on productivity: Firm-level evidence from The Netherlands. *OECD Economic Department Working Papers, 1680*, 1–33.
17. Wang, D., & Shao, X. (2024). Research on the impact of digital transformation on the production efficiency of manufacturing enterprises: Institution-based analysis of the threshold effect. *International Review of Economics & Finance, 91*, 883–897. https://doi.org/10.1016/j.iref.2024.01.046
18. Gebauer, H., Fleisch, E., Lamprecht, C., & Wortmann, F. (2020). Growth paths for overcoming the digitalization paradox. *Business Horizons, 63*(3), 313–323. https://doi.org/10.1016/j.bushor.2020.01.005
19. Guo, X., Li, M., Wang, Y., & Mardani, A. (2023). Does digital transformation improve the firm's performance? From the perspective of digitalization paradox and managerial myopia. *Journal of Business Research, 163*, 113868. https://doi.org/10.1016/j.jbusres.2023.113868
20. Brynjolfsson, E., & Hitt, L. M. (1998). Beyond the productivity paradox. *Communications of the ACM, 41*(8), 49–55. https://doi.org/10.1145/280324.280332
21. Brynjolfsson, E., Rock, D., & Syverson, C. (2019). Artificial intelligence and the modern productivity paradox. In *The economics of artificial intelligence: An agenda* (pp. 23–57). University of Chicago Press. https://doi.org/10.7208/chicago/9780226613475.003.0001
22. Syverson, C. (2017). Challenges to mismeasurement explanations for the US productivity slowdown. *Journal of Economic Perspectives, 31*(2), 165–186. https://doi.org/10.1257/jep.31.2.165
23. Acemoglu, D., & Restrepo, P. (2020). Robots and jobs: Evidence from US labor markets. *Journal of Political Economy, 128*(6), 2188–2244. https://doi.org/10.1086/705716
24. Van Ark, B. (2015). Productivity and digitilization in Europe: Paving the road to faster growth. *Digiworld Economic Journal, 100*, 107.
25. Brynjolfsson, E., & Hitt, L. M. (2003). Computing productivity: Firm-level evidence. *Review of Economics and Statistics, 85*(4), 793–808. https://doi.org/10.1162/003465303772815736
26. Remane, G., Hanelt, A., Wiesboeck, F., & Kolbe, L. M. (2017). *Digital maturity in traditional industries—An exploratory analysis* (p. 10). ECIS.
27. Froger, M., Benaben, F., Truptil, S., & Boissel-Dallier, N. (2019). A non-linear business process management maturity framework to apprehend future challenges. *International Journal of Information Management, 49*, 290–300. https://doi.org/10.1016/j.ijinfomgt.2019.05.013

28. Wu, Q., & Zhuang, Q. (2024). Nonlinear effects of digital development on manufacturing innovation: Evidence from China. *Applied Economics, 56*(52), 6483–6497. https://doi.org/10.1080/00036846.2023.2287555
29. Ahlstrom, D. (2010). Innovation and growth: How business contributes to society. *Academy of Management Perspectives, 24*(3), 11–24. https://doi.org/10.5465/AMP.2010.52842948
30. Surya, B., Menne, F., Sabhan, H., Suriani, S., Abubakar, H., & Idris, M. (2021). Economic growth, increasing productivity of SMEs, and open innovation. *Journal of Open Innovation: Technology, Market, and Complexity, 7*(1), 20. https://doi.org/10.3390/joitmc7010020
31. Romer, P. M. (1990). Endogenous technological change. *Journal of Political Economy, 98*(5), S71–S102. https://doi.org/10.1086/261725
32. Furman, J. L., Porter, M. E., & Stern, S. (2002). The determinants of national innovative capacity. *Research Policy, 31*(6), 899–933. https://doi.org/10.1016/S0048-7333(01)00152-4
33. Bughin, J., Seong, J., Manyika, J., Chui, M., & Joshi, R. (2018). *Notes from the AI frontier: Modeling the impact of AI on the world economy*. McKinsey Global Institute.
34. OECD. (2019). *Artificial intelligence in society*. OECD Publishing. https://doi.org/10.1787/eedfee77-en
35. Lee, Y. S., Kim, T., Choi, S., & Kim, W. (2022). When does AI pay off? AI-adoption intensity, complementary investments, and R&D strategy. *Technovation, 118*, 102590. https://doi.org/10.1016/j.technovation.2022.102590
36. Vijayakumar, H. (2021). The impact of AI-innovations and private AI-investment on US economic growth: An empirical analysis. *Reviews of Contemporary Business Analytics, 4*(1), 14–32.
37. Porter, M. E., Delgado, M., Ketels, C., & Stern, S. (2008). Moving to a new global competitiveness index. In *The global competitiveness report 2009* (pp. 43–63). World Economic Forum.
38. Khyareh, M. M., & Rostami, N. (2022). Macroeconomic conditions, innovation and competitiveness. *Journal of the Knowledge Economy, 13*(2), 1321–1340. https://doi.org/10.1007/s13132-021-00752-7
39. Calvino, F., Criscuolo, C., Marcolin, L., & Squicciarini, M. (2018). *A taxonomy of digital-intensive sectors*. OECD Science, Technology. https://doi.org/10.1787/f404736a-en
40. Su, C. W., Yuan, X., Umar, M., & Lobonţ, O. R. (2022). Does technological innovation bring destruction or creation to the labor market? *Technology in Society, 68*, 101905. https://doi.org/10.1016/j.techsoc.2022.101905
41. Capello, R., & Lenzi, C. (2021). Industry 4.0 and servitisation: Regional patterns of 4.0 technological transformations in Europe. *Technological Forecasting and Social Change, 173*, 121164. https://doi.org/10.1016/j.techfore.2021.121164
42. Markhaichuk, M., & Panshin, I. (2020). The role of digital competence in the impact of digitalization on labor productivity. In *The 35th international business information management association conference (IBIMA 2020)* (pp. 6632–6641). IBIMA.
43. Musimovich, M. V. (2025). Digitalization of the labor market: Potential prospects and risks for participants in labor relations. *Russian Journal of Labour Economics, 12*(4), 31.
44. Morozov, M. A., & Morozova, N. S. (2018). The development of the digital service economy and its impact on the labor market. *Servis Plus, 12*(1), 100–107.
45. Kurnosova, O. A. (2023). Servitization as a modern trend in the development of industrial enterprises. *Bulletin of the Automobile and Road Institute, 44*(1), 81–89.
46. Osei, D. B. (2024). Digital infrastructure and innovation in Africa: Does human capital mediate the effect? *Telematics and Informatics, 89*, 102111. https://doi.org/10.1016/j.tele.2024.102111
47. Grigorescu, A., Pelinescu, E., Ion, A. E., & Dutcas, M. F. (2021). Human capital in digital economy: An empirical analysis of central and eastern European countries from the European Union. *Sustainability, 13*(4), 2020. https://doi.org/10.3390/su13042020
48. Du, Z. Y., & Wang, Q. (2024). Digital infrastructure and innovation: Digital divide or digital dividend? *Journal of Innovation & Knowledge, 9*(3), 100542. https://doi.org/10.1016/j.jik.2024.100542

Organizational Challenges in Digital Transformation: A Review Through the Lens of Organizational Innovation

Umut Ahmet Seyrek, Kürşat Demiryürek, Olga G. Romanovich, and Aizhan A. Rakhmanalieva

Abstract The difficulties encountered in organizational activities during the digital transformation process should be clearly defined and examined. In this way, a concrete step is taken on the contextual effect of organizational innovation. The current qualitative review study draws attention to organizational difficulties faced by industrial enterprises and focuses on solving problems from the perception of organizational innovation during the digital transformation process. In this context, a review was conducted on the literature of organizational innovation, digital transformation and organizational difficulties in the industry. The identified difficulties were grouped and analyzed from the perspectives of labor, management, and supply chain. The findings of the literature review show that the relationships between organizational innovation factors and organizational functioning in order to solve the difficulties encountered by industrial enterprises during the digital transformation process require in-depth research on the specific problems. The study is anticipated to serve as a foundational compilation at a generalized conceptual level, providing a structured overview of organizational challenges within the digital transformation context.

Keywords Organizational challenges · Digital transformation · Organizational innovation · Industry 4.0

U. A. Seyrek · K. Demiryürek (✉)
Faculty of Agriculture, Ondokuz Mayıs University, Samsun, Türkiye
e-mail: 22281409@stu.omu.edu.tr; kursatd@omu.edu.tr

O. G. Romanovich · A. A. Rakhmanalieva
Kyrgyz-Russian Slavic University named after B.N. Yeltsin, Bishkek, Kyrgyz Republic
e-mail: O.G.Romanovich@krsu.kg; a.a.rakhmanalieva@krsu.kg

F. Tao et al. (eds.), *Artificial Intelligence and Digital Transformation*, Lecture Notes in Information Systems and Organisation 78,
https://doi.org/10.1007/978-3-032-00118-4_18

1 Introduction

In the era of accelerated technological development, digital transformation has emerged not merely as a trend but as a critical necessity for the survival and competitiveness of industrial enterprises. The integration of digital technologies into organizational structures is reshaping production systems, managerial practices, and operational processes at an unprecedented scale. However, this transition is far from seamless. While digital tools offer vast potential for efficiency, flexibility, and innovation, they simultaneously introduce complex organizational challenges that threaten the stability and sustainability of enterprises unprepared for change.

At this critical juncture, digital transformation fundamentally redefines both the raison d'être and the operational dynamics of contemporary enterprises. It does not merely entail the adoption of digital tools, but necessitates a profound reconfiguration of organizational structures, workflows, and strategic orientations. Companies that successfully integrate digital transformation into their organizational processes acquire a distinctive capacity to generate industrial value through enhanced agility, data-driven decision-making, and innovative output. Empirical evidence reinforces this assertion. In a study conducted by Teng et al. [1], which investigated the correlation between digital transformation and firm performance, it was demonstrated that organizations completing the transformation process experienced an increase in overall business efficiency by a factor of 8–10. Crucially, the study emphasized that the essence of digital transformation lies not solely in technological adoption, but in the systematic elevation of organizational performance through the innovation of business models, the optimization of internal structures, and the integration of strategic management practices. Thus, digital transformation emerges as a multidimensional process—strategic, technological, and organizational—requiring a holistic rethinking of traditional operational paradigms.

In this context, digital transformation can be conceptualized as a strategic prescription for organizational development and renewal. It provides the necessary framework for enterprises to restructure outdated systems, reconfigure workflows, and align internal capacities with the rapidly evolving external environment. The global crises of recent years have clearly exposed the vulnerability and stagnation of companies that failed to initiate timely digital transformation. Their inability to adapt has resulted in diminished competitiveness, disrupted operations, and even existential threats. According to Vial [2], digital transformation is not merely a technological adjustment, but rather a comprehensive organizational change process that reshapes the fundamental components of a firm's identity, purpose, and functioning. This process includes changes in organizational culture, decision-making structures, and resource allocation mechanisms. Similarly, Huang et al. [3] emphasize that digital transformation triggers a systematic restructuring of organizational characteristics and internal architectures, leading to the emergence of new forms of coordination, leadership, and performance evaluation. A concrete illustration of the strategic significance of digital transformation can be found in national industrial policy initiatives such as "Made in China 2025." This program aims to promote intelligent manufacturing, high-end technological integration, and industry-wide innovation. It exemplifies how digital transformation is employed at both firm and policy levels to drive industrial modernization, enhance value chains, and foster sustainable economic growth [4].

The digital transformation is a complex, multidimensional strategic process, which involves significant risks alongside the potential for substantial organizational gains. It extends far beyond the mere deployment of digital technologies or mechanization, encompassing comprehensive changes in organizational systems, structures, governance mechanisms, and strategic orientation. As Zhou et al. [4] emphasize, technological change alone is insufficient to ensure successful digital transformation; instead, organizational factors such as leadership, internal capabilities, and innovation culture must be addressed in parallel. This perspective is supported by González-Varona et al. [5], who define digital transformation as a fundamental reconfiguration of core business functions—including processes, products, structures, and business models—aligned with long-term strategic goals. Moreover, digital transformation and organizational innovation are increasingly understood as mutually reinforcing processes. As demonstrated by Xiufan and Decheng [6], digital transformation serves as a catalyst for organizational innovation by creating conditions that necessitate the development of new ideas, practices, and institutional arrangements. In turn, effective organizational innovation becomes a prerequisite for leveraging the full potential of digital transformation and ensuring its sustainability and scalability. Kaganer et al. [7] highlight that digital transformation should be viewed as a process of organizational change activated and sustained by digital technologies, requiring a reorientation of structures and routines often hindered by organizational inertia. Similarly, McKinsey's findings [8] indicate that behavioral and cultural adaptation within the organization is critical, as digital transformation exerts its impact through changes in employee mindsets, internal communication, and managerial practices. The interplay between technological, organizational, and social dimensions is further corroborated by empirical research. The study by Al-Ayed et al. [9] identifies a positive correlation between digital transformation and organizational performance, mediated by digital innovation. These findings underscore the importance of adopting a holistic approach that integrates digital tools with structural and cultural transformation.

What we understand from all these facts is that businesses need to structure their organizational structures and operations within a dynamic, universal but unique system for the future in order to carry out sustainable activities within the global innovative transformation processes that occur due to direct and indirect developments within and outside the sector. In this way, they will have a strong corporate identity. Mete [10] emphasized that the market activities of businesses are shaped by institutionalization and that innovation, which enables them to exist in the competitive market, is a part of the corporate movement. In the transformation process of the industrial world, businesses have to innovate and transform innovations into commercial value. In the same study, Mete expressed organizational innovation as the innovation, correction and development activities that take place in the methods that businesses put forward in the operation of their administrative and organizational processes integrated with all their system formations in their active commercial lives.

Innovation, which can be defined simply as the driving force of economic development and competitiveness for businesses, is defined in the Oslo Manual as 'the implementation of a new or significantly improved product (good or service) or process, a new marketing method or a new organizational method in internal business practices, workplace organization or external relations' [11]. The definition given to industrial innovation within the framework of the vision of the future in sustainable digital societies is to provide social and environmental benefits as well as economic benefits. In this respect, businesses that grasp the importance of innovation on the basis of internal processes and departments and implement it by developing it can manage and shape innovation. As can be seen, organizational innovation is one of the main lines of future businesses. At this point, the biggest breakthroughs to be made within the organization, such as commercial practices and workplace planning, fall within the scope of organizational innovation. Toyota is a good example of organizational innovation, offering continuous improvement and development responsibility to the person who does the work as a way of realizing the low cost-high quality principle [12].

In this light, organizational innovation emerges as a critical dimension of innovation activity, particularly in the context of adapting internal structures and processes to the evolving demands of digital transformation. It goes beyond technological upgrades and reflects a deliberate and strategic effort to redesign how an organization functions at all levels. Organizational innovation can be broadly understood as the systematic implementation of new managerial ideas, structural configurations, and operational practices that aim to increase efficiency, generate added value for customers, foster the development of novel products and services, and enhance the organization's overall adaptability and responsiveness to external changes [13]. It entails not only the redesign of business processes, but also the transformation of internal culture, employee engagement, and the diffusion of innovative thinking across departments. As emphasized by Weerawardena [14], innovation within organizations functions through specific mechanisms that enable individuals and teams to identify opportunities, generate creative solutions, and translate them into actionable improvements. These mechanisms form the backbone of innovation management and are essential for embedding innovation into the organizational routine. Morone and Testa [15] further conceptualize organizational innovation as a process of deep structural transformation, including the integration of new knowledge, technologies, and institutional arrangements. Such changes are necessary for organizations to adapt proactively to dynamic market environments, technological disruption, and shifting stakeholder expectations. In this regard, organizational innovation is not only a facilitator of competitive advantage, but also a prerequisite for long-term organizational sustainability and resilience.

Building on this conceptual foundation, it becomes evident that organizational innovation must be operationalized through concrete mechanisms that directly address the practical challenges faced by enterprises in the context of digital transformation. In this regard, the present literature analysis identifies three core organizational domains—labor, management, and supply chain—as critical focal points where structural and functional difficulties tend to concentrate. These patterns represent not only the primary areas affected by technological and organizational change, but also the most promising entry points for innovation-driven interventions. By systematically examining the nature of challenges within these components, the study contributes to the formulation of integrated approaches aimed at fostering resilience, operational efficiency, and strategic alignment in industrial enterprises undergoing digital transformation.

Despite the growing body of literature on digital transformation, there remains a significant gap in the systematic examination of the organizational dimension of this process. Particularly underexplored is the role of organizational innovation as a mediating and enabling mechanism in overcoming the structural, procedural, and cultural obstacles posed by digitalization. Organizational innovation—encompassing new managerial practices, redesign of workflows, and development of collaborative and adaptive cultures—is increasingly recognized as the linchpin of successful digital transition. Yet, the interplay between organizational innovation and the concrete difficulties faced by enterprises in different sectors, regions, and operational contexts requires further investigation.

This study aims to address this gap by offering a structured synthesis of recent scholarly contributions that examine organizational challenges in the digital transformation process from the perspective of organizational innovation. By classifying these challenges into thematic categories—labor, management, and supply chain—the study provides a nuanced analytical framework that not only enhances conceptual clarity but also offers practical value for industry stakeholders.

In line with the outlined theoretical framework and the identified focal areas of organizational innovation, the present study is guided by the following research questions: What types of organizational challenges are encountered by industrial enterprises in the context of digital transformation? How can these challenges be interpreted and analyzed through the lens of organizational innovation as a strategic response mechanism? What evidence-based recommendations can be proposed to effectively address and mitigate the organizational difficulties faced by industrial enterprises during the transformation process? These questions aim to provide a comprehensive understanding of how innovation-oriented organizational restructuring can support sustainable digital transformation in industrial settings.

It is posited that the outcomes of this research will serve as a foundational reference point for further academic inquiry and as a strategic guide for enterprises navigating the path toward sustainable digital transformation.

2 Methods and Data

The present study employs a qualitative, structured literature review approach aimed at identifying and analyzing organizational challenges encountered by industrial enterprises in the context of digital transformation. The primary objective of the review is to classify and interpret these challenges through the conceptual lens of organizational innovation.

2.1 Selection of Sources

The selection of academic publications was conducted using the scientific platform Google Scholar. The keyword combinations used for search queries included: "organizational challenges," "digital transformation," "organizational innovation," "Industry 4.0 and 5.0," "innovation management," and "industrial enterprises." The search was limited to peer-reviewed publications and research reports relevant to the industrial and organizational transformation context. Both qualitative and conceptual studies were included. The language of publication was required to be English to ensure interpretability and methodological consistency. Publication date is not strictly limited but preference is given to recent studies (from 2010 onward) to capture up-to-date developments and trends.

2.2 Inclusion and Exclusion Criteria

To ensure the conceptual coherence and analytical relevance of the literature review, a set of predefined inclusion and exclusion criteria was applied to all initially retrieved sources. These criteria were used to narrow down the scope of the review and select only those publications that provide meaningful insights into organizational challenges within the context of digital transformation, analyzed through the lens of organizational innovation.

Inclusion criteria:

- The study must explicitly address organizational problems or barriers faced by industrial or business enterprises.
- The content must be related to or situated within the context of digital transformation, Industry 4.0/5.0, or innovation management.
- The publication must contain qualitative or conceptual analysis of organizational processes, structures, or behaviors.
- The article must contribute empirical or theoretical insights relevant to one or more of the following organizational domains: labor, management, or supply chain.

Exclusion criteria:

- Studies focused solely on technological, engineering, or IT-specific aspects without a discussion of organizational implications were excluded.

- Articles examining consumer behavior, marketing strategies, or external market factors without linking them to internal organizational dynamics were not considered.
- Publications lacking methodological transparency or analytical depth (e.g., editorials, opinion pieces, blog posts) were omitted.
- Duplicates, inaccessible full texts, or non-peer-reviewed materials were excluded from further analysis.

Following the application of these criteria, seven publications were selected as the final dataset for in-depth examination. These studies provided a diverse but thematically unified foundation for identifying, categorizing, and interpreting organizational challenges relevant to the digital transformation of industrial enterprises. These studies span various sectors and regions, and reflect diverse perspectives on organizational challenges, including workforce dynamics, managerial restructuring, innovation practices, and supply chain adaptation. The final set of publications selected for detailed analysis includes the works of Rinsky-Halivni et al. [16], Bäcklund et al. [14], Agostini and Filippini [17], Namousi and Kohl [18], Kemendi et al. [19], Rodríguez and Lorenzo [20], and Carlsson et al. [21].

2.3 Analytical Framework

To systematize the findings, a deductive thematic analysis was applied. First, the content of each publication was reviewed to extract explicitly stated organizational problems. Second, these challenges were categorized according to three organizational domains, which were determined based on their recurrence and relevance in the reviewed literature: Labor-related challenges (e.g., aging workforce, competency gaps, cultural adaptation); Management-related challenges (e.g., structural inertia, innovation diffusion, leadership overload); Supply chain-related challenges (e.g., integration issues, responsiveness, information asymmetry).

The extracted data were then compared and synthesized to identify patterns, overlaps, and specific problem types, as well as to uncover the underlying mechanisms through which organizational innovation could serve as a mitigating or enabling factor.

2.4 Assumptions and Limitations

This literature review is based on a structured and purposeful selection of academic publications addressing organizational challenges within the context of digital transformation. To ensure methodological transparency, several key assumptions and limitations are acknowledged.

Assumptions It is assumed that the selected sources represent scientifically valid and peer-reviewed contributions, offering theoretically grounded insights into the organizational aspects of digital transformation. The review further presumes a sufficient conceptual alignment across the included studies, particularly with regard to key categories such as organizational innovation, managerial restructuring, and workforce adaptation. It is also assumed that, despite sectoral and regional differences, the organizational challenges identified in the publications are comparable and analytically transferable.

Limitations First, the number of analyzed publications is limited to seven, which, while selected according to rigorous inclusion criteria, may limit the generalizability of findings. Second, the review is qualitative in nature and does not involve statistical or meta-analytical methods, thus limiting the potential for quantitative synthesis or hypothesis testing. Third, the contextual diversity of the sources—spanning various industries and countries—may introduce heterogeneity in the interpretation of organizational challenges. Fourth, the temporal scope includes both recent and earlier studies; although this enhances theoretical breadth, it may also reflect varying stages of digital transformation across cases. Lastly, the analysis is confined to publicly available peer-reviewed literature and does not incorporate empirical data from practice. Future research may extend the analysis by incorporating quantitative meta-analytical techniques or expanding the dataset across additional regions and industries.

These assumptions and limitations define the scope of the current study and should be taken into consideration when interpreting the results and their applicability to broader organizational contexts.

3 Results

The results of the conducted literature review, focused primarily on publications from the last years in light of the accelerated pace of digital innovation, reveal a noticeable research gap in the systematic examination of organizational challenges associated with digital transformation. While a growing body of literature addresses digital technologies and innovation management, relatively few studies explore the organizational dimension of this transformation in a comprehensive and structured manner. Among the available sources, most research tends to concentrate on specific organizational subsystems, such as the workforce or managerial structures, often within particular sectors or national contexts. These studies, although valuable, frequently provide fragmented insights or case-specific conclusions, limiting their generalizability across industries and regions.

The present study analyzes seven selected publications, which collectively encompass a diverse range of organizational problems observed in enterprises across different regions, industries, and operational environments. These works form the empirical and conceptual foundation for the classification and interpretation of organizational challenges through the lens of organizational innovation. The selected publications include:

1. In the study by Rinsky-Halivni et al. [16], data from organizations with varying ownership structures and sectoral affiliations were analyzed through the lens of challenges posed by an aging workforce. The authors identified five levels of organizational difficulties, categorized as follows: *individual employee*, *work environment*, *team relations*, *organizational level*, and *community level*.
2. In their research focused on a large real estate company undergoing multiple initiatives in digital transformation, Bäcklund et al. [14] examined a range of operational challenges. These were articulated as: *top-down over-diffusion of innovation*, *lack of cross-functional innovation*, *lack of user-centered innovation*, *discontinuities in the innovation process and unclear roles of innovators*, *insufficient communication with innovation stakeholders*, *lack of time and resources for innovation and new technologies*, as well as *uncertainties in the implementation of technological solutions*.
3. In a study of Italian manufacturing firms, Agostini and Filippini [17] addressed organizational challenges from a supply chain perspective. The difficulties identified included issues related to *just-in-time (JIT) coordination with suppliers and clients* and *integration of information flows*.
4. The study by Namousi and Kohl [18] investigated organizational challenges arising in the context of rapid growth in startups. Identified problems included *managerial overload*, *absence of clearly defined functional or project leadership*, and *ambiguity in employee roles and responsibilities*.
5. In the study conducted by Kemendi et al. [19] on small and medium-sized enterprises (SMEs) within the European Union, organizational challenges were examined in the context of Industry 4.0 and 5.0 transformations. The key issues included *risk perception in technology adoption* and *ethical concerns in human-robot interaction*.
6. The work of Rodríguez and Lorenzo [20] focused on organizational challenges associated with open innovation practices. Noted problems included *difficulties in seeking external ideas and knowledge*, *networking limitations*, *retention of untapped ideas within the company*, and *barriers to effective commercialization of innovations*.
7. In their investigation of industrial digitalization challenges in manufacturing firms, Carlsson et al. [21] identified critical issues related to *adaptive organizational culture*, *learning processes*, and *competence development*. These were recognized as key impediments to leveraging advanced technologies within organizational settings.

All identified problems were grouped according to their primary organizational actors and associating them with the three components of the organization, namely workforce, management and supply chain. Similar problems in the publications analyzed as data sources were eliminated. As a result, the organizational components expressed as the main actors and the problems presented within these frameworks were grouped in Table 1. Each problem was defined and discussed, and possible solution suggestions were presented by adhering to the relevant literature.

3.1 Organizational Challenges from Workforce Perspective

Individual Employee In terms of individual employees, two basic sub-problems have been identified as health loss and negative attitudes. It has been found that individual decline in understanding, memory, concentration, acquisition, skills and comprehensive data management, which result from age-related health problems, cause a decrease in labor productivity, quality and competence. In addition to health loss, the fatigue felt due to monotonous work for years and the burnout caused by work pressure result in unhappiness and frustration. The physical and psychological decline of employees represents a loss of human capital in terms of improving the

Table 1 Key organizational challenges in industrial enterprises

Groups	Organizational challenges
Challenges from a workforce perspective	Individual employee factors Work environment conditions Team relations and dynamics Organizational-level issues Community-level challenges Undefined or ambiguous employee roles Risk perception in organizational contexts Ethical and operational issues in human–robot interaction Challenges in developing an adaptive organizational culture Organizational learning constraints Competence gaps and skill mismatches
Challenges from managerial perspective	Problem of top-down diffusion of innovation Lack of interfunctional innovation Lack of user-centered innovation Discontinuities in the innovation process and unclear roles of innovators Insufficient communication with innovation stakeholders Lack of time and resources for innovation and new technologies Difficulties and uncertainties in the implementation of technology Managerial overload Absence of clearly defined functional or project management Search for external ideas and knowledge Networking limitations Retention of untapped ideas within the organization Barriers to commercialization of innovations
Challenges from supply chain perspective	Just-in-time coordination with clients Just-in-time coordination with suppliers Integration of information flows

sustainable processes of the business and producing innovative solutions and teamwork. In our age, the complexity, difficulty and various stress factors brought about by the digital revolution led to physical and mental burnout not only in aging individuals but also in working young individuals.

Work Environment We can evaluate today's working world as two poles, which are getting harder and easier in terms of working environments. In geographies that are technologically backward or have not caught up with digital transformation, the existence of mistreatments such as injustice, no worker rights, no work safety, no work health, unhealthy nutrition, inequalities, negative human relations and in hierarchical relations undermine human dignity and psychological well-being, sometimes leading to physical harm. Beyond this negative pole, in geographies where developed or advanced technology exists, in addition to overtime, stress, and work safety problems in businesses that have not yet fully reached ideal ease and comfort, the use of technology itself has, in some cases, become a source of difficulty in some sectors, preventing the productivity of the professional individual.

Team Relations The main problem here is caused by laziness and irresponsibility. Reasons such as deficiencies in sharing, organizing and planning the work and the lack of a sense of duty make the distribution of workload unbalanced among the employees. This kind of organizational problem causes high employee turnover, especially in terms of young individuals, that is, it causes the business to lose employees frequently in the short term. This negative atmosphere spreads to the team or teams in the organization. As relational demoralization, generation conflicts, mutual influence and sharp differences between individuals cause disorder in the organization and ultimately loss in work efficiency.

Organizational Level Negativities such as costs related to health and aging within the organization, unnecessary human resources, incorrect planning and strategic error expenditures, and inability to manage risk are other aspects of organizational problems.

Community Level The problem addressed at this level in the relevant literature is a lack of systematic communication between the occupational physician and the organization regarding the adequacy of the workforce.

Loose Employee Roles Failure to assign the right employees to appropriate positions, the efficiency of the organization decreases. Experienced operations directors and HR specialists are needed to prevent mistakes in recruitment and constant position shifting. Otherwise, managers will be frustrated due to organizational disruption.

Risk Perception Issues Digital transformation is reshaping risk perceptions. The complex technologies that create this are increasing requirements. Industry may see existing and traditional positions and processes at risk. Technological labor shortages are a serious risk. The variation in experience, productivity and physical abilities of employees in production processes in the organization poses a challenge [22]. Risk and control challenges in the organizational structure reinforce the importance of risk management. This requires digital literacy and skills, and the collaboration of digital education with new technological processes. Management needs to redesign tasks and responsibilities within the organizational innovation.

Ethical Issues in Human-Robot Relations In the digital transformation process that is experienced suddenly without certain strategic, planned transformation and change preparations and processes, various psychological and ethical work problems arise between robots that assume integrated, standard, fast and difficult roles and humans. The most obvious example is the decrease in labor demand due to machines replacing humans. Now, digital transformation puts pressure on qualified labor [23]. Digital transformation in businesses in different sectors depends on organizational innovation as well as many quantitative and qualitative changes.

Adaptive Culture Adaptable culture refers to the difficulty of collectively organizing talent, interest, knowledge and understanding to adopt and implement the digitalization initiative. The difficulty in adopting industrial digitalization arises from the indifference, ignorance and inadequacy of the segment that will be adapted to the transformation. A system will be required where indifference can be addressed by participating in digitalization; ignorance will be eliminated by teaching the effects and outputs of digitalization and innovation with the right methods; and inadequacy will be completed with comprehensive technological initiatives in the entire organization in practice. In the perspective of these components, resolving the meaning problem of the organization towards digital transformation comes to the fore. For this, it should be explained what is required for innovation in business, the benefits of innovative production, and the ease, efficiency, quality and savings that digital systems will provide in the organizational structure instead of traditional systems. It is difficult to organize and ensure the sustainability of digital transformation culture adaptation. Employees coming from traditional cultures can transfer adaptation and adaptation responsibilities to others, avoid change or do not trust. The deficiencies in the adaptation roadmap and rules of digital transformation culture should be eliminated.

Learning Learning reveals concepts related to the ways and methods of digital transformation initiatives in the industry. Learning includes understanding decisions, motivation, vision and benefits. We can claim that learning will eliminate the problem of trust in the system and structure. In digital transformation, fait accompli changes and transitions made without training business employees, without measuring their perception, without knowledge and belief in digital systems and without preparing them will create a problem of suspicion and trust in the digitalized organizational structure. At this point, the obstacle of doing nothing will arise against the risk of making mistakes in digital applications with rigid functioning.

Competence The gap in knowing what kind of competence employees in businesses that will adapt technology and provide innovation in the digital transformation process need to have in order to overcome the challenges that will be encountered in industrial digitalization is the competence challenge. In order to acquire and develop competence, time, place and strategy are required. Another problem is the possible disinterest of older employees who come from a classical, or rather manual, culture in acquiring competence. For this, an innovative workforce change may also be required in the organization. For example, in organizational innovation, uncertainty about how I4.0 and I5.0 technologies will be used and how and by whom the applications will be managed and controlled needs to be resolved. It should be clear and explicit who is responsible for industrial digitalization and organizational innovation in the business.

3.2 Organizational Challenges from Managerial Perspective

The Problem of Diffusion of Innovation from Top to Bottom The situation where innovation itself does not spread effectively in the organizational hierarchy due to the difficulties that permeate the organization is defined as the difficulties associated with top-down innovation. In other words, it is expressed as the problem of implementation of innovation. In this context, the most fundamental difficulty is that innovations remain under the control of upper management and units affiliated with upper management and cannot be reduced to the employee level.

To prevent innovation from remaining as a project in the brain of the business in the context of innovation implementation, innovation should be disseminated from top to bottom to the user level in the system that can be described as an innovation pyramid. In the pyramid of needs related to the innovation flow, needs should be systematically determined, and solutions should be sought down to the end user. Innovation should be accessible and applicable at all levels from top to bottom.

The Problem of Lack of Interfunctional Innovation In the organizational structure of companies, when there are multiple development processes for each department and an inclusive innovation process for the entire company, difficulties arise in the coordination of interfunctional innovations. Because the importance given to digitalization varies among business units, uncertainty and cooperation confusion arise in the perception of digitalization. The problem of digital chaos occurs as a result of operational units acting independently and separately in terms of technology application and innovation, which produces multiple independent solutions to the same problem. Thus, the difficulty of controlling multiple independent technological systems and multiple data security risks arise.

Interfunctional coordination should be established in the solution of this organizational problem. For this, the costs for solutions must be determined and new resources must be allocated.

Lack of User-Centered Innovation The lack of purpose, direction and involvement of operational personnel in the innovation process create difficulties in determining and solving needs. The organizational disconnection in the business between the developer and the implementer and inability to understand innovation create a gap in the end users. This situation prevents the development of solution center digital tools such as applications that provide architectural visualization using virtual reality.

At this point, in the technology development process targeting the user, a coordinated connection must be established between the business development and operations unit in the organization.

Discontinuities in the Innovation Process and Ambiguity in the Roles of Innovators The innovation process itself is a challenge. It is difficult to scale organizational innovation in particular. The limitations of basic functions in the innovation process and the uncertainty of responsibilities for innovation projects and applications pose a challenge.

In order to adopt digitalization, it is necessary to clarify every stage of the innovation process from top to bottom. Application duties and responsibilities and application effectiveness should be defined. For example, the effectiveness of using IoT devices in the organizational process should be understood. In this context, new roles will be defined in smart organizations.

Lack of Communication to Innovation Stakeholders The communication frequencies and communication links within the units of a business may be different. For example, the communication patterns of the white-collar project innovation team with each other and the communication structure between the team managing the operational process show contradictory differences. The differences in access to and dissemination of information within the organization create problems in the understanding and implementation of innovation. For this purpose, innovative communication tools and methods should be used in the organization.

The Problem of Lack of Time and Resources for Innovation and New Technologies The chaotic operations of many businesses in organizational, administrative, operational and various areas cause them not to allocate enough time to innovation. For many managers, the time to be allocated for innovation is considered a concept that can be risked or not dared to be spent in the spiral of more production and profit. Innovative ideas in draft form are seen as an even more challenging responsibility to the already heavy workload. In addition, the fact that the digitalization process requires adaptation and adjustment at every level from top to bottom also creates a resource problem.

The direct solution to this problem is to allocate time and resources. This requires a commitment to top-down transformation.

Difficulties and Uncertainties in Operational Processes Related to the Implementation of Technology There may be difficulties in the implementation of innovation and in the subsequent process management within the organizational units. Fundamental issues such as implementation, training and follow-up remain largely unsolved. There is a lack of clarity regarding the implementation and effects of innovation in operational processes. In general, operational employees tend to turn to simple solutions instead of systems that require complex knowledge. Digital functions of the IT system, such as data and passwords, can be a stress burden for personnel. Therefore, the general and familiar operational and organizational process is manual. At this point, it is not desired for digitalization and innovative applications to replace the professional experiences and intuitions that the individual has gained over time.

In order for innovative applications to be included in the organization during the digital transformation process, operational personnel must be included in the organizational innovation process and given holistic adaptation and training on the use of digital technologies.

Management is Overwhelmed by Workload In the growing and developing business world, managing businesses that undergo digital transformation with new information brings an administrative burden that is difficult to follow due to diversified job duties and positions. This situation, which creates stress accumulation on business management, directly or indirectly causes organizational problems. As a result of this problem, suspended projects, unfinished projects, planning problems can be shown. For this reason, potential gains are lost, and even financial losses occur. In addition, this situation can cause managers to burnout, break employee faith and create disappointment. At this point, innovative organizational solutions can be used to analyze and organize the workload.

The Problem of not Having a Clear Function or Project Manager The lack of a specific project manager for a specific plan, strategy and purpose is a serious problem. This lack of leadership will primarily affect team awareness and potential efficiency for the project in question. Indirect assignments without authority to project management cannot be seen as a solution because they mean putting the project at risk. On the other hand, uncertainty of authority between the project management and upper management causes employee insecurity and the project ends inefficiency or failure. This situation also constitutes a usurpation of rights for the project manager.

The only rational way to prevent this situation is to determine the duties and responsibilities of competent managers for each function in the organization through an innovative decision-making process.

Searching for Valuable Ideas and Information Outside This type of problem is the cost of acquiring the information required for innovation. A budget needs to be created for organizational innovations.

Networking Problem The technical knowledge obtained from numerous participating technologies, such as in the aircraft and space industry, the participation of companies in project coordination is a serious function that needs to be handled [24]. In this context, efficient collaboration requires organizational innovation that adds value to innovative companies and customers.

Ideas Left within the Company Potential ideas and information that have not been put on the market and developed need to be evaluated within the organizational process. In addition, the exit of the workforce needs to be prevented. In this way, the escape of ideas and information that can turn into a competitor company will be prevented. It is necessary to prevent the loss of profitability by including the idle capacity inside the company in the transformation process.

Commercialization Problem If innovations are exploited by rival companies, property rights may be damaged, making it difficult to profit from innovations. Self-protection should be ensured in the context of organizational renewal by giving importance to property rights, patent applications and product registrations.

3.3 Organizational Challenges from Supply Chain Perspective

JIT with Suppliers This problem includes organizational problems related to on-time deliveries and the relationship with the supplier. The product exchange processes between the supplier and the buyer must be carried out with smart systems.

JIT with Clients Innovative transformation is required in the organization where smart technologies are used for delivery and production programs that will fulfill the responsibility to the customer against sudden interruptions in production, prevent grievances, and ensure that the manufacturer delivers to the customer on time. For example, ERP [25], defined as advanced systems and software that bring together all the resources of a company and provide end-to-end management and efficiency.

Information Flow Integration The existence of a smart sharing system between production, delivery and supply enables the smooth functioning of the organization by providing real forecasting and data flow between the trade chain partners—distributors, wholesalers, retailers and the manufacturer. Smart technologies that enable monitoring and control of inventory data are an example of this.

4 Discussion

The findings of this literature review provide important insights into the organizational challenges that industrial enterprises face in the context of digital transformation and underscore the central role of organizational innovation in overcoming these difficulties. By synthesizing results from diverse studies, the research highlights how structural, cultural, managerial, and operational factors converge to form complex barriers that inhibit the effective implementation of digital technologies.

A key observation is the systemic nature of organizational challenges, which do not arise from isolated deficiencies, but rather from interrelated constraints within the domains of labor, management, and the supply chain. Issues such as the aging workforce, insufficient digital competencies, resistance to innovation, lack of coordination across functions, and technological fragmentation reflect deeply embedded limitations in organizational capacity and adaptability. These findings reinforce the argument that digital transformation is not merely a technical upgrade, but a comprehensive process of organizational renewal.

From the perspective of organizational innovation, the reviewed studies support the view that internal transformation must precede or accompany digitalization. Innovation in organizational structures—such as role clarity, team-based collaboration, learning mechanisms, and flexible hierarchies—emerges as a prerequisite for sustainable digital change. Notably, several studies emphasized that without a cultural shift and leadership commitment, even well-funded digital transformation initiatives fail to generate lasting impact. This supports prior theoretical work asserting the interdependence between technological innovation and organizational adaptability.

Moreover, the review reveals sectoral and contextual specificity in the manifestation of organizational challenges. For instance, the problems experienced by manufacturing enterprises differ from those faced by service-based or startup firms, particularly with respect to supply chain complexity or managerial overload during rapid scaling. This indicates the need for tailored organizational innovation strategies, sensitive to the institutional, cultural, and operational realities of each enterprise.

The discussion also points to a critical gap in the existing literature—namely, the lack of integrative frameworks that systematically link organizational innovation to digital transformation outcomes. While many studies acknowledge the role of innovation, few offer operational models or strategic roadmaps for its implementation in real-world settings. This suggests that future research should move beyond problem identification toward the development of actionable tools and performance metrics that guide enterprises in aligning their innovation processes with digital transformation goals.

Taken together, the findings suggest that organizational innovation is not only a response to digital transformation pressures but also a strategic capacity that enables organizations to shape and direct their own transformation trajectories.

Building upon the findings of this review, it becomes evident that the successful implementation of digital transformation requires more than isolated technical solutions—it demands a holistic rethinking of the organization's operational logic, human capital development, and value creation mechanisms. While the literature confirms the centrality of organizational innovation as a response to internal structural challenges, it also underscores the transformative power of digital technologies themselves. Thus, a broader view is needed—one that integrates organizational innovation with the strategic deployment of digital tools. In this regard, recent studies emphasize the systemic nature of digital transformation as a process that reshapes not only processes and workflows, but also business models and employee capabilities.

Digital transformation is a comprehensive process in which organizations use digital technologies to fundamentally change their operations, business models and value creation approaches. Digital transformation involves restructuring internal processes, adopting new agile and collaborative working methods and developing digital skills of the workforce [26]. Innovation has an organic life with digital transformation. In the process of innovative transformation, companies cannot remain efficient in current conditions, especially in operational processes, and cannot take a sustainable step into the future without digital applications. Digital transformation enables companies to develop their capabilities, increase their reach and returns across asset and operational value chains. Companies should focus on developing future talent in the digital age to ensure long-term success and adjust competencies to company conditions, global trends, phenomena and organizational urgency to survive and be competitive.

In today's globalizing world, which is transitioning to the space age, innovation is the only way out that provides companies with technological tools to find solutions to organizational challenges, thus making companies competitive and sustainable. Accounting software, organizational tools for information exchange and sharing, scheduling and brainstorming tools, data visualization and next-generation presentations, competitive analysis tools, business models, risk management, Document Management System (DMS), Customer Relationship Management (CRM) Tools, Customer Data Platform (CDP), Business Process Management (BPM) Software, Enterprise Resource Planning (ERP) Software, Content Management System (CMS), Data Analytics Tools, Collaboration Tools, Project Management Tools, robots, sensors, facial recognition technologies that increase human-machine interaction, automatic handling and stocking systems, satellite tracking systems, and many other technologies allow companies to develop their capabilities and increase their asset and operational values. In addition to this reality, the ability to implement trend technologies that shape digital transformation from a technological perspective also brings new challenges to light for companies [27].

In the digital transformation process, innovation optimizes organizational processes, provides cost savings and eliminates organizational problems with its many benefits. Companies know that digital transformation technologies will be used as training tools that will enable employees to make informed decisions. In order to adopt and use digital technologies, employees need to acquire the right skills. This process, which requires investment, can be challenging due to the resources required. For example, in order to digitize customer service management, the company will have to hire experts to ensure that employees acquire the skills and knowledge to use the relevant innovations by providing the relevant adaptation, and to ensure trust, interest and perception in the benefits of digital transformation [9]. At this point, new budget items will arise for workforce renewal and transformation costs.

Therefore, the right plans and strategies are essential to ensure innovation in the organizational structure during the digital transformation process. For example, employees need to understand and experience that artificial intelligence has advanced data processing and decision-making capabilities, and thus optimizes operations and increases efficiency. Similarly, the workforce that understands the necessity of using ISR, which reduces costs and production times by increasing efficiency and precision in production lines and operational processes, will provide innovation in the organization.

Organizational processes such as manufacturing are being transformed by the digital revolution, which enables an efficient and healthy work environment. The use of digital technologies enables operational excellence, risk management and the elimination of managerial deficiencies and inefficiencies. Ultimately, it increases efficiency by improving the workforce, supply and management.

5 Conclusion

This study aimed to examine the organizational challenges that industrial enterprises encounter in the process of digital transformation, and to interpret these challenges through the lens of organizational innovation. By conducting a structured review of selected academic publications, the research sought to address three interrelated questions: (1) What are the key organizational difficulties faced by industrial enterprises? (2) How can these difficulties be understood from the perspective of organizational innovation within the context of digital transformation? (3) What strategic insights and recommendations can be offered to overcome such challenges?

The analysis revealed that organizational problems are concentrated in three major domains: labor, management, and the supply chain. Within these domains, the challenges range from competency gaps, cultural resistance, and role ambiguity to structural inertia, communication breakdowns, and technological integration failures. These difficulties are not isolated or technical in nature; rather, they are systemic and deeply embedded in the internal dynamics of enterprises undergoing transformation.

A key finding of the study is that organizational innovation serves as both a necessary condition and an enabler of successful digital transformation. Innovation-oriented restructuring—characterized by adaptive leadership, collaborative culture, flexible structures, and continuous learning—emerges as a critical response mechanism to the multifaceted challenges identified. The reviewed literature consistently highlights that technological change alone is insufficient; without parallel organizational innovation, digital initiatives are unlikely to be sustainable or effective.

In a rapidly evolving global environment, where digital technologies redefine the principles of industrial competitiveness, the integration of digital transformation with organizational innovation is no longer optional but essential. Enterprises that embrace this dual imperative will be better positioned to navigate complexity, adapt to change, and sustain long-term growth.

The study contributes to the theoretical understanding of how digital transformation interacts with internal organizational processes and offers a conceptual foundation for future empirical research. For practitioners, the results provide a diagnostic framework for identifying critical pressure points and designing targeted interventions aimed at enhancing organizational resilience and performance.

References

1. Teng, X., Wu, Z., & Yang, F. (2022). Research on the relationship between digital transformation and performance of SMEs. *Sustainability, 14*(10), 6012. https://doi.org/10.3390/su14106012
2. Vial, G. (2021). Understanding digital transformation: A review and a research agenda. In *Managing digital transformation* (pp. 13–66). Routledge. https://doi.org/10.4324/9781003008637-4
3. Huang, L. H., Zhu, H. L., Liu, W. H., Dou, Y. F., Wang, J. Z., Cai, L., & Xie, K. (2021). Enterprise digital transformation and management: Research framework and outlook. *Journal of Management Science, 24*, 26–35.
4. Zhou, Y., Chen, L., Zhou, X., & Hu, S. (2024). Key factors and path selection for enterprise digital transformation: Configuration analysis based on fsQCA. *Frontiers in Sustainability, 5*, 1366129. https://doi.org/10.3389/frsus.2024.1366129
5. González-Varona, J. M., López-Paredes, A., Poza, D., & Acebes, F. (2021). Building and development of an organizational competence for digital transformation in SMEs. *Journal of Industrial Engineering and Management, 14*(1), 15–24. https://doi.org/10.3926/jiem.3279
6. Xiufan, Z., & Decheng, F. (2024). Research on digital transformation and organizational innovation of manufacturing firms based on knowledge field. *Journal of the Knowledge Economy, 15*, 15860–15903. https://doi.org/10.1007/s13132-023-01703-0
7. Kaganer, E., Gregory, R. W., & Sarker, S. (2023). A process for managing digital transformation: An organizational inertia perspective. *Journal of the Association for Information Systems, 24*(4), 1005–1030. https://doi.org/10.17705/1jais.00819
8. McKinsey & Company. (2018). *Unlocking success in digital transformations*. Retrieved from https://www.mckinsey.com/business-functions/organization/our-insights/unlocking-success-in-digital-transformations
9. Al-Ayed, S. I., Al-Tit, A. A., & Alashjaee, A. (2023). The effect of digital transformation on organizational performance by a mediating role of digital innovation. *Migration Letters, 20*(7), 380–394. https://doi.org/10.59670/ml.v20i7.4313
10. Mete, N. (2019). İşletmelerde kurumsallaşma ve inovasyon arasındaki ilişkinin incelenmesi üzerine bir araştırma (Master's thesis, Pamukkale University, Social Sciences Institute).
11. OECD, & Eurostat. (2005). *Oslo manual: Guidelines for collecting and interpreting innovation data* (3rd ed.). OECD Publishing. https://doi.org/10.1787/9789264013100-en
12. Marchwinski, C., Shook, J., & Schroeder, A. (2011). *Yalın Kavramlar Sözlüğü: Yalın Düşünürler için Şekilli Sözlük*. Optimist Yayın.
13. Weerawardena, J. (2003). The role of marketing capability in innovation-based competitive strategy. *Journal of Strategic Marketing, 11*(1), 15–35. https://doi.org/10.1080/0965254032000096766
14. Bäcklund, K., Vigren, O., & Carlsson, J. (2024). Implementing digital innovations: Overcoming organizational challenges. *Developments in the Built Environment, 18*, 100436. https://doi.org/10.1016/j.dibe.2024.100436
15. Morone, P., & Testa, G. (2008). Firms' growth, size and innovation: An investigation into the Italian manufacturing sector. *Economics of Innovation and New Technology, 17*(4), 311–329. https://doi.org/10.1080/10438590701231160

16. Rinsky-Halivni, L., Hovav, B., Christiani, D. C., & Brammli-Greenberg, S. (2022). Aging workforce with reduced work capacity: From organizational challenges to successful accommodations sustaining productivity and Well-being. *Social Science & Medicine, 312*, 115369. https://doi.org/10.1016/j.socscimed.2022.115369
17. Agostini, L., & Filippini, R. (2019). Organizational and managerial challenges in the path toward industry 4.0. *European Journal of Innovation Management, 22*(3), 406–421. https://doi.org/10.1108/EJIM-02-2018-0030
18. Namousi, A., & Svenningsson Kohl, D. (2014). Managing organizational problems stemming from successful growth in startups (Report No. E 2014:076). Chalmers University of Technology.
19. Kemendi, Á., Michelberger, P., & Mesjasz-Lech, A. (2022). Industry 4.0 and 5.0—Organizational and competency challenges of enterprises. Polish. *Journal of Management Studies, 26*(2), 165–178. https://doi.org/10.17512/pjms.2022.26.2.13
20. Rodriguez, J. L., & Lorenzo, A. G. (2011). Open innovation: Organizational challenges of a new paradigm of innovation management. *European Research Studies Journal, 14*(1), 75–82.
21. Carlsson, L., Olsson, A. K., & Eriksson, K. (2022). Taking responsibility for industrial digitalization: Navigating organizational challenges. *Sustainability, 14*(2), 866. https://doi.org/10.3390/su14020866
22. Battini, D., Berti, N., Finco, S., Zennaro, I., & Das, A. (2022). Towards industry 5.0: A multi-objective job rotation model for an inclusive workforce. *International Journal of Production Economics, 250*, 108619.
23. Skare, M., de Obesso, M. D. L. M., & Ribeiro-Navarrete, S. (2023). Digital transformation and European small and medium enterprises (SMEs): A comparative study using digital economy and society index data. *International Journal of Information Management, 68*, 102594.
24. Zabala Martínez, J. M. (2009). *El desafío de la innovación abierta*. EL PAÍS. Retrieved from https://elpais.com/diario/2009/12/20/negocio/1261318472_850215.html
25. Haddara, M. (2014). ERP selection: The SMART way. *Procedia Technology, 16*, 394–403. https://doi.org/10.1016/j.protcy.2014.10.105
26. Vărzaru, A. A., & Bocean, C. G. (2024). Digital transformation and innovation: The influence of digital technologies on turnover from innovation activities and types of innovation. *Systems, 12*(9), 359. https://doi.org/10.3390/systems12090359
27. Mahraz, M. I., Benabbou, L., & Berrado, A. (2019). A systematic literature review of digital transformation. In *Proceedings of the international conference on industrial engineering and operations management* (pp. 917–931). IEOM Society.

Sustainable Industrial Development: An Analysis of Trends in the Case of Russia

Svetlana Kudryavtseva, Rustam Nurgaliev, Vepa Kakadzhanov, and Olga Minulina

Abstract The priority task of modern economic science is to search for a new vision on the issues of managing sustainable development of the industrial complex as an advanced link in scientific, technological and economic development, which justifies the importance and relevance of the topic of the article. The aim of the research is to study the trends of sustainable industrial development in the Russian economic system based on the use of economic and mathematical modeling tools. To conduct the study, in particular in the issues of modeling, the methods of descriptive statistics were used (calculation of average values of indicators, mode, median, standard deviation, coefficient of variation, asymmetry, excess, range of variation). To build economic and mathematical models describing trends and patterns of sustainable development of industry, a regression model and correlation diagrams were utilized. In general, the trends in Russian industry correspond to global trends and show an increase in industrial activity, with the exception of some negative aspects (a decrease in the share of knowledge-intensive and high-tech products in GDP in recent years, a slowdown in the growth rate of industrial production). A stable relationship was revealed between the growth of the share of knowledge-intensive and high-tech products in GDP and a decrease in the energy intensity of the Russian economy. The dynamics of industrial production in the Russian economy is characterized as stable and has a positive value, despite the recovery from the pandemic and the effects of anti-Russian sanctions; differentiation in industrial production among subtypes of economic activity is increasing; the manufacturing sector is steadily securing its leading role in the industrial development of the economy; the processes of growth in production efficiency are intensifying based on the use of an integrated lean manufacturing methodology through the transformation of corporate thinking, changes in management methods, modification of production processes and value creation models. The practical significance of the study lies in the development of analytical tools for assessing development trends in relation to

S. Kudryavtseva (✉) · R. Nurgaliev · V. Kakadzhanov · O. Minulina
Kazan National Research Technological University, Kazan, Russia
e-mail: KudryavtsevaSS@corp.knrtu.ru

F. Tao et al. (eds.), *Artificial Intelligence and Digital Transformation*, Lecture Notes in Information Systems and Organisation 78,
https://doi.org/10.1007/978-3-032-00118-4_19

Russian industry, which can be used in the development and improvement of programs for the structural modernization of the Russian economy and the implementation of technological sovereignty projects.

Keywords Sustainable development · Energy intensity of the economy · Industrial production index · Resource productivity · High-tech and science-intensive products

1 Introduction

A significant number of scientific papers are devoted to the issues of achieving sustainable development. In addition, this issue is becoming increasingly rooted in the practical activities of industrial enterprises, whose strategic documents are aimed at reaching the UN Sustainable Development Goals.

The ongoing transformation of technological process models, recognition of technological sovereignty and innovation policy as a key factor in economic and technological development, in this regard, shape the needs of science and industry in the development and implementation in business practice of new approaches to stimulating the achievement of sustainable growth of industrial enterprises and the industrial sector of the economy as a whole. Issues of managing sustainable industrial development in the context of new technical, economic and geopolitical challenges are becoming especially relevant.

It should be recognized that there is a demand for improving industrial policy instruments, forming an effective institutional innovation mechanism for the implementation and use of innovations, creating and developing resource-saving industries. The priority task of modern economic science is to find a new vision on the issues of managing the sustainable development of the industrial complex as an advanced link in scientific, technological and economic development, which justifies the importance and relevance of the topic of the article.

The purpose of the study is to reveal the trends of sustainable industrial development in the Russian economic system based on economic and mathematical modeling tools.

The purpose of the study forms a number of research objectives:

1. To analyze the trends of industrial development in national economic systems;
2. To identify patterns of achieving sustainable industrial development;
3. To study the interrelations of indicators of sustainable industrial development.

A distinctive feature of the proposed toolkit is its comprehensiveness and practical orientation, because, firstly, it has been tested on the example of the real sector of the economy of the national economic system (using the case of Russian industry), and secondly, it combines descriptive-correlation-regression methods of analysis, increasing the level of analytical nature of the research conducted.

2 Literature Review

The literature considers various aspects of achieving sustainable industrial development, their spectrum is very wide and diverse. For example, Sidorov [1] puts uncertainty and risks at the forefront, highlighting the need to develop indicators of sustainable development of the ecosystem, the monitoring of which is aimed at achieving a balance of the economic, environmental, managerial, social and technological subsystems of the enterprise. Theys [2] draws attention to the need to reduce the negative impact on nature by enterprises in the process of conducting production and business activities. In this definition, at the enterprise level, when achieving sustainable development, special attention is paid directly to the environmental component of the activity, which is complemented by the social and economic component [3, 4].

We believe that studying industrial development trends is impossible in the context of modern realities, which are determined by the issues of achieving sustainable development goals in combination with the deployment of the fourth industrial revolution. Here, the focus is on such aspects as positive and negative factors of Industry 4.0 and their impact on achieving sustainable industrial development, the development of an industrial production ecosystem, the introduction of digital industrial management technologies in achieving sustainable development goals and a number of other issues [5–9]. However, we believe that the study of sustainable industrial development trends in these works is more focused on the benefits of using Industry 4.0, which somewhat shifts the focus of the research from sustainable development towards scientific and technological progress and the impact of the fourth industrial revolution on the economic system as a whole.

Recently, such research topics as the role of small and medium-sized industrial enterprises in the development of the industrial complex of the economy, the study of the correlation between the trends of industrial development of individual regions and the global economy as a whole have become popular [10–14]. However, these studies represent a cross-section applicable to a separate geographic territory and their impact on the spatial development of industry as a whole is not clear.

A number of authors (see, e.g., [15, 16]) consider sustainable industrial development within the framework of the circular economy model, defining its advantages and prospects as the best development model in real conditions [17, 18]. However, most studies focusing on sustainable industrial development in the context of the circular economy, firstly, are presented using the example of individual territories, typically China; secondly, they focus on the environmental aspect of this issue, which does not allow for a comprehensive approach to assessing the achievement of sustainable industrial development as a whole.

In continuation of this topic, it seems interesting to study individual characteristics of industrial development from the standpoint of macroeconomic parameters, in particular, the change in energy intensity of economic systems as a collective category that reflects the direction of change in its sustainability from the standpoint of economic and environmental efficiency [19–21]. A number of studies reveal a pattern between the level of efficiency of the economic system as a whole and its energy consumption, resource productivity both in terms of individual geographic territories and in terms of economic sectors [22–24]. We emphasize that the study of heavy industry, its features, efficiency indicators, resource productivity and energy efficiency is more prevalent in research.

The problem of achieving sustainable development in industry is currently considered in a number of priority areas. There are examples of successful practices in the world to reduce the negative impact of industry on the environment. For example, one of the most polluting industries is ferrous metallurgy. The largest emissions of carbon dioxide in ferrous metallurgy are in sintering and blast furnace production. A radical reduction in carbon dioxide emissions in ferrous metallurgy can be achieved by replacing blast furnaces (rejection of coke) with direct reduction units using H2 as a fuel and reducing agent (rejection of CH4) and, as a result, the agglomeration process is eliminated (rejection of coke) and the oxygen converter production is eliminated.

However, we believe that for further improvement of scientific and methodological approaches to achieving sustainable development of industry, it is fundamentally important to reflect and analyze the achieved indicators in this area and study the specifics of the patterns of the relationship between the indicators of sustainable development, which will complement the existing research in this area.

3 Materials and Methods

Data from the World Bank [25] and Rosstat [26] were used as the information base for the study. The dynamic series for the studied indicators comprised the period from 2011 to 2022. Among the indicators, those were selected that characterize the trends in achieving sustainable industrial development: gross value added of industry, industrial production index, energy intensity of the economy, technological and intellectual products in terms of gross value added.

To conduct the study, in particular in matters of modeling, the methods of descriptive statistics were used (calculation of average values of indicators, mode, median, standard deviation, variation coefficient, asymmetry, excess, variation range).

The choice of descriptive statistics methods for analytical purposes is due to the fact that they allow us to identify and reveal general patterns of industrial development, determine the nature of these trends, the strength and depth of their dynamics.

To build economic and mathematical models describing the trends and patterns of sustainable industrial development, the regression model and correlation graphs were used.

The choice of methods of correlation and regression analysis when conducting research allows us to determine the connections between industrial development indicators and their mutual influence on each other.

The use of descriptive statistics methods in the analysis, as well as correlation charts, allows us to identify trends in industrial development, their characteristic features, conduct a comparative analysis in retrospect, and determine the relationships between indicators of industrial complex development.

However, it should be noted that, like any other research methods, the methods of descriptive statistics, as well as correlation and regression analysis, have their limitations. Firstly, it is not possible to build a longer-term dynamics of the estimated parameters of the development of Russian industry, which imposes its own limitations on the reliability of the conclusions obtained. Secondly, the selected methods do not allow taking into account the entire wide range of factors (external economic and internal factors) that influence the development of Russian industry. However, their use in this article can be considered as the first stage of an in-depth study of trends in the industrial complex of Russia, and the results obtained can be used in subsequent studies to identify deeper and more complex patterns and features of development based on more complex economic and mathematical models (VAR models, panel data models, structural equation models, and lagged variable models).

4 Results

The study of issues of achieving sustainable industrial development calls upon researchers to analyze comparative trends in the economy as a whole and individual industrial sectors in particular. The results of the comparative analysis of the general macroeconomic indicator—the growth rate of gross domestic product showed that, on average, for 2011–2021 (comparable official statistical data on international statistics are published with a delay of 2–3 years on average [25]) the average GDP growth rate in the Russian economy was 107%, which among the CIS countries corresponds to the level of Belarus—108.1%, Azerbaijan—109.2%. Among the CIS countries, the highest average GDP growth rates were observed in Uzbekistan—148.7%, Kyrgyzstan—129.8% and Kazakhstan—128.9%. Among the BRICS countries, the leading positions in average GDP growth rates were held by China—157.4%, India—146.4%. Among the rest of the countries, high average GDP growth rates in 2011–2021 were typical for Turkey—145.6%, Romania—122.3% and Poland—121.5%. On average, for 2011–2021, the average rate of industrial production index (IPI) in the Russian economy was 116.6%, which is slightly higher than the CIS successor countries and corresponds to the level of Moldova—113.6%, Kyrgyzstan—109.5%. Among the CIS countries, the highest average IPI rates were observed in Tajikistan—123.3%, Armenia—121.1% and Russia. Among the BRICS countries, the leading positions in average IPI rates were held by India—117.6% and Russia. Among the rest of the countries, high average IPI rates in 2011–2021 were typical for Turkey—149.4%, Romania—130.6% and Lithuania—128.3%. A more detailed analysis of the structure of the economy in the context of countries of the world showed the following results. The Russian economy has the highest values of the average gross value added generated in the industrial sector, including construction. According to the results of 2000–2022, the average share of gross value added of industry in the total value of added value was 30.7%. It should be noted that the BRICS countries demonstrated higher values of the share of gross value added of industry in the total value of added value: for example, the average value of this indicator in China was 29.5%, in Brazil—26.4% versus 20.1% in the USA and 19.3% in the countries of the European Union. Consequently, based on the presented dynamics of the analysis of this indicator, it can be concluded that in countries with high rates of industrial growth and, accordingly, added value, the share of gross value added of industry in the total value of added value of the economy is higher; this trend is more characteristic of the BRICS countries than of developed countries, in which the rate of economic growth is inferior to the similar indicator in the BRICS countries.

According to the results of 2022, the GDP in the Russian economy amounted to 153,435 billion rubles in current prices, but this is 2.1% less than the 2021 level. Gross value added (GVA) amounted to 139,122 billion rubles, which is 3.1% lower than the 2021 level. The slowdown in the growth rate of the Russian economy is associated with the general macroeconomic situation and the geopolitical situation in the world. In 2012–2022, the average GVA growth rate in the Russian economy was 101.1%. An analysis of the dynamics of industrial production rates showed that, in general, it is characterized by positive dynamics; for the period 2015–2022, the average value of the industrial production index (IPI) was 102.2%. However, in 2020, during the pandemic period, the IPP value was below 100% and amounted to 97.9%, in 2021, a rapid growth in production was recorded, when the IPP reached 106.3%. The strengthening of anti-Russian sanctions, as well as the unfavorable general political and macroeconomic market conditions, led to a slowdown in the industrial production index and a reduction in the indicator to 100.6% in 2022. Consideration of the dynamics of the IPP of large types of economic activity showed that, as usual, the highest average IPP value in 2015–2022 was noted in the manufacturing industry—102.9%, followed by enterprises in the energy sector—101.7% and enterprises in the manufacturing sector—101.5%. It should be noted that for all major types of economic activity, the average IPP value for the analyzed period was positive and indicated an expansion of production. A more detailed analysis of changes in the industrial production index by subtypes of economic activity revealed the following results. Firstly, there is a clear trend towards an increase in the average IPP value in 2022 compared to 2015—102% versus 98%, which is also confirmed by visual analysis using a span diagram.

Secondly, the differentiation of the rates of change in industrial production has increased, which is confirmed by the growth of the values of the range—from 84% in 2015 to 209% in 2022, the coefficient of variation—from 12% to 18%, asymmetry—from minus 2 to 5 and excess—from 6 to 40 (Table 1).

Thirdly, there was a shift in the distribution series of subtypes of economic activity—the left-sided asymmetry, in which the median value exceeded the arithmetic mean of the IPP (100% versus 98%) was replaced by a right-sided asymmetry of the

Table 1 Descriptive statistics of the IPP

Indicator	2015	2022
Mean value (%)	98.0	102.0
Median (%)	100.0	101.0
Minimum value (%)	39.0	49.0
Maximum value (%)	124.0	258.0
Range (%)	84.0	209.0
Standard deviation (%)	12.0	19.0
Variation coefficient	12.0	18.0
Asymmetry	−2.0	5.0
Kurtosis	6.0	40.0

IPP that increased in relative terms, in which the average value of the IPP was higher than the median—102% versus 101% (Fig. 1).

Speaking about industrial development trends, it is necessary to analyze its resource productivity. The latest statistics on resource productivity are available for 2021. Thus, in general, starting from 2018, the productivity of fuel and energy minerals increased from 124.2 rubles per 1 kg of standard fuel to 126.3 in 2021, while the maximum value of the indicator was recorded in 2020—132.1 rubles per 1 kg of standard fuel. The productivity of water resources, calculated as water resources taken from water bodies, also increased from 1.86 thousand rubles per 1 m^2 in 2018 to 2.10 in 2021 (the maximum value for the analyzed period); agricultural land—from 20.1 thousand rubles per hectare in 2018 to 20.6 in 2021 (with a maximum value of the indicator in 2020—20.9 thousand rubles per hectare); forest resources—from 4.7 thousand rubles per 1 m^2 in 2018 to 5.7 in 2021 (maximum value for the analyzed period); aquatic organisms—from 112.1 thousand rubles per ton in 2018 to 117.8 in 2021 in 2021 (maximum value for the analyzed period). It should be noted that the greatest increase in resource productivity was noted for forest resources—119.8% in 2021 relative to 2018 and water resources—113.1%. In the context of the analysis of industrial development, we analyze such an important macroeconomic indicator as the energy intensity of gross value added, which shows what volume of conventional fuel is used to obtain 10 thousand rubles of gross value added of the industrial sector. This indicator is inversely proportional, i.e. the lower the value of the energy intensity of GVA, the more efficiently the industry functions. Based on available official statistics, since 2012, the energy intensity of GVA has been steadily decreasing—from 130 kg of conventional fuel/10 thousand rubles to 57 kg of conventional fuel/10 thousand rubles in 2022, the average rate of decline was 7.8% annually. This hypothesis is also confirmed by the obtained linear regression equation with a negative regression coefficient of "minus" 6.5 at a level of statistical significance of the model of $P \leq 0.05$ and a determination coefficient of 0.97 (Fig. 2).

In addition, the descriptive statistics of energy intensity of GVA showed that this indicator has a normal distribution during the analyzed time period, with a low value of the variation coefficient—23% and the absence of asymmetry and excess, which

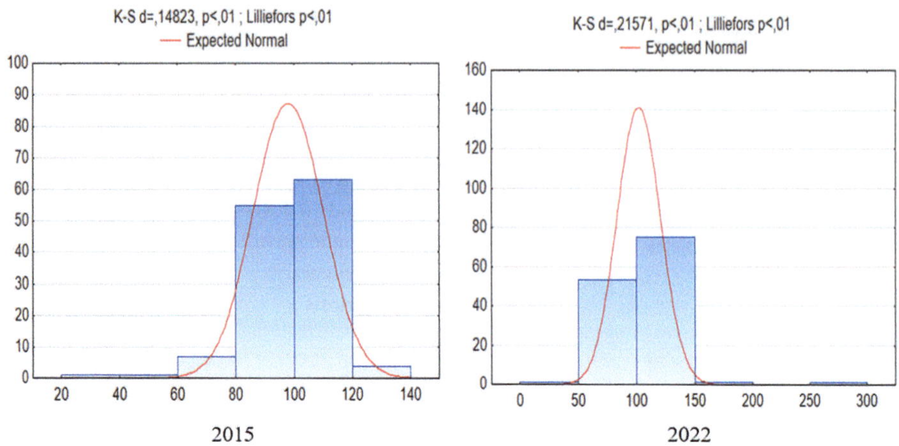

Fig. 1 Visualization of the asymmetry of the IPP distribution series in 2022 relative to 2015

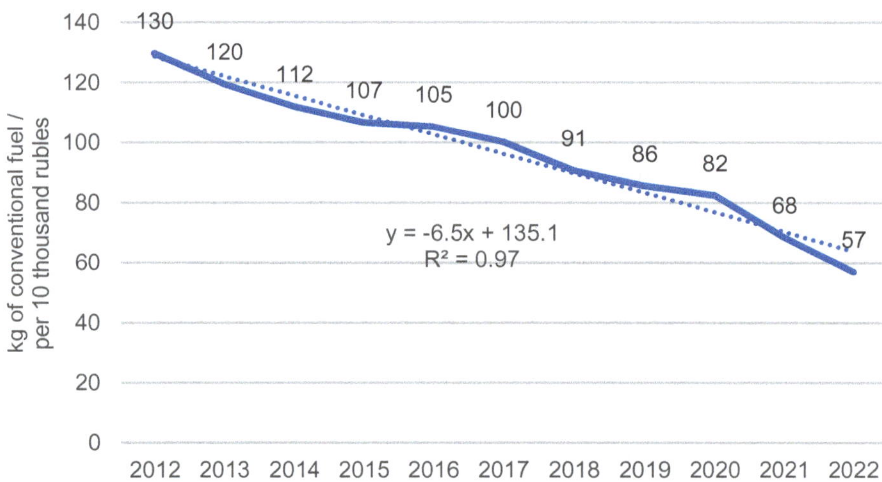

Fig. 2 Dynamics of energy intensity of GVA, kg of conventional fuel/per 10 thousand rubles

allows us to say that the decrease in energy intensity of GVA in Russian industry is sustainable.

The indicator of the efficiency of industrial development, which is the energy intensity of gross value added, is associated with the indicator of the change in the share of technological and intellectual products in the formation of GVA. The share of technological and intellectual products in the formation of GVA increased from 20% in 2011 to 23% in 2022, an increase of 15%. However, the maximum value of the indicator was recorded in 2020—25%, after which a downward trend emerged. In general, it should be said that the dynamics of the share of technological and intellectual products in the formation of GVA in Russian industry has a positive trend, which is also confirmed by the linear regression equation with a positive regression coefficient of 0.3 at the level of statistical significance of the model $P \leq 0.05$ and the determination coefficient of 0.69 (Fig. 3).

In addition, the descriptive statistics of the share of technological and intellectual products in the formation of GVA showed that this indicator has a normal distribution during the analyzed time period, with a low value of the variation coefficient—6.8% and insignificant asymmetry and excess (less than 1), which allows us to claim that the growth of the share of technological and intellectual products in the formation of GVA in Russian industry is sustainable.

Moreover, the calculation of the level of relationship between the two indicators showed a statistically significant correlation between them (Fig. 4).

The value of the correlation coefficient was minus 0.73 ($P \leq 0.05$), therefore, with an increase in the share of technological and intellectual products in the formation of GVA, a decrease in the energy intensity of GVA is observed; at the same time, the converse statement is also true that with a decrease in the energy intensity of GVA, the share of technological and intellectual products in the formation of GVA increases. However, one can try to find an external economic nature in this identified relationship. The Kyoto Protocol and the UN Sustainable Development Goals, one way or another, form models of behavior and business strategies among economic activity participants aimed at reducing the negative impact on the environment, which can be achieved not only by increasing the level of science-intensive production, but also through other intensive factors of production development.

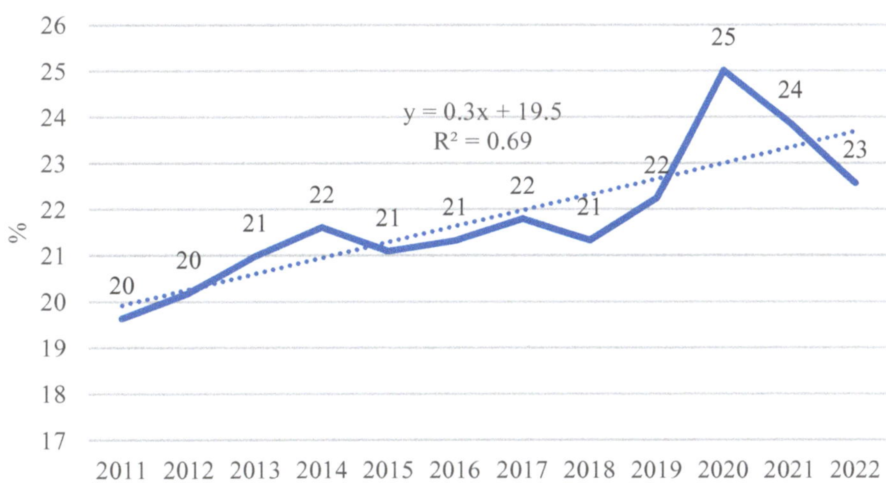

Fig. 3 Dynamics of the share of technological and intellectual products in the formation of GVA, percentage

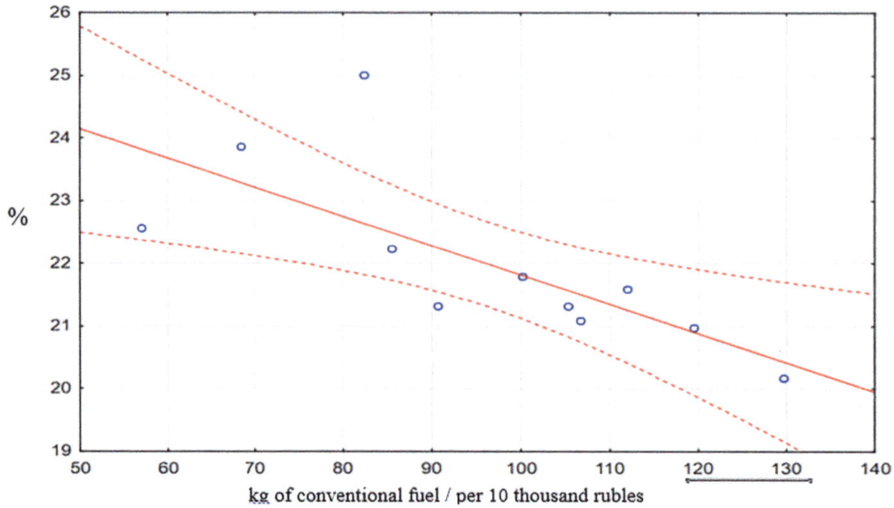

Fig. 4 The relationship between the energy intensity of GVA and the share of technological and intellectual products in the formation of GVA

5 Conclusion

Thus, the Russian industrial sector is characterized by positive development trends, however, adjustments to its sustainable dynamics are made due to the influence of global trends of a geopolitical and macroeconomic nature. In general, it is necessary to point out the favorable outlook for trends in Russian industry, which is confirmed by the dynamics of official statistics and their statistical analysis, which generally indicates the achievement of sustainability of Russian industry.

Currently, industrial development trends are associated with the following geopolitical and macroeconomic factors: sanction pressure, volatility of stock exchange and currency rates, isolation, limited financial resources in matters of industrial lending, etc.

Among the main strategic priorities for the implementation of state industrial policy at present are: focus on the implementation of projects for the structural transformation of the economy, projects for technological sovereignty, development of programs and roadmaps for the development of domestic critical industries and cross-cutting technologies (unmanned vehicles, specialized mechanical engineering, biochemistry, electrochemical industry, etc.).

In this regard, the government of the Russian Federation has defined priority areas for projects of technological sovereignty and structural adaptation of the country's economy.

The first group includes projects in 13 priority areas: aviation industry, automobile manufacturing, railway engineering, medical industry, oil and gas, agricultural, specialized engineering, machine tool industry, shipbuilding, pharmaceuticals, chemical industry, electronics and energy.

The projects for structural adaptation of the country's economy include projects for the creation or modernization of infrastructure that allows for the reorientation of transport and logistics flows to friendly countries.

To summarize, let us highlight the following key points:

1. In general, trends in Russian industry correspond to global trends and show an increase in industrial activity with the exception of some negative aspects (a decrease in the share of science-intensive and high-tech products in GDP in recent years, a slowdown in the growth rate of industrial production). However, among the factors that may restrain the growth of Russian industry in the future, it is necessary to highlight macroeconomic factors (sanctions, limited foreign investment, reduced demand, etc.) and internal factors (low level of innovation activity, underdeveloped sales markets, weak scientific and production base, low level of development of open innovation, etc.).

   However, there has been a decrease in the share of high-tech products in GDP in recent years and a slowdown in the growth rate of the overall index of industrial production (IIP) in 2022. These alarming signals may indirectly indicate possible recessions or adaptation periods that the Russian economy is going through during the period of adaptation to new macroeconomic realities and the implementation of projects for structural transformation of the economy, achieving technological sovereignty.

   A stable relationship was revealed between the growth of the share of science-intensive and high-tech products in GDP and a decrease in the energy intensity of the Russian economy.
2. In general, the dynamics of industrial production in the Russian economy is characterized as stable and has a positive value, despite the recovery from the pandemic and the anti-Russian sanctions; differentiation in industrial production among subtypes of economic activity is increasing; the manufacturing sector is steadily securing its leading role in the industrial development of the economy; processes of growth in production efficiency are being activated based on the use of a comprehensive lean manufacturing methodology through the transformation of corporate thinking, changes in management methods, modification of production processes and value creation models. At the same time, it has to be noted that the strengthening in the future of such trends as a slowdown in the growth rate of industrial production or the share of the knowledge-intensive sector in the formation of GDP may contribute to more negative trends in the medium term—a recession in production and failure to achieve the goals of implementing the policy of technological sovereignty.

   The practical significance of the study lies in the development of analytical tools for assessing development trends in relation to Russian industry, which can be used in the development and improvement of programs for the structural modernization of the Russian economy and the implementation of technological sovereignty projects.

References

1. Sidorov, V. M. (2013). Assessment of sustainable development of the enterprise using the organizational and economic mechanism. *Issues of Regional Economics, 1*(14), 59–62.
2. Theys, J. (2020). Le développement durable face à sa crise: un concept menacé, sous-exploité ou dépassé? *Développement Durable et Territoires, 11*(2), 17468. https://doi.org/10.4000/developpementdurable.17468
3. Nerini, F. F., Sovacool, B., Hughes, N., Cozzi, L., Cosgrave, E., Howells, M., & Milligan, B. (2019). Connecting climate action with other sustainable development goals. *Nature Sustainability, 2*(8), 674–680. https://doi.org/10.1038/s41893-019-0334-y
4. Shinkevich, A., Kudryavtseva, S., & Samarina, V. (2023). Ecosystems as an innovative tool for the development of the financial sector in the digital economy. *Journal of Risk and Financial Management, 16*(2), 72. https://doi.org/10.3390/jrfm16020072
5. Golovina, A. N., Shtykhno, D. A., & Potanin, V. V. (2023). Sustainable development and corporate strategies: The case of Russian metals enterprises. *Journal of New Economy, 24*(2), 66–85. https://doi.org/10.29141/2658-5081-2023-24-2-4
6. Pan, S. L., & Zhang, S. (2020). From fighting COVID-19 pandemic to tackling sustainable development goals: An opportunity for responsible information systems research. *International Journal of Information Management, 55*(3), 102196. https://doi.org/10.1016/j.ijinfomgt.2020.102196
7. Dantasa, T. E. T., Souza, E. D., Destro, I. R., Hammes, G., Rodriguez, C. M. T., & Soares, S. R. (2021). How the combination of circular economy and industry 4.0 can contribute towards achieving the sustainable development goals. *Sustainable Production and Consumption, 26*, 213–227. https://doi.org/10.1016/j.spc.2020.10.005
8. Abbasi, A., & Kamal, M. M. (2020). Adopting industry 4.0 technologies in citizens' electronic-engagement considering sustainability development. In M. Themistocleous & M. Papadaki (Eds.), *Information systems* (pp. 304–313). Springer. https://doi.org/10.1007/978-3-030-44322-1_23
9. Kolotyrin, K. P., Serdyukova, L. O., Bashirzade, R. R., Goryacheva, T. V., & Kiseleva, O. N. (2022). Sustainable industrial development based on digital technology. In A. V. Bogoviz & E. G. Popkova (Eds.), *Digital technologies and institutions for sustainable development. Advances in science, technology & innovation*. Springer. https://doi.org/10.1007/978-3-031-04289-8_42
10. Hernandez-Vivanco, A., & Bernardo, M. (2023). Management systems and productive efficiency along the certification life-cycle. *International Journal of Production Economics, 266*, 109028. https://doi.org/10.1016/j.ijpe.2023.109028
11. Samarina, V. P., Skufina, T. P., Savon, D. Y., & Kudryavtseva, S. S. (2021). Technological windows of opportunity for Russian Arctic regions: Modeling and exploitation prospects. *Journal of Risk and Financial Management, 14*(9), 400. https://doi.org/10.3390/jrfm14090400
12. Ndubisi, N. O., Zhai, X., & Lai, K. H. (2021). Small and medium manufacturing enterprises and Asia's sustainable economic development. *International Journal of Production Economics, 233*, 107971. https://doi.org/10.1016/j.ijpe.2020.107971
13. Shaker, R. R., & Mackay, B. R. (2021). Hidden patterns of sustainable development in Asia with underlying global change correlations. *Ecological Indicators, 131*, 108227. https://doi.org/10.1016/j.ecolind.2021.108227
14. Shaker, R. R., & Mackay, B. R. (2024). The hidden development patterns of Africa and their sustainability correlations. *Environmental and Sustainability Indicators, 24*, 100474. https://doi.org/10.1016/j.indic.2024.100474
15. Stahel, W. R. (2016). The circular economy. *Nature, 531*(7595), 435–438. https://doi.org/10.1038/531435a
16. Zhu, J., Fan, C., Shi, H., & Shi, L. (2019). Efforts for a circular economy in China: A comprehensive review of policies. *Journal of Industrial Ecology, 23*(1), 110–118. https://doi.org/10.1111/jiec.12754

17. Papaspyropoulos, K. G., Liakou, H., & Dimopoulos, P. (2023). Climate change in the biodiversity and forest strategies in Greece using discourse analysis and text mining: Is an integration into a cost-efficient natural resources policy feasible? *Sustainability, 15*(7), 6127. https://doi.org/10.3390/su15076127
18. Kirchherr, J., Reike, D., & Hekkert, M. (2017). Conceptualizing the circular economy: An analysis of 114 definitions. *Resources, Conservation and Recycling, 127*, 221–232. https://doi.org/10.1016/j.resconrec.2017.09.005
19. Sun, S. (2021). Analysis and prospect of industrial internet development in petrochemical industry. *Journal of Internet of Things, 3*, 126–132.
20. Helliwell, E., Choi, D., Merritt, J., & Kreth, J. (2023). Environmental influences on streptococcus sanguinis membrane vesicle biogenesis. *ISME Journal, 17*(9), 1430–1444. https://doi.org/10.1038/s41396-023-01456-3
21. Raifu, I. A. (2022). Examining the time-varying causality between oil returns and stock returns in Norway. *Energy Research Letters, 4*(1), 37693. https://doi.org/10.46557/001c.37693
22. Kane, E. (2021). *Many global chemicals companies trail on carbon-transition goals*. Bloomberg Intelligence. Retrieved from https://www.bloomberg.com/professional/blog/many-global-chemicalscompanies-trail-on-carbon-transition-goals/
23. Tronchin, L., Manfren, M., & Nastasi, B. (2018). Energy efficiency, demand side management and energy storage technologies: A critical analysis of possible paths of integration in the built environment. *Renewable and Sustainable Energy Reviews, 95*, 341–353. https://doi.org/10.1016/j.rser.2018.06.060
24. Malinauskaite, J., Jouhara, H., Ahmad, L., Milani, M., Montorsi, L., & Venturelli, M. (2019). Energy efficiency in industry: EU and national policies in Italy and the UK. *Energy, 172*, 255–269. https://doi.org/10.1016/j.energy.2019.01.130
25. World Bank. (n.d.). *GDP growth*. Retrieved from https://data.worldbank.org/indicator/NY.GDP.MKTP.KD.ZG?view=chart
26. Rosstat. (n.d.). *Technological development of economic sectors*. Retrieved from https://rosstat.gov.ru/folder/11189

Strengthening Digital Trade Integration within BRICS Countries Based on an International Digital Communication Platform

Alla Shcherbina and Liudmila Shabalina

Abstract The study explores the development of digital trade among BRICS countries emphasizing the potential of a platform-based model to strengthen international trade and cooperation. The article analyzes the development of international digital trade in the context of the BRICS integration group countries and considers key aspects, trends and proposals for improving trade relations in digital format. The research highlights five key instruments driving digital trade: business websites, social media, e-commerce, data analytics, and digital platforms. Among these, digital platforms are portrayed as transformative, enabling businesses to streamline operations, reduce costs, and expand into international markets without reliance on intermediaries. A significant proposal in the study is the creation of an International Digital Communication Platform for BRICS. The rationale for this platform lies in its integrative approach, unifying business entities, governmental authorities, regulatory institutions, and civil society within a coordinated, secure, and transparent digital ecosystem. The policy recommendations presented include harmonizing digital trade regulations, investing in digital infrastructure and innovative technologies, and enhancing cybersecurity standards. Implementation of these measures through the proposed platform is anticipated to significantly enhance digital trade efficiency, promote sustainable economic development, and strengthen the competitive positioning of BRICS countries within the global digital market.

Keywords Digital trade · BRICS · Communication platform

A. Shcherbina (✉)
Donetsk National Technical University, Donetsk, Russia

L. Shabalina
Economic Research Institute, Donetsk, Russia

F. Tao et al. (eds.), *Artificial Intelligence and Digital Transformation*, Lecture Notes in Information Systems and Organisation 78,
https://doi.org/10.1007/978-3-032-00118-4_20

1 Introduction

The rapid expansion of digital economy has significantly influenced global trade, particularly within developing markets. The BRICS nations—Brazil, Russia, India, China, and South Africa—collectively represent 41.93% of the world's population and contribute 25.24% to global GDP, recent inclusion of Saudi Arabia, Egypt, the United Arab Emirates, Iran, and Ethiopia has further reinforced the group's economic strength [1]. The expansion of digital trade within BRICS nations plays a crucial role in fostering economic growth and strengthening their integration into the global economy. At present, BRICS countries collectively account for 10% of global services exports and 13% of global services imports, with China and India holding the largest shares of these transactions. However, trade in digital services of BRICS members remains relatively limited, representing just 9% of Brazil's total services exports, 13% for Russia, 6% for India, 4% for China, and 12% for South Africa [2]. Given the rapid advancements in digital technologies and the increasing dominance of e-commerce, there is significant untapped potential for enhancing digital trade and investment among these countries [3, 4].

Digital trade in BRICS countries is rapidly developing, and while the e-commerce market within the bloc is projected to triple within 2025–2030, its current share in the GDP of individual countries (for instance, 0.92% in Brazil and 2.9% in India) remains relatively low. However, regulatory barriers continue to hinder progress in this sector. For example, Russia and India impose restrictions on logistics and professional services, while China enforces limitations on audiovisual and courier services. At the same time, strengthening intra-BRICS cooperation in digital trade is crucial for building economic resilience and mitigating reliance on external markets, especially amidst prevailing geopolitical tensions and economic volatility. Facilitating cross-border e-commerce, harmonizing regulatory standards, and ensuring technological compatibility can significantly enhance the collective economic standing of BRICS nations in the global digital landscape.

The main problem studied is the need to stimulate the development of digital trade between BRICS countries and propose effective digital instrument to promote international economic relations.

The purpose of this study is to analyze current trends and identify barriers within digital trade among BRICS nations as well as substantiate the feasibility of a unified digital communication platform as an effective tool for intensifying intra-BRICS cooperation and enhancing competitive positioning within the global digital market.

2 Literature Review

International digital trade is of vital importance for the global economy, as it helps strengthen economies, improves people's living standards, expands markets and increases competition in business as well as stimulates economic growth and develops the digitalization around the world.

In particular, it is important to distinguish between the concepts of e-commerce and digital trade. While closely related, they differ in scope and economic implications, as e-commerce focuses on online transactions of goods and services, digital trade encompasses a wider array of economic activities enabled by digital technologies, including data flows and digital services. Mentioned distinctions are crucial for formulating effective economic policies and regulations in the digital era. Initially, digital trade was narrowly defined as the online sale and purchase of goods and services. However, contemporary interpretations encompass a broader spectrum, including cross-border data flows, digital services, and the digitalization of trade processes. International organizations the World Trade Organization and the Organization for Economic Co-operation and Development have expanded the definition of digital trade to include transactions of goods and services conducted over computer networks through methods specifically designed for placing or receiving orders and services and data transmitted electronically across borders, such as software, e-books, and online consultancy services. This comprehensive approach acknowledges the integral role of digital technologies in modern trade. The global COVID-19 crisis significantly accelerated the expansion of digital trade, compelling both enterprises and consumers to increasingly utilize online platforms and e-commerce channels. Consequently, this rapid transition underscored critical policy considerations, including the enhancement of frameworks governing digital trade, data security, and regulatory alignment. Moreover, it highlighted the necessity for strengthened international collaboration aimed at overcoming emerging issues like digital protectionism and the fragmentation of regulatory standards.

However, current debates on digital barriers and protectionism within BRICS countries highlight a complex interplay between efforts to achieve digital sovereignty and the challenges posed by such measures. In this way, Ciuriak and Ptashkina [5] analyze the impact of geopolitical dynamics on digital trade restrictions, particularly highlighting scenarios within the BRICS group—most notably China and Russia—where concerns about national security have prompted stronger protectionist measures in digital sector. Their analysis emphasizes the economic implications arising from digital trade barriers, warning of possible disruptions and fragmentation in international digital commerce. To address these challenges, the authors recommend policy approaches aimed to balance economic openness with security imperatives. In parallel, Azmeh et al. [2, 3] provide a detailed assessment of how industrial policies in Brazil, India, and China shape digital trade practices, revealing evidence that domestic support mechanisms for digital sectors can unintentionally encourage protectionism. Their findings illustrate the way in which such policies create market entry barriers for foreign digital companies, potentially hindering integration into global digital trade networks. Azmeh, Foster, and Echavarri propose specific policy adjustments elaborated to foster digital sector development without negatively affecting international trade cooperation. On the contrary, Kapoor and Dey [6] provide a country-specific examination of India's recent shift towards more restrictive digital trade policies, particularly stringent data localization regulations and increased scrutiny of international technology enterprises. The researchers critically evaluate the implications of these policies for India's global and intra-BRICS trade positions, advocating for balanced regulatory strategies that uphold both national security interests and economic openness [7]. Ultimately, the BRICS nations' collective pursuit of digital sovereignty involves strategic initiatives aimed at reducing reliance on foreign technological infrastructure and reinforcing domestic digital autonomy. Although these strategies may bolster national security and nurture local industries, they also risk intensifying digital protectionism, potentially constraining broader international digital trade flows. The fact BRICS develops data protection laws within the bloc reflects a trend towards stricter data governance, as while aiming to protect citizens' privacy, they can also act as barriers to cross-border data flows. Enhanced cooperation among BRICS nations on data protection could harmonize standards, potentially mitigating some protectionist effects [8]. In this perspective, digital barriers and protectionism in the BRICS context underscores the delicate balance between achieving digital sovereignty and avoiding protectionism that could hinder international digital trade [9].

3 Materials and Methods

In line with the established purpose—to identify the key trends, barriers, and opportunities for enhancing digital trade cooperation among BRICS countries, and to substantiate the proposed International Digital Communication Platform model—the study employed a combination of analytical, comparative, and empirical research methods, clearly targeted at assessing the specifics of digital trade interactions within the BRICS bloc of countries.

Initially, to ensure the robustness and accuracy of the analysis, statistical and factual materials were gathered from reputable international databases, including reports and datasets from the UNCTAD, OECD, IMF, World Bank, and international analytical platforms such as Statista and Global Innovation Index. These sources provided comprehensive quantitative data that enabled a precise evaluation of each BRICS country's current positioning, dynamics of digital trade growth, infrastructure development, and innovation capacities.

The comparative analysis approach formed the methodological basis of the research. The process involved systematically contrasting BRICS nations across several key indicators: share of digital trade within total trade, penetration and adoption rates of e-commerce, levels of investment in digital infrastructure and R&D, as well as the regulatory frameworks shaping digital commerce environments. By using the comparative analysis, the authors created an essential basis for recognizing existing disparities, unique strengths, and potential collaborative opportunities within the BRICS digital trade context. Performed evaluation effectively supported the justification for developing Digital Communication Platform proposed to cover all the specific needs of BRICS economies in the field of digital trade. As supportive measure, content analysis of policy documents, national strategies, and regulatory standards related to digital commerce in each of BRICS countries was conducted. Results allowed for the identification of prevailing protectionist tendencies and regulatory inconsistencies that could influence digital trade sphere. Simultaneously, it illuminated opportunities for aligning policy frameworks, vital for achieving seamless integration through the proposed Platform. Furthermore, theoretical insights drawn from contemporary literature on digital commerce, platform business models, and innovation policy frameworks were systematically synthesized to underpin both the conceptual foundation and structural design of the proposed Platform. Theoretical synthesis served as a basis for designing of the Platform's governance structure, operational processes, and expected outcomes for promoting enhanced digital trade cooperation among BRICS countries.

Finally, to ensure methodological consistency and reliability, the study adapted best practices from analogous research within integration blocs such as EAEU and EU, particularly in examining the effectiveness of digital platforms as tools for promoting international economic cooperation. This comparative benchmarking with existing platforms in other integration contexts provided additional validation of the proposed organizational structure and operational logic of the BRICS International Digital Communication Platform.

Collectively, the systematic application of these targeted methods comparative statistical analysis, qualitative content analysis, theoretical synthesis, and comparative benchmarking provided a comprehensive methodological foundation for substantiating the study's recommendations, enhancing the accuracy and practical relevance of the research outcomes.

4 Results

4.1 Digital Instruments of the International Trade Development

In the context of the economy digital transformation, which involves "a radical change in the structure of the economy, the transfer of centers of added value creation to the sphere of digital processes, the use of digital resources and assets," the development of international business occurs with the widespread use of disruptive innovational digital technologies, such as the Internet of Things, cloud computing, big data analysis, Artificial Intelligence, thereby forming a new paradigm for the development of the global digital economy.

Continuous innovations influence the intensification of digital transformation in industries, while the interaction of digital and real economies is becoming more and more extensive. Currently, a large number of digital instruments are used in international business practice, those contributing to increasing the speed and efficiency of digital trade in different countries are summarized below.

The first instrument can be designated as the Website and Online Presence of the business in the digital sphere. As of 2024, the global internet hosts approximately 1.12 billion websites. Notably, only about 17% of them, roughly 193.89 million are actively maintained, leaving the remaining 83% inactive. This fact indicates a substantial portion of the web remains largely dormant [10].

The second instrument is defined as social media. Using social media platforms such as Telegram, YouTube, LinkedIn helps to attract and interact with customers from abroad. According to forecasts, in 2025, advertising costs in social networks will reach 207.10 billion USD, while 26.8% of Internet users aged from 16 to 64 years old discover brands, products and services through advertising in social networks.

By 2027, 247.3 billion USD of social media advertising will be spent on mobile devices, about 81% of businesses will use social media to increase brand awareness, and 72.8% of internet users currently use social media for brand research. Mentioned facts indicate the growing importance of online presence and engaging with potential customers through social media.

The third instrument is e-commerce. It creates the possibility of online shopping and delivery of goods or services to international customers, and it is considered to be the fastest growing segment of online transactions. Based on data of total retail e-commerce revenue worldwide in 2023 (Fig. 1), Asia stands as the foremost e-commerce market globally, with online retail revenues reaching approximately 1.7 trillion USD in 2023. This figure surpasses the Americas' e-commerce revenue by about 800 million USD. In contrast, regions such as Australia, Oceania, and Africa reported significantly lower e-commerce revenues, each is under 40 billion USD in 2023. Asia's dominance in this sector is largely attributed to China, alone generating over 935 billion USD in e-commerce revenue during the same year. The e-commerce market in the Asian region is quite mature and will continue to grow. The market size is projected to grow at over 14% per year between 2023 and 2027.

The fourth instrument is data analytics. The key types of data analysis used in business decision making process count descriptive, diagnostic, predictive and prescriptive types of analytics [13, 14].

The fifth and most transformative instrument of business development is the digital platform, representing a core element of the global digital agenda. Platforms

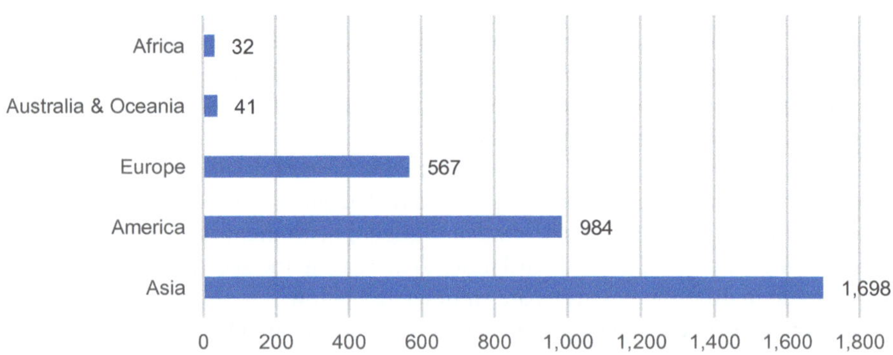

Fig. 1 Total retail e-commerce revenue worldwide in 2023, by region (in billion USD). *Source:* [11, 12]

create a system of algorithmically driven, mutually beneficial relationships between a diverse and significant number of independent participants within a specific economic sector or area of activity. These interactions occur within a unified information environment, where platforms leverage advanced digital technologies to optimize data handling, reduce transaction costs, and reshape traditional labor division systems.

Among the most notable strengths of digital platforms in international business is their communicative function. Platforms serve as dynamic hubs that facilitate seamless connections between various stakeholders, including buyers, sellers, service providers, and regulators (governments), across multiple geographies. The ability of digital platforms to facilitate communication across national borders actively promotes the globalization of trade by overcoming barriers related to language differences, cultural contexts, and operational practices. Specially designed connectivity fosters greater transparency and helps establish trust among international trading partners from BRICS+ economies. Platforms significantly streamline cross-border commerce by directly linking buyers and sellers, trying to exclude the intermediaries, minimizing associated marketing costs, and lowering entry hurdles that previously restricted small and medium-sized enterprises. Additionally, created digital ecosystems gives the possibility to enter new international markets for enterprises efficiently, with usage of real-time consumer data. Basically new approach helps to optimize products and services as well as to address varying customer preferences effectively, thereby stimulating both market growth and innovation. The communicative capabilities provided by digital trade platforms, obviously serve as a critical driver of sustainable global trade growth. While enhancing international connectivity, reducing operational inefficiencies, and fostering broader economic participation, platform models also introduce complex strategic and operational challenges, positioning their continued development as a core notion within contemporary digital transformation discourse.

4.2 Current State of Digital Trade in BRICS Countries

The rapid expansion of global retail e-commerce underscores the increasing digitalization of international trade. As shown in the retail ecommerce sales worldwide graph, demonstrating period 2022–2028 projection, e-commerce sales are expected to grow from 5.1 trillion USD in 2022 to 8.1 trillion USD by 2028, with a steady rise in the share of e-commerce in total retail sales. Despite a gradual decline in annual growth rates from 9.7% in 2023 to 6.9% in 2028, digital commerce remains a dominant force in global trade, driving structural shifts in consumer behavior, cross-border transactions, and supply chain integration [14] (Fig. 2).

Within this context, BRICS countries represent a pivotal group of rapidly digitizing economies, whose potential to influence and benefit from global digital commerce expansion remains substantial yet unevenly realized [15, 16]. Analyzing their current positions against this backdrop provides valuable insights into their future trajectories in international digital trade.

Considering the latest available estimates of digital trade as a share of total international trade for each BRICS+ format country, it is possible to make the following observations. The share of digital trade—broadly including high-technology goods and ICT services—in overall international trade remains relatively modest for Brazil and Russia, but is significant for India. According to the WIPO Global Innovation Index 2024, high-tech exports account for only about 2.1% of Brazil's total trade, and ICT services exports about 1.2%, indicating digital trade makes up just ~3% of Brazil's trade. The Russian Federation shows a similar low share: roughly 2.4% of its trade is high-tech exports and 1.2% is ICT services exports (approximately 3.6% combined). In contrast, India has a much larger digital trade footprint—4.2% of India's trade comes from high-tech goods and an 11.9% share (the world's highest) comes from ICT services exports. This means, nearly 16% of India's total international trade is derived from digital sectors, far outpacing Brazil and Russia. Among BRICS+, China leads by a wide margin in digital trade. Over 26% of China's total trade consists of high-tech exports, occupying the first position in Global Innovation Index 2024 among the 34 uppermiddle-income group economies. However, China's ICT services exports are relatively small (about 2.4% of trade), reflecting China's strength in tech manufacturing rather than services. Thus, China's digitally-delivered services trade reached 371 billion USD in 2022, accounting for 41.7% of China's total services trade. In addition, China's cross-border e-commerce (digitally ordered goods) totaled 295 billion USD in 2022. Combining these, digital trade represents roughly 10% of China's total international trade (goods and services) in 2022. This share is rising as China's digital trade grows faster than traditional trade [16, 17].

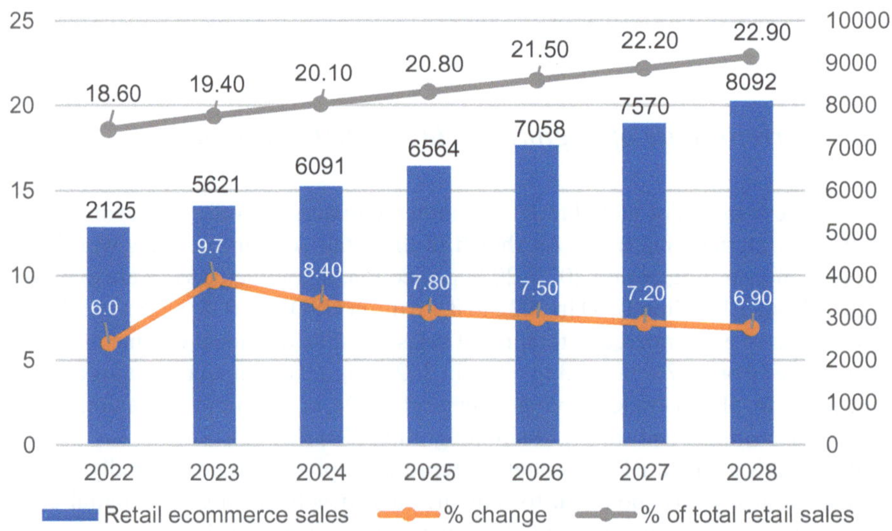

Fig. 2 Projected retail e-commerce revenue worldwide in 2022–2028, (in billion USD)

In South Africa digital trade remains a small fraction of total trade. According to WIPO Global Innovation Index, ICT services exports were only about 0.7% of South Africa's total trade. This low share reflects South Africa's trade is still dominated by commodities and non-digital services. For context, digitally deliverable services are 15% of Africa's services exports on average, and digital goods make up just 13% of Africa's imports. Thus, South Africa is among the continent's largest digital importers, but the overall share is modest [18].

Saudi Arabia's digital trade is very limited relative to its total trade. Estimates by the OECD, only about 4% of Saudi Arabia's exports were in digital form (digitally delivered or ordered). This is unsurprising given oil's dominance in country's trade. While newer data are scarce, the share is still considered to be in the single digits. Saudi Arabia's ICT goods exports, for example, were just 0.4% of total goods exports in 2021, indicating digital trade remains a tiny portion.

Egypt's digital trade is growing but still forms a small share of overall trade. According to OECD data, ICT goods and services combined made up approximately 2.9% of Egypt's total trade. On the services side, 15.7% of Egypt's commercial services trade is digitally deliverable (including IT, telecom, online services). In value terms, Egypt's digital exports (including ICT services and online outsourcing) made 6.2 billion USD in 2023, a growing figure but relatively minor in comparison to Egypt's total trade in goods and services [18, 19].

The United Arab Emirates has a sizable technological sector, but digital trade is not the majority of its trade. In 2022, 8.45% of the UAE's goods exports were ICT products (and 12.2% of its goods imports made ICT goods). The UAE's services trade includes digital services (IT and financial services including), but official breakdowns are not available. Overall, given the large volume of oil and traditional re-export trade, the share of digital trade is well below 20% of the UAE's total international trade.

Iran's international digital trade is negligible. Due to sanctions and an oil-heavy export profile, Iran's digital exports are minimal. For instance, ICT services exports account for only about 0.2% of Iran's total trade (30). Likewise, high-tech/ICT goods are practically nil (ICT goods were 0.2% of Iran's goods exports in 2024. Iran's trade is dominated by crude oil and traditional goods, so digital trade's share remains extremely low (around a fraction of a percent) [20].

Ethiopia (a least-developed, mostly agrarian economy) has very low digital trade as well. Recent estimates show ICT services exports at roughly 1.2% of Ethiopia's total trade (Global Innovation Index Ethiopia, 2023). Ethiopia's goods exports are dominated by coffee and commodities, with minimal ICT or high-tech goods. Its digitally deliverable service exports (like online services) are nascent. In sum, Ethiopia's digital trade share is on the order of 1% (in line with other least-developed countries, which collectively have under 0.5% of global digital services trade).

At the same time, the countries under review are seeing an increase in the number of Internet users, the introduction of digital technologies into business processes and everyday life [21]. The growing potential of the BRICS+ countries in the digital sphere is confirmed by quantitative assessments of digitalization development indicators, including the number of Internet users, the percentage of Internet penetration

Table 1 BRICS+ internet penetration rates and user statistics by country

Countries	Internet users, million people, 2024	Internet penetration, 2023 (%)	% of population using Internet, 2023
Brazil	165.3	84.15	77.1
Russian Federation	129.8	92.25	85.5
India	881.3	43.41	62.6
China	1.1 billion	77.47	77.3
South Africa	31.9	74.7	53.6
Saudi Arabia	34.8	100	96.9
Iran	78.1	81.72	88.8
Ethiopia	36.4	19.38	30.3
United Arab Emirates	8.9	100	95.2
Egypt	80.8	72.7	73.9

Source [12, 22]

of the country's territory and the percentage of the population using the Internet (Table 1). For more effective cooperation in this area, the BRICS E-Commerce Cooperation Initiative was signed in 2017, and the BRICS E-Commerce Working Group was created to coordinate intergovernmental cooperation.

With the purpose to consider a comprehensive basis for evaluating the state of digital trade among BRICS+ nations the selected indicators, such as R&D expenditure as a percentage of GDP, intellectual property payments as a share of total trade, the proportion of high-tech imports and exports in overall trade, and each country's general position in the Global Innovation Index ranking, enable a detailed assessment of the technological and economic environment that underpins digital trade development [21, 23]. Mentioned indicators offer a multifaceted perspective on the structural factors influencing the digital trade landscape, allowing for a comparative analysis that highlights disparities in innovation capacity, participation in high-tech value chains, and engagement with the global digital economy (Table 2).

A critical determinant of digital trade readiness is national investment in research and development, as it reflects a country's commitment to fostering technological advancement and innovation. Countries that allocate a higher share of GDP to R&D typically exhibit greater digital trade intensity due to their ability to develop and commercialize cutting-edge technologies. Among BRICS members, China leads with 2.4% of GDP invested in R&D (ranking 14th globally), which correlates with its dominant position in high-tech exports (28% of total trade, ranking 5th). On the contrary, economies such as Brazil (investing 1.2% of GDP in R&D, ranking 43 in the index), Russia (1.1%, positioning 37th globally), and South Africa (0.7%, 53rd globally) dedicate considerably smaller shares of national resources to research and innovation. This modest investment level directly influences their limited involvement in digital trade markets. The most pronounced gap appears in Ethiopia, allocating just 0.3% of GDP to research and development (81st in global ranking),

Table 2 BRICS+ countries performance in Global Innovation Index 2023, selected indicators

Countries	Gross expenditure on R&D, % GDP (value/rank)	Intellectual property payments, % total trade (value/rank)	High-tech imports, % total trade (value/rank)	High-tech exports, % total trade (value/rank)	General position in Global Innovation Index 2023
China	2.4 (14)	1.4 (24)	22.6 (6)	28.0 (5)	12
UAE	1.5 (26)	0.7 (58)	14.3 (17)	10.6 (16)	32
India	06 (54)	1.4 (25)	10.0 (37)	4.0 (41)	40
Saudi Arabia	0.5 (63)	n/a	7.5 (74)	0.8 (76)	48
Brazil	1.2 (34)	1.8 (17)	13.5 (19)	2.1 (58)	49
Russia	1.1 (37)	1.7 (18)	8.6 (56)	2.3 (55)	51
South Africa	0.7 (53)	1.3 (27)	9.2 (49)	2.1 (59)	59
Iran	0.8 (46)	0.2 (89)	5.1 (114)	0.2 (109)	62
Egypt	1.0 (42)	0.5 (73)	7.4 (75)	0.7 (81)	86
Ethiopia	0.3 (81)	0.0 (111)	9.8 (40)	0.2 (112)	125

Source: [21]

which severely restricts its capacity to develop the innovation-driven sectors necessary for successful participation in the digital economy.

Intellectual property payments as a proportion of total trade also serve as an essential measure for evaluating how actively countries are engaged in global innovation-driven economic interactions. Nations exhibiting elevated intellectual property transaction volumes typically have stronger connections to international innovation ecosystems, either by developing or acquiring technologies and digitally intensive services. Notably, Russia (1.7%) and Brazil (1.8%) display relatively high engagement in intellectual property exchanges, suggesting substantial involvement in digital innovation sectors. However, these figures do not directly correspond to their overall strength in digital trade. China and India, each at 1.4%, reflect moderate engagement, which aligns with their strategic focus on digital innovation and high-tech exports. Conversely, Iran (0.2%) and Ethiopia (0.0%) show minimal intellectual property activity, indicative of their limited roles in the global digital economy.

Furthermore, the competitiveness in digital trade heavily depends on the proportion of high-tech products in a country's overall trade structure, reflecting their degree of integration into global technological value chains. Among BRICS countries, China holds a clear leadership position, with high-tech exports making up 28% of total trade (fifth worldwide) and high-tech imports constituting 22.6% (ranked sixth globally), underscoring its pivotal role in international supply chains. India and the UAE, despite occupying lower ranks, still maintain significant shares of high-tech exports, accounting for 10.0% and 10.6% respectively. In comparison, South Africa (2.3%), Russia (3.5%), and Brazil (3.8%) present substantially lower proportions, highlighting their ongoing dependence on traditional economic sectors rather than digitally advanced industries. Ethiopia has notably marginal participation, with high-tech exports comprising merely 0.2% of its total trade (ranked 112th globally), clearly illustrates structural impediments preventing effective integration into digital commerce networks.

Generally, the Global Innovation Index rankings provide an integrated view of a country's broader innovation environment and its readiness for digital trade expansion. Within this context, China (ranked 12th) and the United Arab Emirates (ranked 32nd) stand out prominently, benefiting from highly advanced technological infrastructure, effective digital governance frameworks, and robust engagement in global innovation networks. India (40th) follows with a strong emphasis on ICT services exports (11.9% of total trade, the highest globally), compensating for its lower engagement in high-tech goods production. Meanwhile, Russia (51st) and Brazil (49th) exhibit moderate innovation performance, yet their digital trade indicators remain below those of leading economies. At the lower end of the spectrum, South Africa (59th), Iran (62nd), Egypt (86th), and Ethiopia (125th) are characterized by weak innovation ecosystems, posing substantial challenges to their ability to expand digital trade capabilities [23, 24].

The development of international digital trade in the founding countries of the BRICS bloc is based on several key factors. The first factor is the rapid growth of digital infrastructure in the group's countries, including expanding broadband and mobile phone coverage laying the foundation for digital trade. An example is the Digital Silk Road Project being the part of the Belt and Road Initiative, designed with the purpose to intensify digital cooperation both within and outside the integration group. The project has made significant investments in the construction of telecommunications networks, including submarine cable systems and satellite networks, helping to improve connectivity between countries. The project supports cooperation in the research and development of new technologies, including artificial intelligence, big data and cloud computing, with the Digital Silk Road placing particular emphasis on cybersecurity and data protection. The Digital Silk Road is an example of a large-scale project aimed at improving digital infrastructure and facilitating digital trade, particularly relevant for the BRICS+ countries seeking to strengthen their position in the global economy [13, 25].

The second factor is the growing middle class population in all BRICS countries and its high level of digital literacy, contributing to the increased demand for online commerce and digital services.

The third factor contributing to the development of BRICS nations digital trade is the active governmental support of the digital economy development by means of various initiatives and programs aimed at stimulating innovation and investment in digitalization (Table 3).

The above factors of international digital trade form the key directions of its development in the BRICS+ countries, namely:

- increase in domestic and international demand, explained by the generated by developing BRICS economies needs both domestically and internationally;

Table 3 Priority areas of the state support for the development of international digital trade in the core BRICS countries

BRICS country/ priority area of state support	Example of the project
India/Development of digital payment systems	India's Unified Payments Interface (UPI) has not only facilitated seamless peer-to-peer and merchant transactions but has also expanded internationally through partnerships with Singapore's PayNow, UAE's Mashreq Bank, and France's Lyra Network, allowing Indian consumers and businesses to conduct cross-border digital transactions efficiently. Additionally, the Reserve Bank of India's initiative on the Central Bank Digital Currency aims to integrate digital rupee transactions into domestic and international trade, enhancing transparency and reducing transaction costs
China/Expanding Global E-Commerce	Government support for internet giant Alibaba actively expanding its presence in the international market. Alibaba platforms such as AliExpress allow small and medium-sized enterprises from China to sell their goods around the world, contributing to the globalization of Chinese digital trade. China's Cross-Border E-Commerce Pilot Zones, established in over 100 cities, are creating a framework for international digital trade by offering tax incentives, streamlined customs procedures, and blockchain-based trade documentation to facilitate global B2B and B2C e-commerce transactions. The Digital Silk Road Initiative, a component of the Belt and Road Initiative, integrates AI-driven logistics and digital trade agreements, strengthening China's role as a leader in global digital commerce
Brazil/ Development of e-commerce	Brazil has launched the Programa Nacional de Exportação via E-commerce, which supports micro, small, and medium-sized enterprises in international e-commerce by providing logistical solutions, training, and digital tools for global trade integration. Additionally, the Mercado Libre Cross-Border Trade Program, backed by government incentives, facilitates exports from Brazil to Latin America, integrating AI-driven analytics for pricing and demand forecasting to enhance the efficiency of digital trade
Russia/Integration of digital technologies into traditional industries	Russian companies, with government support, such as Yandex and Sberbank, are introducing digital technologies into traditional sectors of the economy, such as financial services, retail and logistics. The Russian government is actively developing cross-border blockchain trade solutions, such as the Masterchain system, which facilitates secure digital transactions across Eurasian markets. Additionally, the National Program for Digital Economy, through AI-driven trade facilitation platforms and the implementation of MIR payment systems for international transactions, seeks to reduce dependency on Western financial infrastructures and integrate Russia more deeply into BRICS and Eurasian digital trade ecosystems

(continued)

Table 3 (continued)

BRICS country/ priority area of state support	Example of the project
South Africa/ Strengthening Infrastructure for E-Commerce	Government programs to develop mobile internet and digital payment solutions in South Africa through platforms such as PayFast are driving growth in online commerce, particularly in the small and medium enterprises sectors. The South African Digital Economy Master Plan, launched in collaboration with the private sector, prioritizes the development of blockchain-enabled smart contracts and digital identification systems to facilitate seamless and secure cross-border e-commerce. Furthermore, initiatives such as the African Continental Free Trade Area eTrade Strategy, which South Africa is actively shaping, focus on interoperable payment gateways and harmonized digital regulations to increase trade connectivity with the BRICS bloc

- increase in investment in innovative and technological development, with an emphasis on research and development in the field of digital technologies, contributing to the creation of new instruments and platforms for digital trade;
- expansion of international cooperation within the BRICS founding group with its new members the UAE, Saudi Arabia, Ethiopia, Egypt and Iran.

These development areas provide potential for further growth of international digital trade in BRICS countries, bringing significant economic benefits both to the countries themselves and to their international partners.

5 Development of Digital Trade in BRICS Countries Based on the Platform Model

With the rapid development of the digital economy, where borders are erased and opportunities for international transactions are becoming increasingly accessible, the creation of the International Digital Platform for intensifying trade and developing cooperation ties between the states of the BRICS integration union plays a key role in overcoming restrictions that may hinder digital trade.

Parker [16] defines a platform as "…a business based on creating opportunities for value-based interactions between external producers and consumers. The platform provides an open, participatory infrastructure for described interactions and sets conditions of governance for them".

Since digitalization has a great influence on the development of socio-economic systems, there is a need for innovative approaches to international cooperation and cross-border trade. Digital trade being an important area for the development of international relations, demands special attention. In this connection, the creation of the International Digital Communication Platform for the BRICS+ countries (IDCP

BRICS) can become a decisive step in deepening and expanding trade ties between business entities and government bodies of BRICS countries.

The digital platform is aimed to serve as a universal instrument for strengthening trade relations, facilitating communication and coordination between businesses and governments of BRICS countries [13].

The function of the BRICS IDCP is to ensure the following conditions for the development of international digital trade [25, 26]:

- Global accessibility, helping to enable individuals from all BRICS countries to develop digital trade regardless of their geographic location, which will expand their opportunities in the international market;
- Effective communication by providing the necessary functionality for exchanging messages, video conferencing and forums, allowing participants to promptly resolve issues, discuss the terms of transactions and develop partnerships;
- Simplification of transactions by integrating mechanisms for secure payment, orders processing, logistics and dispute resolution, making the trading process more transparent and convenient;
- Integration with various markets, since the BRICS IDCP provides an opportunity to unite various regional markets of BRICS countries, thereby facilitating the exchange of experience and expanding the range of goods and services;
- Increasing cybersecurity by creating and continuous monitoring a participant verification system, ratings and reviews, ensuring the safety of transactions organized on the platform.

It is proposed, the platform is to be financed by business structures selling their products and services within the framework of the BRICS IDCP, as well as by government funds allocated to support the development of domestic small and medium-sized businesses, membership fees and payments for the use of intellectual property. Such broad approach will balance the interests of all participants and ensure the stability of the platform.

The development of the platform requires active participation of governments and involved business structures, as well as civil society, which is supposed to be the main beneficiary [19]. Sharing responsibilities between actors is aimed to facilitate the interests of all parties and create an effective instrument for the development of digital trade between the BRICS+ countries. The proposed Organizational Structure of the BRICS IDCP is presented in Fig. 3.

The key factor driving the growth of digital platform is the so-called "network effects", meaning the benefits that platform users receive from additional users joining. Thus, in addition to direct network effects, platform also has indirect (pass-through) network effects, where the expansion of the one part of the platform increases the added value for another connected part. The presence of network effects is an incentive for platform to grow rapidly, as additional users joining makes the platform more attractive for the new participants.

Network effects can also generate "lock-in effects". Participants are more likely to remain on the platform rather than switch to competing platforms.

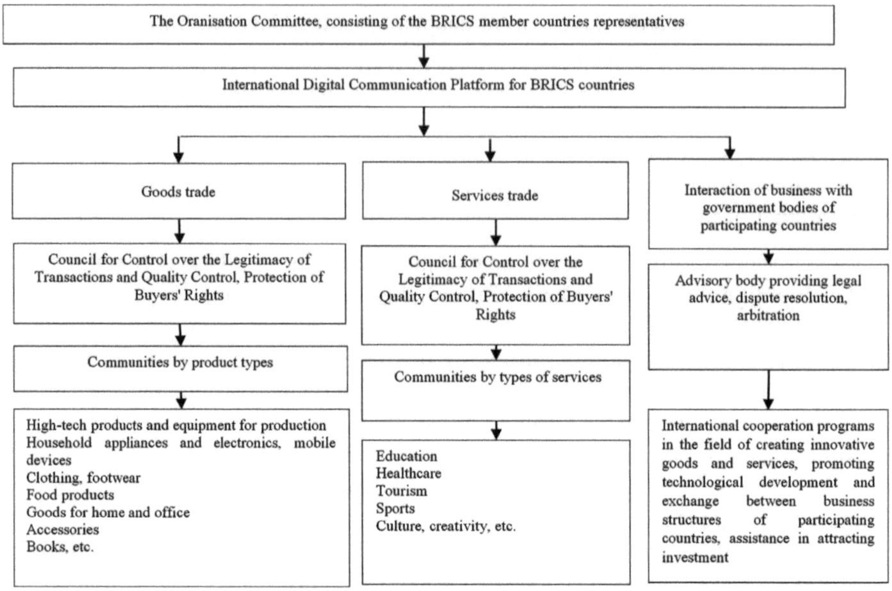

Fig. 3 Organizational structure of the International Digital Communication Platform for BRICS countries

The structural divisions of the platform operate in close interaction, ensuring the execution of deals, exchange of information, and satisfaction of requirements in the field of sale of goods and services, which contributes to the achievement of facilitating the development of cross-border digital trade goal.

It is assumed that business, in addition to trading on the digital platform, will also generate demand for innovative products, thereby stimulating the development of advanced products and innovative technologies that meet the current needs of customers and society as a whole. Ultimately, the international digital platform will stimulate digital trade, growth of exports and imports of goods and services produced by businesses, and, as a result, will contribute to the expansion of international cooperation within the BRICS integration union.

The proposed organizational structure of the BRICS IDCP is strategically designed to address several critical shortcomings identified in existing cross-border digital trade arrangements among BRICS countries. First, the distinct integration of business entities, government bodies, regulatory institutions, and civil society within a single coordinated framework addresses the systemic fragmentation currently observed in cross-border interactions. Such a unified organizational model significantly improves transparency, accountability, and operational efficiency through the clear allocation of roles and responsibilities and the establishment of well-defined communication processes among involved parties. Moreover, the proposed organizational design explicitly integrates features including robust participant authentication, secured transactional procedures, and clearly defined feedback mechanisms, thereby strengthening mutual trust and effectively reducing tendencies toward digital protectionism. Additionally, the structure of the platform is strategically developed to be flexible and scalable, ensuring it can adapt seamlessly to emerging trends in digital commerce. The built-in capacity for ongoing harmonization of regulatory frameworks and technological standards among participating countries further supports long-term collaborative stability and ensures sustained economic advantages for the entire integration bloc.

6 Conclusion

The findings of this study indicate that, despite significant global growth in digital commerce, digital trade among BRICS countries remains unevenly developed. This imbalance is primarily caused by technological disparities, fragmented digital infrastructure, and considerable regulatory differences among member states. Although BRICS economies have substantial economic capabilities, differences in innovation capacities and varying involvement in high-tech trade highlight structural issues that hinder deeper integration and more effective digital collaboration. To address these challenges, an International Digital Communication Platform is proposed as a strategic mechanism explicitly intended to coordinate and unify digital trade initiatives across BRICS countries.

Its implementation is expected to enhance transparency, interoperability, and cross-border transaction security, directly addressing existing obstacles and strengthening economic cooperation within the group. By involving governmental institutions, regulatory bodies, and private-sector stakeholders within a unified system, alignment of digital trade policies can be achieved, promoting joint investment in digital infrastructure and facilitating innovation exchanges across borders. Effective platform operationalization requires targeted policies, including regulatory harmonization, streamlined customs and logistics procedures, increased investment in digital technologies, and continuous enhancement of cybersecurity standards. Successful realization of these measures would significantly accelerate the integration of BRICS nations into the global digital economy, improving their collective competitiveness and economic resilience.

Future research directions suggested by the findings of this study include an empirical assessment of the economic impact of the IDCP BRICS platform on intra-bloc trade flows and developing quantifiable indicators to systematically measure the progress and effectiveness of digital trade initiatives within the BRICS integration grouping.

References

1. Alekseeva, O. A., Bestuzheva, O. Y., Vershinskaya, O. N., & Skvortsova, E. E. (2020). The impact of digital transformation on the modern socio-economic structure. *Narodonaselenie, 23*(3), 36–47. https://doi.org/10.19181/population.2020.23.3.4
2. Azmeh, S., Foster, C., & Echavarri, J. (2020). The international trade regime and the quest for free digital trade. *International Studies Review, 22*(3), 671–692. https://doi.org/10.1093/isr/viz033
3. Foster, C., & Azmeh, S. (2019). Latecomer economies and national digital policy: An industrial policy perspective. *The Journal of Development Studies, 56*(7), 1247–1262. https://doi.org/10.1080/00220388.2019.1677886
4. International Monetary Fund, OECD, UNCTAD, & WTO. (2023). *Handbook on measuring digital trade* (2nd ed.). OECD Publishing. https://doi.org/10.1787/ac99e6d3-en
5. Ciuriak, D., & Ptaškina, M. (2018). *The digital transformation and the transformation of international trade*. International Centre for Trade and Sustainable Development (ICTSD). Retrieved from http://hdl.handle.net/11159/1651
6. Mishra, D., Kedia, M., Reddy, A., Kanwar, S., Manish, M., Das, B., Gupta, S., & Sharma, D. (2023). *State of India's digital economy (SIDE) report 2023*. Indian Council for Research on International Economic Relations (ICRIER). Retrieved from https://www.researchgate.net/publication/370155285_State_of_India's_Digital_Economy
7. Kowalski, T. (2020). Platform revolution: How networked markets are transforming the economy and how to make them work for you. *Studia Medioznawcze, 1*, 139–144. https://doi.org/10.33077/uw.24511617.ms.2017.68.418
8. Belli, L. (2020). Data protection in the BRICS countries: Enhanced cooperation and convergence towards legal interoperability. *SSRN Journal*. https://doi.org/10.2139/ssrn.4390979
9. Belli, L. (2022). New data architectures in Brazil, China, and India: From copycats to innovators, towards a post-Western model of data governance. *Indian Journal of Law and Technology, 18*(2), 3. Retrieved from https://repository.nls.ac.in/ijlt/vol18/iss2/3
10. Kumar, N. (2024). *Website statistics (2024)—Traffic data & trends*. Demandsage. Retrieved from https://www.demandsage.com/website-statistics/
11. López González, J., & Jouanjean, M. (2017). *Digital trade: Developing a framework for analysis (OECD Trade Policy Papers No. 205)*. OECD Publishing. https://doi.org/10.1787/524c8c83-en
12. World Population Review. (2024). *Internet users by country 2024*. Retrieved from https://worldpopulationreview.com/country-rankings/internet-users-by-country
13. Swaminathan, A. (2019). *Digital silk road: How China is creating a new global data highway*. Yahoo Finance. Retrieved from https://finance.yahoo.com/news/digital-silk-road-china-123545748.html
14. ProjectPro. (2024). *Four types of analytics with examples and applications*. Retrieved from https://www.projectpro.io/article/types-of-analytics-descriptive-predictive-prescriptive-analytics/209
15. Cramer-Flood, E. (2024). *Worldwide retail ecommerce forecast 2024 midyear update*. Insider Intelligence. Retrieved from https://www.emarketer.com/content/worldwide-retail-ecommerce-forecast-2024-midyear-update
16. Van Alstyne, M. W., Parker, G. G., & Choudary, S. P. (2016). Pipelines, platforms, and the new rules of strategy. *Harvard Business Review, 94*(4), 54–62.
17. Kuprevich, T. S., & Turban, G. V. (2022). *Digital transformation of international business*. RIVSH. Retrieved from https://edoc.bseu.by:8080/bitstream/edoc/96977/1/Tsifrovaya_transformatsiya_mezhdunarodnogo_biznesa.pdf
18. Weber, R. H. (2010). Digital trade in WTO-law: Taking stock and looking ahead. *Asian Journal of WTO & International Health Law and Policy, 5*(1), 1–24. https://doi.org/10.2139/ssrn.1578139

19. Zhang, D. (2024). Understanding the evolution of China's approach to digital trade: Interests, ideas, and institutions. *Asia Review of Political Economy, 3*, 7. https://doi.org/10.1007/s44216-024-00026-4
20. World Trade Organization. (2023). *Global trade outlook and statistics*. WTO. Retrieved from https://www.wto.org/english/res_e/publications_e/trade_outlook23_e.htm
21. World Trade Organization. (2023). *Digital trade for development*. WTO. https://doi.org/10.30875/9789287075437
22. World Population Review. (2024). *Internet penetration by country 2024*. Retrieved from https://worldpopulationreview.com/country-rankings/internet-penetration-by-country
23. World Intellectual Property Organization. (2023). *Global innovation index 2023*. Retrieved from https://www.wipo.int/en/web/global-innovation-index/2023/index
24. World Intellectual Property Organization. (2024). *Global innovation index 2024*. Retrieved from https://www.wipo.int/web-publications/global-innovation-index-2024/en/
25. Bokova, T. V. (2022). *Development of electronic commerce in the BRICS countries: Features and trends*. InfoBRICS. Retrieved from https://infobrics.org/post/36133/
26. UNCTAD. (2024). *E-commerce and digital economy programme: Year in review 2023*. Retrieved from https://unctad.org/publication/e-commerce-and-digital-economy-programme-year-review-2023

Support for Scientific and Technical Cooperation of the EAEU Countries Through the Creation of a Digital Technological Platform

Liudmila Shabalina, Galina Shavkun, and Mark Timko

Abstract The article analyzes the scientific and technological development of the EAEU countries in the context of digitalization as a key factor in the development of industrial potential. It emphasizes the importance of integrating innovative resources, harmonizing legal and organizational frameworks, and implementing digital technological platforms to enhance the efficiency of interaction within integration associations in the field of scientific and technological cooperation. In this regard, the purpose of the study is to draft proposals for improving the effectiveness of international scientific and technological cooperation by creating a digital technological platform that facilitates the development of international innovative projects, technology transfer and promotion, as well as ensuring the legal protection of intellectual property. Key issues hindering the development of high-tech exports and coordination of scientific and industrial activities have been identified, including differences in the legislative framework and limited resources of the member states. A structure for the Eurasian Digital Technological Platform is proposed, aimed at ensuring the innovation process at all stages, from idea generation to commercialization. The study employs theoretical synthesis and content analysis to identify the principles of integration among countries based on scientific and technological cooperation. Data on the development of scientific and technological cooperation among the EAEU members, collected from open official sources, were preliminarily normalized and processed, with average growth rates calculated based on them. A comparative analysis of the organizational structure of technological platforms and the interaction parameters of their participants was conducted, allowing for the identification of organizational structure elements and the justification of using digital technologies to improve communication efficiency. To develop criteria for evaluating platform effectiveness, a system analysis of interaction indicators among participants was performed. The research results highlight the necessity of promoting international scientific and technological cooperation, contributing to the

L. Shabalina · G. Shavkun · M. Timko (✉)
Economic Research Institute, Donetsk, Russia

F. Tao et al. (eds.), *Artificial Intelligence and Digital Transformation*, Lecture Notes in Information Systems and Organisation 78,
https://doi.org/10.1007/978-3-032-00118-4_21

growth of the EAEU's international industrial competitiveness, which will enable the member states to achieve technological sovereignty.

Keywords Technological cooperation · The Eurasian Economic Union · Digital technological platform · Innovation development

1 Introduction

Under the conditions of intensifying international competition and deepening integration processes, countries face the need to enhance international scientific and technological cooperation (ISTC), which serves as a catalyst for sustainable industrial growth both at the national and regional levels. In this context, ISTC is of particular significance for the Eurasian Economic Union (EAEU), as it aims to develop innovative technologies and facilitate knowledge exchange in addressing complex technological challenges. This process is driven by the adoption of digital technologies that accelerate collaboration and the integration of intellectual property results into economic circulation. The use of integrated information systems within the EAEU is reinforced by the decision of the Eurasian Intergovernmental Council on the "Main Directions of Industrial Cooperation within the Eurasian Economic Union until 2030," which is aimed at accelerating industrial and technological cooperation [1].

It is important to note that the EAEU has adopted a digital agenda designed to harmonize the regulation of the digital economy while taking into account the national interests, economic and technological specificities of the member states, as well as their international obligations until 2025 [2]. Nevertheless, despite efforts to create a favorable environment for scientific and technological cooperation within the union, experts highlight its relatively low level of development [3]. The key reasons identified include the underdeveloped national innovation systems and innovation climate, the absence or weak state of scientific and technological cooperation between member states [4], persistent formal and informal barriers, a tendency to prioritize "traditional national partners," and foreign competition [5].

Political and economic instability, resulting from sanctions and strained international relations, also negatively impacts the development of the EAEU member states and complicates the achievement of long-term goals in the field of scientific and technological cooperation. In this regard, one of the key approaches to overcoming the current challenges is the advancement of innovation and digitalization. This process can be facilitated by the creation of a unified digital technological platform, which will integrate the resources of the EAEU countries necessary for the implementation of joint innovation projects. Such a platform will enhance interactions among all participants in the innovation process by fostering knowledge exchange, technology transfer, and experience sharing, ultimately contributing to the formation of a unified digital space.

The objective of this study is to develop proposals for improving the effectiveness of international scientific and technological cooperation through the establishment of a digital technological platform. This platform will support the development of international innovation projects, facilitate technology transfer and promotion, and ensure the legal protection of intellectual property outcomes.

2 Literature Review

In the context of strengthening global scientific and industrial ties and the formation of international innovation systems, one of the key factors driving their development is ISTC, for which various definitions exist. For instance, Jung [6, p. 235] defines ISTC as the share of articles co-authored with at least one foreign author from any country. According to Wagner [7], p. 11, ISTC occurs when a researcher or a group of researchers of the same nationality reside in different countries but collaborate on a joint project. Zadvumkin and Terebova [8] define ISTC as the joint development of scientific and technical problems, mutual exchange of scientific achievements, industrial expertise, and the training of qualified personnel. This definition largely aligns with the one presented in the Concept of International Scientific and Technological Cooperation of the Russian Federation, which also states that the ISTC system covers the entire innovation cycle—from fundamental research to the commercialization of high-tech products. Its key participants include organizations and teams engaged in scientific research and development, state corporations, development institutions, funds supporting scientific, technological, and innovation activities, high-tech companies, and executive authorities [9, p. 3].

Among the factors determining the success of ISTC, scholars highlight the presence of a regional leader, collaboration with advanced partners outside the integration bloc [10], the reduction of time lags between decision-making and implementation [11], and the full utilization of the territorial potential of member states [5]. According to Shugurova and Shugurov [12], the primary barriers to scientific and technological cooperation within the EAEU include the slow process of legislative harmonization among member states and the absence of a unified strategic document detailing the directions of collaboration.

Regarding scientific and technological cooperation within other regional associations, researchers consider the European Union (EU) to be the most successful example [13, 14], as it possesses the necessary capital, technologies, and human resources that collectively form a high potential for the integration bloc.

In examining the impact of digital transformations on the scientific, technological, and innovation cooperation of the EAEU member states, Shugurov [15] identifies digital platforms as a key tool in this process, as they facilitate the creation of a unified digital scientific and technological space within the union. Dyatlov [16] highlights the main priorities in this area, including the development of a strategy for the digital economy of the member states, the formation of a digital space, and the establishment of a digital platform architecture to ensure the effective functioning of the union's integration management structures and institutions. Popova [17] recommends enhancing coordination between national and supranational levels by synchronizing digital economy strategies and fostering cooperation with international organizations to effectively advance the EAEU's digital agenda.

3 Methods and Data

In the course of reviewing contemporary scientific literature, theoretical synthesis was employed to integrate disparate opinions into a coherent whole, establishing that successful ISTC is determined not only by the exchange of knowledge and technologies but also by the presence of well-structured organizational instruments. The use of content analysis facilitated the systematization of key concepts and the identification of common principles underlying successful integration of countries based on scientific and technological cooperation. Foreign experience, where technological platforms contribute to the effective mobilization of resources, enabled the adaptation of these principles to the specific context of the EAEU countries.

To analyze the scientific and technological development of the EAEU countries, key indicators were selected in the study, including the Global Innovation Index, which reflects overall innovation activity; the number of research personnel, serving as a measure of human capital in R&D; and the volume of high-tech exports, demonstrating the ability of national economies to integrate advanced technologies into production. Additionally, domestic R&D expenditures, costs of technological innovations, and patent activity indicators were analyzed, allowing for the identification of challenges in innovation cooperation among countries.

Data foe analysis were collected from open official sources such as the World Intellectual Property Organization, the World Bank, the RF Federal State Statistics Service (Rosstat), the Higher School of Economics, and the EAEU member states. To ensure comparability, the data underwent preliminary processing, which included currency value adjustments using inflation coefficients and conversion into comparable measurement units. In the next stage, average growth rates were calculated for each indicator, enabling the determination of not only absolute changes but also relative dynamics over the study period. Calculating relative changes facilitated the identification of percentage variations between the initial and final points of the time interval, while data grouping by country provided an opportunity for a detailed comparison of trends within the union.

Drawing on the results of the conducted analysis, insufficient resource integration and existing challenges in scientific and technological cooperation among the EAEU countries necessitated the development of a unified digital technological platform as a tool for bringing together participants in the innovation process. To establish the structural components of the platform, a comparative analysis of the organizational structure of technological platforms was conducted, identifying key functional blocks and highlighting the importance of centralized strategic management.

Based on a systematic analysis of platform participant interactions, evaluation criteria were developed, including R&D performance, the quality of institutional and infrastructure environments, human capital development, the implementation of innovative developments, and the assessment of the network effect. These criteria ensure the objectivity and relevance of evaluating network interactions, tailored to the specifics of scientific and technological cooperation within the EAEU.

4 Results

4.1 *Analysis of the Scientific and Technological Development of the EAEU Countries*

Forming conditions for the implementation of scientific and technological cooperation among the EAEU countries requires a regular assessment of the effectiveness of the measures taken. One of the tools for such an assessment is the Global Innovation Index (GII), which allows tracking the dynamics of innovation development in countries and their integration into international scientific and technological processes. It provides a comprehensive picture of innovation, covering data related to the political situation, education system, infrastructure, and knowledge creation in each country. An analysis of the data presented in Table 1 shows that over the studied period, all the EAEU member states experienced a decline in their GII rankings. However, the Russian Federation continues to hold the leading position among the member states. The decline in rankings for Russia, Kazakhstan, and Belarus is associated with an almost twofold decrease in indicators reflecting the state of government institutions. At the same time, Armenia and Kyrgyzstan experienced a similar deterioration in market conditions. Nevertheless, despite these challenges, the EAEU countries have recorded growth in innovation performance indicators. Moreover, all the member states remain within the top 100 of the ranking, indicating significant potential for the development of scientific and technological cooperation, as well as the creation of prerequisites for improving their positions and strengthening the union's competitive advantages in the field of innovation development.

Table 1 Global innovation index of the EAEU countries

Country	2019	2020	2021	2022	2023	Average ranking	Relative change (%)
Russia	46	47	45	47	51	47.0	−2.61
Belarus	72	64	62	77	80	71.0	−2.67
Armenia	64	61	69	80	72	69.2	−2.99
Kazakhstan	79	77	79	83	81	79.8	−0.63
Kyrgyzstan	90	94	98	94	106	96.4	−4.18

Source: [18]

Table 2 Number of personnel engaged in research and development in the EAEU, persons

Country	2019	2020	2021	2022	2023	Relative change (%)
EAEU	740,966	736,614	719,287	726,683	732,201	−0.30
Armenia	4539	4499	4889	4864	4853	1.69
Belarus	27,735	25,622	25,644	25,233	26,738	−0.91
Kazakhstan	21,843	22,665	21,617	22,456	25,473	3.92
Kyrgyzstan	4385	4495	4435	4260	4523	0.78
Russia	682,464	679,333	662,702	669,870	670,614	−0.44

Source: [19]

Next, we analyze the indicators characterizing the scientific and technological development of the EAEU countries for the period from 2019 to 2023. We begin with examining the data on the number of personnel engaged in research and development (Table 2), which indicate a negative growth rate for this indicator both for the union as a whole and individually in Belarus and Russia. This trend reflects a decline in the attractiveness of the research and development sector, as well as a reduction in the innovation activity of business structures in these countries. Particular attention should be paid to the fact that, on average, about 90% of all personnel engaged in research and development within the EAEU are concentrated in Russia. This underscores its key role in the scientific and technological development of the union and highlights the need for increased efforts from other member states.

The export of high-tech products generates impulses for national economic development, and the importance of increasing such exports by the EAEU countries is determined by the following reasons:

- The production of high-tech products is carried out using advanced knowledge and technologies, which serve as the main source of their added value;
- High-tech exports provide the highest revenue for a country compared to the export of medium- and low-tech goods;
- The volume of exports of knowledge-intensive, technologically complex goods and services creates new comparative advantages and reshapes a country's position in the international division of labor.

The data presented in Table 3 indicate that Belarus and Russia demonstrate the lowest high-tech export volumes. This is due to the integration policy of the Union State of these countries, the expansion of anti-Russian sanctions, and the insufficient utilization of ISTC opportunities within the EAEU. At the same time, it is worth noting the significant growth of this indicator in Armenia and Kazakhstan in 2022, which was driven by the adoption of a parallel import policy following the imposition of sanctions against Russia.

It is important to emphasize that, according to the SITC Rev.4 methodology used by the World Bank, high-tech products include the following categories: aerospace industry, computers and office equipment, electronics and telecommunications, pharmaceuticals, scientific instruments, electrical engineering, chemistry, non-electrical machinery, and armaments. At the same time, in the national statistical

Table 3 Export of high technologies by the EAEU Countries, % of industrial product exports

Country	2019	2020	2021	2022	2023	Relative change (%)
Armenia	9.8	7.1	6.0	22.0	21.0	20.99
Belarus	9.9	9.9	12.5	11.7	15.3	11.50
Kazakhstan	21.79	24.22	22.93	29.55	37.71	14.70
Kyrgyzstan	6.7	8.7	16.3	10.5	19.0	29.77
Russia	5.3	5.7	5.0	5.1	6.0	3.15

Source: [20–24]

Table 4 Domestic expenditures on research and development in the EAEU countries, million USD[a]

Country	2019	2020	2021	2022	2023	Relative change (%)
EAEU	20,771.3	19,113.2	19,747.3	21,947.2	20,333.0	−0.53
Armenia	27.8	29.8	30.8	38.4	42.7	11.33
Belarus	426.1	370.9	346.0	351.1	416.7	−0.56
Kazakhstan	246.1	243.8	277.1	264.0	378.2	11.34
Kyrgyzstan	9.1	7.8	7.1	8.4	8.2	−2.57
Russia	20,062.0	18,460.9	19,086.1	21,285.4	19,487.2	−0.72

Source: [19]

[a] Data adjusted to 2023

agencies of the EAEU countries, high-tech exports may include any products considered innovative for the national market, regardless of their industry classification. These methodological differences affect data comparability and must be taken into account in the analysis.

In addition to the volume of high-tech product exports, a key factor in the development of the national economy and the enhancement of the competitiveness of the EAEU countries is the level of domestic expenditures on research and development. This indicator allows for the assessment of investment activity in knowledge-intensive sectors and their impact on innovation development. According to data from Table 4, the absolute value of this indicator for Russia exceeds 90% of the total expenditures of the EAEU countries. This is explained by Russia's withdrawal from several major international innovation projects involving EU countries, the USA, and Japan due to the imposition of anti-Russian sanctions following the start of the Special Military Operation. As a result, financial flows have been redistributed in favor of national projects implemented within the framework of national development goals. It should also be noted that in the structure of research and development expenditures in Russia, the public sector dominates, accounting for an average of 70% of funding. Government support for innovation activities is primarily provided in the form of subsidies and grants allocated from federal and regional budgets. At the same time, enterprises do not receive funding directly but through government structures responsible for implementing the relevant policies. Many programs supporting enterprise development are financed from multiple sources, with the majority of funding coming from budgetary resources, emphasizing the significant role of the state in stimulating innovation activity and scientific and technological development.

Table 5 Expenditures on innovation activity in the EAEU, million USD[a]

Country	2019	2020	2021	2022	2023	Relative change (%)
EAEU	32,282.8	32,151.7	34,629.8	42,954.9	46,003.8	9.26
Armenia	–	–	–	–	–	–
Belarus	681.2	603.2	467.7	327.6	439.2	−10.39
Kazakhstan	1400.2	1882	1844.2	3156.1	3990.3	29.93
Kyrgyzstan	11.3	3.3	4.9	2.3	1.6	−38.66
Russia	30,190.1	29,663.2	32,313.0	39,468.9	41,572.7	8.33

Source: [24]
[a] Data adjusted to 2023

The next indicator worth attention and forming the basis for the innovation development and modernization of the EAEU economy is expenditures on technological innovations. The data presented in Table 5 indicate an average growth rate of 9.26% across the union. However, Kyrgyzstan and Belarus exhibit a sharply negative trend, which may slow down structural transformations in their economies. The primary goal of these transformations is to enhance the role of industries generating innovations (biotechnology and genetic engineering, robotics and automation, the Internet of Things, renewable energy sources, artificial intelligence, machine learning, etc.). The decline in investments in technological innovations in certain countries of the EAEU may limit their ability to integrate into global technological value chains and reduce their competitiveness on the international stage. This underscores the need to intensify efforts to support innovative industries and stimulate investments in knowledge-intensive technologies.

One of the key metrics reflecting technical and technological achievements in the economy is patent activity (Table 6). This indicator helps identify bottlenecks that hinder the effective utilization of intellectual property results and serves as a basis for planning new research, developments, production modernization, and entry into new markets. Over the studied period, this indicator demonstrated a negative trend in all the EAEU countries. This decline is attributed to the underdeveloped organizational and economic mechanism for interaction in the innovation sector, as well as the reduction in international projects due to sanctions policies. These circumstances highlight the need to establish a common legal framework that will enhance the effectiveness of international scientific and technological cooperation. The creation of unified legal and institutional conditions for the protection and commercialization of intellectual property could be a crucial step in stimulating innovation activity and strengthening the competitive positions of the EAEU countries on the global level. It is important to emphasize that in the EAEU member states, particularly Russia and Belarus, despite a high level of technological progress in developing modern technologies, the latest inventions are infrequently applied. Member countries primarily rely on innovations imported from third countries, while domestic developments lack sufficient demand within the national economy. In most cases, innovation efforts halt at the stage of industrial prototypes and fail to reach large-scale production. This fact indicates the low competitiveness of innovative

Table 6 Dynamics of patent applications and registrations in the EAEU, units

Period	Data type	Russia	Armenia	Belarus	Kazakhstan	Kyrgyzstan	EAEU
2019	Filed	35,511	116	393	805	93	36,113
	Issued	34,008	100	461	709	67	35,345
2020	Filed	34,984	70	394	900	64	36,412
	Issued	28,788	72	447	651	49	30,007
2021	Filed	30,977	48	386	973	87	31,498
	Issued	23,662	27	316	585	39	24,629
2022	Filed	26,924	34	342	838	71	28,209
	Issued	23,315	3	302	492	47	24,159
2023	Filed	26,720	22	359	917	75	28,093
	Issued	23,406	5	248	492	50	23,709
Relative change (%)	Filed	−6.86	−34.01	−2.24	3.31	−5.24	−6.09
	Issued	−8.92	−52.71	−14.36	−8.73	−7.06	−9.50

Source: [25–29]

products produced within the EAEU compared to their counterparts in developed countries.

In industrial cooperation within the EAEU, there remain unused opportunities due to the lack of fully developed interaction practices in the field of bilateral and multilateral industrial cooperation, as well as the lack of understanding of the opportunities and objectives of Eurasian integration by businesses and government authorities, despite the adoption of numerous documents. As a result, fragmentation in cooperation persists, which needs to be eliminated to make it more cohesive and comprehensive. Given the growing need to enhance interstate interaction, an important step toward utilizing the production potential of the union is the development of a digital technological platform that will facilitate scientific and technological cooperation among the EAEU countries. Such a platform will enable the creation of a digital ecosystem where research, educational, and production resources of member states will be integrated, providing a shared environment for the exchange of knowledge, technologies, and expertise. The creation of this platform aligns with the course toward digital transformation and the harmonization of legal frameworks for scientific and technological policy, contributing to the improved coordination of joint projects and active exchange of knowledge, skills, and innovative solutions within the union.

4.2 *The Eurasian Digital Technological Platform*

The term "technological platform" (TP) was first introduced by the European Commission in the report "Technological Platforms: From Definition to a Common Research Agenda," according to which "European technological platforms" are industry-led stakeholder forums that develop short-term and long-term research and innovation programs, as well as "roadmaps" for action at both the EU and national levels, supported by private and public funding [30]. These TPs provide a basis for determining priorities, timelines, and action plans in the field of research and development on important strategic issues within the integration association.

In the Russian practice, the term was first introduced by the decision of the Government Commission on High Technologies and Innovations, where a TP is understood as "...a communication tool aimed at intensifying efforts to create promising commercial technologies, new products (services), attracting additional resources for conducting research and development with the participation of all interested parties (business, science, government, and civil society), as well as improving the regulatory and legal framework in the field of scientific, technological, and innovation development" [31].

The formation of a TP is advisable in the presence of such problems as: multiplicity of potential participants and indirect beneficiaries interested in its formation, as well as the necessity to ensure discussions on the prospects of technological modernization and forms of partnership between business, science, and the state; weak structuring of business interests in the development and implementation of new technologies and personnel training, as well as the need to define requirements for the most important basic technologies; multidisciplinarity of research for the development of promising technologies, uncertainty of existing scientific and technological competencies, and fragmentation of scientific organizations under various executive authorities.

These conditions are characteristic of the innovation process in the EAEU, which determines the positive effect of the integration association from forming such a communication mechanism between business, government, science, and civil society. However, TP is not only a communication tool but also a complex mechanism for transforming the relationships of fragmented participants in innovation activities toward consolidation, the use of shared innovation achievements, and digital technologies. It should be noted that the existing Eurasian technological platforms are designed to accumulate the most advanced achievements in scientific and technological development, mobilize scientific potential for the development of innovative projects, and their implementation in industrial production. Despite the high level of development of existing TPs and efforts to stimulate their growth, the main drawbacks include insufficient coordination of activities in the digital space.

The most relevant tool for digital transformation and the creation of innovation ecosystems is the digital platform (DP), as platform-based development strategies are an effective method of digital change due to the high adaptability of the platform and the effects of network interactions. Despite the growing popularity of this tool, there is no universal approach to defining DP. For example, Dmitrieva et al. [32] define it as a hybrid multilateral structure aimed at creating value through direct interaction between user groups. Lipsett [33] recognizes openness and the creation of public value as key aspects of DP development. At the same time, Smirnov [34, p. 18] defines it as a virtual space, a tool for interaction between innovators from different countries, while Styrin, Dmitriev, and Sinyatullina [35] describe it as a next-generation intermediary institution, a technological structure for interaction.

Consequently, a DP represents a virtual infrastructure that facilitates interaction between market participants and ensures value creation for each participant.

It should be noted that the presented interpretations share several common parameters: the presence of a unified information environment and a corresponding information-technology infrastructure; the algorithmization of participant interactions within the platform; the use of "smart" technologies; mutually beneficial relationships; and increased efficiency of business processes. Thus, a DP is a unified information and communication system consisting of digital infrastructure, digital tools, and digital competencies capable of bringing participants together to achieve economic and/or social effects. The creation of the Eurasian digital technology platform (EDTP) will allow the EAEU countries to consolidate efforts in the scientific and technological sphere, attracting the necessary resources for research and development, facilitating the exchange of knowledge and experience among countries, and actively involving innovation process participants in the development and implementation of innovations. This will be achieved through the integration of information and communication technologies into a unified network for the accumulation and distribution of resources, leading to the formation of the following the EAEU advantages in the field of ISTC:

- increased efficiency of interaction between individuals, legal entities, executive and regulatory authorities of the member states through unrestricted data exchange, meeting their needs without territorial limitations;
- involvement of small and medium-sized enterprises in the innovation sector by enabling data collection and aggregation from various sectors, achieving a synergistic effect;
- reduction of transaction and time costs for all participants;
- enhancement of the competitiveness and innovation development of the member states through the internationalization of activities and the advancement of foreign economic and scientific and technological cooperation to a new level.

In accordance with these advantages, several key tasks of the EDTP can be identified: the accumulation of national and integration achievements in scientific and technological development, the mobilization of innovation potential of member states for work on interdisciplinary projects, the creation of a unified patent database for innovative developments, and the provision of opportunities for the mutual implementation of results in production to facilitate innovation commercialization and enhance the competitiveness of innovative products. For the effective implementation of these tasks, it is necessary to establish a clear organizational structure that ensures the coordination and optimization of platform participants' actions within the framework of scientific and technological cooperation among the EAEU countries (Fig. 1).

The EDTP embraces representatives from science, education, and business, who, at the General Assembly of platform members, the highest governing body (Part 1, Article 29 [36]), determine measures to ensure compliance with the platform's goals, approve strategic directions of activity, develop and implement joint innovation projects, define the roles and functions of participants, as well as the budget and

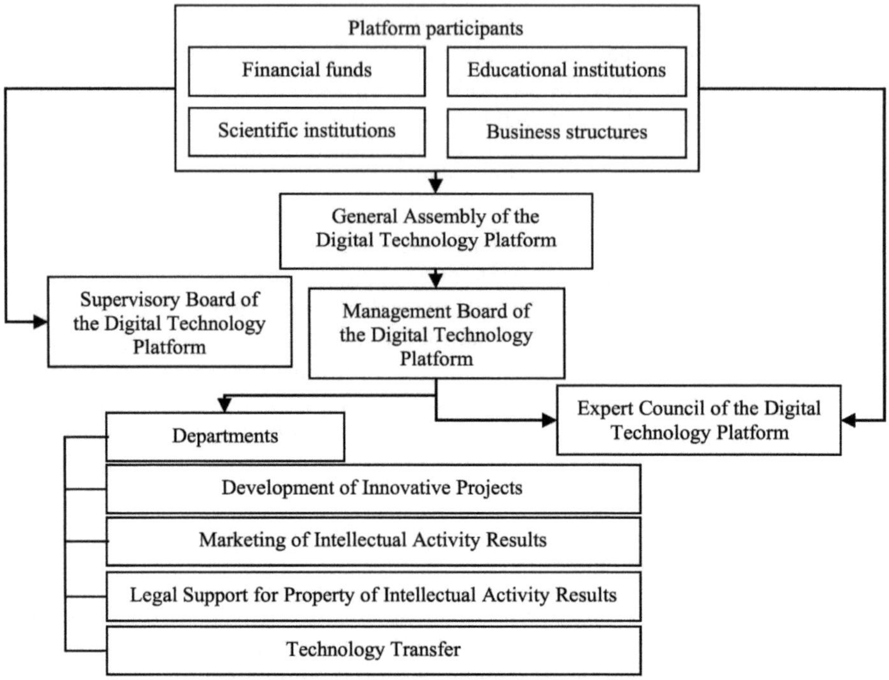

Fig. 1 Organizational structure of the EDTP

resource allocation. The General Assembly coordinates the strategic goals and objectives of the platform, aligning the interests and priorities of all participants and contributing to the efficiency of innovation activity within the EAEU countries.

The Supervisory Board, functioning as a collegial body, oversees the platform's activities. It determines development directions, monitors project implementation and goal adherence, and maintains interaction with external entities, including regulatory authorities and interested companies. The Supervisory Board ensures the implementation of strategic plans approved by the General Assembly and, if necessary, approves modifications, helping to accommodate participant interests while maintaining the strategic priorities of the platform.

The Platform Management Board is responsible for day-to-day leadership and coordination. It develops annual plans and work programs, approved by the General Assembly, distributes tasks among departments, and oversees budget control and project plan execution. As the executive body, the Management Board makes operational decisions on resources and activities, coordinating tasks among participants to achieve the established goals.

The Expert Council performs consultative and expert functions, conducting expert evaluation and assessment of scientific research and innovation projects, as well as developing recommendations for their improvement. The Council ensures the quality and cost-effectiveness of innovations and assists the Management Board and other departments in making strategic decisions. The consultations and reviews carried out by the Expert Council help participants and platform departments enhance projects and minimize risks, strengthening the scientific and technological foundation of innovation initiatives.

The EDTP includes four departments, each of which interacts with the others while performing its designated tasks. The Innovation Project Development Department collaborates with scientific institutions, entrepreneurs, and educational organizations to create projects based on the intellectual property of the participants. It works closely with the Technology Transfer Department to prepare projects for implementation and with the Expert Council for approval and modifications. The Marketing Department for Intellectual Property Results analyzes market conditions, conducts market research, and develops marketing strategies, facilitating connections with potential partners and clients. It also coordinates with the Technology Transfer Department to successfully promote products and technologies developed on the platform in the market. The Legal Support Department provides legal consultation to participants and departments on issues related to intellectual property protection and transaction support, while also working with the Marketing Department to ensure the legal security of operations. It develops and reviews regulatory documents, manages licensing, and provides legal support for projects. The Technology Transfer Department facilitates the transfer and adaptation of new technologies for practical use and their promotion at the national and international levels. It collaborates with the Innovation Project Development Department in planning and implementing technology transfers, as well as with the Expert Council for technology evaluation and market readiness preparation.

The multilevel structure ensures flexibility and the ability to respond quickly to changes, enabling efficient implementation of innovation projects with minimal risks. To maximize the impact of participation in the EDTP for innovation process participants, it is necessary to develop evaluation criteria for their interaction within the platform as a network mechanism. The search for effectiveness and performance criteria is complicated by the complexity of the network environment and the diverse forms of interaction within it. Therefore, criteria should be determined considering the importance of achieving participants' goals and the effectiveness of their cooperation.

It is proposed to define evaluation criteria for the EDTP participant interactions in the following areas (Table 7):

- implementation of R&D—characterizes the processes of initiating and conducting research and development within the platform;
- quality of the institutional and infrastructure environment—reflects the formation of structural ties between ISTC subjects and regulatory and legal frameworks;
- development of human capital—characterizes the scientific, technological, and digital development of the participating countries;
- implementation of innovative developments—assesses the level of commercialization of innovations and their financial outcomes;

Table 7 Criteria for evaluating network interaction of the EDTP participants

Evaluation direction	Criteria
Implementation of R&D	– Number and volume of R&D projects initiated and implemented on the platform – Number of reports on completed research projects – Number of scientific events held (conferences, fairs, webinars, etc.) – Number of scientific materials prepared using the platform (scientific articles, reports, monographs, etc.)
Quality of the institutional and infrastructure environment	– Number of entities registered on the platform, categorized by actor type – Number and size of project groups by research directions of the platform – Number of regulatory documents, projects, and development strategies developed/adopted using the platform
Development of human capital	– Number of training programs jointly developed using the platform – Number of specialists trained under jointly developed educational programs – Number of educational resources jointly developed using the platform – Number of educational events implemented using the platform – Number of specialists employed through the platform
Implementation of innovative developments	– Number of commercialized intellectual property results – Number of new/improved innovative products in the platform's focus areas – Change in revenue of innovation process participants related to the implementation of platform projects
Network effect	– Speed of innovation flow through the platform – Platform capacity – Number of participants in network interactions – Degree of connection involvement; – Share of added value in innovative products

Source: [37]

- network effect—takes into account the features of connections within the platform, defined by its properties, the number of users, and the added value of innovative products.

These criteria will enable the assessment of the current state of network interaction among the EDTP participants, track the structural characteristics and dynamics of ISTC within the EAEU. Additionally, based on the analysis of the EDTP activities over multiple periods, it will be possible to identify "bottlenecks" in various areas of interaction, determine missing elements needed to ensure effective collaboration, and model the expansion and efficiency of the platform. This could serve as a foundation for a new practical direction in economic research on the digital technological platform network of the integration association.

5 Conclusion

The study has identified the significance of ISTC in enhancing the innovation-driven development of the EAEU countries. Based on the analysis of current scientific and technological development indicators of the member states, it has been established that the measures they have adopted stimulate innovation growth, albeit to varying degrees. It has been determined that coordination issues and differences in the EAEU's legislative framework limit opportunities for the exchange of technologies and knowledge in the industrial sector, thereby reducing the effectiveness of ISTC and hindering the promotion of high-tech products in international markets.

To overcome these limitations, it is proposed to improve the interaction mechanism within ISTC through the launch of the EDTP. This platform will allow for the integration of innovation process participants, accelerating innovation activities and commercializing their results. The implementation of these measures will provide the EAEU member states with significant advantages in enhancing their industrial competitiveness in global markets, reducing disparities in innovation infrastructure development, and creating conditions for active participation in international scientific and technological projects.

Evaluation criteria for network interaction among innovation process participants have been defined, allowing for an assessment of the platform's effectiveness based on network effects.

In the future, to further develop scientific and technological cooperation among the EAEU countries, it is advisable to design an organizational and economic mechanism, which should include the development of procedures for the preparation and submission of joint innovation projects involving educational institutions, research organizations, industrial enterprises, national and supranational authorities, and civil society.

References

1. Eurasian Intergovernmental Council. (2024). *On the main directions of industrial cooperation within the Eurasian Economic Union until 2030*. Retrieved from https://pravo.by/document/?guid=3871&p0=F92400279
2. Supreme Eurasian Economic Council. (2017). *On the main directions for implementing the digital agenda of the Eurasian Economic Union until 2025*. Retrieved from https://www.garant.ru/products/ipo/prime/doc/71708158
3. Federation Council of the Federal Assembly of the Russian Federation. (2015). *Scientific and technological cooperation as a factor of Eurasian economic integration: Annual report for 2015*. Retrieved from http://council.gov.ru/activity/analytics/analytical_reports/65859
4. Shugurov, M. V. (2020). Formation of a model of scientific and technological integration within the EAEU: Theoretical and methodological aspects. *Politics and Society, 4*, 50–81. https://doi.org/10.7256/2454-0684.2020.4.34137
5. Shashikhina, T., Barabanov, O., & Tuchina, M. (2024). A decade of the EAEU through the prism of Strategy 2025: Achievements, challenges, prospects. *Eurasian Dialogue, 3*, 670. Retrieved from https://eadialog.com/read/tpost/b670pfrgj1-desyatiletie-eaes-skvoz-prizmu-strategii

6. Jung, J. (2012). International research collaboration among academics in China and South Korea. *International Journal of Chinese Education, 1*, 235–254. https://doi.org/10.1163/22125868-12340005
7. Wagner, C. (2006). International collaboration in science and technology: Promises and pitfalls. In *Science and technology policy for development* (pp. 165–176). Anthem Press.
8. Zadumkin, K. A., & Terebova, S. V. (2009). International scientific and technological cooperation: Essence, content, and forms. *Problems of Territorial Development, 1*, 22–30.
9. Government of the Russian Federation. (2019). *Concept of international scientific and technological cooperation of the Russian Federation*. Retrieved from https://minobrnauki.gov.ru/upload/2021/07/kontseptsiya_MNTS_Rossiyskoy_Federatsii.pdf
10. Krapohl, S., & Vasileva-Dienes, A. (2020). The region that isn't: China, Russia, and the failure of regional integration in Central Asia. *Asia Europe Journal, 18*, 347–366. https://doi.org/10.1007/s10308-019-00548-0
11. Kathuria, S., Shahid, S., & Ferrantino, M. (2015). *Five lessons of regional integration from Asia, America, and Africa*. World Bank. Retrieved from https://blogs.worldbank.org/en/endpovertyinsouthasia/five-lessons-regional-integration-asia-america-and-africa
12. Shugurova, I. V., & Shugurov, M. V. (2019). On the formation of legal foundations for regional scientific and technological cooperation of EAEU states in the agro-industrial sector. *SPJ Dialogue, 1*(13), 62–76.
13. Umarova, D. T. (2021). Foreign experience in scientific and technological integration. *Models, Systems, Networks in Economics, Engineering, Nature, and Society, 4*, 26–40. https://doi.org/10.21685/2227-8486-2021-4-3
14. Gaens, B., Venturi, B., & Ayuso, A. (2020). Differentiation in ASEAN, ECOWAS, and MERCOSUR: A comparative analysis. In *EU Integration and Differentiation for Effectiveness and Accountability Policy Papers*. Istituto Affari Internazionali.
15. Shugurov, M. V. (2020). Trends and prospects for the development of regional scientific and technological integration in the context of the EAEU digital agenda: Political and legal dimension. *Law and Politics, 9*, 119–142. https://doi.org/10.7256/2454-0706.2020.9.33516
16. Dyatlov, S. A. (2018). Digital transformation of the EAEU economies: Priorities and development institutions. *PME, 3*(67), 18–21.
17. Popova, I. M. (2021). Problems of implementing the EAEU digital agenda. *Bulletin of International Organizations: Education, Science, New Economy, 1*, 127–141. https://doi.org/10.17323/1996-7845-2021-01-06
18. World Intellectual Property Organization. (2024). *Global innovation index*. Retrieved from https://www.wipo.int/en/web/global-innovation-index
19. Eurasian Economic Commission. (2023). *Science and innovation: Dynamic series*. Retrieved from https://eec.eaeunion.org/comission/department/dep_stat/union_stat/current_stat/science_and_innovation/series
20. National Statistical Committee of the Republic of Belarus. (2024). *Science and innovation activity in the Republic of Belarus: Statistical digest*. Retrieved from https://www.belstat.gov.by/upload/iblock/4c2/onh6mc8mbf3qr7agmg7hzw9772c0o1nf.pdf
21. World Bank. (2024). *High-technology exports (% of manufactured exports)*. Retrieved from https://data.worldbank.org/indicator/TX.VAL.TECH.MF.ZS?locations=BY-KZ
22. Federal State Statistics Service. (2021). *Russian statistical yearbook*. Retrieved from https://rosstat.gov.ru/storage/mediabank/Ejegodnik_2021.pdf
23. Federal State Statistics Service. (2024). *Russian statistical yearbook*. Retrieved from https://rosstat.gov.ru/storage/mediabank/Ejegodnik_2024.pdf
24. Eurasian Economic Commission. (2024). *Statistical yearbook of the Eurasian Economic Union*. Retrieved from https://eec.eaeunion.org/upload/files/dep_stat/econstat/statpub/Stat_Yearbook_2024.pdf
25. World Intellectual Property Organization. (2024). *Intellectual property rights: Total patent applications (Direct and PCT national phase entries)*. Retrieved from https://www3.wipo.int/ipstats/ips-search/search-result?type=IPS&selectedTab=patent&indicator=10&reportType

=11&fromYear=2019&toYear=2023&ipsOffSelValues=AM,RU,BY,KZ,KG&ipsOriSelValues=&ipsTechSelValues=900
26. World Intellectual Property Organization. (2024). *Intellectual property rights: Total patent grants (Direct and PCT national phase entries).* Retrieved from https://www3.wipo.int/ipstats/ips-search/search-result?type=IPS&selectedTab=patent&indicator=23&reportType=11&fromYear=2019&toYear=2023&ipsOffSelValues=RU,AM,BY,KZ,KG&ipsOriSelValues=&ipsTechSelValues=900
27. Kazpatent. (2020). *Statistical data on Kazpatent's activities for 2020 compared to 2018, 2019.* Retrieved from https://qazpatent.kz/sites/default/files//stat_dannye_2020_rus_1.pdf
28. Qazpatent. (2022). *Statistical data on Qazpatent's activities for 2022 compared to 2020, 2021.* Retrieved from https://qazpatent.kz/storage/app/media/uploaded-files/dannye-1.pdf
29. Qazpatent. (2024). *Statistical data on Qazpatent's activities for 2024 compared to 2022, 2023.* Retrieved from https://qazpatent.kz/storage/app/media/%20сайт%20рус.pdf
30. Council of the European Union. (2013). *Commission staff working document: Strategy for European Technology Platforms: ETP 2020.* Retrieved from https://data.consilium.europa.eu/doc/document/ST-12342-2013-INIT/en/pdf
31. Government Commission on High Technologies and Innovations. (2010). *Procedure for forming the list of technological platforms.* Retrieved from https://base.garant.ru/55188797/?ysclid=lp0iy1ixll997159992
32. Dmitrieva, N. E., Sanina, A. G., Styrin, E. M., Kashanin, A. V., Kvachev, V. G., Gasparyan, D. E., Stepanov, I. M., Minchenko, O. S., Makarov, I. A., Titov, E. A., Rylskikh, E. V., Semyonova, A. M., Vinokurova, M. Y., Rybushkina, Ya, A., Annenkova, K. A., Kozlova, A. A., & Mallyamov, A. R. (2023). *Digital transformation in public administration.* National Research University. https://doi.org/10.17323/978-5-7598-2831-0
33. Lipsett, M. S., & Holbrook, J. A. D. (1996). *Reflections on indicators of international cooperation in S&T.* Simon Fraser University at Harbour Centre. Retrieved from http://summit.sfu.ca/item/13401
34. Smirnov, E. N. (2020). Global digital platforms as a factor in the transformation of world markets. *Issues of Innovative Economy, 1*, 13–24. https://doi.org/10.18334/vinec.10.1.100699
35. Styrin, E. M., Dmitrieva, N. E., & Sinyatullina, L. K. (2019). *Government digital platforms: From concept to implementation.* Issues of Public and Municipal Administration.
36. State Duma. (1996). *On non-profit organizations.* Retrieved from http://pravo.gov.ru/proxy/ips/?docbody=&nd=102039064&rdk
37. Shcherbina, A. Y. (2023). *Development of entrepreneurial structures based on an innovation-digital approach.* Donetsk National University of Economics and Trade Named After Mikhail Tugan-Baranovsky.

MIX
Papier aus verantwortungsvollen Quellen
Paper from responsible sources
FSC® C105338

If you have any concerns about our products,
you can contact us on
ProductSafety@springernature.com

In case Publisher is established outside the EU,
the EU authorized representative is:
Springer Nature Customer Service Center GmbH
Europaplatz 3, 69115 Heidelberg, Germany

Printed by Libri Plureos GmbH
in Hamburg, Germany